Shadow

Bob Woodward

SHADOW

FIVE PRESIDENTS AND THE
LEGACY OF WATERGATE

WHEELER
PUBLISHING, INC.
ROCKLAND, MA

★ AN AMERICAN COMPANY ★

LP
973.92

WOO

Published in Large Print by arrangement with Simon & Schuster, Inc.,
in the United States and Canada.

Wheeler Large Print Book Series.

C1 11/00

Set in 16 pt Plantin.

Library of Congress Cataloging-in-Publication Data

Woodward, Bob.
    Shadow : five presidents and the legacy of Watergate / Bob Woodward.
        p. (large print) cm.(Wheeler large print book series)
    ISBN 1-56895-787-4 (hardcover)
    1. Nixon, Richard M. (Richard Milhous), 1913– —Influence.
2. Presidents—United States—History—20th century. 3. Watergate
Affair, 1972–1974. 5. United States—Politics and government—1945–1989.
6. United States—Politics and government—1989– 7. Large type books.
I. Title. II. Series
[E839.5 W66 1999]
973.92 21

AUTHOR'S NOTE

Jeff Glasser, who graduated from Yale in 1996 and interned at *The Washington Post* that summer, was my assistant and collaborator for the last three years. He tirelessly and resourcefully worked through the presidential libraries of Ford, Carter, Reagan and the National Archives, unearthing key documents, leads and vital new information and corroboration. He also immersed himself in the key memoirs, books, articles—and controversies—of the period 1974 to 1999. A skilled, relentless editor, he repeatedly improved early drafts with detailed comments and suggestions. He assisted in the reporting and writing at every stage. The exhaustive chapter notes are his work, as he made sure the book provided the most explicit attribution where possible and forthrightly stated when the source could not be identified. A child of the information age, he brilliantly used all sources, from the Freedom of Information Act to the Internet. He is wise, intense and independent; I could never have finished this book without him. His friendship and energy made immeasurable contributions to my work and life. He has the highest standards of fairness and accuracy. Jeff was born in 1974, the year Nixon resigned. He is probably one of the few Americans who has a deep understanding of the history of the presidents who have served in his lifetime.

To my daughters, Tali and Diana

CONTENTS

INTRODUCTION

FOR YEARS, I have been struck by a scene in Richard Nixon's memoir, *RN*. Just before Christmas 1967, Nixon, then only a former vice president, wrote on a legal pad: "I have decided personally against becoming a candidate." He would not run for president. He summarized his reasons. Losing again would be, he put it, "an emotional disaster" for his family. He did not relish political combat. After years of campaigning he was tired of having to go begging for support, political and financial, even from old friends. He was bored by the charade of trying to romance the media. "Personally," he wrote, "I have had it. I want nothing else."

By the next month, mid-January 1968, Nixon had reversed course. "I had increasingly come to understand that politics was not just an alternative occupation for me," he wrote in his memoirs. "It was my life." He ran and won ten months later.

The politics that was Nixon's life before he was elected president reflected the 1940s, 1950s and early 1960s. By the time he resigned in 1974, American politics was changed forever because of Vietnam and Watergate.

Although Nixon's responsibility for Vietnam

is large and for Watergate central, he could be forgiven for not entirely understanding the convulsions he had visited upon politics and the presidency. As a result of his actions, presidents not only would be subject to doubt and second guessing, they would be suspected of outright criminality. Nixon's tapes of his office and telephone conversations left an irrefutable historical record that the president abused government power for political purposes, obstructed justice and ordered his aides to do so as well. Watergate ended with unusual clarity and unusual closure because Nixon resigned. The scandal left a series of obvious questions that would come to plague his successors. Could another president be a criminal? Did presidents talk and plot in private like Nixon? Would another president have to resign?

But after more than 25 years of covering presidents, I am still surprised that his successors did not fully comprehend the depth of distrust left by Nixon. New ethics laws, a resurgent Congress and a more inquiring media altered the prerogatives and daily lives of presidents. Congress, made up of men and women whose lives are largely politics, was determined to play a more prominent, inquisitorial role. The media was going to dig deep and incessantly because much had been hidden before. And quite naturally prosecutors and ethics investigators were more and more determined. The habit of deception and hedging practiced by presidents would no longer be acceptable.

This book is not a history of the presidencies of Ford, Carter, Reagan, Bush and Clinton. It is not even a history of all the scandals and investigations that occurred during their administrations.

Instead, it is my examination of the most important moments, small and large, when the honesty and truthfulness of the presidents and those closest to them were challenged. I have tried to single out those times that had the greatest impact on the official and unofficial lives of the five men, their administrations and the inner worlds they inhabited as they struggled to cope with and adapt to the multiple legacies of Watergate. These presidents were inhabiting a new world, but they often seemed not to recognize it.

PART ONE

GERALD FORD

1974–77

1

AUGUST 1, 1974, was a hot Washington summer morning with the humidity heavy in the air, but inside Richard Nixon's air-conditioned White House it was unnaturally cool. The president looked thin, battered, at times almost like a stroke victim. His chief of staff Alexander M. Haig Jr.'s eyes were red. Early that morning Nixon had summoned Haig, a 49-year-old Army general who had been his right-hand man for the previous 15 months, the most grueling, emotionally exhausting and politically unstable of the Watergate scandal. The incessant hangover of sleep deprivation had become a way of life for both.

"Al, it's over," Nixon said in a surprisingly impersonal, even matter-of-fact tone. Nixon, ever the political realist, said he simply couldn't govern. His presidency was collapsing. He could almost hear the air rushing out of it—power leaving. All three branches of the federal government had turned against the president. Although Special Watergate Prosecutor Leon Jaworski worked for the executive branch that Nixon headed, he was conducting an independent, relentless investigation. A week earlier the Supreme Court, in a unanimous decision, had ruled in the special prosecutor's favor that Nixon had to turn over an additional 64 secret White House tape recordings. Two of those tapes, once released, were going to undermine Nixon and show he ordered the Watergate cover-up. In the legislative branch, a lopsided bipartisan majority of the Judiciary Committee of the House of Representatives had days earlier voted three articles recommending his impeachment based on information that Special Prosecutor Jaworski had provided through the grand jury to the House committee. Governing had been reduced to a series of stopgap pretenses.

Typically, Nixon had a plan. He intended to announce his resignation in four days, he told Haig. He needed the weekend to take his family to Camp David, the presidential retreat in the nearby Maryland mountains, and prepare them. He expected his wife and two grown daughters, Julie and Tricia, to resist and fight his decision with every bone in their bodies.

"It might be better to resign tomorrow night and leave town immediately," Haig proposed.

"No," Nixon answered. Nixon's tone was at first gentle. Then he shifted and became gruff, waving a forefinger at Haig as he so often had, demanding his orders be followed. "This is my decision and mine alone," Nixon insisted, warning that he would not succumb to political pressure from Republicans, the Congress or his cabinet. "I've resisted political pressure all my life, and if I get it now, I may change my mind."

"Understood, Mr. President," Haig answered.

Nixon directed Haig to inform Vice President Gerald Ford that he should be ready to assume the presidency, but not to give him all the facts. "Tell him I want absolute secrecy. Tell him what's coming. Explain the reasoning. But don't tell him when."

4

• • •

Watergate had put the presidency in play. The president's hold on the office was loosened as Nixon contemplated resigning. It was a singular moment in American history, creating a dangerous new space in which Nixon, Ford and Haig had to operate. Where exactly was presidential power at that moment? Nixon held the office, according to the law and Constitution. Ford was stumbling to the presidency. For his part, Haig, mindful of his multiple and competing loyalties to Nixon, Ford and the country, was to be the broker and go-between.

There was no steady hand. Nixon was consumed by a simmering, explosive anger that he was getting a bum rap. He was emotionally disabled, depressed and paranoid. Ford had acquired none of the armor that comes with brutal presidential or vice presidential campaigning. He had no real executive experience. He had never run for a national office, having been appointed vice president by Nixon— and confirmed by Congress under the 25th Amendment—to replace Spiro Agnew, who had resigned the previous year in a financial scandal. He was a man of the House of Representatives, where from 1948 to 1973 he had represented his Grand Rapids, Michigan, district.

Haig also was somewhat ill-equipped. He had no legal, constitutional or political standing as a staff man. But as an Army officer he was used to taking orders and getting the job done. He had received his basic bureaucratic education in the school of maneuver and deception run by Henry Kissinger in the National Security Council staff where he had served as deputy.

That same day, Kissinger, now the secretary of state, told Haig, "We've got to quietly bring down the curtain on this charade."

Before he saw Ford, Haig met in his West Wing corner office with Nixon's White House Watergate lawyer, J. Fred Buzhardt, a diminutive, soft-spoken Southerner who had previously worked as Pentagon general counsel. Both were West Point graduates—Haig class of 1947, Buzhardt class of 1946. They had become close over the last year. It was a partnership in survival, forged in one surprise and crisis after another. What was the legal situation if Nixon resigned? Haig asked.

Buzhardt had been working on the issue and had a set of options to present to the vice president. All, with one exception, focused on Nixon—not Ford.

Haig felt it was sensible to concentrate on Nixon. He was still president. They served him, and, as Haig knew, Nixon was an exhaustive explorer of alternatives.

Buzhardt had thought out six possibilities. Five of them were actions that Nixon might take, and two of those included granting a pardon to himself. The sixth alternative: Nixon could resign and hope his successor, Ford, would pardon him. This last one was fleshed out more than the others, spelled out in detail.

"Here's what you should give him," Buzhardt said, handing Haig two sheets of yellow legal paper for the meeting with the vice president.

Ford was on the cusp of assuming the highest office in the land, the leadership of the free world, and Buzhardt was focused on what could be done

6

for Nixon. Haig realized that Buzhardt might be planting a pardon suggestion.

Before 9 a.m., Haig went to Ford's office.

Ford, then 61, had been vice president only eight months. A warm Midwesterner, whose speech was slow, deliberate—and at times awkward—Ford had been grafted onto the Nixon administration as a necessary afterthought. Under the Constitution, Nixon had to have a vice president. Nixon deemed his preferred choices too controversial, ideological or dynamic to win confirmation, especially former Texas Governor John Connally. "This left Jerry Ford," Nixon wrote in his memoirs. Nixon knew that Ford was loyal, a creature of the Republican Party, having served 24 years in the House, nine of those as Republican minority leader. To Nixon, Ford was basically a party chore boy who undertook unsavory tasks such as leading the unsuccessful effort in 1970 to impeach Supreme Court Justice William O. Douglas. With Nixon bogged down in his Watergate defense, Ford had been almost on his own as vice president, peripheral to the administration.

Ford had Robert Hartmann, a top aide and former newspaperman, with him when Haig arrived in the office. Haig detested and distrusted Hartmann. He had received reports from the Secret Service that Hartmann would drink late at night in his office. So Haig told Ford only that a new tape recording about to be released would present grave difficulties for Nixon in an impeachment trial.

Later in the day Haig called the vice president and asked for a second meeting, this time alone. Ford agreed. At 3:30 p.m. Haig entered the vice president's suite. He looked troubled and on edge. He had just read the transcripts of two tape recordings made six days after the June 17, 1972, Watergate break-in. Nixon ordered the cover-up. His case would collapse when the tapes were made public. There was a decorated screen in one corner of the room. Haig later said he was certain that Hartmann was stationed behind the screen to take notes in secret and to protect Ford, a charge both Hartmann and Ford categorically deny. But the air was filled with distrust.

"Are you ready, Mr. Vice President, to assume the presidency in a short period of time?"

Ford, absolutely stunned, said he was prepared.

Haig wanted his assessment of the situation, but Ford did not have a lot to say. "These are what the lawyers think," Haig told Ford, taking out the papers Buzhardt had given him.

The options for Nixon and others in the White House were numerous. Nixon could step aside temporarily under the 25th Amendment, he could just wait and delay the impeachment process, or he could try to settle for a formal censure. In addition, there were three pardon options. Nixon could pardon himself and resign. Or he could pardon the aides involved in Watergate and then resign.

Or, Haig said, Nixon could agree to leave in return for an agreement that the new president would pardon him. Haig handed Ford the papers. The first sheet contained a handwritten summary of a president's legal authority to pardon. The second sheet was a draft pardon form that only needed Ford's signature and Nixon's name to make it legal.

Haig asked for Ford's recommendation about what course Nixon might follow. Haig privately believed that this was a time for mercy if ever there were one. A pardon would be an act of simple humanity. It would spare the country a Senate trial that would create a destructive heritage of hatred and resentment. It would be patriotic and courageous, in his eyes.

Even if Haig offered no direct words on his views, the message was almost certainly sent. An emotional man, Haig was incapable of concealing his feelings; those who worked closely with him rarely found him ambiguous. In fact, Haig not only was incapable of hiding his feelings, he didn't try. It was part of his style—to convey his attitude, and not just through words.

Ford dwelled on the pardon possibilities.

"It is my understanding from a White House lawyer," Haig said, "that a president does have authority to grant a pardon even before criminal action has been taken against an individual." Of course, Nixon was the only major Watergate player against whom the special prosecutor had not taken criminal action.

At the end, the general stood up. The two put their arms around each other and shook hands.

"We've got to keep in contact," Haig said. "Things could break so fast that we have to be accessible to each other."

Haig then reported to Nixon on his meeting with Ford, mentioning that he had presented Ford with the six options as drafted by Buzhardt.

Nixon did not comment.

Ford summoned Hartmann. He extracted another solemn pledge of secrecy.

Hartmann promised.

Ford said Haig had reported that Nixon was going to resign because of new, damaging tapes. Haig had listed some alternatives for the endgame, among them the possibility that Nixon could agree to leave in return for an agreement that he, Ford, as president, would pardon Nixon.

"Jesus!" Hartmann said aloud. "What did you tell him?"

"I told him I needed time to think about it."

"You what?" Hartmann fairly shouted. Ford's willingness to entertain a discussion of a pardon was probably all Haig and Nixon wanted or needed. Even entertaining any agreement of resignation for a pardon, Hartmann believed, was outrageous. Ford had already committed a monstrous impropriety and the damage that had been done was irreversible. Hartmann felt it could taint a Ford presidency forever, linking even a voluntary resignation to discussions of an eventual pardon and perhaps an expectation, at least implied, of a pardon from Ford.

Ford didn't agree. Nothing had been promised. He wanted to talk to his wife, Betty.

Hartmann thought that was a good idea. She was noted for her independence and frankness, and Ford often sought her opinion on important matters. Mrs. Ford would see the danger, Hartmann believed. She could gently turn her husband off Haig more effectively than he could.

Late that night Ford told his wife about Haig's alternatives. She was firm in her view that her husband shouldn't get involved in making any recommendations at all. Not to Haig, not to Nixon, not to anybody. Ford seemed to get the message.

About 1:30 a.m., a late hour for Ford, he called Haig.

"Al, our discussion this afternoon, I hope you understand there was no agreement, no decision and no deal."

Haig hung up and went through about 30 minutes of anguish. Ford thought he had offered some deal? Haig finally phoned Buzhardt, rousing Nixon's lawyer from bed.

"Goddamnit," Haig told Buzhardt at what must have been around 2 a.m., "what did you do to me?" He reported that Ford had called at such an odd hour and what he had said. Haig noted that he had gone over the six alternatives with the vice president and done it all based on legal advice. Now Ford thinks it was some kind of "agreement" or "deal." Haig erupted, "Why did you, if this man thinks there was some deal offered, how the hell did you give me the advice you gave?" Haig felt he had been trapped. He was shocked and worried.

"I didn't do anything to you," Buzhardt replied. "Al, that's all we did was give the options."

Haig concluded there was somebody around Ford who was telling the vice president that he was being snookered. Or maybe it was even worse.

The next morning, Friday, August 2, Haig and Buzhardt discussed at length Ford's late night

11

phone call. They concluded that there was some real trouble brewing around Ford.

Over in the vice president's suite of offices in the Old Executive Office Building that morning Ford brought in a second aide, Jack Marsh, a former Virginia congressman, for advice on Haig's pardon conversation. Marsh, a careful, almost soulful political operative for Ford, was eager to know exactly what had happened. He had dropped in the previous day after Haig's second meeting, and Ford had been sitting alone with his hands on his knees, staring out into space. Marsh had never seen the vice president with such a grim expression. Ford looked like he had just been told that his house with all his family in it had burned to the ground, destroying everything and everyone.

"I want you to swear you will not reveal what I'm about to tell you," Ford said to Marsh.

Marsh assented.

Ford explained that the previous day Haig had said explicitly that new tapes were going to force Nixon's resignation. Ford went through the alternatives that Haig had presented, including the one in which Nixon resigned. "I then, what I would do, I would give Nixon a pardon," Ford said.

Marsh couldn't believe it. He tried to remain calm. He could see that Ford hoped he would say, It's the kind of thing, Jerry, you need to do. But Marsh saw the danger. "Look, you can't do this," he said gently.

Ford was standing. He slowly pulled the two pieces of yellow legal paper out of his pocket and handed them to Marsh. "You could make a strong case for a pardon, that it would be in the national interest," Ford said. He seemed to be advocating Haig's arguments for granting Nixon a pardon.

"You can't do that," Marsh said. It could look like or be a quid pro quo for Nixon's resignation.

Ford didn't see it.

Marsh knew that Ford could be stubborn once he made up his mind. He was concerned that without further advice, Ford might just go ahead with a pardon. Of the alternatives listed by Haig, Marsh could see that Ford was concentrating on the one that involved him. He was going to become president, and perhaps the best and smoothest way was to grant a pardon. Marsh said he had no problem with Ford considering a pardon but not while he was vice president. As the constitutional successor, he couldn't consider a pardon. He knew the law. It was illegal to offer anything of value—as a pardon surely would be—in exchange for a federal office. It shouldn't even be discussed, much less considered.

Marsh and Hartmann talked again to Ford.

Ford was now emotional, saying he had told Haig that Watergate had to stop, that it was tearing the country to pieces. With some contradiction, Ford said he had decided to go ahead and get it over with, so he had called Haig the previous night and told him they should do whatever they decided to do. It was all right with Ford, but there was no agreement.

Hartmann and Marsh were stunned. This version of Ford's call to Haig was significantly more alarming than what they had earlier heard. Both men tried to elicit what exact words had passed between Ford and Haig, but they couldn't get clear statements. Ford obviously just wanted the matter closed.

Marsh wondered if Haig might have concluded that a future pardon was still a viable option. Would he then use it as an inducement to get President Nixon to resign?

Of course not, Ford snapped. Haig knew better than that. There was no commitment, just conversation—and in strict confidence.

Hartmann and Marsh both lit into Ford like Dutch uncles.

Marsh was calmer. He said a Nixon resignation and a possible pardon had to be separated. They had to be de-linked. Discussing the two events in the same conversation made it difficult because that created linkage. It was hard to decouple them.

Hartmann decided that they had to figure out how to unmake an omelette. But Ford would not concede that there was an omelette to unmake.

Hartmann and Marsh left the vice president disturbed.

"We got to stop him," Marsh said. "We got to stop him cold right now."

Hartmann was worried that Ford had already decided to grant a pardon. They drew up a list of ten people that Ford might consult. Who might agree with them and be able to persuade Ford? They put Betty Ford at the top of the list, but they felt it would not be appropriate to enlist her. Second on the list was Bryce Harlow, a former Nixon White House

14

counselor and one of the wise old men of Republican politics.

At their request, Ford agreed to see Harlow.

Hartmann and Marsh poured out their fears to Harlow before he met with Ford. A small, charming, passionate but wordy man, Harlow listened to them and agreed. It was a disaster. The three went to see the vice president.

Haig was carrying out a mission for Nixon, Harlow said, and Ford was in grave danger of compromising his presidency and independence. He said the vice president had to protect himself and ensure that no one could cry deal if Ford later granted Nixon a pardon. "But the most urgent thing, Mr. Vice President," Harlow said, "is to tell Al Haig, straight out and unequivocally, that whatever discussions you and he had yesterday and last night were purely hypothetical and conversational, that you will in no manner, affirmatively or negatively, advise him or the president as to his future course, and nothing you may have said is to be represented to the president, or to anyone else, to the contrary."

It was a lawyer's mouthful. But Ford realized the three men were right. He had been naive. He agreed to call Haig to make it clear that he had never accepted the proffered deal. Harlow wrote out what he should say.

Ford called Haig and told him he had no intention of recommending what President Nixon should do about resigning or not resigning. Nothing they had talked about the previous afternoon should be given any consideration in whatever decision the president might make.

Haig said he agreed. But the second call was

not necessary because he had received the message in Ford's call the night before. Haig believed that the second call was a response to advice from Ford's staff, who in Haig's estimation were continuing to brainwash the vice president.

Afterwards, Hartmann, Marsh and Harlow had a drink together. They celebrated and declared that they had forced Ford to dodge a bullet. Hartmann was convinced that Ford had taken the yellow lined legal paper that Harlow had written outlining what Ford should say to Haig and put it down the toilet.

Ford still didn't want to believe that Haig had offered him a deal, but he accepted the judgment of his advisers that in practical terms the offer was effectively a deal. Whatever it was, Ford believed he had rejected it, an important distinction in his mind. Without acceptance the deal was not consummated.

Ford decided both he and Haig would be better off if they never again sat down and talked about the options. The heart of the matter, Ford believed, was that one way or the other Nixon was going to go. Ford's first concern was that he was about to become president—a job he had never sought. Now it was dropping in his lap. His second major worry was that he really didn't want to become president.

By that evening of August 2, 1974, Haig had a bigger problem. Nixon called to say he had changed his mind about resignation.

"Let them impeach me," Nixon told his chief of staff. "We'll fight it out to the end."

The next day, August 3, the vice president was traveling. In Hattiesburg, Mississippi, he held a press conference. The reporters were interested in Watergate. One noted that Ford's press secretary had mentioned that Ford had met with Haig two days earlier to discuss impeachment. What was going on and what was Ford's attitude?

"I have met with Al Haig," Ford said. "I don't think this is unusual." Rather than evade the question, the vice president lied. The purpose of the meeting, he said, was to discuss "what could be done, if anything, to convince the members of the House that the president was innocent as both of us feel."

Ford was apparently confident that the meetings and discussions with Haig would remain secret. If he answered truthfully, he would effectively declare the Nixon presidency over in Hattiesburg. So he told a whopper.

Later that day in New Orleans, asked again about the meeting with Haig, Ford once more deceived. "It was not an extraordinary meeting," he said, "if that's what you want me to say. It was an ordinary meeting of the kind that we frequently have and has no extraordinary implications."

Ford's statement was, of course, the opposite of what had occurred. It was more than extraordinary. The presidency would probably never be the same. Amid the uncertainty, distrust and secrecy of their small meetings, Nixon, Haig, Ford and three Ford advisers were reshaping the presidency, making the first decisions of a new era. Perhaps for the first time the presidency was to be considered a resignable office.

2

AT 3 A.M. WEDNESDAY, August 7, Hartmann got out of bed. His mind was churning. Nixon was going to resign in two days, and Ford had assigned Hartmann the task of drafting the speech he would give upon assuming the presidency. Hartmann believed it was the most important job he might ever have. He would have to find a way to bridge—but also divide—the Nixon past from the Ford future. In the clarity of the uninterrupted early morning hours, Hartmann came up with what he was certain was the proper rhetorical theme for Ford: "Our long national nightmare is over." It was a work of art, Hartmann believed, the centerpiece of a concept for the new Ford presidency, a firm declaration that America would be different, that Watergate and its multitude of poisons were passing from the governmental system and the political culture.

Proudly, Hartmann gave the speech draft to Ford, who promised to show it to Betty. The next day, Ford pulled the draft from his pocket.

"This is fine," Ford said, "this is just great except for this one sentence." He pointed to "My fellow Americans, our long national nightmare is over."

"Isn't that a little hard on Dick?" Ford asked.

"Oh, Jesus Christ Almighty!" Hartmann shouted in anguish. "Throw the whole rest of it away, just don't throw that sentence away."

His voice cracked. "That's the only thing that you're going to say that anybody will ever remember!" Promising the end of the nightmare will make it true, Hartmann felt. He expected it would be the headline and the lead in every story, or certainly in the first paragraph. Hartmann said it had been a nightmare for Nixon's friends and enemies, torn either by their role in defending a corrupt man or in destroying a Republican presidency. Hartmann virtually got on his knees and begged. He practically wept. He threatened, stopping short of saying he would quit. Hartmann couldn't have been driven out with whips. He saw himself as about to become number one to the new number one.

"Ummm," Ford finally said, "maybe you're right."

On Friday, August 9, 1974, Nixon formally resigned and Ford was sworn in as president. Speaking afterwards in the East Room, Ford promised a new era.

"I feel it is my first duty to make an unprecedented compact with my countrymen.

"I believe that truth is the glue that holds government together, not only our government but civilization itself.

"In all my public and private acts as your president, I expect to follow my instincts of openness and candor with full confidence that honesty is always the best policy in the end.

"My fellow Americans, our long national nightmare is over."

It was the phrase that did end up in all the news stories and accounts—a blunt acknowledgment that Nixon and Watergate were wrong. Nixon's much photographed departure by helicopter from the White House seemed to symbolize the end of the scandal.

The outpouring of goodwill toward Ford in the first week of his presidency was immense. There was a sense of cleansing and simplification. Nixon's crisis had created the feeling of national siege. Ford had punctured the tension. He brought enormous relief, promised to restore trust through his directness and informality. Even before being sworn in, Ford asked Haig to tell the Marine Band not to play "Hail to the Chief" or "Ruffles and Flourishes"; his alma mater's "Michigan Fight Song" would suffice. The morning of his first full day as president, he toasted his own English muffins. The muffins and the "Michigan Fight Song" became symbols of a new approach: the isolated and powerful imperial presidency was over. It needed to be over. The nation seemed to be falling in love with its new Midwestern president.

There was still one lingering matter: Nixon's future. Would the former president be prosecuted? The nation—or at least the media— seemed transfixed by the question. Some of Nixon's former aides went to work to keep him from jail. On August 27, Leonard Garment, a Nixon White House counsel and former law partner who had remained on the Ford legal staff, drafted a memo urging that Ford pardon Nixon the next day when his first press conference as president was scheduled. Garment, probably the most liberal of Nixon's former aides, argued that without an immediate pardon, Ford would lose control. The political costs down the road would be too great as pressure for prosecution mounted and the national mood of reconciliation diminished. "The whole miserable tragedy will be played out to God knows what ugly and wounding conclusion," Garment forecast, implying obliquely that Nixon might even take his own life.

Philip Buchen, Ford's former law partner, friend and now White House counsel, gave the memo to Ford but told the president that it was premature to consider a pardon.

Haig, who had stayed on temporarily as chief of staff, reported to Garment that Ford was going to announce a pardon at the press conference. "It's all set," Haig said, but then later in the day he told Garment that the lawyers had delayed it.

At his press conference, Ford made it clear that a pardon was an option. He also indicated strongly that he was not going to make a premature decision.

"In the last ten days or two weeks," Ford said, "I have asked for prayers for guidance on this very important point."

Hartmann's stomach turned to a knot. If Ford was not going to do anything, what was all the praying about?

After the press conference, Ford was seething with anger. He said to himself, "Goddamn it, I am not going to put up with this." Nixon was still haunting him.

Later that night, Ford was up in the residence clutching a glass of Jack Daniel's. He seemed to be staring 1,000 yards in the distance. He was amazed at all the focus on Nixon and the venom, the hate. Although nine of the 28 questions had been about Nixon's future, Ford thought all the questions or at least 90 percent of them had been about the former president. Ford felt he couldn't function as president if the Watergate obsession persisted. Nothing could compete with the raw drama of a former president, especially Nixon, trying to stay out of jail.

Ford wondered how he could direct the press to other issues. How could he control the emotions of the American people on the subject? What about Nixon? No one ever controlled him. How could he manage the legal process that was in the hands of Special Prosecutor Jaworski? How would he establish his own legitimacy?

Two days after the press conference, Friday, August 30, Ford met with Haig, Hartmann, Marsh and Buchen in the Oval Office. He swore all to secrecy. Pausing, Ford carefully filled his pipe with tobacco. He said he was strongly inclined to pardon Nixon.

There was silence. Hartmann focused on the antique clock. Its loud tick seemed like a burst of machine-gun fire.

Haig couldn't believe the good news. He almost had to pinch himself. He tried to excuse himself. Ford waved him back into his seat.

Ford said he didn't believe the public would want Nixon jailed. If perhaps years down the road Nixon was found guilty, the public might clamor for a pardon. Why wait? "My mind is 99 percent made up," Ford said.

The old Ford hands realized that meant 100 percent; the decision had been made.

Ford had to take a phone call, and Haig left. Hartmann darted into his adjoining office to retrieve the transcripts of Ford's press conference. Waving the papers at the president, Hartmann said, "Here are your own words...'until any legal process has been undertaken, I think it is unwise and untimely for me to make any commitment.' And you answered that 'until it gets to me, I make no commitment.' "

Ford's jaw tightened. He noted that Hartmann had left out the part where Ford had said he wouldn't rule out a pardon.

"Well, okay," Hartmann replied. "Maybe that's what you meant, but that isn't what I heard or what most people heard. What everybody believes is that you may pardon Nixon some day but *not* right away. And not until there have been some further legal steps in the case." A pardon now would seem to be a sudden and unexplainable reversal.

Ford grew testy. Hartmann thought he was going to be physically ejected from the office.

Marsh too was deeply worried. He went to see Ford, who was in his study off the Oval Office, having lunch alone, reading and eating ice cream for dessert.

"You may want to throw me out of this office," Marsh said. "I don't want you to misunderstand me." He reminded Ford of when Haig had proposed a pardon in exchange for Nixon's resignation. Ford had rejected the proposal, but what if he now pardoned Nixon, and the press learned of the Haig proposal? Well, Marsh said directly, it could be a huge problem. "Questions are going to be raised about a deal," he said.

Ford stopped eating. "Jack," Ford said, "I know exactly where you're coming from and I have thought of that and there was no deal."

Marsh was reassured. He tended to believe Ford. But Marsh said there would be a firestorm of public outrage if the press ever learned about the conversation with Haig. A pardon now, so soon after that discussion, would increase the risk of linkage.

"One," Ford said firmly, "I know and understand the risks, and two, there was no deal."

Ford called in Benton Becker, 36, a longtime friend and former Justice Department attorney who had assisted him during his years in the House. He asked Becker to determine exactly what a president's pardon powers were even prior to indictment or conviction. In addition, he assigned Becker to help determine what should be done with Nixon's papers and tapes. Nixon wanted them shipped to him in California. Traditionally a former president owned all his papers.

"You will be writing the history of your presidency in the first weeks," Becker told Ford, "and history is going to say Jerry Ford participated in the final act of the Watergate cover-up." He was intentionally hitting Ford hard, knowing that Ford was the ultimate Republican team player who would want to help Nixon—with a pardon and by sending his papers out to California.

Ford stiffened.

"There will be one hell of a bonfire out there in California and that is *exactly* what the history will write about your administration—no matter what happens for the next two and a half years, whatever you do." Becker kept pounding on the issue.

"That history must be preserved," Ford finally said at another meeting. He put his arm around Becker. "Do whatever you have to do, but it must be preserved. I'm not shipping this stuff out."

In his research on presidential pardons, Becker found a 1915 Supreme Court case, *Burdick* v. *United States*. The Court's ruling stated that a pardon "carries an imputation of guilt, acceptance, a confession of it." Becker explained the Burdick precedent to Ford. If they could get Nixon to accept the pardon, they would have a confession, an acknowledgment that Nixon was guilty of criminal conduct.

"You make sure that Richard Nixon understands that case too," Ford told Becker. "That he understands that our position, the White House position, will be his acceptance is an acknowledgment of guilt." Becker had to get Nixon to accept. "Make sure there's an acceptance," Ford said. "I don't want to be embarrassed."

Ford said he was no longer merely considering a pardon. He had decided to do it if he could.

Herbert J. Miller, one of Washington's foremost criminal defense attorneys, took a call at home on a Saturday from one of Nixon's former aides, Richard Moore.

Would you represent Richard Nixon? Moore asked.

"If I said no," Miller said, "I'd have to resign from the bar." Miller was a lifelong Republican who nonetheless had headed the criminal division of Bobby Kennedy's Justice Department in the early 1960s. He had unusual bipartisan credibility.

In early September, Miller walked into Nixon's office in San Clemente to tell him that Ford was likely to grant a pardon. They began hours and hours of discussion.

Nixon was opposed to accepting the pardon. He felt it would imply some kind of guilt. In the public mind the necessity of a pardon would make him culpable.

Miller knew Nixon's desperate financial situation. If indicted by the special prosecutor, Nixon would have attorneys' fees that would bankrupt him, Miller said. He had taken as much physically and emotionally as he could. He should accept a pardon for the well-being of himself and his family. Given the saturation news coverage of Watergate, Miller said, there was no way the former president could get a fair trial if indicted. "How in God's name could you find an impartial jury?" he asked.

Miller felt any attempt to jail the former president would make the United States look like a Latin American banana republic.

A few days later, Ford decided to send Becker to meet with Nixon and Miller in San Clemente to see what could be worked out on Nixon's papers and tapes, in addition to a possible statement from Nixon if Ford granted a pardon.

Becker and Miller took an Air Force jet and arrived about midnight, which was 3 a.m. Washington time. Nixon's former press secretary, Ronald Ziegler, greeted them coldly at Nixon's compound, the former so-called Western White House situated on a bluff overlooking the Pacific Ocean.

"I can tell you right now," Ziegler told Becker, "that President Nixon will make *no* statement of admission or complicity in return for a pardon from Jerry Ford."

"Can you tell me how to reach the Air Force pilot that brought me here," Becker replied, "so that I can instruct him to take me back to Washington?"

Miller calmed everyone down.

The next day they reached agreement on joint custody of the Nixon papers and tapes. It was a complicated arrangement that would allow Nixon to destroy the tapes after ten years and gain sole custody over his papers after three years.

Ziegler produced a draft of a statement that Nixon would be willing to issue accepting the pardon. The draft emphasized the pressure of the presidency, Nixon's reliance on his staff, how he should have delegated less even though he was focused on foreign affairs.

Becker said no statement would be better.

Miller dictated some ideas. Nixon reviewed it. They went back and forth until a fourth statement was presented to Becker.

In that version, Nixon accepted the pardon and said, "I was wrong in not acting more decisively and more forthrightly in dealing with Watergate."

Becker argued for language acknowledging obstruction of justice.

Miller would not begin to agree since his client categorically denied he had obstructed justice. Miller's goal was to make sure that Nixon did not say that he had committed a crime.

Becker wanted some reference to the period when justice had been obstructed, and eventually Miller agreed to add that Nixon was "wrong," particularly when Watergate reached "the stage of judicial proceedings." Becker thought that phrase at least obliquely meant obstruction of justice.

Miller knew it didn't.

The draft also contained the standard "mistakes were made" language that Nixon had used for years, putting off the blame on others.

Becker insisted that two words be added—"my own."

Miller agreed, but it was in a long paragraph that said: "I know that many fair-minded people believe that my motivations and actions in the Watergate affair were intentionally self-serving and illegal. I now understand how *my own* mistakes and misjudgments have contributed to that belief and seemed to support it."

Many fair-minded people did believe Nixon's actions were illegal, Miller realized, but the statement did not say Nixon was one of them.

Finally, a long, six-paragraph statement was agreed upon about 5 p.m. on Friday, September 6. Becker told Ziegler that he needed to see Nixon to make certain he understood

Ford's position on the acceptance of the pardon.

Ziegler said he and Miller had explained it to Nixon. No meeting would be necessary.

Miller again intervened. There would be no harm if Becker went to see the former president, he said.

Becker walked alone some 40 yards to Nixon's office in the hacienda-style compound. He had never met the former president but had an indelible image of him from decades of watching television. As Becker entered, Nixon rose shakily from behind his desk. The former president's arms and body were so thin and frail that his head seemed disproportionately, even grotesquely large. His shirt seemed too big at the neck. The famous Nixon jowls were exaggerated, the face deeply wrinkled. His hair was disheveled, his fingernails yellowish. Nixon, then 61, looked about 85. He was stooped and seemed to almost jump with fright at seeing Becker.

The walls were stripped bare. Behind the desk were American and presidential flags on either side.

"We've accomplished a lot of very important things here, Mr. President," Becker said, adding that history would benefit from the papers and tapes agreement. "I want to talk with you about the possibility of President Ford issuing a pardon to you."

The mention of pardon seemed to produce anxiety in Nixon, as if he didn't want to discuss it. He walked around his desk, then sat down in a chair next to Becker.

"Big fella," Nixon said, "have you played football?"

"Long, long time ago," Becker replied.

Becker turned back to the matter of pardon. He explained the 1915 Burdick case, noting that it gave Nixon the right to reject the pardon. The full power of the law would back Nixon up if he wanted to reject. However, the case also made it clear that acceptance was a confession of guilt. Becker wanted to make sure Nixon understood. "Acceptance is an acknowledgment of guilt, Mr. President," Becker said. "Those are not my words, those are the words of the United States Supreme Court."

Nixon gave Becker a look of understanding but also puzzlement. "Did you ever work in my administration?" the former president inquired.

"No," Becker said. "But I do live in Washington."

"How are the Redskins going to do this year?" Nixon asked about the capital's professional football team.

Becker said he didn't know. He returned to the Burdick case. "That's what the U.S. Supreme Court says and that's what President Ford's White House will say. I've given a copy of *Burdick* to your counsel. Jack's got a copy, and I'm sure you can read it at your leisure."

"I understand," Nixon said as if dismissing the obvious. "I'm free to say no. Free to say no."

Becker thanked Nixon. He said he appreciated the courtesies they had showed him, and he walked out. As Becker was getting his briefcase and papers together, Ziegler approached.

"The president wants to see you again," he said.

Aw, man, Becker thought, he's going to take

it back, wreck days of intense work. He went back into Nixon's small office.

Nixon, still in his coat and tie, stood behind his chair, which he had pushed to his desk.

"Before you left," the former president said, "I wanted to give you something. You've been a gentleman, and I appreciate that. I've seen enough bullies in the last months." With his frail arms he gestured to the empty walls. "I wanted to give you something," he repeated; in a tone of distress, near tears, he added, "but they took it all away from me. Everything I had is gone." He reached down to a drawer and took out two little boxes. "Pat found these for me in the jewelry box, and I want you to have these. There aren't any more of these in the world."

"Mr. President," Becker said, taking the boxes, which contained a Richard Nixon signature tiepin and a pair of presidential seal cufflinks, "you don't have to do this."

"I want to do this," Nixon said.

Becker shook his hand and turned toward the door. He then glanced back at Nixon, who was leaning forward over his desk. Becker realized that it was a mirror image of the famous picture of Jack Kennedy from the back leaning over in the Oval Office—The Loneliest Job in the World. Kennedy's frailties had been largely hidden in his lifetime. Nixon was exposed, almost naked to the world.

Becker showed the cufflinks to Miller.

"He really is in a very depressed state, isn't he?" Becker said.

"Yes," Miller said, "sometimes he can be very difficult to work with."

31

After returning to Washington, Becker went to the White House to brief Ford on the pardon and papers-tapes agreements.

Ford asked about Nixon's condition.

"Deeply, deeply depressed," Becker said. "More depressed than any person I've ever seen, lacking any will to survive." Noting he was not a medical doctor, and leaving open the possibility that the meeting was a little demonstration to win sympathy, Becker added, "I really have serious questions in my mind whether that man is going to be alive at the time of the election."

"Well," Ford noted, "1976 is a long time away."

"I don't mean 1976," Becker said, "I mean 1974." That was two months away.

Ford read the draft statement that Nixon had agreed to issue: "I was wrong in not acting more decisively and more forthrightly.

"No words can describe the depth of my regret and pain at the anguish my mistakes over Watergate have caused...my own mistakes and misjudgments...."

This was more personal responsibility than Nixon had ever accepted in public, even when he resigned.

Haig asked Becker, only half-joking, "Did you put a gun to his head?"

Later that night Ford leaned back in his large chair, stretched out and placed his hands behind his head. He recited his reasons for granting the pardon.

Hartmann persisted. "What's the rush? Why must it be tomorrow? Why not Christmas Eve, or a year from now, when things quiet down?" Ford had been president for less than a month.

Ford said every time he had a press conference, he would be asked whether he was going to pardon Nixon. "How am I going to answer it?"

"That's easy," Hartmann said. "Just tell them you haven't decided."

"But I *have* decided," the president replied.

Hartmann was amazed, and thought of saying, "Jerry, if you can't be any more of a liar than that you shouldn't be president." But he held his tongue.

Sunday morning, September 8, Ford went to the 8 a.m. service at St. John's Episcopal Church on Lafayette Square across from the White House. He sat alone and took Holy Communion. Back at the Oval Office, he reviewed the draft of the pardon statement he planned to read on television that morning. Taking a felt-tip pen, he inserted a phrase saying that possible prosecution was "threatening Nixon's health."

Ford then turned to Hartmann. "You know, if I decided to do it and then something happened to him and I hadn't done it because I was just waiting for a better time, I would never be able to forgive myself."

An hour before Ford was to go on television, Jerry terHorst, Ford's press secretary and a friend of 25 years, came to the Oval Office. He had just learned of the pardon decision the day before, and he had come to submit a letter to Ford saying he was resigning as a matter of conscience.

Ford read the letter: "Try as I can, it is impossible to conclude that the former president is more deserving of mercy than persons of lesser station in life whose offenses have had far less effect on our national well-being."

Ford saw there was nothing he could do to talk his old friend out of leaving. He knew ter-Horst's resignation would add substantially to the inevitable controversy.

At 11:05 a.m. President Ford turned to the camera. Of Nixon and his family, Ford said, "Theirs is an American tragedy in which we all have played a part. It could go on and on and on, or someone must write the end to it. I have concluded that only I can do that, and if I can I must."

The core reason for the decision, he said, was to put both Nixon and Watergate in the past. In essence, the nightmare was continuing. He called the renewed public focus on Watergate "bad dreams that continue to reopen a chapter that is closed."

He added, "I feel that Richard Nixon and his loved ones have suffered enough." He then read his proclamation, granting Nixon a full pardon for all crimes he committed or may have committed while president.

The new president had misjudged the mood. Rather than sympathy, the public and media voiced outrage at Ford. The pardon seemed to be on Nixon's terms—early, complete and without acknowledgment that he had committed crimes or even impeachable offenses. It also was a total surprise. There had been no preparation with the Congress or the public. Ford's action seemed to contradict his own public statements that suggested he would wait. Ford claimed he acted in the interests of the country. But he included in the announcement the phrase voicing compassion, even tenderness, for Nixon and his family.

One day not long after the pardon, David Kennerly, the new White House photographer and a close Ford friend, was in the Oval Office with the president. Ford had his hands in his pockets and was looking at the seal of office, the large eagle.

"You know the only job I really ever wanted was Speaker of the House," Ford said with a note of melancholy. "I never thought I'd be standing here."

Later Kennerly joked with Ford about the pardon. "What did you think, that by pardoning Nixon on an early Sunday morning no one would notice?"

Ford laughed. He was not defensive at first. He was convinced that it was the right thing to do.

On September 16, eight days after the pardon, Ford held his second press conference. Out of 21 questions, 15 were about the pardon or Nixon. Instead of putting Watergate behind and healing the wounds, Ford had rubbed salt in them, plunging the country back into the nightmare he had declared over.

An outcry in Congress about the pardon and suspicions of a deal or secret reason for the pardon continued, and some House members wanted an investigation. Written questions were sent to the White House for answers.

One question was: "Did you ever discuss the pardon with any member of the Nixon staff prior to the time you became president?"

Phil Buchen, the White House counsel and Ford's former law partner, prepared the draft answers, and to that question he wrote no.

Jack Marsh saw the draft answers and went to see Ford alone. He didn't have to remind the president of the still secret meeting with Haig on August 1, and Haig's offer of a deal. Only Ford, his wife, Marsh, Hartmann and Bryce Harlow knew about the offer. "You can't sign that," Marsh told Ford.

"I know," Ford said.

The questions had come from a subcommittee headed by Representative William Hungate, a Missouri Democrat. Marsh and Hungate had started in Congress the same year.

"You know," Ford said, "the best way to handle this is maybe just to go up there." Maybe he should make a personal appearance before the congressional committee, testify and lance the boil.

Marsh liked the idea.

"How well do you know Carl Albert?" Ford asked, referring to the Speaker of the House, an Oklahoma Democrat.

"I know Carl well," Marsh said. Years before he had served in the House as a conservative Democrat from Virginia. Although he had switched his party affiliation in 1970, he still had a warm acquaintance with the speaker.

Albert was also one of those who had strongly

recommended to Nixon that he pick Ford as his vice president when Agnew resigned in 1973. Marsh felt that Albert's recommendation may have been key to promoting Ford to the vice presidency.

"Jack, go up and see Carl and get Carl's view on what he thinks I ought to do," Ford said. Both Ford and Marsh knew that Albert could control any appearance.

Marsh prepared a one-page summary, including a factual statement that Haig had met with then-President Ford on August 1 to discuss options, among them a presidential pardon. He then took the summary to Albert.

Albert read it and laid it down on the desk.

"Jack," the speaker said, "let me tell you something. The greatest thing that Ford brings to the presidency is integrity and his reputation for honesty." Some of the matters leading up to the pardon are troublesome, he said. "But it's easy to get rid of it. Tell him to come on up here. He isn't going to get hurt, because the most important thing for the United States is the success of Jerry Ford as president. He isn't going to be hurt."

Marsh considered it a firm promise of no rough treatment. The speaker would be watching to make sure nothing got out of hand. Marsh reported to Ford.

"Okay, let's do it," the president said.

Marsh next went to see Hungate, who was getting dressed in the House gym. They found Peter Rodino, the New Jersey Democrat who headed the Judiciary Committee. The three men worked out the arrangements. Ford would take no oath, and the questioning would only be done by subcommittee members with each allowed just five minutes.

Marsh had significant missionary work to do with Phil Buchen, who had not known of the August 1 events. Marsh thought Buchen might resign. Coming in the wake of terHorst's resignation, Buchen's quitting would be a disaster. They had to keep him on board.

When he learned of the August 1 Ford-Haig meeting, Buchen realized that Haig had rather skillfully planted the pardon seed. His biggest concern was what Ford would say in his testimony. He went to see the president.

"You'd better put those meetings up front in your statement," Buchen told Ford. "You've got to tell what you thought of them."

Ford said he did not make a deal with Haig, but that after the Haig meeting, Marsh, Hartmann and Bryce Harlow had convinced him that Haig had offered a deal, although one was never consummated.

Buchen set about drafting Ford's statement, disclosing the Haig meeting and stating Ford's conclusion about the offer of a deal.

Fred Buzhardt, Nixon's White House lawyer who remained on Ford's legal staff, read the prepared testimony. On Saturday morning he called Haig at home. Haig was about to depart for Europe as the NATO commander—the position to which Ford had appointed him.

"Al," Buzhardt said, "I think you'd better come over to the White House. These boys have prepared sworn testimony for the president that could very well result in your indictment."

Furious, nearly out of control, Haig got in his car and drove to the White House to see Buchen and Marsh, insisting he be allowed to read the draft testimony.

Indeed it said that Haig had offered Ford the presidency in return for a pardon for Nixon, and that Ford had rejected the offer in phone calls the night of August 1 and the afternoon of August 2.

"Whoever wrote this testimony," Haig said, "is setting the president up to tell a lie. I won't be a part of it." He demanded to see the president at once.

They told him it was not possible. Marsh said there was no reason for concern.

"I will either see Ford immediately," Haig threatened, "or I will call a press conference right now, right here in the White House press room." He said fiercely he would expose the role of Ford's friends and aides to hurt Nixon and drive him from office. He described "a secret effort by Ford people to hurry Nixon out of the presidency behind Jerry Ford's back."

Within minutes Haig was in the Oval Office meeting with the president.

"Al, what's this about?" Ford asked.

"Did you read the testimony your boys have concocted? They're going to put me in jail for something that's totally wrong." Not only would it lead to charges against Haig but it would fuel suspicions that two presidents—Nixon and Ford—had conspired in a deal.

"What do you want?" Ford asked.

"The truth," Haig replied. "That's all."

"You'll have it, Al," Ford said. He handed Haig a yellow legal tablet. "You write that portion as you remember," the president said.

Haig did. It stated that no deal was offered.

Everything about the conclusions of Hartmann, Marsh, Harlow and eventually Ford, that Haig offered a deal, was excised from the testimony.

Ford and Marsh worked almost every day for the first two weeks of October on Ford's testimony. Just before the hearing, Marsh went with Ford to Kansas and the two worked in the hotel there until about midnight on the opening statement, essentially a speech that ran dozens of pages.

The meetings with Haig on August 1 were laid out in detail, focusing on the benign interpretation of the listing of six options. Nothing about Hartmann's, Marsh's or Harlow's interpretation was mentioned. Nor was Ford's late night phone conversation with Haig included.

"I was determined not to make any recommendations to President Nixon on his resignation," Ford's testimony read in final form. "For that reason, Mr. Chairman, I decided I should call General Haig the afternoon of August 2."

There was nothing about the various concerns of an offered deal.

On Thursday morning, October 17, Ford and Marsh rode up together to the hearing. The stakes couldn't be higher, Marsh thought; it all could go down the tubes here. He looked over at the president, who seemed to be having similar thoughts.

President Ford appeared before Congressman Hungate's subcommittee in room 2141 of the Rayburn House Office Building. It was the first documented appearance of a sitting president before a congressional committee. Ford read his statement for 43 minutes, and he answered questions for an hour.

Ford did say, after Representative Elizabeth Holtzman, a Democrat from New York, raised the issue, "I want to assure you, the members of this subcommittee, the members of Congress, and the American people there was no deal, period, under no circumstances."

"President Denies Any Deal on Pardon," read the banner headline in *The Washington Post*. The news story noted that Ford only added one new fact in the testimony—the Ford-Haig meetings on August 1. "Mr. Ford testified that Haig told him White House staff members were considering half a dozen options that Mr. Nixon might follow," the *Post* story said, "and that one of them was that he might resign and be pardoned."

No one went further. Ford had hidden the real story in plain sight.

That did not end the House inquiry, however. The subcommittee had subpoenas outstanding to a number of the players, including Haig.

But on November 22, the Republicans moved to close down the investigation. Chairman Hungate and two other Democrats joined the Republicans to close the inquiry, and it carried by a 6–3 vote.

Ford, like many presidents, believed what he wanted to believe. The presidency gives the holder a unique power to project an explanation. There was no deal on the pardon because Ford said so. He claimed it repeatedly, and there was no hard evidence to contradict him. But Ford's explanation was never satisfactory.

The new president held powerful cards. Ford could have leveraged his constitutional power to grant the pardon, to force Nixon to make a fuller confession and apology. He could have settled some of the basic questions that Nixon then went on to debate for two decades. A shadow of suspicion was cast over Ford.

3

WATERGATE HAD placed an inexperienced executive in the presidency. Ford was unaccustomed to the high level of scrutiny. He was used to a congressional lifestyle, which often included alcohol at lunch. This habit proved particularly embarrassing for Ford when he gave a luncheon speech. Once, in Denver, he skipped several dozen pages of his remarks because he had what his aides called a few "marts," for martinis, before speaking. Early in the presidency, when Ford put his drink down at a reception, his personal aide took it. Some real friction developed between the president and several of his aides over the issue. Finally William Lukash, the White House physician, went to Ford with some blunt advice.

"You're president of the United States," Lukash told Ford; "stop drinking. Especially stop drinking martinis at lunch."

Don Penny, Ford's professional humor writer, was trying to cure Ford of speaking in his natural, deadly slow, Midwestern, slightly nasal monotone. In one speech Ford had talked about ballistic missiles and deterrence. It came out as if Ford were trying to have "insurance" for the missiles.

Penny asked David Kennerly, the White House photographer, what had happened.

"Well, Don, he had a couple of martinis."

"You mean he drank before the speech?"

Yes, Kennerly said.

Penny forced a confrontation with Ford, who permitted Penny to be both irreverent and frank.

Ford eventually took the advice, and he cut back.

"Why'd you pardon Nixon?" Penny asked Ford once late in the presidency.

"I had to get rid of him!" Ford replied. "I couldn't get the work done. Everybody was busy trying to crucify the guy. And I finally said to people, 'Enough already! Pardon him.' And Phil Buchen said, 'On what basis?' And I said, 'I don't care. Get him out of here. I can't do this job until people stop. Enough.' "

"Well," Penny replied, taken with Ford's

burst of frustration, "if you'd say it to the American people the way you just said it to me, there'd be no doubt."

But Ford never found the voice to say it that way, or to convey how he felt that the public and press outrage over the pardon had weakened his ability to govern.

Ford had to lead in spite of the constraints placed on a president after Vietnam and Watergate. Congress had passed bills limiting the two most important areas of presidential decision making: budget making and warmaking. It was as if the presidency were being penalized for the excesses and sins of Nixon and Lyndon Johnson. One of the most shocking developments for Ford was that his defense secretary, James Schlesinger, a prickly intellectual who had been promoted to the defense post in 1973 by Nixon in one of the Watergate cabinet shuffles, disobeyed his orders—a conclusion Ford avoided in his memoirs.

In late April 1975, as Vietnam was falling, Ford felt that he was powerless. It was almost nine months after he had assumed the presidency, and he could neither mobilize the Congress nor the public. On the final day he sat in the Oval Office receiving reports of the last Americans escaping by helicopter from the U.S. Embassy in Saigon. It was his saddest day as president. He ordered Schlesinger to send U.S. aircraft to evacuate as many South Vietnamese as possible. Schlesinger disagreed with the decision and did not send the aircraft. Ford took note of the flat-out insubordination. There was no question in his mind that Schlesinger had outright disobeyed him. But the fall of Vietnam was tough enough to handle, so he avoided a confrontation.

Two weeks later, in May 1975, Cambodian forces seized the American merchant ship SS *Mayaguez*, which had a crew of 39. During a 65-hour crisis, Ford ordered a successful rescue mission, although 41 American servicemen were killed in the operation. Ford also ordered Schlesinger to launch four military air strikes into Cambodia as punishment. Schlesinger, who did not favor the punitive strikes, reported that the first strike was completed, and Ford assumed his orders would be followed and the other three would take place.

At the end of the crisis, Ford learned through the military reports that none of the strikes had been carried out. Not only had the secretary of defense ignored his orders, he had never given the commander in chief of the armed forces an accurate report. Schlesinger's insubordination was almost too shocking for Ford to contemplate. But the public deemed the rescue mission a huge success, lifting the national mood after the Vietnam debacle. Ford's approval ratings shot up 11 points. Once again he avoided dealing with the defense secretary.

Finally, five months later, Ford decided to fire Schlesinger. He planned to argue that he needed his own team. On Sunday morning, November 2, he summoned Schlesinger to the Oval Office, planning to face him down and list his various acts of insubordination.

"Jim," Ford said, "I'm anxious to get my

own cabinet. I'd like to make some changes and it involves you."

"Are you firing me?" Schlesinger asked directly.

"If you put it that way, yes," the president replied.

Schlesinger got up and walked out before the president had a chance to make his case—a final act of insubordination in Ford's eyes.

For his part, Schlesinger realized that he had disobeyed Ford, so there was reason to fire him. He just felt that these were important enough matters to quarrel with and stand up to the president.

But the unpublicized breakdown of the military chain of command was, as a practical matter, perhaps the worst and most significant scandal of the Ford presidency—one that neither Ford nor Schlesinger should have allowed to continue for a minute. It was the height of the Cold War, and the United States had just lost a war for the first time. The Soviet Union looked strong and formidable, the U.S. military weak and demoralized. That the president and the secretary of defense could not agree on who was in charge was appalling. Someone who had campaigned for president nationally or had come up through the executive ranks as a governor would not have tolerated the situation.

Part of Ford's approach in the 1976 presidential election was to ignore Nixon and Watergate. At an April 29, 1976, press conference, he said, "Well, it's my judgment that is an unfortunate era, certainly the period that took place from 1971 or 1973 on, and I think the more that all of us forget that period and the unfortunate developments, the better.

"I think it's better for all of us to just not remind ourselves of that unfortunate period. I do it deliberately."

In contrast, Ford's Democratic opponent, Jimmy Carter, subtly used Watergate to his benefit, calling the past four years the "Nixon-Ford administration" without specifically mentioning the scandal. Candidate Carter also kept hammering Ford at the slightest sign of ethical wrongdoing. When it was revealed in the summer of 1976 that FBI Director Clarence Kelley had FBI carpenters put up $335 worth of window valances in his house, Carter criticized Ford for letting Kelley stay in his post. "The director of the FBI ought to be purer than Caesar's wife," Carter said. "When people throughout the country, particularly young people, see Richard Nixon cheating, lying and leaving the highest office in disgrace...when you see the head of the FBI break a little law and stay there, it gives everybody the sense that crime must be okay. If the big shots in Washington can get away with it, well so can I."

The Watergate shadow got worse for Ford in September. News leaked on September 21 that the fourth and last Watergate special prosecutor, Charles F. C. Ruff, had subpoenaed records to see if Ford had accepted improper cash payments from a small maritime union. Ford felt the facts weren't there to justify Ruff's action, but he was unsure of what to do. He couldn't talk to the attorney general because he had promised never to interfere with an investigation. He was reluctant to challenge the special prosecutor since that would reek of Nixon and the Saturday Night Massacre. But he thought Ruff was pro-Carter, playing politics and taking more damn time than he should have.

After talking with the influential Washington lawyer Edward Bennett Williams, Ford decided to make his case to the people. On September 30, the president told the press he had complete confidence that Ruff's probe would find him innocent. "There is a saying in the law that 'justice delayed is justice denied,' " Ford said. He wanted Ruff either to shut up or make his case.

Six days later, the FBI interrogated Ford in the president's San Francisco hotel suite, where he was preparing for the second presidential debate with Carter. His aides saw that the president was distracted and upset a day before the most critical moment of the campaign. At the debate, Ford made a serious blunder, claiming, "There is no Soviet domination of Europe, and there never will be in a Ford administration." Carter jumped on the gaffe, pointing out that there were Soviet troops occupying much of Eastern Europe, and Ford plummeted in the polls. Ford's advisers felt the FBI interview was at least in part responsible for the president's poor showing.

On October 13, Ruff finally gave Ford the vindication he had been seeking, declaring the case closed. But the damage had been done. Ford believed the foul aroma of Watergate had been injected unfairly into the campaign, blunting the momentum of his election drive. In

November, Ford lost the presidency by 2 percent, and he left wondering if the pardon of Nixon was the deciding factor.

After the election, Ford had General Haig, now the NATO commander, to the Oval Office for a meeting alone. Haig thought that Ford had grown as president, almost, but not quite, attaining the stature of the office.

For Haig, the pardon had been the seminal act of the Ford presidency. It was above all an act of loyalty to Nixon.

The president threw his arm around Haig. He felt it best that he and Haig not reminisce about the pardon at all. Both would be better off that way.

"Al," Ford said, "this is a very sad time for me. I never really wanted the job. And it was only in the last year or so that I realized that I could do it. And the tragedy is that when I really wanted it, I lost it."

Hartmann published his memoir in 1980 and spoke often on the Ford presidency. He thought that all anyone remembered was that Ford had not been elected in the first place, that he had pardoned Nixon, and that in 1976 he had lost his own election. For Hartmann, the pardon was the hinge on which the understanding of the Ford presidency would open and shut. Ford could never disentangle himself from suspicions about a pardon deal. It was the inhibiting factor of Ford's presidency, Hartmann believed.

In the years afterwards, Nixon campaigned

actively for his version of Watergate. Nixon told British journalist David Frost in a series of 1977 television interviews, "I said things that were not true. Most of them were fundamentally true on the big issues." So he hadn't really lied. "If they want me to get down and grovel on the floor, no. Never. Because I don't believe I should."

"I let down my friends. I let down the country." His political life was over. He had botched things up and had made bad judgments. "I did not commit a crime, an impeachable offense."

Jack Miller, his attorney, realized that Nixon had laid the conditions for his comeback. The launching pad for Nixon's case was simple. He had committed no crimes and no impeachable offenses.

In the end, Ford wasn't sure if Nixon had actually committed a crime. But he was certain that Nixon had committed an impeachable offense—so much so that if Nixon had gone to trial in the Senate and Ford had been in the Senate at the time, he would have voted to convict and remove him from office. Ford felt that those like himself who lived in the arena at the time and had personal hands-on involvement could best understand and judge Nixon.

By 1997—more than 25 years after the Watergate burglary that propelled Ford to the presidency—I had reviewed many of the newspaper stories about his presidency, read the memoirs, had my assistant, Jeff Glasser, spend days reading the files and papers of Ford and his aides stored in Ford's presidential library in Ann Arbor, Michigan, and we had interviewed all the key players. How could it be sorted out? The full story had not been told, as it never is. Was it possible to interrogate this historical record? Attempt to square it all? I arranged to go see Ford. In my years of covering Watergate, even matters that took place during the Ford presidency and all the subsequent years in Washington, I had never interviewed or talked to Ford. We met in a suite at the Waldorf Towers in New York City on September 22, 1997. Ford was there for a board of directors meeting. At the age of 84 he was in good shape and his memory seemed sound. His speech was slow; his mild and decent approach to life was apparent. We sat down and I turned on my tape recorder. No one else was in the room. The Secret Service detail was across the hall.

Ford spoke—there is no other way to describe it—fondly of Nixon. When he had come to the House of Representatives in 1949, a dark-haired fellow, then beginning his second term in the House, came up and said, "I'm Dick Nixon. I'm glad to meet you." They had become friends and stayed friends in the 1950s and 1960s. Yes, Ford said, Nixon committed impeachable offenses. But the real problem with the Nixon presidency, he claimed, was the officiousness and dominance of Nixon's aides—H. R. "Bob" Haldeman, John D. Ehrlichman and Charles W. Colson.

"Fortunately, I knew Dick Nixon better than they did and I knew he didn't operate that way. This was a group of people who were distorting, really, many of the Nixon ideas, plans, etc."

I was astonished, given the monumental record and the dozens of hours of Watergate tapes then available that showed Nixon directing the cover-up and other unsavory activities. We got around to his decision to pardon Nixon. Ford confirmed that Haig had offered a deal, but said he had rejected it when he called Haig the second time. "It was a deal," Ford said, "but it never became a deal because I never accepted."

Of that period in August 1974, Ford said, "Nobody really gets to the heart of it."

"What was the heart of it?" I asked.

Nixon was finished one way or the other, Ford said, either through impeachment, a Senate trial or resignation. "To be honest with you," Ford said, "I had long hoped that would never be the case because he was a friend, I thought he had done a good job and made at least one stupid mistake."

I asked more about his attitude toward Nixon.

"I have a lot more pluses than minuses. I have some strong feelings. He was probably the best foreign policy president in my time. And I liked him personally. We didn't have as much in common as I normally have with a good friend because he wasn't much of an athlete. But socially my wife, Betty, and I liked Pat and Dick." Nixon and Ford were original members of a group of congressmen who formed a club called the Chowder and Marching Society, Ford recalled. "We exchanged family get-togethers. I was dumbfounded by two things, that he let himself get involved with people who misled him—Haldeman, Ehrlichman and Colson. Why he let that coterie of people affect his normal good judgment I never understood."

I had to protest. What about Nixon's tapes? I reminded Ford that they showed that it was Nixon who was in charge ordering illegal activities, using the government agencies—the CIA, FBI, even the Secret Service—to settle scores with enemies or conceal wrongdoing.

Ford looked puzzled. "That's a side I never knew about him."

How might it be explained?

"I think I was a better friend to Dick Nixon than any one of those people, over a longer period of time," Ford said. "It's just non-understandable what I hear and read about in those tapes."

"Maybe he got what he wanted?" I asked. It was possible that Nixon wanted to use the power of his office to settle political and other scores. Wasn't the presidency an instrument of vengeance for Nixon? Wasn't that what the record showed? Wasn't that probably what Nixon wanted?

"I don't know," Ford replied. "It's always been a mystery to me."

Ten months later, the afternoon of May 20, 1998, I visited Ford at his office near his home, which is on a golf course in Rancho Mirage, California. The desert town was hot, but pleasant and quiet. A Secret Service agent greeted me at the end of the road. Ford's first-floor office in a ranch-style building was large and cluttered. The dark-paneled room was conspicuously the office of a former president, full of photos and memorabilia. He was not in a hurry. He stuck to his story about the pardon. More than ever, Ford said, he was sure it was right.

Ford, who had been president during difficult economic times, was taken with the economic boom of the summer of 1998. He actually said, "Two hundred sixty million Americans are prosperous and happy."

I could have reminded him that despite the boom, the entire United States population was not well off—millions in poverty, children hungry, the wrenching despair and horror of life for many. In the two decades since leaving the presidency, Ford had not seen much of this world at the Republican fund-raisers, board meetings or golf tournaments he attended, traveling on private jets from his golf course estate or Colorado ski condo. He was so decent but fully out of touch.

We turned to Nixon once again.

"I've often said, 90 percent of Dick Nixon was first class. But he had a ten percent quirk and that ten percent got exploited by himself and by others."

"But there's something about that ten percent that is more than ten percent, isn't there?" I asked.

If it hadn't been exploited, Ford said, that 10 percent would have been inconsequential.

I asked about some of the stories that he had told Haig and others about not wanting to become president.

"Well, it's absolutely true," Ford said. *"I never wanted to be president."*

I left wondering. A number of presidents

preceding Ford, including Nixon, had made the office itself a victim of their behavior. They had diminished it, caused the Congress and the public to be more and more suspicious about presidential power. Attitudes hardened and new laws were passed that restricted the presidency. In some respects, Ford was a victim of the institution. He had not sought or wanted the job. He had not studied for it. He did not have a theory about it. There seemed to be few, if any, dreams. He had not examined what the presidency was, what it had been in history, or what it could be. Most immediately, he did not understand the history that had played itself out before him. The idea of even a weak modern president being exploited or dominated by his aides is almost impossible. The claim that Nixon was manipulated by his aides, or that the tone of vengeance or criminality in his administration was set by aides, is preposterous and contradicted by the best evidence—the taped record. Ford's suggestion that what happened to Nixon was some kind of 10 percent personality "quirk" is equally unbelievable. The embarrassment for Ford was that he did not understand Nixon—and he did not understand Watergate.

Watergate—and Vietnam—had created the conditions for a diminished presidency. Both the poison of distrust and Ford's own tendency to accommodate held him in check. The unacceptable—insubordination in the military chain of command—became acceptable to Ford. The inappropriate—drinking before speaking—seemed okay. Ford didn't fully comprehend or accept the new rules, and he paid a heavy price for it. He would never experience the heady ether of knowing that a majority of his fellow citizens wanted him, above all, to be their leader.

As the years have passed, I have become more and more convinced that Ford made the correct decision in pardoning Nixon. Nixon had already paid the political death penalty of resignation, and for Ford a pardon was the only way of ending the public and media obsession with his predecessor's future. The problem with the pardon was in Ford's execution. To be successful, the pardon required elaborate orchestration. The public, Congress and the media needed to be prepared. Ford should have mustered all of his sense of decency to explain his actions to the public. He should have seen the danger and avoided the discussions of pardon with Haig. He should have required Nixon to sign a statement admitting his guilt and released it with the pardon. In our second interview I asked Ford why he didn't do this.

"It could have been better," Ford agreed, "but we were under a time pressure." In the initial meetings, Nixon and his lawyers had balked at acknowledging he had committed crimes. "I wanted to get this thing done without a lot of leaks, and the longer it took to resolve some of these things, the more likely, Bob, that the issue would have come to the surface and it could have been a different ball game then."

Like Nixon and all modern presidents, Ford was worried about leaks. The fear is one of the clearest legacies of Watergate, I realized, causing presidents to work with a small, trusted circle of advisers and often to make decisions with undue haste.

But that answered only part of the question. I wanted to know why Ford had not pushed Nixon harder for an admission.

The former president reached into his pockets. "I've got it in my wallet here because any time anybody challenges me I pull it out," Ford explained. He handed me a folded, dog-eared piece of paper.

It was a portion of the Supreme Court decision *Burdick* v. *United States* that Becker had found. Ford had carried it around for years. I began reading aloud. "The justices found that a pardon 'carries imputation of guilt, acceptance, a confession of it.' "

Ford landed on the last phrase, and he repeated it: " 'Acceptance, a confession of it.' " See, he said, Nixon confessed.

"That was always very reassuring to me," Ford said.

PART TWO

JIMMY CARTER

1977–81

4

IN EARLY 1975, Jimmy Carter, the ex-governor of Georgia, began campaigning in Iowa, site of the first statewide contest in the race for the 1976 Democratic presidential nomination. Carter knew almost no one in the state, and his first piece of business was to introduce himself. He set up in a hotel room in Des Moines with soft drinks, crackers and cheese. Then he waited. And waited. No one came to his reception, not a single person. Embarrassed but undeterred, Carter, 50, and Jody Powell, 31, his traveling chauffeur and press secretary, left the hotel room and roamed the streets looking for voters. Anyone with a notebook or tape recorder sent them into ecstasy. As they branched out into the little towns of Iowa, Carter and Powell test-marketed some concepts.

"I'll never lie to you," Carter said one day.

Both he and Powell noticed that Carter's pledge of honesty resonated with the small audience. They stirred, they perked up. People were fed up with the lies that Lyndon Johnson and Richard Nixon had told about Vietnam and Watergate. The appeal of the statement was its power to move the audiences. Carter realized it was one of the most attention-getting declarations he could make.

In the days and weeks that followed, Carter kept saying it, and he went further. "I'll never mislead you," he promised. He told audiences if he did lie or mislead, they should not support him. They should vote for someone else.

Carter's mother, Miss Lillian, told him it was a mistake to make such a bold promise. Small, white lies were a part of life. Charles Kirbo, Carter's best friend, also told him to stop, that no one could stand up to complete scrutiny of his statements and actions. A braggadocio vow to tell no lies, Kirbo said, would arouse a hornet's nest among skeptics. Powell thought the plain statement should not have been surprising, but the media greeted it as a dare. A Carter declaration that he had a secret plan to end war would have been less provocative, Powell felt.

But Carter saw the no-lie pledge was recruiting fervent supporters. It was the backbone of the rationale for his candidacy. He was not Nixon. He was not a lawyer. He had never held office in Washington—the seat of a government few any longer trusted. He was an outsider, and he would tell the truth—always. He would divest himself of the trappings of the imperial presidency. He promised to remain close to the people. He would do what he deemed right, not what was politically expedient. Carter had fashioned a powerful message in the aftermath of Watergate. He was able to use Watergate as both whipping boy and selling point. The diagnosis was that government was corrupt to the core. The remedy was to make the government as good as he was by electing him.

Not only did Carter reject lies. He rejected the description of himself as a politician. When Senator Vance Hartke, the embodiment of the old pol, a three-term incumbent Indiana Democrat with a reputation for cozying up to special interests, repeatedly showed up at Carter's Midwestern campaign stops, Carter blew up at Powell. "If I ever see that son of a bitch again at one of my rallies," Carter told his press secretary, "you can be his press secretary."

Patrick Caddell, a 25-year-old Harvard-trained pollster, signed on to the Carter campaign because he saw Carter as a potential healer. Caddell believed that since the United States did not have a dominant religion, or a prevailing culture, politics was the country's great unifier. The president was the high priest of the political system, but Nixon had been excommunicated, and his misdeeds had damaged the country emotionally and psychologically. Watergate was a wound to America's soul that the new high priest had to fix. Caddell felt Carter could be the antidote to all the venom of Watergate.

Part of Carter's campaign strategy was not just to promise a more forthright approach to politics, but to political scandals. On December 22, 1974, less than six months after Nixon's resignation, Seymour Hersh had published an article in *The New York Times* reporting on an illegal domestic spying campaign by the Central Intelligence Agency (CIA). Idaho Democratic Senator Frank Church and New York Democratic Congressman Otis Pike responded by leading high-profile separate probes into CIA abuses. Their congressional hearings and press reports in 1975–76 uncovered CIA assassination plans, drug testing of unsuspecting persons, domestic spying and other horrors. It looked like another Watergate.

On February 11, 1976, *The Village Voice* published excerpts of the secret final Pike report on the CIA. Instead of acknowledging the misdeeds which the report detailed, the Ford administration denounced the leak. Carter was appalled by the CIA conduct and the administration response, and he took advantage. At a campaign stop in Manchester, New Hampshire, he vowed, "If the CIA ever makes a mistake, I'll be the one as president to call a press conference." It was a pledge that open and honest government in a Carter administration would extend even into the most secret offices of government.

Carter gained national attention by winning the Iowa caucuses in early 1976. Using that victory as a springboard, he prevailed in the New Hampshire primary and a host of others. By the summer of 1976, the unlikely outsider from southwest Georgia had locked up the Democratic nomination. At the Democratic National Convention in New York City, Carter and his handpicked running mate, Senator Walter Mondale of Minnesota, played the theme of moral renewal for all it was worth. On July 15, Mondale spoke to the convention as he accepted the nomination for vice president. "We have just lived through the worst political scandal in our history and are now led by a president who pardoned the person who did it."

Carter was erect and confident as he stepped to the podium for his acceptance speech. A glorious smile was on his face. His message was serious. He reminded everyone that he was there in defiance of the political powerbrokers and he promised a government as good as the nation's people. "It is time for our governmental leaders to respect the law no less than the humblest citizen, so that we can end the double standard of justice in America. I see no reason why big-shot crooks should go free while the poor ones go to jail."

Carter held on to beat Ford. In Carter's view, the good guys had finally won.

Caddell was certain that the mandate was to find out how to heal the country. How do we get over Watergate? he asked. How do we restore confidence in American government? How do we restore a sense of a country together? He was pretty sure these were the problems, but neither he nor Carter, nor anyone in the Carter circle, had a solution—or even a plan. Instead, Carter, the disciplined U.S. Naval Academy graduate and former engineer, turned to managing, proposing programs and legislation, handling the voluminous paperwork, getting briefed and becoming conversant and an expert. He loved to read memos and reports. The presidency was the ultimate final exam, and Carter was going to prove he was the best student.

Caddell haunted Carter with the question about healing. "What do we do about this amorphous thing that we've promised America?" he asked one day.

"I don't know," Carter answered. "We're going to govern as well as we can." He was troubled by the question about healing, but he didn't have an answer.

In February 1977, just weeks after Carter took the oath of office, I learned from a well-placed source that the CIA had made secret payments to King Hussein of Jordan for intelligence and had done favors for the king—sex, money, bodyguards for him and protection for his children going to school in the United States. It was potentially a big story, the first time the new administration would face a scandal and an early test of Carter's proclaimed policy of openness and no lies.

I called the White House. To my great surprise, President Carter agreed to see Ben Bradlee, the *Washington Post* executive editor, and me personally on Wednesday, February 16, at the White House. We arrived, and after a short delay we and Powell, who had become the press secretary, were ushered into the Oval Office.

There standing in the door was Carter, in a perfectly pressed gray, wide-pinstripe suit. Not a crease. He was short and slight—about 5 foot 7 and 160 pounds—and he was smiling on this day, the 28th of his presidency.

Bradlee made his case for publishing the story. Carter listened quietly, obligingly, almost complacently, as in one of his campaign commercials when a voter was making a point.

After Bradlee finished, Carter started to speak. I had a notebook in my lap and prepared to take notes.

"This is off the record," the president said.

Okay, I said, but I'd like to take notes just for our use.

"I want to be honest, fully truthful," Carter said. He looked at the notebook as if it were a contaminant, some barrier to honest communications.

I closed it.

He stared at me hard. I put the notebook in the side pocket of my best blue suit. The momentary tension evaporated. Carter seemed almost to breathe more easily.

"This has been in existence for twenty years," he said of the Hussein payments by the CIA. "It's against my policy...but I can't undo the past or be responsible for all the past."

Jesus, I thought, he's washing his hands of Hussein, the CIA, bailing out on them.

But, the president continued, there is an additional factor: Hussein was a moderate and a key to a Middle East peace settlement. He needed Hussein. His administration's first foreign policy objective was a Middle East peace. Speaking forcefully, raising his eyebrows in sincere emphasis—a stunning presidential performance of "trust me"— Carter said, here are the details. The operation began in 1957. "It was much larger back then." His hand went up and then cut low in the air as he added that the latest payment to the king was smaller, quite smaller.

I mentioned $750,000, the figure I had heard King Hussein was paid yearly.

He nodded. Half of the last payment that went to Hussein, he said, was to pay other officials; the other half went to protect Hussein's children in the United States.

67

The CIA did not want to provide CIA or other U.S. security officers directly because they conceivably might have to shoot someone such as a Palestinian trying to kidnap one of the king's children.

Carter drove to his main point. He had just ordered the payments stopped, he said. "I want to assure you of that."

Why? What happened? Bradlee asked.

You see, Carter said, he had just learned of the payments for the first time that week because of our inquiry.

Bradlee and I half-glanced at each other: the new president had not been told that the king of Jordan was on the payroll. Incredible, I thought.

We asked gently if the payments weren't, when you got down to it, bribes?

"I can't dispute that," Carter said. He added that Secretary of State Cyrus Vance, who was scheduled to arrive in Jordan for talks with King Hussein in two days, would probably not go if the story were printed. The issue would monopolize a Hussein-Vance meeting, and Carter did not want that, he said.

Carter plunged on, saying the current payments were as much an "aggravation" as anything. He didn't specify why this might be. I realized that potential disclosure of the relationship would be an aggravation. Was that what he meant? It didn't seem proper to interrupt.

Other presidents had pushed Bradlee not to publish stories. But Carter volunteered that publication of the story "will not harm the national security." Then the president leaned forward in his chair, bringing his charm totally to bear, tuning it to the maximum, all the goodwill and power of the new leader of the free world. He let the dead, eerie silence in the Oval Office work for him. He would prefer, Carter said, that the story not be published, adding: "I can't tell you how to run your business." And he said he wouldn't. But he said he would like Vance to talk to us.

I calculated that the traveling secretary of state would obviously not be available until his return, after the Hussein meeting, so the president was trying to buy time.

Carter said some other heads of state had used the CIA to communicate with past presidents, instead of using the ambassador. He and Vance were going to put a stop to that practice. Vance, Carter said, did not know about the payments. So Carter said he would like to get 24 hours' notice if the story was going to be published.

Bradlee said that was reasonable and agreed but gave no indication about his decision.

I asked if the president was happy with what he had found at the CIA.

Other activities had been stopped, he said, but he refused to give a hint of what they were.

Overall, Carter said, he was building informal relations with the Middle East leaders. Although he had not yet met King Hussein, publication of the CIA's Hussein relationship in the first month of his presidency would make the other heads of state distrustful of him. They would suspect that the story had been leaked intentionally from his administration or from himself.

At that point Carter briefly discoursed on the importance of trust. Oddly, I thought, he just flat out said he trusted us, adding, "I want you to believe me." A Middle East settlement, he went on, was "a high priority for my administration." If a settlement could not be accomplished in 1977, it would be more difficult, he added.

Out of the blue, perhaps recognizing that Bradlee had not agreed to withhold the story, Carter asked if there were some way to run the story without naming Hussein.

Bradlee and I grimaced, indicating that would not work.

Carter said he knew that was not practical but that he was looking for some way out. He repeated that he was not asking us to withhold the story, but wanted us to fully understand his problem. He paused, sat forward on his chair and said: *"This is your country and mine."*

Bradlee and I nodded. I wondered if that was the final appeal.

Carter quickly added that he hoped Bradlee would come see him on anything.

Bradlee promised not to abuse that offer. "About once a year," he said.

Carter stood. We all rose. Everyone shook hands. Carter turned on his heels and made a beeline out to his small office on the other side of the Oval Office. He had been stately but now seemed to be hurrying to other business. On the way out, Powell promised that he would let us know if anyone else was on to the story.

We again pledged to give him 24 hours' notice before publication.

In the car, I said to Bradlee that it seemed like

the easiest call he'd ever have to make. We had the best source in the world: in the course of the meeting, the president of the United States had confirmed the whole story. The new president hadn't been told and when he had learned of the payments he ordered them stopped. If ever there were grounds for a story, this was it.

By that afternoon, Bradlee told me to call Powell and say we were going to run the story in two days and this was the 24 hours' notice.

So I phoned Powell and told him of Bradlee's decision.

Since a story was going to run some time, Powell said, "the timing does not make that much difference." But they still wanted the 24-hour delay, although it would mean the story would be published the day Vance was arriving in Jordan. That, Powell said with a note of understatement, would be "a little embarrassing to old Cy as he gets off the plane." Powell added that there was a serious debate at the White House about whether the president should have talked to us. Although Powell did not tell me, national security adviser Zbigniew Brzezinski had been strongly opposed to Carter's meeting with us and was railing that the president had not been tough enough. He felt Carter should have asked that the story not be published, in any form, at any time. The intelligence agencies had a vast stake in keeping the story from being published. The story would signal every other paid CIA source or informant that their secret arrangement might not be safe, Brzezinski worried.

Powell also did not tell me why Carter avoided

requesting that we withhold publication. I later found out that Carter was sure that the Hussein story would eventually get out and it could appear as if he were concealing something. After the abuses by Johnson and Nixon of falsely invoking national security to shield information, Carter would not take that chance.

I pressed Powell for more on Carter's attitude toward the payments.

Powell acknowledged that the president was "distressed."

I sensed that the Carter administration's attitude was changing a bit about the entire matter.

It's all more complicated than it seemed at first, Powell said obliquely.

How? Why?

Powell wouldn't say.

I could see that it was now Carter's CIA, and understandably and predictably in the first four weeks of the Carter presidency the world looked different. The campaign statement about calling a press conference if the CIA made a mistake was coming home to roost.

In a later phone call, I asked Powell what the White House would say after the story ran. Were the *Post,* Bradlee and myself in for some trouble?

"Jimmy and I aren't going to do any pissing," Powell said in that rarefied Southern way, vaguely suggesting that someone was, but not them.

We hung up and I told Bradlee what Powell had said. Bradlee took my draft of the story, read it, and for only the second time in the years I had worked for him put a piece of paper in his own typewriter and banged out the first six paragraphs, beginning:

"The Central Intelligence Agency has been secretly making annual cash payments amounting to millions of dollars to King Hussein of Jordan for the last 20 years, *The Washington Post* has learned."

With a few word changes that was what we ran the following day, Friday, February 18, 1977. It was displayed or "stripped" across the entire top of page one under the headline: "CIA Paid Millions to Jordan's King Hussein."

In Amman, the Jordanian capital, the story was out at about the moment Powell had predicted: Vance was stepping off the plane. Vance's reaction was that the diplomatic relationship with Hussein would just have to be written off, that Hussein would never trust the United States again. The king did not cancel their meeting, but he told Vance that the story was embarrassing and dangerous.

At the White House, Powell stepped to the podium for his regular daily press briefing and to general laughter was asked about Hussein.

"It is the policy of this administration not to comment, either to confirm or deny, on these stories concerning alleged covert activities," Powell said stiffly. He added that the administration had been conducting "an intensive and comprehensive review of all sensitive foreign intelligence activities," and called Hussein an "outstanding national leader."

The no-comment posture on covert activities, Powell said briskly, was "a policy statement."

"When was this policy made?" a reporter asked.

"About midnight last night," Powell replied.

After the weekend, Bradlee came by waving a heavy bond piece of White House stationery.

"I'm getting some splatter," he said sarcastically, referring to Powell's no-pissing promise.

I took the note. In Carter's neat penmanship, the note was headed "Personal" and dated February 19—the day after the Hussein story ran:

> To Ben Bradlee
> I think your publication of the CIA story as the Secretary of State was on his Mid East mission and just approaching Jordan was irresponsible.
> This is offered by way of editorial comment.
>
> Jimmy

Bradlee wondered aloud what we were supposed to do. It was not surprising that Carter wished it did not have to be published. But in the meeting, Carter had been friendly and warm and had unequivocally confirmed the payments and his disapproval of them. He had pledged to stop them and clearly stated that the story would not harm national security.

Bradlee slapped at the note. He said a personal message from the president of the United States charging that he had been "irresponsible" amounted to something more. "They didn't piss," Bradlee said. "They shit on us."

The next day, Wednesday, Carter said at a press conference that he had "not found anything illegal or improper" in any ongoing CIA operation, sidestepping the entire issue because he had ordered the Hussein payments stopped, thus they were no longer ongoing.

On February 25, an Associated Press (AP) story revealed that Carter had told a congressional leadership gathering about his meeting with Bradlee and myself. According to a memorandum dictated by one of the leaders after the meeting and obtained by the AP reporter, Carter said Hussein had been "our most reliable source" of information in the Middle East. After he learned that a story might be forthcoming, Carter told the congressional leaders that he had asked Bradlee and myself to the White House and sought to discourage publication.

"I neither confirmed nor denied the account," Carter was quoted as saying. "I told them that if anything had been done, it was not sinister nor did it redound to the personal enrichment of Hussein." Carter told them that he had explained about the great sensitivity of the Vance trip. He said, "The whole thing could be blown up and the trip rendered useless and the chances for peace set back if any news story were to appear during Vance's trip.

"Therefore I pleaded with them on that basis to withhold any story—or at least give us 24 hours before breaking it."

He added, according to the memo, "There was nothing I could do about it, given their attitude....I thought it was irresponsible."

Carter also told the leaders that the Hussein

story and other leaks identifying CIA sources were "drastically disrupting U.S. intelligence-gathering capabilities," and he urged that the number of people with access to such secrets be reduced.

I called Powell to complain and told him that we felt sandbagged, summoned to an off-the-record meeting, led to believe one story and now confronted with a well-publicized version—Carter's own interpretation apparently—that conveyed a rather different impression. Carter had lied about his meeting with us.

Powell said Carter was trying to move Congress to take steps that would curb leaks.

But, I said, the report to the congressional leaders was different from what the president had told us. The drift of the entire meeting had been clear to both Bradlee and myself: Carter did not like the payments and had stopped them.

Powell said Carter did not tell us the payments were improper or against the rules. Carter had stopped the payments, Powell said, because "it is just not his way" to do something like that in secret when it can be done openly.

Hey, wait just a minute, I said. I'm sure there are subtleties in any meeting with the president, but his account of our meeting to the congressional leaders was not accurate and reflected a mood and manner that did not exist. More important, some of the president's claims were not correct, I said, hinting but not specifying his reported statement that he had neither confirmed nor denied the details of the Hussein payments to us.

Powell seemed to sense that a dispute could escalate quickly if Bradlee and I felt that Carter had given his version of the off-the-record session and that now entitled us to give ours. Maybe some effort might be in order to correct the record, Powell said, and at least make it clear that we did not act in an "irresponsible" way, as it now had been characterized privately and publicly.

What Powell did not tell me at the time was that Carter was angry at the way Bradlee and I had handled the story, which in Carter's opinion pulled no punches and was treated with a banner headline and the full flavor of illicit behavior uncovered. From Carter's point of view, the publication on the day of Vance's arrival in Jordan was totally unnecessary, sticking a needle in the administration's eye. Sure, Carter had asked for a 24-hour delay, but why not wait 48 or 72 hours? It was just not decent. He had leveled with Bradlee and me. When informed that Bradlee was upset at Carter's note, Powell reported that Carter had said, "Well, fuck him."

At Powell's noon briefing Monday, he was asked again about the Hussein payments. He said the president had conveyed to the *Post* his preference that the Hussein story not be published. But Powell also told the reporters that "there was no claim on our part that this would in its direct sense endanger the security of the nation."

Because the *Post* had asked for the White House view before publication, Powell said, "there was from the *Post* what I consider to be

77

a good faith effort to try to gain that sort of under-standing. We made a good faith effort to try to provide it while at the same time making explicit our recognition of their right to make their own judgment. That is a very difficult and ticklish situation."

Carter had attempted to have it both ways. He tried to be open with us, but only in a closed-door, off-the-record meeting. He did not want the story published, but refused to say it would harm the national security. He con-firmed he had ordered the payments stopped, but then publicly labeled our coverage irre-sponsible as soon as it was in print. In practice, Carter's policy of openness fell far short of his campaign pledges. Why? I wondered.

A White House intelligence official later offered the best explanation for Carter's con-duct. The Pike Committee's final report said in a single sentence, "Taxpayer monies were spent to provide heads of state with female com-panions...." The reference was to King Hussein. It turned out that during the first years of the operation, when the young king was in his late 20s, the CIA had arranged prostitutes for him here in the United States, the official said. Once the CIA had found, of all things, a Jewish prostitute—a fact that would not have played well, to say the least, in the Arab Middle East. Hussein was enamored and kept insisting on seeing her. Arranging when and how to have these trysts was as difficult, risky and complicated as a covert operation. There was some discus-sion that Hussein was going to give up his throne for her. Finally, the king was weaned from his unlikely obsession, but it had been dicey.

Jimmy Carter liked to read reports and files. He liked the full story. I suspect that the Baptist, born-again new president didn't like this story one bit. No matter how the Hussein operation had changed over the years, I suspect he felt it was fatally tainted. The implicit promise of his presidency was a cleanup. A story about the CIA, a king and prostitutes was exactly the kind of scandal that could blow up. He wanted to put as much distance between himself, his presidency, his CIA and that operation as possible. So he pulled the plug by confirming the story to *The Washington Post.*

Carter, however, soon learned the extent to which the CIA paid people off. As a matter of policy, it might be distasteful, but there is nothing inherently illegal in such payments, especially if it yields cheaper and more reliable information. Most good espionage is about betrayal. The problem is keeping the operation secret, preserving deniability. It is not a great moral or philosophical issue. Obviously, the new president learned, the CIA would buy anyone, from a lowly secretary to the foreign minister. Why not the head of state? If the money purchased good information and a higher degree of knowledge and security, couldn't an argument be made that it was worth it?

Nevertheless, I was left with a feeling of distaste. I had a sickening sense of foreboding, of here-we-go-again with another president. I had seen firsthand that Carter had not been straight at all. Yet the off-the-record agreement about the meeting prevented me from writing a full account. Although he had given a distorted version of the meeting to congressional leaders, I didn't see how I could give ours without launching open warfare. After Watergate, frankly the last thing I wanted was strife with the new president. I decided to turn to another subject, the Supreme Court. But Carter's relations with Bradlee and the *Post* had been soured, and they would not get better.

5

IN THE SPRING OF 1977, Miss Lillian, Carter's mother, tracked down the *New York Times* White House correspondent James T. Wooten in the White House press room.

"I want to talk to you," Miss Lillian said, summoning Wooten for a private chat. A serious, graceful writer, and like Miss Lillian a Southerner, Wooten had covered her son's presidential campaign in depth and was writing a biography of him.

"I'm worried about Jimmy," she confided. "He works these kids to the bone and he never thanks them."

Wooten pressed.

"I know a lot of the kids are not happy because he never says thank you," she said.

Taking this small piece of string—and protecting his source—Wooten went to work interviewing a number of Carter's close aides. The result was a front-page piece, April 25, 1977, headlined "Carter's Style Making Aides Apprehensive, Ways Discourage Dissent, Isolate Office, Some Say." Wooten reported that one of the people who had influenced Carter the most was Admiral Hyman G. Rickover, the legendary and inflexible father of the U.S. nuclear submarine fleet. While in the Navy, young Carter had worked for Rickover, who had never complimented Carter or hesitated to criticize him severely if a job was not done as well as he thought it should be. "The absence of a comment was his compliment," Carter wrote in his 1975 campaign autobiography. Unnamed Carter aides were quoted as saying that like his mentor, Carter could be brutal and intimidating, not given to praise. In the effort to avoid the isolation of Nixon, one aide said of Carter, "He's into almost everything now and once he gets his hands on something he's very reluctant to let go."

Jody Powell went wild, insisting the portrait of what Powell called "the cruel recluse" was totally false. Wooten was ostracized, denied access to top aides and information. The *Times* soon moved him off the White House beat.

Carter continued to have strained relations with both his own staff and the press. Many realized that the only problem with Wooten's portrait was that it was too right, too soon. Gerald Rafshoon, Carter's longtime media adviser, tried to get the president to form personal relationships with major media figures, such as newspaper editors and publishers. He wanted Carter to connect with some of these people. At minimum Rafshoon wanted the president to generate some goodwill, or at least get a break from some of them. In his most optimistic moments, Rafshoon hoped Carter would make some friends. With Carter's permission, he set up a series of little dinners at the White House for Carter and Rosalynn with four to eight people.

Katharine Graham and the other top executives from *The Washington Post* and *Newsweek*, which are both owned by the Post Company, were invited together for one White House dinner. During the evening, Carter told them he would like to have a contact—somebody he could call if he wanted to share something off the record or to get an opinion or advice.

The *Post* executives told him that was not practical. Both *Newsweek* and the *Post* had reporters who covered the White House and the administration, and news should flow through them. The *Post* and *Newsweek* executives didn't want to end-run their reporters.

Standing outside after dinner, Rosalynn said in a whisper that some of the executives overheard, "See, Jimmy, I told you they wouldn't want to help."

Part of Carter's error was addressing such a large group. There is not a single one of those people (including myself or any other reporter) who would not speak off the record with Carter or any other president if requested. The *Post, Newsweek* and other editors or executives have done so many times, basking in the access to a president. But in the macho group atmosphere of a dinner with their colleagues, the executives and editors wanted to show their steel and refusal to be manipulated.

After several of these dinners, Rafshoon

asked Carter, "Anyone you particularly liked?"

"No, no," the president said.

"Anyone you want to see again?"

"No."

"Do you want to continue the dinners?"

"Yes," Carter said.

Rafshoon saw that Carter found strength— and definition—in not compromising, not playing politics, not engaging the various Washington players. He kept opposing congressmen's favorite pork-barrel projects, claiming they were expensive and had little merit.

Representative Jim Wright, the Texas Democrat who later became Speaker of the House, fought with Carter over proposed water projects in his home state. "Every time I see Carter he makes me feel like a political whore," Wright told Rafshoon.

Carter's earnestness was grating. On June 14, 1977, Rafshoon wrote Carter a memo: "You are running the risk of boring the people and you have three and one half years to go."

The president wanted to tackle more issues, have more programs, give more speeches. "Why am I not doing more of this stuff?" he once said to Rafshoon.

"Because every time you do it: *Big Turnoff,*" Rafshoon replied.

At one critical juncture, Carter needed help from some senior senators. The White House arranged for the president to play doubles tennis with several of them, including Senator Lloyd Bentsen, the Texas Democrat.

"Okay, I'll do that," Carter said.

He played two sets of doubles, said good-bye

and left. The next day, Bentsen called the White House. "What the fuck," Bentsen said angrily, "he didn't offer us a drink, lemonade or anything!" There was no conversation, no lobbying, no relaxing.

Rafshoon complained to the president.

"You said play tennis with them, I played tennis with them."

Rafshoon explained that the senators wanted to be able to go back home or to the Senate and say, "When I was having drinks with the president, he said..."

"They want to get home to their families," Carter said dismissively. "They don't want to sit up in the White House on the balcony and have something to drink with me."

Later Carter confided to Rafshoon's wife, "Eden, I think I'm probably antisocial."

Carter, the outsider, didn't understand his own power and appeal, the centrality of the president to Washington, its own peculiar games and power rituals. He was not only removed from the capital city but alienated from it. Watergate had helped produce the most unlikely president: a loner.

Part of Carter's estrangement from the Washington establishment resulted from a painful experience early in his administration. In June 1977, Bert Lance walked over from the Old Executive Office Building to see the president in the Oval Office. An affable big bear of a man, and an ambitious Georgia bank entrepreneur, Lance was Carter's budget director. He was the closest person to a Bobby Kennedy that Carter had in his administration, almost a brother.

Carter considered Lance his key person to deal with cabinet members and the Congress. Officially, Carter didn't have a chief of staff at the beginning because a chief of staff symbolized the imperial presidency in the form of Nixon and the infamous H. R. "Bob" Haldeman. Lance had urged Carter to appoint one, but Carter had said, "I'll just be my own." So Lance had become the de facto coordinator, the deputy president.

Sitting at his desk in the Oval Office behind the copy of Harry Truman's sign "The Buck Stops Here," Carter was all expectation. His open, large, attentive steely blue eyes stared at his friend. Carter found Lance boyish but mature, a man of many dimensions, indispensable. Their 11-year friendship had been forged in the crucible of Southern religion and politics. The two loved to play tennis, and Carter always remembered how Lance described himself as having the grace of a gazelle and the power of an elephant.

"I've got a major problem that relates to my economic viability," Lance confided in his strong, reassuring voice. He was in trouble. He saw immense storm clouds now and in his future. His wealth, as Carter knew, was in millions of dollars of stock in his former bank in Georgia. A bunch of bad loans were going to be written off and the stock was going to drop. Dividend payments to Lance would be cut dramatically, if not entirely. Lance had borrowed heavily against the stock and it was going to be a big mess. *Time* magazine was preparing an article.

"So I think you ought to just let me resign," Lance said. He could go back to Georgia, straighten the bank out, fix the problem and come back to Washington if Carter wanted. "I believe this to be that serious and that important."

"I'm not about to hear that," Carter said, assuming his decisive, presidential mode. "That's foolishness and it doesn't make sense."

"Well," Lance said, "we will continue on." When Carter made up his mind, Lance knew it was fruitless to argue. At least he had warned the president.

As part of Carter's pledge that his administration would adhere to the highest ethical standards, he had required his cabinet appointees such as Lance to make full public financial disclosures and to divest themselves of holdings that might pose potential conflicts. Bank stock obviously was a conflict for Lance, who had such great influence on administration economic policy. Because of Lance's large holdings, he didn't want to sell blocks of stock all at once. A sell-off would drive the bank stock down further. But Lance had promised the Senate committee which confirmed him that he would divest by the end of 1977. If he followed through as promised, he would be ruined because of the depressed stock prices.

Carter proposed that he ask the Senate committee to extend the deadline for Lance to sell his stock. Lance finally agreed, and Carter wrote a letter July 11 requesting the extension.

Lance knew he was a time bomb about to explode. Before he came to Washington there had been a federal investigation of his bank. A number of regulatory agencies were examining various questionable practices. Whether he failed to convey the full seriousness of his problems, or whether Carter failed to hear, as a team they decided to apply for an exception to the new, high ethical standards. They were choosing survival over their own rules.

The Senate committee agreed to the extension, but the request was made public.

William Safire, columnist for *The New York Times* and former Nixon speechwriter, smelled blood. Working in the Nixon White House had given Safire a well-developed sniffer, attuned to the subtle despair of scandal. Personal financial problems and piddling little controversies could absolutely kill a politician, eating away at him, worrying him sick, corroding judgment, he knew. Safire read the article in *Time*, which had done the heavy reporting; then he read a few other articles and made a few phone calls.

On July 21, 1977, Safire published a column headlined "Carter's Broken Lance." He reviewed how banker Lance had the previous year hustled millions of dollars in loans from a Chicago bank and the Teamsters Union pension fund. Safire wrote that these were "sweetheart loans" from those obviously seeking favor and access to one of the future president's best friends. Safire also understood the irony. "Here we have a situation in which the man in charge of the nation's books is deeply, dangerously in hock."

A string of columns followed, and by August, Safire, who had the natural ear of the speech-writer's sound bite, began calling it "Lancegate"—one of the first uses of the "-gate" suffix for a presidential scandal after Watergate. A brilliant publicist and skilled propagandist, Safire believed that Democratic presidents should be held to the same standards and scrutiny that Nixon had faced. He felt it was especially important to point out abuses in Carter's administration, which he believed owed its existence to the exploitation of the public memory of Watergate. So he dusted off the Watergate language. "Cover-up" was used in eight columns on Lance in August and September. "Smoking gun," "stonewalling," "obstruction of justice" and "special prosecutor" were trotted out. Unwittingly or consciously, Safire was framing the language of scandal for the post-Watergate era.

Hamilton Jordan, Carter's top White House aide and former campaign manager, tried early on to warn Carter of the danger that Lance posed to the president and the new administration. "This unfortunate incident—which involves Georgians and close personal friends—could do great damage to your presidency if not handled properly," Jordan wrote in an "eyes only" memo to the president. "You pledged that you would not tolerate wrongdoing or even the appearance of wrongdoing. We cannot allow this or any other incident [to] erode the moral authority of your presidency."

Carter was worried, but he thought the press would judge Lance, who had moved into Georgetown and socialized with some of the Washington establishment, "a pretty good guy" and not deserving of condemnation. But the media saw the inconsistencies and jumped hard on Lance. The Senate held hearings.

Carter did not fully appreciate that his declaration of purity and no lies was being extended to his entire administration. The question was not what Lance was doing in office. It became whether Lance may have lied or cheated or deceived ever, even back in Georgia. Was the president's best friend in Washington, his soulmate in the presidency, somehow corrupt?

Carter alternately perceived and misperceived his own vulnerability. He realized that the Watergate syndrome was still alive in Washington, and that Lance's tangled finances were a dream for both investigative reporters and congressional committees. He didn't fully see that his bond with Lance made the budget director a target, and not because of any real animus toward Lance personally. The question was simple: If Lance is hiding something, what about Carter?

The comptroller of the currency investigated and issued a 394-page report that found no illegal conduct. Citing the comptroller's report, Carter essentially tried to declare Lancegate over at a press conference on August 18.

"My faith in the character and competence of Bert Lance has been reconfirmed. I see no other conclusion that can be drawn from my objective analysis of these findings," the president said. With a giant smile, Carter turned to Lance, who was at his side, and said, "Bert, I'm proud of you."

Reporters soon discovered that the appendix to the report contained damaging evidence about how Lance allowed his family and relatives to overdraw checking accounts at a bank he headed by hundreds of thousands of dollars. The appendix also said Lance had overdrafted bank accounts for his unsuccessful 1974 campaign for governor of Georgia and had used the same collateral on two separate loans.

On September 1, Carter picked up a miniature tape recorder into which he dictated his private diary. *"The Washington Post* is conducting a vendetta against Bert and has apparently ordered two front-page stories about him each day. This morning, for instance, they had nine separate stories about Lance—headline stories—throughout the paper." He noted with little comfort that *The New York Times* had none that day.

Carter had overcounted, but he was right, the story had become a media obsession. Carter and Lance saw it as a campaign against them personally. The scandal and the mounting questions about Lance's personal finances would not disappear. Government agency reports surfaced about hundreds of thousands of dollars of other bank overdrafts by Lance and his family at his bank. Carter realized it was seriously affecting his own reputation and status. But Lance continued to fight, and he agreed to go before the Senate committee again.

Early the morning of his testimony, September 15, Lance asked to meet with Carter. The budget director brought his family Bible. He greeted the president in the Oval Office, and the two went to Carter's small private adjacent study, scene of many important moments in the presidency. It was quiet. Even Carter's regular classical music was not playing. They took turns reading passages that Lance had selected from the Bible. They read passages from the 13th chapter of St. Paul's Letter to the Corinthians:

"For now we see in a mirror dimly, but then face to face."

They read from Joshua and Ecclesiastes about courage and the need to find a time to speak out.

Before the committee later that day, Lance read an opening statement of 49 pages. He asked, "Is it part of our American system that a man can be drummed out of government by a series of false charges, half-truths and misrepresentations, innuendoes and the like?"

It was a powerful performance, but the personal financial house of cards the federal budget director had erected still remained. The incongruity in the face of Carter's clamorous rectitude was unsettling.

Nonetheless, there was a good deal of support for Lance. Carter summoned Lance for a 6:15 a.m. meeting on Monday, September 19. He argued that Lance had finally proved that the system does work and given the chance, an honest man could explain. Given the vindication, Carter presented a surprise ending. All his advisers thought it was time for Lance to resign.

Lance wanted time to think, discuss the matter with his attorney, Clark Clifford, and most importantly with his wife, LaBelle.

Although it would be presented as a joint decision, Carter knew it was his own choice.

On September 21, he brought Bert and

LaBelle to his study next to the Oval Office. The Lances sat on the small sofa adjacent to his desk.

LaBelle argued against resignation, but Carter remained firm. It was the only escape for them all. They had to see they were overwhelmed. If Carter didn't take steps to end the controversy, it would come to define the times and his presidency. He was going to have a press conference later that afternoon.

"You have stabbed my husband in the back after all he's done for you," LaBelle said furiously. She refused to help her husband with his resignation letter, and she went back to their Georgetown home. Lance soon followed.

LaBelle called Carter and vented again. "I want to tell you one thing—you can go with the rest of the jackals, and I hope you're happy!"

They then watched Carter's press conference from their bedroom. Lance lay across the bed spent. He was totally exhausted.

"I accept Bert's resignation with the greatest sense of regret and sorrow," Carter said. "He's a good man." Carter said it was the right decision, and nothing had shaken his belief in Lance or his integrity. The president said the mess was partly his fault by insisting that Lance break his ties with the banking business when he became budget director.

Lance turned off the set.

"Your phone call started his adrenaline and gave him the reserve he needed to make it through," Lance told his wife. "It would have been a disaster to see the President of the United States crying on TV. Imagine how much it would have hurt Jimmy politically."

Lance went back to Georgia. He made peace with Safire and the two became friends. Lance also eventually forgave the prosecutor and the judge in the banking case that was later brought against him. He was acquitted. His lowest moment, Lance said, came when he had to face the question of his own personal responsibility nearly every day for the next 20 years, in one way or another. "Where have I failed?" he asked himself. "Where did I fall short?" He wasn't precisely sure, he said, but he believed Carter, he and other administration figures had failed to understand and manage the powerful forces Watergate had set in motion.

The shadow the two-month Lance scandal cast was long, deepening the alienation Carter felt toward the Congress, the media and Washington. The implicit promise that he would never allow a repetition of the national Watergate embarrassment was in question. Carter realized he had somewhat ostentatiously sought high ethical and legal standards but was quick to seek an exception for a friend. Carter felt it was impossible to overestimate the damage the Lance affair had inflicted on his administration. But to Carter it didn't seem fair or right, and the president was not sure what lessons to draw. This orderly former naval officer and engineer did not take the time to do what they call in the military an after-action report. He did not study the changed circumstances created by Watergate that he had magnified with his own presidential candidacy and words, and so he had not determined how he might manage those new circumstances. For Carter, it was as if the ghosts of Watergate stalked the halls of the White House. As with most ghosts, he wasn't sure they existed, where they were or how to exorcise them.

6

FOUR MONTHS INTO his presidency, on May 3, 1977, Carter called on Congress to pass a new law that would "require appointment of a special prosecutor to investigate and prosecute alleged offenses by high government officials." He took the opportunity to remind Congress and the public of his high-mindedness. "During my campaign I promised the American people that as president I would assure that their government is devoted exclusively to the public interest." A law removing investigations of presidents and other top officials from the Justice Department would be a critical, partial fulfillment of that pledge.

Over at the Georgetown University Law Center, Professor Samuel Dash, who had been the chief counsel to the Senate Watergate Committee in 1973 and 1974, almost whooped with delight. Dash, 52, a Democrat who was an expert on criminal law and on wiretapping, and Senator Sam J. Ervin Jr., the North Carolina Democrat who had chaired the Senate Watergate Committee, had pushed reform for three years.

It had been a long struggle. As Dash saw it,

the need for a new law became clear when Nixon ordered the first Watergate special prosecutor, Archibald Cox, fired on Saturday night, October 20, 1973. Known in Watergate lore as the Saturday Night Massacre, Attorney General Elliot Richardson and his deputy, William Ruckelshaus, refused Nixon's order and they both resigned. Robert Bork, the solicitor general and the number three in the Justice Department, then obeyed Nixon and removed Cox. A firestorm of public protest followed because Nixon had fired his own prosecutor. Hundreds of thousands of telegrams flooded Washington from all parts of the country, and 22 impeachment resolutions were introduced in the House in the days afterwards.

Ervin and Dash felt it was a horrendous act by Nixon—the ultimate obstruction of justice, the elimination of his own investigator and prosecutor. Nixon ordered the FBI to seal off the Watergate prosecutor's offices, jeopardizing the entire investigation. Under public and congressional pressure, Nixon soon yielded and accepted the appointment of another Watergate special prosecutor, Leon Jaworski. But Dash had been shocked that a president could so easily rid himself of a criminal investigator aimed at himself and his inner circle. Nixon's firing of Cox was lawful, and technically Nixon also could have had Jaworski dismissed. As far as Ervin and Dash were concerned, one of the main lessons of Watergate was the need to create, in law, a mechanism so that no future president could control the investigation of himself or his top aides. True independence had to be found, a real remedy to prevent a future Saturday Night Massacre. But how?

Ervin was almost a figure from another era. Born in 1896, he fought in France during World War I and graduated from Harvard Law School in 1922. He had served in the Senate for 20 years. A large man, with a giant face and eyebrows and jowls that shook ferociously when he talked, Ervin regularly quoted from Shakespeare, the Bible and the Bill of Rights, and he carried around a copy of the U.S. Constitution. He could be both stern and funny. His judgment often seemed to carry the extra weight of history.

At the beginning of his committee's televised Watergate hearings in May 1973, Ervin had defined the issue:

"If the many allegations made to this date are true, then the burglars who broke into the headquarters of the Democratic National Committee at the Watergate were in effect breaking into the home of every citizen of the United States," he said. "And if these allegations prove to be true, what they were seeking to steal was not the jewels, money or other precious property of American citizens, but something much more valuable—their most precious heritage: the right to vote in a free election."

Ervin realized that his Watergate Committee had two functions—to give the facts to the public and to make recommendations for new legislation. By early 1974, Ervin concluded that the committee had largely fulfilled its fact-gathering role. The televised hearings of testimony from most of the major Watergate players and the discovery of Nixon's secret taping system would ensure the committee a favorable review in any history of congressional hearings. In some respects they had set the gold standard for investigations.

Ervin summoned Dash to a meeting.

"I think we've got to cut it," Ervin said.

"Why?" Dash protested. They had plenty of new material on Watergate-style campaign dirty tricks and illicit fund-raising requiring weeks if not months more of hearings.

"We've got to get off the stage," Ervin said. His sense of political timing told him that the spotlight had moved to the new special prosecutor, Jaworski, and the House impeachment inquiry. There was nothing worse than a congressional committee, which had occupied the limelight for so long, dwelling on secondary matters, important as they might be. The committee had one more round to fire, and they had to save it for the legislative recommendations. The soundness of their fact-finding would be tested most fully in their proposed remedies.

So in the spring and summer of 1974 Dash scrambled to finish a final report that would contain concrete recommendations for reform.

Ervin was then 77 and about to retire from the Senate, and Dash wanted Ervin's weight as a revered political figure and former judge behind the reform recommendations. The centerpiece was a proposal for a new law that would require the appointment of a "public attorney" who would handle investigations of a president or other top federal officials.

But who would make the appointment to guarantee independence without creating a fourth branch in the federal government? The president obviously couldn't do it. The attorney general had appointed Cox—exposing the fatal weakness and lack of independence for a prosecutor appointed through the Justice Department. Dash researched. The first bills introduced in the days after the 1973 Saturday Night Massacre provided for the appointment to be made by the judiciary. That made sense to Dash. The federal courts in the past had appointed prosecutors in extraordinary circumstances. The Ervin-Dash proposal said the prosecutor would serve a fixed five-year term "and be chosen by members of the judicial branch to ensure his independence from the executive control or influence."

Dash felt their proposal was consistent with the *Federalist Papers*. James Madison had written about "the necessity of auxiliary precautions." Their reform was only one more safeguard.

Ervin and Dash released their final report and recommendations on July 14, 1974. But the July 24, 1974, Supreme Court decision ordering Nixon to turn over his tapes, Nixon's August resignation and the September Nixon pardon consumed the nation and Congress and postponed any meaningful attempts to pass legislation. Hearings were finally held in the Senate in July 1975.

Dash appeared in favor of reform legislation. "I hope the American people do not tire of being outraged and indignant at the kinds of things that occurred in Watergate," Dash said.

All four of the former Watergate special prosecutors, Cox, Jaworski, Henry A. Ruth Jr. and Ruff, opposed the proposal. Ruth, who had taken over from Jaworski, testified that his independence—although conferred by the attorney general and not by law—was the real danger.

"As special prosecutor now," Ruth testified, "I take directions from no one, I report directly on ongoing investigations to no one, and I could easily abuse my power with little chance of detection."

Eventually, President Ford in 1976 came out in support of legislation that Dash found seriously flawed. Under the Ford plan, the president—not the courts—would appoint the special prosecutor.

Dash felt that reform had been crippled. How could favoritism, cover-up or intimidation be prevented if a top White House official, cabinet officer or the president himself was the subject of serious allegations? The attorney general and the Justice Department would have to remain primary, Dash realized, unless the entire system of justice was revamped.

In 1976, the Senate voted out Ford's version of a reform bill by a lopsided 91 to 5, but the House bill was stalled when opponents argued that the concept of a special prosecutor would be a slap in the face of the Justice Department and the attorney general whichever party was in power. Carter's election and his support gave the legislation new momentum, but not enough, and it stalled again in 1977.

Finally, after almost five years of haggling,

Senate drafters developed a passable concept. The attorney general would conduct a preliminary 90-day investigation of serious allegations against a high official. After the preliminary investigation the attorney general could determine the allegation had no merit and drop it. If further investigation was warranted, the attorney general would be required to apply to a new panel of three federal appeals court judges appointed by the chief justice of the Supreme Court. The three judges would appoint a special prosecutor, who would in effect have the powers of the attorney general to investigate, prosecute and issue a final report.

In 1978, as the November election approached, Dash could see that Watergate was still a major political memory, perhaps the dominant one for most of those in the House and Senate. A special prosecutor law was widely seen as a matter of reform, if not honor and integrity. Nearly everyone wanted to be aligned with it. The proposal was no longer controversial. In a way it was almost obvious, even automatic, the only meaningful remedy to a future Saturday Night Massacre. The legacy of Sam Ervin kept it alive in the Senate, where it once again passed by a voice vote on October 7.

On October 12, the ethics bill moved to the floor of the House. A heavyset and amiable two-term Illinois Republican congressman with a forceful voice took the floor. His name was Henry Hyde. He was one of the rare Republicans who had been elected in 1974, which had been in general a post-Watergate disaster for his party. Hyde had tried to extend the special prosecutor's authority to members of Congress under investigation, but his proposal had failed. He still favored the bill sponsored by the majority Democrats. He noted that the Watergate hearings had produced the recommendation, and he supported the special prosecutor provision strongly.

"I will be very candid," Hyde, 54, declared in some wonderment, "I did not think I would ever see the day when the majority party would bring this to the floor."

The bill passed as part of other legislation, 344 to 49.

Carter signed it on October 26, declaring, "I believe that this act will help to restore public confidence in the integrity of our government."

Five years had passed since the Saturday Night Massacre. After the airing of the facts of Watergate and the discovery of the Nixon taping system, Dash and Ervin felt it was the most important byproduct of their investigation. Dash later spoke by phone with Ervin, who was 82 and retired in his hometown of Morganton, North Carolina.

There was no way to put Watergate behind them, Ervin said, and bury it without preparing for the next major scandal. It would surely come. Now, he said, the system would be ready for the next emergency or extraordinary time when someone in high office shook the foundations of government—in Ervin's mind the clear intent of the new law.

7

ON TUESDAY MORNING, November 27, 1979, Arthur H. Christy, a well-to-do attorney with dark, wavy hair and a neatly trimmed mustache, sat at his desk quietly working. Always dressed meticulously, often in a dark business suit, cufflinks, Gucci tie and silk handkerchief, Christy, 56, oversaw a successful corporate law practice from his suite of offices on Fifth Avenue overlooking Rockefeller Center. More than two decades earlier he had been the young U.S. attorney who sent legendary organized crime boss Vito Genovese to jail in a narcotics conspiracy. Christy was by nature direct if not blunt, more streetwise than scholarly. When his secretary buzzed him, he picked up the phone to hear the unexpected but familiar voice of Federal Appeals Court Judge J. Edward Lumbard, his longtime mentor and a former U.S. attorney for whom Christy had worked in the 1950s.

"We need a special prosecutor. We don't know what the hell it is, but how would you like to try it out?" Judge Lumbard asked Christy.

Christy said he couldn't talk. He was in the middle of an important case.

That won't do, Lumbard said sternly. He was sitting with the two other appeals court judges who would make the special prosecutor appointment. They wanted to interview Christy right away. Lumbard suggested rather forcefully that Christy jump on the subway and hasten down to his chambers.

Recognizing the command from his old boss, Christy quickly went downtown to see Lumbard in the federal courthouse at 26 Federal Plaza.

Lumbard introduced Roger Robb, presiding judge on the D.C. federal appeals court, and Lewis Render Morgan, senior judge on the federal appeals court in Georgia. They handed him a copy of the Ethics in Government Act, which the previous year Congress had passed and President Carter had signed into law. They explained that the act, the major post-Watergate reform on financial disclosure designed to make government officials accountable, included a provision for appointment of a special prosecutor when the attorney general received specific allegations of misconduct by a senior government official. The special prosecutor provision of the act had never been invoked, the judges said, but President Carter's attorney general, Benjamin R. Civiletti, had called to say an application for an appointment was forthcoming. They were the three judges under the law who would appoint special prosecutors and oversee their work. Would Christy like the job?

Christy asked if he would have to give up his law practice.

The judges said he could continue handling private cases, and the special prosecutor would be a one-shot investigation.

Christy asked about the case.

Attorney General Civiletti wanted a special prosecutor to investigate whether Hamilton Jordan, now Carter's chief of staff, possessed or used cocaine at the trendy New York disco Studio 54.

Christy was familiar with the allegations, which had been in the newspapers and on television for three months. Steve Rubell, one of Studio 54's owners, had made the charge as part of a last-ditch effort to avoid prosecution for skimming millions of dollars off the disco's profits. A drug-dealing friend of Rubell's, John "Johnny C" Conaghan, had allegedly corroborated Rubell's story, saying he had given cocaine to Jordan in Studio 54's basement. A third witness, a publicist named Barry Landau, had also come forward claiming that Jordan had asked him where he could obtain cocaine. All three had appeared on the ABC Television show *20/20* to brand Jordan a cocaine user.

After some discussion of the intent and operation of the Ethics in Government Act, Christy said he did not think he could accept the appointment, honored as he was, without talking to his law partners.

Lumbard and the others said they understood, but they wanted an answer within two days.

Christy was reluctant but conflicted. A misdemeanor drug possession investigation was incredibly small. The allegation was that Jordan had taken two sniffs. Cocaine possession carried a penalty of a fine up to $5,000 and one year in jail. But Watergate had started out with a third-rate burglary. Jordan certainly had a bad boy reputation. Maybe this probe would lead to much bigger crimes. As a former prosecutor, Christy realized that big cases often started out as small matters. You never knew.

If he took the job, Christy would in effect be

filling the shoes of Archibald Cox and Leon Jaworski, the celebrated Watergate prosecutors. Yet appointing a special prosecutor to investigate allegations made by a tax cheat, a drug dealer and a publicity hound was a little absurd. By the same token, unsavory characters often were the only witnesses a prosecutor might have.

Attorney General Benjamin Civiletti, 44, went to see President Carter at the White House. A special prosecutor in this case was outrageous, he agreed, but his hands were tied by the ethics law. He had conducted a preliminary investigation as mandated. The law said he was required to ask for a special prosecutor unless he concluded that the matter was "so unsubstantiated that it warrants no further investigation." He could not make that conclusion. Some of the witnesses were plea-bargaining and wanted immunity. The law prohibited him from agreeing to such arrangements. So he could not say that no further investigation was warranted. It was the type of case that would not be prosecuted against anyone else. When it was first presented to the U.S. attorney in New York, his response had almost been, So what? Justice Department policy was not to prosecute cases involving simple drug possession.

Carter didn't understand why the case had to be pursued, but he couldn't intervene.

Christy consulted his partners. They found the idea silly but offered no objections. Christy finally concluded that out of respect for Lumbard he had to accept. He called Lumbard on November 29.

That afternoon Christy was sworn in, and the

three judges issued a short order naming him special prosecutor to investigate whether Jordan possessed cocaine on June 27, 1978, in New York or "any other related or relevant allegation" of violations of the federal drug possession law.

At a press conference, Christy pledged to conduct "a very thorough, complete and certainly very impartial investigation as expeditiously as possible in fairness to Mr. Jordan." He noted that there were no geographical limits, but his probe was limited to the drug possession law. "I'm going to call it the way I see it," he said. "Either way there's going to be flak."

The investigation meant that Jordan, 35, the chief political strategist for Carter's improbable 1976 election, a major adviser for the upcoming Carter 1980 campaign, and Carter's chief of staff and top political man, would be mired in a sticky personal criminal investigation for months or longer.

Jordan was sick. He vividly recalled three months earlier when FBI agents had showed up at his doorstep in northwest Washington. They had asked him if he had ever taken cocaine at Studio 54. Jordan waived his right to an attorney, said he recalled going to Studio 54 but claimed it was "absolutely untrue" that he had used cocaine or utilized drugs of any kind.

Although he did not know it at the time of the FBI visit, Jordan was the target of a last-ditch plan to manipulate the criminal justice system and the press for the benefit of the two Studio 54 owners under indictment.

In the summer of 1979, Rubell and a partner,

Ian Schrager, had attempted to trade derogatory information about "a high government official" in exchange for reduced tax fraud sentences. On August 22, Schrager's attorney, Mitchell Rogovin, revealed in a meeting with U.S. Attorney Robert B. Fiske Jr. that Hamilton Jordan was the government official, and that Rubell alleged Jordan snorted cocaine at Studio 54. His message had the sound of a threat. He said, in effect, "We have damaging information about a high government official; we'll tell no one but you if you'll give our clients a break. If not, we'll go public, and there will be severe political and national security implications."

Fiske rejected the bid for leniency, and so Rogovin called officials at the Justice Department. The next day, in a meeting with Justice officials, Rogovin made the same plea. Attorney General Civiletti declined the deal, calling it "blackmail." But Civiletti had to initiate an investigation into the allegations under the Ethics in Government Act, and the FBI agents were sent to interview Jordan.

The investigation leaked to *The New York Times,* which published a front-page story on August 25. After the appointment of Special Prosecutor Christy, Jordan went to the president and offered to resign.

"No," said Carter, "that would be an admission of guilt." Iranians had earlier in the month taken hostages from the U.S. Embassy in Tehran, and Carter was staking his whole presidency on winning their release. "You've got to stay here and help me get the hostages out."

Publicly Carter expressed "complete confidence" in Jordan. The president said he was as confident in the truth of Jordan's absolute denial as he would be if the statement had come from his own wife or children.

After some soul-searching, Jordan concluded that he had set himself up for the troubles he now faced. Coming off the euphoria of the 1976 campaign, he had espoused the anti-Washington sentiments of an outsider intent on taking over the corrupt federal city and cleaning up the politics. Jordan and others in the Carter White House stiffed the Washington establishment and its dinner party circuit with particular relish. He generally avoided telephone repartee with Washington's senior reporters, columnists and editorial writers.

During late 1977, the first year of the Carter presidency, the *Washington Post* Style section ran a long article about the strain between the Carterites and Washington. Included in the last paragraph was an account of a dinner party that Jordan did attend. Seated next to the wife of the Egyptian ambassador, Jordan allegedly at one point grabbed at her front and said, "I've always wanted to see the pyramids."

Jordan flatly denied the account, and the White House declined to challenge it. Sam Donaldson, ABC Television's aggressive White House reporter who was at the table, later said he did not see any physical contact by Jordan but was certain Jordan made the comment about the pyramids. Five others at the table, including the ambassador's wife, denied that Jordan had done or said anything improper. The story and its explicit crudeness received wide attention and became the enduring first exhibit in the case that Jordan was an overbearing, uncouth hick.

The second exhibit came in February 1978 when *The Washington Post* Sunday magazine reported in a gossip column that Jordan allegedly spat a drink of Amaretto and cream down the front of the dress of a young woman at a bar called Sarsfield's on the edge of Georgetown. Jordan denied the account. If the White House had underreacted to the Egyptian pyramids allegation, it overreacted to the Amaretto and cream tale. White House lawyers were deployed to take statements and a 33-page rebuttal was released.

The level of White House effort and the intensity of its denial became the news. No credible firsthand witness ever appeared to support the allegation, and Jordan was probably innocent of spitting on a woman. Jordan was easygoing, but he was a serious person who did not enjoy being a public figure. Yet Jordan—who had divorced in 1978—liked to drink beer and loved chasing women. Jordan himself realized, if only dimly at first, that he put himself in positions that were potentially compromising and became a magnet for allegations. He was not totally innocent. He did go to places like Sarsfield's and Studio 54.

Christy tried to figure out a course of action. There were no guidelines, no paths to follow, no precedents. Nobody had ever been investigated or prosecuted under the act, and Christy was having second thoughts about his role.

He requested a meeting with Attorney General Civiletti and his deputies. He went down to Washington to the attorney general's office in the Justice Department headquarters on Pennsylvania Avenue. Civiletti gave him all the files of the FBI's preliminary investigation and the voluminous so-called FBI 302s, the reports of interviews. It amounted to more than 600 pages. He thought Christy would want any information on possible leads and other nuances not in the reports.

"Why are you doing this?" Christy asked Civiletti. "Suppose I find this evidence, what am I supposed to do? Go get an indictment and try to charge the guy with taking two toots of cocaine?" Christy said no other prosecutor would ever take a case involving a misdemeanor violation and a smidgen of cocaine. Christy wanted Civiletti to be strong and resist the political pressure. The Ethics in Government Act was intended for investigations of serious government malfeasance, not Hamilton Jordan's alleged personal indiscretions. Christy said he did not believe a federal or state prosecutor in New York would bring such a case, even if he could prove it. "Why don't you just decide no way, forget it, decline prosecution, which you can always do?" Christy asked.

Civiletti said his hands were tied. He repeated his belief that the allegations against Jordan were false and the evidence did not warrant prosecution. But the Ethics Act required that he determine that the allegations are so unsubstantiated that no further investigation was warranted. The act did not permit him to grant immunity or use a grand jury in his preliminary investigation. Several of the witnesses wanted immunity from prosecution in exchange for their testimony. So further investigation was warranted. Civiletti and his top advisers were unanimous in believing they had no choice. "Look, it's an allegation that's in the public eye now, we've got this act, how can I just decline to prosecute?" Civiletti answered. "The act mandates me to do this," Civiletti said.

Christy knew that more than legal requirements were at work here. The Ethics in Government Act was in part a Carter administration initiative, and Civiletti could not afford to undermine it the first time it was tested. Civiletti also would be pilloried in the press—which was trumpeting the allegations—if all of a sudden he just declined to prosecute. There had to be a further investigation, and it was already formally in Christy's hands.

"Okay, what you want me to do is pick up your coals and carry them," Christy said.

Civiletti made it clear to Christy that he was not to communicate with anyone in the Department of Justice about the investigation except under unusual conditions. You're on your own, he said.

Civiletti was an expert technician on criminal law. He had been an assistant U.S. attorney in the 1960s, headed the criminal division earlier in the Carter administration, and then became deputy attorney general before taking the top spot. Civiletti felt a special prosecutor investigation was probably unfair to Jordan, but he believed that there could only be justice when the law was followed faithfully. Chaos would prevail if he and others made individual determinations based on common sense or other reasons.

Within a week, Christy was wavering again. He thought about simply announcing that the case was closed on the grounds that no prosecutor would ever bring such a case, and no jury would ever convict. But he quickly decided that having gone through all the hoopla of accepting the appointment as special prosecutor, he could not suddenly reverse field and declare his investigation over, although he had the power to do so. Momentum and prudence seemed to dictate that he continue.

The total independence was slightly unnerving to Christy. Perhaps he could receive some guidance and comfort from the three-judge panel that appointed him? Chief Judge Robb agreed to meet Christy at the Yale Club on Vanderbilt Avenue in New York City.

Would you like me to give you periodic reports on what's going on? Christy asked.

No, Judge Robb replied, we don't want to hear from you until the end of the investigation.

Christy began assembling a staff. He hired three attorneys, a retired FBI agent and an administrative assistant, and he borrowed an FBI agent and a senior man in the Drug Enforcement Agency. He was concerned that the active FBI agent, John Barrett, might feel obliged to reveal everything Christy was doing to his superiors, but Barrett agreed to make no reports. Since it was a drug investigation, Christy felt compelled to inquire of prospective employees if they had used illegal drugs. Once he had assembled his staff, Christy rented office space for them in the relatively cheap Federal Plaza in downtown Manhattan. On January 28, 1980, Christy wrote a letter to the Administrative Office of the U.S. Courts: "The office of the special prosecutor is a temporary government agency that should be operational for a period not to exceed one year."

Christy had a slightly disorganized, clumsy manner that concealed aggressive instincts. He'd gone head-to-head with the New York mob and knew that prosecuting did not always require legal niceties. Christy asked the chief judge of the federal court to impanel a special grand jury that he could use to compel witness testimony and the production of documents. Before taking a witness or a subject to the grand jury, Christy tried to interview the person informally. One of the first was Barry Landau, the public relations executive who had claimed to be in Studio 54 when Jordan had asked for cocaine. Landau had claimed his friend "Ham" had seen his familiar face, started chatting and asked, Where do you get the coke? Christy had discovered that Roy Cohn, the notorious aide to Senator Joseph McCarthy during the 1950s who was a lawyer for one of Studio 54's owners, had arranged for Landau to receive $12,000 the same week in August 1979 that Landau had come forward to support the allegations against Jordan. The money allegedly was to help pay off debts and to finance an Acapulco vacation for two. It smelled to Christy.

113

Christy believed that taking witnesses to the scene of an alleged crime could be revealing. Specifics of where people were standing, what they were wearing and what they said often emerged. Comparing the details, sometimes small, of witnesses helped determine credibility. At 1:30 p.m. on February 6, Christy took Landau into Studio 54.

Where had he first met Jordan on the evening in question? Christy asked.

Landau wasn't sure if it was by the bar, next to the dance floor, or sitting on one of the lounges.

Christy brought Landau down the stairs to an area known as "the cage," with the pinball machine, couches and big pillows. It was a dimly lit, cluttered area reserved for celebrities.

Was that where Ham had asked the question?

Landau wasn't sure.

Christy asked whether he recalled any conversation with Jordan about the drugs.

Landau said Jordan had asked if he could get any cocaine, or if he could get some coke.

Cocaine or coke? Christy asked

Landau could not recall.

If Jordan had used the word "coke," could he have meant Coca-Cola? Christy asked.

No, he could not have meant Coca-Cola, Landau said. The tone of Jordan's voice indicated what he wanted.

What was the tone of Jordan's voice? Christy asked.

Landau could not elaborate on the conversation.

As Christy took him through the details,

nearly every specific Landau had uttered on national television grew more vague.

Finally, Christy flew into a rage. He grabbed Landau by the necktie and threw him up against a post.

"You're a fucking liar!" he shouted.

Next Christy put Landau before the grand jury, and under questioning Landau did not back up his original story.

Christy went to work on Steve Rubell, the Studio 54 co-owner who had recently pleaded guilty to two counts of tax evasion. He had been sentenced to three and a half years in prison and fined $5,000. Christy's main witness— and Jordan's principal accuser—was thus a felon in jail. He brought Rubell in for a series of interviews, asking about statements Rubell had made on national television about Jordan. "Well, he took a hit in each nostril, and that was it," Rubell had said. Christy asked if the statement was true. Had Rubell seen Jordan sniff cocaine?

Rubell could not recall.

Did he have a conversation with Jordan?

Rubell could not recall.

Had Rubell used Quaaludes or cocaine on the night in question?

Probably.

How could Rubell make the revelations on national television if he did not recall any details of the incident?

Rubell said he made the charges on television because he had heard the allegations from the drug dealer named Johnny C.

So, Rubell's information was purely secondhand, but he had presented it as if he had witnessed the cocaine sniffing?

Yes.

Christy took Rubell to the basement of Studio 54 to try to jog his memory. Rubell could not even identify where the incident allegedly occurred.

Rubell then failed a lie detector test. His attorney asked Christy if he would arrange for Rubell to be examined by a hypnotist. If Rubell was not a proper subject for hypnosis, Rubell's attorney asked Christy to have some expert administer sodium pentothal (truth serum) or scopolamine to Rubell.

Christy contacted some experts. The technique looked unpromising. On April 7, 1980, Christy sent Rubell's lawyer a letter. "After consideration, I have decided not to proceed further with any type of examination of Mr. Rubell as you have requested," Christy wrote. He had concluded that Rubell's testimony had no evidentiary value whatsoever.

At 3:45 p.m. on January 18, 1980, Christy had begun interviewing the third main witness, John "Johnny C" Conaghan, at Christy's law office on Fifth Avenue.

You remember, Johnny, that you gave two toots to Jordan? Christy asked.

No, Johnny C said. He wasn't sure at all.

Why did you go on national television and say that if you were unsure?

Johnny C said the interview did not accurately reflect his uncertainty. He never should have mentioned Jordan's name.

What is your knowledge of Jordan's alleged use of cocaine? Christy asked.

Johnny C said he did not know whether the man he had given cocaine to was Hamilton Jordan. He had assumed so because other customers at Studio 54 had told him two days later it was Jordan. Johnny C said he could never be certain that the person he "turned on" was Jordan.

Christy asked about Johnny C's drug use.

I did a lot of coke, at least three to four times a week, Johnny C said. I smoked pot nightly, and it was my custom to drink somewhere around half a quart of Stolichnaya vodka a day, he added.

Later in the interview, Johnny C volunteered that maybe it had all been a setup.

Christy asked what he meant.

Rubell might have had a few customers come up to him within the next few days and say he'd turned on Jordan, Johnny C said.

Christy found him totally unreliable. Johnny C wasn't necessarily a deliberate liar, he just wasn't believable. He seemed too drugged out. After more interviews and a trip with Johnny C to Studio 54, Christy concluded his value as a witness was a perfect zero.

Other allegations about Jordan came to Christy. One was that Jordan had taken cocaine in 1977 at a Los Angeles party. Maxine Cheshire, a reporter for *The Washington Post*, kept asking Christy if he was going to go to the West Coast to look into the allegations. Christy wouldn't answer, because he didn't want to give her a scoop that he was expanding his investigation to California. Cheshire increased the pressure for information. She told Christy during at least three conversations that there was a young woman who could tell Christy about Jordan using cocaine in Los Angeles. On March 13, Christy called Cheshire and pressed for the woman's name, but Cheshire would not tell him.

Christy felt he had been put on notice of such allegations, and thus had a responsibility to investigate. He thought if he didn't probe the allegations and later it turned out there was substance to them, he could be faulted. Within two weeks, he had learned the woman's name, Cynthia Alksne, and brought her in for an interview.

Alksne, who was working for the presidential campaign of Senator Edward M. Kennedy, the Massachusetts Democrat, said she was reluctant to get involved. But under questioning she said Jordan was acting drunk and obnoxious that night.

Christy and the prosecutors pressed her for details.

She said Jordan was loud, telling jokes and slurring his speech a bit.

What about drug use at the party?

She said she had not seen Jordan doing any coke, and she said she had told that to Cheshire during their conversations.

Christy let Alksne go, concluding there was no substance to the allegations.

In the interest of a complete investigation, Christy also brought in Lana Rawls, former wife of singer Lou Rawls, whose attorney claimed to newspapers that she saw Jordan use cocaine at the 1977 Los Angeles party.

Asked under oath, Rawls said she had not seen Jordan take cocaine at any time. Yet another allegation had evaporated.

As Christy dug into the circumstances of the evening of June 27–28, 1978, when Jordan visited Studio 54, a somewhat clearer and disturbing picture emerged. Jordan, two other White House aides and two senior Democratic National Committee officials had flown to New York City for a dinner at "21" with some businessmen and major Democratic donors. After the dinner, Jordan and his group had gone to a party hosted by one of the businessmen, a trucking executive, at an apartment the businessman maintained at the Essex House Hotel on Central Park South.

At the Essex House party were two other women. Christy soon established that they were prostitutes.

Around 11:30 p.m., after the Essex House party, the Jordan group, including the two prostitutes, went with one of the businessmen in his limousine to Studio 54. In the course of the visit, the members of the group visited the Studio 54 basement.

Christy thought the Studio 54 crowd unsavory and decadent. He had not found a truth-teller among them. Truth to them was elusive—exaggerated and hyperbolic story-telling that might or might not have a factual basis. It was a maddening environment for a prosecutor.

But he decided to interview systematically each member of the Jordan group, including Joel

McCleary, a White House aide who had been with Jordan earlier that night.

McCleary and his lawyer came to Christy's conference room on Fifth Avenue.

Christy said he wanted the full story of that evening—honest and complete, spare no details.

McCleary had a remarkable memory. He recounted the dinner and the party at the Essex House. At the party, he said, he went out on the balcony and took a couple of puffs from a marijuana cigarette.

Christy motioned McCleary's attorney to accompany him out of the room so they could confer in private.

"Please shut up your client," Christy requested. "I don't want another case." Christy realized he was dangerously on the road to becoming special prosecutor for misdemeanor drug use in the Carter administration—a role he desperately did not want. But he was glad to have found a truth-teller among the Carter crowd.

McCleary had intentionally implicated himself so he would be credible. He was sure Jordan was not a drug user. Unfortunately for Christy, he had not gone with Jordan to Studio 54.

Christy also learned of some untested allegations that other members of Carter's administration had used illegal drugs. In one case, Evan Dobelle, a Democratic National Committee official, was called to the grand jury. Christy and his deputies had heard that Carter's current campaign manager, Tim Kraft, who had also been at Studio 54 with Jordan, had used cocaine a year earlier in New Orleans. Christy did not want it pursued. "I do not want you to ask any questions about Kraft," he directed his deputies.

One deputy ignored the prohibition. In answer to a question, Dobelle said he had seen Kraft take some cocaine in 1978 at a party in New Orleans. Dobelle also claimed he observed events that suggested to him that Kraft had used cocaine in a hotel suite at the St. Francis Hotel in San Francisco.

Because the allegations were now on the record, Christy felt they had a duty to ask Kraft about drug use. They did so during a January 31 interview. Christy found Kraft to be less than candid in many of his answers. Kraft would not answer if he had smoked pot at any time prior to coming to Christy's office. Through his lawyer he refused in March 1980 to take a lie detector test, even though he had initially been willing.

Although the Kraft allegations had nothing to do with the Studio 54 investigation, Christy decided once they were on the record they had to report the alleged violations to the attorney general.

Civiletti asked Christy if he would consider expanding his investigation. Christy hesitated, but he indicated that he would, provided the three-judge panel approved.

Judge Robb said the three-judge panel would be reluctant to extend Christy's appointment based on Robb's objection. The Kraft allegations were not sufficiently related to the Jordan investigation to justify extending Christy's prosecutorial jurisdiction to include them.

In light of this decision, Christy was off the hook, and Civiletti decided to apply for the appointment of another special prosecutor to probe Kraft's alleged drug use. Kraft resigned as campaign manager, a serious blow to Carter's reelection campaign, but the New Orleans independent counsel, Gerald Gallinghouse, eventually found no basis for prosecution.

Christy called Henry Ruth, the third Watergate special prosecutor, who was now Jordan's attorney.

We have enough evidence, I've reached a point in the investigation where I have to talk to your client, Christy said. He did not say the allegation was not panning out.

Ruth said his client had nothing to hide and would cooperate.

Jordan was wary of Christy. What kind of lawyer would interrupt a lucrative private practice to investigate a misdemeanor drug possession allegation against anyone? It seemed plain to Jordan: a publicity seeker, an ambitious lawyer trying to get his name in the paper. Jordan felt that Christy would turn his investigation into a circus.

On Thursday, March 27, two of Christy's agents met Jordan at LaGuardia Airport in plainclothes and drove him to Christy's Manhattan office. Christy began interviewing Jordan at 10:35 a.m.

Christy advised Jordan that any information he provided would be treated confidentially and would not be turned over to the Department of Justice, the FBI or the media.

Jordan was surprised at Christy's friendly attitude. Christy seemed straightforward, not overly prosecutorial or aggressive. Despite his initial suspicion, Jordan decided to be direct.

"I've got a terrible reputation because there are all sorts of allegations," Jordan said. He recounted the charges about his alleged pyramids comments and the Amaretto and cream. "I'm taking a pasting. I have to tell you, I probably deserve it. I don't think I have behaved as well as I could have." Going to bars or Studio 54 automatically put him in potentially compromising situations, he said, and he should have known better. But he did not have or use cocaine at Studio 54.

Christy quizzed him up and down six different ways. He asked for a narrative of the evening—all the details.

Jordan related what he remembered about the party at the Essex House. Yes, he said, there were two women there who could have been hookers. They were reasonably attractive, but Jordan said he didn't want to have much to do with them.

For Christy, this was an important acknowledgment because it established Jordan's bona fides as a truth-teller. Christy didn't ask any more questions about the prostitutes. It was not part of his investigation. He was dealing with drugs, not sex.

Christy asked Jordan about the alleged cocaine use.

The one thing he was sure of, Jordan said, was that he never had taken cocaine and never asked for it. Not at Studio 54 or at any other time in his life. Lots of beer, lots of women, but no drugs. Drugs were bad for your health, Jordan said, as well as being illegal. People, especially government officials, do not have the right to pick and choose the laws they wish to obey. Jordan added that he would ask anyone working at the White House to leave if he knew that they were using drugs.

Just before 2:30 p.m., Christy decided to take the next step.

"I want to take you over to Studio 54," Christy said.

Jordan said fine.

Christy had his agents arrange for them to enter unseen. In the famous celebrity basement, Jordan looked around carefully.

"I've got to tell you, as I recall it, I may very well have come down here. I don't have any specific recollection." He looked around some more and repeated, "But I may very well have." He said he had a strong impression, a "sense" that he had been there before, but no more precise recollection. He said the basement's blue light triggered his memory. He did not recall ever meeting his three accusers—Rubell, Landau or Johnny C—but he had "a strong hunch" of not being alone in the basement.

At 3 p.m., Christy took Jordan back to his office. They talked for another hour and a half about the California allegations, and Jordan denied he had used or been offered cocaine or marijuana in Los Angeles.

Christy believed him. On the central allegation, he was convinced that Jordan had not taken cocaine. He arranged for Jordan to get back to Washington without any publicity.

About a month later, on April 23, Christy brought Jordan back to New York to appear before the grand jury. Christy had Jordan taken the back way to the grand jury room so again there was no publicity. In the grand jury, Jordan repeated his story and made a fairly good impression with the jurors, who had been skeptical of some of the other witnesses from the White House.

Afterwards, Jordan was unsure if he had been persuasive. Mr. Christy, do you believe me? Jordan asked.

Christy hesitated. That's got to be a matter for the grand jury to decide if they believe you, he said. They're the ones, not me.

Judge Lumbard called Christy. Can't you bring this thing to a close sometime soon? Lumbard asked his protégé. He indicated that although the judges had told Christy they did not want progress reports, they wanted to be rid of the investigation.

I could probably do it by the middle of June, Christy said.

Well, try for the end of May, Lumbard instructed. Six months was enough.

On May 21, 1980, after 19 grand jury sessions and 33 witnesses over two and a half months, Christy called the grand jury together.

He told the grand jury that he believed there was insufficient evidence to warrant bringing criminal charges against Hamilton Jordan. In fact, there was no credible evidence at all. It was impossible to prove a negative, however, and grand juries traditionally did not state absolutely that a charge was not true. So there was no complete exoneration. He recommended that the grand jury vote a "No True Bill," a legal term meaning there is not probable cause to bring charges.

The vote was unanimous.

Christy wanted to issue a public report as soon as possible to make it clear that the investigation was over and Jordan would not be charged. Because of grand jury secrecy rules, he didn't believe he could use grand jury testimony in his report. He had intentionally conducted extensive staff interviews with the witnesses and Jordan so he could use that for the basis of his public findings. He instructed his deputies to cut-and-paste excerpts from the staff interviews with the main witnesses. Terri Duggan, his administrative assistant, began typing up a final report.

On May 28, one day short of six months after he was appointed, Christy's final report was finished in loose paper form. It was 53 pages long. Copies were hand-delivered to the three judges on the special panel, and Duggan handed it out to reporters in brown envelopes. The reporters sat on the floor in the elevator bank and began reading. Murray Kempton, the columnist, came back into the special prosecutor's foyer.

"Where's all the dirt?" Kempton asked.

President Carter attended a champagne celebration in Jordan's office, declaring that his confidence in his top aide never wavered. Jordan was vindicated.

"All you've got in your life is your reputation

and your honor," Jordan said, putting the best campaign face on the matter with the 1980 presidential election only five months away.

Jordan damn sure didn't feel exonerated. All the stories about not bringing charges noted how frivolous and flimsy the allegations had been—a stark turnaround from the breathless front-page headlines and television specials nine months earlier. His reputation had been framed, nearly etching in stone a portrait of recklessness. The taxpayers paid Christy's $181,938 bill for the investigation, but Jordan was $67,553 in debt to his lawyer. He was not independently wealthy, and government pay, while comfortable, could not cover the fees he owed. He spent the next half a dozen years trying unsuccessfully to get Congress to pay for his legal expenses.

Years later, I went to see Jordan at his home in Atlanta. He had made some money and lived comfortably. He was married, had survived two bouts with prostate cancer and had three children.

"I should have just never allowed myself to be put in that situation, never should have gone in there," Jordan said, referring to Studio 54. In retrospect, Jordan felt that his personal behavior had hurt both his professional reputation and the prestige of the Carter administration. "I was a problem back then," Jordan admitted. "I liked to have fun. I used to drink a little bit. Never a whole lot. Never took drugs ever. And I mean I was turned into something very different than the way I am. I'm no different now than the way I was then. I'm a fairly serious person and I was made to look like just kind of a jackass."

President Carter later concluded that the Jordan episode had a greater impact on his administration because of his commitment to a higher moral standard. In 1998, Carter said, "...It was much more serious because of my claiming the high moral ground than it would have been if I had not ever raised the subject that I'm more filled with integrity than others. I mean that was kind of a brash thing for me to do. And possibly a mistake in having done it once I got to be president. But I think that those kinds of claims that I put forward about my moral status and my commitment to the truth got me into the White House. So it cut both ways. It helped me get elected, but it also came back to haunt me later on."

8

PRESIDENTS SET A tone for the country, not only with their politics and programs, but with their style. Although Carter is a Christian and a humanitarian, his manner is all-business. He has a coldness about him. He almost enjoyed presenting bad news to the public and tackling thankless tasks. The 1970s energy crisis was real, and he attempted to sell a program of sacrifice. The treaty giving the Panama Canal back was necessary, although unpopular with conservatives, but Carter was determined to ram it through, as he did. He enjoyed creating a public drama to underscore his seriousness, making the presidency a public stage for the great struggles between good and evil, right and wrong as he saw it.

Other than a handful of Georgians in his administration, Carter never found anyone in Congress or his cabinet who was willing to bleed for him. He never forged the bonds so the leaders in his party or administration or the liberal columnists would follow when he yelled charge. The hallmark of his administration was dutifulness. But this trait was often tethered to self-righteousness. President Carter seemed to be administering unpleasant medicine, not leading or healing with comfortable confidence.

His election was a direct response to Watergate. Ford initially had seemed to cleanse the presidency, but then he had pardoned Nixon, which cast suspicion and doubt on his motivation and action. Ford didn't provide enough of a cleanup. Carter came along and seemed to promise a double cleansing. He was the ultimate anti-Nixon. In his election, Watergate had a distorting impact—channeling media and voter attention almost exclusively to the issues of truthfulness and honesty. Only an outsider with extraordinary ambition and discipline could make it to the presidency, almost foreordaining someone with Carter's driven style. A casual, nice guy wouldn't have a chance in the marathon race for the presidency.

Once in office, Carter had to face a vigilant press intent on finding more Watergates and unmasking the president's weaknesses. Nowhere was that scrutiny more damaging than in the Iranian hostage crisis. On November 4, 1979, revolutionaries in Tehran had seized 52 American hostages in the U.S. Embassy. Carter had taken charge personally of the effort to win their release—again creating maximum public drama, a television spectacle. After public diplomacy and secret missions failed, Carter authorized a rescue mission in the spring of 1980. Malfunctioning helicopters forced the president to cancel the raid. The photographs of the wreckage—an Air Force plane crashed into some of the helicopters in the Iranian desert—became the symbol of America's and Carter's impotence.

Carter's personal obsession with the crisis invited heavy press attention, but one of the offshoots of Watergate was the media's determination to follow every step and misstep of the crisis. ABC Television began an 11:30 p.m. show entitled *America Held Hostage,* hosted by Ted Koppel. The show counted the days, and America Held Hostage Day 365 landed on November 4, 1980, the day of the presidential election. Carter lost to Ronald Reagan by 10 points. The hostages still were not freed.

Carter probably could have sent a large military force into Iran to rescue the American hostages, lost all 52 and dozens or more U.S. servicemen, and likely come out a hero. But the president's humanitarian impulses held him back. "Although I was acting in an official capacity as president, I also had deep private feelings that were almost overwhelming," Carter

wrote in his memoir. "The hostages sometimes seemed like part of my own family." He
knew their names, became familiar with their
careers, and read their letters home. "I knew
and had grown to love some of the members of
their families."

Carter's diplomacy, patience and wrangling
over some $12 billion in Iranian assets frozen
in the United States eventually saved the
hostages. But they were not released until Day
444, just 33 minutes after Carter left office
and Reagan was sworn in as the new president. Carter had won their freedom but lost his
job.

The absence of news about the president
could become news itself in the hothouse of
expectation.

In the midst of the 1979 energy crisis (gasoline prices had increased more than 50 percent
since the beginning of the year), Carter
announced that he would deliver a major televised speech. He helicoptered to Camp David.
On the Fourth of July, he abruptly canceled the
speech scheduled for the next day and offered
no explanation. He then went into ten days of
soul-searching at his mountain retreat. He
invited groups of elected officials, leaders in religion, education and journalism, to speak to
him and his wife about the growing pessimism
and cynicism in America. It was like one giant
therapy session, with Carter and his wife taking
copious notes—once again a high-stakes morality
play with the president at the center.

The White House offered no real public

explanation. The longer the silence from Camp David, the more the mystery deepened. Suspense and speculation grew that Carter was ill or faced some grave foreign crisis. Finally, Carter came down from the mountain to give a speech Sunday night, July 15. Some 65 million Americans tuned in, double the normal audience for a presidential speech. More forceful and assertive than usual, Carter gave a sermon. He suggested that he and his administration had failed. "The erosion of our confidence in the future is threatening to destroy the social and political fabric of America." The speech soon was called Carter's "crisis of confidence" speech or his "malaise" speech—a word he had never used but which captured his mood and purpose.

Carter's popularity rose by 9 percent. But two days later, acting on a suggestion from media adviser Gerald Rafshoon, Carter asked for the resignations of all his cabinet and senior White House staff. The summary action created its own crisis of confidence in Carter's leadership and was widely viewed as a purge of those who seemed disloyal. Soon Carter's popularity was again in the basement with a 74 percent negative rating.

Carter summoned his health, education and welfare secretary, Joseph A. Califano Jr., to his private study off the Oval Office. Califano, a cool Washington operator who had been President Johnson's top domestic adviser, was a fiercely independent overseer of a budget larger than that of all other nations except the United States and the Soviet Union.

Carter said he was going to accept Califano's resignation. "Your performance as secretary has been outstanding," Carter said, according to Califano's memo dictated right after the meeting. "The problem is friction with the White House staff." Carter then twice invited Califano to spend the weekend with him at Camp David.

"Bring your children along," Carter said. "If you want to, you can go up there alone, and I won't go."

Califano shook his head. He was crushed to lose the job running the programs that he had seen put in place by Johnson.

"Then come with me and bring your children. We can leave in a helicopter from the White House lawn Friday afternoon." The Friday helicopter departure was always filmed by the news media, and guests were only those closest to the president.

Califano, who was beginning to hurt, declined again. As he was leaving, Carter renewed the Camp David invitation.

At a press conference, Califano said Carter had praised his work as "superb" and that he had been "the best secretary of HEW." Jody Powell went on record denying that Carter had praised Califano. That weekend, Saturday afternoon, July 21, Carter held a background news conference with reporters. He too disputed Califano, in effect saying Califano was lying. But the president would not allow himself to be quoted.

I spoke with Califano the next year. As a private attorney in Washington, he had represented the *Post* and me during Watergate. He was absolutely and, I believe, genuinely dumbfounded at Carter. Califano produced a handwritten note that Carter sent him in 1980. "You did an outstanding job as secretary," it said in the president's distinctive hand. I recalled my experience with Carter in 1977 on the Hussein story for Califano, how Carter had given one version in private and an opposite version to others. We both noted the eerie parallels. It was not just that Carter wanted, like most people, to have things both ways, Califano and I agreed. It was that Carter regularly broke his most basic promise made when he campaigned for the presidency. He did not always tell the truth.

PART THREE

RONALD REAGAN

1981–89

9

ON APRIL 22, 1986, Theodore B. Olson was celebrating a Supreme Court victory in his law offices on Connecticut Avenue in downtown Washington when Federal Appeals Court Judge George E. MacKinnon called. MacKinnon had sworn Olson in as the assistant attorney general in charge of the Justice Department's Office of Legal Counsel five years earlier. It had been a dream job for Olson, largely above the political scramble, the closest thing to the practice of pure law.

"You know," said MacKinnon, who headed the three-judge panel that appointed independent counsels, "we're going to have to appoint an independent counsel in your case."

Olson, who had returned to private practice several years before, was floored. A House committee had alleged that in 1983 Olson had given false and misleading testimony in a bitter dispute about congressional access to Environmental Protection Agency (EPA) enforcement documents. It was a political wrangle over whether the Reagan administration was adequately enforcing hazardous waste cleanup under the Superfund law. Olson hadn't been under oath in his testimony, and the issue was whether executive privilege covered the documents. The committee had asked Attorney General Edwin Meese III to appoint an independent counsel as the law allowed. It had never seriously dawned on Olson that Meese would go ahead and request one. A full-scale criminal investigation over what was essentially a legal and political argument? With him as the target?

"Would you come see me please?" Judge MacKinnon asked.

Olson found himself saying yes.

The judge said he was in bed with a foot injury at his home in Potomac, a Maryland suburb. He gave Olson the address and directions.

Olson's heart was beating fast. He was stunned. He wondered if he should be driving because he was so distracted.

The judge's wife took Olson up to MacKinnon's bedroom when he arrived. For what seemed to Olson like half an hour, MacKinnon reminisced about Gibson, Dunn & Crutcher, Olson's law firm. Finally, he turned to business—the necessity of appointing an independent counsel. The law gave the three-judge panel no alternative.

"The person we want to appoint," MacKinnon said in a matter-of-fact tone, "we have a person who is just right for this case."

Olson was aghast. Was this attorney going to be his executioner?

"He's an older member of the bar from a prominent firm," MacKinnon said with satisfaction. "I can't say who he is, but he believes there is a possible conflict, but I think that's not disqualifying. If you agree not to object, we'll appoint him."

Olson was almost breathless. He was about

to become the subject of a criminal investigation, and the appointing judge wanted his approval of his prosecutor in the blind? Who was he talking about? What was the possible but not disqualifying conflict? Olson felt he shouldn't even be there talking to the judge. He certainly wouldn't do it—have an ex parte contact with the judge—if he were the lawyer for the subject. But it was worse; he was the subject. What choice did he have? "Of course, Judge," Olson said, "if you think that is correct, that would be acceptable to me."

MacKinnon thanked him and said goodbye.

"I wonder if you'd do a favor for me?" Betty MacKinnon asked downstairs.

Sure, Olson said, wondering, What now? He was dizzy.

"Today is Judge MacKinnon's birthday," she said. "He's 80 years old. Could you write something nice in our guestbook?"

My God, Olson thought, was it conceivable that he was being trapped into making some kind of written record of his visit? Was this summons a plot? What was happening? He picked up the pen and wrote something.

Olson had once done a chart for the Justice Department of the four independent counsels appointed up to that time. All of the investigations had concluded within six months or less, he remembered. This probe is going to be awful and debilitating, he thought, but it would at least be short. The hearing in question had been public, so there would be a record of what he had said.

He was sure he had been careful. No, he reflected, the inquiry was going to be manageable, it would take only several months at most. Other lawyers would probably understand the nature of the dispute, but it was a criminal investigation, liable to be billed as a mini-Watergate.

Two days later the three-judge panel announced the appointment of an independent counsel, James C. McKay. The story made the front page of *The Washington Post*. Olson issued a definitive declaration of innocence: "I deny categorically and unequivocally and without any qualification the charges." Five weeks later McKay resigned because his law partner, Charles Ruff, the former Watergate special prosecutor, had advised the House committee on its investigation of Olson—a potential conflict of interest. The three-judge panel assigned his deputy, Alexia Morrison, to the case.

Independent Counsel Morrison, a dogged and at times uncompromising former assistant U.S. attorney, went into high gear. Olson was summoned to testify under oath before her, half a dozen of her lawyers and FBI agents on her staff for an entire day. He had made comments about the case to friends as they attended a professional basketball game. All were called before the grand jury. In a dispute about document production, Morrison asked Olson to waive his claim to making a constitutional argument against the independent counsel law. He refused and went to court claiming the act was unconstitutional. The six months Olson had expected the investigation to last stretched into years, with no resolution.

While at the Justice Department, Olson had examined the act. He had concluded that it took away executive powers reserved for the president and essentially created a hybrid fourth branch of government. Olson, Attorney General William French Smith, Meese's predecessor, and Kenneth Starr, Smith's chief of staff, had tried to oppose it in 1981–82 when it came up for renewal. Smith and his staff had argued that special prosecutors were used for political purposes and to feed the media appetite for scandal. The high-profile nature of the cases forced the independent counsel to undertake sweeping investigations into remote and irrelevant trivia. Disagreeing, Congress had renewed the law twice with veto-proof majorities. But on January 22, 1988, Olson's attorneys persuaded a federal appeals court that the act was unconstitutional because it "so deeply invades the president's executive prerogatives and responsibilities."

The 2-to-1 decision was made in an 88-page opinion written by Judge Laurence H. Silberman, an ardent conservative on the court. Olson was elated. He felt the opinion was forceful and thoughtful and would give him an edge in the Supreme Court, which would make a final ruling. Olson calculated that they would win Chief Justice William Rehnquist and Justice Antonin Scalia—two who were strong on separation of power issues—another conservative, and likely the two liberal justices, William Brennan and Thurgood Marshall, who often liked to restrain prosecutorial power.

The case was argued before the Supreme

Court on April 26, 1988. Just two months later, on June 29, the Supreme Court upheld the Independent Counsel Act 7 to 1 in an opinion written by Chief Justice Rehnquist. As he read Rehnquist's long opinion, Olson saw that the chief justice made technical legal arguments but outright rejected the separation of powers argument.

Olson found immense emotional comfort in Justice Scalia's dissent, which said the dispute was about one thing: "Power." Since Article II of the Constitution vests all executive power in the president, including the power to investigate and prosecute crimes, Scalia wrote that the law modified the Constitution. "How much removal of presidential power is too much? Many countries of the world get along with an executive that is much weaker than ours—in fact, entirely dependent upon the continued support of the legislature. Once we depart from the text of the Constitution, just where short of that do we stop?" The prospect of an independent counsel turned loose was "frightening....One must grieve for the Constitution," Scalia argued.

"Only someone who has worked in the field of law enforcement can fully appreciate the vast power and the immense discretion that are placed in the hands of a prosecutor with respect to the objects of his investigation."

Scalia quoted from a speech given by Justice Robert Jackson when he was President Franklin Roosevelt's attorney general in 1940: "With the law books filled with a great assortment of crimes, a prosecutor stands a fair chance of finding at least a technical violation of some act on the part of almost anyone." Warming to the subject, Scalia said the result is a "mini-executive...operating in an area where so little is law and so much is discretion....What would normally be regarded as a technical violation (there are not rules defining such things), may in his or her small world assume the proportions of an indictable offense. What would normally be regarded as an investigation that has reached the level of pursuing such picayune matters that it should be concluded, may to him or her be an investigation that ought to go on for another year. How frightening it must be to have your own independent counsel and staff appointed, with nothing else to do but to investigate you until investigation is no longer worthwhile—with whether it is worthwhile not depending upon what such judgments usually hinge on, competing responsibilities."

Scalia directly stated that politics played a role in the enactment and retention of the law. "The notion that every violation of law should be prosecuted, including—indeed, especially—every violation by those in high places, is an attractive one, and it would be risky to argue in an election campaign that that is not an absolutely overriding value....Let justice be done, though the heavens may fall." He noted thankfully that the Constitution spared justices of the Supreme Court, "by life tenure, the necessity of election campaigns." But those in Congress who had to stand for election were trapped. For them, he said, "it is difficult to vote not to enact, and even more difficult to vote to repeal, a statute called, appropriately enough, the Ethics in Government Act. If Congress is controlled by the party other than the one to which the president belongs, it has little incentive to repeal it; if it is controlled by the same party, it dare not. By its shortsighted action today, I fear the Court has permanently encumbered the Republic with an institution that will do it great harm."

Olson's joy in reading Scalia's dissent did not last long. Although the passion was in Scalia's dissent, the law was with the majority. The nightmare would thus continue and intensify. Fearing that Independent Counsel Morrison would be emboldened by her victory, Olson hired James Neal, the Tennessee lawyer who had prosecuted and sent to jail Nixon's top aides in the Watergate cover-up trial after Nixon's resignation. Olson figured that if he were going to be indicted and tried, he better have the best lawyer possible.

Two months later, Morrison announced that Olson would not be indicted, effectively ending the 29-month investigation. Six months after that, her 225-page report was released. Morrison concluded that Olson had been "less than forthcoming" in his 1983 congressional testimony, which was "literally true." Her report also said that the testimony, "while not overly helpful, was not, in most instances at least, designed to conceal Mr. Olson's actual knowledge of critical points."

Olson and his friends proclaimed full exoneration.

"It was as if a horrible presence had come to

144

live with me," he said. The investigation infected his entire life—his legal practice, when he woke up in the middle of the night, when he read *The Bonfire of the Vanities* or *Presumed Innocent,* books about men caught in the web of investigation. His legal fees ran about $1.2 million. The federal government paid about two-thirds and his lawyers absorbed the rest. That was the measurable damage. What he couldn't measure was the toll in distraction, self-doubt, defamation to his reputation, and anguish.

There was also the impact on the country. The 7-to-1 Supreme Court decision ensured that at least for some time the independent counsel law would be a critical part of the national political landscape.

10

IT WAS NOT until well into the sixth year of his presidency that a major scandal touched President Ronald Reagan. Just before noon on Monday, November 10, 1986, Reagan met with nine of his senior foreign policy advisers and cabinet members in a closed-door session. They gathered in the White House Situation Room, a small, windowless chamber with thickly padded tan leather chairs that is the crisis nerve center. Reagan, now 75, was agitated and uncharacteristically engaged.

"We have not dealt directly with terrorists," the president said, a tinge of bitterness in his voice. "No bargaining, no ransom," he insisted.

A week earlier, the leftist Beirut magazine *Al Shiraa* had exposed a highly secret CIA covert operation. For nearly a year the United States had sold military arms to Iran, a supporter of anti-American terrorism engaged in a long and deadly war with its neighbor, Iraq. In return, Iran had used its influence to win the release of two American citizens held hostage by a pro-Iranian group in Lebanon called Hezbollah, or Party of God. It was a risky, preposterous, perhaps illegal bargain between the United States and Iran, two countries that did not have diplomatic relations. Publication of the secret operation had sent the American press into a frenzy, and pressure mounted on the Reagan administration to issue a public response. Reagan wanted it carefully worded. Six U.S. hostages were still being held.

"We should put out a statement to show we want to get the hostages back," Reagan said, insisting again that he had not traded arms for hostages. "But we cannot get into a question-and-answer session with the press regarding the hostages so as not to endanger them."

"Some things we can't disclose," the president continued, "because of the long-term consideration of people with whom we have been talking about the future of Iran." The U.S. and CIA channels were to the moderates in Iran, Reagan's advisers had assured him. These moderates, Reagan hoped, might one day establish a friendly government in Iran, and might somehow win release of the remaining American hostages.

Reagan knew the political price that hostage taking could inflict. He had defeated President Carter in 1980 at least in part because Carter had not found a way to rescue or win release for the 52 Americans taken hostage at the U.S. Embassy in Tehran. Weakness or indecision in the face of hostage taking could be fatal. Reagan had taken a tough public line against Iran. He had declared repeatedly that the United States would not negotiate with terrorists, renegade nations that supported terrorism, or those groups that took hostages. But the covert operation contradicted his stated policy of no deals. For Reagan it was a calculated risk to bring the hostages home and improve relations with Iran.

There were legal problems with the covert operation. One U.S. law banned military arms sales to Iran because of Iran's support for terrorism. Another required the president to give "timely" notice to Congress of CIA covert actions undertaken in the interests of national security. So secret and sensitive was the Iran operation that Reagan had in writing ordered his CIA director, William J. Casey, to delay the required "timely" notification to Congress. Whatever "timely" meant, they realized that a year was a long delay and there was going to be hell to pay. But Reagan and Casey did not trust the Democrats in Congress, whom they believed had assisted the news media in gathering information about other CIA covert operations.

Reagan and Admiral John Poindexter, the calm, pipe-smoking national security adviser, explained now to the participants that earlier in the year, on January 17, 1986, the president had signed a formal top-secret intelligence directive. This so-called finding authorized the covert Iran arms sale operation and project to deal with Iranian moderates and to win release of American hostages.

Secretary of State George Shultz was boiling. A former Marine and veteran of three cabinet posts in the Nixon administration, Shultz, now 66, had warned Poindexter and Reagan for months that arms sales to Iran would be unwise, wrong and illegal. He knew some arms had been shipped to Iran despite his opposition, but he had not known that it had been formalized as a CIA covert operation.

"This is the first I ever heard of such a finding," Shultz said.

He did not believe Reagan's or Poindexter's explanations. In the last two weeks, some 500 U.S. missiles had been shipped to Iran and an American hostage, David Jacobsen, had been released.

"How can you say this is not linked to hostage release?" Shultz asked sharply.

"It's not linked!" Reagan said.

"How else will we get the hostages out?" Poindexter asked, undercutting Reagan's denial.

"Be careful of the linkage between hostages and defense equipment," Shultz warned. He wanted to open Reagan's eyes and then get him to order a halt to the madness.

"The terrorists have not profited," Reagan said, brushing Shultz off. "We let the Iranians buy the supplies and they influenced the terrorists. There were no benefits to terrorists. We are working with moderates, hoping in the future to be able to influence Iran after Khomeini dies." The Ayatollah Khomeini was the Iranian leader.

"I'm not sure what's the difference," Shultz said.

Reagan said he had an obligation as president to do everything within his power to obtain the release of U.S. citizens held hostage.

"I agree our responsibility is to look after citizens," Shultz said. "But we don't deal." The news that the United States had undermined its own policy and had negotiated would make it open season on American citizens abroad, exposing them to kidnapping. It was one of Shultz's worst nightmares. He was an economist, but it didn't take a genius to do the math. If an American held abroad could be exchanged for 500 missiles, it was an engraved invitation to take more hostages. It was absurd. Shultz cautioned against assertions that the shipments were small and inconsequential because they weren't. He had another concern. "I can't help but feel that the Israelis suckered us into this so we can't complain of their sales," Shultz said.

Attorney General Edwin Meese, one of Reagan's conservative loyalists, jumped into the discussion. The president's rationale made sense, he eagerly told Shultz. "Each of these is a set of complex actions not related to ransom." No money went directly to the hostage takers, the Party of God terrorists in Lebanon, he said. "We were trying to help moderates in Iran who also tried to help us."

149

Reagan returned to the question of what they should say publicly. "We must say something but not much," the president said.

Poindexter, who disliked the press intensely, opposed a public statement. The remaining hostages would be abandoned. "If we go with this, we end our Iranian contacts," he said.

White House chief of staff Donald Regan had sat in silence. "We must get a statement out now," Regan said, siding with the president. "We are being attacked and we are being hurt. We're losing credibility."

Shultz was worried about the overall policy. He attempted again to get Reagan to stop the project. "Our policy is what we do, not what we say."

"No statement is needed," Poindexter argued. "The news has leaked." Congress would not be able to hold hearings until the new session in January 1987. "We should not say anything."

The president disagreed. "We must say something because I'm being held out to dry," he said. "We have not dealt with terrorists, we don't know who they are. This is long-range Iranian policy." Then, looking straight at Shultz, he said, "There will be no further speculation of answers so as not to endanger the hostages. We won't pay any money, or give anything to the terrorists. You must support the president's policy but say nothing else due to the danger to the hostages."

Later that afternoon, Poindexter drafted a statement incorporating the president's instructions. "As has been the case at a number of similar meetings with the president and his senior advisers, there was unanimous support for the president's decisions," Poindexter wrote.

He sent the text to Shultz's plane, which was taking the secretary of state on a long-planned trip to Central America. Shultz read the statement.

"That's a lie," Shultz told his executive assistant, Charles Hill. "It's Watergate all over again." As far as Shultz was concerned, Poindexter and Casey had set up their own foreign policy, one based on secret deals and operations. Congress and even Shultz's own State Department were being cut out. Intelligence had too much money and was making policy. The CIA was supposed to be neutral, and it had become a rival in making foreign policy.

By cable, Shultz told Poindexter, "It says there was unanimous support for the president's decisions. That is not accurate. I can't accept that sentence. Drop the last word."

Poindexter grudgingly agreed to the change, omitting the word "decisions" so the statement that was released oddly said, "There was unanimous support for the president." What else would be expected from the chief executive's advisers? The statement also said, "Our policy of not making concessions to terrorists remains intact."

Shultz wished it were so. After key White House meetings or discussions, he would give a detailed oral report to Hill, who took meticulous, verbatim notes in small, readable handwriting. Hill, a career Foreign Service officer, believed in Ralph Waldo Emerson's theory that if someone didn't keep a notebook, thoughts flew off like birds and were never seen again. Notetaking was a pleasant physical act for Hill, who pursued Shultz relentlessly to get the secretary's assessments and recollections.

"They are distorting the record," Shultz told Hill. "There's no end to it. They will ruin a beautiful president, let alone policy." Shultz had fought for four years to establish a hard and fast policy that the United States would not deal with terrorists. He considered it one of his biggest achievements. Now it was being subverted. The biggest danger was falling into a cover-up, particularly because the people behind this operation—Poindexter and Casey—still had their positions of authority. "So I have to call it to account and say I can't be part of it," Shultz said. In Shultz's view, Casey and Poindexter were cornered men. Cornered men were always dangerous, but cornered men with power were extremely dangerous.

Just three months earlier, Shultz had privately offered Reagan a letter of resignation to protest some of Reagan's other policies and the constant sniping he felt from the White House. The president had refused to accept it. Perhaps now the letter would come out of the drawer. "I owe it to the president to give him a hard and unwelcome statement—in Don Regan's presence," Shultz told Hill.

Shultz turned reflective. "This has earmarks of Nixon trying to get me to go after his enemies." When he was secretary of the Treasury for Nixon 15 years earlier, Shultz had refused to direct the Internal Revenue Service (IRS), which he oversaw, to audit Democrats for political purposes or to crack down on tax-exempt groups favoring Democrats. On the Nixon tapes, the president was heard voicing disgust at Shultz's refusal to have the IRS investigate a list of 490 Democratic campaign contributors and staff members. The tapes recorded Nixon telling aides he would fire Shultz if he didn't act. If Shultz raised the issue directly with the president, "It would put me in the position of having to throw him out of the office. He didn't get secretary of the treasury because he has nice blue eyes. It was a goddamn favor to him to get that job."

Shultz told Hill the Reagan White House staff were behaving as Nixon's had, trying to cover up their own projects and lies through press statements and misleading background guidance of reporters. "This is an example—this guidance—of problems they will get into. They are trying by this guidance to get me to lie. What are they trying to pull on me? They're taking the president down the drain. The vice president, secretary of defense and secretary of state should on such occasions prevail on the president. They aren't. So I'm alone." He concluded that he had to raise hell. Back in the Nixon years Shultz had responded somewhat passively by stiffing the White House, ordering that the IRS simply "do nothing." Shultz felt he owed Reagan more. His responsibility as the senior cabinet officer was greater. He had to stand up and confront the president directly. "It's not even a hard decision," he told Hill.

Vice President George Bush had remained silent during the Monday morning briefing,

153

but as was his custom he wanted to offer his views in private to the president. In Reagan's office, Bush found the president sitting alone at his desk. "Let me talk to you about a meeting I had at my house with George Shultz," Bush said. The night before, Shultz had come to his house, worried that Bush was making public statements about the Iran operation that were untrue.

"He feels he's been cut out," the vice president said. Shultz had described being rebuffed at one point by Poindexter. "And he was told that Poindexter was too busy."

Reagan said he was alarmed. The secretary of state could not get in to talk to the national security adviser? That was not good. Reagan said he was suspicious of Shultz's State Department bureaucracy, concerned the bureaucrats were playing games and trying to undermine his policy.

Later, Bush dictated his private views into a tape recorder for a secret diary he was keeping. He said he did not like the concept of arms for hostages, but, "Good things, such as the release of the hostages and contacts with moderates, will in the long run—in my view—offset this."

Bush also noted in his diary that Shultz had warned him about "a Watergate syndrome." The secretary was concerned that the attempts to cover up a bad policy could lead to more legal trouble than the original policy. He had also worried about Bush's political future. "George does not want this to rub off on me for the ...run for the presidency," Bush dictated. "He was very thoughtful about that and very considerate of me. I told him that I didn't see anything in this that would do that."

Shultz felt he had been rough on Bush and probably Bush would never forgive him. But he believed he might have saved Bush's political life. It would likely emerge that the deal was a straight arms-for-hostages operation no matter how it was dressed up as a strategic opening to moderates. Shultz felt that it would come out that Bush had known most of the details. If the vice president was on the record denying knowledge, he might be ruined.

Chief of staff Don Regan had asked the president to talk to the press the previous week when the story broke in the Beirut magazine. The president's strength was direct communication. Speaking through others or by official statement was not personal or credible. "I don't believe we can stonewall," Regan had said.

Reagan had shaken his head, no way, in an adamant tone that was unusual for him.

First Lady Nancy Reagan had already phoned Regan. "He's not going to talk to the press," she said. "My Friend says it's, you know, it's just wrong for him to talk right now."

Regan knew "My Friend" referred to an astrologer, Joan Quigley, whom the first lady consulted. "My God, Nancy," the chief of staff answered, "he's going to go down in flames if he doesn't speak up." Regan glanced down at the color-coded calendar he kept to track the astrologer's predictions. Green ink was used for future good days, red for the bad days, and yellow for those days that would be in between. Mrs. Reagan was right about what the astrology chart predicted, but the secret practice of making scheduling decisions based on astrology was irritating and irrational. Regan believed it was the most closely guarded domestic secret in the Reagan White House.

On Wednesday night, November 12, two days after the closed-door session, Reagan took out a photo-sized album. He too was secretly keeping a diary. In meticulous handwriting, he began to write, his script frugally filling each page completely, with no side margins or space at the top or bottom.

"This whole irresponsible press bilge about hostages and Iran has gotten totally out of hand," Reagan wrote. Television and the newspapers were going wild with breathless, negative coverage of the story. "The media looks like it's trying to create another Watergate."

Patrick J. Buchanan, the communications director in the Reagan White House, knew as much about Watergate as anyone in government. As a senior adviser and speechwriter to Nixon he had watched the Nixon presidency destroyed by the scandal. A loud attack voice among Republican conservatives, Buchanan dashed off a memo to White House chief of staff Don Regan.

"The appearance of things is that we have negotiated with a terrorist regime," Buchanan wrote, "...that we have traduced our policy and violated our principles, that we are now stonewalling. Not since I came here has there appeared such an issue which could do such deep and permanent damage to the president's standing. ...The

156

story will not die until some much fuller explanations—giving our arguments—is provided. Prediction: If we wait three weeks, the president's approval will be down in the mid-fifties at best."

"I agree, and have so advocated for a week," Regan wrote back in exasperation.

The pressure from Congress and the media continued. Reagan reluctantly agreed to give a nationally televised address the evening of Thursday, November 13. That morning, Vice President Bush thought Reagan was showing great tension for the first time. He urged Reagan to be careful.

"I remember Watergate," Bush dictated privately about his concerns. "I remember the way things oozed out. It is important to level, to be honest, to be direct. We are not to say anything. The dam gates are open. Everybody is making judgments based on erroneous information and it is a flood of wrong facts coming out. It really is hemorrhaging and the president is going with his speech."

At 12:45 p.m. that day, Reagan called for Buchanan's current draft of the speech. Writing in the space between the lines and then curling his words around the right side of the page, Reagan wrote: "I KNOW YOU HAVE BEEN READING, SEEING + HEARING A LOT OF HORROR STORIES THE PAST SEVERAL DAYS BASED ON STORIES ATTRIBUTED TO DANISH SAILORS, UNNAMED OBSERVERS AT ITALIAN AIRPORTS + SPANISH HARBORS + ESPECIALLY UNNAMED GOVT. OFFICIALS OF MY ADMIN. WELL NOW YOU ARE GOING TO HEAR THE FACTS

FROM A WHITE HOUSE SOURCE + YOU KNOW MY NAME."

Reagan continued editing and redrafting. "WE DID NOT — REPEAT — DID NOT TRADE WEAPONS OR ANYTHING ELSE FOR HOSTAGES — NOR WILL WE," Reagan inserted.

In an accompanying note to his staff secretary, the president said he wanted the speech to be more forceful. "I didn't try to re-write knowing you were already re-writing but here are just a few little additions," Reagan wrote. "I feel we dwell too much on the Iran history etc. and need *more* flat denials...."

At 8:01 p.m. that night, the president addressed the nation from the Oval Office for 11 minutes. He touted a "secret diplomatic initiative to Iran." He admitted the shipment of a "small amount of defensive weapons," but asserted (falsely), "These modest deliveries, taken together, could easily fit on a single cargo plane. They could not, taken together, affect the outcome of the six-year war between Iran and Iraq. Nor could they affect, in any way, the military balance between the two countries." The lead quote in the next morning's *Washington Post* was Reagan's blanket denial: "We did not—repeat, did not—trade weapons or anything else for hostages—nor will we."

The reaction to Reagan's speech was overwhelmingly negative. A *Los Angeles Times* poll said 14 percent of the American public believed the claim that arms had not been traded for hostages. In private, Reagan was dismayed. He was used to high approval ratings and big boosts after his speeches. Don Regan noticed that the president was flushed and pursed his lips when he talked about the Iran initiative.

Shultz went to see Reagan at 1:30 p.m. on Friday, the day after the speech. Poindexter, furious with Shultz, practically had to be dragged into the president's office to attend. Shultz told the president he wanted to resign, but before doing so he would try to steer him through the crisis.

"I want you to stay," Reagan said. "I want to talk later about it."

Shultz saw Reagan's devastation. He had gone before the American people to make his case and they had not believed him. The next day, Saturday, Shultz tried to get approval for a statement transferring U.S. policy toward Iran to the State Department and for a definitive proclamation that the United States would not under any circumstances sell any more arms to Iran. But he could not get a moment alone with the president for serious discussion.

On Sunday, November 16, Shultz went on CBS's *Face the Nation*. Lesley Stahl, the moderator, asked, "Will there be any more arms shipments to Iran, either directly by our government or through any third parties?"

Shultz replied, "It's certainly against our policy."

"That's not an answer. Why don't you answer the question directly? I'll ask it again. Will there be any more arms shipments to Iran, either directly by the United States or through any third parties?"

"Under the circumstances of Iran's war with

159

Iraq, its pursuit of terrorism, its association with those holding our hostages, I would certainly say, as far as I'm concerned, no," Shultz said.

"Do you have authority to speak for the entire administration?" she asked.

"No," Shultz said, looking her straight in the eye.

Shultz now fully expected to be fired, but the White House blinked. The following day, Monday, November 17, White House press secretary Larry Speakes issued a statement saying, "The president has no desire, the president has no plans, to send further arms to Iran."

For the moment, Shultz felt his gamble had worked. The inconsistency in policy and the sheer irrationality of selling arms to Iran was too great and the White House had to back off.

The media and congressional uproar persisted, and the president agreed to hold a press conference. Nancy Reagan cleared the date, Wednesday, November 19, with her astrologer. That morning, Bush went to see Reagan alone. He encouraged the president to meet with Shultz before his press conference so the secretary got in to see the president at 1:30 p.m. Shultz put his argument to Reagan as gravely as possible. Reagan defended the Iran initiative. "Iran has tempered terrorism," he said.

"It's not so," Shultz replied. "That's a terrible thing to say." He stepped up his rhetoric and became more confrontational. He reminded the president that pro-Iranian terrorists had taken three new hostages as recently as September and October.

"This is news to me," Reagan said.

"You are not fully informed," Shultz continued, "and you have to watch out about saying no deals for hostages." He wanted to make the case that both he and the president were the victims. "We have been deceived and lied to."

"You're telling me things I don't know," the president said.

"Mr. President, if I'm telling you something you don't know—I don't know much—then something is terribly wrong here."

Shultz said he remembered a November 1985 shipment of arms that would be sent only with the return of hostages. An explicit quid pro quo.

Reagan said he knew about the shipment. He did not say whether he would reveal his knowledge at the upcoming press conference.

As Shultz left, he could see he had not convinced the president. "I plead with you," he said, "don't say Iran has let up on terrorism."

The Iran initiative had begun before the top-secret president intelligence finding of January 1986, according to the records. In 1985, secret arms shipments had been made covertly through Israel, which had sold the arms to Iran with an understanding that the United States would restock Israeli supplies and Iran would use its influence to secure release of the hostages. In addition, at least one CIA-assisted U.S. arms sale to Iran had been made in November 1985, as Shultz had reminded Reagan, prior to the presidential finding.

The president disclosed none of these facts

at his press conference. He denied any earlier Israeli role, insisted there had been no shipments in 1985 and downplayed the extent of sales.

Shultz watched from his State Department office and was appalled. He phoned the president, complimented Reagan for handling the pressure but said the president had made a great many factual errors. Shultz could prove it.

Reagan sounded shaken but agreed to listen.

The next morning, Shultz went to the White House to talk with Don Regan. Shultz said the solution was a housecleaning at the National Security Council. "Congress is going to tear this place apart unless changes are made to shape up U.S. foreign policy fast," Shultz said. Poindexter and Marine Lieutenant Colonel Oliver North, the operations officer for the Iran initiative, should resign, he added. The president had too many people who were interested in protecting themselves, not in serving him. Shultz offered to serve simultaneously as national security adviser and secretary of state. He would even temporarily step aside at state to restore order.

Don Regan said the president wanted to leave town and retreat to his secluded mountainside Rancho del Cielo outside Santa Barbara to think it all over.

"That's a formula for catastrophe," Shultz said. "We have to make decisions. Here they are. Make them! The longer you wait, the worse it gets. It's not a matter of getting our lines straight! Think of the future!"

Regan left the meeting for lunch with the president to report that Shultz had issued an ultimatum: "Poindexter has to go or he goes."

Shaken, the president called in Bush for advice. Bush proposed a meeting with all the principal players to lay the disputes on the table, find out what was upsetting Shultz and Poindexter and above all stop the internecine warfare.

At his State Department office, Shultz learned a disturbing new piece of information from his staff. The contractor who was said to have delivered the weapons in the Iran affair—Southern Air Transport—had also been involved in providing support to the Nicaraguan resistance, the so-called contras. Since 1981, Reagan had authorized a covert CIA operation to assist the contras in the overthrow of the leftist Nicaraguan government. Details of the operation had leaked and been publicly debated for years as Congress alternately supported and withdrew the CIA funding for the contras. It was Reagan's and Casey's favorite covert war, and more gritty details were becoming public. Press reports said that after Congress cut off funding, Lieutenant Colonel Oliver North ran private support operations for the contras out of the National Security Council. A possible connection between the Iran operation and the contras set off a warning bell for Shultz.

Shultz prepared to see Reagan again. He directed Hill to dig out contemporaneous notes from the past year. They showed that indeed an Iran arms shipment had been made to get a hostage release in November 1985. The notes matched Shultz's recollection that an arms-for-hostage deal had been made that year, proving that Reagan had erred in his press conference.

At 5:15 p.m. that evening, Reagan finally agreed to see Shultz in the White House residence. They sat in a relaxed sitting-room area upstairs. Don Regan was also present. Shultz realized he would have to cross the line and challenge the president directly. The CIA and the National Security Council staff were giving him false and incomplete information, Shultz argued. The backbone of the foreign policy information system to the president was dramatically fouled up and distorted.

"The press is the problem," the president said.

Shultz said Bud McFarlane, the national security adviser prior to Poindexter, had called him in November 1985 describing the shipment of U.S. antiaircraft missiles to Iran.

"Oh, I knew about that," Reagan contended, "but that wasn't arms for hostages."

No one looking at the record would believe that, Shultz said.

"My material is different," Reagan said. "George, I know what happened, and we were doing the right thing." He said the operation was to pursue a long-term strategic opening to Iran. The weapons sent to Iran were defensive.

"Two thousand good anti-tank missiles disposes of a lot of good tanks," Shultz said, referring to the other main shipment of arms. "Iran is the aggressor party here." The Hawk antiaircraft missiles also could be effective against Iran's opponent, Iraq, which had air superiority.

Reagan was unmoved.

Shultz grew more heated and eventually realized he was on a tirade. He never thought he would talk to a president this way.

But Reagan held his ground. He argued his good intentions to Shultz's claim that they had bad information. For practical purposes, Shultz was saying Poindexter was guilty of bad faith and deception of his president—major crimes in the lexicon of presidential service.

The president and Shultz turned to a proposal to make Pat Buchanan the ambassador to NATO, a post he wanted. Cohesion was the essence of the alliance. Buchanan was noted for his confrontational and divisive methods. It was preposterous to Shultz that it was even being considered. The possible Buchanan nomination to a delicate ambassadorial post was another sign that the administration was adrift.

At 11:30 a.m. the next day, Friday, November 21, Attorney General Ed Meese went to see the president. He told Reagan he was concerned that the administration had not straightened out its story on the Iran initiative. No one was looking out for the interests of the president, Meese said. As attorney general, he wanted to conduct a fact-finding mission.

Reagan asked him to spend the weekend looking into the matter and to report to him on Monday. He said he was concerned by Shultz's remarks and attitude. They were more alarming because he said he respected Shultz and considered him a pillar. Reagan said he would spend the weekend at Camp David, thinking about how to proceed.

At 1:45 p.m. the same day, White House counsel Peter Wallison reported to Don Regan that they were in legal trouble. The November 1985 Hawk antiaircraft missile shipments did not meet the minimum reporting requirements to Congress for arms sales abroad. "A shipment like that would either have to be reported as a shipment by the U.S. or as a violation of the Arms Export Control Act by Israel, and neither was done," Wallison told Regan. "We do not have very good theories to support our position, and the theories we have involve a serious constitutional confrontation with Congress."

Just after 8 a.m. Saturday, Meese went to interview Shultz. "The president," Meese said, "asked me to pull together facts that seem to be eluding us—to get some picture of what you and I didn't know about. Not views but facts."

Shultz warned Meese, "The president says it's small, defensive. It's not true.

"He has been sold a bill of goods," Shultz added indignantly. "He's way out on a limb he shouldn't be on." He attempted to draw a distinction. He was not accusing the president of lawbreaking. "This is a mistake, a terrible one. But done for honorable purpose as the president saw it."

Shultz tried to get Meese, the president's troubleshooter, to see how Reagan had undermined his presidency. "Our president's stock in trade is being straight. He's in a position where he's saying things that are demonstrably not true, although he's not consciously doing so. I told him and he didn't like it at all."

Shultz suggested that they warn the president, "The Democrats will string it along and destroy your presidency." The president has to put the cleaver on it and go on, he told Meese.

"I agree," Meese said. "Certain things could be in violation of law." He said the president didn't remember the Hawk shipment in November 1985. "If it happened and the president didn't report it to Congress, it's a violation," Meese said. "He said to me, 'If it happened I want to tell Congress, not have them tell me.'"

Shultz said he suspected that the worst was yet to come. "Another angle worries me," he said. "This could get mixed in to help for the freedom fighters in Nicaragua. One thing may be overlapping with another. There may be a connection. Our enemies on the Hill would love to wrap the two together."

Meese went to lunch with two of his top assistants working on the inquiry. They ate at the Old Ebbitt Grill just a couple of blocks from the White House. One of the aides, William Bradford Reynolds, reported that as part of the investigation he had searched the office of Lieutenant Colonel North of the National Security Council staff.

"This one you won't believe," Reynolds said. "There's a document that says they would take $12 million from the arms sales to Iran and give the money to the contras."

"Oh shit," the attorney general replied.

CIA Director Casey later sat down in his study to compose a private letter to the president. "The public pouting of George Shultz and the failure of the State Department to support what we did inflated the uproar on this matter. If we all stand together and speak out I believe we can put this behind us quickly. You need a new pitcher! A leader instead of a bureaucrat. I urge you to bring in someone like Jeane Kirkpatrick or Paul Laxalt, who you may recall I recommended for State in 1980. You need this to give your foreign policy a new style and thrust and get the Carterite bureaucracy in State under your control. Otherwise, you will not be doing justice to yourself or to your presidency. Time is short."

Reagan received the letter a day later. After reading it, the president lit a match, turned it on the paper and threw his copy into the fireplace.

On Monday at 2 p.m., Reagan met with his national security team. Meese was still investigating and had not yet told the president what he had found, so he said almost nothing. Poindexter took charge of the meeting as if nothing had happened. He said an emissary would be sent to countries around the world to explain the goals of U.S. policy toward Iran. The Iran project would not change.

Casey gave a positive assessment about intelligence on Iran.

Shultz, a large man who is tightly wound even in relaxed moments and can give the impression that he might explode, could contain himself no longer. He said the Iran operation was wrong and wouldn't work.

"As far as I'm concerned, we were right," the president insisted, glaring at Shultz. "We were successful, and only press activity has thrown it off."

Reagan said the United States had sent only a few million dollars worth of arms to Iran, hardly a ripple when compared to the $9.4 billion in arms sold to Iran by other countries. "Our shipments were only a signal." His anger was directed at Shultz, who had never seen the president so furious.

Reagan pounded the table. "We are right!" he said. "We had to take the opportunity! And we were successful! History will never forgive us if we don't do it!" His anger over the leaks was palpable. "No one is to talk about it. No more anonymous sources!"

Shultz was stunned. The president was enthralled with Poindexter and the operation, seeming to be totally in the admiral's grip. He had never seen the president this way—frustrated, self-righteous, talking about history.

At 4:30 p.m., Meese told Reagan about the document outlining the plan to divert funds to the contras.

The president sat in disbelief. Poindexter and North wouldn't do anything like that without telling him. It had to be a mistake.

Meese assured Reagan he was not mistaken. The memorandum made it clear what had happened. He had interviewed North, who had confirmed the diversion of funds, and Poindexter had confirmed his knowledge of it. The Iran arms sales operation was itself intensely controversial and had been since the public revelation three weeks earlier; the contra operation had been one of the most hotly debated and controversial topics in the nation's politics. Mix the two together and it was a prescription for a maximum scandal. Meese, seeing Reagan's visible surprise, pointedly did not ask the president if he had approved the diversion.

That night Reagan wrote in his journal about the amazing revelation. He used the language of Watergate. "After the meeting in the Situation Room, Ed M. and Don R. told me of a smoking gun. On one of the arms shipments the Iranians had paid Israel a higher purchase price than we were getting. The Israelis put the difference in a secret bank account. Then our Col. North (N.S.C.) gave the money to the contras. North didn't tell me about this. Worst of all, John P. found out about it and didn't tell me. This may call for resignations."

11

THE NEXT MORNING, Tuesday, November 25, the president met with his advisers and Meese. The attorney general had bad news. He reported that perhaps $10 million to $30 million in profits from the arms sales to Iran had been diverted to the contras. Poindexter would resign and North would be fired.

Meese held a press conference and disclosed the diversion. He announced that as attorney

170

general he was making an application to the three-judge panel to appoint an independent counsel to investigate.

Reagan authorized the appointment of a bipartisan fact-finding commission to report on what had happened, who was responsible and what should be done to prevent Iran-contra from occurring again. The three-member board, headed by Texas Republican Senator John Tower, a friend of the administration, was to present its findings to the public as soon as possible, it was hoped within three months.

Congress set up a joint Senate and House committee. Hearings would be held on the arms-for-hostages deals and the diversion of funds from Iran to the contras. The major question was, Did the president know of or approve the diversion? Discussions of impeachment were nearly everywhere in Washington.

Don Regan felt that the press was so excited that the atmosphere had become primal. Many in the briefing room seemed to be having the same thoughts: another presidency would be destroyed, blood and body parts would be floating in the water. Adversaries seemed to be after the presidency itself.

His suspicions confirmed, Shultz was nonetheless shocked and concerned about the diversion. He realized, too, that the revelations would give him immense leverage. He had been right, and Reagan would need his help. The next day he told the president he was ready to sign on for the duration of the administration.

Reagan responded that he would now rely on

Shultz as his point man on foreign policy. They agreed that Shultz could come to the Oval Office without the national security adviser.

Shultz noticed that the president was abnormally subdued. Some of the cheerfulness was gone. Shultz did not want to see another American president destroyed. The only way to prevent that was to make sure the arms-for-hostages policy was dead. But Shultz kept hearing that CIA officers, with Casey's encouragement, were still meeting with Iranian officials in Europe, promising more arms. Casey's men had even used a U.S. ambassador who reported to the secretary of state as a go-between without informing Shultz. It was more of the back-channel, off-the-books operating that Shultz found intolerable.

Shultz insisted on seeing the president again. At 11 a.m., Sunday, December 14, he got in to see him. "We must have a clear chain of command," he said. Casey was making policy, not just supplying intelligence information and analysis. Shultz provided chapter and verse on the CIA efforts and contacts.

Reagan reacted as if someone had kicked him in the stomach.

"I'm glad to be in the position personally of seeing how shocked you are," Shultz said.

But the next day, Monday, Shultz learned that the CIA was still trying to trade arms for hostages. He returned to the White House to confront the president once more. "Mr. President," Shultz said, "you must be decisive!" He later told Bush, "Bill Casey is bad news."

That day, Casey suffered a seizure in his CIA office and was taken to Georgetown Hospital, where he was diagnosed with brain cancer. Three days later, doctors removed a cancerous soft tumor from his brain. They released a statement saying Casey would be able to resume his duties.

Nancy Reagan had distrusted Casey's judgment for some time. Now she made her move. The first lady called Don Regan at least three times that week urging him to get rid of Casey. What had the chief of staff done to find a replacement? she asked.

"Nothing," Regan replied.

"Why not?" Mrs. Reagan said. She was stammering as she did when giving orders. "He's got to go. He can't do his job: he's an embarrassment to Ronnie. He should be out." She was convinced that Casey was deeply involved in Iran-contra. Perhaps it could be written off to his illness.

Don Regan argued that it would be inhumane, even unseemly, to move on Casey while he was this ill. He had received no sign from the president that he wanted Casey removed summarily.

"You're more interested in protecting Bill Casey than in protecting Ronnie," Mrs. Reagan cried. "He's dragging Ronnie down! Nobody believes what Casey says."

With Casey out of action, Shultz and Don Regan noticed that the air went out of the arms-for-hostages scheme. They concluded after looking at the record that Casey had driven the crazy Iran operation.

• • •

Don Regan told the president that he must put one man in charge of responding to the Iran-contra crisis. It was consuming too much of the staff's time and had become an intolerable distraction. In late December, Nancy Reagan suggested they hire Nixon's lawyer Jack Miller, who was representing their friend and former adviser Michael Deaver in another independent counsel case.

Regan thought that was a terrible suggestion. Appointing a famous criminal attorney to defend the president would send absolutely the wrong message to the press and the public. He did not act on Nancy Reagan's suggestion, but the president soon raised Miller's name.

"Mr. President, what are you guilty of?" Regan asked.

Reagan was startled. Well, he said, Miller seems to know a lot about this stuff.

"You bet he does," Regan replied. "That's because he defends people who are charged with felonies. Giving him the job would send all the wrong signals. Imagine what the press would do with an appointment like that."

Reagan saw the point. Miller's appointment would suggest guilt or fear of prosecution that Reagan did not feel.

Reagan and Nancy attended the annual New Year's Eve party in their honor at Walter Annenberg's estate in Palm Springs. Nancy said she was "disgusted" with Poindexter and North. "They should be court-martialed," she declared to Defense Secretary Caspar Weinberger, who along with Shultz had opposed the Iran arms deals.

Shultz rode with Reagan in a golf cart on New Year's Eve. He had never seen Reagan so down, so tentative and humbled. All the discussion and advice seemed to sail over him.

When the president returned to Washington after the holidays, Don Regan said he felt that he should have a press conference soon and he suggested January 20. If Reagan didn't talk to the press, Regan worried, it would look as if he were hiding.

"No press conference for at least three months!" declared the first lady. The astrologer's charts said the president faced danger from late December 1986 through March 1987. Of Regan's proposed date, January 20, Quigley had instructed, "Nothing outside White House—possible attempt" on Reagan's life.

On January 5, 1987, Reagan had a routine but uncomfortable medical procedure conducted for an enlarged prostate at Bethesda Naval Hospital.

The next day, Mrs. Reagan and Don Regan met alone in the waiting room.

"What are we going to do about Casey?" she inquired.

The chief of staff pleaded decency.

"Ronnie could just send him a letter telling him that since he can't perform his duties we're sorry, but that's it."

Regan urged careful consideration.

In the following days, Nancy Reagan seemed more focused on Casey, telling Regan harshly at one point, "I wish that you were as protective of the president's health as you are of Bill Casey's."

President Reagan finally instructed his chief of staff to begin looking for a successor to the CIA director. Mrs. Reagan phoned Don Regan from Camp David to say she had an ideal candidate to replace Casey. She proposed Edward Bennett Williams, the famous Washington trial attorney, leading Democrat and lawyer for *The Washington Post* who had advised Ford during the 1976 election. Williams declined.

On Saturday, January 24, Mrs. Reagan again called Regan from Camp David to say they were going to have to stiffen the president's spine on Casey. "What we're going to have to do," she directed, "is prop up our guy here."

Eventually the president called Regan and gently pushed on Casey. On January 29, Regan and Meese visited Casey in the hospital and Casey resigned.

Minutes after returning to the White House from Georgetown Hospital, Regan picked up his phone.

"What's the news on Casey?" Mrs. Reagan asked.

Regan reported that he had resigned.

"Good," the first lady said.

Nancy was always protective of her husband, but her drive to remove Casey was unusual. Other than removing the obvious architect of Iran-contra from office, she quite likely had deeper suspicions that Casey might allege that her husband was a more willing participant and perhaps even had known about the diversion of funds. The allegation would have less impact and credibility if Casey were out of office, removed because of suspicions about his role. Mrs. Reagan has denied that this was her motivation and has insisted that the president did not know of the diversion. But her full-court press to remove Casey, not one of the high-profile White House aides or public spokesmen, has left unanswered questions. If President Reagan ever learned about the diversion, the one person he might have shared the knowledge with was his wife. Or perhaps she was acting on a suspicion—not of her husband's knowledge but of the danger if it were seriously alleged.

On February 8, Don Regan insisted that the president have a press conference at the end of the month. More than three months would have passed—unheard of silence then for a modern president.

Nancy Reagan was furious.

"It looks like we're shielding him," Regan said, noting the obvious.

"We're not shielding Ronnie," Mrs. Reagan declared, "the press is just writing it that way." Continuing to protect her husband, she added, "He may not be ready."

Mrs. Reagan and Don Regan raced to slam down the receiver and Regan won. The press soon reported that the chief of staff had hung up on the first lady.

That same evening, February 8, Robert C. "Bud" McFarlane, Poindexter's predecessor and a key architect of the Iran and contra operations, poured himself a glass of wine and swallowed 30 Valium, intending to take his life. He lived, however, and nine days later Richard Nixon showed up in his hospital room. As Reagan's national security adviser, McFarlane had spent many hours briefing the former president and seeking his advice—once over dinner and a $300 bottle of 1970 Château Lafite Rothschild, Nixon's favorite wine, at Nixon's New Jersey home just 16 months before.

There was no trust and no necessary secrecy any more for foreign policy operations, Nixon told McFarlane at his bedside. Vietnam and Watergate had rendered such covert actions no longer feasible.

"Your motives were right and your concept was sound," Nixon said reassuringly. An opening with Iran was important and McFarlane would be vindicated. "And you mustn't let this defeat you and end your career."

"Look at me," Nixon said. "I've made a lot of mistakes in my life, Bud, and if I had it to do again I would do things differently. But you don't get that chance." After his resignation he had thought there was no reason to live. "I'm not exactly a public hero." But you have to keep going.

Nixon knew, McFarlane realized. He had glimpsed the abyss, what was in McFarlane's mind and soul: despair and shame, knowing the entire world had witnessed your defeat and weakness.

Michael Deaver, perhaps the person closest to both the president and the first lady, went to see Reagan in early 1987. A public relations and media expert who had left the White House staff a year earlier, Deaver was recovering from alcoholism, and he was about to go on trial for perjury related to alleged influence peddling. He was a man of natural kindness and goodwill, and had grown introspective. He sensed that Iran-contra was sapping Reagan's natural optimism and confidence.

"I think you've got to take an action," Deaver told the president. "I think that action is to fire somebody in order to get the media to believe that you have put this behind you."

"I'll be goddamned if I'm going to fire somebody's ass to save my own," the president said. He threw a pen across the floor.

"Excuse me, Ron," Deaver said, addressing the president by his first name. It was the only time Deaver had addressed Reagan as Ron since he'd become president. "I'm not talking about your ass. I'm talking about the country's ass."

"Well, you know what I think about the country," Reagan said.

"I'm not sure you do at this point," Deaver replied. "I think you're being stubborn."

About 11 p.m., Nancy called Deaver at home. "He has not said a word since you left."

"Good, I hope he doesn't sleep," Deaver said.

"I don't know," Nancy replied. "I've never seen him this quiet."

When he calmed down, Reagan concluded Deaver was right about Iran-contra. He had to take dramatic action and reclaim control. There

179

was too much infighting, too little order in the White House. At 10:10 a.m. on February 23, the president met with Don Regan.

"Where's your head on this?" Regan asked combatively. "What do you think I should do?"

The president leaned back in his chair, a sure sign that he was disturbed. He began talking about the paralyzing disagreements Regan was having with Nancy Reagan. He reminded Regan of his promise the prior November to go quietly on a signal from the president that he had become a burden on the administration.

"I'll stick by that," Regan said. "I'll go whenever you say."

The president said Regan should leave immediately, before the Tower Board released its forthcoming report.

Regan was startled. "You can't do that to me, Mr. President," he said. "If I go before that report is out, you throw me to the wolves. I deserve better treatment than that." Regan's dismay was palpable. "I thought I was chief of staff to the president, not to his wife. I have to tell you, sir, that I'm very bitter about the whole experience."

We'll make sure that you go out in good fashion, Reagan answered softly.

Regan left angry and humiliated, but he believed he had bought himself some time for a graceful exit.

12

THURSDAY, FEBRUARY 26, 1987, was the kind of cold, miserable day better spent in bed, and another low point for the president. The Tower Board that morning issued its report, concluding that Reagan's advisers had traded arms for hostages in violation of administration policy, contradicting Reagan's public denials and his core defense. The board's report, presented in an inch-thick blue cover full of formerly top-secret papers and memos, singled out Don Regan for criticism. "He must bear primary responsibility for the chaos that descended upon the White House," the report said, because he was chief of staff.

The president now wanted Regan out immediately and he delegated the final push to Vice President Bush. Bush summoned Regan, whose corner office was next to Bush's West Wing office.

Bush explained that the president wanted to know the plans for Regan's departure.

"What's the matter," Regan snarled, flashing his temper, "isn't he man enough to ask me that question himself?" What had happened to going out in good fashion, as the president had promised? "If I go now, I'm part of the scandal," he said.

"I know it's rough," Bush replied. "But the president wants it to go smoothly."

"I don't see how it's going to go smoothly," Regan said. Nancy Reagan and her friends were killing him in the press. He felt he had not done anything wrong. It was outrageous, grossly unfair. "I'm being fired like a shoe clerk. I'm bitter, George," Regan said, "and you can tell that to the president."

"I'll tell the president what you said," Bush promised.

Regan poured out the details of his dealings with Nancy Reagan and the chronic ritual of schedule-by-astrology. Talk about chaos.

"Good God," Bush finally said, "I had no idea."

Reagan had to find a new chief of staff. He needed someone to help restore the order and credibility that had been lost. Two of those he first considered—former Transportation Secretary Drew Lewis and Senator Paul Laxalt, a close Reagan friend—were not willing. Laxalt suggested former Senate Republican Majority Leader Howard H. Baker Jr.

Not a bad idea, Reagan figured. Baker was smart, personable, savvy about Washington. He had developed a style that was soothing—a courtly Tennessee gentleman—but tough and businesslike. Friends and foes considered his demeanor a kind of Tennessee Waltz: friendly, flattering, reflective, occasionally wise and dramatic, but often noncommittal and vague.

Baker also had considerable knowledge of scandals and investigations, Reagan knew. His formative political experience had been his service as vice chairman of the Senate Watergate Committee 14 years earlier. He had asked the question during the 1973 televised hearings that cut to the heart of Watergate: "What did the president know and when did he know it?" The answer had been a lot and early, and the experience had made Baker deeply skeptical.

Late Thursday afternoon, Reagan called Baker, who was in Florida with his family, to talk about the possibility of another run for president. He had tried once, in 1980, and lost to Reagan.

Baker quickly discovered that nobody wanted to talk about another presidential campaign—except him. So he had taken his young grandson out for the afternoon.

"Joy," Reagan asked Baker's wife, "where is Howard?"

"Mr. President, Howard is at the zoo."

"Wait until he sees the zoo I've got in mind for him," Reagan said, laughing.

Later in the day, Reagan and Baker talked by phone. Reagan thought Baker accepted the job as White House chief of staff outright. Baker believed he had only agreed to fly back to Washington to see the president the next day at the White House.

On the flight back to Washington, Baker thought through his options. He had been bitten by the presidential ambition bug badly, and he wasn't sure he was ready to give up fighting for the nomination. He was young by presidential standards, only 61, and in a sense he had been preparing all his political life for the presidency. He'd left the Senate three years earlier, after 18 years, including nearly eight years as Republican leader. He ran his own private law practice in Washington, believing it was easier to run for president out of elective office. Baker felt he was ready for the White House, but as the one sitting behind the desk in the Oval Office, not one of the chairs on the side.

He had other reservations. He came from the moderate wing of the party—Reagan from the conservative. He also was wary of taking a job in a scandal-plagued administration. Dealing closely with presidents during a scandal was a treacherous undertaking, Baker had learned. In early 1973 after he had been named vice chairman of the Senate Watergate Committee at age 47, Baker had arranged to see President Nixon privately to offer assistance and establish a secret channel.

The meeting took place in Nixon's office in the Old Executive Office Building late on the afternoon of February 22, 1973. Nixon had just begun his second term on top of the world politically. Few of his major Watergate problems had surfaced.

"Mr. President," Baker recalled saying at the beginning, "I want you to know I'm your friend. I'm going to see that your interests are protected." Baker said it was his absolute conviction at this point that Watergate was a Democratic dirty trick. He felt the stories in *The Washington Post* were political, that the *Post* was carrying water for the Democrats.

Nixon seemed receptive.

"Does my friend John Mitchell have any problems?" Baker asked, referring to Nixon's former attorney general and campaign manager.

Nixon suddenly lowered his voice and sort of

turned away. "He might have a little," Nixon whispered. "Maybe he has a problem of some proportions."

Baker was stunned at the secret news about Mitchell in the face of heated White House denials that there was anything to Watergate. A light bulb flicked on in Baker's head. Nixon didn't need to tell him about Mitchell. What was the whisper about? It was inconceivable that Nixon was taping him, wasn't it? Baker sort of backed out of the room. He realized that there was more to the scandal than he knew, and he decided to keep his head low and be extremely careful. As Watergate Committee vice chairman, the senior Republican, he would ride both horses—protecting the president's interests but also aggressively investigating and seeking the facts.

Years later Baker read a transcript of the conversation with Nixon. It was garbled and unclear, and the voice-activated system had failed to capture the most important parts. Baker was surprised that a transcript could so miss what had happened. Baker read more of the Nixon transcripts and the references to him from the period of early 1973, when he was riding both horses. He was shocked to see how Nixon raged about him, called him a "simpering asshole." Baker felt like a voyeur reading Nixon's fury. "Baker will not be in this office again—do you understand that?" Nixon told Haig on July 12, 1973.

"Never be in the White House again—never, never, never!" Nixon shouted later the same day to his head of congressional relations. "He's finished. Absolutely totally finished....He thinks he's gonna be president. He's finished."

"I don't want anybody in the White House to ever have any contact with him again. Ever. And another thing is this: cut him off. Give him the deep freeze. He thinks this is the way to be president. He loves the adulation of the Georgetown set."

Immediately afterwards Nixon again raged to Rose Mary Woods, his secretary. "Howard Baker, Rose, I have no hatred at this time, I have no hatred here....But I remember loyalty. Howard Baker will never be in the White House again, as long as I am in this office. Never, never, never!" There it was again. "His name will not be on the Christmas list; there will never, never ever be Baker in the White House as long as I'm here."

It was almost the kind of knowledge Baker didn't want to have about anyone, let alone a president.

After the Senate Watergate Committee disclosed the existence of the taping system in July 1973, the stakes increased for everyone. The next month, Baker came home from Tennessee on a Sunday night and found his house had been ransacked. The old safe used by Baker's father had been turned upside down. The most vulnerable spot in the bottom was drilled and the contents were removed. The pockets on all his pants were turned out, as were the cuffs. All his wife's shoeboxes had been examined. A coin collection of his father's and the jewelry were not taken, but they were laid out on the couch on jeweler's paper. Nothing had been stolen. Baker called in a security expert who said the burglars were most likely looking for a key, a claim check or a combination. Why hadn't they taken anything? Baker asked. They had intentionally left everything there, the expert said. They wanted to send a message. What message? Baker asked. "Because they wanted you to know that they were pros," Baker remembered the expert replying.

After the break-in, Baker asked to see his FBI file. The bureau protested, but he insisted. Finally, he was allowed to review his files at the FBI headquarters. Much was marked out, redacted and withheld for one privacy or security or legal reason or another. One part was not cut out. It showed that the Drug Enforcement Agency had wiretapped Baker's home phone for several weeks and found nothing useful or criminal. He could not get a satisfactory explanation. Baker wondered why the FBI had let him see his file. It was almost as if the wiretap information had been laid out on jeweler's paper as another warning.

Baker worried that he actually might be killed. He didn't think he was being paranoid. He was just scared. He didn't know who might be after him. As the Nixon presidency came into increasing jeopardy, Baker realized that Nixon and his aides were fighting for their survival. People had been killed for a lot less. You shoot at the king, Baker concluded, he's likely to return fire.

There was no shooting or killing in Watergate, but the collapse of the Nixon presidency, its emotional and political conflagration, had stamped Baker with an indelible impression of danger and risk, and of human nature, when anyone wanting to serve walked through the gates at 1600 Pennsylvania Avenue.

The great lesson of Watergate was that cover-ups never work. From what Baker had been reading in the news media and hearing from political friends, it appeared that the Reagan White House might be in the middle of one. Overtones of Watergate were all about, and the foreign policy implications seemed immense. Baker felt that the wounds of Watergate had not been healed. By the end of the flight, he had marshaled a number of reasons not to accept any offer from President Reagan.

The next morning Baker went straight to the White House and took the elevator up to the residence. When the elevator door opened, Reagan was standing alone. He looked forlorn and saddened. He was not the jaunty, beaming, confident, bursting-with-optimism Reagan of his television appearances.

"Howard," the president said, "I've got to have a new chief of staff and I want you to do it."

"All right," Baker heard himself saying, quickly ending his careful resolve and determination. He had half expected Reagan to offer him some role as special counsel or senior adviser. Chief of staff was different, the one in charge, Baker felt, too good to turn down. But acceptance was conditional.

The two went to the sitting room.

"Mr. President," Baker said, "if I do this job I've got to have access to everything. I've got to know what's going on. I cannot let myself be taken into a situation I don't understand."

Reagan agreed completely.

Just to be clear, Baker repeated, he had to have absolute access. There could be no secrets. "I want you to issue an order to all people in the White House," Baker said, "and the West Wing in particular, saying that I have access to every record and they should give me total cooperation because I'm going to find out, to the best of my ability, what has happened on Iran-contra, *and everything else.*"

"Okay," the president said. Reagan didn't seem to be hiding.

"Number two," Baker said, "I've got to have my own lawyer." He wanted to bring in a long-time aide and current law partner, Arthur "A.B." Culvahouse, as White House counsel. Reagan hadn't even met the man, but Baker said he had to have him as the top lawyer.

Reagan agreed. No problem.

Third, Baker said he wanted to bring in his own communications person, spokesman.

Reagan said fine.

"Mr. President," Baker also said, "I don't want to make a career out of this, and I'll stay until I think the job's done, but it's probably going to be about a year."

Reagan agreed. He felt that Baker was looking for a graceful way to exit from another presidential race, since Vice President Bush was the likely front-runner.

After Baker left the meeting, he vowed to himself he was going to turn the White House and the CIA and the intelligence agencies and the Pentagon inside out. What the independent counsel was going to do was child's play compared to his plan. If it was bad, they would disclose. If he were thwarted in any way, he would leave.

News that Reagan had selected Howard Baker to replace Don Regan leaked to the media that afternoon. Regan was furious and humiliated. He hadn't formally resigned. He sent the president a one-line resignation letter and stormed out of the White House, not to return.

Regan's ouster destroyed his friendship with the president. It was the bitterest event of his life. The Reagan White House, he believed, had created an appetite for the rise and fall of its courtiers by making theatrical effect its primary objective. Still, Regan could see that the characteristics in President Reagan that drew the most criticism—detachment, delegation, instinct over intellect, and simplicity—might be his strengths.

Culvahouse, 37, a handsome, athletic man, was vacationing in a remote Cancún, Mexico, villa when the maid came running out with four urgent messages to call Senator Baker. One said to phone Baker through operator 1 at the White House.

"The president has asked me to be his chief of staff," Baker said. "I have accepted upon his agreement that he would name you White House counsel. I've tendered our resignations to our law firm, and now that you're out of a job I hope you'll take the one that's offered."

Culvahouse laughed and accepted. He would not have been on anyone's list of the top 100 people to be White House counsel. Probably he wouldn't have been on a list of the top 1,000. Baker said he knew it was a bit of a stretch, but the job of investigating Iran-contra was too important. He needed a friend, someone he could trust, and he didn't have the time to get accustomed to any other lawyer. They were going deep into the bowels of the Reagan White House and CIA, both of which Baker held in suspicion.

On Sunday, March 1, Baker invited Culvahouse, Thomas Griscom, his new communications aide, and James Cannon, a longtime confidant and former domestic policy chief for President Ford, to his house.

Baker had asked Cannon, 69, a sober, gray-haired man, to interview Reagan aides during the prior two days to determine what was happening in the White House. Cannon said the White House staff had described an alarming degree of presidential detachment and drift, not unlike the final months of the Nixon presidency. Reagan's capacity was impaired, according to the staff.

"That's not the man I talked to," Baker snapped.

Cannon persisted. They might have to consider invoking the 25th Amendment, which said the vice president and a majority of the cabinet could declare that the president was unable to function, making the vice president the acting president.

"Well," Baker replied, "we will all observe the president closely and if any of us sees any evidence of that then we'll get back together." They would have to inventory the entire structure of the White House, find out how well it was working, Baker said, including the president's immediate staff and office. He offered part of his initial diagnosis. "The president doesn't have enough to do. We're going to have to get him reengaged."

"There are three goals and we're going to keep them foremost in our mind," Baker said. "We're going to survive Iran-contra if we can and *if we deserve to.* We'll have to live with the facts, but we're not going to make any mistakes." He looked at Culvahouse. "You don't want to be the first White House counsel to have your client convicted in an impeachment trial." Baker told Culvahouse he was going to be a White House counsel with one priority: Iran-contra. "You're going to find someone else to handle everything else until we get our arms around this issue.

"Secondly," Baker continued, "we're going to get an arms agreement with the Soviets." Turning to the next year, 1988, a presidential election year, when the Constitution prevented Reagan from running for another term, Baker said, "And third we're going to elect a Republican president."

The men in the room knew of Baker's presidential ambitions, but no one said anything.

Monday morning, March 2, Baker returned to the White House with his team. They watched Reagan intently, sitting at lunch with him around the cabinet table. Even Cannon agreed that Reagan looked just fine and was in tune with the discussion, especially the jokes they exchanged.

Baker introduced Reagan to his new counsel, Culvahouse. He sat down with the president to discuss the thorough self-investigation that Culvahouse was going to conduct of the White House.

"Mr. President, in my career, I can handle most things politically, but the one thing I can't handle is surprises, and I need your assurance that we will have, particularly Culvahouse, total access to everything. Every document, access to every person to find out what the facts actually are."

"Fine," Reagan said.

Working secretly with John Tower, who had headed the critical Iran-contra review board, and speechwriter Landon Parvin, as well as Nancy, Reagan agreed to give a nationally televised, cleansing speech.

The evening of March 4, Reagan spoke from the Oval Office. "A few months ago I told the American people I did not trade arms for hostages. My heart and my best intentions still tell me that's true, but the facts and the evidence tell me it is not. As the Tower Board reported, what began as a strategic opening to Iran deteriorated, in its implementation, into trading arms for hostages. This runs counter to my own beliefs, to administration policy, and to the original strategy we had in mind. There are reasons why it happened, but no excuses. It was a mistake."

The speech was vintage Reagan—charming, friendly and direct. Overnight, Reagan's public approval rating jumped 9 percentage points.

But political forgiveness was not legal or

193

political exoneration. Baker and Culvahouse knew that impeachment was still in the air. The giant unknown was the anticipated testimony before Congress of Poindexter and North. Both had lawyers and neither was talking. Either one of them could say Reagan had knowledge of or gave approval for the diversion of Iran arms sales profits to the contras—the heart of serious criminal liability and presumably (if true) a serious, impeachable offense.

Culvahouse saw they were fighting blind. Thousands of documents had been turned over to the Tower Board and to Congress without adequate records kept of what they said.

Marlin Fitzwater, Reagan's press secretary, wasn't at all sure what Poindexter might have told the president. Fitzwater, a 44-year-old, congenial, moon-faced career civil servant from Abilene, Kansas, recalled one Air Force One trip to California in the fall of 1986 when Poindexter was still Reagan's national security adviser. Poindexter sat right across from the president, their knees almost touching, and Poindexter whispered.

The engines of the plane roared, the staff was talking and screaming and yelling. Poindexter whispered in the president's ear as if he didn't want even Nancy to hear and certainly not Fitzwater, who was three rows back. The image of Poindexter whispering had stuck with Fitzwater. Poindexter no doubt thought the president would approve of the diversion of funds, and Fitzwater believed that Reagan probably would have.

So one morning, Fitzwater went to see the president.

Mr. President, Fitzwater said, the diversion of funds is the main question. "This is where the press are coming from on this issue, and it all boils down to this question." Fitzwater was prepared for a blank face, or, "Talk to the lawyers."

"I didn't know anything about it," Reagan said. "They never mentioned to me any diversion of funds."

Fitzwater said fine. He felt it was not his job to grill the president—pressing him on whether Poindexter or Casey might have mentioned it, for example. Fitzwater just wanted to hear the denial from the president directly. He realized his own reputation was likely going to depend on that question.

Fitzwater, who still thought of himself as a civil servant, felt he had to keep a certain distance. If the president was guilty, he didn't want him to get off. He was not going to be like the Nixon people—denial and concealment at all costs. He hoped Reagan was innocent; but if he wasn't, he felt that Baker, the lawyers and himself to a certain extent should prove his culpability, not somebody else. Maybe it was selfish, but he didn't want to go down defending a guilty president.

Fitzwater also wasn't going to take a fall for some chief of staff like Baker or some lawyer. As long as he could say that the president told him directly, that he had heard it from his mouth, that was as righteous a cause as a press secretary would get. But Fitzwater was only 90 percent confident in Reagan's face-to-face denial. So he went to Culvahouse.

"This is what the president told me," Fitzwater said, repeating Reagan's denial. "Is that the same thing he's telling you?"

Culvahouse said yes.

"Is that consistent with everything you know?"

Yes.

"Is there any reason to suspect that either he's deluding me or himself or anything else?"

"Now," Culvahouse said, "the thing you want to be careful of, Marlin, is that proving that is not as easy as him saying it." The biggest fear was Poindexter. What would his testimony be? No one was sure.

Fitzwater and Culvahouse began meeting almost daily to discuss possible questions from the media. When Culvahouse proposed answers, Fitzwater at times balked.

"Okay," Fitzwater said to one proposed answer, "that's fine for a lawyer to say who doesn't have to stay there and answer the next damn question, but it's not going to work for me."

At one meeting with Culvahouse, Fitzwater said the press was focused on the diversion, and it was clear that the public probably was going to make its judgment on the issue. If the president did not know about the diversion, Fitzwater said, then they ought to build their public relations strategy around that. "We should have that in everything we say," Fitzwater said. "If that's where we're going to end up making our final stand, then we need to set the stage right now." He proposed a kind of innocence by association

196

strategy. "So that when it's clearly shown that the president didn't know about that, there's also the suggestion that he's innocent of anything else that might be out there."

Culvahouse agreed, so Fitzwater repeated the line whenever possible, dropping it into his briefings at every opportunity, even when it was forced. He realized it was a risky strategy. If the assertion were to be proven wrong, they would all sink. Having lived through Watergate as a press officer in the Environmental Protection Agency, Fitzwater believed that they needed order and direction. It was the only way out, he felt.

Fitzwater was insulated ideologically. He was not a movement conservative. On a number of the litmus test issues, he did not pass. He was pro-choice on abortion and he was for gun control. As a professional spokesman he tried to make sure he made the best arguments on the president's behalf. But he never made it personal. It gave him a little detachment and perspective, and he tried to keep it. He was well aware that if a president felt passionately and strongly about an issue, that in itself set a climate. People with a propensity to act in the extreme could overreact. But he believed it was fair to criticize Reagan, who set the climate in which illegal Iran-contra acts had occurred.

He was aware that Culvahouse and Baker were meeting privately to interrogate the president, but he didn't attend. He didn't want to make it look as if there was a prosecution squad within the White House examining and probing the president.

13

THE REAL THREAT to the Reagan presidency, Baker and Culvahouse knew, lived across town in the Watergate Hotel in a kind of symbolic encampment. The hotel was adjacent to the Watergate office building where the Democratic headquarters had been burglarized 15 years earlier. In room 609 of the hotel, Lawrence E. Walsh, 75, had set up living quarters after being named by the three-judge panel as the independent counsel for Iran-contra. Walsh, a thin, prim, sober-looking man with intense eyes, was a quintessential Eisenhower Republican. From 1938 to 1941, he had been an assistant district attorney. In the 1950s, he had served as a federal judge for three years and then as deputy attorney general for another three years. For the past 27 years he had been in private law practice in New York City and Oklahoma City. He had no recent experience as a prosecutor.

Walsh respected what Reagan had done so far as president. He did not sense public anger with Reagan, as had been the case with Nixon. He decided to move carefully. He would try to make cases against North and Poindexter, and then see what developed. He had no plan to prosecute Reagan, although many in the White House, Congress and the media assumed he was moving to lay the grounds to impeach the president. Walsh suspected that President Reagan knew about the diversion of millions of dollars from the Iran arms sales profits to his beloved contras. But he couldn't project precisely where he was taking his investigation. "I sort of move as I feel," he said. His style was to be deferential to the president, but not to his men.

One of Walsh's first stops was the CIA, which gave his team space and filing cabinets in the basement of agency headquarters in Virginia so they could look at top-secret code-word documents. Early in the investigation, the IRS gave Walsh 11 agents who were experts in tracing hidden money so Walsh could attempt to understand the "Enterprise" that North had set up using Swiss bank accounts for the Iran arms sales, the secret contras resupply and other covert operations.

Iran-contra had dozens of tentacles, and Walsh chose to pursue nearly all of them. He was not sure if he was chasing rabbits or where they might take him. His authority from the three-judge panel called on him to prosecute any related crimes he uncovered, even by underlings. His preoccupation became North and Poindexter, the operational officers.

At the White House, Culvahouse was feeling vulnerable. He read in the newspapers that Walsh was hiring former federal prosecutors for his staff. He called his law school roommate, William B. Lytton III, a 6 foot 1 attorney with large eyeglasses who had been a federal prosecutor in both Chicago and Philadelphia. Lytton, 38, had directed the staff in the investigation of the Philadelphia police firebombing of a house occupied by the radical African

American group MOVE two years earlier. His specialty in Philadelphia private law practice was managing major corporate lawsuits involving dozens of lawyers and file cabinets of documents.

Culvahouse asked Lytton to take the train to Washington to talk. He wanted Lytton to become the deputy counsel, working full time with him on Iran-contra. It was a document and witness management problem, but Culvahouse said he needed someone who would be alert to obstruction of justice issues that might arise. The message was clear: not only was Culvahouse concerned about past obstructions of justice, but he had to make sure that, in defending Reagan, the new team, particularly Baker and himself, did not get entangled themselves. John Dean and other Nixon administration lawyers had gone to jail in Watergate, and it was obvious that it was easy to be swayed by a president who demanded to be protected.

Lytton arrived at the White House in early March to meet with Baker and Culvahouse. Baker said they would defend Reagan, but first he wanted a complete investigation. He assured Lytton that he could hire as many people as he needed. Baker said he had no confidence that what the holdover White House staff had said was accurate. Take whatever steps are necessary to acquire that absolute total confidence, he instructed Lytton. They had to figure out what the administration knew and *when* they knew it. He demanded an aggressive internal investigation the likes of which a White House had never seen. He cautioned that the extent of their effort should be kept secret and out of the media. The general theme of Baker's public posture was that the White House was not concerned about Iran-contra, and a massive self-investigation would betray their worry.

Culvahouse and Lytton tried to focus on the immediate problem. They agreed that if it could be proven, or even forcefully and creditably alleged, that President Reagan had known of the diversion of funds, he would likely be impeached.

Lytton began work on March 16. Finding personnel with the needed top-secret codeword clearances was difficult. They could not wait the months it took for the FBI to complete the necessary background investigations. Someone mentioned that the National Archives had a large staff with the highest security clearances doing historical research. Baker invited the archivist of the United States to lunch at the White House, his first White House luncheon, and soon ten fully cleared archivists were detailed to Lytton's task force.

Lytton discovered that the two White House lawyers working on documents had no records of what they had turned over to the Tower Commission. He was troubled. If the White House's initial response to the scandal became the subject of later scrutiny by the congressional investigators and the independent counsel, Lytton knew they had to be able to prove that they had turned over documents, or the White House could face the kind of obstruction of justice charge that Baker had warned they must avoid.

How do you know whether or not you've actually produced a document? Lytton asked the lawyers.

They said they were sure one of them would remember.

What happens if one of you guys gets hit by a truck? he asked.

By March 25, Lytton had completed a nine-page memo on the organization of a White House Iran-contra legal task force. He divided the staff into special teams on document production, testimony given to the independent counsel and congressional committees, evidence analysis, legal analysis, and evidence security.

The memo directed that all documents would be given control numbers and each page would be assigned a separate number. Copies and a registry would be kept. There would be no relying on anyone's memory.

Lytton moved into a fourth-floor suite once occupied by the secretary of war in the Old Executive Office Building. Soon he had close to 67 people. He called them together.

"The president has said we're going to turn over everything we have," Lytton said. "We're going to do it honestly, we're not going to withhold, we're not going to cover up."

Suppose something incriminates Reagan? someone asked.

"If we find a document that hurts the president," Lytton said, "that is turned over. I want to know about it, but that gets turned over."

Baker came over to talk to the lawyers. Making clear his authority, Baker spoke to the lawyers in a clipped, rapid cadence. "You guys tell us where the lines are," he said. "You make sure that nobody crosses that line. Don't talk about getting close." He did not want to get to the edges of what was legal or ethical. "We will never cross that line and you guys make sure, your job is to make sure."

On April 6, Culvahouse and Lytton went for their first meeting with Walsh. His deputies had made it clear that Walsh liked to be called "Judge," and that he preferred others to come to him in his office.

"I don't wish the president ill," Walsh said, adding that he had great respect for the president. "But you guys are getting documents to us much too slowly and my people have nothing to do."

The White House attorneys promised full cooperation. They would produce documents voluntarily as fast as possible. Subpoenas would not be necessary.

Walsh concurred. Speed was more important than the legal formality of a subpoena.

The president, Culvahouse said, would offer testimony, but they hoped that initially his answers could formally be in writing.

Walsh thought that could be worked out. He wanted to prosecute Poindexter and North. In an open-ended, in-person interview or deposition, Reagan might say he authorized their activities or somehow indicate his support for the Iran and contra operations up to the diversion of funds. It would undermine the prosecution if Poindexter and North could claim presidential authority for their actions.

The immediate problem was the personal diaries that President Reagan kept. Culvahouse said he was going to review them himself. Any relevant passages would be supplied to Walsh, but the president did not want others reading through the diaries.

Walsh agreed to that.

On April 13, when Culvahouse went to the White House residence, Reagan brought out several large volumes that looked like photo albums and handed them over. He asked that Culvahouse alone read them, not even Howard Baker.

Culvahouse took the diaries down to the little dining room off the Oval Office at 9:30 a.m. He sat on one side and Lytton on the other. Lytton would keep a detailed log. When Culvahouse found a passage that might be relevant, he read it aloud. Then he and Lytton discussed it, as Lytton reviewed Walsh's document request for anything dealing with the contras or Iran. Leaning on the side of disclosure, if any diary entry were remotely relevant, Culvahouse dictated it verbatim into a tape recorder.

Culvahouse began with the first volume and an entry for March 21, 1983. For 18 hours during the next week the two men reviewed the diaries. By April 24, they had completed their reading of the current diary in which the president was writing down his daily thoughts. They were relieved to find nothing troubling. They were unsure if Reagan had just forgotten events or had intentionally omitted them or whether there was nothing there in the first place. That evening they went to the White House residence to return the diaries to Reagan, who appeared in his bare feet.

On April 30, six days later, Baker, Culvahouse and Lytton went to see the president in the Oval Office at 1:15 p.m.

Baker reported that they had done a preliminary analysis of the documents. They had reviewed the president's diaries, as he knew, and had assembled the available information on what others in the administration might testify about. They did not know what North or Poindexter would say, but the two almost certainly would be forced to testify before Congress soon under grants of immunity. Given the current state of knowledge, Baker said, Culvahouse and Lytton believed there was no evidence that the president had authorized or known about the diversion of funds. Do you disagree? Baker asked, looking the president straight in the eye.

Reagan said that was correct. He had not known about the diversion, as he had said all along.

Reading Reagan's body language and relaxed tone, Baker thought the president was telling the truth. But who could know for sure? One additional step had to be taken. The lawyers had asked for a series of confidential formal meetings with the president, as their client, to review the law—exactly what Walsh and Congress were investigating—and to take the documents, the diary entries and the statements of others and discuss them with Reagan. They would interview him to obtain his recollections on the key portions of the story.

Reagan agreed.

On May 5, Congress opened public hearings on Iran-contra. The next day, William J.

Casey died in a Long Island hospital. On May 9, the president and the first lady attended his funeral.

Reagan was to hold his first formal meeting with Baker and his new lawyers on May 26. At 1:15 p.m., Baker, Culvahouse and Lytton arrived at the Oval Office.

Culvahouse and Lytton said they believed their discussions would be privileged and would not be disclosed to anyone, including Walsh or Congress. None of them was going to write a book.

By Lytton's count, Walsh had several dozen prosecutors exploring any and every possible violation of the law by Reagan. There were five specific laws that might have been violated, including the Boland Amendment, which had prevented the expenditure of federal government funds for the contras. In addition, they would be looking at the conspiracy laws—whether the president and others worked together in concert to violate any law.

Laurence H. Tribe, a Harvard Law professor and liberal expert on constitutional law, had published an article in *The New York Times* the previous week saying the president had failed in his constitutional duty to "take care that the laws be faithfully executed." Tribe wrote, "In other words, if the puppets are subject to the law and violate it, the puppet master cannot escape accountability."

Reagan noted with distaste that he had read Tribe's comments.

That could become an issue in impeachment, they told him.

Culvahouse and Lytton had assembled every public comment that Reagan had made about the contras.

I believed in the contras, Reagan said. At every possible opportunity I said something to encourage them and those who would give them money.

The private fund-raising for the contras by the president probably did not pose any legal problems, Lytton said.

Culvahouse said the biggest area of vulnerability was if the president had authorized or known in advance about the diversion. "Impeachment would be a possibility," Culvahouse said.

Reagan repeated his denial. "Every day I go to bed," he said, "I realize there are hundreds if not thousands of people out there who say they're speaking on my behalf whom I've never met. I don't know what they're saying, and they're saying they speak for the administration. That's kind of scary."

Lytton asked the president about a phone call he had made personally to Oliver North the day North had been fired from the National Security Council staff. What did the president mean when he called North "a national hero"?

"I was referring specifically to his military service," Reagan said. North had been highly decorated for his Vietnam service, receiving a Bronze Star and a Silver Star as a Marine second lieutenant in 1969. That was all he had meant.

What else was discussed in that phone call which some had interpreted as an effort to keep North on the reservation? Lytton asked.

Reagan said he had avoided any discussion

of Iran-contra or the diversion. "If I had gotten into that I would have said, 'Why the hell did you do this without my approval?' " He said he half-wished he had interrogated North and Poindexter. Maybe they would have explained some of the mysteries.

Culvahouse said they hoped to meet with the president on a regular basis, maybe up to three times a week, during the congressional hearings. They were still combing through documents and gathering the facts.

Reagan seemed to accept that.

Three days later, May 29, Baker and the two lawyers were back in the Oval Office with the president.

By then they had turned over some 200,000 pages from some 12,000 documents to Walsh and Congress. They wanted to discuss some of the documents, including information about a Saturday morning, December 7, 1985, meeting Reagan had with his top national security team in the residence. Secretary of Defense Weinberger had spent nearly a half hour spelling out the folly of selling arms to Iran. He had argued that it would violate the arms embargo to Iran and the Arms Export Control Act. John McMahon, Casey's CIA deputy, was sitting in and he said he was unaware of any moderates in Iran because Khomeini had slaughtered them and any arms would wind up supporting him.

Reagan could recall little of that meeting.

"I feel bad that I keep saying I don't recall," the president said.

They asked about a May 16, 1986, meeting

of the top foreign policy advisers. They had some information which suggested that Reagan had said something about getting North to find some money for the contras when Congress was debating the contra funding.

The president couldn't remember.

They handed Reagan a copy of North's April 1986 memo that explained the diversion project in detail. The $12 million from Iran arms sales would go to the contras, according to the memo.

The president carefully studied the long, complicated memo for several minutes. He finally looked up and said he believed he had never seen it before.

On June 10, Culvahouse and Lytton met with Richard Beckler, Poindexter's attorney. Beckler said the independent counsel was after his client. One solution, he proposed, was that President Reagan grant a pardon to Poindexter, who could then testify truthfully. He suggested that the testimony would be painful for Reagan but hinted that Poindexter would not implicate the president on the diversion.

Brendan Sullivan, North's attorney, also sought a pardon for his client.

Eight days later, the attorneys met with Reagan in the Oval Office at 10 a.m. They brought up the pardon requests. It was a subtle test for Reagan. Presumably pardons would silence Poindexter and North, perhaps forever. Reagan asked for Culvahouse's advice.

People would never believe that the president did not know about the diversion of funds in advance, Culvahouse said, if he pardoned Poindexter or North at this point. It would be a taint on his presidency.

Reagan rejected the request.

On June 23, Baker, Lytton and Culvahouse returned to the Oval Office at 11 a.m.

"I didn't do it," Reagan joked as he greeted them. He threw his hands up in the air.

They focused on the contra support. Back on June 25, 1984, the minutes of his meeting with his foreign policy team showed that Reagan wanted to go to other countries to get money for the contras in place of U.S. funding, which Congress had just cut off. According to the notes, Reagan demanded that their efforts must not leak. "If such a story gets out," he said, "we'll be hanging by our thumbs in front of the White House until we find out who did it."

"Boy," Reagan laughed, "somebody took some pretty good notes at the meeting."

Baker and the two lawyers discussed the problem that Reagan's instruction, as Congress cut off funding in 1984, to hold the contras together body and soul might be cited as general presidential authority.

Reagan listened as his lawyers talked about the issue.

They told him that Walsh was going to be interviewing the vice president, and that he might ask to interview the president. They hoped these meetings would be helpful in preparing him.

The next morning, June 24, the three came in at 10 a.m. They said they needed to talk with Nancy Reagan as part of their review.

What do you have in mind? the president asked.

Culvahouse said they wanted to brief the first lady as a courtesy, but there were also these reports in the news media that Reagan had been close to North. "If you believed some reports," Culvahouse said, "North tucked you in every night."

Reagan laughed. "Mrs. Reagan would be quite outspoken on that," he said. Fine, he said, Baker should call the first lady and set up the briefing.

They turned to the question of whether the Iran arrangement was an arms-for-hostages deal.

Although the president had publicly conceded as much, he reverted to his original argument. "We were working with an intermediary," he explained. "You know, if your kids were kidnapped you would pay somebody to help you get your kids back, not the kidnappers, but you'd hire somebody to go help you get them back." It was clear and simple in the president's mind.

Lytton asked if the president remembered two top-secret intelligence orders or findings that he had signed on the covert arms sales to Iran in January 1986. In the 11 days between the two findings, two or three words had changed.

"Am I supposed to remember the three words?" the president asked.

"There are some people who think that you should," Lytton replied.

"No," Reagan said he didn't remember.

Culvahouse asked if there was anything the

president wished to discuss with them, or that he wanted to brief them on or for them to brief him.

"I'm embarrassed that I have to say so many times that I can't remember things," Reagan said again.

The three came back at 10 a.m. the next morning, June 25.

What kind of staff work was done prior to the time you received a document? the lawyers asked.

Reagan said he assumed the National Security Council staff and some lawyer vetted everything that reached his desk. "It's almost standard the lawyers reviewed things before I see them," he added.

Lytton tried to go through some of the crucial meetings, but Reagan could not recall who said what at a meeting. He just knew that Shultz and Weinberger were opposed to the Iran arms sales. He then repeated his defense: This operation was not a direct transaction with those who took the hostages. "We weren't dealing with the kidnappers, and it was not ransom," he stated.

The president was fixed on that interpretation. Lytton felt it was plausible, but Reagan had lost that argument publicly, and to raise it again would reopen the old wound. Reagan would go to his grave thinking that way, Lytton thought.

Culvahouse asked about CIA Director Casey and his role in the Iran arms sales.

"Casey had very little involvement in it," Reagan said. He didn't recall Casey expressing an opinion. Then he laughed. "I guess he had kind of an alibi because when Casey did talk in meetings he mumbled so much that we couldn't understand or hear him."

Was there any cabinet opposition to the contra policy? the lawyers wondered.

No, the president said. "And there was never any talk of breaking any rules. I was *horrified* that the United States would first encourage the contras to take up arms and then cut off assistance making them wonder whether they'd have enough bullets once we put them in the field."

Baker still wasn't sure they were getting to the bottom. Mr. President, he said, if you ever recall something we need to know, you can rely on the three of us to keep it confidential. "We're the group working on this," Baker added. The president could share it with just Culvahouse, or with Culvahouse and Lytton, or he could raise it just with Baker—any one of them or any combination. He could rely on them keeping any confidence.

"All right," the president replied. They had to understand something. "There was never any time that the contras knew what we were doing in Iran. Iran was a different activity." The opportunity in Iran came up, it was not sought. "The contras was a different item, and much more on our minds than the Iran matter, you know, it was a matter of policy." Reagan repeated that he had first heard about the connection when Ed Meese told him about the Iran operation being used to get money to the contras. Iran and the contras had never before been tied together in his mind, nor did he recall receiving any reports hinting of any connection between Iran and the contras.

Lytton noted that Reagan was firm. He had seen Reagan's movies and did not think he was that good an actor. He believed they had Reagan's guard down—hence Baker's plea about trusting them. Although Lytton felt the standard legal doctrine of not believing your client was a sound practice, he found himself starting to believe Reagan. But he realized that they would never get the full trust of this president.

On June 30 at 11 a.m. Baker and the lawyers returned once more to see Reagan in the Oval Office. North had been granted limited immunity for his testimony and was scheduled to sit down behind closed doors the next day with the leaders of the congressional Iran-contra committees. His lawyers were saying that the Democrats would like what North had to say, Culvahouse reported.

"Oh boy!" Reagan said.

Equally as bad, Culvahouse said, was an article that had just come out in *Washingtonian* magazine, titled "The Ollie We Knew...Here's what he really did, and why he did it." The 17-page article had been written by reporters who alleged they talked to North at least once a week for nearly two years before the Iran-contra story broke. The article described a secret, close relationship between the president and North.

Reagan said just last night he had started rereading his diaries, from the spring of 1983 to the present, and had found no mentions of North.

Culvahouse took a copy of the article and turned to page 141. He read out an account of what North had allegedly done after the 1983 Grenada operation. North had feared the medical students who supposedly had been saved from the communists on the island might publicly criticize Reagan's invasion. North had failed to ensure that intelligence briefers accompanied the students to explain the White House's rationale. North had run up to the Oval Office.

Culvahouse read, "When North met with Reagan, he often entered the Oval Office through the side door, and his meetings were not logged in."

" 'What's the problem, Ollie?' " Reagan asked, according to the article. " 'You appear to be disturbed by something.'

"North told the president what had happened and took responsibility for having failed his commander in chief."

"Come with me," said the president, leading the way into an adjacent room where there was a TV.

"Sit down and let's watch their arrival," Reagan consoled the younger man in a fatherly way. "Everything will be fine. You ought to have faith."

The first student arrived, dropped down and kissed the tarmac.

Culvahouse read on: "Reagan turned to North and said, 'You see, Ollie, you ought to have more faith in the American people.' "

Reagan looked at them and said forcefully,

"This ain't memory with me. That just never happened."

Lytton said they had the movement logs of the president that day which supported Reagan's denial.

Culvahouse read out another passage about the 1986 bombing raid of Libya. Reagan was about to give a nationally televised speech that allegedly contained a mistake: "Seconds before 9 p.m. North burst into the Oval Office and made a direct line for the TelePrompTer. The president looked up from his papers and stared at North, who was erasing a line from the speech on the TelePrompTer."

Reagan frowned. "That never happened," he said. He explained in some detail how changes were made on the TelePrompTer.

The lawyers assumed North's testimony would include details of a close relationship with the president.

"I'd hate to have to stand up and publicly deny it," Reagan said, "because I'd hate to have to do that to him."

"Don't be reluctant to do it," Baker said. "If he were to say what is in this article, he doesn't wish you well." Baker said the records could be used to undercut North's testimony. There might also be a way for Reagan to answer North publicly in a speech or press conference—some appropriate response. But Baker said on constitutional grounds he opposed any formal sworn testimony by the president. Lawyers never wanted their clients under oath if it could be avoided. "It will be over my corpse that the president will testify or give a deposition," Baker said.

The lawyers returned to North. Did the president recall any one-on-one conversations with North?

"No," Reagan said.

Did he ever phone North?

No, only the day last year when North had been fired. Reagan said he didn't recall using North's name.

Lytton said he would interview everyone around the Oval Office, including the Secret Service, to be absolutely certain that North had not been there at these alleged times.

Reagan was trying to remember. He said he recalled seeing North when the hostage David Jacobsen had been released, but that seemed to be the only time.

Lytton gave a copy of the article to Reagan. "After you read the article if you have anything else you want to talk to us about, for us to focus on, let us know." They were going to examine every possible false assertion in the article. "It's a scary article. When you read that article, if that's true, we're in big trouble."

The lawyers said the Democrats on the committee and their staff were not antagonistic. The senior staff was working with the White House lawyers to knock down the article. "They don't believe it either," Lytton said.

At the end of the meeting, Reagan said, "Have a nice day."

On July 2, just after 10 a.m., the lawyers were back.

What about the draft of the first intelligence order or finding in late 1985 authorizing arms shipments through Israel? Because the CIA had facilitated one shipment already, the finding said, "All prior actions taken by U.S. government officials in furtherance of this effort are hereby ratified." This retroactive approval was unusual and questionable. In addition, the finding mentioned arms and hostages. There was no discussion of a broader, strategic opening to Iran—the pillar of Reagan's motivation.

"That's right," the president said.

But this finding had nothing about that strategic opening, one of the lawyers repeated. Did he recall signing it?

"Let me see it," Reagan asked, taking a copy and carefully reading it. "I probably did," he said. He recalled some of the language. "If I didn't sign it, I at least agreed to it orally." He looked down at the one-page document. "I don't remember whether I signed it, but I would have."

Baker said the congressional committees probably would try to show that the president had signed it, and the signed copy was destroyed to protect the president. Did the president, Baker asked, tell anybody to destroy a signed document?

"Hell no!" Reagan said.

Lytton said the committees and possibly Walsh were going to attack him. The reason for selling arms to Iran was to get the hostages back, they could argue. Later references to strategic motives were an after-the-fact rationalization and a cover-up for the real reason—arms for hostages.

"That's not right," Reagan said. "Originally

218

it was an Iranian approach and they never mentioned hostages. They were talking about after Khomeini. We said, 'Well, maybe this is an opportunity.' " Reagan said since coming to office he wanted to establish a relationship with those who would lead Iran after Khomeini. "That's why I jumped at it."

Culvahouse said the president's diaries showed that Bud McFarlane had told him about the moderate elements in Iran, confirming that Reagan was thinking about the strategic aspect of it initially.

Lytton said if Poindexter had destroyed the finding that was signed, it might have been to protect the president because its rationale—arms for hostages—was inconsistent with the strategic opening.

Reagan said it was possible. The day Poindexter resigned he told the president he had made a mistake. But, Reagan added, he had no way of knowing. He hadn't talked to Poindexter since.

Culvahouse asked Reagan if he had ever personally destroyed documents, because they were worried about it. A charge of document destruction could be a central element of obstruction of justice. "Well, I destroyed one," the president said. "Bill Casey wrote me a long letter urging that George Shultz be fired, and I took care of it in here."

"In where?" Culvahouse asked.

Reagan pointed to the Oval Office fireplace.

Reaching into his desk drawer, Reagan removed his diary. He said he had reviewed the *Washingtonian* article, in particular, the account about the alleged meeting with North after the Grenada invasion. He turned to the day in October and read: A National Security Council meeting, Weinberger was off to Europe, meeting with New York Marathon winners—one had only one leg—a meeting with two senators on the crime bill, address to a coalition of Republicans, Bush back from Lebanon, working on a speech for the next day. "Look," he said, "here's what I wrote down that day, guys." No mention of North.

Five days later, Oliver North stood at attention before the joint congressional investigating committee in his Marine olive uniform, his chest covered with medals, his hand raised to take the oath. More than seven months had passed since he was fired from the National Security Council staff. North said he was convinced President Reagan knew everything, including about the diversion of funds. "I believed that the president had indeed authorized such activity," he testified. But North had no supporting evidence. All his personal knowledge was to the contrary. He testified that he never discussed the diversion with the president. Poindexter also told North that he had never raised the diversion with the president. No one ever mentioned to North that they had talked about it with the president. It was a victory for Reagan. North felt that his testimony—and the positive public response to his efforts to fight communism and terrorism—would help save the Reagan presidency.

"We're glad to be able to bring you some good news for once," Lytton said later that day as the trio arrived to see Reagan again in the Oval Office.

Lytton recounted that North had testified that he had never told Reagan about the diversion.

Reagan, beaming, was obviously pleased.

Poindexter was the more important witness because of his position and he was yet to come, but North's statements helped significantly.

"I kind of hope," Reagan said, "that maybe North isn't as bad as some of the media people have suggested. Maybe he really is an American hero." The president wanted to believe. "I guess I'll have to hang a black wreath on the door of Congress since he didn't implicate me."

Turning to contra support, the lawyers asked about a meeting the president had with some ladies who had bought TV ads in support of the contras.

"I really don't know who authorizes people to walk through this door," the president said.

It looked like the former chief of staff Don Regan had approved it.

"Well," the president said, "I don't really know who, you know. If they come in I figure somebody's said that's okay."

Had someone suggested the call to North the day North was fired?

"No," Reagan said, "no one suggested it. I just felt it was the right thing to do to call him and just say good-bye."

For Baker and the others it was a plausible explanation on one level, a simple human gesture to someone wounded in the political warfare, another victim of Reagan's contra war. On another level, the call didn't quite make sense. Reagan had earlier insisted that he wasn't familiar with North's name. Why would a president so remote from his children, cabinet and staff pick up the phone to reach out to this particular lieutenant colonel? By Reagan's own account in his diary, the president realized that "our Col. North (N.S.C.)" had not only given Iran arms sales profits to the contras, but North was the author of "a smoking gun" memo about the money diversion.

They would have to dig deeper, Baker and the lawyers concluded.

On July 10, they came back for another 10 a.m. meeting.

What did it mean when Reagan said in 1984, as Congress was cutting off funding, that he wanted to keep the contras together body and soul?

"Anything we could legally do to encourage the contras so they wouldn't be abandoned," the president replied.

Did that include North on the NSC staff creating an elaborate resupply effort?

Reagan said he never pictured the idea that the NSC was set up to do that. They were a staff, not operational. "It would be the CIA doing it," Reagan said.

But the evidence showed the high level of NSC effort by North directly and daily supervised first by McFarlane and then Poindexter—Reagan's two national security advisers.

"Maybe this is inattention on my part," the president admitted.

They went into the mechanics of the Iran arms transfers and hostage release. No plane carrying arms would land until a hostage or hostages were released, correct?

Reagan said that was his understanding. He recalled a specific time when a plane carrying arms didn't land because the hostage was not freed. Seeing the obvious implication that it was arms for hostages, the president added, "We were not buying our hostages, we were not dealing with the people holding the hostages." He went through his whole rationale, noting the triangular nature of the transactions. He again said he was seeking a strategic opening with Iran. "You know people were telling me that Khomeini was going to die any minute. We expected him to be dead in the next 24 hours." Khomeini was still alive. "Maybe it was a scam," Reagan wondered aloud. "Maybe Khomeini was in on it all along?"

Culvahouse said apparently Khomeini had made an amazing recovery.

The White House records showed only a few one-on-one private meetings with Bill Casey.

"That's right," Reagan said. There were regularly scheduled meetings with Shultz and Weinberger, but nothing regular with Casey. He would just stop in, Reagan said.

Did the president ever talk alone with Casey about Iran or the contras?

"No," Reagan said.

"Well, what did you talk to Casey about?" Culvahouse asked skeptically. It was not believable that the president would not discuss the two most important covert operations with his CIA director.

"There weren't many discussions," the president replied. He was trying to recall. "There were so few discussions." Casey had once complained about personnel, thought some cabinet and other senior posts should change. Reagan said he kept Casey's confidences on his recommendations but never acted on them.

Did Casey ever say he was keeping things from the president?

"No," Reagan said. He said he agreed it was possible that Casey and North had a close relationship since the records showed dozens of meetings, and both had offices on the third floor of the Old Executive Office Building.

Baker had arranged for the lawyers and himself to interview the first lady that same day. They arrived at the residence at 4:50 in the afternoon.

Baker introduced Culvahouse and Lytton.

"We're all lawyers, we're working for the president and conversations with you will be confidential," Baker said.

After outlining the efforts of the task force, Baker said they operated under the principle of no surprises. What about your husband's relationship with Poindexter?

"It wasn't close," Nancy Reagan said. The mention of Poindexter made her tense up slightly. Poindexter had never been in the living quarters to her knowledge, never been to Camp David. She was emphatic.

What about North?

After four days of televised testimony, she said,

she now knew who he was. But she wasn't sure she would have recognized him before.

Had North been in the residence of the White House?

"Never. Never. Never." Never at Camp David, she said.

What about Bill Casey?

Never been to the residence, she said.

The Secret Service entry logs showed seven Casey visits to the White House residence from 1984 through early 1986, but they didn't challenge her.

Casey never came to Camp David either, she said. "Not a close friend," she added. They did not see the Caseys socially.

What happened right after the November events of last year when the diversion of funds to the contras was made public?

Mrs. Reagan said she and Ronnie had gone to Camp David. She referred to her own diary. Ronnie was upset and disappointed because North had done something wrong with the funding and Poindexter had never told him.

Did her husband believe he was swapping arms for hostages?

No, she said, repeating his argument about dealing with intermediaries in Iran who were moderates. The American hostages weighed heavily on Ronnie, she said. "We have met too many airplanes with too many coffins." Ronnie had not told her about the Iran arms sales initiative until the story broke publicly, she said.

After half an hour they left. During the interview the first lady's dog had been barking and licking a superficial wound on Baker's hand covered by a Band-Aid.

"That yappy little dog," Baker told the lawyers as soon as they had exited. Lytton could see that he had wanted to kick it but had resisted the temptation.

They were satisfied. The first lady confirmed her husband's information. Apparently there would be nothing coming out of Nancy's shop— always a potent channel of information to the media—that might contradict what they had gathered.

The morning of July 15, Admiral Poindexter testified in public for the first time. He said he had intentionally not told President Reagan about the diversion. At noon, Baker and the two other lawyers went to the Oval Office to tell the president, who was having lunch in the adjacent dining room with Vice President Bush.

Reagan laughed when they entered. "See. I've been saying the same thing for seven months. What was everyone worried about?"

Baker again asked what Reagan might have done if he had been told about the diversion?

Reagan repeated that he would have questioned whether the money wasn't technically our money, the United States's money, so it could not be used without congressional authorization.

Bush reminded everyone that North had said it was Ayatollah Khomeini's money, although Bush acknowledged it was a lawyer's technical argument as to whose money it was.

Feeling confident, a major burden removed, Baker said he now believed that based on his own observations, he didn't think the president would have approved the diversion if he had known about it.

"Well, neither do I," the president said with mounting self-assurance. "I don't want to play hero here, but if I had been told I would probably have said, send the excess money back to Iran as an aid to help establish that strategic relationship."

It was a nice neat little package, Lytton thought, joining in the smiles of the others. Maybe true, maybe untrue; but with unfettered access to files, people and the president himself, they had found nothing to contradict it.

"You know," Bush said, "if the committees had given these guys immunity a couple of months ago, we wouldn't have had to go through all these months of waiting and uncertainty."

No one asked the obvious question: If it had been clear for months that the president was telling the truth and the full story from the beginning, why was there uncertainty?

Baker felt that the Congress he knew so well was on the run and losing its appetite for the investigation.

What do you have with a lawyer buried up to his neck in dirt? Reagan asked the lawyers, who were back in the Oval Office July 20 at 11:35 a.m. Not enough dirt, he answered. They all laughed. The tone had loosened. The meeting was more relaxed.

Baker said the perception of the congressional hearings had changed. Everybody now seemed to agree that no one was going to implicate the president in the diversion. So the remaining efforts by anti-Reagan Democrats, Baker said, would be focused on destroying the credibility of Poindexter and North—and by extension the president's credibility. The argument would center on the improbability that Poindexter, the model chain-of-command Navy admiral, hadn't told the president about the diversion. So even though no gun existed they would try to create enough smoke to prove the same thing.

A giant housefly had flown into the Oval Office and began buzzing loudly. Baker rolled up a memo and tried to swat it, missing numerous times.

"Wow," Reagan said, the fly had evaded White House security and now no one could stop it.

Baker said the committees would use the notes of Shultz's executive assistant Charles Hill to try to show in a dramatic way that the president was willing to risk jail or impeachment to carry out his policy. His congressional detractors would use the notes from the December 7, 1985, meeting in the residence, in which the president was quoted saying, "The American people will never forgive me if I fail to get these hostages out over this legal question." Reagan then, according to the notes, had quipped that if laws were broken and people went to jail, the visiting hours were on Thursday. Baker said that was the worst case scenario, but they had to be prepared. They were not trying to scare him.

The Sunday talk shows the day before, Reagan said, made it evident that the focus was shifting from the diversion and back to the arms-for-hostages issue.

Returning to the December 7, 1985, meeting notes, the lawyers then went over some of them. It sure was contentious?

"Yes, it was," Reagan said. His memory of the debate that day was that they—Shultz and Weinberger—didn't give in and he didn't relent. He added that he was not familiar with the Charlie Hill notes, hadn't seen or heard about them before.

They read some more, including a rather inflammatory Weinberger statement that the president could not unilaterally lift the arms embargo to Iran and to do so would be illegal. They quoted some of his remarks. Did that sound like him?

"Yeah," he said. He then remembered a later meeting when Shultz and Weinberger—and he recalled where they were sitting—fought hard against direct arms sales to Iran, that it would appear to be arms for hostages. "That wasn't so, we weren't giving Hezbollah [Party of God] a damn thing. Iran could influence the Hezbollah but could not give orders." He noted that Hezbollah, the kidnappers, did not receive weapons; Iran did. "I've got this meeting coming up with George Shultz, I'll remind him of it," the president said, referring to a scheduled meeting with Shultz on foreign policy matters.

No, no, no, the other three said. Shultz was going to testify before the congressional committees soon. The president most certainly should not talk to him about his testimony. "That

229

could be misinterpreted," one of the lawyers said. Someone might think they were trying to keep their stories straight. "Don't say anything to him until after his testimony."

Reagan then brought up an article in that day's *Washington Post* (July 20, 1987), raising the argument that it was arms for hostages because the first finding Reagan signed in December 1985 mentioned that and had no reference to a strategic opening. The press was saying if the president signed the finding, he should have known it was arms for hostages. The three said they thought it was a cheap shot.

"It sure is," Reagan said. "It's a three-way arms deal for hostages. We're providing arms to the Iranians, the Iranians getting Hezbollah to free the hostages. They got two hostages out. And that was it."

That evening Baker, Culvahouse and Lytton had dinner to celebrate at Mr. K's, a downtown restaurant.

Afterwards, Lytton came back to the White House to review more Charlie Hill notes. During the next two days, he won agreement from the congressional committees not to use the personal material in Hill's notes. The Democrats also pledged not to raise the discussion of impeachment if Shultz didn't mention it in his testimony.

The closest to a real investigation of presidential involvement in Iran-contra was conducted not by Independent Counsel Walsh, the Tower Board or Congress, but by Reagan's White House lawyers. I am not at all certain the lawyers would have turned the president in if they had discovered incriminating information. But their inquiry was perhaps unique in a modern White House. Baker, Culvahouse and Lytton conducted 13 long interrogations of Reagan, set up practically a legal defense firm of 67 people within the White House, and vetted more than 12,000 documents. In the end, the lawyers did not prove Reagan had no knowledge of the diversion. They did not, however, discover any information to challenge Reagan's assertion.

14

SHULTZ APPEARED BEFORE the committee on July 23, 1987, to begin two days of nationally televised testimony. He criticized the Iran arms sales, the contra diversion, the National Security Council staff, the CIA, Poindexter, North and Casey. But he found a way to praise Reagan. The others were responsible for the deception, not the president. "I developed a very clear opinion that the president was not being given accurate information," Shultz testified. "His judgment is excellent when he is given the right information and he was not being given the right information."

Shultz recounted that when he first came to Washington as a member of the Nixon cabinet, he received some important advice. Bryce Harlow, then a top Nixon adviser, had taken him, then the young secretary of labor, under his wing. Harlow, he said, was "a wonderful man, very experienced in the ways of Washington, and, boy, nobody was sharper at figuring the angles and getting his way. He was sensational. But everybody listened to him, there was never a mark on Bryce. Why? He drummed it into me when I first came here. He said, 'Remember George one thing: Trust is the coin of the realm; trust is the coin of the realm.' "

Shultz believed he had made the case that the Reagan administration could still be trusted. There was an explanation for Reagan's behavior. Reagan was kidding himself, not facing the facts, when he denied he had traded arms for hostages. But, Shultz concluded, some basic, primordial instinct prevailed on Reagan to keep Shultz and listen to his voice of dissent. He didn't feel personally proud that Reagan had not fired him. It was simply Reagan operating in his own interest. It was called survival.

Shultz realized he had been used, but he knew of no better way. He had at least maintained his basic integrity and his office. So many others had lost one or the other—or both.

Since no one had implicated the president in the diversion of funds, the congressional hearings were, for practical purposes, over. Ten days later, they ended formally. Reagan gave a 15-minute nationally televised speech.

Lawrence Walsh, television clicker in hand, tuned in to watch. Walsh had the mute button ready in case the president made any direct reference to the testimony of Poindexter and North. The committees had granted Poindexter and North limited immunity. Their testimony couldn't be used against them, but Walsh planned to prosecute them based on evidence he had gathered independently. He had to be able to prove that he and his prosecutors had not used their immunized testimony, so he was not even supposed to listen to it or any references to it.

"I want to talk about some of the lessons we've learned," Reagan said, casting Iran-contra as a great national civics lesson. "These past nine months have been confusing and painful ones for the country. I know you have doubts in your own minds about what happened in this whole episode."

Rather than debating the specifics of the hearings, Reagan concentrated on general themes. "I was stubborn in my pursuit of a policy that went astray," he said.

He said he supported the contras. "Let me put this in capital letters. I did not know about the diversion of funds. Indeed, I didn't know there were excess funds." Walsh noted that Reagan flashed a wry smile, suggesting none of the indignation or anger the president claimed to have felt.

"Yet the buck does not stop with Admiral Poindexter, as he stated in his testimony; it stops with me. I am the one who is ultimately accountable to the American people."

Reagan said the nation could draw positive lessons from the Iran-contra mess. "Probably the biggest lesson we can draw from the hearings is that the executive and legislative branches of government need to regain trust in each other. We've seen the results of mistrust in the form of lies, leaks, divisions and mistakes. We need to find a way to cooperate while realizing foreign policy can't be run by committee. And I believe there is now the growing sense that we can accomplish more by cooperating."

Walsh awakened in the middle of the night. He took out a pen and a notebook and went to the coffee table in his Watergate suite to jot down his thoughts. He wrote that he was now convinced that Reagan did know of the diversion. In his speech, Reagan had also called Poindexter an "honorable man." Poindexter or Casey must have informed the president in some way, no matter how indirect or veiled. Poindexter would not have gone ahead without giving the president some indication. Reagan was the kind of person who did not want or need an operation like that spelled out in detail. There was one lingering problem: How to prove it? With Casey dead, and Poindexter and North denying, Walsh needed a storytelling witness who could lay out all the details. But who?

Richard Nixon, in the 13th year after his resignation, also watched Reagan's speech. Afterwards, he sent a personal, private "Dear Ron" letter to Reagan.

"The speech last night was one of your best," he wrote. "What was even more important than what you said was that you sounded and looked *strong*. You gave the lie to the crap about your being over-the-hill, discouraged, etc.

"If I could be permitted one word of advice: Don't *ever* comment on the Iran-contra matter again," Nixon continued. He proposed a total Iran-contra blackout. "Have instructions issued to all White House staffers and Administration spokesmen that they must never answer any question on or off the record about that issue in the future. They should reply to all inquiries by stating firmly and categorically that the president has addressed the subject and that they have nothing to add.

"The committee labored for nine months and produced a stillborn midget. Let it rest in peace!" The letter was signed, "Sincerely, Dick."

Reagan left for a 25-day vacation in California believing the worst of the scandal was behind him. He could spend the days riding his horse, chopping wood, clearing brush and avoiding interrogation.

Walsh, however, had only just begun. He and his team of prosecutors continued down the many investigative trails. They pursued the CIA angle and the classified information. They tried to understand the money trail. Poindexter and North were tried and convicted, but the verdicts were overturned on appeal. Walsh's team discovered that Shultz had not produced all of Charlie Hill's notes, and Walsh thought of indicting him. He felt bad about indicting and trying some of the CIA people, and even worse about convicting some of them for lying to Congress. But he felt he had to do it. He couldn't let the CIA get away with it.

As the probes multiplied, Walsh and his team moved further away from the president rather than closer. The many-headed hydra of Iran-contra kept yielding up more mysteries and subjects. No one provided them, Walsh believed. They discovered them. Each had its own seductive, time-consuming momentum.

It wasn't until August 1990, more than three and a half years after Walsh's appointment, that the independent counsel's prosecutors stumbled back onto the cover-up trail of President Reagan's inner circle. John Barrett, a young prosecutor, had spent a year rereading the fabulously detailed notes of Hill, Shultz's notetaker. The Hill notes, some 10,000 pages long, had fascinated Barrett. His compulsive reading of them forced him to have his eyeglasses strengthened several times, and his thoroughness paid off when he deciphered a reference to Caspar Weinberger's notes. According to Shultz, Weinberger "never referred to them" and so he "never had to cough them up." It was a tantalizing lead.

Walsh tried to subpoena Weinberger, but Weinberger avoided being served the subpoena. Walsh's senior FBI agent caught up with the former secretary of defense as he left his office building through the service entrance and threaded his way through barrels of refuse toward a waiting car. Weinberger repeated his earlier denials in an interview with Walsh's prosecutors, claiming he hadn't really taken any notes since 1981. Anything that he had scribbled could be found on the back of his classified briefings, he said. Walsh sent a young associate to look at Weinberger's classified notes, which were stored at the Library of Congress, but he came back with nothing.

Finally, in November 1991, another young associate working for Walsh, Tom Baker, discovered among the unclassified section of Weinberger's files stacks of boxes containing handwritten notes. Baker soon saw that some of the notes contained references and information on the nation's most sensitive military and intelligence secrets. In all there were 7,000 pages, nearly 1,700 of them from the Iran-contra period.

"Very smart," Walsh thought upon receiving the news of the new treasure trove of notes; "hide in plain sight."

The voluminous notes contained no smoking gun, but they showed, as only compulsive note-taking could, the intensity of Weinberger's personal argument to Reagan that the initial arms sales to Iran, through Israel, were illegal because of a U.S. law preventing them.

"I argued strongly that we have an embargo that makes arms sales to Iran illegal & president couldn't veto it + that 'washing' through Israel wouldn't make it legal."

The notes also stated, "President said he could answer charges of illegality, but he couldn't answer charge that 'Big strong President Reagan passed up a chance to free hostages.' "

The notes seemed to establish that Reagan was willing to break the law to maintain his image of strength.

Robert Bennett, Weinberger's lawyer, argued that since the notetaking was habitual, "like brushing his teeth," Weinberger's repeated denial of having notes was innocent. He simply forgot about them. Bennett produced a report by a so-called memory expert who argued that the notetaking was routine and virtually unconscious so it was not stored in the memory bank for easy retrieval.

Walsh was amused and astounded. When he threatened indictment, Bennett looked at him and said, smiling, "Of course, you know this means nuclear war."

On June 16, 1992, Walsh had his grand jury indict Caspar Weinberger on five felonies, including obstruction of justice, making false statements and perjury.

More than five and a half years into his investigation, Walsh and his deputies finally began to realize that they had spent years chasing the underlings—Poindexter, North, various CIA men, and others at the middle or bottom of the operations. They had forgotten to follow and probe the people who were making the decisions—the senior people who made policy like Weinberger and Shultz. And Ronald Reagan, who had been out of office for three and a half years.

The Weinberger indictment was designed to bring to justice someone who had, in Walsh's eyes, consciously and deliberately concealed his notes. A Harvard Law graduate with Weinberger's experience did not forget his own toothbrush. Lurking self-righteously in the background of the scandal as one of the most outspoken opponents of the Iran arms sales, Weinberger had skated by as one of the good guys. Walsh believed that behind the notes was potential testimony that might incriminate others. Even such a compulsive notetaker as Weinberger could not or would not always write it down. What did the former secretary of defense, now age 74, really know? What could his truthful testimony show?

In the summer of 1992, Walsh called former President Reagan's private personal attorney—Ted Olson, the same attorney who had fought the independent counsel law as unconstitutional and lost in the Supreme Court.

Although Reagan did not seem to be a target in the endless Iran-contra investigation, Olson noted that during the last three years, news stories in *The New York Times* and *The Washington Post* consistently implied, often quite darkly, that Walsh might be zeroing in on the former president.

Walsh told Olson that he intended to get the former president's sworn testimony. After five and a half years of investigation, he wanted to hear from Reagan himself.

What is the purpose? Olson asked.

Walsh said he wanted to interview Reagan as a potential witness in the Weinberger trial.

Olson replied that Reagan wasn't going to be a witness called by Weinberger in the trial. He could promise that. The sworn written answers he had given in 1987 were as true now in 1992 as they had been at the time. His testimony for the Poindexter trial was the same. The former president had nothing of value to add and there was no reason to interrogate him.

Walsh said he was going to have to insist.

The words and tone almost gave Olson the cold shivers. He knew all too well the power of an insistent independent counsel.

Walsh would not back down. Privately, he wanted to give Reagan one last chance to tell the truth. Walsh alternately felt a drive to complete his work and escape home to Oklahoma, but also to leave no stone unturned and leave Washington triumphant.

Barrett was assigned the task of negotiating with Olson. "We want to close the loop," Barrett told Olson. "We want to protect ourselves from criticism. When the investigation that's gone for years is closed down, people will say, 'Well, Walsh never interviewed Reagan.' "

As a preliminary step, Walsh and Barrett demanded access to the actual pages of Reagan's personal diaries—not the typed excerpts that White House Counsel Culvahouse had prepared back in 1987. Having been burned by Shultz and Weinberger, they threatened to subpoena the diaries. Finally, Barrett flew to Los Angeles and was allowed to review the full photocopied pages from Reagan's handwritten diaries. Working meticulously with the excerpts, Barrett conducted an exhaustive double check. Amazingly, he did not find that a single relevant entry had been overlooked or concealed. What struck Barrett was how Reagan had adopted the cause of the seven American hostages. The diaries had constant references to each of the seven by name, almost as if they were members of Reagan's family. Equally striking and more important was that there was not a single mention of a strategic opening to Iran. The arms sales were vividly a hostage rescue operation in Reagan's eyes.

Walsh and Barrett continued to insist on taking Reagan's testimony.

Olson argued that Reagan was not going to be some kind of surprise rescue witness at Weinberger's trial.

Walsh and Barrett said there were some questions that had never been squarely asked or answered. They offered to do an interview in the president's hometown, Los Angeles, rather than compelling Reagan to testify before a grand jury in Washington.

Olson said Mrs. Reagan was deeply concerned and had asked, "What is this all about?"

Barrett said it was basically a witness interview.

"You've got to understand the mistrust there is out there about your office and Walsh," Olson said. "How am I supposed to explain to Mrs. Reagan what this is about? It looks like you're going to prosecute her husband." She had said Walsh should leave her and her husband alone in retirement.

Barrett assured Olson that he was interested in what Reagan had to say as a possible witness. He was not a target of the investigation and he did not face indictment.

Olson said Reagan was not going to have any recollections that would be useful to them. A doctor could come talk to Walsh to show that Reagan didn't remember anything of consequence about Iran-contra. Barrett wouldn't agree.

Olson felt like he was handling a poisonous snake. In his view, the Walsh investigation was a travesty. It had gone on for more than half a decade, and Walsh had insisted on prosecuting matters that Olson was sure were not violations of law. A prosecutor could twist just about anything if he wanted, Olson felt.

Still, Olson had to consider how it would affect not just Reagan but the presidency. They might get an adverse court decision that would have a significant impact on all future presidents. There was a grave danger in trying to stiff Walsh. The independent counsel could issue a subpoena. There probably were no legitimate grounds for a former president to resist a sub-poena in a criminal investigation. To contest would make it look like Reagan was hiding. Olson also did not want to anger Walsh, who had the upper hand. It was important to get a statement from Walsh that Reagan had been fully coop-erative—important to ending the Iran-contra affair on the most favorable terms to the history of the Reagan era. He wanted to get Walsh to a point of maximum comfort about Reagan.

Olson examined the Iran-contra record care-fully, spoke with Culvahouse, Lytton and others. He was confident that Reagan had done nothing unlawful, that he had not known about the diversion of funds to the contras and could testify truthfully. Olson finally relented, but insisted on a four-page written protocol about who would be present at the interview, where it would take place, what subjects would be cov-ered and that it would be limited to a single day of questioning.

The agreement was signed July 21, 1992. "As we have informed you," Olson wrote to Walsh in their letter of understanding, "there are aspects of these matters about which the president's memory may be regrettably but understandably vague, uncertain, possibly inaccurate, or faded entirely. In fairness to President Reagan, it is important that you be aware of this condition before you undertake the interview." At a 3 p.m. meeting with the lawyers on the same day, Olson stressed again that there were going to be lots of things that Reagan couldn't recall.

"You are going to get imperfect memory," Olson said, "and if he says he remembers something, that's really not going to be valid because there are going to be so many other things surrounding the same matter that he can't remember."

In an accompanying note, Olson warned that Reagan had a hearing problem. "He does not always hear questions completely, but he is somewhat reticent about saying anything if he has not fully heard a question," Olson wrote. They agreed to speak loudly.

Two days later, Walsh, Barrett and Christina Spaulding, an associate who compiled volumes of the information they had on Reagan, flew to Los Angeles. They spent the night at a hotel in Century City near the office that the federal government provided Reagan as a former president. Barrett prepared a rough outline of 12 areas of probable interrogation, from the president's response to the taking of the hostages to the administration's missteps after the operation was revealed in November 1986. He also drafted an "A" list of Reagan advisers about whom he planned to ask Reagan. The list included Meese, Weinberger, Shultz and Casey.

The next morning, July 24, Walsh and his two associates walked over to Reagan's office carrying thick binders of documents in legal evidence briefcases. They had elaborately prepared tabs and chronologies and a comparative analysis of notes, memos and testimony. None of them had ever met the former president.

Around 10 a.m., the three attorneys from the independent counsel's office took seats in Reagan's suite around a large table in the ceremonial conference room on the top floor, with large floor-to-ceiling windows overlooking the city.

Five minutes later Reagan entered the room majestically through a back door with Olson and his law partner, John Mintz. The former president was dressed in a perfectly tailored suit, tie and shirt. He wore gold, square cufflinks with a colorful blue rippled-pennant design in the center. He looked radiant and relaxed, his face flush with a California tan. He firmly shook hands with Walsh and the two associates, greeted them warmly with the television-familiar voice, deep and confident, and sat down at the long conference table directly across from Walsh.

Reagan was sworn in. The court reporter, repeating the questions and answers into a large microphone strapped on as a mask, began taking down the verbatim record.

"I will start by asking a very simple question and that is that you were president of the

United States from January 1981 until January 1989?" Walsh began.

"Yes," Reagan answered.

"The State Department was headed by Secretary Shultz, George Shultz? Would that be correct, sir?"

"I think so, but I can't swear anymore," Reagan said.

"And Ed Meese started as counselor to the president during your first term of office and then became attorney general during the second term of office?" Walsh asked.

"I take your word for it here," Reagan answered.

"When Ed Meese became attorney general, Don Regan moved into the White House as your chief of staff?" Walsh continued.

"You know," Reagan said, "this is awful for me to say but with this lapse of time I don't recall."

Walsh asked about Reagan's time in California as governor and some of his associates who had come to Washington with him, chief among them Michael Deaver, the longtime friend and media adviser.

Reagan looked blank.

"Was he in the California administration with you?" Walsh asked.

"I'm going to have to think," Reagan said. He couldn't place the name. "I honestly can't swear to that. I'd hate to have him hear me say that."

Walsh's cheeks turned a crimson red, his embarrassment and discomfort fully apparent.

Barrett shot a glance at Chris Spaulding.

She was bug-eyed in disbelief. Barrett looked at Walsh, who was not making eye contact with anyone else but Reagan. Walsh appeared gentle and deferential, even solicitous.

Reagan was sorry. It was genuine, straight.

Olson felt frustrated, but the best way to be protective he was sure was to endure.

Walsh tried to get something, the loosest or vaguest recollection.

Reagan didn't have it. The political and personal magnetism were still there—affable, direct—and his speech was fine and coherent. But he seemed to have nothing that could help them.

Walsh continued with more random questions, chucking notes and question sequences, the entire game plan.

Walsh had Reagan read aloud a diary entry in which Reagan discussed convincing Syrian President Hafez al Assad to make an effort to get four kidnap victims back from the terrorists. "Does that come back?" Walsh asked.

"No, and you know something, I'm trying now to remember who was Assad."

Walsh gently reminded Reagan who Assad was.

"Well, again, this is something I don't remember."

Walsh next asked about the famous June 14, 1985, hijacking of Trans World Airlines Flight 847 to Beirut, Lebanon, and whether Iran had been instrumental in getting some of the 153 passengers and crew released. It was one of the most publicized terrorist incidents of his presidency.

"I don't have a memory of that," Reagan said.

Who would you work with to recover the American hostages? Walsh asked.

"Oh, Lord, it was very much on my mind and I think I talked to everybody about it in trying to find a way that we could get them freed," Reagan said. "We knew we couldn't go in and try to kidnap them or something. They would be dead before we got there."

"You had a task force on counterterrorism," Walsh asked. "Do you remember that?"

"I had forgotten about that," Reagan said.

"I was just thinking of things that you did to try to reduce terrorism in the world," Walsh said.

"I'm embarrassed here," Reagan replied. "I don't want it to seem to be that I wasn't aware of any of these things that were going on. I just don't have any memory of the specifics."

Walsh asked a question about Bud McFarlane and his efforts with the Israelis.

"I have to tell you that my memory with regard to names is just terrible," Reagan said. "You know there was something like, wasn't it 1,200 people that surrounded me there in the office as part of the staff and I didn't remember names."

Walsh read another Reagan diary entry in which Reagan wrote about Japanese Prime Minister P. M. Nakasone's attempts to intervene with the Iranians.

"I don't know what that would have been about," Reagan said. "I'm very embarrassed. I'm sorry." The former president almost blushed. "It's like I wasn't president at all," he said sadly.

Sensing everyone's unease, Olson asked, "Would this be a good time for a break?"

"Oh sure," Walsh replied.

Before leaving the conference room, Reagan tried to explain why he couldn't remember and why he kept a diary. "When I left the governor's office, Nancy and I talked about how little we could remember of all the happenings and the things that went on because it was a busy life and so forth and yet we had no memory of much of the things we had accomplished and all that.

"That was why when the presidency came along," he said, as if it were an accident, "...Nancy and I reminded ourselves of this thing of the governorship and that's when we decided we'd better keep diaries of what went on and we kept the diaries. But as I told you, I read them now and I still can't remember the happening that I've written about."

"It's very difficult," Walsh responded. "Mr. President, if it makes you feel any better, just in trying to write a final report on the last five years, I'm having more trouble than I think you're having."

Olson went off with Reagan to the former president's office and tried to relax him. Reagan was more than willing to just talk. He offered no protest. Olson said it was the kind of day they would have to get through, let the clock run out.

After about 20 minutes, everyone reconvened in the conference room.

Reagan was so uncomfortable. The distress was almost physical. He groped desperately for anecdotes he could remember about his days as president. If he couldn't remember his lines, he would ad-lib. He remembered talking with Soviet leader Mikhail Gorbachev in Geneva, Switzerland, about arms reduction in November 1985.

"Why don't we let our two teams start this discussion about the reduction of the weaponry and all and why don't you and I get some fresh air?" Reagan recalled telling Gorbachev.

They had walked 150 yards across the lawn to a beach house adjacent to a lake. "It was cold, a real wintry day," Reagan testified, "and the beach house had a big roaring fire going in the fireplace." Reagan said he had stopped Gorbachev right before they sat down and looked at him. "I'm going to give you a quotation that's not mine," Reagan recounted telling Gorbachev. "Someone else has said that we mistrust each other because we're armed. I believe we're armed because we mistrust each other. Wouldn't it be fine if we would spend just as much time trying to find out the reasons for our mistrust?"

The prosecutors sat quietly enthralled by Reagan's performance, absorbing the story and allowing the president to talk for five minutes without interruption.

"They kept dying on me," Reagan said of the Soviet premiers, three of whom had died before Gorbachev took over. "But he was different, seemed different."

Reagan said he looked Gorbachev straight in the eye again and said, "The only alternative to this is we resume the arms race. That is a race you can't win. There is no way we're going to permit you to be superior to us in weaponry."

Reagan said they had talked for another hour

and a half and finally returned to the main house where the Soviet and American staffs were negotiating. The president said he had quickly told his advisers that he had negotiated a second summit. "They couldn't believe it," Reagan said proudly.

"That's really remarkable," Walsh told Reagan after he had finished, "just the beginning of this tremendous achievement that is due to you."

"Now, there are a few things I guess like that that I can remember because of their very oddity," Reagan said, "but the rest of it I'm not fooling around when I say that when I started reading the diary the other day, I couldn't even remember writing the things that I was writing about."

Walsh tried reading from the notes of Weinberger and Shultz. Could the president confirm any of his contemporaneous statements on Iran-contra developments? "Does that sound like you?" Walsh asked hopefully.

"Yes, it does," Reagan answered. "I don't have a memory of it all taking place, but I can see that, yes, that would be my attitude."

The president began to talk about his anger at Congress for passing the laws restricting aid to the contras and the arms embargo with Iran. "I was just madder than the devil about them and their doing this to us," Reagan said. "I felt that as far as being the president that a thing of this kind to get back five human beings from potential murder, yes, I would violate that other—that law."

Finally, Walsh had something. But there

was no confrontation. Instead, Walsh asked deferentially, "In other words, to avoid responsibility for the death of the hostages, you would explain to the American people why you violated that law?"

"Yes," Reagan said.

On one level, it was an astounding admission. Reagan had essentially said he had violated the law. In the context of Reagan's memory, though, even Walsh saw it meant nothing.

Olson asked for another break.

Walsh, Barrett and Spaulding retired to a room together.

"He's really diminished," Walsh said. "He doesn't remember any of this. What do we do? How do we sort of bring him back in?" Walsh wasn't going to beat up on the former president, and he wasn't going to ridicule him.

They decided to stick with the concrete evidence they had. He couldn't deny his own handwritten diary, for instance.

"I'm just going to really go through the president's diary entries with him just to see if it helps pick up a thread or any sort of recollections as we go along," Walsh said after the break.

Walsh tried some specific references, long chunks of diary entries or meeting notes kept by Weinberger and others.

Reagan apologized. It sounded right, but he had no memory of such events, or people or decisions or conversation at meetings. "Well, again, that's a party I must not have been at," Reagan said at one point. "I don't recall any of this." About the only thing that Reagan could remember was the story about the Danish sailor "who claims to have served on a ship carrying arms from Israel to Iran" that he had referred to in his November 13, 1986, speech.

Barrett almost wanted to go over and hug Reagan and tell him it was okay and say they were sorry. It was painful, but Barrett stayed silent.

Walsh tried to draw Reagan out, but the former president had only distant fragments of memory unconnected to Iran-contra and of no use to the independent counsel.

"I hate to sound so ignorant," Reagan said, "but it's just that the life was so damn busy—"

"Mr. President," Walsh interrupted, "those of us who are a lot less busy have the same trouble. I hope you feel comfortable with that. I want you to be fully relaxed here as though you were talking to Ted instead of to me."

"You're nicer than I am," Olson interjected.

"Well, I don't have the long relationship," Walsh said. "I'm just trying to start one."

Reagan then launched into a long story filled with anecdotes about Margaret Thatcher, not from her days as Britain's prime minister but before, when Thatcher was head of the Conservative Party. At the end, Reagan said, "I hope I didn't take up your time with that."

"Oh, no," Walsh replied. "This is far more interesting than the subject matter of the testimony, but we have to keep coming back to it."

Olson called another break.

Reagan took Walsh over to one of the windows. He pointed to and spoke about some of the various buildings. The airport out in the distance, Reagan said. He pointed his finger and

252

said, That's the Santa Monica airport. He paused for a moment and added, They've got a new airport now over by the water. What do they call the thing?

Somebody said LAX.

Right, Reagan said.

Walsh was moved by Reagan's pride and affection for the city. Reagan took Walsh and the others to a side of the room that had a collection of artifacts, sculpture and Western art. He showed them the knickknacks he had collected and pointed to a well-known American folk art painting of the south portico of the White House. All the presidents were in the picture, interacting with each other—Franklin Roosevelt talking with George Washington, Carter with Jefferson. Reagan pointed proudly to his portrait.

"That's me," he said, beaming.

It had been a long time since any person had captivated Walsh so fully.

When they resumed, Barrett asked Reagan about testifying 18 months before in the trial of John Poindexter, the former national security adviser.

"Good Lord, I don't have any memory of that," Reagan said.

"You gave a deposition," Walsh reminded him.

Barrett read some of Reagan's testimony from the trial.

With a pained expression, Reagan said, "I had totally forgotten all about that. Oh my gosh."

Barrett asked about Reagan's effort to ask Saudi Arabia to contribute millions of dollars to the contras when Congress had denied U.S. funding.

Again Reagan had nothing.

Barrett brought up his testimony in the Poindexter trial again.

"I can't even remember that I was testifying."

"That was about two, two and a half years ago," Walsh said.

"For heaven's sake," Reagan sighed.

"February, 1990," Walsh reminded Reagan.

"Good Lord."

At 3:25 p.m., Walsh decided it was time to call a halt. "Well, thank you for helping us," he said. "We understand the position you took and how you felt about it."

"Oh, dear," Reagan replied.

As they said their good-byes, Reagan offered Walsh and the others some of his presidential jelly beans, which had been sitting in the middle of the table.

The prosecutors walked back and awaited the arrival of their litigation bags out front of the hotel. Their weeks of careful research and preparation had been totally useless.

What are we going to do with our jelly beans? Spaulding asked.

Barrett said he was going to save his. This was his first presidential jelly bean, he said.

Walsh had the jelly bean in his hand. He popped it into his mouth and ate it. "I've met a lot of presidents," Walsh said.

For Walsh, the Reagan interview was both a disappointment and a relief. He had been so caught off balance he had not asked a single question about the diversion of funds—the supposed focus of his inquiry. The independent counsel knew he was dealing with an actor, and in a sense Reagan had created a character whom nobody expected ever to know the details. Yet after 60 years of seeing and examining witnesses, Walsh was sure the appearance that day was not an act. He was ready to stake his reputation on that conclusion.

Two days later, on July 26, a front-page *Washington Post* article was headlined "Walsh May Seek Indictment of Reagan in Iran-Contra." It said Walsh would decide in the next ten days whether to indict Reagan and some former aides for concealing President Reagan's role in the 1985 Iran arms deals through Israel.

Mrs. Reagan was hysterical. She called Olson in tears and demanded to know what was happening.

Olson promised to find out. He called Walsh.

"It's not true," Walsh insisted. It was obvious that the president had declined mentally. Prosecuting him would be absurd and cruel. Walsh flatly denied the story, and he insisted that it was not leaked by him or anyone in his office.

"You better goddamn well fix it," Olson said furiously, "wherever it's coming from. If it's coming from you, fix it. If it's not coming from you, fix it!" He reminded Walsh of Reagan's total cooperation. "It's time for you guys to live up to your part of the bargain."

A few days after the article appeared, Walsh wrote Olson another letter stating again, "This office regards President Reagan as simply a witness and not as a subject or target."

On August 17, more than three weeks after his testimony, the 81-year-old Reagan appeared in Houston at the 1992 Republican National Convention. Olson, who was general counsel to the Republican platform committee, stood in the audience holding his breath. His heart thumped loudly as he thought what a shame it would be if the nation's final memory of Reagan was as a figure of pity.

"Tonight is a very special night for me," Reagan said. "Of course, at my age, every night is a very special night." The crowd roared.

He put on display his upbeat version of conservatism—tolerant and open. "In America, our origins matter less than our destination."

He mocked the 1988 vice-presidential debate barb of Lloyd Bentsen that Dan Quayle was no John Kennedy. In a clear reference to Democratic candidate and Arkansas Governor Bill Clinton's goal of becoming Thomas Jefferson, Reagan said, "I knew Thomas Jefferson. He was a friend of mine. And Governor, you're no Thomas Jefferson."

The Houston Astrodome crowd went wild.

Olson almost wept with joy.

The timing, the voice, the cadence were all there. The *Washington Post* television critic Tom Shales wrote that the golden age of television had returned for Reagan's flawless 35-minute speech.

"Gippericious, Gipperacious, Gipperific," Shales wrote.

The next morning, Walsh, Spaulding and Barrett ran into each other in the hallway.

Were we had? one of them asked.

They all laughed. It was almost a joke. Reagan surely had read from a TelePrompTer. He had fallen back on his acting ability to read the lines others wrote and placed before him. After all, to do that he didn't need his memory, did he?

Two years and three months later, on November 5, 1994, Reagan wrote a letter addressed to "My fellow Americans."
"I have recently been told that I am one of the millions of Americans who will be afflicted with Alzheimer's disease." Reagan said he and Nancy had struggled with the decision whether to go public, but had decided to share his condition with the American people in the hope of raising public awareness. "Unfortunately, as Alzheimer's disease progresses, the family often bears a heavy burden. I only wish there was some way I could spare Nancy from this painful experience. When the time comes, I am confident that with your help she will face it with faith and courage."
"I now begin the journey that will lead me into the sunset of my life. I know that for America there will always be a bright dawn ahead. Thank you, my friends. May God always bless you."
The letter was signed, "Sincerely, Ronald Reagan."

On February 18, 1998, I went to see Judge Walsh at the Watergate hotel where he had lived on and off during the Iran-contra investigation. The judge was 87 years old, a contemporary of Reagan's, but he still had considerable energy and memory. He had closed his investigation finally in 1994 and had written an angry book published in 1997 justifying his long inquiry. He was in Washington for a conference at Georgetown University on the independent counsel law, one of many he attended around the country defending his investigation. He was bleary-eyed but friendly when I arrived. He explained that his flight had been delayed and he had not made it to Washington until 2 a.m. that morning.

I was interested in discussing his attitude toward Reagan. Over the years Walsh had been portrayed widely as an unrelenting prosecutor hellbent on punishing the president. My reporting and the files my assistant had read, copied and summarized suggested somewhat the opposite. Walsh had been deferential to Reagan, accepting written interrogatories instead of live testimony in 1987, chasing operational officers North and Poindexter instead of the president's senior advisers during the crucial first years of his probe.

"Well, I admired him as a partisan Republican," Walsh began, "because he carried success with him and he was terribly likable, at least from the outside." Walsh said there was a generational connection between himself and his wife, Mary, and the Reagans. They were both retired, home watching old movies on television. "So there was just a natural feeling of admiration and even some affection for him, from a distance, although I never met him until I took his deposition."

Why had he waited so long to interview Reagan, an incredible five years into his investigation? I wondered.

"I figured I'd only get one shot at him,"

Walsh said. He wanted to be respectful. "One, I didn't think I should go back repeatedly, although I would have done it if I had to, and second, I thought there would be a public reaction if I started, you know, did anything that looked at all like I was heckling him."

I asked about the decision to accept written answers instead of deposing Reagan in 1987. Reagan's own attorneys said they would have demanded live testimony if they had been the prosecutors.

Walsh said Reagan already was showing a lack of memory. "And you can't beat up on a president. I mean if he says he doesn't remember, you could try to refresh his recollection, but you can't ridicule him for it."

Reagan had seemed to be in big trouble during the first months of Iran-contra in 1986–87. The press and Congress were abuzz with discussions of possible impeachment. But Walsh said he wasn't concerned. "I never had the feeling that he was going to go down," Walsh said.

We went into the details of his investigation. I asked about possible vulnerabilities Reagan might have had to impeachment. "See, if he knew about the diversion and it could be proven," Walsh said, "then we're talking about stealing money in large amounts and that could be an impeachable offense. The only way to get there for me was through North and probably Poindexter."

Walsh had pursued a traditional prosecutorial strategy. He had built his case up from the bottom, trying to gain convictions and then turn the smaller players into witnesses against the higher-level officials. But on that road Walsh had lost the way to his destination.

In retrospect, Walsh admitted the problem. "So you know going into a lawsuit you sort of have a feeling," Walsh said, "you've got all these possibilities, but as you're drifting along you don't have any feeling that you know exactly where you're going to go. I'm not that good at it. I never can project precisely where I am, I sort of move as I feel."

"You come in," I said to Walsh, "and have authority to make the president accountable for what happened. So then they kind of throw North and Poindexter, two logs on the fire, and you try them and go through all the ups and downs of that. Then you get into Shultz's notes, you get into Weinberger's notes, Don Regan's notes, George Bush's diary, and every time you've gone through one of these cases, they throw another log on the fire to absorb your energy. And your anger."

"Well, they didn't throw the log on the fire," Walsh protested. He was full of pride. "We found 'em. None of this was done voluntarily."

"Whenever your energies needed to be refocused," I asked, "they found a target that was not Ronald Reagan?"

"I think that's a fair statement," Walsh said. He realized he had been too deferential to Reagan. For example, they had interviewed Shultz several times, he said, and tried to shake him up. "And we never dealt that severely with Reagan."

I summarized some of what Reagan's lawyers

had done during their internal White House investigation. "They think they saved the Reagan presidency," I told him.

"They saved it by searching all of the records," Walsh replied, noting that he also never found a smoking gun that would implicate Reagan.

"How will Iran-contra be remembered in history?" I asked.

"I think it'll be remembered as a non-sordid disregard of constitutional restraints," Walsh said. "I think the president was wrong, he was defiant, he was deliberate, but he wasn't dirty."

PART FOUR

GEORGE BUSH

1989–93

15

GEORGE BUSH, 64, in his seventh year as Reagan's loyal vice president, was uncertain how to respond to the unfolding Iran-contra scandal. Allegations of wrongdoing were deeply unsettling. They threw him off stride. He winced at trouble or disorder—anything that was at odds with his patrician, gentlemen's-club view of the world with everyone and everything in its designated place.

Fifteen years earlier, in 1973 and 1974, Bush had drawn duty as the Republican National Committee chairman during Watergate. These were tumultuous times for Bush as he traveled the country, the party front man defending Nixon, sometimes passionately and stridently. In his blue GOP elephant necktie, Bush tried to hold the party apparatus and faithful in line. But he took a pounding while Watergate built to its conclusion. As party chairman, he reported to Nixon White House chief of staff Alexander Haig. Bush kept sending in negative poll results to Haig. In a July 10, 1974, memo, he wrote: "The news is *not* encouraging." One Friday night near the end, Bush appeared in Haig's office to complain.

"How can I be expected to hold this party together," Bush demanded, "with that evil man down the hall?"

"George," Haig replied, weary of being Bush's case officer, "you owe everything you have to that evil man down the hall. I was there when he picked you out of the gutter after Lloyd Bentsen waxed your skis for you." In 1970, Bentsen had beaten Bush in the Texas Senate race, a crushing defeat for Bush. "You were finished," Haig reminded Bush. "And *he* put you up at the UN against the better judgments of Henry Kissinger and, for whatever voice I had, me." Nixon had appointed Bush United Nations Ambassador in 1971, and it was a critical rescue post for a defeated candidate for the Senate. "You get back to work and support your president and let the system decide," Haig ordered.

Haig thought Bush was weak. When the final "smoking gun" from Nixon's tapes was disclosed in early August 1974, Nixon counselor Dean Burch reported Bush's response to White House colleagues: "He broke out into assholes and shit himself to death." At Nixon's final cabinet meeting, Bush expressed doubt that Nixon had the ability to govern. Haig and Kissinger almost stomped on him for getting out of line. The next day, August 7, Bush wrote Nixon a letter recommending resignation—a course on which Nixon had already settled.

Bush was often tagged with the weakness label, variously dubbed by critics as "the wimp" or "a lapdog." The vice president's handling of Iran-contra in late 1986 and 1987 reinforced the image. Bush was looking for a way out. Panicky and unsure where the scandal was going, he moved in contradictory directions. Publicly, he backed Reagan as much as possible while claiming he was "not in the loop," that he had no operational role. Privately, Bush wanted to get the bad news out early and explain what he knew about the scandal so it would be largely forgotten by 1988 when he ran for president.

I was a beneficiary of some of this last effort. On Friday, February 6, 1987, Bush dispatched one of his top aides to my house to deliver a copy of a three-page top-secret memo. It outlined how a senior Israeli official had briefed Bush in detail about the Iranian arms sales during a meeting the previous summer at the King David Hotel in Jerusalem. The memo showed that Amiram Nir, the Israeli counterterrorist specialist and the Israeli equivalent to Oliver North, had told Bush that they were "dealing with the most radical elements" in Iran because "the moderates can't" deliver the American hostages. The memo contradicted Reagan's claim that the Iran arms sales were to the Iranian "moderates."

Two days later, Sunday, February 8, Bush read the lead story in *The Washington Post* that ran under the headline, "Bush Told U.S. Arms Deals Were with Iran Radicals." Administration officials and congressional investigators were quoted saying the Iran arms sales were in practice a cynical trade of weapons for American hostages. That Sunday morning, Bush called the aide who had delivered the memo to my home.

"Congratulations," he said.

It was perhaps a shrewd use of the news media by Bush. The memo would be released at some time anyway, so why not take the hit early? By pitting his knowledge of the true nature of the arms-for-hostages deals against Reagan's public claims up to that point, Bush put himself closer to the camp of the realists. At the same time, he could adhere to his practice as vice president of insisting that he would not reveal what he had said or recommended to Reagan.

For moments in 1988, Iran-contra threatened to derail Bush's quest for the Republican nomination. Was he or wasn't he in the loop? The records showed that Bush had attended many meetings on the Iran arms sales, but Independent Counsel Walsh felt at that point that his role was not central. In interviews outside the grand jury, some of Reagan's key national security people, even Secretary of State Shultz, supported this view. They dismissed Bush as a decorative yes man, a heartbeat away from the presidency but miles away from heavyweight decision making.

The pressure on Bush came largely from the news media, which was trying to sort out the confusing, often arcane details of Iran-contra. Bush scored in a big way on January 25, 1988, during a live television interview with *CBS Evening News* anchor Dan Rather. Instead of allowing himself to be trapped in the details of Iran-contra, Bush shot back at Rather and displayed an unusual toughness. "How would you like it if I judged your whole career by those seven minutes when you walked off the set in New York?" Bush asked Rather. The anchorman had no answer, and Bush was a temporary hero in Republican circles.

Bush won the Republican nomination and the presidency in 1988. It was in part an exercise in survival. He'd shown up with the strongest résumé and had benefited from the weaknesses of his Democratic opponent, Massachusetts Governor Michael Dukakis.

Annoyed by talk that his administration was effectively going to be Reagan's third term, Bush was determined to be his own man. One of his first decisions was to nominate his old Texas Republican friend, former Senator John Tower, to become secretary of defense, perhaps the most sensitive position during the Cold War after the presidency. Tower, who had chaired the presidential commission that had looked into Iran-contra, had been among the first major Republican figures to endorse Bush for president. As a member of the Senate for 23 years, Tower was a fully anointed member of the one club that Bush had never made. Bush's father had been a senator from Connecticut from 1952 to 1963, and the son had lost Senate races in Texas in 1964 and 1970.

A small man, who dressed in British three-piece suits and expensive flashy neckties and carried a brass cigarette case, Tower loved the good life. Drinking and womanizing formed part of his background story. His impending nomination brought rumors of his carousing to the surface. The FBI began an intensive background investigation. Many allegations appeared in the initial FBI background report sent to the White House, including some from Tower's ex-wife.

C. Boyden Gray, 45, the White House counsel and Bush's lawyer during the eight years of the vice presidency, was scrambling to keep up with the allegations and help Tower win confirmation. Gray, a 6-foot-6 North Carolinian who had graduated from Harvard, was so thin he looked like he might break in half. He seemed to walk with a permanent stoop, and his natural facial expression was a scowl. Gray went to Bush, still president-elect, to recommend that Bush not go ahead and nominate Tower. There was way too much smoke.

Bush wanted to know if any of it was real.

Gray said there was no hard, disqualifying information at that point.

Bush insisted they make the formal nomination. He announced his total confidence in Tower at a press conference on December 16, 1988. He brushed aside a question about Tower's "alcoholism." The FBI background report was made available to the Senate Armed Services Committee, which was going to hold the confirmation hearings. More stories about Tower's behavior were printed and broadcast.

"It's so damn ugly," Bush confided in his private diary February 9, 1989. People were tarnishing Tower, thinking it would endear them to the media. "Rumor after rumor," he dictated. "Insinuation after insinuation, investigation after reinvestigation, and it's damned unfair." Specific sexual liaisons were being reported, "one salacious bit of gossip after another." No ironclad firsthand witness appeared to verify any of the allegations, but Tower had left a trail of stories and enemies.

Later, when an allegation surfaced about Tower's role in a long-running defense contracting probe, Gray went again to Bush to recommend that the nomination be pulled. It meant another two-week delay as they chased down and answered the allegation, Gray said. Practical politics dictated that they end the fight.

Bush glared at Gray. "It's none of your business," he told the man who was in charge of overseeing the legal aspects of the nomination. "I'm not going to pull it!"

At one point, Tower called Gray at 11 p.m. "I think I'm going to withdraw," he said. The next morning Bush insisted that they keep fighting. In late February, Gray went to the Senate to meet with Senator Sam Nunn, the Georgia Democrat and Armed Services Committee chairman who was leading the charge against Tower. Although Tower himself had chaired the Armed Services Committee, Nunn opposed him on the grounds that a drinking problem was disqualifying for a potential secretary of defense.

"Have you ever seen him drunk in all the years of intimate contact with him?" Gray asked.

Nunn said he had not but noted that he never knew about other senators whom he later learned had significant clandestine drinking problems.

"There is no accusation that Tower is a secret drinker," Gray replied angrily. "The allegation is that he has been altogether too public about it. It can't be both."

Gray never got his hands around a specific allegation that he could track down and authenticate, although one former staffer who was now a congressman from Texas, Larry Combest, had come forward with stories about alcohol abuse. Anecdotal descriptions of drinking binges by unqualified observers did not constitute evidence.

Bush and Gray complained about the hypocrisy of the Senate and the media. Battering and defeating a nominee in a confirmation fight had become a new sport, Bush believed, and using the raw FBI files was only one more tool in the battle. Tower went on national television and pledged never to drink hard alcohol if he were confirmed as defense secretary. Bush still couldn't believe that the Senate was going to make drinking an issue. He almost couldn't deal with it. Finally and uncomfortably, he decided that loyalty was the issue he needed most to demonstrate. "I owe Tower a lot from Texas days," the president said. "I'm going to stick with him."

On March 9, the Senate turned down Tower's nomination, 53 to 47. It was the first time in 30 years that the Senate had rejected outright a president's cabinet choice.

It was a baptism by fire for Bush, Gray could see. The president did not want an analysis of how the fiasco could have been avoided or how the White House could have done better. Gray knew the answer: let the FBI complete a full investigation, study it, check it and only then go ahead with the nomination if all the questions had been answered and the allegations cleared up. But Bush had been in a hurry to announce his cabinet.

Afterwards, Bush blamed the news media for the onslaught of rumor and doubt that he believed had infected Washington. He also blamed them for wantonly circulating the rumors. It seemed to Bush that if the news media showed some forbearance and didn't publish or broadcast such rubbish, it would be given no weight. He traced some of this poison to Watergate and the climate it had created.

Bush asked Marlin Fitzwater, Reagan's press secretary for the last two years, to remain in the job. Fitzwater had worked as Bush's vice-presidential press secretary from 1985 to 1987.

"Now CIA, Skull and Bones," Fitzwater told Bush when he was offered the job, referring to Bush's past service as CIA director and membership in a Yale secret society, "I know you like secrets. How are we going to operate here?"

Bush reminded him that they went way back.

"I'd like to have the same kind of access and openness that I did with President Reagan," Fitzwater asked, adding that he was willing to demonstrate that he could be trusted. "I need to know all these things."

"Well," Bush said, "I don't know about national security."

"Let's just see how it goes," Fitzwater said.

Bush said okay, and gave him his CIA look.

Fitzwater began attending every meeting, no matter what it was, especially National

Security Council sessions. As long as he didn't speak but listened, he found that the members of the cabinet or the White House staff accepted that he wasn't trying to share in their power or authority. Soon Fitzwater was operating the way Bush had when he was vice president. He would remain silent in the large group, and then go privately to the president and tell him what he thought.

During the first weeks of his presidency, at a large Oval Office meeting, Bush ranted and raved about some personnel decision that had leaked to the media. "Who's leaking this stuff?" he asked. "Where's this stuff come from? This is an outrage."

Sitting on the couches or chairs, they all nodded their heads in sympathy, appearing to agree. How terrible it was.

Later that day, Fitzwater went to see Bush.

"Mr. President," Fitzwater said, "it's fine for you to get angry every morning." But the time to do it was when Fitzwater came in at 7 a.m. to see him alone. "Yell at me, don't yell in front of the whole staff, because those people will all leave and every one of them hates the press, and worse, they will think they have a greater license to hate the press because you do." The president, he said, wanted those people out working the press, being positive, directing coverage, not hating the reporters.

"Oh, I understand," Bush said. He rarely complained about the press in large groups after that. He confided his criticism to small groups of aides he trusted.

Fitzwater discovered that Bush had an enormous capacity to steel himself against public criticism if he thought he was right. His code for dealing with the media seemed to be: "If I'm doing the right thing, I can take any punishment." But Fitzwater rarely could convince Bush to see the value of leaking decisions in advance to set the tone and lay the foundation in the print press before television got to it. So he could not always build sufficient public support for Bush's programs and positions.

Bush's third son, Neil, four years earlier had joined the board of Silverado Savings, Banking and Loan Association, a high-flying Colorado S&L. Hoping to make a big financial killing, Neil, the shy and dyslexic son, became entangled with other Colorado businessmen. One of them extended Neil Bush a $1.2 million line of credit for a petroleum development company in which Neil had invested only $100 of his personal funds. When the S&L bubble burst, in a scandal that would cost taxpayers hundreds of billions of dollars, some Democrats and some reporters attempted to make Neil the public face of one of the largest financial disasters in American history. All three newsmagazines, *Time, Newsweek* and *U.S. News & World Report,* referred to Neil as the "poster boy" of the scandal. One business magazine put Neil on the cover, and a writer published a book, *Silverado: Neil Bush and the Savings & Loan Scandal.*
President Bush was sick, almost reduced to tears. He fully realized that his son was paying part of the price for his father's presidency. Neil's problem created a Bush family crisis that cast

a sour pall over the White House years. Bush was protective of his least capable son.

"They're out to get my boy," he told Fitzwater, "they're out to get me."

Brent Scowcroft, the national security adviser, saw how the focus on his son wounded Bush.

"You know," Bush told Scowcroft, "they don't have guts enough to come after me, they go after my son who was an innocent victim."

Scowcroft realized that Bush was just stewing about the treatment of Neil, stewing more about it perhaps than about anything else. Had there not been Watergate, Scowcroft felt, there would have been no legs for almost any of these mini-scandals. Watergate had created the atmosphere that nourished them.

Who is your candidate? White House chief of staff John Sununu asked Boyden Gray in a phone call during the summer of 1990. Supreme Court Justice William Brennan had announced that he was going to retire. From the first days of the administration, Bush had insisted that Attorney General Richard Thornburgh and his counsel Gray have a list of qualified nominees to the high court who had been initially screened. He did not want to be unprepared and allow the media to pressure him into a hasty selection.

"Ken Starr," Gray told Sununu, referring to the administration's solicitor general, the number three post in the Justice Department. "He's the most conservative, confirmable person we have." He added that Starr had been placed as solicitor general, the lawyer who argues Supreme Court cases for the government, for the express purpose of moving him to the Supreme Court if a vacancy occurred.

But Thornburgh and the Justice Department opposed Starr because he didn't seem conservative enough, and soon Sununu opposed him also.

Bush was first interested in naming Clarence Thomas, an African American conservative on the D.C. federal appeals court. But Thornburgh and Gray argued that Thomas was not ready, having just joined the appeals court.

Another top candidate was David H. Souter, a 50-year-old federal appeals court judge in New Hampshire and a bachelor. Early in the administration, Gray had spent a long lunch with Souter and had been impressed by his low-key intellect, humility and knowledge of the law. Sununu, an ex-governor of New Hampshire, assured Gray that Souter was okay on the administration's issues, including abortion. Senator Warren Rudman, a New Hampshire Republican and Souter's best friend, was his chief sponsor.

Bush nominated Souter. The press began to investigate. In an August 6, 1990, cover story on Souter, *Time* magazine reported on "speculation that Souter is homosexual." *The Washington Post* in a Style section profile noted that there was "a flurry of speculation that the Supreme Court might be getting its first gay justice." There were never any specifics or details, simply that the bookish, gentle Souter and his lifelong bachelorhood seemed to fit the stereotype.

Rudman was outraged. He had known Souter for 20 years. The printed rumors were irresponsible and reflected a grotesque intolerance not just for homosexuality but toward anyone who might choose to live alone and differently. Rudman was convinced that Souter loved the law and his privacy above all else. It would be monstrous if this issue somehow became part of the Senate or public debates. Rudman had already dropped everything to focus on his friend's nomination. He made the Souter nomination his single cause, escorting him for personal sessions with most of the 100 senators, counseling him and pouring his considerable energy into getting his friend confirmed. Before the formal confirmation hearings were to begin in September, Souter and Rudman got word that a New York gay newspaper was planning an "outing" of Souter's alleged secret gay life.

That night Souter and Rudman went to Rudman's apartment at the Harbour Square in Washington that overlooked the Potomac River. Souter had a salad, Rudman a sandwich. Souter was unusually quiet. About 10 p.m., Souter's frustration spilled out.

"If I had known how vicious this process is," Souter told his friend, "I wouldn't have let you propose my nomination." He wished he had not accepted Bush's nomination. It had been a mistake. The anguish of scrutiny was too great a price to pay. Souter said he was going to phone President Bush and insist that his nomination be withdrawn.

Rudman was beside himself. He argued forcefully that Souter had to be tough. He should not throw away the nomination on these side issues, even though they might strike at his soul.

At that particular moment in history, the future of the 1973 Supreme Court decision *Roe* v. *Wade,* which established abortion rights, hung in the balance. The newest member of the Court was likely to be the deciding vote. The Supreme Court had four members hostile to *Roe,* and President Bush was nominally in favor of overturning. Although Rudman had not talked directly with Souter about *Roe* v. *Wade,* he was certain that Souter would not vote to overturn the decision if he made it to the high court. Rudman, who was pro-choice, felt strongly that abortion was in part a matter of compassion, and he believed that Souter was compassionate and would see the brutality in taking away a woman's right to choose abortion. Rudman also knew that Souter believed in the principle of not overturning Supreme Court precedents unless there was an overwhelming argument. For practical purposes, Rudman was planting a pro-choice mole on the high court. Much more than Souter's future was at stake.

But Souter was determined to withdraw.

"It's your destiny to serve on the Supreme Court," Rudman argued. "This is your destiny. The court needs you."

No, Souter said, he was taking himself out. He was going to call President Bush that moment, and he moved toward the telephone in the small third-floor apartment.

Rudman, a large man who had served in

combat during the Korean War, grabbed Souter's small, wiry frame and restrained him physically.

Souter resisted, trying to make his way to the telephone. Rudman felt he had no choice. He physically held onto his friend or blocked his access to the telephone for what seemed like nearly half an hour. Wait, ride it out, think, Rudman argued vehemently. His phone was not going to be used to withdraw. Souter, for all his mildness, was tough and he fought back. He eventually had a scotch, and Rudman, still keeping him from the phone, drank a bourbon. It took hours before the storm finally passed. By 3 a.m., Souter had agreed to stay and fight.

When President Bush heard indirectly that Souter had almost withdrawn, he shuddered. What in the world was happening to America? The gay newspaper never published an article, and nothing concrete had ever surfaced about his alleged sexual preference, but what if it had?

At his Senate confirmation hearings, Souter declined to take a position on the *Roe* abortion decision, but he explained his understanding of the duties of a judge and a justice of the Supreme Court in what he called the "stewardship of the Constitution." Souter added, "At the end of our task some human being is going to be affected. Some human life is going to be changed in some way by what we do....We had better use every power of our minds and our hearts and our beings to get those rulings right."

The Senate confirmed Souter by a vote of 90 to 9.

Two years later, Souter and two other justices wrote a highly unusual three-justice signed opinion, joined by two others, upholding *Roe* v. *Wade.* Rudman was coming back from New York by train the day the decision in the case, *Planned Parenthood* v. *Casey,* was announced. He was overjoyed, certain that Souter had played a pivotal role. The efforts of the Reagan and Bush administrations and the religious right to overturn Roe were probably defeated forever, Rudman calculated. In the train station, he ran into Senator Joseph Biden, who had chaired the Senate Judiciary Committee during the Souter confirmation hearings. Biden, a Delaware Democrat, was equally delighted that *Roe* had been affirmed. The two senators embraced, laughed, yelled and even cried.

"You were right about him," Biden said. "Did you read that opinion? You were right!"

The next summer, 1991, Justice Thurgood Marshall announced his retirement, and Bush selected Clarence Thomas to replace him. Bush anticipated a strong ideological attack from the liberals, and he called Thomas to warn him.

"We'll stand by you," Bush said from his summer home in Kennebunkport, Maine. "I hope you'll stand by us. This will be one of the most difficult journeys you will ever make. Hope you know what you're getting into."

Thomas accepted the warning and the nomination. The Senate had already confirmed him four times for lesser posts, and he had testified before Congress some 50 times.

Bush was astounded when at the confirmation hearings, Anita Hill, a former employee of Thomas's in the Department of Education and at the Equal Employment Opportunity Commission, came forward to testify that Thomas had sexually harassed her.

Gray, again responsible for squiring an important nomination through the Senate, saw the daily toll the battle took on Bush. The president was glued to the television as the hearings proceeded into Hill's allegations. Everybody was ganging up on Thomas, he said. He did not understand the discretionary power of the media or a congressional committee to inquire into whatever they chose—the most personal and unsubstantiated accusations. But he was determined to fight. It was now us against them, the president said.

On Sunday, October 13, 1991, Bush played golf at the Holly Hills Country Club near Camp David. He brought along a small television so he could watch the Thomas-Hill coverage as he moved from hole to hole. Bristling with anger as he watched, he walked over to a group of reporters.

"My heart aches for him and his family," Bush said. "The American people know fairness when they see it and they know that this process is ridiculous and they know it's unfair." He praised Thomas's resilience and toughness. Of the hearing, he said, "I think it's outrageous."

Bush's aides had cautioned him not to attack

Anita Hill personally, fearing that he would be accused of insensitivity toward women. But Bush could not stay out of the fray. "How come the normal behavior for ten years? How come the last-minute charge brought before the American people? I don't understand that. She didn't have to come forward at the last moment." He could barely contain his disgust.

Bush described the hearings as "the ultimate in trying to drag someone through the mud and tear down his family." He said many Americans, including himself and his own family, "felt kind of unclean watching this."

Two days later, on October 15, the Senate voted. Thomas was confirmed by a slim 52-to-48 margin.

Gray, who was close to Thomas, later observed that it took five years for Thomas to become a whole person again.

For Bush, the lesson was clear: no one was safe from a battering, either by a congressional committee or the media. No subject, no matter how far in the past, was out of bounds.

In August 1990, Iraqi President Saddam Hussein's forces invaded and took over neighboring Kuwait, which triggered a major international crisis. During the next five months, President Bush ordered more than 500,000 American military men and women into the Middle East. It was the largest deployment since the Vietnam War. By early January 1991, Bush, with the full backing of the United Nations, was poised to launch a war to drive Iraq out of Kuwait.

The president met with his national security team, including Secretary of State James A. Baker III, Chairman of the Joint Chiefs of Staff Colin Powell and national security adviser Brent Scowcroft. He was about to send Baker to meet with Iraqi Foreign Minister Tariq Aziz in Geneva to try to negotiate a last-minute pullout of Saddam's forces from Kuwait. It was risky. He hoped to demonstrate to the world and to his critics that he was determined to go the extra mile to achieve a peaceful resolution. He could not have a war without maximizing his effort to at least speak with the Iraqis. Congressional and public support hinged in part on such a demonstration.

"So if he gets out without a war, that's okay?" Bush asked Powell.

"Yes, sir," Powell replied. That was the goal of both the United States and the United Nations: Iraqi withdrawal from Kuwait. If there was no war, no U.S. servicemen would be killed, Powell stated, speaking like a good military leader looking out for his troops.

Baker agreed. A talented, ambitious close friend from Texas and a subtle rival of the president's, Baker wanted to bring home victory through diplomacy. If he could negotiate an Iraqi withdrawal, it would be a monumental personal achievement. Several days before, Baker had pressed Bush to allow him to go to Baghdad to meet Saddam himself, but the president had refused to authorize the mission. Now Baker said he was determined to negotiate.

Next Bush and Scowcroft, almost together, jumped on Powell and Baker.

"Don't you realize that if he pulls out, it will be impossible for us to stay," Scowcroft asked. Bush nodded in agreement as Scowcroft spoke. The massive U.S. force, based mostly in Saudi Arabia, could not remain in the region indefinitely, Scowcroft said. It would be politically and logistically impossible—and politically insupportable in the United States— to keep the troops there for an extended period or even probably well into the year. The nightmare would be for Saddam to pull out of Kuwait and move back into Iraq but stay on the border. "There would be 400,000 to 500,000 Iraqis," Scowcroft said. They could wait indefinitely, threatening to invade again, effectively holding the United States hostage to the actions of the vast Iraqi Army. A diplomatic victory could wind up a huge strategic loss, he said. They needed the chance to destroy Saddam's army or at least to devastate it so it would not be a threat in the near future—to Kuwait or other countries in the region.

It was sobering, the president agreed, the most sobering reality of the crisis. He had to play all the diplomatic cards. But, he made it clear, a diplomatic solution would in fact bring about a larger crisis. There was no diplomatic victory that could destroy Saddam's army. Looking squarely at his advisers, the president said plainly, "We have to have a war." His words hung in the air as heavily as any he had ever spoken.

Scowcroft was aware that this understanding could never be stated publicly or be permitted to leak out. An American president who declared the necessity of war would probably be thrown out of office. Americans were peacemakers, not warmongers. But the president's words reflected the stark reality of the Gulf confrontation. In addition, Bush couldn't afford to wait because the coming summer heat in the desert would make ground operations untenable. So it was now or never.

It was a simple and obvious conclusion, and it was one that could not be spoken. During World War II, the stated wartime goal of "unconditional surrender" had been widely accepted—the destruction of the German and Japanese regimes was the only long-term solution. But Americans now wanted easier remedies, neater and surgical. In that moment, Scowcroft came to glimpse the full and horrible weight carried by the president.

The risk to the country and to Bush was growing daily. Simultaneously, Bush was asking the Senate and House to pass resolutions supporting the use of force. The vote was going to be incredibly close in the Senate. If any reliable information got out that Bush felt, for strategic reasons, he needed a war, the resolutions could fail.

Baker met with Tariq Aziz on January 9, 1991, in Geneva for more than six hours. Bush feared the Iraqis would come up with some kind of gimmicky proposal or maneuver. He was nervous; it was one of his toughest and tensest times as president. Finally Baker called on the secure telephone.

"It's over," Baker told him; the Iraqis would not budge.

Bush had to suppress his relief. He sat down

with his closest advisers before a television to watch the conference at which Baker was scheduled to appear.

Fitzwater realized the box that Bush was in, the extent to which diplomatic victory could be the nightmare. He asked if Aziz simply announced that Saddam intended to pull out, what would they do?

Bush didn't answer.

"Let's say Tariq Aziz says, 'Okay, we'll pull out,' and he pulls one tank around. Do we call this off?" Fitzwater persisted.

Bush moved in his chair, deeply unhappy, but he didn't say anything.

"What about 10 tanks?" Fitzwater asked. "Or 100 tanks?"

Bush sat stone-faced and silent. His mortal fear was that Baker would succeed even a little bit at the last moment.

Finally, Baker appeared on the television screen for the press conference.

"I heard nothing that suggested to me any Iraqi flexibility whatsoever," Baker said. The negotiations were over.

In part, Bush was jubilant because it was the best news possible, although he would have to conceal it publicly. The other part of Bush was totally drained and full of anxiety because he knew the failure of negotiations meant war.

Bush had written his five children a personal letter two weeks earlier on New Year's Eve from Camp David trying to express the agony and burden he felt about risking the lives of so many. "When the question is asked, 'How many lives are you willing to sacrifice'—it tears at my heart," he wrote. "The answer, of course, is none, none at all." He said he had tried to achieve a peaceful resolution, "but the question of loss of life still lingers and plagues the heart."

"My mind goes back to history:

"How many lives might have been saved if appeasement had given way to force earlier on in the late 30s or earliest 40s? How many Jews might have been spared the gas chambers, or how many Polish patriots might be alive today? I look at today's crisis as 'good' vs. 'evil.' Yes, it is that clear."

Bush knew his course. He had his reasoning in place.

The Senate and House passed resolutions supporting the use of force, and an air war was launched January 15, 1991.

The massive air war directed against Iraq and its military forces lasted 38 days. The day before ordering the final ground assault, the operation that risked the greatest number of American lives, Bush met in the Oval Office with his advisers.

Again the issue of half measures arose. Powell reported that the Iraqi Army was beginning to crack. Referring to the commander in the Middle East, General H. Norman Schwarzkopf, Powell said, "Norm and I would rather see the Iraqis walk out than be driven out. There will be costs. We will lose soldiers in substantial numbers at a time." Powell sounded a harsh alarm. "There is a high probability of a chemical attack. It involves an American attack on an Arab country. We will get more of their tanks and stockpiles by attacking, but the cost in lives and later problems is not worth it."

"Would you prefer a negotiated settlement?" Bush asked.

"If it met our conditions totally, yes," answered Powell. "They will crack."

"If they crack under force, it is better than withdrawal," Bush said.

"But at what cost?" Powell asked.

There it was again. Even at that point, Bush saw the danger of an Iraqi withdrawal before their army was destroyed in some form. He ordered the ground war. After four days, the intelligence showed that only two to six of the Iraqi 42 divisions in the theater were functioning, and Bush called a halt to the war as the remaining Iraqis fled Kuwait.

"It hasn't been a clean end," Bush confided to his diary that night, February 28, 1991. "There is no battleship Missouri surrender. This is what's missing to make this akin to WWII...."

It was a stunning victory for U.S. forces and their commander in chief.

The big secret went undisclosed. Bush was viewed as a president who had been forced into war by Saddam's total refusal to negotiate. That was true, but Bush and Scowcroft knew that by January 1991 it was a war they had to have.

Bush didn't want the turmoil of after-action analysis, and he declined to talk in depth to reporters or authors about the Gulf crisis or the war while in office.

"This is not something I want second-guessing on," Bush told Fitzwater. He wanted the war judged on the outcome, not the process of how he got there, or on who said what to whom. "Hell, they'll be writing about this and before you know it, they'll have us losing the war."

Bush did not trust the Congress or the media to sort out or explain his dilemma and responsibility without sensationalizing it. Watergate had made a sober account of the truth by the president almost impossible.

"Let's leave sleeping dogs lie," Scowcroft said. In their book, *A World Transformed,* published in 1998, Bush and Scowcroft did not reveal the problem or their reasoning.

Following the war, Bush was criticized for failing to march to Baghdad and bring down Saddam. If Saddam was a modern Hitler as the president had claimed, why was he left in power? Bush had a solid answer. The United Nations resolutions and U.S. war aims, he argued, were focused on expelling Saddam from Kuwait, a mission they had accomplished. Bush felt stung by the criticism. On March 13, 1991, he confided to his diary that the press drumbeat continued—what he called the "sniping, carping, bitching, predictable editorial complaints." It was, the president dictated, "the cynical liberalism that comes down on any president," even though the march-to-Baghdad critique was coming from the right. He said he resented cartoonist Garry Trudeau, a fellow Yale graduate who routinely ridiculed Bush in his "Doonesbury" comic strip. He called Trudeau "a little elitist who is spoiled, derisive, ugly and nasty."

To his dictation machine, he added, "Sometimes I really like the spotlight, but I'm tired of it. I've been at the head table for many years, and now I wonder what else is out there."

16

IN APRIL 1991, Patty Presock, Bush's secretary, reported to Dr. Burton Lee III, the White House physician, that Bush's handwriting had changed. The president's sleep patterns were erratic. He had lost 15 pounds. The next month while jogging at Camp David, Bush collapsed from shortness of breath. His heart was beating irregularly. The diagnosis was Graves' disease, an overactive thyroid. Bush lost some of his zest and stamina. Fitzwater watched for any changes, knowing the press would notice them. He saw that Bush had some mood swings and was not as engaged in his presidency. The president kept delaying his decision to run for reelection in 1992.

The Walsh investigation of Iran-contra had dragged on well into Bush's presidency. One of the lions of the Washington legal establishment, Jacob Stein, himself a former independent counsel, had warned three of Walsh's prosecutors five months before, "This office has been in business too long." Stein had investigated Ed Meese for alleged conflict of interest violations in 1984, and had filed a report finding no basis for prosecution in six months.

Stein asked the three young prosecutors to consider the following hypothetical about his client, Colonel Sam Watson, who had worked for then–Vice President Bush:

"Suppose Watson takes you up on your offer to come in here and write on a clean slate. He says he went to the vice president and volunteered, 'I know all about Iran-contra, and here are four or five documents.' Suppose the vice president, now the president of the United States, says to my client, 'These documents must be destroyed.'

"Now what the hell could you do with that?" Stein asked indignantly. "What might have been possible three and a half years ago is not really a possibility now because public interest has moved on to other issues, and this man was elected president of the United States."

Walsh's prosecutors disagreed and continued to pursue the investigation. By April 1991, Boyden Gray was sufficiently alarmed to call Bill Lytton, the attorney who had helped bail President Reagan out of Iran-contra four years earlier. The endless Walsh investigation was continuing, of course, Gray noted sarcastically, and Walsh now, of course, wanted to interview Gray about Gray's internal fact-finding in the early stages of the Iran-contra investigations. Of particular interest to the independent counsel was Don Gregg, a former CIA officer who had been Bush's national security adviser during the vice-presidential years. There was documentary evidence that Gregg knew more about North's contra resupply operation in the 1980s than he had acknowledged. In addition, there were some questions about attorney-client privilege on some documents which Walsh had requested.

On April 9, Lytton arrived at the Bush White House and was appointed special counsel to assist on Iran-contra. Lytton brought himself up to date and then met with Deputy Attorney General William Barr, who said the Bush White House was not paying sufficient attention to the Iran-contra investigation. The focus and discipline of the Reagan effort were gone, Barr said. Walsh was still out there dragneting every issue. There was a dangerous lack of strategy on these matters, Barr said. Aggravation and anger had replaced a cool-headed defense. Gray was too involved and should recuse himself.

Lytton called around and found out that a number of the defense attorneys in the case were concerned that Gregg could be indicted. Walsh had two secretaries ready to testify that Gregg's deputy, the same Colonel Sam Watson whom Stein represented, had dictated a memo putting the issue of "resupply of the contras" on the agenda for a meeting Bush and Gregg had in May 1986 with a CIA operative. Gregg said it was a dictation or transcribing mistake, that it should have read "resupply of the copters." He categorically denied that he or anyone else mentioned, or intended to discuss, resupplying the contras.

On May 14, Lytton went to meet with Bush. After a delay because Queen Elizabeth II was visiting the White House, Gray and Lytton were ushered into the Oval Office complex at

293

2 p.m. The White House chief of staff, John Sununu, showed up also.

What are you doing here? Gray inquired of Sununu.

Sununu said he was going to attend the meeting.

Gray said only lawyers could be present.

Sununu asked Lytton to explain.

A non-lawyer at the meeting, Lytton said, would destroy the lawyer-client privilege of confidentiality.

Okay, Sununu said, and he left.

Gray and Lytton went into the small study by the Oval Office where Bush was waiting. The president was fiddling on his computer, which he was learning to use.

Gray reintroduced Lytton, who in 1987 had helped Bush with his Iran-contra testimony. A photographer took a picture, and Gray left.

Walsh was intending to interview Gray, Lytton explained. It wasn't a formal subpoena yet, but that couldn't be ruled out in the future. The president had three options on Gray, Lytton said. The president could invoke attorney-client privilege, executive privilege, or both. Second, he could let Gray talk about anything and everything. Third, he could try a middle path, let Gray talk about subjects that were not privileged, avoid a fight and hope to satisfy Walsh.

Bush asked what the prosecutors wanted from Gray.

Focusing on the early fact-gathering during Iran-contra more than four years ago, they were after what others on Bush's staff, particularly Gregg, had told Gray, Lytton said. As best

294

Lytton could tell, the conversations they were trying to learn about were meaningless, non-substantive or had never happened. Lytton said he didn't want Walsh spending a lot of time spinning his wheels in search of nonexistent conversations.

Bush said he didn't think he should assert any privilege because he would be accused of trying to cover up. He preferred the middle path.

Lytton said he felt he could work it out—make it clear a privilege existed, but since what Walsh asked about didn't happen, Lytton would be able to convince Walsh not to press the issue.

Bush said that was fine.

"Mr. President," Lytton said, "as best I can tell Walsh is really coming after you." Walsh was working through all the people who were close to Bush. The effort to interview Gray was no doubt designed to somehow get Bush entangled in something. Walsh was even zeroing in on Robert Gates, the Bush deputy national security adviser whom Bush had nominated that day to be the CIA director. Lytton wanted to wake Bush up to the danger.

Bush responded that it was an outrage that the Walsh investigation had dragged on for so long. "If they want to come after me," the president said, "let them come, but get it over with."

Even if Walsh didn't indict anyone else, Lytton said, Walsh would file an unpleasant, accusatory report.

At 2:25 p.m., Sununu poked his head in the door.

"John, come in," Bush said.

"I can't," Sununu said, pointing at Lytton, "he won't let me."

Lytton briefly re-explained that Sununu's presence would undermine the attorney-client privilege, and Sununu said he would come back when they were finished.

At the end of the meeting, Lytton urged the president to take Walsh seriously.

In the next several weeks, Lytton systematically canvassed the lawyers who were representing Walsh's targets. He identified 17 areas of focus that might touch on Bush. He divided up responsibility to lawyers in and out of the White House to ensure they had their hands around the issues and could establish where Walsh might be taking his investigations.

At 3 p.m. on June 12, Gray and Lytton went to see Bush again. The president was seated at his desk in the Oval Office with his jacket off. He was wearing a striped shirt with a white collar. His tie was loosened. It was his 67th birthday. One of his gifts had been a stuffed toy that included a plastic mallet. Upon seeing the lawyers and knowing the subject, Bush removed the mallet.

"Take that, Walsh!" Bush shouted, hitting the plastic mallet on his desk. Bang! Bang! Bang! "Take that, Walsh!" He hit the desk some more, a look of relish and anger on his face. "I'd like to get rid of this guy," the president said.

Gray and Lytton didn't think Bush had a plan or did intend to fire Walsh, but Bush was visibly frustrated. Lytton could see that his wake-up call had aroused the sleeping president.

"Let them come after me," Bush said, "if they want to come after me." Walsh had a vendetta, he said. Their investigation was a waste of time and money. It's politics, he said.

The performance was George Bush, the competitor and fighter. But the lawyers were there to urge the president not to fight. They wanted him to take hard stands and then negotiate so Walsh would get some of what he was requesting.

Bush and Gray chatted briefly about a tennis game. Gray, who was divorced, said *Mademoiselle* magazine had an article reporting that he was dating beautiful women. "I'd like to know who they are," Gray joked, noting that some time back the same magazine had named him one of the least eligible bachelors. Gray then left Lytton alone with the president.

The two moved back to the private study. Lytton handed Bush some memos outlining the 17 areas of Walsh's investigation.

Bush read. The issues included a 1987 production of documents, Bush's interviews with the Tower Board, Bush's travels to Central America. Why the hell was Walsh interested in some of these areas and people? Bush asked.

"In my view," Lytton replied, "they have a wish list and George Bush's name is on the top of it."

"They're barking up the wrong tree," Bush snapped.

Lytton proceeded down each avenue. He said he had assigned lawyers to each of them. He believed they had found a way to resolve each issue so that Walsh would be satisfied with explanations, testimony or documents. If everything stayed on track, Lytton said, he probably wouldn't have to bother Bush again. They were going to play a little harder than Reagan had, he said. They had made it clear to Walsh that they were not going to turn this White House upside down once again.

Bush agreed but still showed his anger at Walsh. As Lytton was leaving, Bush asked, "What kind of guy is he?"

"He is 79 years old, had been a federal judge years ago for a short period of time." Walsh had served as a judge from 1954 to 1957. "And he still insists that people call him 'Judge.' And whoever gets to him last will usually win the argument."

Bush shook his head.

In the middle of the summer of 1991, Bush met with nearly 20 of his key political advisers at Camp David. "I haven't made up my mind to run yet," he said. Several aides told the president he was vulnerable on the economy, that the Persian Gulf War victory cloaked real economic problems. Bush lashed out at "a bunch of whiny Team 100 members," referring to some of the group of big Republican donors who were worried about the economy. But he said he wanted ideas. In an unintended illustration of his isolation, he said memos and proposals for the campaign could be sent to him the next month at his summer home in Maine. Bush read aloud an address that would forward mail only to him personally: "Box 492 in zip code 04046." The former CIA director said it was a clandestine "eyes only" mail drop to which no one else had access. "Only I will get them," he said proudly.

Since the spring chief of staff John Sununu had been embroiled in a scandal about using government planes for personal trips, which had cost taxpayers $500,000 over two years. There were few easier targets than Sununu, the former New Hampshire governor who virtually crackled with overconfidence and bluster. The media demanded all the information on each trip and also was looking for Sununu to say uncle, apologize, come clean and acknowledge a lapse of judgment.

"I'm not going to give them a damn thing," Sununu roared at Fitzwater. The chief of staff grew red and puffed up. Later he screamed, "They will never get me!"

But the story didn't go away, and it was quickly dubbed "Air Sununu." On many days Fitzwater went to see the president in private to brief him on the latest Sununu story or reaction.

In late November 1991, Bush brought in Fitzwater for an evaluation. "Can Sununu get through this?" he asked. "I'm getting calls from friends saying he's hurting the presidency."

"Mr. President," Fitzwater answered, knowing this moment was his chance, "you've got to decide whether you need him and whether he's the best person to do certain things for you, but I can tell you in a press sense, a public sense, that it's hurting really badly. Now what it's done, it's emboldened all your enemies to be your enemies because they were afraid of him, now they're not anymore." Second, Fitzwater said, it had created a new class of enemies willing to criticize both Sununu and Bush. "It makes us just look like we're foolish. There's no single issue that the American people hate more than stupid, frivolous expenditure of taxpayer dollars."

Expecting a tough reelection campaign, Bush could not afford to have any staff member become a campaign issue. He moved on Sununu, forcing his resignation. Sununu was in tears when he finally had to submit his letter in December 1991. He blamed the media. "They'll be celebrating, I suppose," he told Fitzwater. "I didn't think they could get me."

For Bush it was again another scandal that had taken him too long to understand or fully grasp. The outcome deprived him of his chief of staff. Again it was the media machine in full frenzy that seemed to grind up whomever it wanted and whatever the president needed.

Bush saw the scandal inflation and escalation more and more in personal terms, Gray, Fitzwater and the others on the White House staff realized. He felt the scandals hurt his ability to govern, and they were going to be aimed at his most important task the next year—his bid for reelection.

After finally declaring his candidacy, Bush faced a loud challenge from Pat Buchanan, the conservative former Nixon and Reagan speechwriter and communications director. The final public opinion polls before the New Hampshire Republican primary showed Bush with a comfortable lead—60 percent to 33 percent, according to CNN, 54 to 26, according to the *Boston Globe.*

About 5:30 p.m. on February 18, 1992, the day of the primary, Samuel Skinner, who had replaced Sununu as chief of staff, Bob Teeter, the campaign chairman, and Rich Bond, the Republican National Committee chairman, filed into the Oval Office.

The latest exit polling showed Buchanan and Bush running even with 49 percent each, Teeter reported. Incredible as it might seem, it was possible that Bush could lose. "What happened to all these polls?" Bush asked sarcastically.

"They were wrong," Teeter answered.

Suddenly Bush swiveled in his chair at his desk, turned his back to the three men and stared out the window in silence. The three sat quietly for what seemed like several minutes. It was embarrassing, torture.

"Well," Bush said, turning back to them, ending the misery only momentarily, "then this means, I guess we're all going to have to work harder." He was stern and glaring. He dismissed them with a wave of his hand.

Bush won the New Hampshire primary with 53 percent of the vote to 37 percent for Buchanan, but he refused to attend his own victory celebration. He knocked off Buchanan in the subsequent primaries and prepared to face Arkansas Governor Bill Clinton in the general election.

In the summer of 1992, the U.S. Navy was being torn apart by the investigations and cover-ups of the debauchery at the annual Las

Vegas Tailhook Convention for naval aviators the previous year. The convention's infamous wild parties and organized harassment of women had shaken Bush, a former naval aviator in World War II.

Bush asked his military national security leaders to lunch—Secretary of Defense Dick Cheney, Powell, Scowcroft. The question was what to do with Navy Secretary H. Lawrence Garrett, a man who had risen from mess cook to the top job in the Navy.

"Do I need to fire Garrett?" Bush asked.

The others weren't sure, and they hedged. Garrett had been at the Tailhook Convention only briefly, and no one had implicated him in the misconduct. But he was the person at the top. Didn't he have to pay with his job?

"Should I talk to Garrett?" Bush asked.

No, the others said, if the president had a face-to-face meeting with the Navy secretary and then he did not fire him, it would be read as an endorsement. If Garrett was going to be fired, someone else should do it.

On Wednesday, June 24, Paula Coughlin, a former Navy lieutenant and admiral's aide who had filed the original Tailhook complaint, told ABC News, "I went down a hallway where every man in that hallway got a shot at me. They knew I was an officer. They knew I was an admiral's aide. And I think that made the sport that much more rewarding."

The president and the first lady invited Coughlin up to the White House residence for a private meeting. Coughlin told the story again in vivid detail, bringing both the Bushes to tears.

Two days later, on Friday, June 26, Cheney fired Garrett.

Garrett felt he had done nothing wrong, and he could not believe he was not given a chance to protest or talk to Bush. Devastated and in despair, Garrett saw 30 years of government service end in disgrace. That day he literally watched his entire life pass before him. "It's as if someone died," his wife wrote in her daily calendar for that day. Garrett was convinced it was a bald political decision. Bush was not doing well with women voters and the gender gap was widening, a potentially fatal blow to his campaign for reelection.

The next morning, Saturday, Garrett was at home, his life in shambles. His wife answered the phone about 10:30. It was the White House operator for Garrett. At last, Garrett thought, Bush was calling to say thank you for your service, to apologize for what had to be done.

Garrett picked up the phone, and the White House operator said something about the president.

"Congratulations on a job well done!" said the voice. But it was not President Bush. The voice was that of former President Richard Nixon. Garrett barely knew Nixon.

Nixon said Garrett had served the country well and he had the gratitude of the country. His service was what was important, Nixon said. It would be remembered, not his leaving. "Hang in there," Nixon said.

The Buchanan challenge, Tailhook, and the other inevitable controversies surrounding the election campaign continued to frustrate Bush. On July 24, Bush snapped at a heckler, "Shut up and sit down." Later that day, campaigning in Ohio, Fitzwater was worried. Dr. Lee said Bush had an irregular heart episode that morning. The doctor told Fitzwater he was having trouble regulating the president's medication. The dosage, he said, affected mental acuity. Fitzwater was shocked. When Bush appeared looking terrible and pale, he asked Bush's photographer what he was seeing. The photographer confirmed that the president seemed to be drained. Later Bush's shirt soaked through and his voice was weak. Fortunately, Saddam Hussein was acting up again, and Bush was able to cancel weekend travel and go to Camp David. Fitzwater concluded that Bush was sick, but he seemed to recover. The insane five-mile runs in the morning stopped, though he occasionally went for a mile jog later in the day.

When Fitzwater questioned Bush about his health, the president claimed everything was perfect, no change. But the staff had to push the president, set up special meetings to get him focused. The more Bush denied any problem, the more Fitzwater and Dr. Lee realized it was real. There were lots of difficult discussions. The president eventually shut down on the topic and said he did not want to hear any more.

Barbara Bush, who also suffered from Graves' disease, was upset and angry. She faulted Dr. Lee for not getting on top of the problem and regulating her husband's medication more effectively.

Regardless of who was to blame, the drive and vitality went out of Bush and his presidency.

On September 24, two months before the election, Bush's personal secretary Patty Presock opened the third-floor White House residence safe. Sitting there were stacks of transcripts and tapes dictated by Bush. It was the president's long-hidden diary. Presock began reading and realized that some of the daily dictations touched on Iran-contra matters. She highlighted and paperclipped relevant passages, wondering if the notes should be given to Independent Counsel Walsh, who more than five years ago had requested any relevant Iran-contra records from Bush.

The next day, Presock found the president in the room adjacent to the Oval Office and told him about her discovery. The material is relevant to Walsh's investigation, she argued. Bush disagreed and called Gray.

"We've got something we didn't know we had," the president said. "Call Patty."

Presock explained to Gray that Bush had dictated a daily diary and then had it transcribed. Normally the tapes of Bush recollections were sent to his private office in Houston, his hometown.

Gray was shocked. It surely was something Bush knew he had. Gray started going through the material. Bush had begun dictating the diary the day the Iran arms sales were publicly disclosed—November 4, 1986. Gray was terrified. Walsh had indicted Weinberger for failing to disclose his notes. Gray was shaking as he read.

"I'm one of the few people that know fully the details," Bush had dictated. Gray was astonished that he could feel so close to Bush and at the same time be so far removed. Here were hundreds of pages, a virtual record of the last two years of the Reagan administration and then of the entire Bush presidency. Was there some secret life in here? Legal problems?

Gray found that the diary material was largely exculpatory, but some of it was relevant. It likely would be read to counter Bush's claim that he had been out of the Iran arms sales loop.

If the diaries were suddenly turned over after all these years, charges of cover-up would be made. In light of Weinberger's indictment, it could be a disaster for the president. All of Walsh's endless requests to Bush had been informal or had been made by letter. There were no subpoenas. In the face of recent requests, Gray and the other White House lawyers had promised to respond to Walsh after the election. Gray decided to take a calculated risk. He felt it was his job as counsel to develop the legal rationale and take the heat if necessary. He went to see Bush.

Gray told the president that the immediate jeopardy was political and public relations, especially before the election. The race against Clinton was close. It seemed as if it could go either way, although Clinton was ahead at the moment. Gray was worried that the existence of the diaries would leak and harm Bush's chances for reelection if they told Walsh. They could delay until after the election and then face the consequences. Gray said he planned to tell no one.

"If that's your judgment, fine," Bush said.

Nine days later, on Sunday, October 4, *Newsweek* put out a press release about a short item it was carrying that week in its Periscope column. The FBI was investigating whether someone at the State Department had tampered with Clinton's passport files. "For weeks news organizations have been chasing an unsubstantiated rumor that Clinton, as an anguished young Rhodes scholar, faced with the draft, considered applying for citizenship in some other country." Three news organizations had filed Freedom of Information Act requests seeking the file. "When State officials pulled Clinton's file late last week, they discovered that it had apparently been tampered with—that several pages seemed to have been ripped out."

Bush dictated in his diary the next day that he was following stories about Clinton's anti-Vietnam protests, especially reports that Clinton had protested against the war while traveling abroad. "According to the press," Bush dictated bitterly, "the debate on the draft, the lying and all of that have no bearing on the character issue." Three days later he dictated, "We cannot get this smoking gun on Clinton and his demonstrations, demonstrating against his country. There are all these rumors of him carrying a coffin. There are rumors that there was something in his State Department files that now apparently has been tampered with. All kinds of rumors as to who his hosts were in Russia, something he can't remember anything at all about. He hasn't come forward with his draft records and the press doesn't hone in on it. The press let up and they're not focusing on it, but I just can't help believe that the American people don't care about this."

At the October 15 presidential debate in Richmond, Virginia, Bush was caught on camera looking at his watch in the middle of questioning. Afterwards, Jim Baker, who had relinquished his job as secretary of state to return as Bush's chief of staff for the campaign, told Rich Bond that the president was down. Come to the White House for lunch with him, Baker requested.

"What can I do?" Bush asked Bond.

Bond said Bush seemed passive in the campaign. He had to show the voters he intended to win and get fired up for the last three weeks.

Out on the campaign trail, Bush began calling Al Gore—Clinton's vice-presidential running mate—"Ozone Man" or just "Ozone" because of Gore's strong positions on the environment. Then the president called Clinton and Gore a couple of "bozos." On a campaign swing in Ohio, Bush said he would trust his dog Millie for foreign policy advice over the Democratic ticket. "I'd go to Millie before I'd go to Ozone and Governor Clinton."

Baker, beside himself, blamed Rich Bond. "You goddamn little shit!" Baker said to Bond.

For his part, Baker didn't go on television to campaign or defend his friend and boss. Baker wanted to return to his post at the State Department if Bush were reelected. If he became part of the public Bush campaign, he argued, he would anger Democrats. Baker would need the Democrats in a future confirmation hearing. The key to a successful foreign policy was to get, and keep, the partisan rancor out. Bush had agreed that Baker shouldn't be the television spokesman for the campaign, but Baker seemed more focused on his future than the president's.

Iran-contra would not go away for Bush. Although on September 29 the judge in the Weinberger case dismissed a key obstruction charge, ruling the independent counsel had not shown that Weinberger corruptly worked with others, he demanded a proper reindictment within the next month.

Walsh himself had insisted on the obstruction count. He had hoped to try the case as an effort by Weinberger and others in the Reagan administration to hide and conceal an illegal operation. Walsh also had rejected his staff's advice that the indictment include charges of making false statements against Weinberger with direct quotes from Weinberger's notes. Walsh didn't want to be seen as piling on charges against Weinberger. "No, I'm not going to do it," he had said. Walsh was now in the doghouse with his deputies and staff, and he immediately approved a reindictment that was going to resurrect the false statement charges.

While Walsh stayed in Oklahoma, he had John Barrett, one of the prosecutors who had questioned President Reagan, help prepare a new Weinberger indictment in Washington. Since they were charging Weinberger with making false statements, Barrett included specific quotes from the notes. One Weinberger note recounted a January 7, 1986, meeting at which President Reagan approved a large sale of arms to Iran "in return" for hostages. Weinberger's notes stated that he and Secretary of State Shultz "opposed," and then the notes said of Bush, "VP favored."

On Wednesday, October 28, six days before the election, Barrett faxed a copy of the new indictment to Walsh in Oklahoma. It was hard to read, but Walsh got through it. He still didn't like the long quotes from the notes because they would have to read the damn thing to the jury at trial, and it didn't have a narrative flow. But he had gotten himself into trouble on the first indictment by opposing the staff. The next day, Walsh talked with Barrett by phone.

For five years Bush had denied that he was fully aware of the intensity and extent of the Weinberger-Shultz opposition, and had made general claims that he was "out of the loop."

"Nobody believes Bush when he says that," Walsh said. He didn't consider the reference that "VP favored" was a big deal. The congressional committees had long ago concluded that. Poindexter had testified about it publicly, and the Weinberger-Shultz opposition was all over the record despite Bush's denials.

"But this is a new note," Barrett said. "As long as you're okay with it."

"It's okay," Walsh said.

Stephen Ellis, 28, the youngest attorney on Walsh's staff, was disturbed about the timing of the reindictment just days before the presidential election. He approached Barrett.

"It would be a political bombshell," Ellis said, "a really big deal."

"Look, Steve," Barrett said, "you're new. We know this." The judge in the case and Weinberger's attorney had been pressing for the new indictment as soon as possible because the trial was scheduled for January 1993. They had promised the judge the new indictment by the end of the month, and the judge was showing no flexibility. "What would you have us do? Sit on it until after the election and then release it?"

Yes, Ellis said. If the judge complained they could explain the reasoning.

Barrett recommended that if Ellis had such serious reservations, he should go talk with James Brosnahan, a senior Walsh deputy who had just joined the staff to try the Weinberger case.

Ellis vividly recalled a long protest meeting with Brosnahan. Brosnahan does not recall the meeting. He was preparing for the case, trying to sort out the dozens of players and transactions. He asked Barrett whether they should include the Bush note.

Barrett had checked the Department of Justice guidelines on the question since the independent counsel's office was bound by them. The guidelines said prosecutors were not supposed to take political positions or political activities into account. They should not delay or expedite actions because of the political calendar.

Brosnahan called a meeting of the Weinberger prosecution team that included Ellis.

Ellis protested, saying they had to act and appear as if they had no political motivation.

Brosnahan said he read the guidelines to mean

311

that they should do what they would do in the ordinary course of business. Delay could be an improper political act. Suppose Bush won narrowly, and then they issued the reindictment with the notes? People might be furious that they had been deprived of this information. The promise to the judge should determine their course.

Ken Parsigian, another of Walsh's prosecutors, had read the draft indictment and thought the "VP favored" reference was a real problem. He was worried that the note could precipitate a dangerous reaction from the Bush White House, perhaps even a pardon for Weinberger. He didn't get anywhere with the Weinberger prosecution team, so he went down to the courthouse to see Craig Gillen, Walsh's deputy. Gillen had been the main prosecutor in the Weinberger case, but he had to withdraw because years before he had attended one of the meetings at which the defense secretary allegedly made false statements.

Parsigian asked Gillen to weigh in with Walsh, that the reference to Bush was not a necessary piece of evidence to convict Weinberger. They should convince Walsh to call a special meeting of all the staff to flush out the issue, Parsigian said.

Gillen agreed that the Bush footnote was a "nuclear bomb." But he said it wouldn't be fair to second-guess or undercut Brosnahan, who had replaced him as the lead attorney on the case.

Without Gillen's active support, Parsigian concluded he couldn't discuss the issue one-on-one with Walsh. He decided to drop the matter.

The polling showed that the race was narrowing. Gallup had it 41 percent for Clinton, 40 for Bush—a dead heat, too close to call. Other polls showed Bush further behind, but apparently he was in a last-minute surge.

Brosnahan called Walsh twice in Oklahoma. He was not inclined to give Bush a break, and there was no discussion about the concern that some lawyers in the office had expressed. Instead, he asked Walsh for his opinion.

Walsh said the substance in the new indictment was not new, it would not be newsworthy, despite the reference to Bush. He had no problem.

On Friday morning, October 30, the Bush campaign daily tracking poll had the race a dead heat at 39 percent for Clinton, 39 percent for Bush and 12 percent for Ross Perot, the outspoken Texas billionaire. That afternoon, Walsh's grand jury voted the new indictment of Weinberger and it was released. The first wire story came out about 1 p.m. The Friday before a Tuesday election normally begins one of the most sacred four-day news vacuums in American journalism. Most news organizations have a strong policy against publishing or airing new issues or charges in the final days of a campaign. News is usually a rehash or an account of the last campaign appearances by the candidates. But the Weinberger reindictment was an official grand jury action, and the "VP favored" was technically new. It was the first documented evidence that Bush had known the arms were a direct exchange for hostages and that Bush had been privy to the strong opposition of Weinberger and Shultz.

Gray was stupefied that Walsh would intrude in an election. It was one of the most outrageous public acts he had ever seen. Some people thought that Bush himself had actually been indicted, he realized.

George Stephanopoulos, the Clinton campaign spokesman, jumped on the issue: "It is never pretty to see a defense secretary question a commander in chief, but this is conclusive evidence once and for all that George Bush was as deep in the loop as you can get on Iran-contra. This is the smoking gun." Clinton's running mate, Albert Gore Jr., picked up the Watergate analogy, calling it "a true smoking gun."

In Oklahoma City, Walsh had worked well into the evening at his office and came home late.

"You were all over the news," his wife Mary said.

"What news?"

They turned on CNN's *Larry King Live* where Bush was appearing to insist that there was "nothing new."

Walsh thought Bush was taking a pasting. He seemed uncertain and hesitant, ducking the specific questions about his own conclusions and knowledge, still half-clinging to Reagan's defense. Almost as a reflex, Walsh considered calling the Bush campaign to help them outline a better defense. Bush should have noted that Attorney General Meese had been at the meeting in question, had favored the transaction and had deemed it legal. Walsh did not place the call. He found himself recalling Tolstoy's description of the role of luck in battle and unintended consequences at the turning points of history. Was it possible, Walsh wondered, that after nearly six years of battle, his most recent actions, which he considered incidental, might influence a presidential election?

Front-page stories ran almost everywhere. The *New York Times* headline read: " '86 Weinberger Notes Contradict Bush Account on Iran Arms Deal." *The Washington Post:* "Bush Stance, Iran-contra Note at Odds, Weinberger Memo Says President 'Favored' Arms-Hostage Plan."

Bush was on a campaign train in Wisconsin the next day, Saturday, October 31. His daily tracking poll was a shock. Clinton was still at 39 percent, but Bush had dropped 7 points to 32 percent, with the last 7 percentage points going straight to Perot, putting the Texas billionaire at 19. It happened to be Halloween. When Bush stopped in Chippewa Falls, a single-engine plane circled overhead with a fluttering banner streaking behind: IRAN-CONTRA HAUNTS YOU. The president nearly flew off his hinges.

"Today is Halloween, our opponents' favorite holiday," Bush declared to the crowd. "They're trying to scare America." If Clinton was elected, Bush said, "every day is going to be Halloween. Fright and terror!" In Oshkosh, the president shouted, "Fright and terror! Witches and devils everywhere!"

A radio reporter asked Bush what he thought about the large and enthusiastic crowds.

"Great!" Bush said. "I've only been mooned once!"

The next day, Sunday, November 1, Bush

appeared on CNN to be interviewed by Frank Sesno, who asked about the polls, which had several days earlier showed a narrowing of the gap. They now showed Clinton moving ahead.

"You don't live or die by an overnight poll, trick or treat, you know what I mean, last night," Bush replied.

Sesno pulled out a copy of a local Wisconsin newspaper and read the headline, "New Notes Confirm Bush Not Telling All on Iran Scandal."

"Who wrote the story there?" Bush asked, apparently hoping it was one of the Eastern newspaper reporters.

"The *LaCrosse Tribune,*" Sesno answered.

"Well, the headlines don't help," Bush said, "but I don't think people believe this. This is the same old charge that's been refuted...but it does seem a little weird on a Friday before an election that something like this is elevated."

"The polls consistently suggest that a majority of the American people don't believe you," Sesno said.

"Well, too bad," Bush said, "because I've told the full truth."

Sesno asked about Walsh. "If you're reelected, would you fire him?"

"I am not going to discuss what I'll do about that," Bush said.

When Sesno pressed on Iran-contra, Bush bristled. "I thought you might bring all this up and dwell on it." He later added, "I think most people concede that the media has been very unfair." The president returned to the news coverage again. "I think the press has been the worst it's ever been, ever!"

• • •

The Bush campaign tracking polls showed that Bush's chances of turning it around had evaporated. He was cranky, his vitality sapped. When Mary Matalin, a senior spokeswoman, handed him a sheet with some numbers, the president threw it across the table. "I don't want to see them anymore," he snapped. The news Friday night, Saturday and Sunday had largely been one version or another of Bush's Iran-contra role. The complexity of the scandal—arms shipments, the CIA, Lieutenant Colonel Oliver North, contra resupply, missiles, a strange blur of shady middlemen, Swiss bank accounts— had for years shielded Bush from providing a full accounting. Now the simplicity of an indictment and his own contradictions exposed him, probably unfairly.

On Monday, November 2, Nixon, in retirement in New Jersey, knew the outcome. He faxed Bush a copy of a letter that he had received 32 years earlier on election day 1960 when he had lost the presidency to John F. Kennedy. The letter was from Thomas E. Dewey, who had lost to Harry Truman in 1948. It read: "If you are defeated, pay no attention to the Monday morning quarterbacks. Everybody knows how to conduct a campaign better after the event. No one could have worked harder with higher fidelity to duty and integrity; no one could have done more for Party and Country. You have earned the best and the nation will always be in your debt."

On Tuesday, November 3, Clinton won the presidency with 43 percent to Bush's 38. Ross

Perot took 19 percent of the vote. The next day a defeated Bush returned from Houston to the White House, where he was greeted by more than 1,000 supporters, cabinet members and staff watching in a drizzle.

"Let's finish this job with style," the president said in brief remarks, standing without a coat on a platform on the South Lawn. As he walked into the White House, he spotted Attorney General William Barr in the crowd. With an index finger motion of "follow me," the president summoned Barr. The affable 42-year-old intellectual, conservative legal strategist stepped in behind Bush and walked with him up to the Oval Office.

Eighteen months earlier, Bush had elevated Barr from deputy attorney general to the top post at the Justice Department. Since the beginning of the Bush administration, when Barr had started out as head of the Office of Legal Counsel at Justice, he had worked assiduously to prevent further erosion of presidential power. Barr thought Watergate had hurt the presidency by causing cutbacks on executive privilege, increasing congressional micromanaging, generating more cynicism, and virtually forcing passage of the independent counsel law.

When they were alone in the Oval Office, Bush exploded about the Weinberger reindictment.

"It appears this was very political!" he bellowed, following up with a string of very pungent remarks. "Cost me the election," he said furiously. He felt he had been tricked. A pivotal event, he said, citing the polls and the loss of momentum. "What is your reaction?" he finally asked.

Barr said he thought it was a crude political act with a political motive. Career Justice Department prosecutors would never bring out such information in an indictment just before an election. Barr said he wanted to dismiss Walsh. He knew the law well. He could remove Walsh for "misconduct."

"Walsh has abused his power!" Bush said, inviting the attorney general to fire Walsh.

"I've had an itchy finger," Barr replied. During the last 18 months, he had been tempted. The most recent outrage only renewed his interest. He said he had asked himself, "What is the standard that applies to this guy?" He had consulted his most trusted and confidential advisers in the department. They worried that if Barr terminated Walsh, there would be a new firestorm. A firing would trigger a reaction like the Saturday Night Massacre. Since Walsh was appointed under the independent counsel law, Barr said, the courts would replace him with another person. The investigation would continue. They wouldn't be rid of the problem.

Neither man had to mention the obvious: a presidential pardon. They both knew that would be absolute, that it would be best for Weinberger and perhaps for Bush. Barr agreed to talk to Boyden Gray.

Jim Baker stayed put in Houston after Bush's defeat. The next day he appeared in the garage of the hotel where Bush had stayed, wearing his bird-shooting outfit. It was one of his favorite hobbies. He was going hunting in Texas and then vacationing at his ranch in Wyoming. "I'm not going to mind calling him George anymore," he confided to a top Republican. "I'm kind of tired of calling him Mr. President."

Walsh voted against Bush. He would have been glad to accept credit for his defeat because he felt Bush was covering up. But he didn't think he had ever effectively investigated Bush, who never seemed to have played a key role in Iran-contra. It was right that Bush had been defeated, Walsh believed, but he maintained that he felt bad about the role of his investigation and the Weinberger indictment.

Bush remained convinced that Walsh issued the indictment to influence the election. If not Walsh, it was at least some of the liberal Democrats who worked for him, Bush said.

"Walsh had that phony indictment come out just before the election," Bush told Fitzwater. "Probably cost me the election."

After the election, the flap over Clinton's passport became a major sore spot for Bush and his administration. It turned out that Elizabeth M. Tamposi, an assistant secretary of state, had led the pre-election search of Clinton's passport files. Tamposi had contacted Janet Mullins, the top White House political aide to Bush, and Baker, the chief of staff.

Secretary of State Lawrence Eagleburger, who had succeeded Baker, advised Bush that he was planning to fire Tamposi.

Bush told Eagleburger that he had to do it.

"WHITE HOUSE TIED TO PASSPORT SEARCH," said the *Washington Post* front-page story Monday, November 16, by Walter Pincus.

Bush dictated to his diary, "The Tamposi passport deal is raging....I talked to Jim Baker from Florida and he said, 'I don't want to talk to you about this at all,' and then when I got home last night he said he wanted an hour to discuss it." Bush then added, "It's a bizarre case and one that needs to be squashed."

Pincus had another story the next day on the *Post*'s front page. Bush dictated, "Indeed the whole discussion yesterday was dominated by this silly little incident regarding Betty Tamposi and the passport file. Walter Pincus is on the war path, and Jim Baker is very, very worried....He's worried that it's going to end up on his doorstep."

Baker's concern stemmed from his own conduct. At a meeting of his chief campaign aides on September 16, 1992, the aides had discussed a rumor that Clinton had actually written a letter renouncing his U.S. citizenship because of the Vietnam War. The Freedom of Information Act requests from the media for Clinton's files could turn up information that might be a major bombshell. Baker and his aides had wondered if there was a way to expedite the requests so any information would be released before the election.

Bush continued to complain to his diary about the media focus on what came to be called "Passportgate" and its failure to question the political motivation of the Weinberger reindictment just before the election. "The damn Post is hostile to a core—nasty to the core," Bush dictated November 19. "What difference does it make if Tamposi fouled up the passport system on Bill Clinton—it's nothing." Bush had sat and held his mother's hand for hours that morning in Greenwich, Connecticut, before she died. Her death put losing the presidency two weeks earlier and the scandals in perspective. Bush reflected, "It's immaterial when you think of Mother, love, faith, life and death."

The next day, Friday, November 20, about 10:30 a.m. Baker came to see Bush in the president's private study off the Oval Office. Baker was depressed about the passport matter. He told the president that his career was ending in embarrassment. "Who needs this?" Baker said. He did not want to tarnish the president. Baker then took out a long letter of resignation and read it aloud to Bush. The passport matter was a blot on himself, on the president, and on the entire administration, Baker said.

Bush saw that the magnitude of the loss of the presidency was taking an emotional toll on Baker. He told Baker where he could stick his resignation. He would not accept it. Get rid of the resignation letter, he directed. This was crazy and out of proportion. Baker was overly worried about perceptions and the news media and was torturing himself for no reason.

Five days later, Secretary of State Eagleburger came to see Bush. "He's really down," Bush dictated later. "He told me nothing had gotten to him more than this, all this damn *Washington Post* and their mean little approach and their investigations."

In December, Gray realized he was going to have to do something about Bush's diary, which he had been sitting on for several months. He called Bill Lytton.

"It turns out the president dictated some notes," Gray said, describing the extensive daily diary.

"You'd better get him a lawyer," Lytton said. "If I were you, I'd find a Democrat. Call Griffin Bell, you need him."

Bell, a former federal judge, had been Jimmy Carter's first attorney general. In all his time representing President Reagan, Lytton had never felt that Reagan needed a personal attorney. Now Bush did. "At this point you're not representing the office," Lytton told Gray. "Now the individual has a personal problem, and you've got to get counsel that focuses on that."

Gray was distressed but agreed and called Griffin Bell, who was hired to represent Bush.

Gray had one of his assistants, Paul Beach, call Walsh's office. Beach left a message for John Barrett. They exchanged several phone calls before hooking up on December 11.

"There's a document that may be responsive to the request that you said we could answer after the election," Beach said.

"Wait a second," Barrett replied. "The election thing was about the answer being no. If the answer is yes, that wasn't the deal." If they had something, Walsh wanted it right away.

Walsh sent some of his lawyers over to the White House to begin reading the diary. They saw instantly how politically damaging it was to Bush. They were furious. They interrogated Beach, who said he was not told by Gray about the diary until recently, that month, December. How was this possible?

Beach was uncomfortable, almost in tears, almost hyperventilating. "Boyden made a very difficult judgment call," Beach said, "and I'm not going to second-guess him."

Walsh was apoplectic. In one entry in the diary, Bush voiced astonishment that Shultz had turned over 200 pages of notes. Bush said he would never do that.

17

"THIS IS A LOAD of bullshit!" Attorney General Barr shouted to the attorneys from the public integrity section, which handled corruption investigations in the Justice Department. They were recommending that he seek an independent counsel in the passport case. The attorneys had developed the theory that even if the search of records of Clinton and his mother was conducted properly, it was theft if someone had a political motive. Under that notion, any legal action—the president signing a bill or going on a trip that had a political motive—could be subject to investigation, Barr said. "Bullshit," Barr declared again, "bullshit!"

He was about tapped out on the issue. He felt the independent counsel law was a travesty. "The independent counsel law prevents anyone from exercising common sense," he said. He was still going to try.

"Jim Baker is still all uptight about the passport mess and there is nothing else that he can think of," Bush dictated on December 9.

The next day, December 10, Barr's deputies again requested that he seek appointment of an independent counsel in Passportgate. They believed that Janet Mullins, the top Bush and Baker political aide, had lied. She had refused to be interviewed. Under the law, further investigation was warranted.

Barr asked the lawyers to send her a message. Tell her that the attorney general specifically and personally asked that she cooperate. Mullins refused.

The independent counsel law was due to expire on December 15, 1992, because Congress had placed an automatic sunset provision in the law. It had not been renewed, to the delight of Bush and Barr. All Barr had to do was ride out a few days and let the law lapse, which would render the Passportgate recommendation from his deputies moot. But he realized that if he did so he would be accused of a cover-up. It would smell and would make the matter worse for Bush, Baker, Mullins and himself. Someone was going to have to investigate. It would be better that the investigation not be conducted in an atmosphere permeated with suspicion and allegations of Justice Department or Bush administration cover-up. On December 11, Barr filed a secret request to the three-judge panel asking them to appoint an independent counsel.

Three days later, Joseph E. diGenova, the former U.S. attorney for the District of Columbia, took a call from Judge David B. Sentelle, head of the panel that appointed independent counsels.

DiGenova, 47, a tough-talking Republican, had extensive experience in Congress working as counsel for the Senate Judiciary and Intelligence Committees. As chief federal prosecutor, he had spent years investigating Washington, D.C., Mayor Marion Barry, only to have the next U.S. attorney make the case, catching Barry on videotape smoking crack cocaine.

Sentelle asked if diGenova was interested in being appointed independent counsel. The case involved the allegations that Bush White House political aide Janet Mullins had acted illegally in the State Department search of Bill Clinton's passport files.

DiGenova said he was interested.

Sentelle asked a series of questions about diGenova's political activities. Yes, diGenova said, he gave small amounts in political contributions to Republicans and a few Democrats.

Later, Sentelle hooked the other two judges on the panel into a conference call with diGenova.

Judge John D. Butzner Jr. said he had two questions for diGenova. "Do you have the guts to indict somebody no matter how powerful they are?"

"Yes, sir," diGenova replied.

"Do you have the guts not to indict somebody if the evidence doesn't support it?" Butzner asked.

"Yes, sir."

The next day, Bush dictated to his diary, "Jim Baker has lost all interest in what's going on at the White House. There isn't much for him to do and he's worried about this passport deal still. He's got a lawyer [former Carter White House counsel Lloyd Cutler], and the lawyer tells him that they can't find anything that he could even be charged with and that it's most unlikely a special prosecutor will be appointed. He seems somewhat relieved but still totally preoccupied." Bush noted that Baker was working with him on some speeches. "But his heart isn't in any of that. It's just gone. He wanted to leave but doesn't feel he can as long as this passport is beeping along out there."

The passport independent counsel was announced. "Baker is a nervous wreck," Bush dictated December 17.

Bush met with Gray, who told him diGenova was a fair person. Barr probably felt that he could not stand up to all the pressures from the career people at Justice, Gray speculated. He said he couldn't talk to Barr and get answers. Gray had a potential conflict of interest because Baker's lawyer, Lloyd Cutler, was Gray's former law partner.

The next day Bush noted, "It's ruining Jim Baker's life. Of all the clean honorable decent guys to have his Christmas ruined by this guy, it's too bad."

Bush arranged to have a meeting with Gray and Barr. He said he had decided—"no ifs, ands or buts"—that he was going to pardon Weinberger.

"You have outrageous behavior by Walsh," Barr agreed. The Weinberger prosecution was a deep injustice. If the president was going to pardon Weinberger, Barr said, he might as well pardon the others. He recommended pardons for Weinberger, former CIA officials and the former State Department assistant secretary Elliott Abrams, who had been pressured to plead guilty in the Walsh investigation. "In for a penny, in for a pound," he said.

Barr could see the same determination and fury that Bush displayed when Iraqi President Saddam Hussein invaded Kuwait the previous year. Then Bush had told the nation on the White House lawn in one of his more memorable moments as president, "This will not stand." Now Bush was saying Walsh would not stand. The president seemed to like the idea of pardoning the others, too. If he pardoned only Weinberger, he would invite charges that he was protecting himself from a trial where his diary and possible personal testimony might be required. Extending the pardons to others might help shield the president from that charge. It would stick it to Walsh more completely.

Bush read Mary McGrory's *Washington Post* column on December 22. Headlined "Missing and Presumed Injured," McGrory quoted Republicans as saying Baker had virtually dropped out. The passport flap had hurt Baker's reputation and his own aspiration to be president some day, she wrote, tainting him with a Republican dirty trick and a failure to properly manage the campaign.

"An ugly editorial by Mary McGrory," Bush confided to his diary, although Bush knew it was basically true that Baker had withdrawn, "and it will have Jim Baker climbing the wall....I feel sorry for Jim Baker. Mary McGrory tries to act like Barbara and I are opposed to him in some way—the meanest, nastiest, ugliest column. She has destroyed me over and over again and Jim is so sensitive about his own coverage that he will be really upset."

Walsh was determined to proceed with the Weinberger trial. He approved an expenditure of $52,600 for Brosnahan to conduct a mock trial before 36 citizens who were paid to act as jurors. After the presentation of the prosecution and defense cases, the 36 people were divided into three separate juries. Two of the mock juries found Weinberger guilty on all four counts; the other found him guilty on three of the counts. The story leaked, unleashing a fresh attack on Walsh. Many Republicans were now publicly urging President Bush, who would be leaving office in January, to exercise his constitutional power to pardon Weinberger.

Bob Bennett, Weinberger's attorney, told Gray his client's trial could be embarrassing for Bush, who might be called as a witness.

Gray said he was exploring the pardon option.

"What can I do?" Bennett asked.

"Get some Democratic cover," Gray said, "and I've got to be convinced it's a one- or two-day story."

Among others, Bennett recruited House Speaker Tom Foley, the Washington State Democrat, to phone Gray pledging his support for a Weinberger pardon. Bennett also enlisted Senators Daniel Inouye, a Democrat from Hawaii, and Warren Rudman, who headed the Senate Iran-contra probe, to write a letter of support. Bennett wanted to have anyone in touch with Bush, down to the janitor changing a light bulb in the Oval Office, lobbying for a Weinberger pardon.

Bush had some reservations. On Tuesday, December 22, he dictated into his diary, "The pardon of Weinberger will put a tarnish, kind of a downer, on our legacy."

Before going to Camp David that Christmas weekend, where he planned to make the final decision on pardons, Bush was in the Oval Office closing the briefcase on his desk.

"Okay, Marlin," Bush asked Fitzwater. "What's your final recommendation?"

"Pardon all of them."

Why? the president asked.

"In my view the Weinberger indictment, whether it's legitimate or not in terms of what he did," Fitzwater answered, "shows that Walsh has become vindictive." Weinberger objected to all the arms sales. "Now he's the last victim. I think it's just gone on long enough and my advice is just put a stop to it."

Gray was strongly in favor of pardons. It would end the Walsh investigation. He had his deputies call around to the lawyers for other convicted Iran-contra figures to see if they would accept pardons. Four did: two CIA officers, Elliott Abrams, and former national security adviser Bud McFarlane. Gray helped draft a three-page executive order explaining the reasoning. Bush signed it on Christmas Eve, December 24, 1992.

Concerning Weinberger, Bush said, "I am pardoning him not just out of compassion or to spare a 75-year-old patriot the torment of a lengthy and costly legal proceeding, but to make it possible for him to receive the honor he deserved." Anticipating a strong reaction from Walsh, Bush added, "Some may argue that this will prevent full disclosure of some new key facts to the American people. That is not true. The matter has been investigated exhaustively."

Bush said, "All five have already paid a price—in depleted savings, lost careers, anguished families—grossly disproportionate to any misdeeds or errors of judgment they may have committed.

"In recent years, the use of criminal processes in policy disputes has become all too common.

"Now the Cold War is over. When earlier wars have ended, presidents have historically used their power to pardon, to put bitterness behind us and to look to the future."

At midafternoon, Gray called Walsh's office and reached one of the assistant prosecutors, Kenneth Parsigian.

"I *must* speak with Judge Walsh," Gray said.

The newspapers had carried stories about possible pardons and Parsigian realized what the call meant. He muffled the telephone to his chest and screamed, *"Fuck!"* He connected Gray with Walsh in Oklahoma.

Half-laughing, Gray said he understood no one had informed Walsh of the pardons.

Walsh thought it was just dirty. Bush had decapitated his investigation. Furious, he called a press conference in Oklahoma City. Breaking a gentleman's agreement with Bush's lawyers, Walsh stepped in front of the cameras and revealed for the first time that Bush had concealed his own diary for five years. "The production of these notes is still ongoing and will lead to appropriate action. In the light of President Bush's own misconduct, we are gravely concerned by his decision to pardon others." Walsh said Ford's pardon of Nixon stood in stark contrast. That was an act of statesmanship. Nixon had not been indicted and was not ten days away from trial.

Walsh justified the Weinberger prosecution and said the delay in obtaining Weinberger's notes "forestalled a timely impeachment of President Reagan."

Later, Walsh made a Christmas Eve appearance on PBS's *MacNeil/Lehrer NewsHour.* Was it possible that Bush would be prosecuted?

"I could not comment on that," Walsh said. "He's a subject now of our investigation."

Did Walsh think this pardon was part of a continued cover-up by Bush himself?

"I think it's the last card in the cover-up," Walsh said. "He's played the final card."

On ABC's *Nightline* that same evening, Walsh wanted to hurt Bush. He said, "He has shown an arrogant disdain for the rule of law."

Two days later, Bush asked Griffin Bell's law firm, King & Spaulding, to investigate whether there was "misconduct" as Walsh had alleged in Bush's failure to turn over his diary earlier. From now on he would do his own investigating.

Bush found no joy in the final days of his presidency. "Having it end up on this note—" he dictated December 29, "is absolutely sickening. I can understand why Jim Baker feels as he does on that awful little passport pimple, but that's the ugliness of it all."

On January 15, 1993, King & Spaulding issued a 14-page report on the Bush diary. Bush's self-investigation cleared him and anyone else of any misconduct. In three weeks Bell's lawyers had interviewed all the relevant participants—a clear contrast to the sprawling seven-year Walsh probe. Walsh was at fault, not Bush, the report said, because of "the overly broad personal document request." The real problem was that Walsh had not subpoenaed Bush for documents, which would have allowed Walsh to allege concealment or obstruction. Instead, Walsh had been so anxious to get documents from the Reagan White House that he agreed in 1987 to make informal "documents requests" as Reagan's lawyers Culvahouse and Lytton had proposed.

Walsh had no leverage. The wheels had come off his investigation, and now Bush was trying to preempt him. Walsh called a meeting of the ten attorneys who remained in his office on April 1. Poised and dignified, he explained that he wanted to take Bush's sworn deposition and, if necessary, issue a grand jury subpoena.

One by one the attorneys sitting around the table offered strong objections. Attempting to prosecute Bush would look like retaliation. The president wouldn't remember anything anyway. No indictable offenses were likely to come out of it. Another investigation could take years and cost millions of dollars. The you-can't-do-this chorus echoed around the room, a sense of defeat casting a pall over the discussions. The staff attorneys were unanimous.

"I know everybody's tired," Walsh said, "tired of taking a beating, but I'm not going to make a precipitous decision. I have a job to do and I'm going to do it."

Walsh was still angry about the pardons, and he wasn't about to shut down because his attorneys were demoralized. He felt he had a duty to interview Bush and find out what he knew. Walsh said the attorneys had made strong arguments. "But don't I have an obligation to close this last loop?" he asked.

The attorneys were insistent. There were no more criminal cases to make. It was time to call it quits.

Walsh left without making up his mind. Distrusting decisions based on talk, he asked Parsigian, who had opposed including the Bush note in the Weinberger reindictment, to write a memo explaining the pros and cons of using a grand jury to question Bush. Parsigian saw that Walsh was put off by some of the arguments made at the staff meeting. He decided to use a gentler approach in his memo. Walsh could legally and ethically bring Bush before the grand jury, he wrote, but there were practical reasons why he shouldn't. "You are probably right that some people would accuse you of not fully completing your task," his April 2 memo to Walsh said, "but they would be an extreme minority. I do not believe that your mandate requires you to lift every possible rock and investigate it in every possible way. Given the timing, the incredibly low probability of getting Bush in the grand jury and getting anything useful if we do, the expense, and the current lack of interest in our investigation, I think it would be a proper exercise of your prosecutorial judgment to terminate the investigation."

Walsh read the memo and thanked Parsigian for his thoroughness.

The same day, two of his other attorneys sent Walsh a memo on the factual findings of their investigation of Bush's diaries. The prosecutors concluded that what they learned was largely consistent with the King & Spaulding report two and a half months before. But their findings differed with Bush's attorneys in one important aspect. Bush's lawyers had written that he had no recollection of reviewing any document requests. "To the contrary," the independent counsel lawyers wrote, "our investigation has revealed substantial evidence that a copy of the March 1987 document request was received by Vice President Bush and that the requirements of the request, including the demand for personal materials and documents, were communicated to Bush by his Counsel, C. Boyden Gray.

"Whether or not Bush actually reviewed the document request, the evidence strongly suggests that he understood the request encompassed personal notes and diaries."

Despite this conclusion, Walsh could not act. The original 1987 documents requests to Bush had been voluntary, so there was no criminal case. Walsh concluded he had made a mistake in not issuing a subpoena. But faced with the unified opposition from his own staff, Walsh, a proud fighter, finally gave up.

He took another six months to finish his final report. On January 18, 1994, the courts released his findings to the public. Still stately in appearance and manner, Walsh faced the press for the final time as independent counsel. "I think President Bush will always have to answer for his pardons," Walsh said. "There was no public purpose served by that." He could barely conceal his disdain for Bush. "President Reagan, on the other hand, was carrying out policies that he strongly believed in. He may have been willful, but he, at least he thought he was serving the country in what he did, and the fact that he disregarded certain laws and statutes in the course of it was not because of any possibly self-centered purpose."

Passportgate still lingered on for Bush. DiGenova had set up a team of five lawyers and nine FBI agents to investigate. He went to Houston to interview former President Bush.

"Oh by the way there's a little problem," Griffin Bell, Bush's attorney, said when diGenova arrived.

"What's that?"

"We have discovered some documents which have not been produced pursuant to your subpoena," Bell explained.

"What are those?"

"It's the president's diary."

DiGenova said he didn't know any of Bush's diary entries related to Passportgate.

Bell explained that they consisted of brief recollections, sometimes non-sentences, little phrases and descriptions of his feelings. They were just laden with remarks about Passportgate, filled with recollections of conversations with various people, including Jim Baker and a host of others.

"Is there any reason why these weren't produced?" diGenova asked.

"Well," said J. Sedgwick Sollers III, the other attorney working with Bell, "we're not even sure they're covered by the subpoena." They had just found the information two days earlier.

"You're not going to suggest to me that these are not covered by the subpoena that this office issued?" diGenova said, virtually shouting.

Sollers tried to raise a technical objection, perhaps there was a privilege.

DiGenova, hot by nature, went ballistic. "We can settle this in one of two ways!" he screamed. "I can issue another subpoena and then it becomes part of the final report that this case has been over-lawyered. Or you can just get out of everybody's way and let's get on with this." DiGenova said there was no way that Bush could claim executive privilege or attorney-client privilege. "He's talking to himself, for Christ's sake! He's not talking to somebody else and nobody's talking to him."

"Ah think we can work this out," Bell finally said in his deep Southern accent.

"We can do two things," diGenova said. "We can interview the president or we can go home." Upon reflection, diGenova said, "We're going to go home as a courtesy to him. We're not going to sit around here and ask questions because I'm not going to waste his time." DiGenova said he was not going to interview a witness without having looked at the documents relevant to his testimony.

DiGenova turned to Sollers. "There is nothing worse in this world than young lawyers over-lawyering and that's what you're doing on behalf of your client. Listen to Judge Bell and let's get on with this. We don't have to decide this today but don't embarrass the president and don't embarrass yourself. Just let us look at the documents." Then diGenova delivered the important news. The former president was a witness, not a target of the investigation. "Let's get on with this, we don't have to litigate this question, just give me the damn documents." The potentially relevant portions of diaries were eventually transcribed and copies were given to diGenova.

He pored over them. The most intriguing discovery was that Baker, in near despair, had offered to resign over the issue. DiGenova had already interviewed Baker, who made no such disclosure.

DiGenova spoke with Baker's lawyer, Lloyd Cutler.

"Surely you don't suggest?" Cutler said, taking offense that something might have been deliberately concealed.

"Yeah," diGenova said, "I do suggest. We're going to talk to him again, and this time I want it all. You guys are being dumb, you're over-lawyering. I am not a marauding prosecutor, I'm

338

not out to make a name for myself. I already have one. I don't need this case, and neither do you. You can either cause your client trouble or you can help me find out the truth, and then we'll end this matter." DiGenova said he wanted to be candid since he had spent months investigating already. "We all know that if there was a crime committed here, it isn't worth very much."

Cutler agreed completely.

"I'm telling you where I'm going," diGenova continued. "I don't think a crime's been committed, but if one had been it may not be a crime that's worth prosecuting. Everybody needs to think about that before they start lying and forgetting and losing documents."

Cutler promised cooperation. Baker was interviewed again. He said he didn't think his offer to resign was important.

DiGenova realized that rarely had the stakes been so low and the anger so high. He passed the same assurances to Bush's attorneys that he wasn't after anyone.

On October 28, 1993, diGenova went to Houston to interview Bush. FBI special agent Laura M. Laughlin filed a 13-page 302 report on the interview.

Bush was gracious. DiGenova thought that the former president discussed the 1992 presidential campaign as if somebody else had been running. The way Bush talked it was almost as if the campaign had been a remote, out-of-body experience. There was a race for the presidency and somehow he was involved. Bush actually said he did not need to ask "permission" from the campaign people to bring up Clinton's character. But the media had decided that character wasn't important, Bush said, because the media were Clinton's peers and agreed with Clinton that the Vietnam War was morally wrong. Bush said he followed the media because he lived and died by these reports, including the ones about the passport matter. These articles drove politics, he said.

At one point Bush said he was indignant that his campaign people did not find out what Clinton was doing when he traveled abroad as a student. Bush also showed how angry he was about the independent counsel law. He was especially incensed at the FBI. During the campaign, the bureau had tried to pull one of their famous undercover sting operations on Bush's Texas campaign chairman, James Oberwetter, who was a friend of his son, George W. Bush. After complaining that the Republicans had bugged his office, Ross Perot had given the bureau a recording of his own voice. An undercover agent had then called Oberwetter and said he had tapes of Perot's conversations. Oberwetter met the agent outside his office, quickly realized he was being set up and turned down the offer. When he learned what the FBI had done, Bush was as angry as his advisers had seen him in 12 years.

Recalling this affair for diGenova, Bush said bitterly that Perot was a "bastard" and "very dangerous." The former president said he would never forgive the FBI. "I always defended the FBI, but not anymore," he said.

It took three years before diGenova completed his investigation. He decided to bring no charges. He released his report in December 1995. In all, they had interviewed 147 witnesses, examined more than 60,000 pages of documents and analyzed the hard drives of some 200 White House computers. The cost was put at $2.2 million.

Bush administration officials had been "stupid, dumb and partisan," diGenova said, but he had found no crimes. Those subjected to the process were due an apology, he said.

But diGenova realized that given the concealments and dodges and attempts at being too cute, he could have made a criminal case somewhere against someone. It would have been a nasty and injudicious use of the federal criminal law in his opinion, but he had seen firsthand the all too powerful weapon in the hands of an independent counsel.

In early 1998, I talked with Jean Becker, Bush's chief of staff who had been a newspaper reporter, about interviewing the former president for this book. She suggested that I write Bush a letter, explaining as precisely as possible what I was attempting to do.

I sent the letter January 27, 1998, just as the Clinton-Lewinsky scandal was breaking. Three weeks later I received a three-page "Dear Bob" letter from Bush, dated February 12. It was in an envelope with only his post office box number as a return address. PERSONAL was written over the back seal, apparently in his hand, with two pieces of Scotch tape over the seal.

President Bush wrote: "I know that you and my trusted Jean Becker have been going back and forth, trading calls, chatting. Now I have your letter of January 27th. Let me be very frank—I am disinclined to have the conversation that you suggest. There are several reasons for this position.

"First, I do not think you and I had a very pleasant relationship."

We in fact had no relationship. Bush had declined numerous requests I made to interview him throughout more than two decades. I was not surprised that he had never agreed to be interviewed by me, since I was looking for behind-the-scenes accounts of decision making—a style of reporting he disliked. I also felt that if he had agreed to be interviewed, he would not be particularly helpful. But I did want to give him a chance to respond and to add whatever he chose. He no doubt knew that I talked to many of his senior aides and cabinet members.

Bush continued in his letter, "You were the aggressive investigative reporter, I the office holder who knew that his every move, his every experience in business, or personal life or politics no matter how long ago would come under intrusive scrutiny. In the old days this would not have influenced me. That aggressive adversarial relationship went with the territory. Today, happily retired and trying to stay away from the Beltway media, it does influence me.

"Back then experts would tell me, 'You better talk to him/her, they'll write the story anyway and you better get your side of it told accurately.' But now at 73 and having been through some ups and downs with the Washington press I am inclined to stay out of the story, out of the interview business. Instead I favor letting the writers themselves make the call, letting the chips fall where they may without my spin.

"Perhaps I am being unduly influenced by today's frenzy, a frenzy of sleaze and alleged tawdry behavior, but for me my reluctance is far deeper than that.

"When I read books by today's new school journalists I see my name in direct quotes, words in my mouth I never uttered. I talked to our publisher at Knopf about this method. 'Literary License,' says he. But I don't like it.

"Watergate was your watershed. For you it was an earthshaking event that made you....For me Watergate was a major event, for as you correctly point out, I was chairman of the GOP during those tumultuous times. I am sure I learned from Watergate, but it did not have the major effect that your letter seems to imply. Watergate had absolutely nothing to do with how I conducted myself during the Iraqi crisis."

(In my letter to Bush, I had said that I thought Watergate had taught him an important lesson, namely, to narrow the gap between his statements and actions. In other words, to speak as close to the truth as possible, and I wrote he had done that in his public statement about Iraq's invasion of Kuwait: "This will not stand.")

Bush continued, "I think Watergate and the Vietnam War are the two things that moved Beltway journalism into this aggressive, intrusive, 'take no prisoners' kind of reporting that I can now say I find offensive.

"The new young cynical breed wants to emulate you. But many of them to do that question the word and the integrity of all in politics. It is almost like their code is 'You are guilty until proved innocent.' I gave a speech on the media in New York last fall and that is all I think I should say on the subject.

"Having said the above the bottom line is I really don't want to get into any of this with any reporter or writer any more than I want to discuss the current scandal about which I would inevitably be asked to comment.

"Another reason for 'just saying no' is that I do not want to try to direct history. I am not writing a memoir. With Brent [Scowcroft] I have co-authored a book on several significant changes that took place in the world when I was president. Incidentally some of what we have written will agree with what you have written in *The Commanders*—some will not.

"Barbara's memoir gave our family history and did it well. That's enough for me now. Oh there may be a handful of additional interviews, but if they re-live ancient history and reopen old wounds I'm sorry but I want no part of it.

"I told the truth on Iran-contra, but I have been plagued by a press determination to prove otherwise. I listen to revisionistic leftists flail away against our action in Panama. I see respected columnists constantly criticize me for not 'getting' Saddam Hussein, going in, finding him, killing him. They, of course, are free to do their thing; and I am free to do mine. Mine is to stay the hell out of Dodge and do as the old Chinese mandarin adage says 'Stand on sidelines hands in sleeves.'

"I hope you do not find this letter personally offensive. Out of office now, away from Washington, out of national politics I have a freedom now that I treasure. I am turned off by what you appropriately call a 'climate of scandal and mistrust.' I am deeply offended by much of what I read, having tried to show respect for the offices I was proud to hold. But I know that comments by me would not help change things, indeed would probably be seen as piling on by a poor loser. So, Bob, we better leave things as they are.

"I suppose it might have a ring of hypocrisy if I, unwilling to pitch in, wish you well on your new project; but I do."

The letter was signed "Sincerely, George Bush."

I recognized the voice from Bush's diaries. Bush's political skills were interpersonal—the chummy heads of state club he managed so well and loved even more. Struggle, name-calling, digging into a motivation or person's life deeply offended him. He generally didn't make noise or protest. He had built his career as the patron of other Republican presidents, turning setbacks into opportunities. Nixon had rescued him from defeat in 1970, after he had lost the Texas Senate race, appointing him United Nations Ambassador. Ford had made him director of central intelligence, his first major executive post and one with mystique. Reagan had selected him to be vice president after he had lost the nomination.

Bush had played by the accepted rules of

the Republican Party and gentlemanly restraint had served him well. But the same qualities that had helped Bush reach the presidency hurt him once he became president. He had not acquired the political skills that many politicians develop through struggle and adversity. As a new president, he was not as well equipped as he should have been to handle the inevitable scandals. The investigations and conflicts were distasteful to him. The controversies almost dazed him. In the presidency and the years afterwards, he never seemed to reach a state of peace, relaxation or happiness. He stayed the hell out of Dodge, but the emotional inner life of his presidency was at times consumed with anger and private warfare with the various inheritances left by Watergate.

I sent Bush one more request for an interview, but then I backed off entirely. The First Amendment includes a right not to speak.

PART FIVE

BILL CLINTON

1993–

18

Bernie Nussbaum, a slightly built, well-dressed New York lawyer with intense eyes, flew on January 8, 1993, to Little Rock. He was a tightly wound individual, a bit jumpy. Well organized and spectacularly self-involved, Nussbaum was one of the veterans and masters of the corporate takeover wars.

Many men and women were taking the flights to the town of 132,000 on the Arkansas River as power in a new national government was being divided up. Nussbaum, at 56, was set to have a key place. He believed he was ready, at his prime. He had the perfect résumé to become the chief lawyer to the president of the United States, the counsel in the White House. Two decades earlier he had managed the staff of the House Judiciary Committee during the Nixon impeachment investigation. He understood Watergate as few others. He had been among the first to clamp on headphones to listen to the Watergate tapes as Nixon destroyed himself. Watergate, the great swamp, was not only a failure of character and morality, in Nussbaum's view, but a failure of lawyering. From Nixon's naive, young and criminal White House counsel John W. Dean III to the legal team during the final days, not one lawyer had been able to get hold of and manage the corrosive forces in the Nixon White House—paranoia and hate.

Nussbaum had special status. In 1974, one of the compilers of information on the House Judiciary Committee staff had been a young, fragile-looking female attorney, Hillary Rodham, now in 12 days to become the first lady. He didn't remember exactly what Hillary's role had been in the Nixon case—something about reviewing and summarizing information. She was one of dozens who did the scut work. But she did her job well, with a Yale Law School graduate intensity. He had found out that she was anything but fragile. Nussbaum had assumed the role of mentor to Rodham. For many years he had provided occasional advice, another New York contact, and fund-raising as Hillary's husband shot improbably through 1992 to victory.

Nussbaum went straight to the Governor's Mansion and met with Hillary. Reality checks had long been one of Hillary's assignments in Arkansas, but she would need help in Washington.

They walked downstairs to the basement of the mansion to see Clinton. It was a kind of family room, scene of many important meetings and encounters throughout a dozen years. It was hard for Nussbaum to believe that Clinton, just 46 and so youthful in appearance and manner, was about to become president.

"Tell him your notion of the job of White House counsel," Hillary said.

"We've had experience with the last four or five presidents," said Nussbaum, who was almost a decade older than the president-elect. "Small problems which can be handled properly and should be handled properly mushroom into huge political problems." He cited the Bert Lance problem for Carter in the 1970s and the Iran-contra scandal of the 1980s for Reagan and Bush. "It seems that every president since Nixon has had their problems—this theme of legal problems becoming huge political problems that debilitate the president."

Clinton, who had followed the ups and downs of each presidency like a child charting the baseball box scores waiting for his turn at the record books, nodded comfortably.

"My job will be to look out for these things so they don't explode," Nussbaum said. Legal brush fires would flare, and his job would be to contain them. He would provide early warning.

"I understand," Clinton said. "I'm looking for you to be my lawyer, and I'm looking for you to keep me out of trouble." It wasn't just law or politics—it was trouble whatever its origin. He knew enough history. There was no forecasting trouble, but a good lawyer could help.

Neither the Clintons nor Nussbaum had any need to mention Watergate and its lessons. Watergate was ingrained in them all, Nussbaum felt. They had experienced it, lived it, watched the Nixon presidency fall with a sense of relish, even vindication. There was an immediate sense of how great things, a presidency even, could falter on what, at first, seemed small.

Nussbaum went to the Justice Department to meet with President Bush's attorney general, William Barr.

"We killed the independent counsel statute,"

Barr said. "Take my advice, don't breathe new life into it. As a Republican, I'd love to see you live under it, but as an American, I can tell you it would be bad news if you get that thing going again."

Barr said it was a terrible law that made it impossible for the executive branch to function at times. He advised that the new Democratic administration should let the Republicans take the hit for killing it.

The Saturday night of January 16, Clinton, Hillary and their daughter, Chelsea, flew out of Little Rock to begin a week of inauguration festivities. The next day, they boarded a bus with the license plate "Hope 1" for a last exultant bus tour, this time tracking Thomas Jefferson's 1801 inaugural ride from Monticello to the capital.

Three days later, the opening day of the Clinton presidency—January 20, 1993—Nussbaum was summoned from lunch to the Oval Office to deal with the first small crisis.

"We have got a problem with Zoë Baird," the president said. Baird, Clinton's nominee for attorney general, had failed to pay Social Security taxes for her nanny until after she had been nominated. Even Democrats in the Senate, which would have to confirm her appointment, were leery. The chief law enforcement officer of the nation couldn't be confirmed if she had broken the law, Clinton said.

"She'll have to defend herself," Nussbaum said.

George Stephanopoulos, Clinton's young

communications aide, said it was serious, that her nomination might have to be pulled.

"Let me tell you guys," Nussbaum said, working himself up, "remember what happened with Jimmy Carter? He pulled the nomination of Ted Sorensen for the CIA and that gave an impression of weakness."

No, Stephanopoulos said, that had been a political fight; the Zoë Baird problem was about the ethics of the nominee for the top law enforcement officer in the administration. They would make a mockery of themselves after proclaiming that the administration was going to have the highest ethical standards, insisting that the Reagan and Bush standards had not been sufficient.

"When you abandon your people," Nussbaum insisted, "you send a message that you can be rolled."

Six hours later, Clinton concluded that the appointment was too politically damaging and pulled Baird's nomination. By the end of the day, Nussbaum felt weaker. He knew Hillary could be tough, but he wondered about the president. Toughness was part of the job. Strength grew from acting strong, sticking with decisions.

During the next months, Nussbaum watched as variations of the theme of weakness played out. Clinton had wanted his close friend and Yale Law School classmate Lani Guinier, a striking black law professor, to head the civil rights unit of the Justice Department. When her academic writings became a source of controversy, Nussbaum told the president he should stand firmly behind her. Clinton bailed out again. A long Senate fight would be futile, he told Guinier. He pulled the nomination, and many on the White House staff blamed Nussbaum for having failed to read and understand Guinier's published work. Nussbaum figured that it was part of his job to take the hit.

That spring seven members of the White House Travel Office were fired after independent auditors at Peat Marwick, an accounting firm, found "gross mismanagement." The small office arranged for hundreds of members of the media to accompany Clinton on trips. Billy Dale, the head of the office, was dismissed for depositing $68,000 in news media money into his personal account. The business was going to be transferred to a distant cousin of the president's and to a Little Rock travel agency.

The White House brought in the FBI to investigate the Dale operation. Initially the FBI planned to issue a statement saying simply the White House was going to forward to the bureau the audit report on the travel office. At a meeting with Nussbaum, Stephanopoulos and others at the White House, John Collingwood, the senior press spokesman for the FBI, agreed to alter the proposed FBI statement. The new statement said "additional criminal investigation is warranted." It was a technical violation of FBI procedures to announce a criminal investigation, and it left the strong impression that the bureau was being used for political purposes to cover a hasty or nepotistic decision at the White House.

Behind the scenes, Mrs. Clinton had voiced unusual interest in the travel office situation, which gave the issue added significance. The White House didn't have, or was unwilling to provide, detailed answers to reporters. Instead, an internal White House investigation was launched. The president and White House chief of staff Thomas F. "Mack" McLarty, Clinton's childhood friend and former chief executive of a natural gas company, Arkla Inc., told Nussbaum that since the counsel's office had been involved in the initial review, Nussbaum had a conflict and couldn't participate in the internal inquiry. Nussbaum realized that to make the White House self-investigation credible, the report would go overboard and criticize White House officials.

"This is nuts to reprimand our own people," Nussbaum told the president. It was damage control designed to satisfy the news media. "We'll wind up feeding the beast, the press."

Clinton disagreed. A critical, no-holds-barred report would show they were trying to get to the bottom of the affair. It would show they were acting in good faith.

Nussbaum saw a copy of the first draft of the report on the self-investigation. William Kennedy, a lawyer in the counsel's office and former Little Rock Rose Law Firm partner of Hillary's, was reprimanded for actions that "risked creating the perception" that the White House had improperly pressured the FBI to investigate. Nussbaum thought the report was absurd. Kennedy worked for him and the deputy counsel, Vince Foster. Foster, also a Rose partner, was exceptionally close to Hillary. He was a handsome, quiet lawyer whom the Clintons had imposed on Nussbaum as deputy. Nussbaum had grown to like and respect Foster. In the counsel's office the main work was divided so that Nussbaum handled the president and the main White House issues, and Foster handled the Hillary account.

At their first meeting in early 1993, Nussbaum and Foster had agreed to do informal background checks on each other.

"What's the worst thing they can say about you?" Nussbaum inquired.

"People claim I had an affair with Hillary," Foster said.

"Is it true?" Nussbaum asked.

"No, it's not true."

After stewing over the first draft of the travel office report for a few moments, Nussbaum burst into chief of staff Mack McLarty's office in a corner of the West Wing.

"I demand that you reprimand me and Vince Foster," he said. If one of their subordinates was to be censured, it was only reasonable and brave that the bosses take criticism also.

"Do you really think so?" McLarty asked.

"Yes."

"Okay," the chief of staff replied. It would be done.

Nussbaum went to see Foster.

"I just did a good thing," he reported. "They were going to reprimand Bill Kennedy, but now you and I are going to be reprimanded."

Foster gave him a faint, wan smile.

Two hours later, Foster came to see Nussbaum. The president and McLarty had overruled him. "They're not going to reprimand us. They decided we're too high up."

In early July the White House report on the travel office was released, criticizing staff management. Although Foster was not formally reprimanded and Hillary barely mentioned, Foster took it badly. He stopped functioning. On one occasion, Nussbaum told Foster to take a vacation and on another to go home and rest. Foster wanted to hire lawyers. He was worried that Hillary was going to be dragged in further, that she would be attacked and smeared. Nussbaum thought Foster was acting as if he were Hillary's shield.

On July 20, Foster was found shot to death in Fort Marcy Park in suburban Virginia. From all indications it was a suicide. Clinton called his mother, Virginia Kelley, in Arkansas to tell her. He was crying. She wept also. What a waste. How did it make sense? What a price to pay. Both remembered Vince from Bill's kindergarten class.

"Every man has his breaking point," Kelley told her son. "We just don't know where it is."

Hillary was also depressed and angry—a common reaction for someone close to a suicide victim.

"How could he have done this?" Hillary asked Nussbaum. "Why didn't he tell us? We could have helped him." In retrospect, the signs of withdrawal and overreaction had been there. "We could have known," she added. "We should have known."

It was Nussbaum who oversaw the search of Foster's office. He kept the FBI and the Justice Department at arm's length, refused them unfettered access, did it his way. It was not a crime scene, and attorney-client privilege protected many of Foster's documents.

Phil Heymann, the deputy attorney general, was angry that the FBI had been excluded from the search. "How could you have misused me this way?" Heymann said in a tense after-hours call to Nussbaum. "Bernie, are you hiding something? Is there some horrible secret here that you're hiding?"

Nussbaum insisted absolutely not.

But the suspicions of the administration's deputy attorney general added to a sense of siege.

Nussbaum sent some Foster documents he deemed personal to the White House residence. Included were small files relating to a personal land deal the Clintons had made 15 years ago in Arkansas. Whitewater was a sprawling 230-acre tract on the White River in the Arkansas Ozarks. The land deal with two old friends, James and Susan McDougal, was supposed to give the Clintons a comfortable nest egg. Instead, it had gone bust and cost them some money. During the 1992 presidential campaign, *The New York Times* had published a story raising a number of questions about the financing and about Hillary's legal work for the McDougals' savings and loan, which was regulated by the state while Clinton was governor. Nussbaum insisted that Whitewater was on no one's mind in the immediate aftermath of Foster's suicide.

The mysteries surrounding Foster's death seemed only to deepen. Nussbaum belatedly discovered a note Foster had written that described the displacement and despair he felt in Washington. "I was not meant for the job or the spotlight of public life in Washington," he had written on yellow legal paper nine days before his death. "Here ruining people is considered sport."

Nussbaum brought Hillary into his office to read the note.

"I can't deal with this," Mrs. Clinton said. "You deal with it."

When Nussbaum took a copy of the note to Clinton, the president said he had been told about it, and he didn't want to see the copy.

By the fall of 1993, the government organization investigating failed savings and loans, the Resolution Trust Corporation, had referred a case to the Justice Department for possible criminal investigation. The company under review was Madison Guaranty, the S&L run by the McDougals. The Clintons were listed as possible witnesses. *The Washington Post* reported the referral in a front-page story October 31, 1993: "U.S. Is Asked to Probe Failed Arkansas S&L." With a possible criminal investigation of Whitewater pending, the Clintons realized they would have to hire private lawyers. Nussbaum and Bill Kennedy interviewed four candidates from the Washington bar and settled on David Kendall from the law firm of Williams & Connolly. The Clintons agreed.

Kendall, 49, had known both Clintons at Yale Law School. Scholarly, a bit stiff, Kendall was a rare Washington lawyer with a genuine interest in culture, music and art. While a college student he had spent the summer of 1964 registering black voters in Mississippi, where he had been briefly jailed. After law school he had worked for the NAACP, attempting to save some of the most notorious men on death row, including the Florida murderer John Spenkelink, from execution. Kendall had as prestigious credentials as any lawyer in Washington. Besides Yale Law School, he, like Clinton, had won a Rhodes scholarship. He had clerked for Supreme Court Justice Byron White. He had ten years' experience defending clients in savings and loan cases.

Williams & Connolly lawyers defended their clients with an aggressiveness that rattled, at times outlasted and almost always infuriated prosecutors. Kendall was a believer.

A couple of months after Kendall's hiring, on December 20, *The Washington Times* ran a front-page banner headline: "CLINTON PAPERS LIFTED AFTER AIDE'S SUICIDE." The story alleged that papers from Foster's office on Whitewater had been removed to the White House residence.

The July White House suicide, the October disclosure of a criminal case touching on the Clintons and the December allegation that Whitewater files had been spirited from Foster's office were a formula for a media frenzy. Washington was ablaze with speculation and doubt about the basic integrity of the Clintons and their White House. Had they brought a small state land deal scandal with them? What the hell was going on?

Certain key Republicans began calling for an

independent investigation, then the calls came from some key Democrats. Nussbaum went on a crusade around the White House against an independent investigation. The 1978 Ethics in Government Act had expired. It was, with Clinton's backing, expected to be renewed later in 1994. The single remaining mechanism was for Attorney General Janet Reno to appoint a special counsel who would function with essentially the same independence as the court-appointed independent counsel under the old law.

In any form, Nussbaum was opposed. "Here is an institution I understand," he told Clinton. "It is *evil*. They have one case. They have unlimited resources. They have no time limit. Their entire reputation hinges on making that one case."

Nussbaum recalled for the president that when he had worked as a prosecutor, he had many cases going, often simultaneously. If one didn't work out, he could turn to another in the stack. The process naturally drew the prosecutor's attention to the most obvious and important crimes—the ones with the best evidence. In contrast, an independent prosecutor closed the office only when no crimes were found. It becomes a magnet for allegations, Nussbaum said. The office might as well be an advertisement for people to bring in dirt. The Justice Department is at least accountable to the president and in a sense on a president's side, he argued. The Justice Department would at least receive and evaluate allegations with a presumption of innocence. An independent prosecutor can and often does operate with a presumption of guilt, he maintained.

Nussbaum's campaign against independent investigations and the independent counsel law was not getting a receptive audience in the White House or in particular the Oval Office. When the Democratic leaders in Congress reported that fall that the renewal of the act could be put on the back burner, Nussbaum suggested to Clinton they jump at the chance.

"No, nah, Bernie," Clinton said. "This is good. And I promised it in the campaign."

The White House could not contain the Whitewater problem. The press would not let go. A formal "Whitewater Response Team" was created, headed by Harold Ickes, the White House deputy chief of staff, chief political operative and damage control specialist for the Clintons. Ickes was a profane, skinny and high-strung 55-year-old lawyer from New York who had known Clinton from the anti–Vietnam War movement. He held team meetings twice a day to discuss the aggressive Justice and FBI investigations which had begun looking at Whitewater.

"Those guys are fucking us blue," Ickes complained at one meeting.

At another damage control team session, Hillary turned to her husband and said, "We need a plan, and we're diddling around."

Tentatively, the president agreed that the solution was to turn over all the Whitewater documents to *The Washington Post*, which was pressing for them. But Hillary didn't want anyone poring through the details of their past, their investments, her legal work in Arkansas. The past could be a time bomb in the hands of the wrong people—especially reporters who were determined to put the most negative interpretation on their behavior and documents. She had a compelling exhibit. Five days before Christmas, the *American Spectator* had released an 11,000-word article quoting former Arkansas state troopers who alleged numerous sexual escapades by her husband. The article was titled "His Cheatin' Heart," and reporters began referring to it as "Troopergate." Hillary vetoed the documents' release.

Stephanopoulos was convinced it was the wrong strategy. He did not know what was in the documents or what precisely lay in the long Arkansas past, but he didn't think it was that bad or that it was criminal. Hillary's manner convinced him that she wanted at all costs to avoid petty embarrassments. It was nothing more than that, he concluded.

The evening of January 5, 1994, Clinton learned that his mother, Virginia Kelley, had died in Arkansas. Clinton had never known his father, who died three months before his birth. At another time with another president, humanity and courtesy would have dictated a modest political timeout. But the culture had changed. Within hours, Senator Bob Dole, the leading Republican and Senate minority leader, went on the three network morning television shows and castigated Clinton for Whitewater. "It cries out more than ever now for an independent counsel," Dole said. He continued his public criticism for two days, including the day of the funeral. Clinton could not believe it. Political attacks on the day of his mother's death and then again on the day of her funeral were unforgivable.

Calls for an independent Whitewater investigation apart from the Justice Department increased from the Democrats. On January 10, Senator Bill Bradley of New Jersey joined Senator Daniel Patrick Moynihan of New York and seven other Democratic senators urging a special counsel.

The next day, Clinton was in Europe. Reporters chiefly wanted to ask about Whitewater. Clinton was furious. That night a Whitewater Response Team assembled in the Oval Office, including Mrs. Clinton and Kendall. They got the president on a speakerphone from Prague.

Ickes set up a formal debate. Stephanopoulos favored asking the attorney general to appoint a special counsel; Nussbaum opposed. Nussbaum was certain that one of the reasons he had been brought to the White House was this moment.

Stephanopoulos said no one wanted a special counsel, but they had no choice. The Justice Department had started an investigation, but that had heightened suspicion that the fix was in. Regular process was not enough. The conditioning of Watergate required an independent prosecutor. The press attention on the subject would not abate until there was a credible independent investigation. They had to get the Whitewater story off the evening television news and front pages. They needed the issues out of the White House. An independent investigation would allow them to say no comment legitimately.

Nussbaum warned, "You'll quiet *The New York Times* and *The Washington Post* for one week."

Stephanopoulos countered that of the dozen independent or special counsels, most had not come up with indictments. Investigations in Carter's administration had taken a maximum of six months. "This will be over in six months," he said. Janet Reno would recruit a fair person. For two weeks, there had been nothing else in the news other than Whitewater. Could they halt the presidency to continue a fight about an old land deal? They expected criticism from the Republicans, but now it was coming from the Democrats—the same Democrats who had made it possible to pass their economic plan by a single vote in the Senate months earlier. Everything would stall. "This is the presidency," Stephanopoulos said. They were powerless now.

"I've lived with this institution," Nussbaum replied, repeating his anthem. "It is an evil institution." The special counsel's reputation would ride on the one case. "The world has changed since Carter. Iran-contra lasted seven years. You will create a roving spotlight which will examine your friends and everyone you've ever had contact with." Some of those people no doubt did something wrong somewhere, and the investigation will be expanded to those areas—ones that can't even be contemplated.

Others protested, saying the probe should be limited to and focused on Whitewater.

No, Nussbaum answered, they did not understand the law or the pressure that develops to get something, someone. "Mr. President," he said, shopping the room for a likely candidate and landing on Bruce Lindsey, Clinton's long-time aide, "one year from now Bruce Lindsey will be under investigation. Your friends, your family will be chased to the ends of the earth."

"Goddamn it, Bernie," Clinton said, his voice coming disembodied over the speakerphone, "I can't give a press conference without being asked about this." It was now about 2 a.m. in Prague. Clinton was tired and frustrated and angry. "I can't take this," he declared. "One question after another. God damn it!" Then he settled down. "Give me an alternative."

"Mr. President," Nussbaum replied, answering off the top of his head, "you think this is important. This is about before you were even governor, this land deal. The alternative is turn over everything. And then you and Hillary demand to testify before Congress within 30 days to tell the whole story." The key was to act quickly, he said, citing President Ford's testimony to Congress after he pardoned Nixon. That appearance extinguished the pardon inquiry. Although the pardon remained a lasting and destructive political issue, there was no official investigation. "What you have to do is ensure that there's no special staff assigned to this." Special congressional staffs such as the one Nussbaum and Hillary worked on during the Nixon impeachment investigation take on a life of their own. Testify only once. "You control it, the Democratic Congress. That's the alternative."

"Are you crazy?" Stephanopoulos almost shouted. "Can you imagine the publicity?" An appearance would add daily fuel to the Whitewater media fires already raging, creating more damage.

Nussbaum said they could take adverse publicity because it could only last so long if they testified only once. "If you create a special counsel, it will last as long as your presidency and beyond."

James Carville, Clinton's chief political strategist, took Stephanopoulos's side. "Get somebody," Carville said, "have Reno appoint somebody. It's just a pile of shit, you know, it'll all blow over. But if we don't, we're going to be totally distracted."

Stephanopoulos argued again that Reno would appoint a good person as special counsel and then the independent counsel law would be reenacted and the three-judge panel would appoint the same person.

"I don't think so," Nussbaum said. The judges on the current panel were conservative and this process was perniciously political. They would disapprove of Reno's choice. Reno had made the same point publicly.

"This is the craziest thing you've said," Stephanopoulos replied. "This demonstrates how off-the-wall Bernie is."

The others in the room agreed.

"Okay," Nussbaum conceded, "Janet will get a good person, but the idea that the same person will be appointed by the three judges is only fifty-fifty."

Stephanopoulos accused Nussbaum of being hysterical.

Nussbaum realized that at this point he was hysterical.

Stephanopoulos reminded them again that the independent counsel law was going to be reenacted and the president was on record saying he would sign it into law. When that happened, he said, they would be back at square one because Whitewater would trigger the act and they would get an independent counsel anyway.

"She will not appoint one," Nussbaum said. The reenacted law would only require the appointment if the attorney general found specific and credible evidence that a crime might have been committed. "I know her. She will stand up if there's nothing there."

"You are wrong," Stephanopoulos replied sharply. "It will happen anyway and we've got to appoint our own and get out front."

Hillary stood up. "Let's end this now," she said, briefly summarizing the main positions. She assured her husband that he had heard all the arguments.

"I'll sleep on it," Clinton said.

The next morning, Hillary walked into Nussbaum's West Wing office and put her arm around her old mentor. "The president feels compelled to ask for a special counsel," she told him. He has concluded that he has no choice if he is going to get on with his agenda. She was going to reform the health care system. That required laser focus. In the name of health care reform, they were going to get White-water off the news.

"This is a great tragedy," Nussbaum replied. He was not a gracious loser. He was certain the Clintons were giving their opponents a giant weapon. "Why are you going to put your head in that noose?"

Hillary didn't reply.

Nussbaum drafted a letter to Reno. He made it clear that he was acting under orders. "The president has directed me to request you to appoint as special counsel a respected, impartial and qualified attorney, who is not a member of the Department of Justice or an employee of the federal government, to conduct an appropriate independent investigation of the Whitewater matter and report to the American people."

19

AT THE JUSTICE DEPARTMENT, the letter was received with some chagrin. Attorney General Reno had taken the position, privately and publicly, that if the Republicans and Democrats in Congress wanted an independent investigation they should reenact the independent counsel law so a three-judge panel would appoint someone. If she, working for the president, selected somebody, that person would be suspect, destroying the whole notion of independence. So her answer had repeatedly been no, no, no, no. Now, given the president's request, it would have to be yes. She did not like to be in the position of giving such an emphatic, logical no and then having to change course.

But those were the orders. She asked three of her top deputies to find a special counsel who would be distinguished by his credibility. The person didn't have to be a Republican, but it would obviously be a plus. During a Saturday lunch the three deputies settled on Robert Bishop Fiske Jr. Fiske, 63, a moderate Republican, had practiced law in two places—eight years in the U.S. attorney's office for the Southern District in New York City, first as an assistant and then as the U.S. attorney for four years during the Carter administration, and 32 years at Davis, Polk, one of the premier New York City law firms. Small, lean, gentle-mannered, Fiske was careful and meticulous and hard-nosed. Reno's assistant in charge of the Justice Department's criminal division, JoAnn Harris, had worked as an assistant U.S. attorney for Fiske back in the Carter administration and considered him the best. She called him later the next day.

Is there any way you could do this? Harris asked her former boss.

"Yeah, if you want me, I will," he replied. That weekend there were more calls to Fiske, who was at his vacation retreat in Vermont, where it was about 20 below zero. Fiske accepted the job. On January 19, 1994, he flew to Washington. One of Harris's deputies gave him a draft of the statement outlining his jurisdiction. They wanted Fiske to be comfortable with his charter, so they told him to take the draft into another room and edit it.

Fiske knew the importance of broad prosecutorial jurisdiction, and he rewrote the document. The focus of his inquiry would be the Clintons' "relationships" with the Whitewater Development Corporation. But he added sections empowering him to investigate any possible criminal or civil law violation that might arise. He also specifically included authority to investigate obstruction of justice, perjury and conspiracy. The meaning of this provision was clear to Fiske, as it would have been to any other criminal lawyer or legal expert. It would give him the authority to investigate any person or possible witness for any crime ranging from tax matters, drug charges to unrelated financial transactions. In other words he would be able to squeeze and plea-bargain with witnesses for testimony—the key tool of a prosecutor. It would give him access to the agents and records of the IRS, Customs, the Drug Enforcement Agency, bank regulators—essentially the resources of the entire federal government.

When attorneys in the criminal division read the redraft, they realized they were giving Fiske the kitchen sink, the authority to investigate anything that came his way or that he might stumble on, no matter how remote, if it was connected to Whitewater, the Clintons or any possible witnesses. In effect it was the power to investigate anyone for anything, and by extension everyone for everything, a much broader jurisdiction than had been granted other special or independent counsels. It was breathtaking. But

Reno's instructions were to let Fiske have all the running room he wanted.

Fiske told Reno's deputies that he was immediately taking a leave of absence from his law firm and would work full time as special counsel. He didn't see how he could possibly concentrate, much less think about anything else.

He was taken to see Reno. They had only met once before at a conference of trial lawyers.

"Are you satisfied that you have all the authority that you need and the jurisdiction you need?" Reno inquired.

"Yes, I am," Fiske said. He told her he had basically written the charter himself.

"Well, that's wonderful," Reno said. "I want you to be completely independent. I don't expect to talk to you again until this is all over."

"That's certainly fine with me," Fiske replied.

The next morning, January 20—a year to the day after Clinton's inaugural—Reno and Fiske met with reporters to announce the appointment. Reno reminded the reporters of what she required in the Whitewater special counsel: "Someone who would be fair, and impartial, who has a reputation for integrity and skill, someone who would be ruggedly independent, and I think Mr. Fiske fits that description to a 'T.'"

Fiske said, "I have been told time and time again by the top officials of the Justice Department, including the attorney general, that there are *no limits* on what I can do."

Although Fiske didn't say it, in his mind he expected that it would take about a year to determine if there were indictable offenses. If there were indictments of others to win their cooperation, then the landscape would change and it would be more than a year. Fiske had voted for George Bush in 1992, but he felt confident that he didn't have any strong feeling about Clinton one way or the other. With significant time as both prosecutor and criminal defense lawyer, he felt there was a way to proceed, to jump in and see what might be there, to cast a wide net but to quickly clear out the investigative underbrush—leads and suspicions that would not lead to real, credible evidence or witnesses. The culture was awash in these low-grade speculations, conspiracy theories and links. As part of his charter, the Justice Department attorneys told Fiske that he would take over a case that was scheduled to come to trial in two months.

David Hale, a former Arkansas municipal judge who had run Capital Management Services, Inc., a federally licensed lending operation for disadvantaged small businesses, had been charged with defrauding the Small Business Administration. He had alleged publicly that in 1986 then-Governor Clinton had pressured him to arrange a $300,000 federal loan to Susan McDougal, and that some of the money had gone to help bail out the Whitewater land deal. Fiske immediately hired an experienced prosecutor to take charge of the Hale case.

They quickly entered into plea-bargaining negotiations and arranged to talk with Hale under an agreement called "Queen for a Day," meaning the prosecutor could learn directly from the target of the investigation what he knew about others.

They could use the information he gave about others for leads, but they could not use the information against Hale directly. The day lasted three weeks. Two of Fiske's attorneys and two FBI agents almost lived with Hale. They found no wobble in his story. An important test of his credibility was that Hale resisted the temptation to pile on, to take his story to the next step with new allegations. This moderation made Hale a more critical witness and put him in position to get a better deal from the prosecutors. In the end, Hale agreed to plead guilty to two felonies that would mean a minimum of six years in jail.

Fiske realized that it was a long jump to say they might eventually be bringing a case against the president of the United States based on this one allegation, but it was obvious they were in the realm of the serious.

The *American Spectator* editors had decided not to name any of the women in their long 1993 Troopergate article about Clinton's alleged sexual liaisons. The *Spectator* copy editors were empowered to remove the names of all Clinton's alleged mistresses "so as not to exploit them more than Clinton already has, or to punish innocent family members." But there was a small reference that the editors failed to excise. Clinton had met in the Little Rock Excelsior Hotel in 1991 with a woman named "Paula." A state trooper, later identified as Danny Ferguson, allegedly had taken Paula, a 24-year-old, $10,270-per-year clerk in the Arkansas government, to a hotel room to meet the governor. Afterwards, as he escorted her back to the conference, Paula had offered to be Clinton's girlfriend, Ferguson said.

Paula Corbin Jones went public at a Washington press conference February 11, 1994, stating she was the "Paula" of the story. Rather than accede to Clinton's sexual advances, as the *Spectator* article strongly implied, Jones said she had rejected Clinton and felt humiliated by the experience. She said Clinton had kissed her, reached under her clothing and asked for oral sex. The allegations were explosive, but the mainstream press largely ignored them because the conference was sponsored by the right-wing Conservative Political Action Conference, which was promoting a "Troopergate Whistleblowers Fund."

Jones might never have gone public had her first name not been used in the article. *Spectator* editors later said that under their own policy not to name the women, the "Paula" should have been deleted.

In February, *The New York Times* ran a Man in the News profile of Nussbaum, headlined "Litigator on a Tightrope." Yale Law School Professor Geoffrey C. Hazard, an expert on legal ethics, openly criticized Nussbaum. Hazard said any attorney worth his salt would not have transferred the Whitewater papers found in Vince Foster's office back to the Clintons without realizing that government investigators had an interest in them. "Anybody who reflected on Watergate should know that."

Before the first news story on the Madison

Guaranty criminal referral appeared in early October 1993, Nussbaum and the White House staff had learned of it from the Treasury Department. By early March 1994, news stories detailed White House officials' efforts to find out more about the criminal referrals on Madison Guaranty, the McDougals' failed savings and loan. In all there were 40 contacts between the White House and Treasury officials who oversaw the Resolution Trust Corporation (RTC), which was investigating Madison and McDougal.

Nussbaum insisted that the discussions were intended only to prepare the White House to respond quickly and intelligently to media inquiries. He had personally attended just three meetings arranged by others. Treasury was giving the White House a heads-up so they could respond. But the extent and emotions displayed in the contacts suggested that the White House was applying pressure, even if indirect and subtle. It was Nussbaum who had argued earlier that the White House should not be so concerned, let alone obsessed, with what the media was saying. He had even advised others on the White House staff, "We can't let leaks drive us crazy. It's the seed of Watergate." But he maintained that the media and leaks had driven him and others to try to glean what the Treasury officials knew.

Given Nussbaum's detailed knowledge of Watergate, including the Nixon White House's efforts to interfere with the Justice Department and FBI investigation, it is somewhat odd that Nussbaum didn't stay out of the matter entirely, or that he didn't issue an order, preferably in writing, to the entire White House staff informing them that no one should seek information, pose any questions or discuss any Whitewater matter with the RTC or those overseeing it in Treasury. The president and his wife also knew the pitfalls of Watergate, but neither intervened to get the White House staff to stay out of a criminal investigation that touched on them.

The news stories portrayed a White House staff crawling all over Treasury officials. It had the aroma of a political fix. In early March, the president publicly criticized the White House–Treasury contacts. "I think it would be better if the meetings and conversations had not occurred," he told reporters.

Nussbaum talked with Hillary. She spoke of appearances. "Things look so bad," she said.

"It looks bad," Nussbaum conceded, "but there was nothing wrong. I didn't call the meetings."

One of the first indications of problems for Nussbaum came when he heard that his deputy, Joel Klein, who had replaced Vince Foster, had told Vice President Al Gore that Nussbaum's contacts appeared to be improper. As the White House lawyer, Nussbaum should have been more careful.

"We're going to go see Gore about this," Nussbaum told Klein. The two lawyers went to Gore's office. Nussbaum said he had heard that Klein had alleged that he had acted improperly. "I have not," Nussbaum said.

"Bernie," Gore said stiffly, "your moral compass should always point north, and your compass hasn't always. I feel compelled to recommend to the president that you resign."

"You can tell the president any fucking thing you want," Nussbaum said. He stormed from Gore's office.

Gore told the president that Nussbaum had to go.

Nussbaum knew his head was on the chopping block, but he was determined to stay the execution. Late Friday, March 4, Clinton called Nussbaum to the Oval Office.

"This does not have to do with friendship," Nussbaum told Clinton. "This has to do with the strength of the presidency." Nussbaum argued that his actions had been proper and consistent with an aggressive legal representation of the president and his office. The White House could not run on appearances.

Clinton looked at Nussbaum with a blank stare. He said he did not want to argue about the appropriateness of the meetings and contacts.

"If me resigning makes the presidency stronger," Nussbaum said, "I'll do it."

"If you go," Clinton said, "there will be peace. We'll pass health care."

"It will feed the beast," Nussbaum countered. The media should not govern. "I've done nothing wrong. I acted properly to protect your interests, and it will hurt the presidency if Bernie Nussbaum can be driven out. It will show this is the price of loyalty. It will give off a message that if a person is close to you and loyal, he can be driven out."

Clinton let his counsel have his argument.

"What message are you giving to Janet Reno if I have to resign?" Nussbaum demanded. He had played a big role in her selection and confirmation. What about the message to FBI Director Louis Freeh, whom Nussbaum had essentially found for Clinton to take over the bureau? Everyone would act to protect themselves from doing something that might appear bad rather than to act properly to watch out for the president. Who could afford to look out for Clinton?

Nussbaum defended himself. He wanted to debate the president. Nussbaum loved debate—thinking on his feet, getting caught on the wave of his own enthusiasm and righteousness, rolling it out, chopping the air with his small hands. "If you believe I acted inappropriately, yes, I should resign," he said finally.

Clinton was silent.

What do you think? Nussbaum asked.

"I'm not sure," Clinton said. "It looks bad."

"At those meetings, no one said fix this. We were worried about leaks....I didn't call the meetings." Nussbaum was getting more upset. He turned to the impact on his reputation. "This will tar me," he declared. "If you fire the White House counsel for inappropriate meetings, you give off the impression of massive wrongdoing." Nussbaum admitted that it sounded as if he were trying to save his own skin. "If I truly believed it was best for you, I'd go back immediately. But it's about you and the presidency. It will send a message to everyone that no one can count on you. It will hurt you as president. It will hurt your ability to govern."

Clinton sat, absorbing the litigator's final summation. Nussbaum sensed he had not won. So he made the last argument, digging into Clinton's manhood. "Mr. President," Nussbaum said sharply, "if you do this, history will consider you a wimp. And I hope that doesn't come to pass."

Clinton looked straight up at him, paused and contained his words. "Let's think about it some more."

Kendall called Clinton to argue strongly that Nussbaum not be fired. Nussbaum had been aggressive. That was lawyering. Nussbaum had been impetuous, but he had done nothing wrong or illegal. The lesson of Watergate was that if a president needed to chop off somebody's head, he should do it early, Kendall believed. But in this case the head didn't need to go.

Several hours later McLarty told Nussbaum he would have to resign.

The next day, Nussbaum wrote out his resignation letter, fully defending his actions. He was distraught and defensive, and he was certain that Clinton had violated a basic principle of human relations and politics. The president abandoned his friends but did not penalize his enemies. In contrast, Nussbaum knew he was a hater. So was Hillary to some extent. They could identify their enemies and knew about payback. "You should do harm to enemies if you can," Nussbaum once said. Now Clinton was harming his friend.

As Nussbaum reflected on his 14 months as counsel, he realized that he had been used and was now disposable. Clinton hadn't genuinely confided in him. The president would moan and complain out loud, but Nussbaum had seen the interior walls in Clinton going higher, getting thicker.

20

LLOYD CUTLER, who began practicing law in Washington in 1946, the year Clinton was born, shuddered as he watched the Clinton presidency falter. It was precisely the kind of mess that was unnecessary—and, in his view, avoidable. Perhaps the most senior and experienced fixture of the Washington legal establishment, Cutler had acted for decades as an adviser to presidents. From his perch at the law firm that he had created, Wilmer, Cutler & Pickering, strategically placed between downtown Washington and Georgetown, Cutler, 76, fielded phone calls from an array of contacts about the mounting troubles of the new Democratic administration. A sense of mild panic was in the atmosphere. A gray-haired figure with thick glasses and a slight stoop, Cutler exuded an air of patience.

One call Cutler received was from Vernon

Jordan, the former civil rights attorney and President Clinton's main Washington confidant. Cutler knew that a call from Jordan was a call from the president. They agreed to meet at Cutler's Georgetown home.

When Jordan arrived, he explained that the president needed better, more sophisticated lawyering. Nussbaum's irascible style had antagonized too many people, especially in Congress and the press. With Congress planning summer Whitewater hearings and the special counsel gearing up, the president needed a counsel who could make peace and reach out. "If we asked you," Jordan asked, "would you accept?"

Cutler said he did not want to do it. He reminded Jordan that he was 76 years old. He had done his service as Jimmy Carter's White House counsel in 1979 and 1980, coming in as part of a rescue operation because Carter too had alienated the Washington establishment.

Would you stay a year? Jordan asked.

"Well, I'd stay six months if I can do it as a special government employee," Cutler said. That way he would not have to sever his relationship with his law firm. He was sure it was an offer the president couldn't accept. An interim counsel wouldn't do much good for anyone. By the time he unpacked he would be out the door.

At 8 p.m. Sunday, Cutler was sitting in the White House residence. Clinton turned on the charm for two hours. Everyone was saying he needed a Lloyd Cutler type as his counsel, the president said, and he figured he might as well get the real thing if he could.

Cutler said his wife, Polly Kraft, was fed up with politics and would permit only the limited six months.

The president accepted the offer of six months.

Cutler told the president that he wanted the same role that he had enjoyed in the Carter White House 15 years earlier. One similar to that performed by Clark Clifford for President Harry Truman—the inside lawyer and counselor who has access to every person, every transaction, every meeting. Carter had made the pledge in writing.

The president said Cutler would have full access. He said he was innocent of any conceivable criminal offense relating to Whitewater. It was proper and legal for his White House staff to find out about the criminal referrals in Whitewater, Clinton contended, repeating Nussbaum's arguments.

Cutler thought that Nussbaum had been too good a soldier for his prince. It was a matter of style: defend but don't antagonize. He told Clinton that he felt Nussbaum had misinterpreted his job as that of the president's personal attorney. The White House counsel should protect the institution of the presidency, rather than the president's personal interests. David Kendall, the Clintons' attorney, should handle the private Whitewater-related issues. He would concern himself with official White House legal problems, focusing on the long-range impact on the presidency.

Clinton told Cutler that a major problem was producing the documents requested by

Special Counsel Fiske and the congressional committees. "We've got to cooperate, and I've got to go on being president," Clinton said.

His old Arkansas enemies were feeding the flames. "The press is after me unfairly," the president said. He'd had bad press back in Arkansas, too. Clinton reminisced on Vince Foster's suicide. Cutler could see that it was still painful. In moments of anguish, Clinton's eye contact and body language were shockingly intimate. "Look," the president said, "frankly I'm genuinely worried that Congress and the press and my enemies are going to make life miserable for me." Clinton talked about the investigations and the need to find a coherent defense.

Will I just be forced to play defense, Cutler asked, and react only to investigators, or am I going to be able to play offense, be involved in the daily political and legal issues that affect the presidency?

Of course, Clinton answered, indicating the latter.

Cutler formally accepted the job. He found himself liking Clinton. Having known and dealt with ten previous presidents going back to Franklin Roosevelt, he was mesmerized. Clinton seemed to focus totally on each of Cutler's words.

At 4:15 Tuesday afternoon, March 8, Clinton appeared with Cutler in the White House briefing room. All four television networks went with live coverage. It looked as if Clinton was bringing his father or grandfather to the White House—a gray eminence who had the bearing and manner of a judge without actually wearing the robes.

While Clinton made it clear he was using Cutler to bolster his message of cooperation and accommodation, he declared, "Let me emphasize this point: On ethics, as with every other issue, it is the president who must set the standard."

"In government, as in other aspects of life," Cutler said, "trust is the coin of the realm, and Mr. President, I pledge myself to do what I can to assure that trust is maintained."

"Are you bitter about this, sir?" one reporter asked the president.

"No," Clinton said.

"Why not?"

"Because I think as you grow older, bitterness is something you have to learn to put aside."

"I want the American people to see that this White House is different," Clinton said. "If there's a question here about conduct, we're open, not closed. There's no bunker mentality." From the sidelines, Stephanopoulos could see that Clinton was trying to say he was not Nixon.

Cutler felt that the guts of the Whitewater problem would be showing good faith cooperation. He hoped to advertise, in bright lights, the Clintons' willingness to get as much material out as possible to Fiske. As best he could tell, the documents Fiske wanted were years of routine banking, tax and other financial records that were generated from loans and real estate deals.

Cutler met with Fiske and found him to be like the first Watergate special prosecutor, Archibald Cox—honest, frank but hard-nosed.

Fiske needed documents, especially the White-water files found in Foster's office, so he could fully reconstruct the many transactions and troubled financial arrangements.

David Kendall argued they should provide the documents as they were subpoenaed. This criminal investigation could become a criminal case against his clients. Why should the president and the first lady show their hand without seeing the hands of the others who were involved or might be potential witnesses? Kendall said the documents were not incriminating in themselves, but they were full of leads and names of others for the prosecutors to interview.

Cutler reviewed the material. He agreed the documents were not incriminating, but he felt that withholding nonincriminating material made zero sense. He appreciated Kendall's caution, and he knew there were legitimate arguments for not turning them over. But Fiske was eventually going to get to the names of possible witnesses. It was in their interest to lead him there if there was no problem. If they fought they wouldn't win in court, and a fight for privilege could be a public relations disaster.

Hillary Clinton was in no mood to cooperate. *The New York Times* had just published a story on March 18 disclosing that Mrs. Clinton had made nearly $100,000 in 1978 and 1979 trading commodities futures on a meager $1,000 initial investment. A flood of editorials followed, pointing out the contrast between Hillary's earlier denunciations of greed during the Reagan years and her own secret profit making. Hillary believed that the *Times* reporters had unearthed the story because many years earlier the Clintons had released their tax returns for the ten previous years. But those years didn't include 1978 and 1979. The *Times* had pressed for those returns and came to think of them as "missing" because they had not been voluntarily disclosed.

Hillary believed that the generous disclosure of the ten years of returns—way beyond what was legally required of candidates—had helped focus attention on the 1978–79 returns. Somehow the *Times* had learned enough about the two returns to discover the $100,000 commodities profits. To her lawyers, the first lady lamented the unintended and damaging consequences of releasing documents. Not surprisingly, she said she did not want to turn over any more documents voluntarily.

An argument followed. Cutler told Kendall and Hillary they had to live with the new atmosphere of suspicion and try to manage it. The commitment to scrutinizing the Clintons would only intensify. The mystery surrounding records not produced would cause greater damage than revealing whatever they contained. These documents were nothing.

Clinton sided with Cutler. He agreed to turn over the documents to Fiske.

Cutler wanted to go an extra mile with Fiske's request. One of the Whitewater documents mentioned on the list of files taken from Foster's office could not be found. It was finally discovered near the desk of one of Cutler's secretaries, a large, intense woman named Linda Tripp. Cutler immediately sent the file over to the special counsel.

On Thursday, April 21, the *Los Angeles Times* published a poll showing a drop in Hillary's approval rating of 12 percent—from 56 percent in January to 44 percent. In the same period, the president's approval rating had stayed relatively constant at 54 percent. The next day, Friday, her staff spread the word to the media that the first lady would hold a press conference in several hours. Television cameras were welcome. She would answer any and all questions about Whitewater, Vince Foster's death, her commodities trading or any other issue. It was in effect the first full-scale news conference by any first lady.

The major television networks broke into their afternoon programming for live coverage several hours later as Hillary walked into the State Dining Room of the White House wearing a pink sweater and long black skirt. Her hair was carefully combed back, exposing her ears and large round earrings. She sat down in a wooden armchair by the fireplace and folded her hands in her lap. A large portrait of Abraham Lincoln hung in the background.

A reporter asked Mrs. Clinton how she squared her criticism of the 1980s as the decade of greed with her own efforts to make money in Whitewater and the commodity trading. Wasn't it hypocrisy?

"I do think you raise an important question that I would like to talk about a little bit," Mrs. Clinton said. "You know, I was raised to believe that every person had an obligation to take care of themselves and their family." Her father had her read the stock tables when she was a little girl, she said, and she did that with her daughter, Chelsea. "I don't think you'll ever find anything that my husband or I said that in any way condemns the importance of making good investments and saving or that in any way undermines what is the heart and soul of the American economy, which is risk-taking and investing in the future. What I think we were saying is that like anything else, that can be taken to excess—when companies are leveraged into debt, when loans are not repaid, when pension funds are raided. You know, all of the things that marked the excess of the 1980s are things which we spoke out against. I think it's a pretty long stretch to say that the decisions that we made to try to create some financial security for our family and make some investments come any-where near there....We obviously wanted enough financial security to send our daughter to col-lege and put money away for our old age and help our parents when we could."

Did her opposition to a special counsel in Whitewater or to the release of their tax returns create problems? the next reporter asked. "Do you think that that helped to create any impres-sion that you were trying to hide something?"

"Yes, I do," Mrs. Clinton said directly. "And I think that is probably one of the things that I regret most and one of the reasons why I wanted to do this."

"I'm wondering," the 23rd questioner asked, "what kind of toll, if any, this has taken on your and the president's personal and political lives. And do you ever look in the mirror and wish that you just never got into this?"

"No, never, never," Mrs. Clinton said. "This is really a result of our inexperience in Washington, if you will, that I really did not fully understand everything that I wish now I had known." She said she didn't fully appreciate the need to answer questions from the media. "And I'm certainly going to try to be more sensitive to what you all need and what we need to give you." On Whitewater and the related issues she said, "I feel very confident about how this will all turn out. This is not a long-term problem or issue in any way."

Shouldn't she and her husband have been more aware of the Whitewater investment debts and loan?

"Well," Mrs. Clinton said, "shoulda, coulda, woulda, we didn't."

Next, the 34th reporter asked, "Considering what you've been through, do you have any greater appreciation of what Richard Nixon might have been going through?"

Three days earlier, Nixon, 81, had suffered a stroke and was in a deep coma.

"What I think we ought to be doing is praying for President Nixon," Mrs. Clinton said. "And from my perspective," she said, her voice cracking and tears filling her eyes, "you know, it was a year ago April that my father died at the age of 81, and so, you know, I'm just mostly thinking about his daughters right now."

Nixon died that evening at 9:08 p.m. Two hours later Clinton went to the Rose Garden to make a formal announcement of Nixon's death. "It's impossible to be in this job without feeling a special bond with the people who have gone before," Clinton said.

In private to his staff, Clinton had voiced deep ambivalence about Nixon, at times calling Nixon a war criminal because of Vietnam, at others noting the difficulties faced by any president.

Several days later, Clinton met with his senior staff in the Oval Office to discuss a draft of remarks he was to make at Nixon's funeral later in the week in California. A sentence in the draft said that "the day of judging Richard Nixon based on one part of his life alone has finally come to a close."

Stephanopoulos was aghast. He said the subtext would be lost on no one. It could be interpreted as a self-serving plea by Clinton that he too be judged in totality and not just for Whitewater and the other scandals. "We just can't say that," Stephanopoulos said.

Clinton said he wanted to say something like that. They began playing with the language. On Wednesday, April 27, Clinton delivered careful remarks at Nixon's funeral. "Let us say, may the day of judging President Nixon on anything less than his entire life and career come to a close," he declared.

By May of 1994, the scandals were multiplying. Cutler was worried about Paula Jones. The press had begun to pay attention when Jones threatened to file a federal civil lawsuit against Clinton. She had until May 8, 1994, to file before the statute of limitations expired, three years to the day after the alleged incident.

David Kendall wanted to handle the case, but Cutler was convinced that Kendall was already overburdened with the Whitewater allegations and investigations. Since it was a civil matter, meaning it could only lead to monetary damages and embarrassment, Cutler recommended that Clinton hire another private lawyer from a different firm. He told the president to find an attorney who would practice an aggressive press policy, who might be able to settle the case, a lawyer with a sense of politics.

"Settle the suit if you can," Cutler advised the president, "because even if you win, it will be damaging." A Jones suit could drag Clinton through the sticky mud of his sexual past. Cutler recommended Robert S. Bennett, one of Washington's most pugnacious defense lawyers. A heavyset, swashbuckling master of the sound bite, Bennett naturally and regularly roiled with indignation when his clients were under attack.

Cutler invited Bennett for a Saturday lunch at the Four Seasons Hotel in Washington. The president and Cutler wanted Bennett to represent Clinton in the Paula Jones case, Cutler said. Kendall was opposed to bringing in Bennett because Kendall liked to litigate behind closed doors. The Jones allegations needed to be met in public pro-actively, Cutler told him, and the president was on board.

Bennett, 54, settled into his chair. A former amateur boxer and admirer of Muhammad Ali's pugilistic and oratorical talents, he liked the spotlight and loved to talk. He had been involved one way or another in many high-profile Washington scandals for the last 25 years. Flattered, nodding yes, Bennett recounted how he had worked with Boyden Gray, Bush's White House counsel and Cutler's current law partner, in the Iran-contra indictment of his client Caspar Weinberger. Bennett said he had convinced Bush to grant a pardon to Weinberger, using Gray as an intermediary. Gray had wanted assurances that Bush would not encounter a firestorm if he pardoned Weinberger and other Iran-contra figures. "You've got to show us that a pardon would not be a problem," Gray had told him, Bennett recounted. So he recruited key Democrats to say publicly that they favored a pardon or would not oppose it.

The resulting Christmas Eve 1992 pardons of Weinberger and the other Iran-contra figures virtually had died as a political story by the New Year, Bennett said. The pardon had saved Weinberger the $2 million in legal fees that he would have spent on a trial. Bennett said he hoped to replicate that kind of success with his newest potential client.

Bennett went to see Clinton, whom he did not know.

"I want you to represent me," Clinton said. He said he would find a way to pay Bennett's $475-an-hour rate.

Bennett accepted. "I'm not going to treat you differently because you're president of the United States."

"I swear to God, it didn't happen," Clinton said adamantly, denying Jones's charges. Quite frankly, he said, it was not his style to be so aggressive or crude with a woman. When he was governor, they would bring people to meet him. Hundreds, perhaps thousands over the years. Yes, in hotel rooms, everywhere. Clinton said he did not remember Paula Jones but had to concede that it was possible he had met her. "Bob," Clinton said to his new lawyer, "dig deep enough and you'll find my enemies in Arkansas are behind this. They are trying to redo the presidential election."

Bennett agreed with Cutler that even winning the case would be losing. His initial task would be to try to settle with Jones before a lawsuit was formally filed. It was the kind of political negotiation that he relished. On April 30, he spent eight hours at the White House.

Bennett called one of the newly hired attorneys for Jones, Gilbert K. Davis, whom he knew from Washington legal circles. "Jesus, Gil, I'm in the case, but before you file against the sitting president of the United States you've got to make sure you're right. Because before you know it we'll be off to nuclear war."

Davis said all Jones and her family wanted was an admission that Clinton and she were there in the hotel room and that she had done nothing immoral.

Bennett had sent lawyers to Little Rock. They had located an old boyfriend who alleged that Jones had many sexual partners. One former boyfriend had taken at least half a dozen photographs in which Jones posed provocatively in the nude.

"I understand there are some nude photos of her," Bennett told Davis.

An experienced former federal prosecutor who was no stranger to legal gamesmanship, Davis countered that Jones had recently recalled new details about the encounter with Clinton. "Jones can identify certain distinguishing characteristics in the president's genital area," he said.

Bennett began drafting an acceptable settlement statement. In one of his proposals, Clinton was willing to say, "I do not challenge her claim we met there." The president was also willing to say she did not engage in any improper or sexual misconduct, and he regretted any assertions or suggestions by others that she had. Clinton also wanted an agreement to state that he had made no improper or sexual advances. They seemed close to settling. Statements would be exchanged, no money would be paid, and Jones would not file suit.

But on Thursday, the negotiations began to unravel. Davis told Bennett that the family wanted Clinton to make the agreed-upon statement personally and not issue it through his press secretary. After that was done, neither the president nor his staff would be allowed to make any further comment about the issue.

"That's a deal-killer," Bennett said.

Later in the day Jones's sister, Charlotte Brown, gave an interview to a Little Rock television station. Brown maintained that Jones had confided in her about the Clinton encounter but said Jones "smelled money" if she made public her sexual harassment allegations against Clinton.

Jones told her lawyers she wanted an agreement from Clinton that she could reinstate a lawsuit if anyone from the White House or Bennett's office bad-mouthed Jones in public or orchestrated a public campaign against her.

For Bennett, that kind of an agreement was impossible. There was no way he or Clinton could enforce it and it would be laughable to try.

But Bennett felt settlement before a lawsuit was still possible. The lawyers seemed to be getting along. Davis agreed to delay filing the suit for a day so they could continue to talk.

By Thursday night, Bennett had learned that a draft of the possible lawsuit included the alleged "distinguishing characteristics" language about Clinton. Bennett felt that was pretty ugly. A settlement now would lead the press to conclude that he and Clinton had been scared off by the draft lawsuit. They were at an impasse.

The next day, Friday, May 6, Jones filed suit seeking $700,000 in damages.

At 2 p.m. Bennett held a press conference. "The president adamantly denies the vicious and mean-spirited allegations in this complaint," he said. "This complaint is tabloid trash with a legal caption on it....This suit is about publicity, it's about talk shows, it's about money." Echoing the president's private remarks, Bennett said the lawsuit was "really about trying to rewrite the election results."

"Are you prepared to have the president testify under oath?"

"That's a very premature question," Bennett replied, adding confidently, "which I don't think is going to happen."

Bennett met with Clinton and Cutler to develop strategy. The first goal, he said, had to be postponement. They wanted to get the lawsuit caught in the courts beyond the 1996 presidential election, more than two years away.

Cutler agreed. It had been his idea for some time. "The institution of the presidency deserves it," he said. The issue was whether a sitting president could be dragged into court by a citizen in a civil case. If Jones could do it, then any citizen could bring suit. The potential disruptions to the presidency were mind-boggling. At heart, Cutler judged, it was a constitutional issue. The Constitution needed to protect a sitting president from civil lawsuits while serving in office. The office required it.

Bennett conceded that his motive was baser. As the lawsuit proceeded, the lawyers for Jones would be allowed to seek evidence and interview witnesses under oath, including eventually the president himself. They could ask just about anything that might potentially lead to admissible evidence. "Discovery in a civil suit is a form of extortion," Bennett told Clinton.

Bennett saw no tactical disadvantage in going to federal court to make the claim of constitutional immunity. If they lost, they could appeal, tying the matter up in the appeals court and even the Supreme Court if necessary. The court process would take Paula Jones off the front burner. The press would lose interest. "Only Linda Greenhouse," Bennett said, referring to *The New York Times*'s intellectual Supreme Court reporter, "would be writing about it."

The court challenge, Bennett said, would offer another important advantage. It would consume time and be expensive, and it would test the staying power of Jones and her legal team. They were looking for a political score. A multi-year battle in the courts might dampen if not obliterate their enthusiasm.

"Bob," the president directed, "you've got to get this shit beyond the election."

On June 27, Bennett filed a motion in federal court in Little Rock asking that the Jones suit be dismissed while Clinton was in office. He was careful not to seek total immunity. The suit could be reinstated after the Clinton presidency was over, he said.

Bennett began meeting frequently with the president. He told Clinton they should not apologize or pay money that could be interpreted as an apology. He said if they paid $400,000 or $500,000 to Jones, other women would come out in search of money. On the other hand, if they could settle for some bullshit, vague language and a small amount of insurance money, they should consider.

Clinton agreed but was conflicted. One moment he favored a settlement, considering the impact on his family. At other times he refused to concede, protesting his innocence.

Bennett assured the president that if they had to get in a legal fight on one of these woman issues, "There is no better case than the Paula Jones case." He was optimistic that they could win on the law and the facts.

Bennett came to feel that he wanted to protect Clinton. "I feel like I'm your older brother," he said at one point. At another meeting, Bennett told the president, "Most of my cases, I can get my clients out from under the underlying conduct. What happens is they flunk the investigation. They do things during the investigative phase to cause the trouble." So Clinton had to be careful. "Don't do your own investigation. Don't contact witnesses. Don't do anything. If you have a bright idea, pass it on to me." Bennett said he had to know what was out there, what might come back to haunt them. Since this case might likely evolve into an exploration of Clinton's sexual past, Bennett needed to know.

Eventually Bennett sought the president's confidence about his past. "My handling of this and dealing with it is going to be only as good as the information I get," he told Clinton. If other women from Arkansas surfaced, it might create a domestic problem with Hillary and be a political nuisance or more, Bennett told Clinton, but it wouldn't necessarily be a legal difficulty.

One day, Clinton and Bennett went for a stroll on the White House grounds. Both had cigars. Bennett lit his. Clinton did not. Bennett took the matter a step further. Rumors persisted in Washington connecting Clinton sexually with various women. For all Bennett knew, they were total garbage.

Perhaps it was the intimacy of the walk, the perfectly tended White House grounds or the male party and communion suggested by the cigars, even though the president's was unlit.

"If you're caught fucking around in the White House," Bennett said, "I'm not good enough to help you."

"This is a prison," Clinton responded. "I purposefully have no drapes on the windows." As for women, "I'm retired," the president of the United States declared, repeating himself emphatically. "I'm retired."

21

ONE COMPONENT of Fiske's investigation was the death of Vincent Foster. All the speculation, some wild, cast a cloud over Clinton, the White House and even Fiske's own investigation. Fiske decided that if possible he not only had to look to see if there was a crime involved, his primary mission, but he had to go further. There was a real public interest in explaining Foster's death. Fiske decided to order the FBI and prosecutors to do their interviews not in the grand jury room. That way he could issue a public report without violating grand jury rules. Fiske also wanted to complete the investigation quickly. If it dragged on for a year or more, people would think, My God, there must be a huge question about this probe. They would ask, Why is it taking them so long? Time would increase the mystery.

Four pathologists were selected to review the case—the chief medical examiners used by New York City, Seattle, the U.S. armed forces and the FBI. In May, Fiske met with them to hear their preliminary report.

Charles S. Hirsch, for five years the chair of New York University's Department of Forensic Medicine, said it was a no-brainer. The evidence overwhelmingly showed it was a suicide. The speculation, some of it published, that Foster died elsewhere and his body was moved was absolutely not true. It was impossible, Hirsch said.

Fiske stopped Hirsch, reminding him that for years he had heard expert witnesses testify about conclusions. Experts always left themselves an escape hatch, Fiske said, an on-the-one-hand, on-the-other-hand analysis. But Hirsch had just come out and said flat-out impossible?

"Yeah, flat-out impossible," Hirsch said. On a scale of 100, this is a 99. He said he had done hundreds of these investigations, exploring whether deaths were homicides or suicides. "There are always questions. You're never going to finish one of these things where there aren't questions. There are always questions. But you know this one, compared to others, this is easy, this is simple."

The others agreed.

Their analysis and conclusions rang true to Fiske. Reaching conclusions—or deciding whether to prosecute—was a process of aggressive investigation, applying maximum suspicion to everything, but then taking the bulk of information and making a judgment. Fiske agreed with Hirsch, you never got all the relevant information. Decisions had to be made and prosecutors had to move on. When he worked as U.S. attorney for the Southern District in New York City, he had a Saturday morning meeting once a month with all the assistant U.S. attorneys. Going around the table, each had to review his or her cases while Fiske took notes.

If there was insufficient progress after several months, Fiske would shut down the case and direct that the prosecutor devote his or her attention to other cases. They could shift cases easily because the investigations most often were not public. But Fiske realized he had to be extra careful in the matter of Foster's death because a public accounting would be required.

Fiske spoke with David Kendall. He said he wanted to talk with both Clintons for his investigation.

Do you mean just an interview? Kendall asked.

No, Fiske said, I think it's best for everybody if we do it under oath. He would be willing out of respect for the office to do it at the White House, in lieu of a formal grand jury appearance. He then would read the testimony to the grand jury.

Kendall asked what precisely did Fiske want?

The session would not involve the Arkansas aspect of the Whitewater investigation, Fiske said. He would confine questions to Vince Foster's suicide, the handling of the papers from Foster's office after his death and Treasury's heads-up to White House officials about the Whitewater criminal referrals to the Justice Department. He made it clear that he wanted to dispose of the Washington end of the investigation so Congress could proceed with its own inquiry and public hearings.

On Sunday, June 12, Fiske came to the White House. In part he wanted to get a read on the Clintons—an essential, routine step for any prosecutor.

Kendall and Cutler had prepared the president for his deposition. They reminded him of the fundamental rule: Answer yes or no and then shut up. Don't volunteer information, don't give speeches.

Fiske found Clinton cooperative. He answered every question. There were lots of "I-don't-recalls." Sometimes Fiske found a way to ask the key questions more than once.

The president said he had not had a sense that Foster was deeply depressed. He said he knew little about the documents taken from Foster's office, or about the White House–Treasury contacts on the Whitewater referrals to the Justice Department. He wasn't argumentative, but he gave a number of incredibly long answers—the length, not the content, making his lawyers uncomfortable.

After the session was over, the president gave Fiske a tour of the Treaty Room. President Ulysses Grant's table was there. Grant's cabinet used to meet there. There were seven drawers in the table, one for each cabinet member to store his government papers. Wouldn't it be nice if government were like that today? Clinton joked. Fiske sensed that Clinton was trying to be his friend.

Hillary was next. Her tone was direct. She said often that she didn't remember. She carried the same sort of studied detachment in the interview with the prosecutor as she had in her now famous meeting with reporters two months earlier, an event that had been dubbed her "Pink Press Conference." Because the questions didn't deal with the old Arkansas end of White-

403

water, it was a lot easier. She confidently and even somewhat breezily told how little she knew about the White House–Treasury contacts, Vince Foster's death and his documents. When Fiske left, Hillary met with her lawyers. The attorneys told Hillary they felt Fiske would soon wrap up his Foster and White House–Treasury investigations.

On Thursday, June 30, Fiske issued two reports. After an extensive grand jury investigation, he said he had found that no crimes had been committed in the White House–Treasury contacts. His report on Foster stated: "Vincent W. Foster, Jr. committed suicide by firing a bullet from a .38 revolver into his mouth. The evidence overwhelmingly supports this conclusion, and there is no evidence to the contrary." He also wrote, "We found no evidence that issues involving Whitewater, (related issues) or other personal legal matters of the president or Mrs. Clinton were a factor in Foster's suicide."

Cutler was pleased, and he went to see Clinton. The president didn't like to talk about Foster's death, but he indicated he was content that an independent investigation had established once and for all that Vince had taken his own life. It's painful, Clinton told Cutler, but at least it ends that chapter. The determination on the White House–Treasury contacts would finally lift the cloud that had enveloped the White House.

Cutler issued a statement: "This should put to rest the irresponsible speculations—many of them politically motivated—that something more sinister had occurred. We hope these rumormongers and the media that published their rumors will now leave the Foster family in peace."

That same day, the president was sitting at his desk in the Oval Office about to sign the reauthorization of the Independent Counsel Act. It was several hours after Fiske had released his report on Foster. There was a moment of hesitation. Clinton turned to his new chief of staff, Leon Panetta, a former California congressman and Clinton's first budget director, who had taken over from McLarty three days earlier.

"Do I have to?" Clinton asked. He was more serious than not. It would be extraordinary for a president to begin a bill-signing ceremony and then change his mind.

"Mr. President," Panetta said to Clinton, "you don't have any alternative. It's been passed overwhelmingly by the Congress." By margins of about 3 to 1, both the Senate and House had passed versions of the legislation, and the administration had pushed it. Panetta had been elected to Congress in 1976 as part of the backlash against Watergate and Republicans. Aggressive independent counsels or prosecutors had basically performed well, enforcing higher ethical standards and keeping Republicans in line, Panetta felt.

A statement was handed out in which the president called the law "a foundation stone for the trust between the government and our citizens. It ensures that no matter what party controls the Congress or the executive branch, an independent nonpartisan process will be in place to guarantee the integrity of public officials and ensure that no one is above the law."

He added, "This is a good bill that I sign into law today."

Afterwards, Clinton asked Panetta, Could it be misused? Have we started down a path we are not going to like? He and Hillary were already under investigation by Special Counsel Fiske, but would this law somehow make it worse? "I hope this doesn't present trouble for the future," Clinton said.

The next day, Attorney General Reno made an application to the three-judge panel for a Whitewater independent counsel under the new law. She formally requested that Fiske be selected for the post "so that he may continue his ongoing investigation without disruption and with the full independence provided by the act." She added, "Appointment of a different independent counsel would seriously disrupt the investigation."

Senator Lauch Faircloth, a North Carolina Republican, immediately jumped on Reno, declaring it "highly improper" for her to recommend Fiske because she herself had selected him as the initial Whitewater counsel. Instead, Faircloth said Reno should have asked the judges "to appoint a new, truly independent counsel."

Indiana Representative Dan Burton and nine other Republicans wrote to the three-judge panel to complain about Fiske, particularly

his report ruling that Foster had committed suicide. Despite the partisan objection, Fiske was
confident that he would be allowed to continue. He felt there was a need to expedite the
investigation, and his Republican credentials
would stand him in good stead.

Justice Department attorneys passed word to
Fiske that he could not use the grand jury or
operate under the new law because the three
judges had not selected him. A department
lawyer called the clerk assigned to the three-judge
panel and asked that the judges act as quickly
as possible because Fiske was in limbo.

As a month passed Fiske grew worried. He
didn't like the waiting.

On August 5, Fiske arrived in Florida to
visit his ill mother-in-law. As he walked off
the plane and greeted his wife, his beeper went
off. The return number was his special counsel's
office in Washington. He reached Mark Stein,
one of the attorneys in his office.

"What the heck is this message?" Fiske asked.

"You won't believe this," Stein said. "The
three-judge court just picked Ken Starr to
replace you."

Fiske was surprised, disappointed and angry.

The three-judge panel said, "It is not our intent
to impugn the integrity of the attorney general's
appointee, but rather to reflect the intent of the
Act that the actor be protected against perceptions of conflict."

Kenneth Winston Starr, 48, was not surprised that he was asked to be the new inde-

pendent counsel. He had been on the short list for a number of appointments recently, including the Supreme Court. He had been one of Attorney General Reno's finalists for the Whitewater special counsel the previous year when she had selected Fiske. He was one of the Republican Party's leading conservative legal figures—law clerk to Chief Justice Warren Burger in the mid-1970s, chief of staff for Attorney General William French Smith from 1981 to 1983. Reagan had appointed Starr a judge on the District of Columbia Federal Appeals Court in 1983 at the age of 37, then the youngest appointee to that court.

In 1989, Bush asked Starr to leave the appeals court to become solicitor general to argue the administration's cases before the Supreme Court. Starr loved being an appeals court judge but heeded the president's call. In 1993, after Bush lost, Starr had considered running for the U.S. Senate from Virginia, but did not when polls showed that Oliver North was the favorite among Virginia Republicans. Starr was in private practice in the Washington office of Kirkland & Ellis, a large firm based in Chicago, earning about $1 million a year.

The son of a Baptist minister from Texas, Starr was a dutiful, even pious figure, balding, with glasses, a Mister Rogers manner and a reputation for patience. He tended to think and talk abstractly. He had only one major problem with the opportunity to serve as independent counsel. He not only thought the law was unconstitutional, he felt it was bad policy, harmful to the orderly administration of justice.

During the early Reagan administration, when Starr had served as the attorney general's chief of staff, he had been among a group of conservative lawyers who wished to overturn a series of laws and court rulings. Among them were school busing for racial balance, the ban on organized school prayer and the independent counsel provision of the Ethics in Government Act. Since the high court ruled in 1988 that the independent counsel law was constitutional, Starr agreed to take the Whitewater post. It did not seem to give him pause to accept a post created under a law he opposed and thought unconstitutional. He spoke of duty. His former colleague on the court of appeals, Judge David Sentelle, had asked him to serve.

Kendall read the order from the three-judge panel naming Starr. It implied that Fiske's investigation was tainted and had to be dumped. Kendall thought that it would probably force Starr to start from scratch. He felt Starr would have a huge learning curve taking over the case. Starr had never been a prosecutor or criminal defense attorney, and he was not familiar with the facts. We're going to have a big, big, big delay, Kendall surmised. Still, he thought Starr would be fair. Any White House effort to demonize the new independent counsel would be a mistake, he believed.

Kendall's career had already intersected with Starr. Seven years earlier, in 1987, Kendall had represented *The Washington Post* in a libel case brought by the president of Mobil Oil, William P. Tavoulareas, who was incensed by an investigative article alleging that he had helped his son win millions of dollars in Mobil shipping business. Starr, as an appeals court judge, had written a First Amendment opinion giving the *Post* its biggest libel court victory. Kendall had been overjoyed at the Starr opinion, which concluded that the disputed article was largely true and endorsed aggressive investigative reporting.

Kendall had a passing acquaintance with Starr and liked him. The two shared a sense of decorum that others might consider stuffy. Kendall found Starr smooth, witty, polished, hardly a Republican zealot.

"Who is Ken Starr?" Harold Ickes screamed at one of Lloyd Cutler's deputies. Ickes was livid when no one had an immediate answer. They had been caught by surprise.

Panetta convened a meeting in his office to consider a response. The group tried to put together a fact sheet.

Cutler called the president.

Clinton said he was disappointed. Look at Starr's political background, he said.

Cutler tried to allay Clinton's concerns. He said Starr had an excellent reputation. He had been a good judge, not overly doctrinaire. He had been a good solicitor general. Recently Cutler had debated Starr on television about presidential immunity in civil cases. Starr didn't believe there was immunity, but he was not a right-wing kook. The problem, Cutler said, was that Starr probably would have to revisit everything that Fiske had done.

Clinton was heartsick. That could mean months more of investigation.

Cutler said it would be madness to criticize Starr. He issued a terse statement promising full cooperation.

"Wait a minute! Just wait a goddamn minute!" James Carville shouted. Starr had once criticized Clinton to Carville's face in the U.S. Air Club at Washington's National Airport. He called Clinton and recounted his chance encounter with Starr. Carville said he wanted to challenge Starr publicly as an obvious partisan. Starr had been appointed by the three-judge panel headed by Judge David Sentelle, a conservative Republican. Sentelle's patron had been Senator Jesse Helms, the arch-conservative Republican from North Carolina. It was so obvious it hurt, Carville said. Starr was a partisan pawn. Nothing happened in Washington that was not political, Carville believed. Their strategy had to be clear: politicize the appointment now from the beginning. He planned to attack.

Clinton wanted both to mollify and attack. Caught between Cutler's caution and Carville's belligerence, Clinton called Bob Bennett, who in a way represented both schools. Bennett was in Montana on vacation when Clinton reached him. Although Clinton was asking Bennett for advice, he made it clear that Starr's appointment should not go unanswered.

Kendall soon called Bennett conveying instructions from the president. "The client," Kendall said, wanted Bennett to go public with his own critique of Starr. Both Clinton and the White House had to be insulated.

"I think Starr should decline it," Bennett

said publicly on Sunday afternoon, because of his partisan connections. "I think there is a real appearance of unfairness. If Starr found anything wrong, I don't think anybody could have any confidence in that."

Attending the American Bar Association's annual meeting in New Orleans, Starr dismissed Bennett's concerns and said he would approach the inquiry "with an open mind." He spoke of himself as if he were still a judge.

"Judges are accustomed to setting aside their views and proceeding apace with a fresh perspective and saying that was yesterday and this is today and my duty is to go forward with an open mind. That's what judges do, and I believe Congress intended that independent counsel conduct himself or herself in that same manner."

Cutler, upset, argued to the president and Panetta that public criticism of the new independent counsel would antagonize Starr and wind up hurting the president. The key to maneuvering through these investigations was accommodation, not confrontation. The independent counsel could make life miserable for the Clintons and their aides.

On Monday, Cutler slipped the knife to Bennett. Bennett was speaking for himself, not the president, he said. "We have no reason to doubt the fair-mindedness of Ken Starr. The president does not think that Starr should step aside."

When Cutler's statements were published the next day, Tuesday, August 9, Carville decided he was not going to sit still. Everything in his gut said Starr was bad news. Carville called his friends in the White House. "Y'all better get ready, this guy is bad, bad, bad!" He had a letter hand-delivered to Panetta.

"I am convinced that the appointment of Kenneth W. Starr as independent counsel represents a historic and unconscionable violation of fairness and justice," Carville wrote. Because he was a consultant to the White House and the Democratic National Committee, Carville noted that he was constrained from speaking out. No more. "I am relinquishing my White House pass (it is enclosed with this letter)." He was also terminating his retainer fee with the Democrats. Starr had been appointed because of "political pressure from virulent opponents of the president." Carville said he had agonized and realized he had become ineffective in defending the president. "This is an intolerable situation and I plan on saying it often; speaking only as an individual citizen and not on behalf of the White House or of the Democratic Party."

Panetta showed the letter to Cutler. The counsel argued that no one would believe that the president's former campaign strategist, a highly visible figure such as Carville, was acting alone or without tacit presidential approval. He threatened to quit if Carville went ahead.

Panetta and Stephanopoulos concluded that the president could not afford to have Cutler, the man Clinton had brought in to restore his credibility, quit. Even if Cutler were bluffing, they couldn't play it out.

Panetta talked to Clinton.

Clinton was still suspicious of the Starr

appointment. "Things like this don't just happen," Clinton said.

Panetta agreed that it was strange and likely meant trouble, but it would not be smart to unleash Carville. If Cutler resigned, it would be a disaster.

Clinton said his first instinct was to punch Starr in the stomach, but he agreed that the Carville approach was not workable. "Where are the Democrats to attack this appointment?" he asked. "Who will attack?" Only Republicans seemed to know how to attack, he lamented.

Carville had drafted his letter as much for public consumption as for Panetta. He had given a copy to Ann Devroy, the White House correspondent for *The Washington Post,* with an agreement that he could pull it back before 6 p.m. After six, she could use it and call the White House for comment.

Stephanopoulos called Carville.

"Please, God, man," Stephanopoulos said. "Lloyd Cutler says he's going to resign."

Stephanopoulos begged and pleaded, and Carville finally promised to send someone to pick up his letter from the White House. "You have got to call Ann to tell her to spike the fucking story," he added.

Stephanopoulos called, and the story did not run.

But Carville was not going to be muzzled. He attacked Starr publicly for giving a $1,000 contribution to a Texas Republican who was running regular "Whitewater update" radio commercials criticizing Clinton. He also lashed

out at Judge Sentelle. "What is a political protégé of Jesse Helms doing appointing a potential senatorial candidate to a position like that?"
Carville said. "... Partisan politics is driving this
whole thing."

On Sunday, August 7, Fiske was in Arkansas,
where he had his main office. A rebellion was
in progress. The ten prosecutors who had
worked round the clock wanted to resign, and
the 25 FBI agents were demoralized. Fiske
gave them a pep talk.

They could not quit, he said. He appreciated
the loyalty. "I appreciate it but that's wrong.
This is for the country, we've got to keep this
thing going and you guys, everyone has an
obligation here to stay on at least until Ken Starr
has a replacement that you've had a chance to
fully debrief so that they can pick up the baton
and not lose any speed.

"The investigation is going to go on," Fiske
said. "Ken Starr is a very capable person."

Monday, August 8, Starr went to Little Rock
to meet the special counsel's staff.

"My people are going to leave," Fiske said.
"Don't count on them staying." They were
loyal and emotional. "No reflection on you, but
they just don't want to stay."

Fiske took Starr to meet his deputies. Going
around the table the attorneys presented their
main cases.

Within the next six months, Fiske expected
seven indictments naming 11 people. His prosecutors told Starr about David Hale, the former
municipal judge who had said Clinton pressured

him to make a $300,000 loan to Susan McDougal. They were undertaking a number of investigative steps to determine whether Hale's charge could be corroborated. Fiske said he found Hale credible. He was believable and would be an effective witness.

Fiske's prosecutors had also turned up evidence indicating that Webster Hubbell, the president's close friend, a former associate attorney general in the Justice Department and a former partner of Hillary's in the Rose Law Firm, had bilked the firm out of hundreds of thousands of dollars. Fiske said they were also preparing a criminal fraud case against the sitting governor of Arkansas, Jim Guy Tucker.

Starr said he was impressed with the investigations and how far they had come in a relatively short period of time.

Fiske could hardly take Starr's compliment as vindication. His two public reports had been construed as favorable to the Clinton administration. Fiske wished he could have stayed and shown the judges and the public the serious criminal cases he intended to bring.

On the morning of August 10, Clinton was first asked in public what he thought about the Starr appointment.

"Everybody else has talked about that," he said, without revealing his own role in the positive and negative statements coming out of the administration about Starr, contradictory as they were. "I'll cooperate with whoever's picked. I just want to get it done."

After reviewing what Fiske had accomplished, Starr concluded he had to reopen the Foster death investigation. Starr felt it was still ambiguous. He would have to walk over every inch of ground to assure the public that Fiske's findings had been correct. He increased the number of lawyers working on the case from two to four and the number of FBI agents from four to 12.

As Cutler's six-month tenure was coming to an end in the summer of 1994, he was experiencing his own disillusionment. He found the working situation within the White House untenable. The Clark Clifford role hadn't materialized. All too often Clinton's staff did not bother to tell Cutler about meetings, and he couldn't attend meetings he didn't hear about. Cutler also felt crippled in performing his lawyerly tasks. He couldn't take notes since the independent counsel and multiple congressional committees could subpoena any piece of paper that was created. The committees wanted drafts of his investigative report on the White House–Treasury contacts, internal memos, exchanges of correspondence. He felt as if there were hidden cameras placed in every office in the West Wing.

All presidents needed running room to ask questions and get recommendations, options and the potential negative consequences of any decision. Lawyers had to issue warnings, perhaps even overstate that certain actions could be against the law, casting arguments in hyperbolic, apocalyptic language. In a memo or notes obtained by political opponents, such matters could be easily misconstrued.

Cutler also found it distressing that the president was constantly shaping his views about policy and other matters to attract the largest number of people. These course corrections, Clinton protested, were minor and consistent. Cutler thought that too often they looked calculated and manipulative.

Watergate had heightened all these inherent problems, Cutler believed. The simple, perhaps tragic bottom line was that the public no longer trusted the presidency. It wasn't just the person in the office. It wasn't just politicians or public figures. It was the presidency itself.

Cutler felt he had never achieved an intimate relationship with Clinton. Intimacy was the main building block for getting a client to confide in a lawyer. Cutler hadn't come close.

In those six months, Cutler noticed how the White House had changed dramatically. With the end of the Cold War and no major external threat or economic crisis, Clinton was not being tested. The major crises were the personal and private business scandals. As the questions mounted and investigations proliferated, Clinton had turned more and more inward. He was not seeking the guidance and advice he needed for the great missions of the U.S. presidency.

If Franklin Roosevelt had been a 10 on a scale of 1 to 10, Cutler concluded, Clinton was only a 7 or an 8.

Cutler began to search for his replacement. He knew that he had to recruit and get a successor in place or he wouldn't be allowed to leave.

He wanted to find someone with a commensurate knowledge of Washington. He soon landed on Abner J. Mikva, chief judge of the U.S. Court of Appeals for the District of Columbia, which after the Supreme Court is perhaps the most important court in the country. Mikva, 68, had served on the court for 15 years and previously had spent ten years in Congress, representing a liberal Chicago district. A Chicago politician and a serious legal analyst, Mikva had clerked on the Supreme Court and had taught law. He was intimately familiar with Congress, the federal courts and the issues. Cutler invited Mikva to lunch at his club, the Metropolitan, just two blocks from the White House West Wing. He did not tell Clinton what he was doing.

"How would you like to come be White House counsel?" Cutler inquired almost at once, smiling, mildly laughing and shaking his arms at his sides. He liked surprise, and he liked to sell. "It's the most exciting lawyer's job in the country, if not the world," Cutler told Mikva. It was better, more interesting and more at the center of events than attorney general. "As counsel, you're on the cutting edge of every issue. You're occupied with what will be in the next day's news." Yes, Cutler said, you have to make quick decisions, more often than not based on inadequate information. "But it's truly exciting."

Mikva had one reservation. He barely knew the president.

Cutler said it was easy to get to know Clinton. He indicated that Mikva's name had been run by the president, who liked the idea and knew and respected Mikva's background and reputation.

Mikva said he would have to think about it and talk to his wife. He found his wife surprisingly nonresistant. About an hour after lunch he called Cutler to say that he would do it if the president asked him.

The next year Mikva would have to retire as chief judge of the appeals court, and he liked the idea of capping his career with a senior position in the executive branch. He would then be one of the few individuals who had served near the top of all three branches of government. Clinton offered the job, and Mikva accepted.

During a transition of seven weeks, Cutler acquainted Mikva with the details of the job. They agreed that for practical purposes they had no attorney-client privilege that would guarantee the confidentiality of their papers or discussions with the president.

"Don't take notes," Cutler advised.

The president told Mikva that he wanted all the information on Whitewater delivered to the investigators. "Get it all out," Clinton directed. "I'm not covering up," he said at another point. "Put everything out." On Whitewater, he said, he and Hillary had one problem—the McDougals, their Whitewater business partners. "The only mistake we made is who we went into business with."

1. Gerald Ford never wanted to become president, and First Lady Betty Ford advised her husband that he shouldn't get involved in making recommendations to Nixon about when or how to resign.

2. General Alexander M. Haig Jr., White House chief of staff in the final year of the Nixon presidency, acted as broker and go-between with Vice President Ford in the dangerous days when the presidency was in play.

3. Ford with Jack Marsh, a former congressman. As a top Ford aide, Marsh told Ford he couldn't agree to grant Nixon a pardon because it would look like a quid pro quo for Nixon's resignation.

4. Bryce Harlow, one of the wise old men of the Republican Party, told Vice President Ford that he was in grave danger of compromising his independence by having discussions about a possible Nixon pardon before assuming the presidency.

5. Benton Becker, a former Justice Department attorney, was sent to California to work out the statement Nixon would issue accepting the pardon. He reported to Ford that Nixon was "more depressed than any person I've ever seen, lacking any will to survive."

6. Ford with Robert Hartmann, his top aide. Hartmann tried to talk Ford out of granting Nixon a pardon in the first month of his presidency. "What's the rush?" Hartmann asked.

7. Secretary of State Henry Kissinger, Ford and Defense Secretary James Schlesinger. Ford found that Schlesinger outright disobeyed his orders.

8. "I'll never lie to you," Jimmy Carter said as a candidate. His mother and closest friend told him to stop making the pledge because no one could stand up to complete scrutiny of his statements and actions.

9. Bert Lance, Carter's budget director, warned the president that he was in financial trouble before the story broke and urged, "I think you ought to just let me resign." Carter refused, declaring, "That's foolishness and it doesn't make sense." Carter didn't understand that the investigations of his closest Washington friend and adviser would become an obsession that would engulf his administration until Lance left office. Three months later Carter forced Lance to resign.

10. Arthur Christy, the first special prosecutor under the 1978 ethics reform law, was reluctant to undertake the investigation of Hamilton Jordan for allegedly taking cocaine. After six months Christy found zero evidence to support the allegations.

11. Hamilton Jordan, Carter's top aide and chief political strategist, became the subject of a special prosecutor investigation required by the 1978 Ethics in Government Act. He allegedly had used cocaine at New York's trendy Studio 54. For six critical months in 1979 and 1980 when Carter was running for reelection and managing the Iranian hostage crisis, Jordan was under a cloud. He was finally cleared. "I was turned into something very different than the way I am," he said.

12

12. President Reagan allowed a full-scale internal White House investigation of Iran-contra by his attorneys, and Nancy Reagan pressured White House Chief of Staff Don Regan to replace CIA Director William J. Casey after Casey fell ill. She told the White House lawyers that Casey was "not a close friend" of the Reagans and had never been to the White House residence. Secret Service logs show seven Casey visits to the White House residence from 1984 to early 1986.

13. On July 15, 1987, President Reagan and Vice President George Bush with White House lawyers A. B. Culvahouse and William Lytton. Former National Security Adviser John Poindexter had just testified that the president did not know about the diversion of profits from Iranian arms sales to the Nicaraguan contras. "What was everyone worried about?" the president asked the lawyers.

13

14. Former Senate Republican Leader Howard Baker accepted the job as Reagan's new White House chief of staff in February 1987 but insisted he learn all the secrets. He told the president, "I want you to issue an order to all people in the White House, and the West Wing in particular, saying that I have access to every record and they should give me total cooperation because I'm going to find out, to the best of my ability, what has happened on Iran-contra, *and everything else.*"

15. Secretary of State George Shultz felt that National Security Adviser Poindexter and CIA Director Casey were covering up Iran-contra. "It's Watergate all over again," Shultz said.

16. Iran-contra Independent Counsel Lawrence Walsh insisted on taking former President Reagan's sworn deposition six years into his investigation, in 1992. Reagan couldn't remember the names of some of his key aides or former world leaders. He told Walsh, "It's like I wasn't president at all." In 1998, after his Iran-contra investigation was finally completed, Walsh said, "I think the president was wrong, he was defiant, he was deliberate, but he wasn't dirty."

17. White House press secretary Marlin Fitzwater, who served Presidents Reagan and Bush, watched Bush rage at media leaks early in his presidency. "Yell at me," Fitzwater recommended, "don't yell in front of the whole staff, because those people will all leave and every one of them hates the press, and worse, they will think they have a greater license to hate the press because you do."

18. Attorney Theodore B. Olson, the subject of an investigation, challenged the independent counsel law in the Supreme Court and lost. He was not charged and later represented former President Reagan during the sixth year of the Iran-contra investigation.

19

20

19. President Bush and First Lady Barbara Bush. Scandals and investigations threw Bush off stride from the beginning to the end of his presidency, including Iran-contra and an investigation into alleged tampering with Clinton's passport file during the 1992 election. "Having it end up on this note—" Bush dictated to his diary December 29, 1992, "is absolutely sickening."

20. Brent Scowcroft, Bush's national security adviser, saw the possibility of a diplomatic settlement in the 1991 Gulf crisis as an unacceptable risk. The United States had committed more than 500,000 servicemen and -women to drive Iraqi President Saddam Hussein out of Kuwait. Bush and Scowcroft concluded that they had to have a war to destroy a significant portion of the Iraqi military.

21. Joseph diGenova, the independent counsel for the investigation into allegations that Bill Clinton's passport file was improperly tampered with during the 1992 presidential campaign, brought no charges. But he realized that the various efforts to conceal matters by Bush officials could have been the basis for prosecution. DiGenova saw the powerful weapon in the hands of any independent counsel and the opportunities for abuse.

21

22. C. Boyden Gray, Bush's White House counsel, was shocked to learn in September 1992 that Bush had been dictating a daily diary for six years without telling him. Gray, who was also Bush's counsel during his vice-presidency, saw how scandals and investigations affected Bush emotionally.

22

23. Bernard Nussbaum, Clinton's first White House counsel, didn't want to resign and argued vehemently with the president in March 1994. "I acted properly to protect your interests," Nussbaum told Clinton, "and it will hurt the presidency. . . . It will show this is the price of loyalty. It will give off a message that if a person is close to you and loyal, he can be driven out." But Clinton insisted Nussbaum resign.

24. Lloyd Cutler, Clinton's second White House counsel, found the working situation within the White House untenable. He couldn't take notes because they would be subpoenaed. No advice was private or confidential.

25. Former federal appeals court judge Abner Mikva, Clinton's third White House counsel, tried to give all the Whitewater information out to the prosecutors. The president told Mikva that the only mistake he and his wife made in Whitewater was the selection of their business partners, James and Susan McDougal, their longtime Arkansas friends.

26. Jane Sherburne, the White House special counsel who handled scandals in 1995 and 1996, developed the strategy of avoiding confrontations with congressional committees or the independent counsel. If there was no confrontation, there was little or no scandal news, she concluded.

27. Jack Quinn, the fourth White House counsel, was aggressive in defending the Clintons. He confronted Congress and told Independent Counsel Ken Starr that the subpoena of Mrs. Clinton to testify before the grand jury in 1996 was a "political act," but he was unsuccessful in his effort to persuade Starr not to call the first lady.

28. Charles F. C. Ruff, the fifth White House counsel, gave the main arguments for the president in Clinton's impeachment trial in the Senate. He did not submit his remarks to anyone for review or comment, including the president. There were no practice sessions. It was a stunning delegation of authority by Clinton.

29

29. Paula Corbin Jones, shown in
1998, filed the sexual harassment
lawsuit that set in motion a chain of
events and concealments that led to
Clinton's impeachment by the House.

30. Washington attorney Robert S. Bennett defended the president in the Paula
Jones sexual harassment lawsuit and told Clinton that if he engaged in any sexual
activity with other women while president, it would be difficult to defend him.
"I'm retired," the president said, "I'm retired."

30

31. David E. Kendall, the Clintons' personal Whitewater lawyer, on February 6, 1998, denounces illegal grand jury leaks by Independent Counsel Ken Starr's office. When the president was later subpoenaed to testify before Starr's grand jury, Kendall thought it was a real alternative for the president to invoke his Fifth Amendment right against self-incrimination.

31

32. Robert B. Fiske Jr., the Whitewater special counsel appointed in 1994, rewrote the definition of his jurisdiction so broadly that it gave him the authority to investigate anything that came his way—an authority that was later extended to his successor, Ken Starr.

32

33. Vernon Jordan, Clinton's personal friend, who was enlisted to help former White House intern Monica Lewinsky obtain a job in New York City. He told Starr's grand jury that he asked Monica Lewinsky only if she had had sexual relations with the president. "Period," he testified. "Did they hold hands? Did they kiss? Did they dance? Did they stand on top of the table? I didn't get into that."

34. White House press secretary Michael McCurry was appalled at Clinton's risky personal behavior, and James Carville, Clinton's longtime political strategist, stood by the president and helped keep the partisan fires raging during the Lewinsky inquiry.

33

34

35. Ken Starr testified before the House Judiciary Committee on November 19, 1998, when he believed he regained some of his reputation. Charles Bakaly, Starr's spokesman, sat in the background (left).

36. The Whitewater prosecutors in June 1997—deputy independent counsel John Bates, associate independent counsel Brett Kavanaugh and Independent Counsel Kenneth W. Starr.

37. House Judiciary Committee Chairman Henry Hyde, the Illinois Republican. As his committee was voting to recommend impeachment on December 11 and 12, 1998, he suggested a backchannel maneuver to get a censure resolution of President Clinton onto the House floor.

38. The president and First Lady Hillary Clinton before the Whitewater
investigation engulfed their White House years.

39. President Clinton on January 26, 1998, wagged his finger and told the nation, "I did not have sexual relations with that woman, Miss Lewinsky."

40. President Clinton in the Map Room of the White House, about to deliver his speech to the nation on August 17, 1998. He acknowledged he had a relationship with Lewinsky that was "not appropriate" and "wrong." He criticized Ken Starr during the speech. "I intend to reclaim my family life for my family. It's nobody's business but ours."

41. The Clinton family departed the White House the day after Clinton acknowledged an "inappropriate intimate" relationship with Lewinsky. On the ride to Martha's Vineyard, Massachusetts, for a two-week vacation, the president and the first lady were basically not speaking to each other.

42. President Clinton apologizes September 11, 1998, at a breakfast for religious leaders. "I have sinned," he said. He bit his lip and tears came to his eyes. "I will instruct my lawyers to mount a vigorous defense. . . . But legal language must not obscure the fact that I have done wrong."

Weather

Today: *Variably cloudy,*
showers. High 53. Low 44.
Monday: *Variably cloudy,*
warmer. High 62. Low 45.
Details, Page **B2.**

The Washington Post

Inside: **Book World, TV Week,**
The Post Magazine, Comics
Today's Contents on Page A2

$1.50

122ND YEAR No. 15   ••• ••   c   SUNDAY, DECEMBER 20, 1998

Prices may vary in areas outside
metropolitan Washington. (See box on Page A2)

Clinton Impeached

House Approves Articles Charging Perjury, Obstruction

43. Mrs. Clinton, the president, Vice President Al Gore and House Minority Leader Richard Gephardt after the House voted to impeach Clinton. On the South Lawn, the president told Democratic House members, "We must stop the politics of personal destruction."

43

Weather

Today: *Partly sunny, cold.*
High 38. Low 24.
Sunday: *Afternoon snow.*
High 38. Low 30.
Details, Page **B10.**

The Washington Post

Inside: **Real Estate**
Today's Contents on Page A2

142ND YEAR No. 70 · · ·

SATURDAY, FEBRUARY 13, 1999

25¢

Clinton Acquitted

2 Impeachment Articles Fail to Win Senate Majority

44. The president on February 12, 1999, walks to the Rose Garden after the Senate acquitted him of the impeachment charges. "I want to say again to the American people how profoundly sorry I am for what I said and did to trigger these events," he said, adding, "I believe any person who asks forgiveness has to be prepared to give it."

44

22

ON TUESDAY, NOVEMBER 8, 1994, the Democrats lost control of both the Senate and the House. It was a devastating defeat, especially the loss of the House, which the Democrats had controlled for 40 years. The Clintons went into a deep funk and withdrawal.

Harold Ickes was deeply worried. He wanted a plan of action. Now the White House would not only have to contend with Ken Starr's Whitewater investigation. The Republicans were going to use the new chairmanships of the key committees to investigate the Clinton White House inside and out. The new Speaker of the House, Newt Gingrich, was talking tough and was quoted saying 20 task forces or subcommittees might investigate corruption in the Clinton White House, although he later backed off on the number 20.

"Washington just can't imagine a world in which Republicans have subpoena power," Gingrich said. Ickes could. Because Panetta was more interested in policy than scandal, and Mikva didn't have the stomach for a bare-knuckles defense, Clinton and Panetta told Ickes to set up a special unit within the White House. Ickes contacted Jane Sherburne, a 43-year-old law partner of Cutler's, who had worked at the White House during Cutler's six months. A specialist in internal investigations, Sherburne was a petite version of the

Hillary Rodham Clinton of the 1970s, with thick lenses in her glasses and long hair.

"I want you to come back here and manage this for the next two years and get us through the election," Ickes told her. The "this" was Whitewater and all related scandals. It was obvious that Congress was going to exploit its investigative authority to try to defeat the president's reelection, he said.

Sherburne said she would have to think about what she would require, what it would take to do the job effectively.

Kendall liked the idea of bringing in Sherburne. Gloom and apprehension about Gingrich had overcome the White House. They needed a pro-active strategy, a quick response team such as the 1992 Clinton campaign "War Room." He talked with Sherburne, who identified 39 areas of investigation or concern ranging from Whitewater, Vince Foster and Paula Jones to Mrs. Clinton's various problems. She filled 12 pages of notes and then summarized her approach. "Nothing to hide, stick to the facts, get right the first time, keep it simple, resist harassment, govern America."

Sherburne went to see Ickes at the White House.

Ickes said scandal had absorbed too much attention of the key, day-to-day players—chief of staff Panetta, White House counsel Mikva, spokesman Michael McCurry. Ickes wanted scandal out of all of those offices and concentrated with her.

Her requirement, Sherburne said, was that she would get to hire her own people—other lawyers, congressional relations experts and a special spokesman. She would have to have complete control. It would be too high-risk any other way.

"Fine," Ickes said. He would guarantee her portfolio. "I'll protect you."

She was to report directly to him. He would be her real boss, but she would have to keep Mikva informed about what she was doing since technically she would be assigned to the White House counsel's office.

Sherburne conceived of her new group as a little strike force. The strategy was going to be simple, straight out of Lloyd Cutler's Washington legal playbook: never join the issue, never have an all-out fight with Starr or the congressional committees. Never say no to requests for documents or testimony. Always say, We'll get back to you, we'll get you what we can. Let's talk about this, Let's meet, Let's negotiate. Always keep something on the table. Avoid confrontation. Write conciliatory letters. The reason for the strategy was also simple: if there was no confrontation, there was no news. Conflict was news. White House–Congress to meet tomorrow to work out a compromise was not news. Delay and continuing negotiations were boring. The less scandal news, the better for the president and his reelection.

Ickes arranged for Kendall to bless Sherburne's operation and then took her to meet the president in the diplomatic reception room of the residence. Other senior staff members were there, including Stephanopoulos and McCurry. Ickes gave a little speech about Sherburne's duties and her authority.

Clinton put his arm around Sherburne and walked her over to the corner for a little private conversation. He made small talk, and he said he was glad to have her on the job. The point of Clinton's gesture was a demonstration of his support, and the message about her authority seemed to have been conveyed. They all were like dogs, Sherburne thought, each marking their territory. Scandals were now hers.

Early in 1995, Sherburne went to see Hillary in the first lady's West Wing office. She had met Mrs. Clinton several times during Cutler's tenure but didn't know her well. Maggie Williams, Hillary's chief of staff, was present.

Sitting on a small stool, Sherburne outlined her responsibilities and her theory of scandal management. The White House staff had let themselves be surprised too often, did not know the facts, often spoke or released information prematurely, Sherburne said. They did not appreciate how important it was to move quickly, get information out before a story built. Things were going to change. Her new team was going to be organized. They were going to plan in advance.

Mrs. Clinton, listening intently, could barely contain her skepticism. Sternly, she asked, who was Sherburne going to hire?

Sherburne said she was in the process of recruiting six to eight people—congressional, media and political components, and more lawyers.

Mmm-hmm, Mrs. Clinton said, assenting. She was weary. She suggested that nothing was ever right. What did Sherburne see coming and when?

Sherburne had some idea about what the congressional investigators had scheduled, but there was no telling in many respects. They would follow events and new disclosures. They didn't know where the Starr investigation was going, and the media operated on its own timetable. The rhythm was unpredictable.

Mmm-hmm. Hillary said she would want to be reassured from time to time, and would need to understand what Sherburne was doing.

Sherburne left feeling she could not read the first lady well, and what she could read said, in effect, Prove it to me, this scandal management has been fucked up for two years.

Ickes and Sherburne thought deep and hard about who should be the public face and voice for the new scandal management team. It was a critical link. Ickes had heard of a Harvard-trained attorney and former debate champion working at the Housing Department named Mark Fabiani. As counsel and then deputy mayor of Los Angeles under Mayor Tom Bradley from 1985 to 1992, Fabiani had steered Bradley successfully through federal and city legal probes of Bradley's personal finances. He had also helped organize Bradley's response to the 1992 Los Angeles riots. Ickes figured that anyone steeped in crisis management in Los Angeles might be able to handle Washington. Ickes asked Fabiani to the White House.

Fabiani, 37, went to Ickes's small West Wing office. He looked like a 1990s version of an *L.A. Law* attorney, handsome, tall, smooth. He was fresh from a honeymoon in Florence, Italy, and happy with his job at the Department of Housing and Urban Development, managing the empowerment zones program that was designed to help inner cities economically.

What would you do with Whitewater?

The public and the press find Whitewater a stale issue, Fabiani said. It was so long ago and so far away. The fuel to the controversy has been the subsequent actions and the mystery surrounding them—Vince Foster's death and the documents in his office. The response to trouble or a crisis was often more damaging than the underlying events, he said. They needed a fresh approach. If there was nothing to hide, the White House had to organize itself to be the agent of disclosure—explaining and getting all the information out. Fabiani said that in law school he had been the chief research assistant to Alan Dershowitz, the activist professor and lawyer. In the process he had developed a healthy respect for the press. Good reporters could be steered with solid information and arguments.

Ickes liked what he saw and heard, and he summoned Fabiani for a second meeting.

"Look, I've told the president and the first lady you're going to take this job," Ickes said.

"I don't think I want it," Fabiani replied. He loved his job. Being recently married, he did not want a position that would take up his whole life.

"You've got to take this job," Ickes said.

Fabiani continued to resist.

"It's done," Ickes said.

Fabiani would not go along. Ickes was not accustomed to being rebuffed, especially by a mid-level bureaucrat from the Housing Department. This offer was a request to serve the president of the United States. It was not to be taken lightly. Ickes soon wound himself into a rage, his ears sticking out, veins bulging, eyes almost popping.

Fabiani was not responding.

"People are unhappy with the empowerment zones and you may not have a job at HUD," Ickes said.

Fabiani was stunned at the implied threat. "You ought to want a person in this job who's not afraid of losing another job," he replied sharply.

"Look," Ickes said, "the president *needs* to be reelected." They were fighting for the future of the country, the Democratic ideas that Fabiani supported. "There are going to be all these investigations. How we handle it could be the difference. You're part of a team in this administration, and if we need you to move from one position to another, you ought to do it."

Fabiani thought that was a more reasonable argument. He said he'd think about it.

Mulling it over, Fabiani decided he had to get beyond Ickes's threat about losing his current job. It was despicable, but Ickes's later arguments were compelling. Someone else was the coach and Fabiani was just a player to be moved around. Perhaps he had an obligation to the administration and the president he served to be a team player. He agreed to the assignment.

During the next weeks, Sherburne recruited members for her team. Mikva asked what she was doing. He reminded her that he was the counsel and he, not she, reported to Panetta. That meant Sherburne reported to him, not to Ickes, and she should be working with him on these appointments.

Sherburne was surprised. She had diagrammed it for everyone, showing that she reported to Ickes while keeping Mikva informed. She believed she was doing that.

Mikva disagreed.

Ickes arrived in Mikva's office with Sherburne in tow.

The conversation began in a friendly tone on the subject of exactly how they were going to function. It deteriorated when Ickes explained that one of Sherburne's positions was going to be filled from the counsel office slots, and Mikva would not be involved.

I'm not going to be told what to do by *that woman*, Mikva said.

"Ab," Ickes screamed, "you better get this fucking straight and listen up!" He said he had Panetta's approval, and this was the way he was doing it. He had hired that woman, he wanted his team and he wanted it to work this way. Ickes totally lost it and flew into a blinding rage. "You better keep your fucking nose out of it! And if you don't like it you can just go fuck yourself!" he told Mikva.

Okay, Mikva said.

Sherburne thought of Mikva as a federal judge and no one talked to a judge that way, but she also believed that Ickes had rescued her. Wow, she thought, was there some way to bottle that? In her entire life nobody had ever defended her with such clarity and authority.

428

Ickes later told Sherburne to try to walk the line, to keep Mikva informed, but foremost she had to do the job.

Mikva was aware that Sherburne was also cultivating Mrs. Clinton, seeking out the first lady as another protector.

"Why doesn't Jane get to sit in on some of these meetings?" Mrs. Clinton asked a surprised Mikva one time, suggesting that the old boys' network in the White House was operating behind Sherburne's back.

"You can't do that!" Clinton screamed at Mikva.

Mikva had just told the president that they would have to pull his nomination for CIA director, Michael P. C. Carns, a retired four-star Air Force general, because he had failed to pay Social Security taxes for a Filipino houseboy he had brought to the United States.

"Why are you doing this?" Clinton raged. "How can you do this?"

Mikva said he was just reflecting what would happen in Congress. The Senate was not going to confirm someone as CIA director who had perhaps broken the law. It was the equivalent of a male nanny problem. The cry of a double standard would be too loud.

"The sad truth," Clinton said the next day, March 11, 1995, announcing that Carns was withdrawing voluntarily, "is that we live in a time when even the most exemplary individuals like General Carns—who has already given so much to his country—are deterred from serving by the fear that their records will be distorted, their achievements ignored and their families maligned."

"Oh my God," Clinton told Panetta upon hearing the news that Reno had asked for another independent counsel, this time to investigate his friend and Housing secretary Henry Cisneros for allegedly lying to the FBI about payments made to a former mistress. "Where are we headed with this?" He reminded Panetta that he had spotted trouble with the independent counsel law the day he signed it. "I told you," the president said. "Is Janet exercising good judgment here?" He said Cisneros was a dedicated, decent guy whom everyone liked. Years earlier as mayor of San Antonio, Cisneros had paid a huge price because of the affair. He had to admit publicly that he'd had this mistress, and then acknowledge that he had paid money to her. Now the issue was, what had the exact price been? It was too absurd. This was one where Janet Reno should have done the right thing, Clinton said.

Mikva said his hands were tied. There was no way he could get information from Reno, but he had heard from others at Justice that the FBI had forced Reno's hand. FBI Director Louis Freeh had effectively slammed his fist down on Reno's desk, insisting that lying to the FBI had to be treated with the utmost seriousness and could not be kissed off. Part of the effectiveness of the FBI in gathering accurate information was the threat that anyone lying or deceiving agents could be prosecuted.

"I wish she had resisted the pressure," the president said.

In a phone conversation that day, Clinton told Cisneros that he would not have to resign. They should stick together, the president said.

Mikva began privately calling Clinton "the good-news president." The president didn't like to hear about problems and scandals, and at times he took out his anger on the bearer of the bad news. It was a key feature of Clinton's personality that Mikva realized few people understood. It was also a potentially dangerous character flaw in a president.

In contrast, Hillary seemed to be drawn to bad news, seeing conspiratorial maneuvering in sometimes benign behavior. Mikva came to see her as a center of paranoia. He had served on the court of appeals with Ken Starr for seven years and followed his work as solicitor general. In many respects, he felt the Clintons were lucky. Starr tended to spread himself too thin. He loved to travel and make speeches, and at times, Mikva felt, he had underprepared for his arguments before the Supreme Court. Mikva also felt that Starr was the opposite of a street fighter, and that was good for the Clintons. He told the Clintons that Starr was a decent, moderate conservative. "A model of what an appellate judge should be," Mikva said.

"Your friend Ken Starr," Hillary snapped derisively several times when Starr did something she didn't like.

Aware of Hillary's power, Mikva ran major legal decisions by her to get her opinion or approval. As the Clintons' personal legal bills began to mount, he tried to get some decisions about the private legal defense fund that had been set up for them. Hillary was nervous, and Mikva kept pressing her.

"Well," she finally told him, "you have to talk to the president about that."

With Hillary and Sherburne heavily involved in White House legal business, Mikva began joking that he did not leave a lifetime appointment on the federal appeals court to be *deputy* White House counsel. In a sense, if Clinton had fired his wife as his chief domestic policy adviser after the failure of health care reform in the fall of 1994, he had rehired her as his chief legal adviser. Granted, it was natural for anyone to consult a spouse, and she was entangled in many of the investigations, if not at the center of them, so her role was perhaps inevitable. But Hillary's paranoid style added to the suspicions that secrets were being kept, Mikva felt.

Mikva wanted to satisfy the investigators, create an atmosphere of comity. Taking the president at face value to disclose what was available, Mikva decided that he would try to expedite the Starr investigation as much as possible. He called Mark Tuohey, Starr's top deputy in Washington. Tuohey was a Democrat, and the two had known each other for years.

"We want you guys to get what you want," Mikva said. "We're not afraid of the facts." A prolonged inquiry would hurt the president. A multi-year investigation would be particularly distracting and hurt Clinton's ability to govern. To make it clear that he was operating with Clinton's authority, he said, "The president told me, 'Give them what they want.' "

Starr and Tuohey asked for the documents from Vince Foster's office, and other documents relating to Foster.

Mikva considered it a back channel, although he had Clinton's approval. Three or four deliveries of documents were made.

In the spring of 1995, Starr called Mikva.

"We would like to examine the president and the first lady under oath at their convenience," Starr said.

Mikva proposed that Starr take the testimony at the White House on a weekend, as Fiske had done the previous year. Starr said that would be fine. He agreed it would be in lieu of formal grand jury appearances.

Mikva was delighted. That way he could release a statement after the testimony was given and it would appear in the back pages of the newspapers.

They agreed to begin at 1 p.m. Saturday, April 22. Mikva called Starr that morning. "Can we do it at noon?" he asked.

Starr agreed. They gathered at noon in the Treaty Room of the White House. The president was first. He was direct in his answers. He didn't seem particularly put out or unhappy. It took two hours. Mikva was surprised. Am I missing something here? he thought to himself. The questions were mostly trivial. He almost felt sorry for Starr, that the independent counsel should be embarrassed to be asking the president such questions. Many didn't seem to border on anything that could possibly be criminal. Only a few were pointed about the $300,000 loan David Hale had made to Susan McDougal after allegedly being pressured by Clinton. Clinton denied it.

Mikva could also see that Clinton seemed to like Starr. They almost hit it off. At the end, Starr, a history buff, made some comments and asked some friendly questions about the White House.

"Ab," Clinton said, "when we're through, make sure Judge Starr sees the Lincoln Bedroom."

As the president was saying that, Hillary entered the room.

"Don't you dare show him the Lincoln Bedroom," she whispered to Mikva.

Mikva decided to obey the last order. Starr did not see the famous room.

The president left, and Hillary sat down. She was measurably cooler. She was sworn in and the interrogation began. After a few minutes, there was a knock at the door. A White House steward entered the room.

"Golf clubs! Golf clubs!" the steward exclaimed, running to the other end of the room. He opened the closet, took out a set of golf clubs and exited with them hurriedly.

Starr and Tuohey realized suddenly that Mikva had called to advance the session an hour so Clinton could get in a full round on the spring Sunday. Mikva was looking at the ceiling.

Hillary's sworn session lasted two hours. She made it clear she was not happy to be there as she struggled to try to answer how much legal work she had done on Whitewater and related matters.

Kendall was wary of Starr's questions, some of which seemed to stray far afield into the Clintons' political life.

• • •

The president was disbelieving on May 17 when his attorney general announced she was seeking appointment of yet another independent counsel to investigate the business dealings of Commerce Secretary Ronald H. Brown. Brown was another close Clinton political ally and friend, a possible candidate to run his reelection bid the next year.

The entire administration was now a target, Clinton told Panetta. He reminded his chief of staff of his premonition the day he signed the independent counsel law. Reno was dead wrong on this decision, Clinton said. Brown had done nothing wrong. The president told Brown that he would not have to resign during the inquiry.

The Senate Whitewater hearings were scheduled to begin in July. Sherburne heard that Chairman Alfonse D'Amato, a New York Republican senator, was going to open with Vince Foster's death and the handling of the documents taken from his office. Sherburne thought D'Amato had made a smart tactical decision— a White House suicide had all the attendant mystery, grief, supposedly missing documents, the ancient Arkansas past resurfacing like an old ghost in the White House. Various pieces of the story had been told, but no one had presented the public with a coherent picture of what had happened. She was determined that D'Amato and his partisan committee should not be the narrators.

Mark Fabiani had spent months fielding Whitewater questions from reporters and getting to know some of them. Few cared about the basic Whitewater land deal and all its convoluted, small-potatoes intricacies. The questions were focused on suspected connections between the Foster death and suspicions about the removal of Whitewater documents from his office that might have incriminated the Clintons.

"Let's get this stuff out there and take the mystery out of it," Fabiani argued to Kendall. He wanted to include about 30 of Foster's personal files, 100 pages dealing with Whitewater, that had been removed from Foster's office after his death. He met a wall of resistance.

Mrs. Clinton said no matter what they did, they would get negative stories. But she passed the decision off to Kendall. "You've got to work with Kendall," she said.

Kendall was worried that the documents would provide ammunition to the Clinton critics, and that some might contradict previous statements made by the Clintons.

Fabiani pulled out his trump argument. They were about to give all the documents to Senator D'Amato and his committee. Surely D'Amato would release them and place them in an unfavorable light. The White House ought to get out front.

Sherburne felt that Kendall and Mikva and many of the others didn't understand. Why would you want to do that? Mikva had asked.

White House stories about wrongdoing, scandal, inconsistency or mystery took on a life of their own, Sherburne believed. The basic elements were going to find their way out one way or another. The choice was not disclosure or nondisclosure. The stories were either going to come out in some grotesque form with the White House noncooperation intensifying the suspicion or the stories were going to appear in an orderly way with their interpretation. They could cushion even the worst stories.

Kendall finally agreed.

Fabiani decided that one reporter should get exclusive access to the documents. An exclusive could be controlled more than a general release, and the chances of a long, more carefully nuanced story were increased. Fabiani didn't want to give the material to some pro-Clinton reporter or someone who covered politics. Instead, he selected Michael Isikoff, a hard-nosed junkyard-dog investigator who worked for a publication, *Newsweek*, with wide national circulation. If they could convince Isikoff, who was famously skeptical of Clinton, his story and his conclusions would carry weight with other reporters and perhaps set the tone of the coverage.

Stephanopoulos called Fabiani.

"So you're doing this to take D'Amato's thunder away?"

"Yes."

"Great," Stephanopoulos said. "Good idea."

Sherburne and Fabiani wanted a complete, coherent package to supplement the Whitewater documents they would show to Isikoff and would later share with other reporters. They wrote a script, starting with the night Foster died. They summarized what each witness said, stating where their stories differed rather than trying

437

to hide the differences. They tried to give reasons or possible explanations for conflicting testimony. They also addressed the points where the differences couldn't be reconciled. Included were records showing that alarms in Foster's office had been secure much of the time after his death.

On Sunday, July 9, Isikoff's *Newsweek* story appeared. It wasn't a cover story, but it had a small headline on the cover as a teaser: "The Night Foster Died."

Sherburne and Fabiani were generally content because Isikoff made the key point: the decoupling of Foster's death and Whitewater. "*Newsweek* has uncovered no evidence that Foster's death was in any way connected to the Whitewater scandal." His story incorporated the White House defense, that after Foster's death, panicked, grief-stricken Clinton aides had been sloppy. They bungled the investigation, leaving a mess behind, but they were not covering up. Embarrassment was no crime. The 52 pages of documents were mostly routine, only curious and perhaps embarrassing details such as notes about the Whitewater financial records being in shambles. "But there is no document, memo, note or scrap of paper suggesting that Foster, the Clintons or anyone else was orchestrating a cover-up."

Isikoff's story disclosed that a uniformed Secret Service guard, Henry O'Neill, had testified that he saw Maggie Williams remove a box of documents from Foster's office that night. But he wrote that Williams denied it, that she had passed a lie detector test, and that others in the White House supported her account. The account took the sting out of one of D'-Amato's planned surprises.

All that weekend, even before *Newsweek* appeared, Sherburne and Fabiani briefed reporters from other major news organizations, one at a time, on the documents and their information. It took about one and a half hours to go through the entire script. Part of the strategy was to bore the reporters, show that the D'Amato hearings would not produce much that was new, that the hearings would be essentially old news. The sessions led to generally favorable stories in *The New York Times*, the *Los Angeles Times*, and *The Washington Post*.

Still, in the White House on Monday, there was some second-guessing. Hey wait a minute, the D'Amato hearings do not begin for a week, why is the White House generating Whitewater news? the skeptics asked. The important issue was that investigations were in progress, and how could they be slowed or stopped? But others in the White House generally viewed it as a success.

The one missing piece from "The Night Foster Died" was Hillary's account of what had occurred. As the months had passed, Sherburne had come to realize that people were constantly putting words in Mrs. Clinton's mouth. Hillary said this, or Hillary wants that. Half the time it wasn't true or was distorted. Because she was a formidable independent force in the White House, the staff liked to invoke her name as their authority. Or they tried to read or interpret her wishes, and then attribute their interpretation as "Hillary wants."

Sherburne asked Mrs. Clinton if she could interview her.

"Of course," Hillary said. Mrs. Clinton asked David Kendall to attend. Kendall was not fully schooled in the Foster document-handling issue. It would be part of his education and preparation since Starr sooner or later was going to interview both Hillary and the president on the issue again.

On July 11, Sherburne interviewed Hillary. She, with her staff, had already questioned the major players. In the course of responding to the subpoenas from Starr and the Congress, Sherburne and her staff believed they had all the relevant Foster documents.

Mrs. Clinton began her narrative. She was standing in the kitchen of her mother's house when she was called and told that Foster was dead. She described coming back to the White House. She was devastated, overwhelmed and depressed, she said. She just couldn't make herself function. She didn't want to get out of bed. Then several days later she said to herself that she had to overcome her depression. "I'm going to go over to my office." She pulled herself together and returned to her office in the West Wing. Almost immediately, Bernie Nussbaum came running in, saying, "Come here, come here. I've got to show you something." She said she walked over to Nussbaum's office and he showed her the note he had found in the bottom of Foster's briefcase. It was pieced together on the table. "I just flipped out,"

Hillary said. "I just looked at him and said, 'I can't deal with this,' and I walked out."

D'Amato was livid when he saw the stories appear. The White House had pulled a fast one. His staff passed word that the reporters had been had by the White House. Fabiani had released only part of the Whitewater material from Foster's office. Reporters called Fabiani. He went back to Kendall. Yes, Kendall said, there were some 100 pages relating to Whitewater tax matters that he still had.

Embarrassed, Fabiani insisted on seeing and then releasing the tax material. Kendall sent it over to the White House. In the 1992 campaign, the Clintons had released a report claiming $68,000 in Whitewater losses. Foster's notes showed he could only account for some $5,800 that was lost—a major discrepancy. Worse, there were handwritten notes that Foster had made for himself worrying about an IRS tax audit and describing Whitewater as "a can of worms you shouldn't open." It was precisely the kind of cover-up language that Fabiani dreaded, but on Thursday, July 13, he released the tax documents. He had to claim to reporters that they had misunderstood him and Sherburne over the weekend when they had told the reporters that they were seeing all the Whitewater files from Foster's office. These were tax files, he said. The mess triggered a new series of front-page stories.

On Monday, *The Washington Times* began an editorial, "Poor Michael Isikoff," and criticized the White House. "It is this very sort of too-clever-by-half game that has created the climate of suspicion surrounding the Whitewater scandal." *Time* magazine's story was headlined "Whitewater Tricks; New Hearings Prompt the Clintons to Make New Revelations—Only to Be Caught Short Again."

The New York Post headline that day: "TARGET HILLARY."

"Well," Ickes told Fabiani acidly, "people aren't giving us credit for being open."

Although they had taken a hit, the tax documents revealed inconsistencies that had no legal consequence, Fabiani answered. They wouldn't get credit with just a single effort, he added. "Look, we've got to build our reputation for openness."

After the short-lived success in preempting D'Amato, Fabiani didn't give up. He proposed that they take all the documents that had been given to D'Amato, put them in a room at Kendall's law firm—a kind of Whitewater library—and open it to the media. Eventually D'Amato was going to make everything public and cast it in the most unfavorable light, he argued again. This effort would put them a step ahead.

Kendall said he would rather take his chances that the committee would miss things. Make it accessible and the sheer novelty of it would attract all the reporters who would compete to find negative nuggets, Kendall said. The reporters and the nuggets would make it death by a thousand cuts. It would just be awful, he said. "No way."

Starr requested a second session with the Clintons. Saturday, July 22, was agreed upon.

The president testified for three and a half hours, and Hillary for another two hours. It was professional and civilized—again no bombshells in the questions or answers.

Afterwards, Mikva walked out of the White House with Starr to the independent counsel's car. It was a hot, muggy summer day.

"Ken," Mikva said, "I appreciate the civility and the attitude you have taken in dealing with the president and the first lady." They had avoided creating a circus atmosphere with no advance notice—or leak—to the media. Overall, the session had gone well and been fair. "I know your job is not to make the president look good. I appreciate that nothing has been done to embarrass them."

"Well, some day we'll have a Republican president," Starr said jocularly, making it clear he understood that it then would likely be his party's turn in the independent counsel box.

"You will," Mikva replied.

"Seriously," Starr said earnestly, "I would do nothing to demean the presidency."

Hillary picked up the August 7, 1995, *Newsweek* and read Joe Klein's column. An early admirer of Clinton, Klein was now disillusioned with both Clintons and the administration.

"The Body Count, The Real Whitewater Scandal May Be How the Clintons Treat Their Friends," the headline said. While belittling D'-Amato's hearings, Klein wrote that Whitewater had exposed the character of the Clintons. "They are the Tom and Daisy Buchanan of the Baby Boom Political Elite." The Buchanans were the 1920s-style careless people of F. Scott Fitzgerald's *The Great Gatsby*.

"They smashed up lives and didn't notice," Klein wrote. He laid out in harsh terms how Hillary's chief of staff, Maggie Williams, had broken down in tears while testifying the previous week. Williams was saddled with large legal bills, virtually abandoned by her patrons in the White House.

"How could the first lady allow her chief of staff to spend $140,000 on legal fees?" Klein asked. "Why hasn't she come forward and said, 'Stop torturing my staff. This isn't about them. I'll testify. I'll make all documents available. I'll sit here and answer your stupid, salacious questions until Inauguration Day, if need be.' "

Hillary was sobbing when she called Jane Sherburne.

Had Jane read the Klein column?

Yes.

"It's killing me to let this happen," Hillary said. She wanted to testify, to make it better, to take care of it. "Every bone in my body tells me that's what I should do." She could not stand by and let Maggie be hurt so, have others dragged in. "How is Maggie?"

Sherburne said they both knew Maggie was both vulnerable and tough. She was willing to throw herself in front of any train and get beat up.

Hillary's voice caught and she gasped in short breaths.

Testifying, Sherburne said, would be a mixed blessing. It would be such a sensation. The pure spectacle of the first lady appearing before Congress would overshadow anything she said. Were there words she could say that would resolve the issues and answer all the questions? They would always find more questions.

"I got to do this," Hillary said, gaining strength, taking deeper, measured breaths. "I'm going to do it."

Kendall was against it, they both knew—vehemently opposed in the midst of Starr's grand jury investigation of Whitewater. Public testimony by the first lady before D'Amato's committee might play into the Republicans' hands. Hillary would not be testifying on health care reform as she had done brilliantly. It wouldn't be a Pink Press Conference for an hour. There would be rounds of questions with all the Republican senators honing in. Potentially very ugly. Hillary was good but, you know, hey.

"Am I really that powerless?" Mrs. Clinton asked. The portrait of her as heartless and selfish was tearing her apart. It was awful to stand silently by as those she cared about were being hurt, she said.

Sherburne mentioned that it was all taking place outside the personal arena. Her testimony would have multiple legal ramifications. What about Starr, his investigation and grand juries? Politically, how would D'Amato and the other Republicans handle her? Her husband's reelection bid was a little more than a year off. The basic strategy on Whitewater was to calm the waters, avoid confrontation, minimize news coverage.

Sobbing again, Hillary took the issue to the next level. As she had said a number of times, her parents had always told her not to be guided by the opinions of others. "You have to live with yourself." Well, now the law and politics had cornered her. It wasn't a matter of appearances—appearing cold and indifferent to her friends and staff. If she stood by silently, she would be that person they accused her of being. "That is not who I am!" Hillary said, crying, pleading. "I take care of people."

Sherburne realized that Hillary had become the person she, at all costs, did not want to be. It was not simply a loss of identity. It was worse. She seemed to have fully realized the price that had been paid, and the identity that had been lost. She had become the person she hated.

Mikva's relationship with Sherburne deteriorated further. With the patronage of the first lady and Ickes, Sherburne was making too many legal decisions that had broader implications for Clinton and the presidency. The daily struggle was debilitating for Mikva. With Sherburne operating somewhat independently and David Kendall in charge of the case from his law firm downtown, Mikva never had the feeling that he knew enough of what was going on to function as counsel. He wasn't in charge.

More to the point, Clinton coped with Whitewater by not dealing with it. He often railed that Hillary was taking the hits and getting the heat, and all of it was unfair. But there was never a plan or a disciplined structure to the decision making or an overall theory about how to get on top of the issue and right the ship of state.

Most important, Mikva came to feel that many people just didn't find Clinton credible. People didn't trust his morality or his leadership. It wasn't that Mikva ever really saw anything bad, it was just that he didn't see enough that was good.

There were other problems. Sherburne and some of her assistants were keeping notes, and the Republican Congress and Starr were going to subpoena them. The notes would eventually provide a work list for the Republicans. Mikva decided not to present an ultimatum to the president that either he or Sherburne had to go, although Sherburne believed he had. Instead, he just yielded the floor to Sherburne on these issues. For practical purposes, he disengaged. He was now 70. He was sleep-deprived. It was time to leave. On Wednesday, September 20, he announced that he was resigning as soon as a successor was found. Publicly, he emphasized that it was retirement after 40 years in government, rather than the single year in the Clinton White House. Mikva said, "This is a good time for me to travel and devote more time to my family."

Starr's conflicts of interest were galling and worthy of further inquiry, Fabiani told Sherburne that summer. At the same time that Starr was conducting an investigation of the president, he continued to earn $1 million from Kirkland & Ellis. He represented tobacco clients and other groups opposed to the president. He had a heavy Republican speaking and travel schedule. Fabiani said he wanted to collect negative background information on the independent counsel and give it to reporters.

Sherburne was uneasy. This was different from waging a war of words with D'Amato. Starr was still largely thought of as a respected legal figure, straightforward and judicious. If Starr's ethics were attacked publicly on the basis of comments from Fabiani or the White House, they could be accused of tampering with or obstructing Starr's investigation. Sherburne told Fabiani there could be no White House campaign or private investigation. He could give publicly available facts to reporters on background with no White House fingerprints. Let the reporters decide on their own what information, if any, to use, she instructed. Ickes concurred.

Fabiani talked with Sam Skolnik, a reporter for the *Legal Times,* a legal newspaper covering Washington. Skolnik indicated that he was interested in probing Starr's alleged conflicts of interest. Fabiani got reams of press clips and background information from the Democratic National Committee research office and gave them to the reporter.

Skolnik's article appeared in the October 23, 1995, edition under the headline "Kenneth Starr's Conservative Conflict?" He wrote that the Lynde and Harry Bradley Foundation, a conservative group with ties to some of Clinton's biggest critics, had retained Starr. On behalf of the foundation Starr was advising Wisconsin Republican Governor Tommy Thompson, "a potential 1996 presidential candidate," about a Milwaukee school voucher court case, a favorite conservative cause. Skolnik also noted that other conflict of interest questions about Starr had already been raised, such as his work for the conservative Brown & Williamson Tobacco Corporation, which strenuously opposed Clinton's antitobacco efforts. Absent from Skolnik's story was any mention of Fabiani's or the White House's role in providing him with information. In the article's 35th paragraph, Skolnik wrote, "A White House spokesman declined comment for this article."

Fabiani was elated. He could show Skolnik's piece to other reporters and urge them to look into Starr's background and find other conflicts of interest. In that way Fabiani could build up a record on Starr's conflicts entirely in the independent media. Fabiani and his staff even came up with a name for the stealth effort: "pollinization."

In the fall, Fabiani called in his assistant, Chris Lehane, a 28-year-old Harvard Law School graduate who had worked on the 1992 Clinton-Gore campaign as the Maine political director.

At the end of the day, the two liked to have a drink together in Fabiani's fourth-floor EOB office or at the Bombay Club across from the White House where their favorite bartender was Norman. Fabiani pulled out two shot glasses with the White House insignia and a bottle of Maker's Mark, an expensive Kentucky whiskey, and poured some for each of them. Life in the damage control operation often called for a stiff drink at the end of the day—if there was time. A late-breaking story would often put them in what they called their "Submarine Mode." They would be hunkered down, waiting for the depth charges to hit, in their case the phone calls from reporters. Often at 5 or 6 p.m., all six lines on the phone would light up simultaneously.

This day had been quiet.

"What would you think if I told you the Riadys paid off Hubbell?" Fabiani asked.

Lehane was new, but he understood. Whitewater was all about the Arkansas past, the intrigues and interconnections. Hubbell, of course, had been the president's close friend and Hillary's law partner; and Hubbell had gone to jail for stealing some $400,000 from the Rose Law Firm.

The Riadys were an Indonesian family worth at least a billion dollars. They controlled the Lippo Group, a conglomerate with interests in the United States, Asia and China. James T. Riady, the son of the family patriarch, Mochtar Riady, had been only 20 in 1977 when he went to Little Rock, where he met and became friends with the young Arkansas attorney general, Bill Clinton. In the 1980s James Riady ran the Worthen Bank in Little Rock and formed a close association with the governor. Hubbell had been the attorney for both James Riady and the Worthen Bank.

The interconnections were explosive, Fabiani said, especially if money had been paid to Hubbell after he was caught stealing. Fabiani said he had heard that Jeff Gerth, a *New York Times* investigative reporter who had written the original Whitewater story, was making inten-

450

sive inquiries about Hubbell, the Riadys and money. Gerth had not yet come to the White House for a response, but something serious was brewing, Fabiani said. "If you think the D'Amato hearings are bad," he added, "just wait till this story gets written by Jeff Gerth."

But Gerth did not write the story for nearly two years.

23

IN MID-NOVEMBER 1995, the federal government literally shut down because of a budget impasse between Clinton and the Republican majority in Congress. It was the biggest gamble of Clinton's presidency. On the second day of the crisis, November 15, amid the chaos of having no regular employees on duty, Clinton wound up alone in the chief of staff's office with a young intern who caught his eye. They began flirting. She teasingly raised her navy blue jacket in the back. The straps of her bikini thong underwear were visible just above her matching navy pants. It was a trick she had learned from an old boyfriend. Nobody but the president could see.

About 8 p.m., the intern walked near the Oval Office toward the ladies' room. As she passed by Stephanopoulos's room adjacent to the Oval Office, she glimpsed the president inside alone. He gestured for her to come on in.

She told Clinton she had a crush on him.

He laughed. Would you like to see my private office? Clinton asked.

She nodded.

Clinton took her through his private dining room toward his study. He stopped in a small, windowless hallway. It was the only room in the White House which afforded him some privacy.

They kissed passionately. Before leaving, she wrote on a piece of paper her phone number and her name: "Monica Lewinsky."

Around 10 p.m., at Clinton's invitation, Lewinsky was back. Clinton began talking with a congressman on the telephone in the darkened study, the one with no drapes, while she performed oral sex on him. He finished his call and told her to stop. He said it was too soon to do that. He did not know or trust her well enough.

At one point, Clinton tugged on her pink intern pass. "This," he said, was going to be a problem. Interns were not allowed in the West Wing without an escort.

Lewinsky tried to make Clinton more comfortable. She said she knew the rules. She had had an affair with a married man before, she told him. She was sending a signal that she knew how to keep quiet.

The president went upstairs to the residence to have dinner with his wife.

Two days later, the president ran into Lewinsky as she came out of the restroom. He invited her back to his office.

She asked if he remembered her name.

He said he did.

She told Clinton she had secured a full-time job in the White House legislative liaison office. She would be able to see him without an escort.

They embraced. Lewinsky said she had to get back to her desk. She didn't want to raise suspicions. He suggested that she return with some slices of pizza, which had been ordered for a snack. A few minutes later, Clinton's secretary, Betty Currie, knocked on his door. "Sir, the girl's here with the pizza," Currie said.

He told Lewinsky to come in. He said he liked her smile and her energy. "I'm usually around on weekends, no one else is around, and you can come and see me," he told her.

Lewinsky was on cloud nine, but she was worried that perhaps Clinton's regular girlfriend was furloughed and would be back as soon as the government shutdown ended.

Jane Sherburne was enjoying a rare day at home December 29 when the phone rang. Natalie Williams, a junior lawyer on her staff who was handling the subpoenas from the House of Representatives in the investigation of the White House Travel Office firings, was on the line.

"You won't believe what our cleanup effort has uncovered," Williams said. She had been going through files sent in by the Federal Records Center—one of the countless government document archives—and she had found a nine-page memo in the files of Patsy Thomasson, the deputy White House administrator, that had been written by her boss,

David Watkins, the assistant to the president for management and administration. The memo contradicted earlier denials by Watkins and Mrs. Clinton that the first lady had no role in the firings of the travel office staff. Williams's first reaction to discovering the memo had been "Oh shit! Oh damn!" It was that kind of memo. Williams had only been at the White House for six months and had not been around during the initial travel office flap, but this was the kind of memo that should have been found at the beginning of a document search, not the end. The delay of more than two years was sure to cause trouble.

Addressed to White House chief of staff McLarty, Watkins had written: "This is a soul cleansing....It is my first attempt to be sure the record is straight, something I have not done in previous conversations with investigators—where I have been as protective and vague as possible." While previously stating that he was responsible for the decision to remove the seven employees, he said he acted at Mrs. Clinton's "insistence," declaring that there would be "hell to pay" if he "failed to take swift and decisive action in conformity with the first lady's wishes."

"Foster regularly informed me that the first lady was concerned and desired action—the action desired was the firing of the travel office staff," Watkins wrote. In a phone conversation directly with Mrs. Clinton, Watkins said, "She conveyed to me in clear terms her desire for swift and clear action."

Sherburne thought there had to be an explanation. "Make a copy of it and just put it under my door," she told Williams.

Sherburne fretted. What was this memo, and why now? She eventually went down to the White House and read the memo. It was a classic in the annals of cover-up documents— a rare find with someone stating in writing that he had not been straight, but protective and vague. Before calling in her colleagues, Sherburne wanted to find out more. She went home and called Watkins's attorney. He said he knew about the memo and was stunned to learn it was in the files. It wasn't supposed to be. Watkins had wanted to bare his soul, get the matter off his chest. He had drafted something and told his lawyer about it. Don't be a fool, the lawyer said, if you feel like you have to do that, write a memo to me so at least it's protected by attorney-client privilege. But apparently an earlier version had survived.

Yes, apparently.

Sherburne called Maggie Williams to report the bad news.

Williams had learned from Hillary to be action-oriented. Okay, what was the plan? How could they handle it? The first lady had written a book on children called *It Takes a Village and Other Lessons Children Teach Us*. She had worked hard and poured her soul into it. Hillary's book tour was beginning on January 16, 1996, and Williams noted that the implications were enormous for the tour and other scheduled events in the coming weeks.

Sherburne called Ickes.

He was quiet at first. "Man, how are we

going to get through this?" Ickes asked. "How are we going to survive this? This is really bad." Had Sherburne told Maggie Williams?

Yes.

When would it have to be produced? he asked.

Soon.

Sherburne called Mark Fabiani, who was in California visiting his in-laws. "You better get back here," she said.

"What happened?"

"You just better get back here," she answered. "We'll talk about it when you get here."

Hillary dismissed the memo. She had been concerned about incompetence in the travel office, but it was hardly an obsession.

After the weekend, Kendall, Sherburne, Fabiani and the other attorneys held long discussions that lasted several days. Since D'Amato and William F. Clinger, the Republican House chairman of a committee investigating the travel office firings, were breathing fire and were the most immediate political problem, Sherburne would concentrate on them. Starr was not focusing on the travel office specifically. Sherburne and the other attorneys had many documents that were going to be sent to the committees. It was her practice not to produce a document every time one was discovered. Normally they would wait until a critical mass of documents had been gathered and then send up a box. They could just stick the Watkins memo in the box. Bury the diamond. Maybe it would not be found, or it might take them days or weeks. Maybe the committees would miss the political significance.

Fabiani bet that the memo would become instant news. By the fourth day after its discovery, he was getting worried about the delay, concerned that they, the lawyers, could get in trouble.

"We have *got* to put this out," Fabiani told the others. "We can't wait another day." He threatened to take matters into his own hands. "I'm not going to wait even till tomorrow morning to put it out." Waiting 12 hours more would make him uncomfortable.

Finally the others agreed, but it was late in the day, making it impossible to get copies to all the news media. Fabiani called the Associated Press wire service. The AP story went out the night of January 3, 1996. The following morning Fabiani figured he could make copies for everyone else and they would be off to the races.

Sherburne sent documents, including the nine-page Watkins memo, to the Hill the same day. It was her 45th birthday, and her children were fixing dinner for her. At 9 p.m. she was still not home, so she ran out of the White House.

At about 4 a.m., Sherburne sat straight up in bed. Oh, no! she realized, she had not sent the Watkins memo to Starr. She sent it over to Starr's office first thing in the morning.

D'Amato's and Clinger's staffs found the memo in about an hour. "There was a cover-up here," Clinger said, promising more subpoenas and a new round of hearings. D'Amato cited a "troubling pattern that keeps recurring involving Hillary Rodham Clinton."

Starr and John Bates, his deputy, read their

copy of Watkins's "soul-cleansing" memo. At first glance they agreed it looked like a smoking gun, someone finally coming clean, acknowledging he had been "as protective and vague as possible." In Foster's last note he had mentioned his concern that Hillary would be blamed for the travel office firings, and here Watkins was saying she had insisted on it. Starr decided to issue an unusual public statement, voicing "distress" at the delay. "The White House had an obligation to turn this memorandum over to the Office of Independent Counsel as soon as it was discovered."

Bates didn't think that Sherburne would intentionally hide documents, but he knew that she, like any lawyer, made decisions about timing. Bates wanted to put her on notice that they needed information earlier rather than later.

After reading the statement, Sherburne called Bates. She was furious. Bates had a family, children. He knew the pressures, the confusion. She was sure that Bates did not think she was involved in hiding or holding back documents.

"Goddamn you," Sherburne said. "After all these months we worked together and you know how careful I am, and you can't even cut me 24 hours!"

Bates gave a sheepish reply.

Fabiani was unsure about how to handle the fallout from the memo. On one hand it was in stark contradiction with Hillary's statements that she had "no role" in the decision to fire the travel office employees. But on more detailed examination, he found that Watkins had made some of these claims before. Going through the precise statements, Fabiani also found that Watkins's versions contradicted each other. Watkins had given somewhat different accounts to the first 1993 internal White House review, the General Accounting Office, the investigative arm of Congress, and then to the FBI. Watkins also was somewhat a discredited figure. He had been fired from the White House in May 1994 after using a government helicopter for a golf outing. So the question was, should the White House try to discredit Watkins and take him on? Could they suggest that Watkins wrote the memo as an act of retaliation? Or even as an act of potential blackmail? Or, in the other extreme, should they embrace him or some of his statements?

Before noon on January 4, the day after the Watkins memo had been turned loose, the Clintons' personal assistant, Carolyn Huber, sent a message to David Kendall.

"David," she said, "would you come by my office. I have a document I would like for you to see that I have found."

Huber handled all the Clintons' personal correspondence and bills and maintained their personal financial records. She had served as administrator of the Governor's Mansion in Arkansas for Clinton's first term in 1979–80 and then gone on to be administrator of the Rose Law Firm for a dozen years before coming to the White House to serve as their closest aide on personal matters. She was almost family, one of four special assistants who worked in the East Wing for President and Mrs. Clinton. Her title

459

was special assistant to the president and director of correspondence for the White House. Among her duties she attended to the Clintons' personal guests in the White House residence. She had driven the Clintons' cat, Socks, from Little Rock to the White House in 1993 as a favor to Hillary.

About 1 p.m., Kendall went to Huber's office in the East Wing of the White House, room 214 on the second floor.

"David," she said, "I have some documents for you." She handed him a sheaf of paper—Rose Law Firm billing records. Kendall could see 116 pages, records of Mrs. Clinton's work in the 1980s for Madison Guaranty. The records had been subpoenaed years ago.

Huber was agitated and flustered. She said she had found the records in a box of memorabilia in her office when she had moved a table. There was red handwriting on the some of the pages. Whose was that? Kendall asked.

Huber said she believed it was Vince Foster's handwriting.

Kendall told her to keep the records, safeguard them, and he would return with White House counsel. She ought to call her own personal attorney, Henry Schuelke, he recommended.

I felt I had to tell you, Huber said. Have I done the right thing?

Absolutely, Kendall said, she had done the right thing.

Kendall left, went to the National Gallery. He had tickets for the Vermeer show, which he was determined not to miss.

Before 5 p.m., Kendall called Sherburne.

"I've just got a call from Carolyn Huber," Kendall said, "and she says she has found some documents that she thinks that I ought to look at. And so I'm on my way over." Kendall did not tell Sherburne that he had already seen the documents.

Kendall soon showed up at Sherburne's West Wing office, the old White House barber shop.

"Well," Kendall said, "let's go see what she's got."

Kendall, Schuelke and Sherburne arrived in Huber's East Wing office.

"Well, here they are," Huber said. She handed Sherburne a half-inch sheaf of large 11-inch-by-17-inch computer paper that was folded over.

Sherburne took the computer pages in both hands and opened them. "Madison Guaranty," she read. "Client Billing & Payment History." On the first page and some other pages she noticed the handwriting in red ink. Sherburne recognized Foster's distinctive thick, crimped handwriting. Here it was—precisely what D'Amato and the suspicious investigators thought had been taken from Foster's office.

"And where were these?" Sherburne asked.

They were from a table in the Book Room on the third floor of the residence, Huber said. She didn't have to add that that was where the documents from Foster's office had been sent in 1993 after his death. In fact, two days after Foster's death, Hillary had asked Huber to transfer the documents to a locked closet in the personal quarters of the White House. This Book Room was adjacent to a room that Hillary used occasionally as an office.

Sherburne set the records down and turned to Kendall and Schuelke. "We've got to talk."

The three attorneys stepped out into a hallway.

"We have to be completely comfortable with every move we make," Sherburne said, "in the way we respond to this because we will be testifying about every single minute from this moment forward, and we better be damned sure that we can defend our actions." Once again the White House would be under investigation. "I don't know that we should be handling these records because they're obviously Foster records." What about fingerprints? she asked. Do they stay on paper? What about her fingerprints?

Schuelke, a former prosecutor, and Kendall, who had dealt with fingerprint evidence when he handled death row inmate cases for the NAACP, both said yes, fingerprints could be detected from paper, but they did not know how long the prints lasted.

Then the lawyers turned to the question of how many subpoenas were outstanding for these documents. Starr was the first priority. Yes, they agreed. Also D'Amato and the House Banking Committee. Also the two regulatory agencies that were investigating Madison— the RTC and the Federal Deposit Insurance Corporation (FDIC). The total was five they could think of right away.

Sherburne was for immediately turning them over to Starr.

Kendall said they just couldn't release them to Starr without making copies so they could comply, even belatedly, with the other sub-

462

poenas. How could he possibly hand them over without retaining a copy for himself to analyze? He had one of the most basic and obvious ethical obligations to his clients.

They discussed using rubber gloves while copying to protect the existing fingerprints, but Sherburne was afraid the gloves might smudge them. Would the copying conceivably be considered an obstructive act? Destroying evidence inadvertently? Could they be accused, especially in the current atmosphere?

Kendall insisted on making copies. He could not turn over documents, especially something this complicated, without having his own copy. It was standard, routine and Starr would understand.

The three lawyers then returned to quiz Huber.

Where were these? How did they get to your office? When? How? Why?

Huber was more than flustered. Her hands were shaking. She had picked them up on the table in the Book Room, which was where the Clintons stored things such as gifts after a foreign trip. It was the residence junk room, and Huber regularly removed gifts or papers for filing, trying to keep order. One of her New Year's resolutions was: bring order to her own office. She had recently been organizing photographs, the Clintons' personal papers, even Chelsea's stuff. Some material was in boxes they had brought from Little Rock. She had been going through the room two or three boxes at a time. Then Hillary had hired an assistant to help with her book, and it had to be cleaned out more. Huber found the records on the table, more like a card table in the room, and had just plunked them down in a box which she had brought to her own office. She showed them the box. It contained a pair of old shoes and a coat hanger.

When? What was the sequence?

She had brought them over from the residence three months ago, she thought. No, maybe five months ago, ten months ago, maybe eight months. In the summer, she said. She had the ushers bring their dollies up to the residence to carry back the boxes.

Boxes? There were more?

Yes, four or five. Maybe two or three. She had new built-in shelves made for her office and just that morning she had the movers take out a large table, six feet by three feet, and back under the table were these boxes. Moving the table out exposed the boxes, and she started to reorganize her office, move the stuff out of the boxes onto the shelves, and she had found the records. Her hands were still shaking.

Kendall wanted to get pictures of Huber's office to show the clutter. He went out and got a disposable camera and snapped off pictures—a box on a chair, a row of other boxes on the floor, a messy desk, disorder, pictures, files, junk.

He insisted he needed a true copy of the billing records, same size, 17 by 11, and made on a color copier to show the red handwriting. They could not find an oversized color copier in the White House complex or the Old Executive Office Building. They finally located one in the New Executive Office Building across Pennsylvania Avenue. Sherburne didn't want anyone else to know what they were doing or what they had found. So all three attorneys and Huber went over to the New Executive Office Building. It was about 7 p.m.

Kendall and Schuelke had to wait to get clearance into the building, so Sherburne and Huber went in and began the copying. When the men arrived they seemed to deem it a task for the two women, who were struggling with the copier, which needed new powder. Soon powder was flying everywhere. It was a tedious process, making sure everything on each page was fully and clearly copied.

At one point, Sherburne went to a phone and called Fabiani.

"Don't go anywhere," she said in hushed tones, there were new developments.

"Where are you calling from?" he asked, noting the display on his telephone console was an extension unfamiliar to him.

"I'm calling from a remote location," she said.

It took about three hours to make two copies that satisfied Kendall. He took the original and one copy. Sherburne took the other.

Kendall and Sherburne determined that the subpoenas had been issued to both the Clintons personally and to the White House officially. Since the records had supposedly been found in the residence, the personal subpoena applied, but since Huber, an official employee, had them in her official office, the White House subpoena also applied. So they decided that both Kendall and Sherburne would call Starr in the morning to tell him they were coming. It was another classic hybrid issue in which the personal and the official could not be pulled apart.

"Jane," Kendall said, "this is going to turn out to be nothing."

"David," she replied, "you are so wrong." The climate was perfect to make this discovery a big deal—the D'Amato hearings, the election year, Foster's handwriting, Hillary, Starr and everyone already suspicious about the Watkins memo on the travel office.

"I will bet you dinner," Kendall said in his precise way, "with you and your husband. Anne and I will take you out, nicest restaurant in town, that six months from now this will be a big nothing."

"You are on."

It was about 10 p.m. when they left. Kendall and Schuelke went off, and the two women walked back though the darkness and cold the two blocks to the main White House complex.

"I hope I did the right thing," Huber said in a high-pitched, distraught, almost childlike voice.

"What do you mean by that?" Sherburne asked.

"I didn't know what to do when I found these today," Huber replied. "Maybe I should have just thrown them out."

Many lawyers are happy to have their clients make that decision on their own, but once the lawyers are asked, they had to stick to the rules.

"Carolyn," Sherburne replied, "you did the right thing. It would have been wrong to throw them out."

Back at the White House, Sherburne finally called Ickes to inform him. It was about 11:30 p.m. when she gave the deputy chief of staff the details.

"What are we going to do?" Ickes asked.

"We're going to send them to Starr. We're going to analyze them as quickly as we can," she said. They were going to determine what issues the records might raise and what could be said.

Ickes, for one of the few times in his life, was speechless.

Sherburne and Fabiani met late. She filled him in on the details and showed him her copy. Fabiani thought that Sherburne at times over-reacted, but this time he was suitably impressed with the gravity.

"We have to give these out," Fabiani said. All the reporters had to get copies. "And we have to show them to people the minute we send them over to D'Amato. We can't let D'Amato get the first crack at this."

Kendall spent much of the night analyzing the 116 pages. They showed that in the period 1985–86 Mrs. Clinton billed about 60 hours for Madison—89 tasks, including 33 conferences or phone calls with Madison officials on 53 separate days. Kendall felt it could be argued that the records were consistent with her testimony that she had done minimal work. Some 60 hours was not a lot of time in a lawyer's life. Law firms might overbill, but they never under-billed. The 60 hours was an absolute upper limit, Kendall felt. In the morning he arranged to have more copies made to comply with the other sub-

467

poenas. He wanted to properly stamp and number each page.

In the White House, Sherburne and Fabiani asked each other, What is this? What does this mean? How could this happen? Where could these billing records have been all this time? They realized there were no good answers. The two knew each other well enough to explore larger questions. Were they being told the truth? Fabiani was worried that as the person who would have to be out front explaining the unexplainable, he might destroy his own credibility. Was this the point where he would have to say, Look, I'm not going to do this anymore, I'm out of here. Was he getting sucked in? Was he seeing things clearly? Did he have the courage, the will to say good-bye? He hoped he wasn't missing his chance to get out. In the summer of 1974 as a high school student, Fabiani had studied debate in Washington at Georgetown, and he had watched Nixon and his spokesman Ron Ziegler go down the tubes. He didn't want to be the next celebrated scandal victim.

But the basic mechanics of getting the copies, releasing the records and doing their work overtook their discussion. Sherburne focused on the next step. Starr was her primary concern. As the morning wore on, she was getting hotter and hotter about the delay.

Kendall said he didn't want to send them to Starr until he had a set ready for D'Amato. He didn't want to get caught in the crossfire again.

"We've got to call Starr right now!" Sherburne finally insisted. "I don't care what we tell him, that they're coming at two or three or whenever."

She wanted them to make the first notification to Starr. It was too hot, it could leak, placing everyone, including the lawyers, in a vulnerable position. She set 10 a.m. as the deadline for them to call Starr.

Finally, at 11 a.m., they called Starr but didn't reach him. Kendall phoned John Bates.

"We found some materials in the White House residence," Kendall said. "We found Rose Law Firm billing records."

Bates said they would need to see them right away.

Kendall promised to send them over.

"Okay," Bates said coolly, "we'll be here." When the documents didn't arrive after several hours, Bates called to ask where they were.

24

KENDALL CALLED Mrs. Clinton that morning and informed her about the discovery of the billing records. He then met with her at the White House later in the morning. She voiced surprise but no alarm.

"Who Is Hillary Clinton?" the first lady had read that morning, January 5, in *The Wall Street Journal.* She shuddered. A month before Vince Foster's suicide, the *Journal* had run a similar editorial headlined "Who Is Vincent Foster?"

The editorial on Hillary filled the entire space normally used for three or four separate editorials. The 1,600-word article focused on the Watkins memo, asserting that Hillary's denials and contradictions fit a pattern.

One dart was aimed at the question of what work Hillary had done years ago as a Rose Law Firm lawyer for the McDougals' Madison Savings and Loan. "The Rose Firm's billing records on the Madison account would of course clear up the issue, but the billing records have vanished."

Was it possible the *Journal* knew something?

The parallel construction with the famous Foster editorial took her breath away. Foster had singled out the *Wall Street Journal* editors as those who "lie without consequence" in his famous suicide note in which he had concluded that he was not meant for the spotlight of public life in Washington.

Sherburne went to see the president. She outlined the discovery, Kendall's initial analysis and the decision to get the records to Starr. The main problem was that they would be suspected of obstructing justice. Oh yeah, this was going to be a big problem, she said. D'Amato would have a field day. He was desperate to legitimize his investigation and hearings. They might have handed him the weapon he needed. Starr would investigate at once, treat it as if the keys to the kingdom suddenly had been discovered.

The president said he didn't see the logic in any suspicion of obstruction of justice. "Why would we be producing them now," Clinton asked, "if we have been trying to hide them and obstruct? That doesn't make sense. And why would we have been hiding them if it was turning out that they're helpful or support what we have been saying all along?"

Sherburne explained that the convergence was too perfect, the combination of Foster's handwriting, Whitewater. D'Amato and others would say these were the documents that they believed Maggie Williams snuck out of Foster's office that night, documents the White House was concealing all along.

The president said he understood. "But as a rational matter here," he added, "why should this be a problem?"

Sherburne said they were good points, but she didn't think it was rational anymore.

So here we go again? the president asked.

Oh yeah.

Kendall finally sent the original of the billing records over to Starr and copies to the other investigations.

Mike McCurry wanted Kendall to make a public announcement that the records had been found and turned over to the investigators. Kendall didn't want to say anything at first. McCurry almost had to bludgeon him. Finally Kendall appeared late in the day in the Williams & Connolly conference room and said the records "confirm what we have said all along about the nature and amount of the work done by the Rose Law Firm and Mrs. Clinton for Madison." He contended the records were consistent with Mrs. Clinton's statement that her work for Madison was "very limited." "With public release of these records, yet another set of baseless allegations can be laid to rest," Kendall said. But he added he could not explain why the office records were not found earlier and said he had previously searched for them himself.

At Starr's office, the billing records were logged in and handled by people wearing gloves as they began an intensive fingerprint and forensic examination of the 116 pages. It would be 24 to 36 hours before Starr and his deputies could meet to examine the records.

Starr and Bates met with their senior attorneys.

Bates said if Kendall had called them the previous day, when the records had been discovered, they would have reached an accord to send over FBI agents and forensic experts for the originals. They could have reached some accommodation so that Kendall could have obtained copies.

For Starr, the one-two punch of the Watkins memo and the billing records raised serious questions about the ability of their investigation to get information. Here relevant, significant and even startling information had been missed. Was the White House operating in good faith or bad faith? he asked. He wasn't sure. But this discovery was now an issue of potential national significance. He wanted to proceed carefully. He said they risked having an impact on the functioning of government and the presidency as an institution. So they had to make sure what they did was right.

Some of Starr's deputies held the theory that all roads led to Hillary, and to them the handling of the billing records was proof. Others thought that many of the events pointed to obstruction of justice, and the actions, especially by Mrs. Clinton, were all connected and designed to conceal. The two theories were not mutually exclusive.

Bates noted that important evidence about a prime suspect in the Whitewater case—the first lady—had been concealed in the home of the prime suspect. Kendall had in effect said previously that these billing records either didn't exist or couldn't be found. A huge subinvestigation would have to be launched, probing where the records had been found, who had access to the space, why and when. The question of where they were found was potentially more important than what was in the records.

Starr's attorneys discussed the possibility of obtaining Mrs. Clinton's testimony—an obvious crucial step. They would have to give her the opportunity early on. It was conceivable she would resist or even take the Fifth Amendment against self-incrimination. But that would tell them a lot in itself.

Starr said he preferred to subpoena her to testify before the grand jury in person. No more special treatment. The appearance of deference, acceding to testimony in the White House residence, the Clintons' home turf, would end.

They discussed options. Perhaps they could have the grand jurors come to the White House. But that might create more of a spectacle. They discussed a neutral site but felt that would be difficult.

Starr solicited the views of the grand jurors.

They, too, wanted to see Mrs. Clinton in person. Starr informed Kendall that a subpoena would be issued.

Kendall was upset. "If you do this," Kendall said, "this will fundamentally change the nature of our relationship."

Starr and Kendall had basically gotten along well. Both were slightly nerdy former Supreme Court law clerks who followed the Court's cases regularly. Small talk between the two before a meeting several times turned on a discussion of the latest cases, down to obscure footnotes. But now their relationship was becoming more tense.

On Friday, January 19, Starr issued the subpoena for Mrs. Clinton to appear the next Friday. He told his deputies that Mrs. Clinton was a citizen like everyone else. She should not be treated differently. Yes, he knew, the White House probably would escalate its criticism. But he was going to proceed.

Around this time Hillary spoke by phone with Bob Bennett. The plan was for Bennett now to have a seat at the table on all scandal issues, not just Paula Jones, advising on the overall legal and public relations strategy. She and her husband had been impressed with Bennett's public defense on the billing records discovery.

The Sunday before, on *This Week with David Brinkley,* Bennett had defended her, with no hedging. Noting that the White House had voluntarily produced the billing records, Bennett said, "I've read every word of them. These documents do not undercut the position of the first lady or the president. Rather—and I'm willing to discuss that at great length, because I've spent a lot of time dealing with it. They, rather, are supportive. They *are* supportive." He gladly attacked Billy Dale, the fired former head of the travel office, who was becoming a right-wing martyr. "Billy Dale," Bennett said in full basso profundo, "was willing to plead guilty to embezzlement and serve four months in jail. So let's not all cry about Billy Dale." In sum, "Partisans are now becoming assassins."

What should they do? Hillary asked Bennett.

Timidity was a problem, Bennett explained. Kendall's firm, Williams & Connolly, looked at it as 80 percent law and only 20 percent politics when it should be the opposite.

Why was the culture of scandal so out of control? she asked.

Bennett said the media felt misled during the 1992 campaign by Clinton's denials of draft dodging, a sexual affair with Gennifer Flowers and his infamous "I didn't inhale" comment about marijuana use. It was payback time, Bennett claimed.

Their talk lasted about 45 minutes. Bennett was delighted that he was now fully in the loop. That weekend he was going on television to once again defend the Clintons.

"Where did these come from?" Leon Panetta asked. Was this just another screwup? Or was there something more here? Stephanopoulos reminded Panetta that these kinds of problems had happened in the 1992 campaign all the time and Panetta had to get used to it.

They had to launch their own inquiry, Panetta said. Unlike the lawyers, he could not draw some distinction between the White House office and the White House residence.

McCurry agreed strongly. He argued the White House should launch its own billing records inquiry. He was the one who was going to have to go before the press corps and explain. He needed answers, he couldn't stonewall. If he didn't have answers, he had to be able to say they were making a full-speed effort to get them. To do less would suggest the White House wasn't treating the discovery of the billing records seriously.

Panetta met with some of the key White House lawyers. McCurry did not attend.

"I am the chief of staff here," Panetta said. "I can't have things turning up like this without getting answers."

Fabiani argued against another White House investigation. Whatever they did would *not* be credible. Whatever they did would be subject to monumental amounts of second-guessing. Any mistake would be seen as a cover-up. Their investigation would soon be the subject of the next investigation. The issue was already in Starr's hands. That would be sufficient.

"You're going to have to get another press secretary," Panetta said.

What do you mean?

"McCurry will not agree to that."

Fabiani cited the White House Travel Office investigation, which slowed the press criticism of the administration only for a short period of time. Look at what a huge source of controversy it later spawned. The questions were endless. Why hadn't they asked the first lady this question? Why was the report written this way? Ultimately wasn't the self-investigation a mechanism for a cover-up and limiting disclosure? Witness the Watkins memo, now discovered two and a half years later.

Panetta still favored an inquiry.

Well, Fabiani asked, who would do it? What kind of staff? They couldn't use the FBI. Who would be competent enough to do it? Would they be willing to follow the investigation wherever it might lead? Was anyone prepared to follow an investigation to the door of the first lady? Or of the president?

The answer was obvious, and no internal investigation was launched. Fabiani continued to put out the position that the White House was fully cooperating with Starr and Starr would find out the details that the White House didn't know. Surprisingly, that line held up, and out of inertia no White House probe was begun.

Carolyn Huber testified before Starr's grand jury and D'Amato's committee. Her position on when she first found the billing records in the Book Room hardened—August 1995, she was now sure. In contrast to the sketchiness and inconsistency earlier and on other matters, the date of discovery was her one moment of definitive clarity. Mrs. Clinton, Sherburne and Fabiani concluded that the billing records had probably been sitting around in her office all along and there had never been a thorough search of her material and files.

Fabiani felt that the search of the files to comply with the various subpoenas had been so inadequate that Starr would be justified in serving a search warrant on the White House. He worried that Starr would be able to make a credible case for taking that extraordinary step. Kendall and Sherburne didn't take the possibility that seriously, but Fabiani began sketching out what they might say if it happened.

Hillary planned an 11-city book tour for *It Takes a Village and Other Lessons Children Teach Us*. *Newsweek* was going to run excerpts of the book. Part of the agreement with *Newsweek* called for an interview about her work, but the discovery of the Watkins memo and then the billing records prompted many questions about the scandals.

On January 8, a *Newsweek* cover story on Hillary was headlined "Saint or Sinner?" over a frumpy picture of the first lady. The same day, columnist William Safire of *The New York Times* wrote that Hillary was a "congenital liar." The column probably would have been lost to the blizzard of '96, since many newspapers had not been delivered in the Northeast, but White House press secretary Mike McCurry responded by saying that if Bill Clinton were not president he would deliver "a more forceful response to the bridge of Mr. Safire's nose."

A big media flap ensued. Part of the intense discussion, to Hillary's discomfort, focused on whether she had told the truth. She wanted to discuss her issues—children's issues—but she agreed to answer questions about the scandal. On January 15, she appeared on the Diane Rehm show, a serious, popular Washington talk radio program. She said she and her husband had always acted in "good faith." Even during the 1992 campaign her staff had made the Whitewater documents available, she said. "We actually did that with *The New York Times*," she claimed. "We took every document we had—which, again, I have to say, were not many, we laid them all out."

Hillary was treading on sacred ground with *The New York Times*, which had broken the initial Whitewater story in 1992 and since then had been trying to get the full story with backup documentation.

The *New York Times* Washington bureau chief called Stephanopoulos to note that Mrs. Clinton was wrong. The clearest example was the computer run of the Rose Law Firm billing records—the same records that Carolyn Huber had recently found and that caused so much trouble. The Clinton campaign had these records in 1992. They hadn't been turned over. Mrs. Clinton's current claim of total Whitewater disclosure in 1992 was incorrect. There was going to be a front-page, above-the-fold, first-lady's-a-liar story.

Stephanopoulos wanted Fabiani and Sherburne to smooth over this problem.

Sherburne called Susan Thomases, Hillary's close friend, who had helped with the initial *Times* story. She reported what Hillary had said.

"Oh, my God, we didn't," Thomases explained, recounting how they had severely limited the documents they made available in 1992.

Sherburne and Fabiani reviewed the information. Mrs. Clinton had overstated. What could they say? They drafted a convoluted three-paragraph statement that effectively said nothing. Stephanopoulos tried to rewrite it. Fabiani said it was incomprehensible. They needed to say that the first lady had made a mistake and was now correcting her comment based on new information, but she had not intended to mislead anyone. They finally just drafted a short statement with the key word "mistakenly" in it.

Sherburne had to phone Hillary, who was on the road promoting her book, to clear the statement-retraction with her. Just before Sherburne placed the call, she learned about Starr's grand jury subpoena for the first lady.

When she reached her, the first lady was profoundly upset about all these matters stacking up. Watkins, billing records, the grand jury subpoena and now the coming first-lady-is-a-liar story. Fine, she said, issue the statement, but call Diane Rehm to let her know the statement is coming.

Hillary poured out her emotions. Sherburne had never heard her so distressed. She was at wit's end, under siege, in despair. She dwelled on the ugly, ugly sequence of events. "Saint or Sinner?" "Congenital Liar."

"I can't take this anymore," Hillary said. It was the voice of someone at the end of her rope. "How can I go on?" she asked. "How can I?"

At the end of the call, Sherburne was truly upset herself. She didn't have an answer. How could Hillary go on? At what point did you stop? Hillary was so talented, so vibrant, so effective, Sherburne believed. When she was on her own message with her children and family agenda, she was a dynamo. Now this nastiness. The first lady was being forced to find a resilience in herself that no one, including Hillary, had known was there.

But the acknowledgment that Mrs. Clinton had "mistakenly" spoken cooled the *Times,* and a short, 11-paragraph story ran on page 10: "Aides Say Mrs. Clinton Erred in Claiming Press Got All Files." The issue disappeared, and the White House never again heard about it.

For the election year, Clinton felt he needed a more political White House counsel to replace Abner Mikva. He decided to hire Jack Quinn, Vice President Gore's chief of staff. He had heard about Quinn's testimony the previous summer before D'Amato's Senate investigating committee.

Quinn, an intense, compact, 45-year-old attorney, had met D'Amato speech for speech. He had worked with Nussbaum in the review of Foster's records, and he gave an effective justification for the way Nussbaum handled them. Quinn virtually invoked national security to defend Nussbaum. He produced a copy of the oath he had sworn when granted a top-secret codeword security clearance, and noted that Nussbaum had the same legal obligation to protect the documents in Foster's office.

Quinn said he had practiced law in Washington for 17 years. "In that time I can tell you I have simply never heard of a lawyer opening up an office or a set of files to investigators without undertaking any effort to determine whether there might be among those files sensitive or privileged materials—and in this case classified information.

"It would have been absolutely improper and negligent for Mr. Nussbaum to have done so without first conducting the kind of review he did," Quinn testified.

Some Republicans complimented Quinn's performance, and D'Amato finally conceded, "Okay, I'm not going to press this."

Clinton too was impressed. After several meetings, the president hired Quinn. The new counsel seemed tough and aggressive without being crazy. Since he was not a practicing litigator, Quinn was not caught up in the mumbo jumbo of the legal profession. He could speak in plain English sentences.

Quinn thought he would be able to perform political tasks for the president because Mikva had told him that Whitewater had turned out to be a bust. "There is nothing there," Mikva had said. But Quinn soon found much of his time was preoccupied with responding to the ever-expanding investigations.

Kendall wanted a meeting with Starr about the subpoena for Mrs. Clinton. On the Sunday before the scheduled grand jury appearance, Kendall, his co-counsel Nicole Seligman, Quinn and Sherburne went to Starr's office on Pennsylvania Avenue. Starr, Sam Dash, the former Senate Watergate chief counsel, now 70, who was Starr's ethics adviser, and four other deputies were present. All the men were in jacket and tie except Starr.

They sat around a large conference table, Starr and Kendall across from each other. Starr said he was there to listen. Appeals court judges were always willing to hear the argument.

"Is this necessary?" Kendall asked. "This will taint Mrs. Clinton in the eyes of the public for no reason." Starr would get his evidence, Kendall promised. Mrs. Clinton would again testify under oath at the White House. "There is a common law in this investigation," he said. "There are three precedents when Mrs. Clinton gave testimony at the White House. Seldom do you have three precedents." A grand jury appearance would have no more weight. There was no venality here, only a baffling mystery, he said. If there was some wrongdoing, why turn the billing records over in the first place? Kendall repeated his conclusion that the records supported Mrs. Clinton's previous testimony, showing she had done about an hour a week during 15 months. The only reason to compel this appearance would be to insinuate some culpability on the part of the first lady, Kendall said. The fact that Starr and Fiske before him had taken her testimony in the White House would send a message that this grand jury appearance was different. If grand jury appearances had been routine from the beginning, then this decision would be okay.

Starr noted that the substance of what was in the billing records was subject to interpretation. Privately, he found that the billing records showed that Mrs. Clinton's testimony was kind of shaky, but the contradictions were not clear. Starr played it close to the vest and only said the grand jury was the regular course. No one should take offense. He said he had great respect for the office of the presidency, but this discovery was serious. The grand jury in a matter this serious was entitled to face the witnesses.

Quinn, steaming, played the bad cop. "Subpoenaing the first lady before a grand jury will be a political act!" he charged. No other first lady had been compelled to testify before a grand jury ever as best they could tell. Quinn was offended. It would be an affront to the first lady—and to the president. By subpoenaing the first lady, they would impact the functioning of the presidency. It would obviously have an impact on her, and that would distract the president.

Dash took the floor. A lifelong Democrat, he liked to lecture. Subpoenaing any witness who might have knowledge of a crime was normal, routine and proper, he said, seconding Starr's comments. No one should be exercised or offended. No one would draw negative implications.

"This will be demeaning," Quinn contended. On the heels of the discovery of the billing records and all the publicity and outrage, the necessary public implication would be that she had done something wrong.

Dash insisted it was the way criminal investigations worked and was perfectly consistent with Justice Department guidelines, which the independent counsel was required to follow if he could.

Quinn was more angry at Dash. In his view, Dash had rented himself out to provide the echoes of Watergate and surround Starr's investigation with a sense of propriety and nonpartisanship.

Dash said, "When something of this magnitude happens...," referring to the sudden discovery of important evidence.

Sherburne interrupted. "Of what magnitude? What is the basis for this?"

"There's no evidence that she had anything to do with this," Dash replied. They were investigating and routinely calling witnesses before the grand jury.

"So what you've described, Sam," Sherburne said, "is what you do with a target, or somebody who you're about to indict, or somebody who you believe has committed a crime or you have evidence....You don't have any evidence of that here. No one has said that she knew where these billing records came from, that she had anything to do with them. Nothing. You don't know anything that makes this different from the way you've handled her in the past."

Dash replied that this was normal process and they shouldn't be so exercised.

Quinn and Sherburne said it would be an absolute circus.

"This won't be a circus," Dash insisted.

"Where have you been living?" Sherburne asked.

Starr said they would handle every part of it with decorum. He worked his hands together at times when he spoke. Sherburne thought he was being so pious and sanctimonious. It was driving her crazy. She recalled Lloyd Cutler's admonition not to politicize Starr, that he had been a good federal judge, a good solicitor general, that he couldn't be a bad man, he was just doing his job. No, Sherburne concluded, something out of bounds was occurring here, something unprincipled. Starr had no sufficient legal justification. This is just evil, she thought.

Starr said the grand jury process was important. The 23 citizens on the grand jury needed to see the witnesses in person so they could assess their credibility. Ominously, he said credibility was the key in an investigation into possible perjury and obstruction of justice. "I know you think that the grand jurors aren't significant here," Starr said, "but in fact this is a very hard-working grand jury and the grand jurors are very interested in this and do pay attention." They should not be constrained. They needed to be active and have the opportunity to question the witness.

At one point, Quinn raised a question about security for Mrs. Clinton at the courthouse. Could she come in a back door? The basement?

Some of Starr's deputies quietly laughed at this remark.

Quinn also asked about Mrs. Clinton's Secret Service protection. Would agents or an agent be allowed into the grand jury room with her?

Starr said no, but he said he would ensure her absolute security.

Starr took his deputies to another room to caucus. He told them he was more determined than ever to go forward. Grand jury testimony had more weight if it turned out to be perjury. It would be harder to lie, to look those 23 people in the eye and lie, he believed. Much harder than to lie to a bunch of lawyers—half on your side—sitting around the Treaty Room in the White House residence on a Sunday afternoon. Since a grand jury witness was not allowed an attorney in the grand jury room, Mrs. Clinton would be alone. He wanted her alone. "We are required to do this," Starr said. "We need to do it." There was no objection from his deputies.

They returned to the conference room. Starr informed Kendall, Quinn and Sherburne that the subpoena to the grand jury would stand. He said he would not announce anything publicly about the subpoena or the testimony. He promised that he would do anything and everything to keep it confidential. It would be up to the White House and Mrs. Clinton to decide what to say, if anything.

Back at the White House a classic internal debate began. Should they announce the grand jury subpoena or try to hide and do it secretly, even having Mrs. Clinton slink in through the basement?

Sherburne and Mark Fabiani were worried that information about the subpoena would leak to the news media. They felt a leak would likely have a negative spin. They wanted to announce it from the White House and shape the story.

Bob Bennett learned about the subpoena on Monday also. He ignited. Hillary had known on Friday and had not told him in their 45-minute conversation. Unbelievable. He had appeared on television as their defenders. He couldn't be surprised or uninformed. It would demolish his credibility. Had he been asked about the likelihood of a subpoena to the grand jury for her, he probably would have dismissed it.

He was continuing to urge Hillary to testify before D'Amato's committee. Maggie Williams thought they should get all the lawyers together—Kendall, Bennett, White House attorneys Sherburne and Fabiani and some outside advisers—to discuss the possibility.

Kendall was opposed to even having a meeting on the subject. As far as he was concerned, the issue was decided. Hillary would not testify before D'Amato. It was an obvious decision, driven by Hillary's interests as a person involved in a criminal investigation.

Maggie Williams, however, forced a meeting on Wednesday, January 24, at 10:30 a.m. in her conference room, just two days before Hillary's scheduled grand jury appearance. Mrs. Clinton wasn't going to attend, but she authorized a full airing of the arguments.

Kendall arrived late and said he could stay for only ten minutes. He felt embattled. He was having difficulty getting time to prepare the first lady for Friday's grand jury testimony, and he had two sessions scheduled with her later that day.

Bennett began by saying he had drafted a letter to D'Amato. He planned to pass out copies.

Kendall was astonished and angry that Bennett would presume to put something in writing on a matter way beyond his legal representation and knowledge. He objected. It was finally agreed that Bennett would summarize his argument. Bennett proposed that they announce the next day in a letter that the first lady would voluntarily testify before D'Amato, perhaps as early as the following week. This television spectacular would totally overshadow Friday's grand jury appearance, Bennett said. Hillary should go up there and slay the dragon, lay it to rest. She looked like she was hiding, and this move would prove there was nothing there.

Kendall thought the proposal was lunacy. There would be no time to prepare the first lady. Congressional testimony would be open-ended. She couldn't duck any questions. An appearance would require days, weeks of careful preparation.

The tension between the two lawyers electrified the room.

Bennett said he was absolutely sure that testifying was the course of action in the best interests of the client. The first lady needed to be out there. It was nuts to hold her back.

Kendall, seething, folded his arms. "Well, that's all very interesting," he said. "Some interesting points," he said. "I'll think about those. And now I have to leave." He walked out.

The others stayed and talked awhile, but the meeting was over. Thereafter, Bennett stuck to the Paula Jones case.

Kendall believed that the D'Amato hearings had no credibility and no traction. He was not going to have Hillary feeding a hungry dog. If Hillary had to go public, the D'Amato committee was absolutely the last forum he would choose.

The issue died as the D'Amato hearings sputtered on. Bennett told Fabiani that it was inconceivable that Kendall had let relations with Starr break down to the point that the first lady was subpoenaed. "If you're a white-collar defense lawyer," Bennett said, "you have a very close relationship with the prosecutor and you can prevent something like this from happening."

For Kendall, the grand jury subpoena was a turning point. As far as he was concerned, Starr was now overseeing a politically motivated investigation. Hillary was angry but less so than the others. "Then I'll get ready," she said.

Kendall presented her with a number of options for going to the courthouse. She could take a limousine into the courthouse basement or even sneak in covertly.

"Nope," she said. A past master of putting the best face on disaster, she decided that it was best not to attempt to sneak into the courthouse through the basement like some Mafia suspect or engage in some other subterfuge. This appearance was going to be a television spectacle no matter what she did. The day of her testimony, she chose a fashionable black coat with an Art Deco swirl in silver beads and two large gold buttons. She walked in, head held high, smiling, comfortable, putting on the air of just doing her citizen's duty.

Mrs. Clinton went to the witness room with her attorneys. She and Sherburne were lingering at the doorway. First the 23 grand jurors walked by into the grand jury room. They were mostly black and about half women. Then suddenly a group of men led by Starr paraded by into the secret room. Hillary and Sherburne both mentally counted out, one, two. Nine altogether. All white males in suits. Sherburne looked at Hillary, then Hillary looked at Sherburne. Both registered the same reaction—but-of-course.

"God," Mrs. Clinton said, noting she and Sherburne had the same reaction, "I'm looking in the mirror."

Hillary was summoned. Her look was I'm-going-to-let-'em-have-it.

Inside the grand jury room, Hillary was a strong but not defiant witness. She tried to be direct, assured. The questions focused on where the billing records had been previously, when she had last seen them and how they might have turned up in the White House residence. She said she may have seen them during the 1992 campaign when the computer run was made, but she had no idea how they had wound up in the residence. She was as mystified as anyone. There were many questions about how she and the White House had complied with the subpoenas, searched for documents and turned them over. It was as if they wanted there to be a kind of procedural purity and completeness to every step, all by the rules, all by the numbers, no mess. Well, any White House, especially her husband's, was messy. The Starr subpoenas—

vital and important to Starr and his lawyers—were not the only business before them. She tried to convey the sweep and variety of White House business and life without suggesting they had not been thorough and careful. But the work on the subpoenas was delegated to the lawyers. She was not asked a single question about the substance of what the billing records showed—her work for Madison and various related enterprises.

At several points, grand jurors nodded at her testimony. She believed she had won over her audience. One member of the panel of 23 brought along a copy of her book, which had reached number one on the best-seller lists, and asked her to autograph it. She wasn't sure what to do. Go ahead, one of the prosecutors said. She took the book and signed: "To Donald, best wishes, Hillary Rodham Clinton." The grand juror was later dismissed from the panel by the judge overseeing the grand jury. Grand jurors weren't supposed to talk with or seek anything from witnesses.

Outside, after dark, after four hours of secret testimony, Hillary walked up to an array of microphones.

"Well, you are all still here, I see," she said coyly to the hoard of reporters, photographers, cameramen and onlookers. She loved to fight, and the best fight here was to be upbeat, almost exuberant, fully on top of the situation. "Glad to have the opportunity to tell the grand jury what I have been telling all of you: I do not know how the billing records came to be found where they were found, but I am pleased that they were found, because they confirm what I have been saying."

"Would you rather have been somewhere else today?" she was asked.

"Oh," Hillary said, "about a million other places."

As she came under increasing attack, Hillary pressed Fabiani and Sherburne. "Why is Starr getting a free ride? I don't understand this. Everything we do gets put under a microscope and look at this guy! No one says anything negative about him. How can he get away with this?" Hillary wanted the White House to call attention to the potential conflicts of interest and Starr's part-time status, the types of criticisms that she kept hearing on the news and reading in the newspapers.

Fabiani did not believe they dared declare open war on the independent counsel. The White House's relationship with the independent counsel's staff would deteriorate rapidly. Fabiani also felt a public attack was what many would expect, and to a certain extent that would mitigate any potential damage to Starr.

Sherburne decided not to tell Hillary about Fabiani's work with the reporters on Starr's background and conflicts. She hoped to protect her and the president. But Hillary continued to vent in private about the administration's failure to attack Starr. "We're out there," Sherburne told her, hoping she would get the message.

Back at Starr's office, just a few blocks up

493

Pennsylvania Avenue, attorneys were poring over the transcript. They still needed a witness to explain what had happened. Although Starr subpoenaed Carolyn Huber and the lawyers, including Kendall and Sherburne, the mysteries of the disappearance and sudden reappearance of the billing records remained.

On March 15, Starr got word that he had won an important ruling in the 8th Circuit Court of Appeals. The court reinstated a tax fraud indictment that Starr had brought against Arkansas Governor Jim Guy Tucker. The year before, U.S. District Court Judge Henry Woods, a friend of Hillary Clinton's from Arkansas, had thrown out the indictment on the ground that it was not related at all to Whitewater. Starr had been incensed and suspected a fix. The appeals court agreed that Starr's jurisdiction included prosecuting wrongdoing he found in the course of his investigation. The court took the further step of removing Woods as Starr had requested because of the close friendship between the judge and Mrs. Clinton.

"A complete and total victory," Starr told his deputies. The high risk of asking the court of appeals to oust Woods had worked. The rightness of Starr's legal conclusions only reinforced his conviction that the forces trying to thwart him would contort and twist the law to have their way.

Starr asked for the first lady's fingerprints to compare with prints they had found on the billing records. Kendall hoped Hillary could be spared an additional humiliation. Didn't the government have her fingerprints on file some-

494

where, somehow, going back to when she worked on the Nixon impeachment inquiry or chaired the Legal Services Corporation during the Carter administration? Nothing was found. So the FBI sent an agent over to the residence. Mrs. Clinton had to give a full roll of each thumb and finger getting both sides, the sides of the hands and the palms.

Again Fabiani worried that the story would leak. He wanted to put it out publicly.

"We can't tell people whenever Starr does something," Kendall said. "We can't get in a situation where people expect us to say whatever it is that Starr has asked us for. What happens if he asks us for the president's fingerprints?" No.

Nothing was put out about the fingerprinting, and at the time it did not leak. But Starr did ask for and soon obtained the president's fingerprints.

In May, John Bates called Sherburne.

"I've got something sensitive we need to discuss," Bates said in his best official voice. "We have a need to search the residence, and I don't know how to do it other than by having a search warrant executed."

"You are out of your fucking mind!" Sherburne almost shouted. The election was six months away. It rushed through her mind—another historic first, the FBI, suits and rubber gloves carting out boxes from the White House, a full television spectacular. "That is not going to happen!"

"There is an alternative," Bates said.

"Okay," Sherburne said, calming down. "What's that?"

"You do it," Bates said.

Sherburne thought, Really, really clever, putting her in the ridiculous position of White House lawyer acting as agent for the prosecutors.

Why? Sherburne asked. What's the reason? What are you looking for?

A box, Bates said, that has "Vince Foster" or some form of Foster's name on the top of the box.

Perfect, Sherburne thought, of course. The 18½-minute gap of Whitewater, she thought, recalling the famous 18½-minute erasure on one of Nixon's tapes.

What was in this alleged box? she asked.

Bates said he didn't know.

Size? A jewelry box, shoebox, document box?

Bates didn't know or wouldn't say. Obviously they had some witness making an allegation about a box.

Where in the residence? she asked. Where was she supposed to look if she undertook such a search?

Bates said he couldn't limit the search. "It's up to you to search and verify that you searched for a box and this is the only description I can give you, and you search wherever you think you need to search in order to verify that there is no such box in the residence."

Bates said he wanted her to search the entire second and third floors. She didn't need to search the first floor where all the official reception rooms were located. Bates said Kendall couldn't do the search because if he found something that was a problem, his obligation was to his clients, to defend and protect them. But Sherburne was the official lawyer, and as they had discussed, she had an obligation to report any possible crimes. Bates had one other requirement. He wanted Gary Walters, the chief usher in the White House, to accompany Sherburne on the search.

Sherburne called Kendall. Previously, she and Kendall had a rigid division of real estate. She was responsible for legal matters involving the White House offices, and Kendall the residence. This search was going to cross the line.

Kendall was outraged, but he said she had to do it. There wasn't much to talk about. Better her than the FBI.

Sherburne wanted to do it right away and didn't want anyone to know or for it to leak out. The president was not there, so she spoke with Hillary.

"Oh for heaven's sake," the first lady said. "Well, come on in and get it done." She agreed that it should be done right away and kept secret. She didn't seem disturbed at this latest invasion of their privacy. "What will they think of next?" she asked.

Sherburne got her assistant Miriam Nemetz and Gary Walters and went to the residence. They started on the third floor, which has a single cedar closet and old clothing and boxes stored from Arkansas and elsewhere. Sherburne and Nemetz worked closely together, opening closets and drawers and boxes. That way each could act as a witness to the other if something turned up. Walters hovered stiffly at their side. He would not search or touch. They moved to kitchen areas, a laundry room and an exercise room. It was the equivalent of the president's attic. Since the Clintons had no private home of their own, it was the accumulation of a lifetime. The old and new, the necessary and what was apparently unnecessary, all of their belongings.

They found no Foster box on the third floor. Moving to the second floor, the living quarters, was suddenly more personal and intimate. Sherburne found herself alternately horrified and fascinated. She realized she was scared to death they would find something. Then what?

They went into the Lincoln Sitting Room, off the Lincoln Bedroom. Walters, who had been at the White House since 1970, related stories about how Nixon had regularly at night sat alone in the room and often fell asleep. One night, incredibly loud music was coming from the room. Nixon was sitting alone in the dark, the curtains drawn, keeping out all light, a brooding solitary figure. No Foster box here.

In Chelsea's room, Sherburne even got down on her knees to look under the bed. No Foster box there either. "I can't believe this," she said. "There are dustballs under Chelsea's bed."

"Oh, my God," Walters gasped. He was in charge of housekeeping in the residence, and he went to make a phone call.

It was eerie. A sign on Chelsea's desk said, "Don't touch anything." Her Sidwell Friends School biology book was out. Sherburne recognized it because her son, although a year behind Chelsea at Sidwell, was in the same biology class. It was exam time.

On to the Clintons' bedroom. Walters refused to enter Hillary's closet. "You do this one by yourself," he said. Sherburne and Nemetz went through every drawer.

At one point, Hillary came into the residence and went to read in the living-room area. The search continued. Furniture was moved, drawers opened, boxes searched. The desks and drawers in the offices of both the president and the first lady were searched. On and on, the two lawyers, plunging their hands where probably no outsider had been. Walters had to get keys for several locks.

Sherburne was amazed what lawful authority could get out of her, how she had been co-opted.

After several hours, they finally finished. Sherburne went back to her office and called Bates.

"I did it," she said, "and I didn't find your fucking box."

Bates just wanted to make sure that someone in the White House counsel's office was accountable for the search.

Sherburne was humiliated, disgusted and exhausted, but relieved. She said she would send him a letter certifying that she had conducted the search and found no box or anything relating to Vince Foster. "I just feel like standing in the shower," she said.

25

In early May 1996, Sherburne read a copy of a letter Quinn had sent to William Clinger of Pennsylvania, chairman of the House committee that was investigating the travel office firings. In the course of the endless battle over documents, procedures and testimony, Clinger had threatened to hold the White House in contempt, an ultimatum he had issued at least threes times before. This time, Quinn had pushed back. "Let me be blunt," Quinn had written. "This threat can only be characterized as a desperate political act meant to resuscitate interest in a story that long ago died."

"What the fuck are you doing?" Sherburne asked Quinn. As he knew, the White House strategy was always to say, Let's get together and talk through the problem, leave something on the negotiating table. Quinn's letter was a declaration of war. Bombing Clinger would only give him credibility—and visibility. "I've been managing this problem for months, and where do you get off just doing this without even telling me?" Sherburne shouted.

Quinn reminded her that he was counsel to the president. The letter had come to him, and he had responded appropriately. Clinger had demanded working papers the White House had generated for the earlier investigations. Once again they were investigating the investigation. The circularity was ridiculous, and he didn't have to check with Sherburne if he didn't feel like it.

"All right," she replied, "then I'm out of here." Sherburne's agreement was that she was in charge of responding to the investigations.

Panetta summoned them to his office.

Sherburne said she was either running the scandal response or she wasn't staying. She had bottled up the investigations for nearly 18 months. The success of her strategy spoke for itself.

Quinn said they couldn't let the congressional committees push them around. They had to fight back. The political and legal issues didn't occur in a vacuum. As the president's counsel, he needed to know and be in charge of overall policy. It was unworkable to have central legal functions handled separately.

"You may not like the deal you inherited," Sherburne snapped, "but that's my deal and that's how I do it."

Now children, Panetta almost said. "There's got to be a way to work this through. Jane, can't you find your way clear to working with Jack on this?"

"I don't think so," she replied. "Our approaches are too different."

"I really want you to think about it," Panetta said. "This isn't for me. It's not for Jack. It's for the president." He didn't have to remind them the election was six months off. Containing scandal was paramount.

Sherburne said she would think about it.

Late that night, Maggie Williams called Sherburne at home to inquire about the meeting.

"It didn't go very well," Sherburne said.

Williams said she and Hillary agreed—Jack Quinn had to stay out of this stuff. Their strategy could be jeopardized by confrontation. What are you going to do?

Sherburne said she thought she would quit.

"Do you want to sleep on it?" Williams asked.

"I don't think so because then I won't sleep well. I think I'm okay with this." She slept well.

Hillary called Williams that night to find out about the meeting in Panetta's office. When she was told the details, Hillary erupted and then she told the president what was happening. Soon Clinton was in full orbit. The scandal containment strategy was about to blow up.

The president called Ickes, Kendall, Panetta and Maggie Williams. He had one late night message: Fix it.

In the morning when Sherburne arrived at the White House, Ickes was impressed. He reported on his call from the president.

Kendall called Sherburne. "You just," he said, "you can't do this."

Sherburne went to see Panetta, who seemed almost willing to give her the South Lawn if that's what she wanted.

The imperatives of presidential service required accommodation, Panetta argued. This dispute was not merely some staff or turf fight, he said. Clinton wanted her to handle the problems. "The president really doesn't want you to leave," Panetta said. Her departure could do significant damage.

"I don't want to do anything to hurt the president," Sherburne replied.

What were acceptable terms?

"I'll stay as long as I'm working my own way, so this is my beat and Jack stays out of it."

It's a deal, Panetta said.

Quinn and Sherburne just stopped interacting with each other. But Sherburne's deal didn't hold because Quinn had already thrown himself into the dispute with Clinger. Quinn was now the named adversary; he was on the road to being cited for contempt by the House. If he were found in contempt, he could be fined $1,000 or sent to prison for up to a year.

The committee had already received some 40,000 documents, and the few that remained were internal documents from the counsel's office. On May 9, Quinn wrote another belligerent letter to Clinger declaring, "You have unilaterally determined that this president is not entitled to any confidential legal communications, and therefore, any defense."

Later that day, Clinger's committee voted 27 to 19 along party lines to hold Quinn in contempt. Sherburne thought that Quinn was worried about going to prison. He seemed to be losing weight. He looked pale.

Quinn was confident he wouldn't be sent to jail. Lawyers in the Justice Department had assured him they would not prosecute even if the full House of Representatives cited him for contempt. No one had ever gone to jail in such a dispute. Finally, a compromise was worked out. Most documents were provided, and Clinger was permitted to see the others at the White House. Quinn was not cited for contempt or jailed.

On Tuesday, June 4, Sherburne was dealing with the story of the day—FBI tests showed Hillary's fingerprints on the billing records. The White House argued that this finding was consistent with Mrs. Clinton's statement that she might have handled the records during the 1992 campaign. Although as expected Huber's and the lawyers' fingerprints were there, Mark Fabiani said the absence of the fingerprints of Maggie Williams and other top officials showed it was another dry hole. "Yet another Whitewater allegation has evaporated," Fabiani told reporters.

At 8 p.m., Sherburne was reading the news wire stories. One said Clinger wanted to know why the White House had sought and received the confidential FBI background file of Billy Dale seven months after he had been fired. What the hell is this? Sherburne asked herself. She called around the White House and couldn't find out much. Just that day they had turned over 1,000 pages of documents about the travel office to Clinger's committee. It was part of the compromise effort to appease the full House and smooth over the friction between Clinger and Quinn.

Sherburne had reviewed the 1,000 pages, but one of the other lawyers—Wendy White, whom Quinn had hired—had found the Billy Dale FBI file in the middle of a file in Box 8 of the documents. She threw it in the pile they were sending to Clinger at the last minute without Sherburne's knowledge.

Six months earlier, Clinger's committee had issued a detailed and sweeping subpoena. It listed 21 categories of records with a two-page definition demanding all documents relating to the 12 previous or ongoing investigations of the travel office. The subpoena was oppressive. Clinger's approach supposed that the White House had nothing to do other than answer his requests for records. The problem was that the fishing expedition had obviously worked, and now three years after the firings he had something.

The next morning, June 5, Sherburne met with Craig Livingstone, the director of personnel security at the White House, to inquire how the White House could have requested the Billy Dale file so many months after Dale left.

Livingstone, a large, effusive former bar bouncer, explained that at the end of every administration all the FBI files were cleared out and sent to the archives of that president. So they had to get a new set of FBI files for holdover employees such as Billy Dale.

Huh? It still didn't make sense. Sherburne asked Livingstone to get some answers. She was worried that it would turn out that the committee had asked for the FBI files on the other six travel office employees who had been fired. The next day Livingstone reported that the Billy Dale file had been requested as part of what was called the "Update Project." Anthony Marceca, an Army detailee to the White House, ran it. The project was designed to update the security files of employees from the previous administration who maintained their positions in the Clinton administration or had official reason to continue to have access to the White House complex. This explanation sounded innocuous to Sherburne. But why would he have pulled Billy Dale's file after Dale was fired?

"I've figured it out," Livingstone reported later by phone. "I've figured it out. Let me come over and show you this list I've got." He soon came barreling in, sweaty but enthusiastic that he had an explanation.

"Look, here it is," Livingstone said, pointing to Billy Dale's name on a multi-paged list. "There's his name. This is the Update Project."

Sherburne glanced at some of the other names on the first page. James Addison Baker. Was that the former secretary of state in the Bush administration? Anthony Blankley. The same Tony Blankley, press secretary to House Speaker Newt Gingrich? Why would these former officials, prominent Republicans, need regular access to the Clinton White House? "Wait a minute," she said, "did you get all of these?"

"Yes."

"You mean this administration asked the FBI for all these files?"

"Yes."

"You mean we have them?" It looked like there were several hundred on the list.

"Yes." Livingstone said they were archived up in records management on the top floor of the Old Executive Office Building.

Sherburne went upstairs to find Ickes. This screwup was so bad, it had to be a mistake, she thought. Who would ever be so stupid? She explained the situation to Ickes, who started laughing at the absurdity. After Sherburne's report, Ickes marched her down to chief of staff Panetta's office, grabbing Stephanopoulos on the way. Sherburne had not been on top of the situation. She didn't know what they had sent to Clinger, who was now clobbering them over Billy Dale. From Panetta's office, Sherburne called one of the lawyers, Sally Paxton, to ask her to go up to the old records management office and get the boxes, to make sure that in fact they did exist, that the White House had hundreds of FBI files on Republicans.

Paxton soon reported that they did. The files were detailed bureaucratic summaries for all the FBI information that might be relevant. They included derogatory allegations that might come only from one source, a neighbor or co-worker, at times unnamed, raw and unverified allegations.

Who had made these requests to the FBI? Quinn wanted to know. Bernie Nussbaum's name appeared on the request for Billy Dale's file at a time when Nussbaum had been counsel, the lawyers in his office explained. There was a form sent to the FBI liaison. Quinn had never heard or seen the form. "You mean that requests to the FBI go out in my name as counsel that I never see?"

Yes.

"That ends today," Quinn said.

Quinn also suggested that Sherburne call the FBI general counsel, Howard Shapiro, and send the files back. Sherburne reached Shapiro.

"I'll send someone over tomorrow," Shapiro said.

"No, no, now," Sherburne said. "I really don't want these here, now that I know they exist." Next, Sherburne called Paxton, who reported the files were in five or six boxes.

"Don't touch it," she said, "don't open them." The FBI was on the way. "We're going to wait until these guys get here." The records management people were nonpolitical civil servants, she noted. "Make sure those records management people never leave the room when you're in it."

The FBI agents came, put on rubber gloves and did an inventory of the records. The records personnel signed affidavits, and the boxes were carried back to the FBI.

The next morning, Panetta, Ickes, Stephanopoulos and Sherburne went to inform the president.

"What!" Clinton said. He disparaged the terrible ineptitude of the first year and a half of his administration.

Panetta, who had come in as chief of staff after those first 18 months, joined in the criticism.

Clinton blew up. Here were the travel office firings, like old ghosts, jumping out of the closet again. What was the explanation?

Sherburne said she didn't have one.

Clinton interrogated her. Why didn't they know what happened?

The only way to stop his anger was to be blunt. "If I had an answer, Mr. President," she said, "I'd give it to you, but I can't make it up."

They discussed what the president's public

response might be. Because of the uproar, he was going to have to say something. Stephanopoulos had already sought to frame it as a bureaucratic blunder. The president was scornful of that approach.

Sherburne still thought it was too fantastic for anyone to believe it had been done intentionally.

No, no, Clinton said. This file-gathering was going to be a mess, another big mess.

Mark Fabiani was worried that they didn't have it nailed down, not even close. He refused to make a statement in his name. But the pressure to say something was intense, and so Sherburne issued the statement in her name later that day, June 5. "We believe Mr. Dale's records may have mistakenly been sought," she said.

Sherburne informed Hillary about the discovery of the FBI files.

"You know," the first lady said, "before this is over I'm going to be responsible for this too."

"Oh, come on! You're not anywhere near this."

"Just wait," Hillary said, "they'll find a way."

At one White House meeting, the president asked, "Why aren't we investigating this?" He again wanted to know what had happened. But a White House self-investigation was no longer possible, as the travel office fiasco had proven.

Attorney General Reno immediately announced that her deputy, Jamie Gorelick, would coordinate a review of how Billy Dale's FBI file was sent to the White House so long after his dismissal. Gorelick had been a white-collar criminal defense attorney for 18 years at the firm of Jack Miller, private attorney for Richard Nixon. Prior to becoming deputy attorney general in 1994, Gorelick had served for a year as general counsel at the Defense Department.

At the Pentagon she had found that the principle of civilian control was ingrained in even the most crusty and hidebound generals and admirals. One of her jobs as deputy in the Justice Department was liaison with the FBI. Unlike the military, the FBI viewed itself as an independent power, the neutral investigative arbiter. Stung badly in the Watergate investigation when Nixon and his White House had manipulated and attempted to control the bureau, the FBI bristled at direction from the Justice Department or the White House. FBI Director Louis Freeh regularly proclaimed that he had institutional interests and had to protect the FBI scrupulously from the slightest appearance of political taint. Freeh assigned his general counsel, Howard Shapiro, to investigate, and a team set out to try to figure out what happened.

Freeh presented his findings on Friday, June 14. Gorelick read the report, and it showed, conclusively in her opinion, that there was no political motive.

Gorelick was surprised to hear Freeh was issuing an accompanying statement on the inquiry. She hadn't known the FBI director was going to comment publicly. She read the statement. "Unfortunately, the FBI and I were victimized,"

Freeh said. "I promise the American people that it will not happen again on my watch."

The Republicans were already having a field day with the issue. Now the FBI was proclaiming it had been "victimized." The White House was stunned, and Mike McCurry said publicly he did not understand the FBI statement.

Gorelick, who has a bad temper, was furious when she reached Freeh. She pointed out that his statement about being "victimized" was inconsistent with his own report. "This is not right!" she yelled at the director.

Freeh said he did not know about the statement himself. Someone in the bureau press office had drafted and released it.

"Fix it!" Gorelick shouted.

Within hours, Freeh issued a clarification. "The FBI and I fell victim to my lack of vigilance," he said, taking responsibility.

Because Starr had jurisdiction in the travel office investigation since the Watkins memo had been found six months before, he had his deputies do a preliminary study of the Billy Dale FBI file issue. Starr decided he didn't want to go further and issued a statement that someone else should be assigned. He had enough work.

Reno and Gorelick concluded that the solution was a quick, credible and thorough investigation that would be made public. But everyone was hopelessly compromised. The FBI couldn't investigate itself. The White House was at the center, and the Justice Department also would have zero credibility investigating its own bureau or the White House.

"This is impossible," Reno told Gorelick.

511

Experts in the criminal division noted that many of the witnesses in the FBI files were already being interrogated by Starr in his probe of the travel office. They didn't want two prosecutors stumbling over the same witnesses.

At 7 a.m., Gorelick called John Bates in Starr's office. It would be impossible for anyone else, she said. Reno needed Starr to take full jurisdiction to investigate the entire FBI files question.

Starr found it hard to say no to the attorney general.

On June 20, Reno made application to the three-judge panel, requesting that the FBI files be assigned to Starr. The next day the three-judge panel agreed and issued the order.

Once again, the third time that year, Starr was obliged to change his structure and increase his staff.

On July 15, the FBI passed on more bad news to Sherburne. According to Livingstone's own FBI file, Bernie Nussbaum told the FBI agent doing Livingstone's background security check that Hillary Clinton had "highly recommended" Livingstone. Hillary was a good friend of Livingstone's mother, according to the file.

Sherburne couldn't believe it. She informed Hillary.

"What did I tell you?" Hillary said. "What did I tell you?" She flatly denied that she had recommended Livingstone, or that she knew him or his mother.

Sherburne talked to Livingstone, who denied

any connection with Mrs. Clinton. Livingstone's mother said she only met Mrs. Clinton once and after her son had been hired. Mrs. Livingstone had helped decorate a White House Christmas tree, and Hillary had come to thank the group. Nussbaum denied he had claimed Mrs. Clinton had recommended Livingstone.

Sherburne told the FBI she found the alleged statement inexplicable. It was denied by all.

Over in the scandal management shop run by Fabiani, his young deputy, Chris Lehane, found the Watergate references no longer just fun office jokes. The gathering of hundreds of FBI files on the political opposition was deadly serious, full of overtones of misusing the most misused of agencies, the FBI. Lehane thought the reporters were picking up that Clinton was not treating the matter with seriousness.

Clinton missed an opportunity to stop or at least tame one of his scandals. Many who dismissed Whitewater itself realized the legal and constitutional horror if the administration were found to have used FBI material for political purposes. The president might have gone on national television and announced what had been found in his White House and declared that he had nothing to do with it. He might have given an impassioned speech about privacy rights and written letters of apology to the Republicans whose files had been obtained. He could have sent a powerful message if he had said bureaucratic snafus involving the FBI and invasions of privacy would not be tolerated in his White House. A little outrage would have gone a long way.

But the matter was under investigation. Neither Clinton nor anyone else in the White House could be sure what Starr might find. The lawyerly approach prevailed. It was dangerous to put out an explanation or show a reaction. They couldn't explain what they didn't know for sure. The idea had gradually developed to use Starr's office as a shield of sorts. Let Starr find out what had happened and explain it.

With this approach, Clinton abdicated responsibility. It looked as if he were hiding. Clinton, who was so often willing to take risks in other areas of his life, did not take a chance to regain some of his credibility. Rather than allying himself with those supporting disclosure, he sided with the lawyers.

There was another factor. Dick Morris, Clinton's chief political strategist for the president's campaign, decided to submit the decision to what he once called "the ultimate master of the Western world—the polls." He conducted a public opinion study on the impact of the FBI files revelation.

A total of 52 percent found it resembled a "Watergate-style cover-up." Only 26 percent bought the White House explanation that it was a "simple mistake."

In a June 12 memo, Morris wrote, "Conclusion: the issue is a loser for us no matter how we argue it. Best course is to distract attention with other issues." That is exactly what Clinton did.

Morris had used the Republican takeover of Congress in 1994 as his personal moment to regain a foothold with Clinton. At 47, he was the Republican consultant who had helped orchestrate Clinton's rise in Arkansas politics going back to 1977. He knew Clinton was desperate for political advice on how to reinvigorate his presidency. The moment had thrown them together once again.

Morris was obsessive, erratic and certainly brilliant. His one goal was victory. Clinton and Morris were like two alcoholics, and their drink of choice was politics. Morris had come to realize that the dynamic in the relationship included periods in which Clinton showered love, punctuated by periods of intense abuse.

A defining moment in Morris's understanding of Clinton's personality dated back to the 1990 governor's race. One late night before the election, as Clinton was dropping in the polls and blaming Morris, his campaign consultant, they were talking at the Governor's Mansion. About midnight, Clinton, who rarely drinks, had a glass of wine. He flew into a rage out of exhaustion and the fear of defeat.

"You got me into this race," he screamed, "so you could make some extra money off me." Clinton felt Morris was neglecting him and his campaign. "You're screwing me!" Clinton shouted at Morris. "You're screwing me!"

Morris stormed out. Accounts differ about what happened next, but all include a bizarre physical confrontation. One has Clinton tackling and slugging Morris. In his own book, *Behind the Oval Office,* Morris wrote that Clinton grabbed him and wrapped his arms around him to stop him from leaving. Morris added that he wound up on the ground because he slipped there. But in a more detailed account, Morris said the encounter was frightening. He also gave this account at the time to his wife, Eileen McGann. She said she wanted Morris to file a criminal complaint against Clinton because Clinton was out of control. According to Morris and McGann, Clinton had tackled Morris from behind, thrown him to the ground bodily and cocked his fist, about to slug his consultant. Hillary had intervened by grabbing her husband's arm. Hillary then walked Morris around the grounds and apologized on her husband's behalf. She made three points—forgive him, he didn't mean it and he needs you.

She offered Morris a telling explanation for Clinton's behavior. "He only does that to people he loves," she said. "He only does that to people he loves." In other words, the love went hand in hand with the abuse. You buy in for one, you get the other.

Morris was not sure whether abuse was a form of love or how they fit together, but taking the abuse was certainly the price of admission to Clinton's inner council. Morris found there was no more exciting, even thrilling professional interaction than with Clinton. He was willing to pay.

By July 1996, Morris was fully enshrined as Clinton's chief political strategist for the presidential reelection campaign. The polls showed Clinton comfortably ahead, but one night at a weekly strategy session held in the White House residence, Clinton blew up about the scandals.

"You can't tell me," the president said, "that the drip, drip, drip of this innuendo, of lies and defamation and slander and totally concocted, fictitious stories, one after the other after the other, that this isn't going to have an impact!" He was red in the face, screaming and even shrieking, pounding the arm of his chair.

Morris said none of the negatives from the scandals were showing up in the polls. "None of this is having any effect on you," Morris said, "and it won't have any effect no matter how long it continues." As long as Clinton didn't mention the scandals, the public thought Whitewater was remote. The other matters involved his staff or at worst Hillary.

Clinton would not hear of it. He raged about how the media covered nothing else—mistakes became supposed crimes, innocent members of his staff were dragged through costly investigations. "The hammering, the pounding, the garbage, the lies, the dirt," Clinton yelled. "You can't tell me that these aren't going to kill me!" The scandals were on television all the time. It was all the press cared about. Their sole interest was in destroying as many people as they could and making careers off it. The media was anxious to win Pulitzer Prizes by posting scalps. "They want their own president they can hang," Clinton said. "How can you say it's having no effect?" he demanded, still shouting. "How can you say nothing ever will have an effect? How can you say that?"

Morris said he gave up and held his hands high in the air. "If you," he said, pointing at the president, "you, *you* are indicted and *you* are convicted and

517

you are impeached and *you* are removed from office, they won't vote for you again."

The room filled with laughter and relief, Clinton slumping back in his chair, emotionally spent for the moment.

Panetta had joined the laughter and wondered to himself why the president always had to present himself as the victim. Whatever the reason, Panetta felt the outburst was a form of therapy for the president, perhaps one of the only opportunities he had to express his rage.

Later, in private, Clinton raised the subject with Morris.

"I get the sense that you don't believe that I'm innocent," he said. He sounded hurt and wounded. "I get the sense that you don't believe me."

"Mr. President," Morris replied, "my job is to run the pump and the motors, not to fix the hole in the bottom of the boat."

Clinton appeared not to like that answer one bit. He sought to convince Morris several other times of his innocence. He and Hillary, the president said, were being framed. People were making up stories.

Morris wouldn't give him a yes or no. As the scandals proliferated, he had begun to have doubts. He asked himself, Why is it that the travel office firings take place and Clinton has nothing to do with it? Why is it that the FBI files get delivered and Clinton has nothing to do with it? Is this a carefully constructed web of silence? Are these Clinton friends, aides and confederates willing to take a fall for him and go to the ends of the earth until the last dog died or was jailed?

Morris concluded it was not either of these,

nor was it innocence. It was more subtle. It had to do with Clinton's style. Clinton had a marvelous capacity to walk through the snows of scandal without leaving footprints. He would complain to those closest to him of the miseries inflicted on him, and his aides often responded to his whining by doing something or saying something publicly. But when they reported back, Clinton's frequent reaction was to listen without comment or indicate he was thinking about it or wasn't sure. Projecting vagueness had been raised to a high art form. Clinton did not explicitly approve or disapprove. The listener was free to make his own interpretation. So in fact Clinton never asked anyone to do anything. It was, Morris believed, an elaborate pattern. He was deceiving everyone—including himself—because he didn't authorize any of his aides' actions. That absented him from many of the scandals.

Morris had seen it in 1980 when Clinton was defeated in his reelection bid for Arkansas governor. Up until that time, the Clintons were really a two-career family, and Hillary didn't pay much attention to his political career. After the defeat, she changed. She said, "Oh, shit, I've got to step in and manage this thing because this guy is too naive, he's too nice, he's too sweet, he's too general, he just couldn't manage, he couldn't be tough." She had taken control.

In many respects Hillary had been in charge until 1994, when her health care reform proposal was defeated in Congress and the Democrats lost the midterm elections.

"I'm just confused," she told Morris in

November 1994. "I don't know what I ought to do anymore. I don't know what works or what doesn't work. I don't know why this is happening. I'm just so confused."

It was Hillary's doubts and the ensuing vacuum that had provided the opportunity for Morris to return to Clinton's political fold. Morris believed that Hillary and he were the conceptualizers in Clinton's life. But in November 1994, Hillary was damaged goods. As the family lawyer and investor she had screwed up Whitewater, and then in 1994 she had lost what was supposed to be the crown jewel of his presidency: health care reform. Clinton's reelection was in jeopardy. So Clinton had, in effect, fired her or she fired herself.

But Mrs. Clinton's scandal-managing role continued. Morris felt she was a disaster in this role. She was brittle, paranoid, she overreacted.

One day Morris was meeting with Hillary and her staff in the residence to review the 1996 campaign and the schedule. Several days earlier at an event for the president, a group of demonstrators had stood up opposing domestic gay marriage.

"Did you notice where those demonstrators were standing?" Hillary asked Morris.

"Yes," Morris answered, "just a few rows over from me."

"Exactly," she said, "the $500 seats. Now how many of those demonstrators do you think could afford the $500 to be there? Could they come up with the $10,000–$15,000 to get those seats?"

No, Morris said. He had the impression they had just moved into some empty seats nearby.

"No way," Hillary said with certainty. "There were security guards. They bought those tickets. Now, who do you think paid for those tickets for them?"

Morris didn't know.

"The Republicans," Hillary said. "They're going to do this to us at the convention. I'm raising it with you because at the convention we're going to face this on a massive scale." She was emphatic, she was absolutely certain. "They will have hundreds and thousands of people in the galleries just for the purpose of disrupting our convention. And we need a system of passes and background checks to make sure that this doesn't happen and we know who's in that gallery."

Afterwards, Morris told Harold Ickes about Hillary's plan. "She's really off the wall about this," Morris said. "You're not going to do that?"

Ickes said he didn't think they needed such a system.

Morris took the issue to the president. "Hillary's really got a bug up her ass about this," Morris said, "and we better be careful about it because if you do background checks and stuff, it's going to get out and it's going to look awful."

Clinton seemed to agree and the idea went away, but Morris could see that given the new siege mentality, such ideas did not die quickly.

Hillary seemed to believe now that toughness and confrontation were the right answers. Charm wouldn't work for her. In 1993, Morris had urged her to soften her image. "One of the most appealing things about public figures is when they lead with their vulnerabilities," Morris said. "They talk about their defects and people cut them a lot of slack." He cited Eleanor Roosevelt's shyness, or even Reagan's jokes about his poor memory. Defects and weaknesses can be assets, he argued.

"I can't think of any," Hillary had said. "I'm not good at that. What do you want me to do?"

Only once in a major way had she taken this approach. In 1994 at the Pink Press Conference, she had acknowledged her mistakes, and it had been a tremendous success.

But now in the campaign and under siege the old Hillary was back.

Although Clinton was viewed as a hands-on president, heavily involved in detail, Morris knew there were many matters he delegated. Those in the close Clinton circle loved working for him because of the massive grant of authority they received from him and the lack of second-guessing. Clinton could be like the Freudian psychiatrist who didn't let himself be a factor in the discussions and didn't respond. Clinton had set up his White House so it could run on automatic pilot. He could intervene when he wanted or when it was absolutely necessary in a crisis or political opportunity.

After giving testimony in the White House to Starr and his deputies, Clinton told Morris how awful it was. "They were just the sleaziest, filthiest people you could imagine. I wanted to take a shower after it was over."

Failing to win agreement from Morris about his innocence, Clinton developed a broader theory about what was happening to him. Elections no longer settled anything in America, the president said. He would have to endure a permanently insecure incumbency because he had won with only 43 percent of the vote and the Republican opposition was so filled with bile. They regarded him almost as an illegitimate president.

At one point Clinton said as a practical matter the country didn't have elections any more. What they had were photographs of public opinion polls, a kind of over-the-counter market quotation of the polls in an ongoing partisan war that would last all four years. But the numbers in those polls were the most important numbers in the world for Clinton.

Morris also knew that Clinton rarely admitted mistakes. Clinton took responsibility for the 1980 defeat for governor, the defeat of health care reform and his handling of the 1994 midterm elections when the Republicans took over the House and Senate. But those were mistakes of a magnitude that could not be ignored, and Clinton worried about them endlessly.

On the campaign trail, Clinton had snapped at a reporter, and Morris called him to say it didn't look good.

"No wonder I snapped at that reporter," Clinton replied, "the way McCurry lets them have access to me." He blamed others for over-scheduling him. "Every minute I turn around there's another microphone in my face."

When Clinton and Morris discussed the Whitewater investigations, Clinton's cry was loud. Senators Helms and Faircloth were out to get him. They had put Judge Sentelle on the bench, and Chief Justice Rehnquist, a Nixon-Reagan conservative, had chosen Sentelle to head the three-judge panel. Sentelle had chosen Starr, who was out to get him. Helms, Faircloth, Sentelle, Starr and the system—all of the above—were after him, he said.

In August 1996, the *Star* tabloid revealed that Morris had an ongoing, pay-for-sex relationship with prostitute Sherry Rowlands. He was forced to resign in disgrace.

26

SIX WEEKS before the election, September 23, 1996, Clinton gave an interview to Jim Lehrer for his public television *NewsHour*. Lehrer asked, Did the president agree with Susan McDougal, his former Whitewater partner who was refusing to testify, that Starr was out to get the Clintons?

Clinton replied that Susan McDougal and her attorney claimed that Starr and his attorneys urgently wanted to find something incriminating about the Clintons. "They wanted her to say something bad about us, whether it was the truth or not," he said. "And if it was false, it would still be perfectly all right."

Asked if he believed that, Clinton said, "There's a lot of evidence to support that."

"But do you personally believe that's what this is all about, is to get you and Mrs. Clinton?" Lehrer asked.

"Isn't it obvious?" the president replied.

"You obviously believe that, right?"

"Isn't it obvious?" Clinton repeated.

Asked about a possible pardon for Susan McDougal, Clinton said he had given no consideration to it but also said it would have to be handled through routine Justice Department channels for pardons.

When Starr saw Clinton's words, he felt cut deeply and personally. The idea that he would encourage or knowingly accept—suborn—perjured testimony was outrageous. On a more practical front, Clinton seemed to be holding out the promise of a possible pardon to Susan McDougal, who two weeks earlier had refused to testify before the grand jury and had gone to jail under a contempt charge.

Starr was as angry as some of his key deputies had ever seen him. The president had accused the independent counsel of egregious ethical and even criminal misconduct. Starr wanted a retraction from Clinton, and he felt the president should publicly encourage Susan McDougal to testify at once and truthfully. Starr was almost fulminating on the issue. He directed that a letter be written to the White House counsel. In all, Starr sent five letters on this topic to the White House.

In September, the first newspaper stories appeared about large foreign campaign contributions to the Democratic National Committee. A number of the contributions were connected to the Lippo Group, the Indonesian conglomerate owned by the Riady family. James

Riady had made about 20 visits to the White House since Clinton was elected and had continued to pursue close ties with his old friend the president.

Sherburne and Fabiani had known for more than a year that *The New York Times* was asking some questions about money, apparently $100,000 that Riady had given to Webster Hubbell. The payment had been made to Hubbell after he had resigned from Justice but before he had plead guilty to bilking his former partners, including Hillary, and clients of $400,000.

The matter was explosive, Sherburne and Fabiani had realized for some time. Hubbell was the nexus of Bill Clinton, Hillary Clinton, the Rose Law Firm, their Arkansas past and the first year of the Clinton Justice Department when he had been the number three official. Starr and his investigators believed Hubbell could provide damaging testimony, and they found they had not been aggressive enough back in 1994 when they had accepted a plea from Hubbell in the Rose billing fraud. They should have squeezed Hubbell and forced him to spell out exactly what testimony he might have been able to provide against the Clintons. While he was serving his 18-month prison term or afterwards, Hubbell provided versions of "I don't know" or "I can't recall" when questioned by Starr's prosecutors.

A $100,000 payment to Hubbell by Riady had overtones of hush money—money paid for Hubbell's silence, Sherburne realized. The payment of hush money to the Watergate burglars was one of the most explicit crimes in the Watergate cover-up.

As Sherburne was attempting to sort it out, she decided that it was best not to talk directly to the president. If Clinton had been involved in some way, had said something to encourage paying Hubbell, he could be personally implicated in some kind of obstruction of justice. Because she did not have an absolute attorney-client privilege with the president, she didn't think she should bring it up with Clinton.

Sherburne called Kendall. Could he ask the president whether he knew about any payment to Hubbell from Riady's Lippo Group? Did Clinton instruct anybody to help Hubbell? Did he facilitate, in any way, the payment, or know about it?

Kendall said he would ask.

Once you've done it, Sherburne said, only tell me what I need to know.

Kendall agreed. He knew what to protect. He got back in touch with Sherburne later. "I've checked it out," he said convincingly. "It's not a problem."

The week after the first presidential debate in October, some reporters began posing the first direct questions about Riady to Sherburne and Fabiani. Their questions were about the relationship between Clinton and Riady and the campaign contributions—nothing yet about the alleged $100,000 Riady payment to Hubbell.

Bruce Lindsey, Clinton's friend and deputy counsel, said he would go to Clinton himself, get the answers about Riady and Hubbell, and report back to her.

Sherburne wanted to be sure, to touch it and feel it herself, ask the follow-up questions of the president and make sure everything was buttoned down. She hoped to ask directly, Could you have ever said anything to anyone that they could ever have construed to encourage assistance to Hubbell? Who did you talk to about it? How often? What was said?

Lindsey said he would handle it. He reported back that there had been some meetings. Riady had said he was glad China was being given favorable trade status. He also had stressed the importance of good relations between the two countries. But Lindsey said the relationship between the president and the Riadys was routine and basically social. There is nothing there about Hubbell, he said.

What exactly did the president say?

There is nothing there, Lindsey repeated.

On October 9, Fabiani told reporters that the three or four meetings between the president and the Riadys amounted to nothing more than an "informal chat." Sherburne said they were "casual, drop-by visits."

Sherburne and Fabiani were getting exceedingly antsy. More Riady questions were coming in, and Lindsey was giving them nothing more. Sherburne asked the records management office to provide all the correspondence between the president and the Riadys. They sent down a big stack of documents as she was leaving for Albuquerque, New Mexico, where Clinton was going to prepare for the next presidential debate October 16 in San Diego.

On the plane out, Sherburne sat next to Sandy Berger, then the deputy national security adviser. She asked him for a short course on Indonesia and the Riadys. She read through her stack of papers. Included was a March 9, 1993, letter to the president from Mochtar Riady, the head of the family. It was four pages, single-spaced, urging Clinton to normalize relations with Vietnam and pursue better economic ties with China. There was also a reference to seeing the president at his inauguration, and a request to allow the Indonesian president to attend a G-7 economic meeting. This certainly was not an exclusively social relationship.

In Albuquerque, Sherburne went up to Ickes's suite, where Lindsey and Ickes were discussing the Riady questions.

"It's social," Lindsey said. "They were social meetings."

"Bruce," Sherburne said, "look at this stuff." She showed him the letters and documents. "This isn't going to hold. We can't describe this stuff as social. Why can't we just say what happened and let everybody else characterize it? Just give them the facts?"

That would be crazy, Lindsey said. "If we give them the straight facts," Lindsey said, "they'll turn it into something much more substantive than it really was, and it really was offhand, very casual." To recharacterize it would be to mischaracterize it, he said.

Based on the letter, Sherburne said the press would never believe the characterization of the meetings as social.

Lindsey said he didn't care what the press believed.

Clinton and his staff went to San Diego for the debate. A *Los Angeles Times* reporter asked Lindsey about two meetings in 1995 and in 1996 that Lindsey and Clinton had attended with Riady.

"It was basically a drop-by social visit," Lindsey said. U.S. policy was not discussed. Asked if one meeting was about campaign fund-raising, Lindsey declared, "I'm not going to tell you what the meeting was about."

Fabiani read the story and paged Sherburne.

What is going on here? Fabiani said.

They went over Lindsey's comments. It was a complete in-your-face, fuck-you, I'm not going to tell you what happened.

Fabiani felt Lindsey was putting him in a corner with a declaration that would not hold. The truth would surely come out. The White House would be seen as lying. His greatest asset was his credibility with the press. He dreaded becoming the White House mouthpiece who lied. He was planning on leaving after the election anyway so he just checked out and gave up. He never briefed the press or issued another statement in his name.

"You know," Sherburne said, "I give up too." She decided to leave soon.

Ickes and Lindsey proposed that Cheryl Mills, a deputy counsel who occupied Vince Foster's old office on the second floor of the West Wing, take over responding to campaign finance allegations. Mills, a 1990 Stanford Law School graduate, was one of the senior blacks on the White House staff. She was close to Lindsey, and the two appeared together at various social occasions. She agreed to the new assignment.

Sherburne turned over all her campaign finance files to Mills.

On November 5, 1996, Clinton won the election by 49 percent to 41 percent for Dole. Ross Perot received 8 percent. But the electoral vote was 379 for Clinton and only 159 for Dole—not close but also not a ringing endorsement or public mandate for the incumbent.

The New York Times called Sherburne. They understood that she believed Lindsey had lied to her about the Riady meetings. Sherburne tried to find a middle ground. There was a miscommunication and a misunderstanding, she said. In describing what had happened, she believed she didn't give away the store to the *Times* or rat out on Lindsey.

On November 19, the *Times* ran the story about the Sherburne-Lindsey dispute. It followed up with an editorial entitled "An Instinct to Deceive," and suggested that Lindsey ought to resign.

Sherburne realized she was in the soup. There it was. She was publicly contradicting Bruce Lindsey, who was as close to Clinton as anyone.

The best defense was a strong offense. Sherburne went to Cheryl Mills.

Mills said she had been in the car when Bruce had been on the phone to Sherburne answering questions about the meetings, and Bruce had never said the meetings were social.

There had been countless other conversations with Lindsey in which he had said precisely that, Sherburne said. It had appeared in the press. All kinds of people could confirm that.

Mills proposed that Sherburne send a letter to the *Times* saying they had it all wrong.

Unfortunately, the *Times* had it just about right, Sherburne said.

Mills drafted a letter for Sherburne to send and handed it to her after 9 p.m. the next night. Sherburne decided that if she read it, she wouldn't be able to sleep. The letter could wait until morning. When she read it the next day, she was appalled. It was completely wrong. Sherburne had to take her daughter out to the Potomac Riverside farm stables across Whites-Ferry. When she got there, she called Maggie Williams on her cellular telephone.

"I was so glad to see that letter," Williams said.

"What do you mean?"

"Cheryl dropped off that letter and said that you were prepared to send it."

"Maggie, that's not true."

"What do you mean it's not true? I already sent it to the Philippines to tell the president and Bruce that you were prepared to send this letter."

No, no, Sherburne said. She could not and would not send it. Maggie had better call back all of the copies of the letter. Just then Sherburne's cell phone went dead. Unbelievable. She dropped off her daughter and got a flat tire on the van out in the middle of nowhere. Then she couldn't find the jack to change the tire. She was ready to explode. She was lost, immobile and without communications. Then she looked around. It was a gorgeous day. Maybe, she realized, there was a message in her travails. If she had been able to get home, to get to a phone, maybe she would have done something stupid, pulled the plug and self-destructed.

As Hillary had suggested to her many times, she took a deep breath and tried to think. She eventually found the jack and changed the tire.

In the next days at the White House, no one of any importance talked to Sherburne. As long as Ickes was strong in his position at the White House, she was strong. But Ickes had been cast aside, passed over for chief of staff—the post he had coveted.

For some time, the president had talked with Erskine Bowles, a pro-business New Democrat who had been deputy chief of staff earlier, about returning to the White House as the number one White House aide.

Bowles, a tall, calm, wealthy 51-year-old from North Carolina, said he had no desire to return to Washington and urged the president to select someone more attuned to scandals and partisan warfare.

The second Clinton administration, the president said, needed someone who would build bridges to the Republicans and cut the necessary legislative deals.

"I don't do scandals," Bowles said.

Clinton said the investigations were basically done.

There could be no more shenanigans in the White House, Bowles told him. Poor administration like the travel office or FBI files fiascos could not be tolerated. There could be nothing that would trigger more investigations.

The president promised. That's exactly why he was recruiting Bowles, a tough manager who would enforce discipline.

Bowles accepted. It didn't dawn on him to ask Clinton about women.

Ickes had learned of the decision to give the chief of staff post to Bowles from the media. All his efforts managing scandal, campaign money and politics had made him radioactive. Now his weakness was Sherburne's problem.

Sherburne turned to her computer. She knew the truth. Certainly some day she would be testifying about the Riady episode—the inevitable sequence of scandal, investigation of scandal and then the investigation of the investigation of the scandal. Since she knew what had happened, she decided to put down on paper what was true, what she would be saying under oath, so the others could accommodate themselves to it and not make the mistake of getting in the way of the truth as she believed Cheryl Mills had. Since no one was talking to her, she would write it down so there wouldn't be any doubt.

She typed out a six-page memo dated November 26, 1996, detailing her efforts to disclose the content of the Riady meetings.

Sherburne showed it to Ickes, who confirmed its accuracy as far as he knew.

Sherburne took the memo to Maggie Williams and stayed while Williams read it carefully.

When she finished, tears were in her eyes. "I can't breathe in this memo," the first lady's chief of staff said.

"What do you mean?"

"You've got everything covered. You can't breathe in it. There's no room for any other explanation." It was airtight.

"Well, I want it to be complete, clear."

"But you know it's possible that Bruce wasn't lying to you," Williams said.

Sherburne said she had never said in the memo that he was lying. But they both knew that was the implication. A White House lie, especially by one so close to the president and so wrapped in mystery, was powerful stuff.

"There could be an explanation for this that could account for his views," Williams said. Was there not some way out? Could not this memo be turned into a joint memo from Jane and Bruce?

Sherburne said she would think about it. She felt misused at this point, but she promised to make one last effort. She phoned Lindsey. He didn't call back. She paged him several times. He didn't return her messages. Sherburne gave up, but she sent the memo to Panetta, who was leaving, Bowles, and other key White House aides, including Jack Quinn.

Cheryl Mills responded, calling Sherburne's account inaccurate.

Lindsey wrote to Quinn, "Jack, this is mostly crap. Bruce."

The president told Lindsey, "I don't know how these people can characterize the meetings since you and I were the only two people in them."

For months, friends in and out of the White House had advised Sherburne on the importance of devising an exit strategy—a way to depart the White House on an upbeat note or at a timely moment when things were good or heading up. How you left was often how you would be remembered, several suggested. Sherburne realized she had blown it completely. It was a case study in how not to exit. She had broken a rule.

Nonetheless, at the end of the year, Clinton thanked Sherburne warmly for all her hard work. The Lindsey incident went unmentioned, as did the bad blood that remained. "I couldn't have done it without you," the president said.

The ties with Hillary were not broken. On December 19, the first lady threw a good-bye party for Sherburne and her family in the residence.

Panetta came, as did Maggie Williams and David Kendall. Ickes came and held Sherburne's hand, and he cried.

Hillary said nice things. She voiced no judgment on the dispute with Lindsey or the issue of truth-telling from the White House. But she went out of her way to say that whatever had happened, it would not affect her personal relationship with Sherburne. Hillary signed and sent a picture of the two of them at the party, writing, "My fearless friend, With gratitude and affection."

At a press conference on January 28, 1997, a reporter asked Clinton about the reports that the Riadys had paid at least $100,000 to Hubbell.

"I didn't personally know anything about it until I read about it in the press," the president said.

Sherburne, out of the White House but following all the scandal events, thought, Wait a minute. She called Kendall to remind him that before the first news stories about the Riady money given to Hubbell, she had asked Kendall to check it out.

Kendall said he recalled.

536

"How deep into this are you, David," she asked, "because the president made this statement, but how could that be true given the conversation we had?"

Kendall reacted angrily, suggesting that there was some disconnect.

"You better get in this because people are saying things that are going to cause problems," Sherburne said. She remarked that the president had potential personal exposure on this issue if he had encouraged or instructed that the Riadys pay money to Hubbell.

Kendall indicated that he would straighten it out but was vague.

Sherburne thought that Kendall was one more person who didn't tell her the full story.

27

ON JANUARY 20, 1997, Clinton was sworn in for his second term by Chief Justice William Rehnquist. Clinton later told Quinn that he and Rehnquist shook hands. Rehnquist, Clinton said, had looked at him almost with pity and said, "Good luck!" The inflection was dismissive, with an edge of sarcasm, that good luck would be impossible.

Quinn was skeptical.

No, the president said, he detected a definite animus on the part of the chief justice.

Quinn was told that a woman who did the makeup for the president before his television appearances had claimed that the president had flirted with her. Since his job was to protect the president, Quinn went to Clinton to report the alleged incident.

"What!" Clinton bellowed.

"That's what they're saying," Quinn said. "This kind of crap can get passed around and I know you're being careful. I just wanted to report to you that that's one of the rumors that's circulating."

Clinton wagged his head in disbelief as if to say, Oh, it's all unfair. How can they think that of me?

Clinton still had to contend with the Paula Jones case. His lawyers would have to argue his immunity claim in the Supreme Court. Quinn preferred to settle the Jones case before a decision was made. "Can't we find a way?" he asked the president. It was still Russian roulette, Quinn felt. They had a good case arguing for presidential immunity in a civil suit, but it was not a slam dunk. Quinn felt that Bob Bennett was hungry, perhaps too eager to try the case.

Clinton was noncommittal.

In another discussion, Quinn suggested the president hire someone other than Bennett to make the oral argument to the Supreme Court. Bennett had never argued a Supreme Court case. Quinn said Clinton, and the presidency, deserved a seasoned advocate for such an important issue. Quinn originally had hoped to arrange for Rex Lee, the independent conservative former solicitor general in the Reagan administration, to argue the case. But Lee had died in March

1996. Others in the White House told Clinton to find someone other than Bennett. The only vote for Bennett was Clinton's, and that was the one that mattered.

For months Clinton and Bennett had prepared for the Supreme Court hearing of the Jones case. The issue of settlement had come up once again. The Jones lawyers had asked for some form of apology.

Clinton said he would not apologize. It was a deal-breaker. "Hillary is adamant about no settlement," the president said.

Bennett realized that was crucial. So he got everyone pumped. He was going to win.

Just after 10 a.m., Monday, January 13, 1997, Chief Justice Rehnquist said, "We'll hear argument now in No. 95-1853, *William Jefferson Clinton* v. *Paula Corbin Jones.*"

Bennett stepped before the Court. "I am here this morning on behalf of the president of the United States, who has asked this court to defer a private civil damage suit for money damages against him until he leaves office." Bennett wanted badly to get the justices to see how in the modern world civil litigation could become hand-to-hand combat.

Justice Souter asked whether a civil suit against the president would take that much of the president's time. "It's going to keep you busy," Souter said to laughter, noting the president would not have to attend the depositions.

"But in the real world of litigation," Bennett began. Jesus, he thought to himself, the justices had no idea that modern litigation was an all-consuming war. They lived in a bubble. Bennett said the attorneys for Jones were essentially investigating "any time the president of the United States has come into contact with a member of the opposite sex."

"Don't you think I'm going to have to talk to the president of the United States about all those events?" Bennett asked.

"Mr. Bennett," Justice Antonin Scalia interrupted, "do you think all those events are relevant to this case?"

That was part of the problem. It would be up to the judge who had the case. A civil suit was a free-for-all.

"How long do you think it will take to try this case?" Justice John Paul Stevens asked.

"It's impossible to say," Bennett answered. "I can tell you the president has spent—personally spent a substantial amount of time on this case already." He added, "The very nature of this case is so personal that it would require his heavy involvement."

Later in January 1997, Kendall concluded that Whitewater was finally in remission. The original investigation was a bust as best he could tell. Starr's prosecutors thought Webb Hubbell was a tomb of secrets, but that had not turned out to be the case. William Kennedy, Hillary's former law partner who had come to the White House counsel's office, knew more than Hubbell, Kendall believed, but Starr had not shown interest in him.

Kendall still talked with the president and Hillary regularly. Clinton frequently expressed rage about Starr and the prolonged inquiry. The Clintons had answered more than 20 document requests from Starr, various congressional committees and federal regulatory agencies. The president had testified under oath three times at the White House for Starr; so had Hillary in addition to the billing records grand jury appearance. The president had provided sworn videotaped testimony in two of Starr's Arkansas trials. He had provided 60 pages of answers to Resolution Trust Corporation questions. Hillary had provided 100 pages, answered questions in writing from the House and Senate and given a deposition to the FDIC. They had spent days on preparation, evenings and weekends.

The time and energy of both Clintons that had been diverted could not really be measured. But it hung over them, a permanent psychic energy drain, Kendall believed. If Starr were seriously thinking of indicting either of them, he would have given some indication or asked to meet with Kendall to try to plea-bargain. But that had not happened. Starr had never sent a letter informing Kendall that either the president or Hillary were targets, again proving to Kendall that three years of investigation was headed nowhere.

Out of the quagmire of charges, the FBI files appeared on the surface potentially to be serious. But the evidence showed that it was about two mid-level staffers on a lark—Livingstone and Marceca. Kendall wanted a quick resolution to all of the scandals, and hoped that Starr would announce that he had found no indictable offenses and then issue a detailed report. There would come a point when the prolonged investigation would erode Clinton's legitimacy, Kendall worried, and he wanted to make sure they never reached that point, though it was dangerously close. The investigation was becoming increasingly intolerable, in his view.

For Kendall, despite the remission, it was still full-scale war with Starr. The independent counsel asked for the notes that Sherburne had taken with the first lady. Kendall felt they had given Starr everything that was reasonable. Now the prosecutor was demanding the client's notes. "Fuck you!" Kendall thought to himself. He couldn't give in. This request was a proxy for other issues. It was the right principle to resist, Kendall believed to the core. Let the prosecutors put their nose under the attorney-client tent, and there would be no limit. Starr was after a John Dean, a White House lawyer who would turn. Kendall could imagine Starr finding something in the notes, some stray phrase in the margins such as "the first lady is guilty." The reference might look incriminating, and he could see Starr trying to use it as leverage with Sherburne or some other White House attorney. Kendall believed that Starr's ultimate strategy was to break into Kendall's own attorney-client privilege.

Out of distrust, pride and a lifetime of protecting his clients, Kendall would not make an overture to Starr to close down the investigation. Kendall thought that kind of effort would be rebuffed. His phone number was well known. Let Starr call him.

In addition, Starr and his prosecutors kept sending signals that they still had unanswered questions. God, the unanswered questions! If only Starr had worked as a trial lawyer at some point in his life, Kendall wished. The living, working metaphor for a trial lawyer is the famous Japanese movie *Rashomon,* which demonstrated that people in perfectly good faith see different things and have different recollections. In the real world, the pieces don't always fit together. Exhibit A was the discovery of the billing records. There are just lots of mysteries out there, Kendall believed, and it was a shame that Starr and his people didn't understand that basic, simple truth.

In February, Starr met with his Washington deputy, John Bates. Starr said he had decided to accept an offer to become dean at the law school of Pepperdine University in California, beginning in six months. He would be resigning. "This is what I've decided to do," Starr said, not asking Bates's opinion. Bates had already chosen to leave the office himself and go back to the U.S. attorney's office in Washington, D.C., but he voiced some concern for the continuity of the investigation. Starr's departure would send signals that the serious part of his investigation was over.

Starr said he had talked with his family, and the decision was made.

Who would take over? Bates asked.

Starr didn't know. That would be up to the three-judge panel. He made the announcement February 17, Presidents Day.

Kendall would never forget the day. I have won, he thought. I have outlasted him. He was somewhat surprised but not totally. Hubbell was no John Dean, and Starr seemed to be pounding sand down a rathole. It was not illogical for him to leave.

Republicans, counting on Starr to vindicate their deep suspicions about Clinton, called on the independent counsel to reconsider his decision. Bates had a nasty confrontation with Starr, arguing that the move bordered on abandonment.

A tidal wave of criticism engulfed Starr. James Carville and the White House—despite admonitions from McCurry to stay quiet—taunted Starr. "Deep down inside, everybody knows he's a quitter now," Carville said. White House aides were quoted on background saying Starr's departure meant he had no case, and no indictments of the first lady or the president would be forthcoming. The *New York Times* editorial page criticized Starr for a "selfish indifference to his important civic obligations." Pennsylvania Republican Senator Arlen Specter, a former prosecutor, sent Starr an angry letter: "Your departure will have a very serious, if not devastating, effect on the investigation."

After four days of withering rebukes, Starr called a press conference. He promised to stay until the investigation was completed. He cited Specter's letter as influential in the reversal. He apologized to Bates and the staff for not consulting them. Quoting the legendary New York City mayor, Starr said, "As Fiorello LaGuardia would say, when I make a mistake, it's a beaut. I try not to make mistakes. I do make mistakes."

Despite the skepticism of the justices during oral arguments, Bennett expected a big win in the Supreme Court. He believed the White House had the best constitutional scholars on their side. The president agreed. Bennett could not imagine the Supreme Court would allow such cases to go forward. He was crushed on May 27 when the Supreme Court ruled 9–0 that a private civil suit can go forward against a sitting president. The ruling permitting *Jones* v. *Clinton* to proceed provided no guidelines, leaving it all up to Judge Susan Webber Wright, the Arkansas federal judge who had been assigned to the case.

Clinton was disappointed but said the Supreme Court was largely conservative, not his friends, and he had anticipated an adverse ruling.

A friend told Bennett he could have done worse than losing 9 to 0. Losing 5 to 4 would have been tougher, the friend said, because then he might have made a difference in the briefs and oral arguments, convincing one justice and shifting the case to a 5-to-4 victory. But this ruling had not been close.

For three years, Starr and his prosecutors had looked for the elusive witness who would provide the compelling story of White House wrongdoing and obstruction—the aide who would lay it all out much as John Dean had blown Watergate wide open in 1973 with his incredible memory. The Supreme Court had ruled in the famous 1974 Nixon tapes case that Nixon could not protect the tapes of his conversations with Dean and others. So Starr argued that

Clinton could not protect the notes his White House lawyers on the government payroll had taken in various Whitewater matters under investigation.

Many times Starr had requested notes from White House lawyers. A pattern had developed. The White House would resist, Starr would threaten to go to court, then the White House would cave in, often in stages. First a White House lawyer would read the notes to a Starr prosecutor. After a kind of back and forth, they would eventually supply the notes. In one matter, however, the White House was inflexible. The attorneys would not let go of notes that Jane Sherburne had taken of her interviews with Hillary Clinton.

Starr finally went to federal court. The Justice Department filed a brief joining in part of the White House argument against producing the notes. Starr exploded. His deputies had rarely seen Starr so angry or emotional. Starr said it was outrageous that the Justice Department was jerking him around and teaming up with the White House. The Nixon case provided that a prosecutor was entitled to the evidence in a criminal investigation. Starr won in the 8th Circuit Court of Appeals. In June, the Supreme Court declined to take the case, allowing Starr's victory to stand.

The White House immediately turned over Sherburne's notes, approximately 15 pages. Starr was stunned. There was nothing of significance. "If there's nothing to hide," Starr told his deputies, "you try to expedite." White House tactics were designed to delay and thwart his investigation, Starr concluded. He vowed not to be stopped.

Starr had used his legitimate power to overcome what was surely a frivolous claim of privilege by the White House. But it had yielded nothing. Starr's effort looked like he was overreaching and being abusive.

The independent counsel convened a formal meeting of his attorneys to review the evidence against the first lady. His prosecutors from Little Rock joined in on the speakerphone.

"She's the queen," Hickman Ewing, Starr's hardball Little Rock deputy, said from Arkansas. He had drafted an indictment of the first lady.

"It is not appropriate to refer to Mrs. Clinton that way," Starr said, interrupting. He went on a tirade in his schoolmarmish, prissy way. He said he would not have such talk. They had to respect the office of the presidency. "She is the first lady," he declared indignantly, as if the others might have forgotten.

After hours they concluded they had a circumstantial case but no direct, compelling evidence, no witness alleging specific crimes by Mrs. Clinton.

To indict a first lady, Sam Dash argued, they would have to have unusually strong evidence. In the area of perjury, they had a high burden and would have to show a clear intent to lie. Mrs. Clinton had made self-protective, evasive and misleading statements, but they were far short of perjury. Dash said the world had changed. President Clinton had been reelected. If Starr was going to do something that would shake the world, he had to have proof that would convince the public that something was truly rotten and wrong. Dash thought Starr agreed.

547

But Starr seemed more willing to continue than others on his staff. He was reluctant to close anything out while there was still a possibility.

When Starr decided to stay on as independent counsel, he became more determined to find a criminal case to make against the Clintons. He authorized his prosecutors to pursue lines of inquiry delving into every aspect of the Clinton past.

In June 1997, I received a tip that Starr's prosecutors and FBI agents had questioned Arkansas state troopers about their knowledge of extramarital relations that Clinton may have had while governor. I called Ronald B. Anderson, a 12-year veteran of the Arkansas force. He had been one of the four troopers who had alleged in the 1993 *American Spectator* story that he helped facilitate Clinton's clandestine liaisons.

Anderson allowed me to tape a long interview on June 19. He said Starr's prosecutors and FBI agents had recently contacted him and gone through a list of about a dozen women, including Gennifer Flowers and Paula Jones. Anderson said he had refused to answer the questions about personal relationships. "I said, 'If he's done something illegal, I will tell you. But I'm not going to answer a question about women that he knew because I just don't feel like it's anybody's business.' " The questioners seemed to want to find out if any of these women had been Clinton's mistress, he said, but he had declined to answer specifics.

The next day I called Roger Perry, a trooper who had worked on the Clinton detail from 1988 through 1992. A 21-year veteran of the Arkansas force, Perry said he had been questioned about 12 to 15 women. "All they wanted to talk about was women." The lead attorney had said, "We would like to know if Bill Clinton had any contact with these women or if he had any extra-marital affairs with any of them."

Perry said, "They asked me if I had ever seen Bill Clinton perform a sexual act. The answer is no." One focus was Paula Jones. "They asked me about Paula Jones, all kinds of questions about Paula Jones." He said the Starr investigators had asked him if Clinton had provided one of the women with gifts from a named Little Rock department store. They also wanted to know if another woman had given birth to Clinton's child and whether the child looked like Clinton.

In two previous interviews over the years with Starr's investigators, they had focused on Whitewater and possible crimes, Perry said. "This last time I was left with the impression that they wanted to show he was a womanizer, and that they wanted to show some support with Paula Jones."

With Starr's permission, Ewing had initiated the questioning. Neither Bates nor any of the Washington attorneys working for Starr were aware of the new line of inquiry, which was formally called "The Trooper Project." Bates and some of the other attorneys were upset. They felt it was an extremely unwise project, casting their investigation as a sex probe.

When I called Bates at the time, however, he defended the practice and said it was "perfectly appropriate to establish the circumstances of the contact" between Clinton and a potential witness, whether male or female. He said if Clinton's hobby was playing poker, they would have interviewed his poker buddies. The purpose of the interrogation was to interview the women in Clinton's past to see if they knew anything about Whitewater or could recall anything that Clinton might have said about the land deal or money.

On Wednesday, June 25, Susan Schmidt, the *Post*'s lead Whitewater reporter, and I wrote a front-page story in *The Washington Post* detailing the interrogation of the troopers with the headline "Starr Probes Clinton Personal Life." Starr, furious, issued a denial. He claimed he was not investigating Clinton's sex life, but merely using "well-accepted law enforcement methods" to find witnesses associated with Clinton who might know something. "We have no control over who those persons might or might not be."

In downtown Washington, Kendall wondered if Starr had finally perhaps found a thread for his case. The independent counsel knew about Clinton's alleged sexual vulnerabilities, and his investigation had become an all-out attack. The question was whether the line of inquiry was merely an ice cube floating in the vast sea of Starr's multifaceted investigations or whether it was an iceberg, concealing much. Kendall thought it was most likely an iceberg, but he wasn't sure how or why.

Carville was delighted. Once again he savaged Starr in public. The investigation was now not only in the ditch, he declared, but in the sewer.

"This guy's out to get you, man," Carville told the president in private. "Starr's got one way out and it's you." Starr would investigate and prosecute and embarrass the president any way possible. "He will stop at nothing! There are not limits for this man."

"You know, I understand what you're saying," Clinton responded, without indicating whether he agreed. He took a few swipes at Starr, then added, "Starr will probably be after me after I even leave office."

In July, Starr announced that after an exhaustive investigation, he had concluded that Vince Foster committed suicide. Three years earlier Special Counsel Fiske had reached the same conclusion, and now four years had passed since Foster's death. A 114-page final report on Foster was released in October. "Mr. Foster," according to the report, "told his sister four days before his death that he was depressed; he cried at dinner with his wife four days before his death; he told his mother a day or two before his death that he was unhappy because work was 'a grind'; he told several people he was considering resignation; he wrote a note that he 'was not meant for the job or the spotlight of public life in Washington. Here ruining people is considered sport.' The day before his death, he contacted a physician and indicated he was under stress."

Foster's sister, Sheila Anthony, issued a statement accepting Starr's conclusions but criticizing the length of his investigation. She said, "In my view, it was unconscionable for Mr. Starr for so long to allow the American people to entertain any thought that the president of the United States somehow had complicity in Vince's death."

28

IN LATE SEPTEMBER 1997, James A. Fisher, a 41-year-old Dallas attorney, and two of his law partners flew to California to meet with Paula Jones. Jones was looking for a new attorney, and Fisher, a practitioner in commercial, real estate and employment discrimination law, believed she had a strong case. Arkansas trooper Danny Ferguson helped substantiate her allegations. He established that Clinton had asked for a hotel room and that Jones be brought there. Ferguson confirmed that Clinton had initiated the 1991 meeting. Jones, Ferguson said, stayed for a significant period of time. These facts alone—a sitting governor and a low-level clerk in a hotel room alone in the middle of the day at the governor's request—laid a strong foundation for suspicion. In that context, Fisher found Jones's allegations about Clinton's advances to be more than plausible. Clinton had failed to offer any reasonable or even remotely credible alternative explanation for the encounter.

Fisher and his partners took the Jones case—a big decision for their firm, Rader, Campbell, Fisher & Pyke, which has only six lawyers.

The Rutherford Institute, a conservative legal aid society based in Charlottesville, Virginia, had asked them to handle the lawsuit and agreed to fund it partially. The new Jones lawyers decided to attack Clinton in every lawful way. Fisher believed that the previous attorneys, who had wanted to settle the case before dropping out, had neither the resources nor the courage to tear fully into Clinton. They did.

Within a week of taking over, the lawyers requested a session to take Clinton's sworn deposition. Bob Bennett stalled. The case brought out all of Bennett's aggressive instincts. "I'll kill her," he told his associates, and they had searched into Jones's sexual past. Bennett was convinced she was no innocent neophyte. They obtained a sworn affidavit from a man who said Jones had performed oral sex on him in a car after meeting her at a bar; the alleged event took place just months before she met Clinton in 1991. Bennett had tried to trade the information about Paula's sexual history with Jones's lawyers in 1994 to obtain the details from the statement Jones had made about Clinton allegedly having "distinguishing characteristics" in his genital area. It hadn't worked, but Bennett wanted to make sure there were no such characteristics.

At first Bennett thought it might be a mole or birthmark. So he started asking longtime male Clinton friends who might have seen him in the shower at one point or another in his life. Had they seen anything? No one had.

Later, Bennett was in the Oval Office with

Clinton, and the president had to go to the washroom. For a moment, Bennett thought of following the president into the Oval Office bathroom to see what he might see, but he decided against it.

"We can't have the president of the United States's penis on trial," Bennett finally said to Clinton directly. "There is an ugh factor in politics."

"It's an outrage," Clinton replied. "It's totally not true. Go to all my doctors. It's just false!"

Bennett obtained sworn statements from a former doctor and the current Navy doctor that Clinton was normal. Bennett asked the urologist who had treated Reagan, Bush and Clinton to take a second, detailed look. The doctor did so and swore out a strong statement that Clinton had no abnormalities in terms of size, shape, direction or whatever Bennett felt a devious mind might suspect. A thorough dermatological examination disclosed no blemishes, no moles, no growths. The only step that was not taken was to ask the doctor to induce an erection to reduplicate the circumstances that Jones had alleged. That was unthinkable. Yet Bennett was confident enough.

On October 1, the new Jones attorneys served Clinton with a second set of interrogatories, requesting sworn answers in writing. Questions 8 and 9 asked the president to give the names of medical doctors who had performed any surgery on or otherwise examined the president's genitalia.

"It's a sham," Bennett said during an October 12 television appearance. The alleged "distinguishing characteristics" were part of a marketing plan to make the trial into a circus. He told the Jones attorneys that he wouldn't say those things if he were not certain. In public, the issue soon died. But it was not put to rest until Bennett supplied the names of the doctors who had examined Clinton to the Jones lawyers in a December 2 telephone conference run by Judge Susan Webber Wright. Bennett also declared that none of the doctors or anyone else had performed any surgery on the president's genitalia.

In line with their total war strategy, the Jones lawyers explored any allegation, tip, article or book suggesting some kind of Clinton sexual liaison. They came up with a broad list of 146 possible witnesses and arranged an alphabetical listing. Not all were women, and some were obscure.

One possible witness they based on a phoned-in tip that had come in November. The tipster, Linda R. Tripp, 48, was a former assistant in the White House counsel's office and current $88,000-a-year Pentagon public affairs specialist. She told Jones's attorneys she had tapes of conversations with a female co-worker in which they discussed the woman's affair with the president. The Jones lawyers were scrambling, so they put the woman on the list. They misspelled her name, leaving out the "n." Witness number 80 was listed as "Monica Lewisky."

In the fall, Clinton called Lewinsky about 2 a.m. and recalled that she had promised she would be no trouble for him.

"Tell me when I've caused trouble for you," Lewinsky responded.

"I've never been worried you would do something to hurt me," said the president, who had broken off the sexual relationship in May.

Lewinsky said she wanted a job in New York. She needed his help.

The president promised to do what he could. He enlisted chief of staff Erskine Bowles to see if he could find a job for Lewinsky. He described her as a good friend of Betty Currie, his personal secretary.

Tripp and Lewinsky discussed the involvement of Bowles on the phone.

"I'm going to tell him that I don't think Erskine should have anything to do with this," Lewinsky told Tripp. "I don't think anybody who works there should."

Instead, Lewinsky followed Tripp's suggestion that Vernon Jordan should help her find a job in New York. She told Tripp, "Somebody could construe or say, 'Well, they gave her a job to shut her up. They made her happy....And he [Bowles] works for the government and shouldn't have done that.' And with the other one [Jordan] you can't say that."

At 5:40 p.m. on December 5, the Jones attorneys faxed their list of 146 potential witnesses to Bob Bennett. It included some 15 to 20 women who might be suspected Clinton girlfriends as best Bennett could tell as he glanced down at the sheet. There were many familiar names going back deep into the Clinton past. The Jones lawyers had easily traced the names from details in the *American Spectator*, the conservative, anti-Clinton magazine that had published the original Troopergate story—with the initial mention of a "Paula." The list only gave weight to Clinton's claim that the Jones case was a vicious attack by political enemies and Clinton haters, Bennett thought.

Judge Wright had scheduled the trial for the following year. The taking of depositions and gathering of evidence would be cut off in about seven weeks.

Bennett immediately sent a copy of the witness list to Bruce Lindsey at the White House and another to Clinton. The Jones attorneys were going to take Clinton's sworn deposition on January 17, 1998.

"Bruce," Bennett said, "here's the witness list. Get back to us."

The next day, December 6, Bennett sat down with the president and Lindsey at the White House.

"I've been doing this shit for 30 years," Bennett said. "The key thing is, don't go in and perjure yourself." They needed to prepare for each possible witness, each woman, to establish the facts. Since this case was a rummage through Clinton's entire sexual past and any encounter with any of these women might be the subject of inquiry, they had to probe Clinton's memory. "Maybe some of these things will present a problem with Mrs. Clinton," Bennett said. That was something the president would have to deal with privately. "But the American people elected you twice, and they know you're not a choir boy."

Bennett noticed that Lindsey kind of went, Phewww, as if he were glad somebody was pressing the president.

To underscore his seriousness, Bennett said, "Look, my handling of this and dealing with it is going to be only as good as the information I get."

The list was long, and Bennett was hoping to get the judge to somehow limit the inquiry, but they had to go through it. One of the names was Gennifer Flowers. Flowers had publicly alleged a 12-year affair. What was the real story here?

Clinton said he only had sexual relations with Flowers a single time—in 1977.

Bennett next asked about Lewinsky, whom he had discovered was a former White House intern and then an employee.

"Not a problem," the president said.

Bennett pressed. Clinton reminded his attorney that the problems were in the past. "I'm retired," he repeated. "I'm retired."

Bennett went through the list in more detail with Lindsey. Bennett considered Lindsey the person who knew everything about the president, or close to everything.

When Bennett mentioned Lewinsky again, Lindsey said, "Absolutely no problem."

Bennett wasn't worried only about the witness list. In sealed requests, the attorneys for Jones had requested sworn interrogatory answers from Clinton. They had asked the president "to state the name, address and telephone number of each and every individual (other than Hillary Rodham Clinton) with whom he has had sexual relations or with whom he proposed or sought to have sexual relations" during the last 20 years. Bennett had objected loudly and formally in sealed motions. Judge Wright was due to rule soon.

Betty Currie called Vernon Jordan to enlist him in Lewinsky's job search.

In the nearly five years of the Clinton presidency, Currie had passed messages and requested small favors for Clinton. But it was the first time she'd asked Jordan to help someone get a job. Jordan knew that a call from Currie was a call from the president. He quickly agreed.

On December 8, Lewinsky sent a copy of her résumé by courier to Jordan. He read: Lewinsky, age 24, had attended Beverly Hills High but graduated from a private school, Bel Air Prep. She graduated from Lewis & Clark College in Oregon. She had been a White House intern beginning in 1995, then had been hired in the White House legislative affairs office in late 1995. But that didn't last long, and in April 1996 she had gone to work in the Pentagon public affairs office—a job she had recently quit.

Three days later, Lewinsky came to see Jordan in his 12th-floor law office at Dupont Circle.

Jordan found her a bit flaky and chubby, not his type. Lewinsky was confident and aggressive beyond her years and experience. You're a friend of the president's? Jordan asked.

Lewinsky said she didn't really look on him as the president, but reacted to him more as a man and got angry at him like a man.

Why? Jordan asked.

"When he doesn't call me enough or see me enough," she replied.

Take your frustrations out on me, Jordan told her, rather than on the president. Clinton had competing obligations. Jordan saw that Lewinsky was deeply infatuated.

Jordan sat on the boards of directors of ten companies. After the meeting with Lewinsky, he called senior executives he knew at Revlon and American Express, where he was on the boards. He also phoned Peter Georgescu, the chairman and chief executive of Young & Rubicam, and asked him to take a look at a bright young person from the White House. Georgescu set up an interview for Lewinsky with Burson-Marsteller, the firm's public relations subsidiary.

Later that day, December 11, Judge Wright ruled that Clinton would have to answer questions about women who were either state or federal employees during the time frame 1986 to 1996. That was five years before and five years after the alleged Jones incident on May 8, 1991. Judge Wright also decided that Clinton would have to respond to a second category of women during that ten-year period, "Those whose liaisons with Governor Clinton were procured, protected, concealed and/or facilitated by state troopers assigned to the governor."

Bennett found the ruling reasonable. Judge

Wright had a rough sense of justice. She was fair. He began drafting a response for Clinton to give to the interrogatories.

Jim Fisher and his partners thought Judge Wright's ruling was rather typical for a sexual harassment case. Obviously there were going to be some limits on the questioning. The five years after the 1991 Clinton-Jones hotel meeting were critical. If they got the case to trial before a jury, it would be vital to establish that after 1991, particularly during his presidency, Clinton had continued to make sexual advances or have some kind of sexual relationships with subordinates. Jurors, like the public, might have the impression that Clinton had cleaned up his act after coming to Washington. It was essential in a trial to undermine that perception or disprove it. The reason was simple. Large punitive damage awards were normally awarded to deter somebody's future behavior. If the Jones attorneys could not prove the alleged behavior continued with subordinates and needed to be stopped, they would likely not win punitive damages—which were normally the big monetary judgments that could run in the millions of dollars for egregious behavior.

This aspect was particularly important in the Jones case, Fisher thought, because proving actual damage was going to be difficult. Jones had not lost her job or been demoted.

Fisher and his partners had to find a woman from Clinton's White House years. They continued to get and seek information about Lewinsky and her alleged relationship with Clinton from Tripp. On December 15, the

561

Jones lawyers served Clinton with another subpoena asking for documents relating to communications between Clinton and Lewinsky.

About 2 a.m. on December 17, the president phoned Lewinsky at her apartment. He had two pieces of news. Betty Currie's brother had died in a car accident, and Lewinsky's name was on the witness list in the Jones case. Clinton said it broke his heart that she was being dragged into the proceedings. She might not have to testify if she could sign a sworn affidavit that would satisfy the attorneys for Jones. She could say she was visiting Betty at the White House. On occasion, while working, Lewinsky had brought him letters when no one else was around. He said she should come by soon so he could give her Christmas presents.

After 3 p.m. on Friday, December 19, Lewinsky was in her office in the E-Ring of the Pentagon when she was served with a subpoena. It ordered her to appear for a sworn deposition at 9:30 a.m. on January 23, 1998, and required her to turn over gifts she had received from Clinton. The subpoena was specific, requesting "each and every gift including, but not limited to, any and all dresses, accessories, and jewelry, and/or hat pins given to you by, or on behalf of, Defendant Clinton." It asked for all documents showing communications with the president, including letters, cards, notes. It also demanded her telephone records.

She burst into tears. The president had given her a cotton dress, trinkets, a hat pin, and many other gifts. She realized the Jones lawyers knew a lot. Only Lewinsky knew what had probably happened. Over the course of her relationship with the president, she had told at least ten people about it. She had opened her heart to many girlfriends, including hours and hours of talks with Tripp.

Lewinsky went to a pay phone and called Jordan.

Jordan immediately phoned Clinton at the White House.

"Monica Lewinsky called me up," Jordan said. "She's upset. She's gotten a subpoena. She is coming to see me." Jordan said she needed a lawyer. He would try to arrange it. He had in mind Francis D. Carter, the former head of the D.C. Public Defender Service from 1979 to 1985.

"You think he's a good lawyer?" the president inquired.

Jordan said he was.

When she arrived at Jordan's office, Lewinsky was disheveled. She was highly emotional and crying. She showed him the subpoena. She was going to have to testify. How could the Jones attorneys have known about the gifts? she wondered. The specific reference to a hat pin was alarming.

Subpoenas are generally sweeping. The specific reference was highly unusual. Jordan nonetheless told her it was standard. He said he would be seeing the president that night.

Be sure to tell him about her subpoena, Lewinsky said.

Jordan promised.

Lewinsky asked Jordan if he thought Clinton was going to leave the first lady at the end of his presidency.

"That's a really crazy notion on your part," Jordan said. He claimed the Clintons would be together 'til death do us part. But he drew the obvious implication of her question. He asked Lewinsky, "Did you have a sexual relationship with the president?"

Lewinsky was sure that Jordan knew. She felt he was asking the question with a wink and a nod, almost as a trial run for what she might say to others. No, she said, she did not.

Give the president a hug when you see him, Lewinsky said at the end of the meeting.

That evening Jordan went to see the president in the residence while his wife, Ann, caught the tail end of a White House dinner. Jordan's friendship with Clinton had boosted his reputation and status in Washington and his legal business. But he had paid a price. In one way or another Jordan was caught up in most of the investigations. He had already testified or provided documents in the probes of three Clinton cabinet members he knew. The FBI had interviewed him at length about a $100,000 consulting contract he had arranged for Webb Hubbell to receive from Revlon before Hubbell went to jail. It seemed almost every week Jordan had to do something for one of the inquiries. He was worried about further entanglement.

At the White House, Jordan and Clinton met alone. They reviewed what had happened with the subpoena. Jordan said he was concerned with Lewinsky's fascination with Clinton, her near fixation, her hope that the president would leave his wife. Jordan gave Clinton his best and most dramatic, level-with-me gaze, staring him in the eye.

"You aren't boffing this kid, are you?" Jordan asked.

"No way," Clinton said, according to Jordan. "Absolutely not."

Despite his close relationship with the president, Jordan felt uncomfortable interrogating his friend further after Clinton's firm denial. He said, "I'm going to try to be helpful to her as much as I possibly can."

Clinton thanked Jordan and made it clear that he wanted him to continue to try to get Lewinsky a job, preferably out of town.

On Monday, December 22, before Jordan and Lewinsky were scheduled to see Francis Carter, she asked Jordan to meet her alone. She explained to him that she was worried that someone might have eavesdropped on her phone conversations with the president.

Why the concern?

"We've had phone sex," Lewinsky replied.

At 11 a.m., Jordan and Lewinsky arrived at Frank Carter's office. Jordan offered no thoughts or advice, took a piece of candy and departed. Lewinsky retained Carter as her attorney. She told Carter she had no sexual relationship with the president.

Carter said she could swear out an affidavit stating her denial categorically. He then might use it to persuade the Jones attorneys to withdraw the subpoena. The affidavit would put the Jones attorneys on notice that they would be wasting their time to question her under oath in a formal deposition.

The next day, December 23, Carter called Bob

Bennett to say he represented Lewinsky and to report that she had been subpoenaed. Carter and Bennett knew each other from Washington legal circles. They met for an hour. Carter said he was contemplating a sworn affidavit.

Bennett told Carter that Judge Wright was allowing him to give lawyers representing possible witnesses the predicate, or reason, they had been subpoenaed. Obviously the one that applied to Lewinsky was that she had been a federal employee during the time frame 1986 to 1996. The questions were about whether there had been a sexual relationship or whether the president had proposed or sought one.

What does she say? Bennett asked.

She says no, Carter replied.

"Frank," Bennett said, "tell me if I'm not asking the right question."

Carter said Lewinsky had told him there was nothing.

Bennett suggested that Carter dig into it a little further. "I can't be blindsided," the president's lawyer said.

That day Clinton reviewed his sworn answers to the questions about the names of those state or federal employees with whom he "had sexual relations or proposed or sought to have sexual relations" from 1986 to 1996. The answers were "None." Under penalty of perjury, he signed William J. Clinton.

On Sunday, December 28, at 8:30 a.m., the president and Lewinsky met at the Oval Office. They played for a moment with Clinton's new dog Buddy and went back to the study. The president gave her six Christmas gifts—a stuffed animal, a marble bear's head, a Rockettes blanket, a New York skyline pin, joke sunglasses and a small box of chocolates. According to Lewinsky, the president said Christmas kisses were an exception to his earlier statement that there would be no more intimate contact between them. He gave her a passionate kiss. Lewinsky asked how she might have been placed on the witness list for the Jones case.

Clinton said he thought it might be someone from the White House staff, a former White House staffer or the Secret Service.

Lewinsky did not warn him that she had told many others about their relationship. But since the Jones subpoena called for her to turn over all gifts, she asked if she should get them out of her possession. She could give them to someone, perhaps Betty Currie.

"Let me think about that," Clinton replied. He then packaged up the new gifts for Lewinsky to take home.

Later that afternoon, Lewinsky and Currie talked by phone. Lewinsky was sure that Currie offered to come retrieve the gifts. Currie hazily recalled that she believed Lewinsky had raised the question of the return of the gifts. In any case, they agreed Currie would come get them.

Lewinsky took about 13 gifts she had received from Clinton and divided them into piles. She put ten of the gifts in a box for Currie to take. She kept some of the more sentimental items such as an old copy of Walt Whitman's *Leaves of Grass,* the marble bear's head and the pair of joke sunglasses.

Currie drove over to Lewinsky's, took the box home and wrote, "Please do not throw away!!!" on the top. She put it under her bed.

29

ON JANUARY 7, 1998, Lewinsky signed a sworn affidavit declaring in unambiguous terms, "I have never had a sexual relationship with the president, he did not propose that we have a sexual relationship, he did not offer me employment or other benefits in exchange for a sexual relationship." Lewinsky turned over to her attorney some of the items listed in the subpoena, including three Christmas cards, some letters and a copy of Clinton's campaign book. Carter didn't send her affidavit to the Jones lawyers. He was still hoping to talk them into voluntarily withdrawing the subpoena.

Lewinsky told Jordan, who called the president and informed him that she had signed the denial affidavit.

The next day, Lewinsky flew to New York for an interview with a senior vice president at the holding company that owned Revlon. It went poorly. She called Jordan, who promised to call Revlon chief Ronald Perelman on her behalf. She thought he was joking, but he wasn't. Jordan couldn't go any higher or any richer. About 5 p.m. he reached Perelman and recommended this bright, terrific young girl.

The next day, three Revlon executives interviewed Lewinsky. They offered her a $40,000-a-year public relations position, and she informally accepted.

Lewinsky called Jordan with the good news. Jordan informed both Currie and the president. "Mission accomplished," he said.

On Saturday, January 10, Donovan Campbell, the lead Jones attorney, took the sworn deposition of Kathleen E. Willey behind closed doors. The allegation that Clinton had groped her during a 1993 White House meeting had appeared in *Newsweek* the previous summer. Tripp, then a White House employee, had told *Newsweek* that she had seen Willey disheveled after she left a meeting with Clinton. A former White House volunteer, Willey had met with Clinton in late 1993 to ask for a full-time job. She was in desperate financial circumstances. Willey testified to the Jones lawyers that Clinton had groped her in the hallway outside the Oval Office during the meeting. She also testified that during the encounter the president had taken her hand and put it on his genitals when, she contended, he was sexually aroused.

The Jones lawyers were elated. Willey was a Democrat, a mature woman and Clinton supporter who had nothing to gain. She was credible, they believed, a crucial witness in establishing a continuing pattern of harassment by Clinton—their ticket to punitive damages.

On Monday, January 12—five days before Clinton's scheduled sworn deposition in Washington—Bennett, his team and the Jones lawyers, including Fisher, met in Pine Bluffs, Arkansas, in a closed session with Judge Wright.

The judge asked the lawyers who they were going to call as witnesses at the trial. "You're probably not going to win on the merits," she told the Jones lawyers in an unusual criticism of their case. "Everyone in Arkansas knows he plays around, but you'll never get 12 people to believe he harassed her."

Fisher and his partners were dumbfounded that the judge would offer such a blunt assessment of their case. Fisher felt that Bennett had long ago won the battle for the judge's heart and head. At times, he thought, Bennett seemed to have her eating out of his hand. It had become clear to Fisher that Judge Wright detested Paula Jones and thought the new legal team was reviving a suit that was without merit. This expression of her views was the most emphatic declaration of her animosity, they believed. But Fisher and the others didn't want to mess with the status quo by complaining. Judge Wright was letting them take Clinton's sworn deposition—a key part of their effort. None of them wanted to derail that moment in history or the opportunities they would have with the president under oath.

Given the potential witness list of 146, Wright continued, it was time to whittle it down. "I'll allow a few women to be called, but not a lot."

Bennett had a practical problem. "I want to know the names of the women that you are going to ask the president about," Bennett said.

Judge Wright concurred. She told the attorneys to explain in general terms the reasons for inquiring about each of the women they wanted to question.

The Jones lawyers knew they had to do what the judge asked. They narrowed their list to nine. They began giving the names as Bennett and his associates scribbled furiously:

• Kathleen E. Willey. Bennett knew what Willey had alleged in her sealed deposition, which he had attended. Fisher considered Willey their number one woman in the effort to establish Clinton's ongoing harassment of subordinates.

• Beth Coulson, an attorney whom Clinton appointed to the Arkansas Court of Appeals in 1987.

• Sheila Lawrence, widow of M. Larry Lawrence, a major campaign contributor to the Democrats whom Clinton had appointed ambassador to Switzerland.

• Gennifer Flowers, the former television reporter and nightclub singer who alleged she had a 12-year affair with Clinton. Flowers got a job working for an Arkansas state agency after she was named in 1990 in a lawsuit as one of Clinton's alleged lovers.

• Juanita M. Broaddrick, an Arkansas nursing home owner, who had told friends that Clinton had raped her in a hotel room in 1978 when he was Arkansas attorney general.

• Dolly Kyle Browning, a childhood friend of Clinton's who alleged a running affair with him over 30 years.

• Marilyn Jo Jenkins, a longtime Clinton friend who was a utility marketing executive for the power company in Little Rock.

• Cyd Dunlop, the wife of an Arkansas Clinton supporter; she alleged that Clinton had inappropriately pursued her in 1986.

• Monica Lewinsky.

One of the Jones lawyers said of Lewinsky, "Our information is that she had an affair with the president."

Bennett felt he had a pretty good chance of preventing questions about some of these women because they fell outside the judge's own guidelines: they didn't come into the ten-year period 1986 to 1996. Some of the women had never been state or federal employees. He went back to Washington and to the White House to ask more questions.

What about Willey? he asked Clinton. Anything in the White House years would be trouble.

Clinton categorically, up and down, denied that he had groped Willey. Maybe he had kissed her on the forehead. She was in distress. He tried to comfort her.

As they went through the list, the president denied them all, except the one encounter with Gennifer Flowers.

Why were they asking about Lewinsky? Bennett asked the president and Lindsey again. What might be the basis for alleging that Lewinsky had an affair with you? Has she ever been to the Oval Office?

Clinton said Lewinsky had brought a pizza to the Oval Office during the government shutdown. She delivered mail. No problem, he said. Absolutely nothing, no difficulty.

Were there any other Oval Office visits by Lewinsky?

"Betty Currie had invited her church group to look at the Christmas decorations," Clinton said, "and Monica tagged along and maybe she poked her head in." Nothing more.

Is there anything I'm not asking about her? Bennett asked.

Clinton said no.

Could there be a rumor or a part of this story we don't understand? Some misunderstanding? A misinterpretation of some sort? Bennett wanted to see if he could trace the origin of the information the Jones lawyers claimed they had about an affair with Lewinsky. What haven't I asked?

Clinton was blank.

Bennett figured that short of hitting the president with a chair, he had posed the hardest questions. They reviewed the rest of the list.

"After this case is over," Bennett joked, "your reputation as a womanizer may go down the drain."

Paul Rosenzweig, one of Starr's newly hired lawyers, went to see Jackie Bennett, the deputy independent counsel. Rosenzweig said he'd had dinner with an old friend from the University of Chicago Law School who was secretly helping the Jones lawyers with their case. The friend, Jerome Marcus, had told him about Lewinsky's

573

alleged affair with Clinton and about Tripp's tapes of their conversations. Were they interested? Jackie Bennett said Tripp had to come in the front door with her story. Starr concurred. Rosenzweig sent word back to Marcus.

On Monday, January 12, Tripp called the independent counsel's office. Briefly, she said she had information that Lewinsky was going to lie about an affair with Clinton in a sworn statement. The president and Vernon Jordan had encouraged the perjury. Tripp said she had some 20 hours of telephone conversations she had secretly tape-recorded.

Within an hour, at 11:45 p.m., six of Starr's deputies and an FBI agent were in Tripp's living room in suburban Maryland. They heard the story and listened to some of the tapes of the conversations with Lewinsky. In the taped conversations, Lewinsky described a sexual relationship with the president and how she planned to lie in the Paula Jones case.

Back at Starr's office, the deputies expressed their amazement. This was huge. The allegation on the tapes that Vernon Jordan was trying to silence Lewinsky with a job was the perfect link to their investigation of Jordan, whom they suspected was trying to silence Webster Hubbell by helping him get a lucrative contract with Revlon. They were now plugged into an apparent ongoing conspiracy with the president's sworn Jones deposition just five days off. Starr saw the Tripp-Lewinsky tapes as a chance to break into the ring of silence that had surrounded Clinton for years. They gave Tripp immunity from prosecution, and she agreed to

574

wear a wire in a meeting with Lewinsky. They had a lunch scheduled for the following day.

The next day, January 13, Lewinsky met Tripp for lunch at the Ritz-Carlton Hotel near the Pentagon in Virginia. They talked for three hours while upstairs the FBI listened in and recorded the conversation through Tripp's microphone.

Lewinsky said Vernon Jordan had encouraged her to lie. Lying in her own sworn affidavit in the Jones case was essential to protect the president. "I could not live with myself if I caused trouble," Lewinsky said. "That is just—that is not my nature. I am a good person. I think no matter what—no matter how he has wronged me, no matter how many girlfriends he had, no matter how many people he abused, no matter how many, it—it was my choice."

"I know that," Tripp said.

"That is what I would do for you," Lewinsky said. "I know a secret about every single one of my friends." Not harming your friends was important. "To me, that's integrity. To me, when I meet my maker, and my maker says, 'Did you harm people who were good to you?' if I say no, that's what integrity is to me."

The next night, Wednesday, January 14, Jackie Bennett paged Deputy Attorney General Eric Holder Jr., who was at a Washington Wizards professional basketball game.

"Something has come up," Jackie Bennett said, "and it could be serious." They had to meet the next day, he said.

On Thursday, January 15, Starr's legal team

met with Holder. They played portions of the FBI's recording of Lewinsky telling Tripp that Jordan had encouraged her to lie under oath. Starr then formally requested that the attorney general ask the three-judge special division to give him jurisdiction to investigate. The independent counsel was already probing whether Jordan had tried to buy Webb Hubbell's silence by helping Hubbell obtain the $100,000 Revlon contract shortly before going to jail.

Holder was uncomfortable with the independent counsel looking into the president's private life and wanting to expand his investigation formally. But the allegations deserved further inquiry. Since they involved the president, the Justice Department couldn't do it. Holder considered recommending that Reno seek appointment of another independent counsel, but Starr was already in business and had argued that delay would ruin the entire probe.

Starr's urgency grew that morning when Michael Isikoff of *Newsweek* called his office. Isikoff had learned about the Tripp-Lewinsky lunch that the FBI had audiotaped. He was going to call Jordan and Lewinsky for comment. Requested to delay making those calls, Isikoff said he would wait until the next day at 4 p.m., which gave Starr less than one day and a half before his investigation was blown for sure.

Carter was getting nowhere with the Jones attorneys. They would not withdraw the Lewinsky subpoena. He sent them Lewinsky's sworn affidavit denying the Clinton relationship.

· · ·

On Friday, January 16, Bennett trudged rapidly up the White House driveway. These two days were going to be the most important in his three decades of practicing law. He was on edge. *Am I really going to say this to the president of the United States?* he asked himself. He rarely shied away from blunt exchanges with clients. In truth he relished forcing his clients out of their corners of untruth. But he worried that a direct confrontation with the president might be stepping over the invisible line separating ordinary mortals from—what might they be called—figures of real history?

Fuck it, Bennett concluded. He knew the old adage: "The worst defense lawyers are the ones that believe their clients."

Bennett, radiating equal measures of ego, self-confidence and bluster, and one of his law partners entered the White House West Wing. They were soon ushered into Clinton's inner sanctum, the private study off the Oval Office, to meet with Clinton and Bruce Lindsey for the final preparation session before Clinton's deposition.

Every case, every witness, every client had a point of greatest vulnerability—an Achilles heel. Locating it was a lawyer's, and ultimately the client's, insurance policy.

Of the nine women on the list he had located the real problem. It was not Kathleen Willey, because that had never been a relationship. It was not Monica Lewinsky. It was totally improbable that the president had taken up with a young woman, age 23 or 24, who apparently brought pizza and mail to the Oval Office.

No, Bennett believed, he had smoked out the real liability on the list—Marilyn Jo Jenkins, a beautiful marketing executive whom Clinton had known for more than a decade. Jenkins was a longtime employee of the Arkansas Power and Light Company. Her name had been linked to Clinton in published reports but only in vague references.

Danny Ferguson, the Arkansas trooper who was Clinton's co-defendant in the Jones case, had sworn under oath that he had brought Jenkins four times for private basement office visits with Clinton at the Governor's Mansion in the less than three months between Clinton's election in November 1992 as president and his January 1993 inaugural. Three of the meetings with Clinton had happened at about 5:15 a.m. or 5:30 a.m., and one in the evening. Each lasted about 45 minutes. During the early morning visit on the day Clinton was leaving for Washington, Jenkins had arrived in a long coat and baseball cap. Ferguson had brought gifts to Jenkins from Clinton. Phone records showed that in the period 1989–91, Clinton had placed 59 calls to Jenkins's home or office. One call was for 94 minutes and had been placed at 1:23 a.m.

Bennett had learned from another lawyer that Clinton had asked Ferguson to cover for him and take responsibility for the phone calls; the trooper had declined. Ferguson also had said that in a discussion at the state capitol nearly a decade ago, Governor Clinton had confided that he loved both his wife, Hillary, and Marilyn Jo.

"It's tough to be in love with two different women," Ferguson quoted Clinton as saying.

Clinton had denied to Bennett that he had a sexual relationship with Jenkins. Bennett was not buying it. He noticed that Clinton reacted differently when Jenkins's name came up. The president paused in a forlorn and wistful way. Bennett couldn't quite put his finger on it, but Clinton's manner seemed to be a definite tip-off. In poker, it was called a "tell"—an unconscious physical reaction to bad cards or good cards, a distinctive way of stiffening in the chair, twitching in the face, or handling of cards. Bennett loved poker. He played in a monthly low-stakes game with a group of Washington lawyers, including Chief Justice of the United States William Rehnquist. Besides knowing the rules and the odds, poker, like the law, at times required going with pure gut instinct.

In the quiet study, Bennett looked squarely at the president. Bennett's eyes were largely hidden behind his glasses so he had to work with his body and his voice. He leaned close to the president, nearly touching him.

"Mr. President," Bennett said in his aggressive baritone, "I find your explanation about one of the women frankly unbelievable." He summarized the connections to Jenkins, the 5:15 a.m. meetings. Jenkins attempted to explain away one early morning encounter by claiming that she had to catch a plane and wanted to say good-bye to Clinton. Bennett shook his head in consternation. "This is what impeachment is made of. Your political enemies will eat you alive if there's anything in that deposition that isn't truthful." There can be no fudging or finagling. It would be better to have to deal with the first lady if there is a problem, Bennett repeated. "If..." Bennett said, stopping for effect, making it clear there could be no evasion. He shook his head, almost feeling electricity in the air. "You are dead. You are dead!"

"I hear you," the president said.

Bennett believed he had hit home, and he was certain that he was right about Jenkins. He reminded the president that the judge would make a final ruling the next day at the deposition about the questions relating to the nine women. Supposedly, Clinton was going to be asked only about women who had been state or federal employees, and Jenkins had never worked for either government. Bennett was going to object, but the judge could rule either way, Bennett said. It probably was a fifty-fifty shot whether questions would be allowed about Jenkins, he said. The president had to be ready to answer, Bennett said, inviting Clinton to share with his lawyers his possible responses.

"I hear you," the president said again, without elaborating.

Afterwards, Bennett met alone with Bruce Lindsey.

"He needed that," Lindsey said.

Down Pennsylvania Avenue that same day, Attorney General Janet Reno asked the three-judge special division to expand Starr's jurisdiction to cover the Lewinsky inquiry. The judges later in the day issued a sealed, secret two-page order giving Starr power to investigate "whether Monica Lewinsky or others sub-orned perjury, obstructed justice, intimidated witnesses or otherwise violated federal law." Neither the president, nor Jordan, nor anyone covered by the Independent Counsel Act was mentioned.

That morning Tripp, once again wired, met Lewinsky at the Ritz-Carlton. Two FBI agents quickly appeared. They told Lewinsky that attorneys for the Whitewater independent counsel wished to discuss her culpability in criminal activity. They took her to room 1012 upstairs in the hotel at 1:05 p.m. She was crying.

They told Lewinsky that she couldn't call Frank Carter, her attorney. They worried that he might be part of the conspiracy to keep her silent. But they said they could give her the number for another criminal attorney.

Lewinsky declined.

The prosecutors laid out the evidence for two hours. They told her they had her on tape saying she had committed perjury, that they knew she had signed a false affidavit. They told her she could go to jail for 27 years. But they said there was a way out. If she would cooperate fully and wear a listening device in conversations with others who were under investigation, they would offer her complete immunity from prosecution.

Lewinsky said she was going to talk it over with her family. They had to wait hours for her mother, Marcia Lewis, to arrive from New York City.

Jackie Bennett told Lewinsky that at age 24 she didn't need to consult with her mother.

About 10:15 p.m., Lewis finally met with Michael Emmick, the prosecutor who was in charge of the Lewinsky task force. She explained that her daughter was younger than her chronological age, and that six years ago Monica had talked about suicide.

Lewis phoned her ex-husband, Monica's father, Bernard Lewinsky, in Los Angeles. He recommended an old family friend, attorney William Ginsburg.

Ginsburg, a bearded, self-important and successful medical malpractice attorney with a deep voice, was at his club, the Jonathan, when he received a call saying his legal services were required at once. He asked two doctors he was meeting with to leave the room and took the phone.

Emmick identified himself. He explained the immunity proposal.

Ginsburg said he had to have the offer in writing.

Emmick said they had no computer or fax available because he was in the hotel, not at his office.

Go to the concierge floor at the Ritz-Carlton, Ginsburg said. It was on the 16th floor; he knew it well. Take out some letterhead stationery, write out the immunity offer by hand and fax it to me. Ginsburg said he would stand by for the fax at his club. Emmick didn't even have to put his name on it. "I'll trust you," Ginsburg said. He would sign it and send it back.

Emmick said no. Agreement had to be reached at once. He didn't say *Newsweek* was about to break the story and they needed Lewinsky to make some phone calls immediately that would be recorded.

Ginsburg said he couldn't spend the thousands of dollars it would cost to charter a jet to get him to Washington in four or five hours.

The conversation ended with no deal.

While the negotiations were going on between the lawyers, Lewinsky asked if it were possible for her to cooperate just partially.

No.

If the Paula Jones case went away, she asked, would this investigation go away?

"No," Emmick said.

At 12:45 a.m. on Saturday, January 17, nearly 12 hours after the FBI agents had approached Lewinsky, she and her mother were escorted to her car in the parking garage adjacent to the Mall and released.

In ten hours, the president was going to be questioned under oath by the Jones lawyers. Lewinsky realized Clinton could be set up. Should she signal the president? Call Betty Currie or Jordan or Clinton himself to report what had happened? She was distraught and exhausted. If she made a call, she feared she might be arrested or the phone might be tapped. She sent no warning.

That night Tripp had met with an attorney for Paula Jones and provided further details about the Clinton-Lewinsky relationship—detailed information that might be useful during the president's interrogation the next day.

30

BENNETT HAD DECIDED to ask Judge Wright to attend the deposition of the president. That way she could rule immediately on whether Clinton would have to answer certain questions, especially about other women. If the judge were not present physically and were just listening by phone, Bennett reasoned, her tendency might be to allow the Jones lawyers more latitude and more questions. The lines of inquiry that probably wouldn't be allowed at a trial might creep in, and these would surely leak. Judge Wright's presence would ensure a tighter rein on the proceedings, Bennett hoped.

Charles F. C. Ruff, the White House counsel who was going to sit in on the deposition, agreed to ask the judge to attend.

Fisher and the other Jones lawyers didn't take a position. They knew they couldn't prevent it. If they objected, it would look as if they were planning to do something improper. So their position was that they welcomed Her Honor.

Judge Wright was reluctant at first. But when Bennett made it clear that the president asked her to be there, she said she would come.

Bennett felt well prepared. He and his team of lawyers had made sure they were getting everything that might be reasonably obtained about Jones and the other women. Most comforting was Bennett's conviction that they were dealing with a past buried in Arkansas. Bennett also felt physically well. He had stopped drinking at night. The president often would call between 10 p.m. and midnight, and Bennett had to make sure he was up to talking business.

Before 10 a.m., Paula Jones and her attorneys piled into two taxicabs at their hotel on Capitol Hill for the five-minute ride to Bennett's office. Photographers swarmed, blocking Jones's exit from the taxi. After considerable pushing and shoving, Jones and her attorneys made it upstairs to the 11th floor. They were shown to a spartan holding room. Water and coffee were on a table.

Bennett arrived early at the White House. He approached Lindsey about what the president might say about Marilyn Jo Jenkins.

"Has he worked it out?" Bennett asked.

"Yeah," Lindsey said, providing no details or information on a strategy.

Soon the president and Bennett were together before the deposition began.

"I appreciate what you said yesterday," the president said, "and I've worked it out."

Bennett's final advice to Clinton was to give short answers and not to attempt to take the case into his own hands. Let the lawyers run the deposition, he counseled.

At 10:18 a.m., Clinton left the White House in his limousine. Bennett and Lindsey accompanied the president for the two-block ride to Bennett's office.

About 10:25 a.m. Jones and her lawyers were escorted into the conference room, where the judge and the president's lawyers were waiting. All sat down. With a great flourish, the double doors were opened. They could see Clinton coming down the hall alone. It was as if he were entering the East Room of the White House for a press conference—everything but the red carpet. The president was wearing heavy makeup for the videocamera. He entered and sat down. There were no introductions.

The deposition began at 10:30. Clinton was sworn. Bennett said the president had a meeting at 4 p.m. They expected the deposition to conclude by then. He wanted the Jones lawyers to realize this deposition was their one shot, and that the judge agreed.

Fisher introduced himself. He had a surprise. He said he had developed a definition of sexual relations, because the judge had hammered on both sides to keep the depositions on as professional a level as possible. He had created a three-part, 92-word definition of sexual relations focusing on any contact with "the genitalia, anus, groin, breast, inner thigh, or buttocks of any person." It was drawn from the federal criminal law on sexual abuse and the Violence Against Women Act that President Clinton had signed into law in 1994.

Seeing the risk, Bennett objected vigorously to every part of the sweeping definition.

"What I'm trying to do is avoid having to ask the president a number of very salacious questions," Fisher said, "and to make this as discreet as possible."

Judge Wright said it was confusing, but she didn't rule at this point. "Embarrassing ques-

586

tions will be asked," she said, "you may go into the detail."

Fisher's first questions were about Kathleen Willey.

Clinton denied having any form of sexual relations with her. Asked if he recalled meeting Willey in the hallway outside the Oval Office, Clinton said he did. He began adding details about Willey's attempts to meet with him later.

"Mr. President," Bennett interrupted, "just answer his question, please, sir."

Clinton had read a summary of Willey's sworn statement.

"You're aware that she testified that you took her hand and put it on your penis?" Fisher asked.

"I'm aware of that," the president replied.

"And you deny that testimony?"

"I emphatically deny it," the president said. "It did not happen."

"Do you know why she would tell a story like that if it weren't true?"

"No, sir, I don't," Clinton answered. He testified that Willey had come to see him because she was in great financial trouble. "When she came to see me she was clearly upset. I did to her what I have done to scores and scores of men and women who have worked for me or been my friends over the years. I embraced her, I put my arms around her, I may have kissed her on the forehead. There was nothing sexual about it."

As the questioning continued, the president lowered his voice.

"Keep your voice up, Mr. President," Bennett said.

587

More than an hour into the questioning, Fisher turned to another woman.

"Now," Fisher asked, "do you know a woman named Monica Lewinsky?"

"I do," the president replied.

"Is it true that when she worked at the White House she met with you several times?" Fisher asked.

"I don't know about several times," the president answered. "When the Republican Congress shut the government down the whole White House was being run by interns, and she was assigned to work back in the chief of staff's office, and we were all working there, and so I saw her on two or three occasions then, and then when she worked at the White House, I think there was one or two other times when she brought some documents to me."

After a break, Fisher asked, "At any time were you and Monica Lewinsky together alone in the Oval Office?"

"I don't recall," the president answered. "It seems to me she brought things to me once or twice on the weekends."

"It's possible that she, in, while she was working there, brought something to me and that at the time she brought it to me, she was the only person there. That's possible."

"Did it ever happen that you and she went down the hallway from the Oval Office to the private kitchen?"

Bennett interrupted. "I'm going to object to the innuendo. I'm afraid, as I say, that this will leak....I question the good faith of counsel, the innuendo in the question. Counsel is fully aware that Ms. Lewinsky has filed, has an affidavit which they are in possession of saying that there is absolutely no sex of any kind in any manner, shape or form, with President Clinton."

"No," Judge Wright said, "just a minute, let me make a ruling." She told Mr. Bennett not to comment on other evidence or coach the witness.

Bennett said, "In preparation of the witness for this deposition, the witness is fully aware of Ms. Lewinsky's affidavit, so I have not told him a single thing he doesn't know."

"I am very confident there is substantial basis," Fisher said.

"I'm going to permit the question," the judge ruled.

Clinton proceeded to give his longest answer, directing himself to the lack of privacy in his office. "The private kitchen is staffed by two naval aides," he said. "They have total, unrestricted access to my dining room, to that hallway, to coming into the Oval Office. The people who are in the outer office of the Oval Office can also enter at any time.

"I was, after I went through a presidential campaign in which the far Right tried to convince the American people I had committed murder, run drugs, slept in my mother's bed with four prostitutes, and done numerous other things, I had a high level of paranoia.

"There are no curtains on the Oval Office, there are no curtains on my private office, there are no curtains or blinds that can close the windows in my private dining room."

For Fisher, this monologue seemed like a

prepared speech that Clinton had been going to give at some point no matter what the question.

"Now, to go back to your question," Clinton said. "She was back there with a pizza that she brought to me and to others. I do not believe she was there alone, however. I don't think she was. And my recollection is that on a couple of occasions after that she was there, but my secretary Betty Currie was there with her. She and Betty are friends."

"Have you ever met with Monica Lewinsky in the White House between the hours of midnight and six a.m.?"

"I certainly don't think so," Clinton testified, then quickly added, "there may have been a time when we all—we were up working late....I just can't say that there could have been a time when that occurred, I just—but I don't remember it."

"Certainly if it happened, nothing remarkable would have occurred?" Fisher offered.

"No, nothing remarkable," the president testified. "I don't remember it."

"When was the last time you spoke with Monica Lewinsky?"

"Probably sometime before Christmas. She came by to see Betty sometime before Christmas. And she was there talking to her, and I stuck my head out, said hello to her." He modified that to sometime in December. "That may not be the last time. I think she came to one of the Christmas parties." He made this statement even though he had said earlier that he did not recall Lewinsky at any White House social event such as Christmas parties.

"Did you ever talk with Monica Lewinsky about the possibility that she might be asked to testify in this case?" Fisher asked.

"I think Bruce Lindsey told me that she was, I think maybe that's the first person told me she was," Clinton said, adding, "I want to be as accurate as I can," although he had just answered a Lewinsky question by diverting to what Lindsey had done.

"We got sidetracked," Fisher said, returning to his question. "Have you ever talked to Monica Lewinsky about the possibility that she might be asked to testify in this lawsuit?"

"I'm not sure, and let me tell you why I'm not sure," Clinton replied. "It seems to me the, the, the—I want to be as accurate as I can here. Seems to me that last time she was there to see Betty before Christmas we were joking around how you-all...were going to call every woman I'd ever talked to, and I said, you know . . ."

"We can't hear you, Mr. President," Bennett said, interrupting.

"And I said that you-all might call every woman I ever talked to and ask them that, and so I said you would qualify, or something like that." He said he had seen her name or had heard her name was on the witness list.

"Within the past two weeks," Fisher asked, "has anyone reported to you that they had had a conversation with Monica Lewinsky concerning this lawsuit?"

"I don't believe so," the president answered. "I'm sorry, I just don't believe so."

"You know a man named Vernon Jordan?" Fisher asked.

591

The president said he knew Jordan well and had known him for a long time.

"Has it ever been reported to you that he met with Monica Lewinsky and talked about this case?"

"I knew that he met with her," Clinton answered.

What! Bennett thought. Bennett had never heard of this encounter. Vernon Jordan meeting with Lewinsky? Incredible. Some two months earlier Jordan had called Bennett one night and asked to come to see Bennett at his house. "I'm here as a friend," Jordan said that night. "I want to know if it makes sense to settle this." Jordan, one of Clinton's closest friends, then added, "I'd be happy to raise money." Bennett had replied with his standard line. "Yes, it is a good idea, but you agree we shouldn't pay more than $1 million and apologize." Jordan had agreed, "Oh, no, no," they couldn't pay a huge sum or apologize. Bennett had thought nothing more of the visit, but now he could see that Jordan's role might be much larger.

As the questioning continued, the president said he thought Currie had reported to him that Jordan was giving Lewinsky advice about what to do when she moved to New York.

"Have you ever given any gifts to Monica Lewinsky?" Fisher asked.

"I don't recall," Clinton replied. Incredibly, he then turned the tables on Fisher, asking the lawyer, "Do you know what they were?"

"A hat pin?" Fisher asked.

"I don't remember," Clinton answered, "but I certainly, I could have."

"A book about Walt Whitman?" Fisher continued.

"Let me just say," the president responded, "I give people a lot of gifts....So I could have given her a gift, but I don't remember a specific gift."

"Do you remember giving her an item that had been purchased from the Black Dog store at Martha's Vineyard?"

"I do remember that," the president said. He went into a long explanation about how the store had sent him a selection of items, T-shirts, sweatshirts, shirts. He had bought more and had Currie distribute them.

"Has Monica Lewinsky ever given you any gifts?"

"Once or twice," Clinton testified. "I think she's given me a book or two."

"Did she give you a tie?"

"Yes, she has given me a tie before."

"Well, Mr. President, it's my understanding that Monica Lewinsky has made statements to people, and I'd like for you . . ."

Trooper Ferguson was also a defendant. His attorney, Bill W. Bristow, objected. Fisher was in essence testifying and providing information. Bennett joined the objection. Judge Wright sustained it.

"I understand," Fisher said. "Did you have an extramarital sexual affair with Monica Lewinsky?"

"No," the president testified.

Fisher said he used the term "sexual affair" as limited by the first part of his definition of sexual relations that Judge Wright had approved.

There had to be "contact" with the erogenous zones of any person.

"I have never had sexual relations with Monica Lewinsky," Clinton repeated. "I've never had an affair with her."

"Have you ever had a conversation with Vernon Jordan in which Monica Lewinsky was mentioned?"

"I have," Clinton replied. "He mentioned in passing to me that he had talked to her, she had come to him for advice about moving to New York." Clinton stressed that it was "advice" and Jordan "suggested where she ought to go for interviews."

"Is it your testimony that you had nothing whatsoever to do with causing that conversation to take place between Monica Lewinsky and Vernon Jordan?"

Bennett objected at this strategic point. The judge suggested that Fisher rephrase.

"Did you do anything, sir, to prompt this conversation to take place between Vernon Jordan and Monica Lewinsky?"

In a long answer, Clinton said he believed that Currie initiated the contact. "I didn't think there was anything wrong with it. It seemed like a natural thing to do to me. But I don't believe that I actually was the precipitating force."

Fisher asked if the president had ever discussed Paula Jones with Jordan.

"I'm sure I have," Clinton replied. "I don't remember what it would have been."

Bristow could not help but interject. "It is now almost 12:30 and to my knowledge this is the first moment in the deposition that the word 'Paula Jones' has been mentioned."

At a break, Bennett told the president that they had to think ahead to a possible trial. The judge had said the video testimony was possibly all the Jones lawyers might get of Clinton. The video would have to be used in the trial. Therefore Bennett said he wanted to read Lewinsky's affidavit denying a sexual relationship to Clinton and get his sworn agreement. He would need that video clip if the case ever got to a jury. In arguing before a jury it would be useful.

The president, Lindsey and Ruff agreed.

After lunch, Fisher asked Clinton about his relationship with Marilyn Jo Jenkins.

Clinton testified that he could recall only two meetings, including a 5:15 a.m. good-bye meeting the day he left Little Rock for the inauguration.

Fisher asked if the president had ever had sexual relations with Jenkins.

Bennett objected strenuously. Jenkins did not fit the definition of what relationships could be probed. She did not work for the state. Even though a meeting may have been facilitated by state troopers—one of the categories that the judge ruled Clinton could be questioned about—Bennett argued that the troopers routinely escorted visitors. It was their job.

Judge Wright ruled that Fisher could not ask about Jenkins—a huge victory for Clinton. They had escaped, Bennett thought.

Later Fisher asked, "Did you ever have sexual relations with Gennifer Flowers?"

"The answer to your question," the president said, "if the definition is section one there in the first piece of paper you gave me, is yes." Clinton said what he had told Bennett—it happened once, in 1977.

Near the end, Bennett began to carry out his plan to build the record of sworn videotaped testimony of Clinton denying certain allegations. "I'm going to read you certain portions of Miss Lewinsky's affidavit, and ask you about them."

"In paragraph eight of her affidavit, she says this," Bennett said, reading, " 'I have never had a sexual relationship with the president, he did not propose that we have a sexual relationship....' Is that a true and accurate statement as far as you know it?"

"That is absolutely true," the president testified.

The deposition ended about 4 p.m. Clinton left with Bennett and Ruff.

"How do you think it went?" the president asked.

"Great," Ruff said. Only about 10 percent of the questions had been about Jones.

"Great," Bennett said. He felt they hadn't laid a glove on him.

The atmosphere was almost one of celebration, just short of breaking out the champagne. Bennett believed that the president had made the essential, core decision in the case that set the strategy: namely, that the only way to deal with the Jones lawsuit was to go to war. It looked like they had won. There were so many allegations about women out there that they had to be tough. Once when Clinton had been most angry about the lawsuit and they were discussing strategy, he had said something that had left a profound impact on Bennett, who is the father of three daughters. "How would you like it?" Clinton had said. "What would you think if your daughter had to listen to this stuff about you?"

After the deposition, Paula Jones was alone with her attorneys. She burst into tears. Fisher believed they were real tears of pain—hard weeping, not the tears of joy or relief. He had consulted Patrick Carnes, an expert on sexual harassment and editor of the journal *Sexual Addiction and Compulsivity*. Carnes had said they should anticipate such a reaction. It would be typical. The tears, according to Carnes, reflected the pain of reliving the experience and seeing that the perpetrator of the harassment was unrepentant and was going unpunished.

Fisher thought that Jones was not smart enough to fake such a reaction.

Back at the White House, Clinton canceled plans to go out for the evening with Hillary. Later he called Betty Currie. He asked her to come to the White House the next day, Sunday, to go over something important.

David Kendall was in New York City with his family for a leisurely weekend making the rounds of various plays and art shows. His cell phone kept ringing with calls from Viveca Novak, a Washington reporter for *Time* magazine. She was panicked about some big story *Newsweek* had about Whitewater and tapes.

Kendall told her he had no idea what she was talking about.

"Viveca," he said in the final call, "get a life! It's Saturday afternoon."

Just after midnight at 1:11 a.m., Sunday morning, the Drudge Report was out on the Internet with a big scoop:

BLOCKBUSTER REPORT: 23-YEAR-OLD, FORMER WHITE HOUSE INTERN, SEX RELATIONSHIP WITH PRESIDENT.

★★World Exclusive★★

"At the last minute, at 6 p.m. on Saturday evening, *Newsweek* magazine killed a story that was destined to shake official Washington to its foundation."

At 5 p.m. Sunday, the president met Betty Currie at her desk outside the Oval Office. At the Jones deposition, he said, they had asked him questions about Lewinsky. He then peppered Currie with a series of questions.

"You were always there when she was there, right?"

"We were never really alone?"

"Monica came on to me, and I never touched her, right?"

"You can see and hear everything, right?"

At 5:12, Currie left a code-name message on Lewinsky's pager, "Please call Kay at home." Lewinsky did not call back. Three more times that evening Currie paged Lewinsky, but no call came back.

At 11 p.m. that night, Clinton called Currie at home.

Had she spoken with Monica?

No, Currie said.

The next morning Currie made eight unsuccessful attempts to reach Lewinsky. The last time she sent an urgent page: "Please call Kay re: family emergency."

31

KENDALL HAD BEEN out of town on another case and returned home about 8:30 p.m. Tuesday. He was sitting down to dinner and a bottle of wine with his wife when McCurry called.

"Can you take a conference call in 20 minutes?" McCurry asked. *The Washington Post* is going with its Monica Lewinsky story."

"Mike," Kendall said, pausing, "who is Monica Lewinsky?"

McCurry brought Kendall up to speed. The *Post,* he said, was going to report that the Justice Department and the three-judge panel had authorized Starr to investigate whether Clinton and Vernon Jordan had encouraged Lewinsky to lie about a sexual relationship with the president.

Kendall thought he might be able to head off the article, even at this late hour, if he could establish there was something inaccurate about it. The story seemed far-fetched to him, the Justice Department role strange. Kendall called one of his Justice contacts, who sent definite signals that Kendall should not rush out to deny the existence of an investigation.

Kendall took in the indirect confirmation and

the possible consequences. So the probing into Clinton's personal life was an iceberg after all. Starr's moralism had crested and reached a dangerous new high. In Kendall's view, Starr was not stark raving mad, but he had adopted religious rhetoric and was applying it to the law. An experienced prosecutor would have avoided this zealotry. Starr had commenced the final battle, the death struggle, Kendall thought, and someone was going out the door feet first.

"Jesus! Jesus! Jesus!" Jordan shouted into the phone at the St. Regis Hotel in New York City at 11:30 p.m. Tuesday, January 20. "I never told her to lie."

He was speaking to his law partner and personal attorney, William Hundley, who had just called to inform him about the *Post* story. Hundley and Jordan agreed to say nothing except to promise that Jordan would cooperate with any investigation.

Hundley, 72, one of the most experienced figures in the Washington legal establishment, thought it was virtually inconceivable that the Whitewater investigation could have reached this outcome.

The *Post* story, headlined "Clinton Accused of Urging Aide to Lie," hit the wires about midnight. The president talked to Bennett for half an hour, then Currie for 20 minutes, and twice briefly with Bruce Lindsey. At 2:30 a.m., he left a wake-up call with the White House operator for 7 a.m. Two minutes after being awakened, Clinton called Kendall and later reached him at 7:30. They talked for half an hour. The president seemed wobbly but denied it all.

Since the White House lawyers didn't have a clear attorney-client privilege, they agreed Kendall would take charge of this aspect of the Starr investigation. Kendall's advice was to stick with the tried and true strategy of volunteering nothing.

The president talked with Bennett from approximately 8 a.m. to 8:15 a.m. Clinton denied everything.

Ruff drafted a statement for McCurry to issue. It said the president was "outraged by these allegations," and that "he never had an improper relationship with this woman."

McCurry went to see the president, who was subdued.

"Here's exactly what I am going to say on your behalf," McCurry said, showing the president the statement. "And you know I'm going to make it clear that I'm saying this on your behalf."

Clinton read it.

Is that satisfactory? McCurry asked.

Yes, Clinton said, that would be fine for the public statement. He indicated that what he was going to say next was not to be part of any public comment by McCurry. "And now you understand," the president added, "they set me up." The deposition in the Jones case five days earlier was all part of a design. "They brought me in there because they were convinced I was going to lie about Monica Lewinsky, and they couldn't believe it when I told them the truth."

McCurry didn't understand.

"They were going to try to get me to perjure myself," the president said, "and they couldn't believe it when I went in there and acknowledged

601

some kind of relationship and didn't lie to them."

McCurry was even more confused. But the president was done. As McCurry left he wondered, What was the relationship? That's what no one was telling him. He realized that he was on shaky terrain. He was determined to stick to the formulation about nothing "improper." He was not going to interpret it or expand on it.

His press briefing was disastrous. McCurry, determined not to crack, wouldn't explain further. The formulation about no "improper" relationship left open the question of whether Clinton was denying any sexual relations with Lewinsky. "I'm not going to parse the statement," McCurry said. "You all got the statement I made earlier, and it speaks for itself."

Asked if he was "absolutely confident" the allegations were not true, McCurry answered, "My personal views don't count. I'm here to represent the thinking, the actions, the decisions of the president. That's what I get paid to do." McCurry was not offering a ringing endorsement of the statement he had just delivered.

"Mike, what's your next move, or counsel's next move, or president's next move?" a reporter shouted.

"My next move is to get off this podium," McCurry said.

Clinton told Bowles and his top deputies that he did not have a sexual relationship with Lewinsky. He went further in a meeting with John Podesta, the deputy chief of staff, denying any oral sex.

Dick Morris had left a message at the White House that he was available to talk. About noon he reached the president and offered sympathy.

"There's a vast capacity for forgiveness in this country," Morris said. Ask the country for forgiveness, he suggested. "The one thing you've got to avoid is getting trapped like Nixon into a rigid posture of denial because that gives you no flexibility, no room to maneuver, and you get stuck. And presidents only get killed when they get stuck."

Morris volunteered to conduct a poll about the possible impact.

That afternoon, the president had a previously scheduled television interview with Jim Lehrer for the PBS *NewsHour*. It began at 3:30 p.m. in the Roosevelt Room.

Lehrer asked about Starr's investigation of the Lewinsky allegations. Clinton's eyes were baggy, and he was tightly wound.

"There is not a sexual relationship," the president said, "an improper sexual relationship, or any other kind of improper relationship."

Listening, McCurry was confused and upset. It seemed that Clinton was leaning heavily, even exclusively, on the present tense "is." Reporters accustomed to parsing Clinton's language would seize on it.

"Well, that was a disaster," the press secretary told the others on Clinton's senior staff. "We've got to do something."

They went to Clinton.

"Look," McCurry said, "you used the present tense, were you meaning to communicate anything?"

"Oh, no, no, no, no," the president said.

An hour later in a telephone interview from the Oval Office with Morton Kondracke of *Roll Call* newspaper, the president again addressed the question of his relationship with Lewinsky. "It is not an improper relationship, and I know what you mean, and the answer is no."

"*Was* it in any way sexual?" Kondracke asked, leaning hard on the 'was.' "

"The relationship *was* not sexual," the president replied.

In Los Angeles, James Carville had been on the set of the television comedy show *Mad About You* when he heard about the investigation. Carville believed when you're there in the good times, you have to be there in the bad times. He also thought he couldn't use the media when he needed them but avoid them when they asked him about something he didn't want to talk about. At the same time, he did not want to become the president's sex defender—a role that made him uneasy. But Clinton had been awfully good to him, had put him on the map.

On CNN's *Larry King Live* that night, Carville said, "I think in the end, the people are going to conclude the president didn't do anything improper, and when that happens, he'll probably be the most popular human being on earth for what these people have put him through."

Carville talked to all his old friends in the White House. He and everyone else was sure that Clinton would take a big hit in the polls, perhaps his approval rating would drop 10 to 15 points. At least that.

Mary Matalin, Carville's wife and a Republican, disagreed. "Oh, Clinton will survive. Of course Clinton is guilty." But, she said, her husband and the others in the White House spin team would think of something to help Clinton weasel out of this jam too.

At 11:30 p.m. that night, Morris reached Clinton with the results of a quickie poll conducted by Action Research (of Florida) of some 400 to 500 people.

"Well, I'm wrong," Morris said. "You can't tell them about it, they'll kill you." The public was concerned about perjury and obstruction of justice, although less about adultery, Morris said.

The next morning, January 22, Clinton met with his senior staff: Bowles, Podesta, senior policy adviser Rahm Emanuel, Paul Begala, Ruff and McCurry. They agreed that the media was in a fever pitch—television specials, round-the-clock coverage of Lewinsky. It was like nothing they had encountered, and it was essential to provide some details about the Lewinsky relationship.

"Unless we go out there and say what it is," McCurry said, "you have said what it isn't, but unless you say what it is, they're going to pound you on it."

"We can't do that," Ruff said, obliquely suggesting that until they knew what Lewinsky was going to say and do, there could be some kind of legal jeopardy. Lewinsky might cooperate with Starr; her mood was uncertain. Until they knew her status, they couldn't be more forthcoming. Ruff was lining up behind the standard Kendall defense. Starr and his team were like an organized crime strike force, and any tactic would be used to get the president.

The others said if Clinton didn't explain, he would not be able to get the issue behind him. This scandal was going to go on and on and on.

"We don't have the privilege," Ruff said. "Kendall does and will handle this case."

"You're going to have to address this at some greater length," McCurry said of Lewinsky. "Let's sit down and talk about it at some point."

"I agree," Clinton said. "You guys are right. We really will have to get this all out there." He said he would make a more accommodating statement at the photo opportunity with Yasser Arafat of the Palestinian Authority, with whom he was meeting.

Just after 10 a.m., Clinton had the brief photo opportunity in the Oval Office. The president was trying to make peace in the Middle East. The sixth question was about the Lewinsky investigation.

"Let's get to the big issues there, about the nature of the relationship and whether I suggested anybody not tell the truth. That is false. Now, there are a lot of other questions that are, I think, very legitimate. You have a right to ask them; you and the American people have a right to get answers."

"I'd like for you to have more rather than less, sooner rather than later."

· · ·

McCurry, Begala and Emanuel went to see Ruff in the counsel's office on the second floor of the West Wing. They were the ones out in public defending the president. "We got to know if we're on sound ground here," McCurry said.

"You can be firm and unequivocal on the president's statement he did not have sexual relations," Ruff said, "he did not obstruct justice, he didn't tell anyone to lie about it." They could take that to the bank, Ruff added. "Don't go speculating about the nature of the relationship." Keep within the boundaries of the statement, he said. "We're not going to be in a position to go beyond this and say any more on it. We can't. We're just going to have to hunker down."

McCurry didn't like it but felt he could stay operational. Clinton had been elected twice, and the public suspected he was a womanizer in one way or another. McCurry also had seen Clinton flirt with women. He was a grabber, he sought physical contact. Clinton was often draping his arms around someone—male or female—and he seemed unconscious of how inappropriate that might look or be. Whatever the nature of the relationship with Lewinsky, McCurry figured, it could be in this kind of zone.

Can I be completely confident in what I said? McCurry asked himself after another rancorous briefing. He realized that he didn't trust the information he was getting, because there wasn't enough of it. The information vacuum led him to one obvious commonsense conclusion. McCurry had met Ron Ziegler at a conference and been on a panel with him, and he was determined not to turn out like him. So McCurry said less and less at his briefings.

Clinton received word that McCurry was shaky. As the press secretary, McCurry had to be out there every day taking the heat. After one Oval Office meeting, the president had a private chat with him.

"I just want you to know that this is really unfair," the president said sincerely, "and there's so much more that I can't tell you right now, but you should not worry. It's going to work out okay."

The press secretary didn't know what to believe. He wanted Clinton's denial to be true, or close enough to the truth that the president would be able to defend it. McCurry hoped that in some contorted way it was the truth, and that was how the president was going to get through it. But there was an ominous sign. When Starr was mentioned, the tonal quality of Clinton's outbursts about the independent counsel were more modulated and less vehement than in the previous years.

McCurry also realized that as press secretary he wasn't doing his job—getting the press and public real answers. Most importantly, he couldn't take Clinton any more. McCurry had told Clinton that he wanted to leave after the State of the Union Address on January 27. Now he raised the issue again.

"This has been a great honor doing this," the press secretary said, "but it's time for me to get on with my life. I've got to get off that podium because I'm going to go crazy one day and just start screaming at the press."

"I think there are some positive things to this," the president replied. He asked McCurry to be a defender on the outside and for him to offer a much needed critique of the media. "I think that you're probably worn out, but you're going to get out on the speaker's trail, and you can raise some of these issues that need to be raised better from that position than you can here."

But McCurry couldn't leave in the middle of the scandal. It would look like he was backing out on Clinton in the president's time of need. He stayed.

Sam Dash read in the newspaper about how Starr's prosecutors had used Tripp to wire Lewinsky secretly before they had jurisdiction in the case. He went to Starr.

"If this is true, you guys have really, really screwed up," Dash said. He was outraged, and he threatened to quit as ethics adviser.

Starr said they had done nothing wrong. He told Dash to investigate. Starr ordered everyone in the office who had anything to do with the Lewinsky probe to turn over their paperwork and notes. Dash found that they had used the initial wiring of the Lewinsky-Tripp meeting to persuade the Justice Department that some inquiry was needed. Jackie Bennett's notes showed that he had reported to Justice that these "messy" allegations had come to them and someone ought to investigate—a new independent counsel or Starr. Starr had not seized the case improperly. According to the notes, Reno had determined that it should be given to Starr.

"Yes," Dash said in an oral report to Starr later, "you did nothing wrong."

Harry Thomason, a Hollywood producer and longtime Arkansas Clinton friend, flew in from Los Angeles. He felt the key to Clinton's survival was better stage management and command of the theater. Clinton needed to make a stronger denial.

Bob Bennett also weighed in, telling Clinton, "You got to be so fucking indignant that you're almost seething."

On Monday morning, January 26, at about 10:30, Clinton and Hillary appeared for remarks on after-school care, a proposal he would present in the State of the Union Address to Congress the next evening. After 15 long paragraphs, Clinton turned more intently to the cameras.

"I want to say one thing to the American people," he said, scowling and wagging his finger. There was pain and anger on his face, a posture the public had not seen. "I want you to listen to me. I'm going to say this again. I did not have sexual relations with that woman, Miss Lewinsky. I never told anybody to lie, not a single time—never. These allegations are false."

At 5 a.m., Tuesday, January 27, Hillary awoke in her hotel suite at the Waldorf-Astoria in New York. She dressed in a dark blue business suit and spent a brief time preparing for a long-scheduled morning television appearance on NBC's *Today Show*. Her chief of staff, Melanne Verveer, found the first lady relaxed but not completely natural. Deep circles beneath Hillary's eyes showed the strain she was under. On the limousine ride over to NBC Studios at Rockefeller Center, Hillary and Melanne talked about how odd it was that so many press people had covered her speech at a UNICEF dinner the night before in Harlem, as if she would interrupt a children's benefit to respond to the brewing scandal.

At 7:05 a.m., Hillary appeared on camera sitting back calmly in a chair.

"We appreciate you honoring your commitment, even in light of recent events," Matt Lauer, the show's co-anchor, began. "There has been one question on the minds of a lot of people in this country, Mrs. Clinton, lately. And that is, what is the exact nature of the relationship between your husband and Monica Lewinsky? Has he described the relationship in detail to you?"

"Well, we've talked at great length," Hillary replied. "And I think as this matter unfolds, the entire country will have more information. But we're right in the middle of a rather vigorous feeding frenzy right now, and people are saying all kinds of things and putting out rumor and innuendo."

Lauer noted that Clinton had described to the American people what this relationship was not—

"That's right," Hillary interjected.

"Has he described to you what it was?"

611

"Yes," Hillary answered. "And we'll find that out as time goes by, Matt. But I think the important thing now is to stand as firmly as I can and say that, you know, the president has denied these allegations on all counts, unequivocally. And we'll see how this plays out."

Hillary said she was calm because she had been through so many investigations. "I mean, Bill and I have been accused of everything, including murder, by some of the very same people who are behind these allegations. So from my perspective, this is part of a continuing political campaign against my husband."

"This is pretty devastating," Lauer said.

"Well, just think about it," Hillary said, her voice rising. "And this is what concerns me.

"We get a politically motivated prosecutor who is allied with the right-wing opponents of my husband, who has literally spent four years looking at every telephone—"

"Spent $40 million," Lauer said, encouraging Mrs. Clinton.

"More than that now," Hillary noted. "But looking at every telephone call we've made, every check we've ever written, scratching for dirt, intimidating witnesses, doing everything possible to try to make some accusation against my husband."

Lauer pointed out that she was criticizing Starr.

"It's not just one person," Hillary contended. "It's an entire operation."

"If he were to be asked today, Mrs. Clinton, do you think he would admit that he again has caused pain in this marriage?"

"No, absolutely not," Hillary replied sharply.

"And he shouldn't. You know, we've been married for 22 years, Matt, and I have learned a long time ago that the only people who count in any marriage are the two that are in it. We know everything there is to know about each other and we understand and accept and love each other."

Hillary went back on the attack. "The great story here for anybody willing to find it and write about it and explain it is this vast right-wing conspiracy that has been conspiring against my husband since the day he announced for president," Mrs. Clinton said. "A few journalists have kind of caught on to it and explained it, but it has not yet been fully revealed to the American public. And actually, you know, in a bizarre sort of way this may do it."

"I don't know what it is about my husband that generates such hostility, but I have seen it for 25 years," she added a moment later.

"Let me take you and your husband out of this for a second," Lauer said. "Bill and Hillary Clinton aren't involved in this story. If an American president had an adulterous liaison in the White House and lied to cover it up, should the American people ask for his resignation?"

"Well, they should certainly be concerned about it," Hillary said.

"Should they ask for his resignation?"

"Well, I think if all that were proven true, I think that would be a very serious offense. That is not going to be proven true."

It was one of Hillary's strongest television appearances, and it made major news. If she had settled accounts with her husband, why should anyone else dwell on it? With the single interview, she had managed to refocus media attention on Starr.

Top Clinton aides almost danced in the corridors of the White House. That night as the president left the White House to give his State of the Union Address to Congress, his friend Harry Thomason told him, "Just remember, you've got the biggest balls over there. Just go over and kick their butts." Clinton spoke for 90 minutes, sticking to his government themes. He gave no sign he was rattled.

The next day, Starr was furious. He told his deputies that in his opinion the first lady had almost threatened potential witnesses. She was sending a message: This is war and anyone perceived to be hostile will be killed. He had to be calmed down. Starr eventually issued a statement in his own name: "The first lady today accused this office of being part of a 'vast right-wing conspiracy.' That is nonsense." He spelled out how his investigation had the blessing of Attorney General Reno and the three-judge panel. "We are working to complete the inquiry as quickly and thoroughly as possible."

Two of Starr's deputies argued that they should issue a formal subpoena calling the president before the grand jury to get his testimony locked down.

Starr said it would be rash. The normal procedure was to gather evidence in a case and then go to the subject or target and ask for his testimony. "It would be more proper to invite the president," Starr said. The White House could raise constitutional questions and go to court and try to block and delay a subpoena, he said. He authorized Bob Bittman, one of his deputies, to call Kendall and on behalf of the grand jury invite the president to testify the next week.

Kendall told Bittman that he would get back to him.

Clinton grew more emphatic in his denials in private. On February 2, he was standing in the Oval Office with Gore and Bowles. He apologized for the disruption but grasped Bowles by the right forearm. "I'm telling the truth on this," Clinton said.

32

WILLIAM GINSBURG submitted a ten-page proffer that Lewinsky had written in her own hand on February 1 stating what her testimony would be if she was granted immunity. She would testify to an intimate sexual relationship with Clinton that "included oral sex, but excluded intercourse." At the same time, she wrote, "neither the president nor Mr. Jordan (or anyone on their behalf) asked or encouraged me to lie."

The proffer contradicted what Lewinsky had told Tripp. Starr and his deputies were deeply suspicious. Encouraging someone to lie was at the heart of their investigation, the major felony of obstruction of justice. They asked Ginsburg to allow Lewinsky to meet face-to-face with the prosecutors—a routine requirement before immunity is granted. Ginsburg refused.

Starr was exasperated with Ginsburg, who became the most sought after television talk show guest. The Los Angeles attorney willingly accommodated, appearing on five shows one Sunday. He contradicted himself. Off air he relished telling the latest oral sex jokes. At one point Ginsburg said he didn't think Clinton should resign because of the president's positive policy toward Israel and the Jews. At another he said all 24-year-olds embellish.

On February 5, Starr wrote Ginsburg a scathing four-page letter. In one breath Ginsburg was claiming he had acquired immunity for Lewinsky, Starr wrote, and in the next saying, "We would like immunity."

"In the many years of prosecutorial experience represented by attorneys in this office, we have *never* experienced anything approaching your tactics....You terminated one negotiating session at our offices by hurtling from the room and shouting obscenities."

Kendall courted Ginsburg, had lunch with him and talked to him frequently. In Kendall's view, Ginsburg was properly keeping Lewinsky out of Starr's clutches. Ginsburg didn't hand out a copy of Lewinsky's proffer, but he conveyed its contents to Kendall. Sex but no obstruction. Starr and his team desperately needed Lewinsky to provide evidence of obstruction, Ginsburg said, and she could not. No orders or even hints that she lie. She had figured out what to say for herself.

Starr heard about the Kendall-Ginsburg lunch. He was convinced that the attorneys were working together to protect Clinton.

At a White House dinner for British Prime Minister Tony Blair on Thursday, February 5, the president's team received word *The New York Times* was publishing a damaging story in its first editions. They read a copy on the Internet. Headlined "Aide's Statements Are Said to Differ from President's," the two-column lead story said the president had called in Betty Currie to go over his recollections of his relationship with Lewinsky. Damning, carefully written, it suggested that the president was trying to enlist his secretary to corroborate his version. On television, the story was repeated, saying the president had "coached" his secretary, an action that could be the crime of obstruction.

Currie had just appeared before Starr's grand jury, and Kendall was sure it was a calculated leak. Whatever the president's relationship with Lewinsky—and Kendall wasn't sure at that point, Clinton had been emphatic in denying that he had encouraged anyone to lie or that he had coached anyone—these would be serious felonies. The media stories about the Lewinsky matter were obviously coming, at least in part, from Starr's office. Reporters frequently cited "sources in Starr's office," or "prosecutors," or "sources close to Starr." The leaks could have immense impact, Kendall felt, convincing possible witnesses that Starr had more hard evidence than he actually possessed.

The stories made it appear that Clinton's secretary had turned on the president as a witness for the prosecution. Currie's lawyer insisted that was untrue.

The only strategy for the White House was to attack and make war, Kendall believed. Mickey Kantor, the former commerce secretary whom Clinton had brought in for personal legal advice, concurred. They would have to inflict real pain on Starr and his deputies. One way to throw a lawyer off balance is to malign his integrity. Kendall put together a 15-page letter to Starr specifying alleged leaks from his office.

Late in the day on February 6, Kendall appeared outside his office for a rare press appearance. It was bitter cold, but his friends had advised him to ditch his trench coat, which had become a symbol of his nerdiness. He denounced these criminal leaks and said he was going to court to stop them. He cited 50 excerpts of broadcast and newspaper reports that attributed information to unnamed prosecutors, investigators and sources close to the investigation. He released copies of his letter to Starr.

"These leaks make a mockery of the traditional rules of grand jury secrecy," Kendall said, jutting his jaw, carefully reading his statement. His sound bite was the lead on all the major television network broadcasts that evening.

Carville was dancing. Finally, Kendall had joined in the public attack on Starr. In Carville's hometown in Louisiana, a man named Stanley Stein had written a book called *Alone No Longer* about a community of people who had leprosy. Carville called and left a message on

Kendall's answering machine describing Stein and his work. "Alone No Longer!" Carville yelled joyfully.

Kendall's goal was to deter future leaks, which with a prosecutorial spin could be devastating. He took the unusual step of asking the court to allow him to question Starr and his deputies under oath. In large part, major leaks of grand jury testimony ceased.

In the White House, some of Clinton's political advisers—including Emanuel, Begala and political director Doug Sosnik—were urging the president to give a longer public explanation and for the White House to attack Lewinsky. Stonewalling had not worked for Nixon.

Kendall dug in. He was told his strategy would cause the Clinton presidency to die. The appraisal of his recommendations grew bitter and personal. It was the most difficult time for Kendall in his four years representing the Clintons. The internal criticism lasted three weeks. But he finally prevailed—no comments and no attack.

Kendall didn't read the polls, but he heard about them constantly from the White House and Clinton. Clinton's approval rating had climbed from 59 percent during the first week of the scandal to 67 percent at the end of the second week, according to a *Washington Post* poll. Another poll with a comparatively small sample on February 8 found the president's approval rating to be even higher—an astounding 79 percent. What was the public responding to? Kendall wondered. Did they dislike Starr?

They liked the good economy? Did they consider lying about sex understandable? He wasn't certain at all.

"When the poll numbers defied gravity," Kendall said, "I got control."

Starr issued second and third invitations for the president to testify before the grand jury. On February 13, Kendall responded with a "Dear Bob" letter to Starr's deputy, Bittman. He wrote that he was unable to respond "because I was in the process of dealing with prejudicial and false leaks about your investigation."

Kendall continued, "The president has the greatest respect for the grand jury. However, under the circumstances it is impossible to accept this invitation. The situation in Iraq continues to be dangerously volatile, and this has demanded much of the president's time and attention. The president also has a heavy travel schedule at present. Our access to him has necessarily been limited." He added that "in light of the well-publicized and questionable investigative techniques of your office," the president would have to be fully prepared by his lawyers and the time was not now available.

The letter was greeted in Starr's office with considerable mirth and ridicule. In regular daily 5 p.m. meetings that Starr held with his deputies, several attorneys urged with increasing passion that the president be formally subpoenaed. The Supreme Court favored their side. The 1974 decision directing Nixon to turn over his secret recordings and the 1997 high court ruling in the Jones case that made Clinton answerable to a civil suit meant a president could not escape the law. Clinton had already voluntarily testified three times at the White House, sworn testimony that was equivalent to grand jury appearances.

Starr agreed that there was no question they had the law on their side, but he was still reluctant. He seemed determined about Clinton but squeamish about the presidency. He directed that another invitation be sent on February 21. A fifth invitation was sent March 2. In that letter, which Starr edited, Bittman wrote: "We fully acknowledge that the president has immense and weighty responsibilities. We want in every way to take fully into account those grave duties of state. Yet since this matter arose, the president has—with all respect—found time to play golf, attend basketball games and political fundraisers, and enjoy a ski vacation. We assure you that the grand jury's inquiry of the president will not take long."

Bill Hundley spent days reviewing his client Vernon Jordan's story. Jordan had dealt with Lewinsky for just eight weeks. Most fascinating was Jordan's relationship with Clinton. It went back far and deep, reminding Hundley of his former client, Attorney General John Mitchell, and Mitchell's relationship with Nixon. Hundley recalled riding in a limousine in 1975 to the courthouse where Mitchell was going to testify in his own defense in the Watergate cover-up trial.

"You got any final instructions, coach?" Mitchell had asked.

"John," Hundley said, "I know you love Nixon, and I don't want you to say anything bad about him, but please don't defend him. Your testimony should be to defend yourself."

About 15 minutes into his testimony, Mitchell began lionizing Nixon. Back in the car, Mitchell asked Hundley, "What's the matter, coach?"

"You didn't defend him," Hundley said. "You eulogized him."

"What difference does it make?" Mitchell replied.

Hundley found it much the same with Jordan. Jordan didn't express any disappointment or feeling that Clinton had misused him. To the contrary, Jordan spoke of Clinton as if he were a god.

Starr hired Thomas H. Bienert, a California prosecutor with 11 years experience, to focus on Jordan. After a month of preparation, Bienert and Bittman scheduled a March 3 appearance for Jordan before the grand jury.

"Let's go up there," Hundley recommended to Jordan. "We'll gamble you're not a target." No formal target letter had been sent to Jordan, which meant that an indictment was not imminent. It was against Justice Department guidelines to subpoena a target before the grand jury without notice. "They're not just going to slap a target letter as you go into the grand jury because then you wouldn't testify." In his review of Jordan's story and the records that were available, Hundley couldn't find any criminal exposure for his client. He knew from Ginsburg that Lewinsky would not testify that Jordan asked her to lie or do anything illegal.

Who else might testify against you? Clinton? Hundley laughed.

Jordan and Hundley went to the courthouse.

"What's my guy's status?" Hundley asked Bittman.

"Subject." That meant Jordan was being investigated seriously, but the prosecutors did not have evidence that would lead to imminent indictment.

About 9:50 a.m., Jordan began his grand jury testimony.

Bienert asked about December 19, when Lewinsky received her Jones case subpoena and had come to see Jordan quite disturbed. "I thought quite honestly that I was listening to a bobby-soxer who was mesmerized by Frank Sinatra, who was quite taken with this man because of his position, because of who he was, because he was tall and he was handsome and because he was president." Having discovered this fondness and intense interest, he testified that he asked Lewinsky, "Have you had sexual relations with the president?" She said, "No."

"Without you needing to be graphic," Bienert asked, "what did you mean when you said that?"

"My view of it was sexual intercourse," Jordan said. "Period. That's my definition of sexual relations is sexual intercourse."

Since the Jones case was specifically about Clinton allegedly asking for oral sex, why did Jordan not ask Lewinsky about oral sex?

Jordan said he didn't understand the question.

"Let me ask it again," Bienert said. "We'll do it as many times as we need to."

"Oral sex never entered my mind," Jordan said.

"Let me finish my question," Bienert said.

"Let me interrupt you to say that to you, unequivocally, indubitably so that you will understand it. The concept of oral sex never entered my mind when I asked her the question."

They went round and round. Bienert insisted he didn't want to get specific.

"Well, I don't believe that," Jordan said.

Bienert pressed.

"I think what is included in the term sexual relationship is defined by the two people in the relationship," Jordan testified. He had asked Lewinsky about sexual relations, he said. "Period. Did they hold hands? Did they kiss? Did they dance? Did they stand on top of the table? I didn't get into that." Jordan wouldn't go any further. By 4:30 p.m. he was done for the day, and expected to return the next day.

He had a message to deliver on the courthouse steps—a message to the prosecutors, the media and the president. "To those of you who cast doubt on my friendship with President Clinton, let me reassure you that ours is an enduring friendship, an enduring friendship based on mutual respect, trust and admiration. That was true yesterday. That is true today. And it will be true tomorrow."

Starr's prosecutors were infuriated that Jordan had sent a signal to the president of complete and total loyalty for the present and future.

Kendall continued with his strategy of trying to make Starr's conduct the issue. Bittman's

624

acknowledgment of the president's "grave duties of state" triggered a four-page March 4 letter from Kendall. "The buck really does stop with the president for decision-making on a vast range of issues that are critical to the country's safety and economic security," Kendall wrote. He presented a catalogue of the foreign policy problems: Iraq was still "highly volatile," as was the "Southeast Asian economic crisis and the Bosnia situation."

On the domestic front, Kendall wrote, "the president's schedule is equally congested." His budget proposal demanded time, as did Social Security, a possible tobacco settlement, the president's race initiative, health care proposals, highway legislation, and an auto safety bill.

Kendall reminded Bittman that they had access to a copy of the president's January 17 deposition in the Jones case. He then complained about reports that Linda Tripp had briefed the Jones attorneys on the eve of Clinton's deposition. Kendall peppered Starr and his deputies with more letters criticizing Starr's possible conflicts because one of his Kirkland & Ellis partners, Richard Porter, had secretly helped the Jones attorneys. Another letter accused Starr of improperly wiring Tripp with a microphone during the January 13 meeting with Lewinsky before Starr had jurisdiction in the investigation.

On March 18, Kendall claimed there were so many issues about Starr and his office that he believed the investigation was "a campaign to embarrass and harass the president." In a

625

follow-on letter, Kendall wrote that the number of issues and questions outstanding meant "we cannot, as a matter of professional duty to our client, allow the president to give further testimony at the present time. The issue remains open, however, and depends on your office."

On Wednesday, April 1, Bennett took a phone call from Barry Ward, Judge Wright's law clerk. Ward said the judge had granted summary judgment on the Jones case. She had thrown it out completely and declared it had no merit.

Bennett was ecstatic. He called Ruff at the White House with the good news. Bennett phoned the White House signals operator to get the president, who was in Africa. While Bennett was waiting for the president, he thought to himself, Oh shit, it's April Fool's Day! Could it be a joke? Yes—he had a partner who could imitate the judge's law clerk. Worried, he asked one of his associates to call Ward directly. It was soon confirmed.

"Mr. President," Bennett said when Clinton came on the line, "this is not an April Fool's joke. It wouldn't be a good career move for me." He then explained the total victory, 100 percent.

"Wow!" Clinton said. "Unbelievable, fantastic."

They agreed to handle their statements coolly. The most eloquent testimony to the victory would be the judge's opinion.

But Clinton was ebullient. He was photographed chewing on an unlit cigar and banging on an African drum as the sun set in Dakar, Senegal.

Ginsburg was still spending his time in Washington making the restaurant scene with his famous client. That night Lewinsky and Ginsburg accepted an invitation from Carol Joynt, a CNN producer and the owner of Nathan's Restaurant in the heart of Georgetown, to dine as her guest in one of the red-leather banquette booths in the back.

Lewinsky and Ginsburg ate heartily, and he ordered a 1985 Château Haut Brion at $190 a bottle.

Lewinsky expressed disgust at the Jones lawsuit and said it should have been thrown out long ago.

The CNN camera crew asked to come in to take a minute or two of film.

"No audio," Lewinsky said, approving, "and no pictures of me eating."

The CNN crew quietly took some footage.

Lewinsky looked voluptuous in a pink sweater, with a lovely complexion and gorgeous hair. She reminded Joynt of a 19th-century porcelain doll.

Lewinsky made several vague references to the president. She didn't speak of him with awe. She was more forthcoming about herself. "I'm a sensual person," she said. "I'm in touch with my sexuality and I'm not ashamed of it."

Ginsburg's beeper and phone went off regularly during the dinner. Joynt easily persuaded him to call in to *Larry King Live*. One call that Lewinsky took was from Marcia Lewis, her mother.

"My mother said I looked fat on the six

o'clock news," Lewinsky said after the call. "She says I better wear a jacket."

The ABC camera crew wanted to come in to film. Ginsburg said it was okay with him.

"No, I don't want it," Lewinsky said, as if she were turning down dessert.

Joynt loaned Lewinsky her Armani jacket for the well-filmed exit.

"I've never had an Armani on before," Lewinsky said as she departed.

Starr realized that he was taking a thrashing in the media. His natural smirk was a television disaster. He began searching for a spokesman to put a professional but tough face on his investigation.

He settled on Charles Bakaly, a 43-year-old attorney who had worked for Jim Baker in the Reagan administration. Baker had one of the all-time successful media operations in post-Watergate Washington, and Bakaly had at least served on the fringes of it. Tall and somewhat debonair, with swept-back hair, Bakaly had a deep, perfectly pitched radio announcer's voice. He had spent the past two years as the deputy independent counsel under Don Smaltz, who was investigating the former agriculture secretary, Mike Espy.

In mid-April, Bakaly began work in the offices at 1001 Pennsylvania Avenue. He thought Starr did not understand the value of momentum in a high-visibility political struggle. Momentum could carry them through the mistakes and inevitable stumbles. But there was a rhythm to battle, and Starr lacked the prosecutorial instinct for the kill. Because the Lewinsky case was going to be slow, Starr needed to avoid perceived conflicts of interest. Starr had left open the possibility that he would take the Pepperdine job at some future date. Bakaly persuaded him that Clinton's defenders had scored political points by tying him to Richard Mellon Scaife, an ultraconservative who funded many projects at Pepperdine, including the new public policy school that Starr was to head. Starr agreed to write a letter withdrawing completely.

The White House was controlling the public relations playing field, Bakaly argued, and Starr had to get into the game. It was proper for them to defend their investigation—its integrity and fairness—from White House attacks. It was important to project fairness to possible grand jury witnesses, potential jurors and even to the judges who might be involved in any cases. Starr allowed Bakaly to open a public relations offensive.

The Secret Service was now asserting a new privilege, refusing to be interviewed in the Lewinsky investigation. The Secret Service chief said testimony by agents guarding the president would heighten the risk of assassination and destroy the trust they needed to protect the president.

Starr reacted emotionally to this claim, certain that it was merely an effort to delay and obstruct. No one could find any basis in law or court rulings to support the contended privilege.

The independent counsel's office was also

under siege for trying to get information on Lewinsky's book purchases from two local Washington bookstores to confirm Lewinsky's claims on the Tripp tapes about book gifts to Clinton. The office was instantly accused of defiling the First Amendment.

In addition, the White House was asserting executive and attorney-client privileges for many White House witnesses, most notably Bruce Lindsey. At one point Lindsey appeared at the courthouse with ten attorneys.

Anger was driving the president's strategy, Starr believed. A scorched-earth attack would work if the White House knocked off the prosecutor, but if it didn't, Starr still had his power. Perhaps he had failed to understand his own strength. He was, after all, still standing.

Convinced more than ever of a pattern of obstruction and cover-up from the White House, Starr was not going to let go of the basic Whitewater case. His analysis was simple. Six people, he believed, knew what had happened. Two were now dead—Vince Foster and James McDougal, who had died March 8. Two more were in the White House—the president and the first lady, and he believed they were not telling the truth. That left two who had defied their every effort to get them to talk—Susan McDougal, who was still in jail, and Webster Hubbell, who had served 18 months in jail.

Moving on the live witnesses, Starr's prosecutors questioned Hillary Clinton under oath April 25 for 4 hours and 40 minutes on Whitewater and Arkansas matters. She stressed how little knowledge she had of Whitewater finances.

"I've never seen these documents before and I have no information about them," the first lady testified at one point. "I never spent any significant time at all looking at the books and records of Whitewater." She invoked her right not to answer two questions relating to discussions she had with her husband.

On April 30, Starr indicted Hubbell and his wife on tax evasion charges relating to $1 million in income that Hubbell received before going to jail.

Five days later, Starr's Little Rock grand jury indicted Susan McDougal on criminal contempt charges for again refusing to answer questions about Clinton. Among the matters she refused to discuss was a 1983 check for $5,081 that had the provocative written notation on it: "Payoff Clinton."

After the indictment, the Arkansas Whitewater grand jury disbanded without further action. In the end, Starr did not have what he believed was a cooperating, truth-telling witness—not the president, not the first lady, not Susan McDougal, not Hubbell.

On May 25, Memorial Day, the president played golf and that night attended a Washington Capitals play-off hockey game with Vice President Gore. He was the first sitting president to go to a professional hockey game, and he watched from the luxury suite of the owner Abe Pollin at the new MCI Center in downtown Washington.

Early in the game, Clinton went to the back area, which was filled with drinks and food. He walked up to Jack Quinn, his former counsel, and Housing Secretary Andrew Cuomo. The subject of what Clinton called his "troubles" finally came up.

"Goddamn it!" the president said. He said he knew he was paying a price for the Lewinsky investigation. Then Clinton launched into a three-minute tirade against the Jones lawsuit and Starr. "It's a hokey, trumped-up, baseless lawsuit," he said. All his problems stemmed from that lawsuit, he said. Starr had set a perjury trap for him, he said, seething. The attempt to question the Arkansas troopers the previous year about his sex life was directly connected to the conspiracy against him. "What this guy is doing is discovery for the Paula Jones case. That thing they were doing last year was about discovery." Starr and the Jones attorneys were working together hand in glove. The president said he was fed up, had had it up to here, putting his hand up to his eyes. "That guy's on a mission to get me!"

During the second intermission, Clinton, smiling, told a TV interviewer, "I'm having the time of my life. I love this. It's fascinating."

33

STARR HAD CAREFULLY STUDIED section 595(c) of the Ethics in Government Act, which dictated his duties in a possible impeachment. The law directed that an independent counsel "shall advise the House of Representatives of any substantial and credible information...that may constitute grounds for an impeachment."

He interpreted the law to mean he had no choice but to advise the House if he had evidence that "may" be grounds for impeachment. The "may," Starr felt, was an incredibly low legal standard. It meant the "likelihood" or "chance" that the information might be grounds for an impeachment. He believed they had met that standard. He directed a team of three lawyers to begin drafting a document outlining the information gathered in the Lewinsky probe for possible referral to the House on Clinton.

In early May 1998, Starr persuaded Brett Kavanaugh, one of his young protégés, to return to work at the independent counsel's office. Kavanaugh, 33, had worked in Starr's office from the early stages of the Whitewater investigation in 1994 until October 1997, when it appeared everything was winding down. He had graduated from Yale Law School, worked for Starr in the solicitor general's office and then at Kirkland & Ellis, Starr's law firm. In 1993–94, he had clerked for Supreme Court Justice Anthony Kennedy. He looked somewhat like a dark-haired version of the movie actor William Hurt, and he had a similar soft style. He was to handle some appeals on privilege issues and to act as a kind of legal counsel and adviser.

Kavanaugh had sometimes wondered if Starr had made a mistake taking the Lewinsky investigation. It had dragged Starr down in the muck and undermined public confidence. But Kavanaugh had heard from some of the lawyers in the office that they had built a strong case, and he was eager to review it. He went through the Tripp tapes, the testimony of a number of Lewinsky's friends who said she had told them about her sexual relationship with Clinton, Jordan's and Currie's testimony, and the backup documents.

Huh? he thought when he'd finished. There was no direct testimony from anyone implicating Clinton in wrongdoing or illegal activity. They had no testimony from Lewinsky. They had nothing from Vernon Jordan that incriminated Clinton; nor from Betty Currie, whose recollections had grown more hazy and vague with each subsequent grand jury appearance. Everyone in the office seemed focused on how to obtain the testimony of the key witness, Lewinsky. But how?

Michael Emmick, a senior prosecutor, who had headed the public corruption section of the U.S. attorney's office in Los Angeles, was in charge of the small Monica task force. He argued that they should subpoena Lewinsky before the grand jury, give her immunity and force her to testify. That move would create more hostility with Lewinsky, but Emmick and others feared that if they struck a voluntary deal with her, she might undermine their entire case, as Hubbell in some ways had done after agreeing to cooperate. All Lewinsky would have to do was come to the grand jury and say that everything she had said to Tripp on the tapes and to her other friends was her exaggeration.

The other possibility was to indict Lewinsky for obstructing the Jones case, take her to trial and then after a possible conviction force her to testify with immunity. They had used that tactic with other subjects of their investigation such as Jim McDougal, but Starr realized he and the entire office could face an avalanche of public criticism if they prosecuted Lewinsky.

After his review, Kavanaugh urged Starr to find some way to induce Lewinsky to talk. But Starr continued to have an intense distrust of Ginsburg that seemed to override everything.

Kendall followed Starr's every action and word, including his public speeches. He read the text of Starr's June 1 remarks to the Charlotte, North Carolina, bar group. Kendall's head was almost spinning after he finished. The speech was a clear attack on defense lawyers. Starr had said, "At what point does a lawyer's manipulation of the system become an obstruction of the truth? A good lawyer, acting as a counselor, must urge the client against steps that are likely to impede the quest for truth." Starr seemed to be calling on attorneys to turn in their clients.

My God, Kendall thought. It was so grotesque. Starr had invoked Atticus Finch, the fictional defense attorney in Harper Lee's novel *To Kill a Mockingbird* (1960). "Atticus Finch strove to find the truth while defending a black man who was wrongly accused of rape in a segregated community," Starr had said. It was unbelievable to Kendall. Starr had turned Finch's role on its head. In the famous novel and the movie version in which Gregory Peck played Finch, the lawyer was defending his lonely client *against the power of the state.* Kendall had been arrested in that segregated South in the mid-1960s, and he understood the potentially dangerous power of a police state.

Kendall turned to his word processor. "The attempt to make Atticus Finch into a docile figure who bows to the prosecutor's will simply won't do," Kendall wrote. The barrier was the Bill of Rights. If Starr had gone after Atticus Finch's unpopular client, Tom Robinson, Kendall wrote, then a football buddy would have taped phone conversations secretly. In that scenario, Robinson would have been questioned for hours without a lawyer, Robinson's mother would have been hauled before a grand jury, records of Robinson's purchase of a Bible from the local bookstore would have been subpoenaed, and the newspapers would have been full of prejudicial leaks.

"Truth, as Atticus knew, emerges from an adversarial judicial system that includes a vigorous defense as well as a vigorous prosecution," Kendall wrote. He quoted Justice Brandeis's words about the danger of "men of zeal, well-meaning but without understanding."

Clinton liked Kendall's draft editorial, as did the White House political advisers, who saw it as a shot in the public relations war. Kendall sent it to *The New York Times*, which agreed within 15 minutes to publish it as an op-ed piece June 3.

The editors didn't require any changes but insisted on writing the headline: "To Distort a Mockingbird."

Over in Starr's office, the reaction of some

of the prosecutors to his North Carolina speech was not that different from Kendall's. Unfortunately, they had seen Starr's criticism of defense lawyers harden. He had argued in the office that it was best for a guilty person to confess and accept punishment so the guilty would be, as he once put it, "better off in this life and the life after." Starr was behaving as a preacher and father confessor, not as a lawyer. Some of the attorneys joked that Starr wanted the defense lawyers, who were bound to protect their clients and their rights, to commit malpractice.

"So defense lawyers are supposed to confess," one Starr deputy joked.

Starr seemed to suggest that Kendall knew his client, the president, was guilty in the Lewinsky case, and therefore Kendall shouldn't invoke privileges that deflected Starr from his path to the truth.

Plato Cacheris, the ultimate good old boy of the Washington legal fraternity, picked up his phone in late May. It was Billy Martin, the attorney for Marcia Lewis, Monica's mother.

"I've been asked by the family to see if you would be interested in representing Monica Lewinsky," Martin said.

"I can tell you I'm not interested if this Ginsburg fellow is involved," Cacheris said.

"He's out."

Cacheris, 69, was winding down a long career as a criminal defense lawyer, but he loved high-profile cases. He phoned Jake Stein, 73, who had offices on the 11th floor of the same D.C. office building, and asked him down to talk.

Stein, the thin, well-dressed former independent counsel who had declined to prosecute Ed Meese, went down to Cacheris's office. The two walked to a small, well-lit, comfortable alcove in the corner that invited intimacy. Stein sat on a colorful couch, Cacheris at a chair before a small table.

Cacheris mentioned the call from Billy Martin.

"I got a call from Billy Martin too," Stein said, smiling.

Cacheris roared with laughter, his beefy frame shaking. Should we work together? he asked.

On June 1 at 11:30 a.m. Cacheris went to the Washington Court Hotel to meet Lewinsky for the first time. Billy Martin and Marcia Lewis were also present. Lewinsky looked fresh, she seemed bright and intent.

"If you want somebody to negotiate a guilty plea with the independent counsel," Cacheris said, "I'm not the person you want." He paused. "But I would be available to do a trial if you're indicted or I can negotiate immunity. A guilty plea would be just stupid. It's not in their interest to destroy their witness." He believed that Starr's tactic of indicting his potential witnesses, such as Susan McDougal and Hubbell, had been a disaster. Looking directly at Lewinsky, Cacheris said, "You should be a witness in this case." He suggested a team approach to representing Lewinsky, maybe with Stein or somebody else.

Cacheris and Stein were invited together back to the hotel the next day, June 2. Monica, her mother and Billy Martin were there. They got Bernard Lewinsky, Monica's father, on a speakerphone. He agreed to hire both of them and pay them each $350 an hour.

"I want my daughter protected," Lewis said. She became emotional, jumped up and hugged the lawyers. "Oh, thank you. Oh thank you."

Later that afternoon, Cacheris called Bob Bittman, whom he knew, and requested a meeting. At 2 p.m., Cacheris and Stein arrived at the independent counsel's offices. They explained that as of today they together now represented Lewinsky.

Bittman and Jackie Bennett seemed both surprised and slightly amused that Ginsburg was gone, replaced by two old Washington hands.

"We have substantial evidence on your client," Bittman said.

Neither Stein nor Cacheris responded. They sat looking hard at the prosecutors. Silence was the opening note in the bargaining minuet. They were seeking nothing, offering nothing. They said they were making a courtesy call— just to keep the Office of Independent Counsel informed—and left.

"Thank God," Starr said when Bennett and Bittman reported to him. "It's a new day." Starr knew Stein well. Just last week he had presented a Council for Court Excellence award to Stein. At last Starr had legal professionals to work with who would not jerk him around.

Lewinsky came up to Cacheris's office. She and her new attorneys were going to have a brief press conference out front to announce the new legal team. She told them how angry she was at Ginsburg. The final straw, she said, came when Ginsburg wrote an open letter in *California Lawyer* magazine. He had called on Clinton to fire Starr and had written that the independent counsel "may have succeeded in unmasking a sexual relationship between two consenting adults."

She said she didn't understand Ginsburg. "He should have talked to me," she said. "He should have consulted me." She also said she had been pissed off when Ginsburg claimed that he had kissed her inner thighs when she was a baby. "He never knew me when I was a baby," she said in disgust.

At 5 p.m. they held the brief press appearance. The story was big news.

Clinton was on a fund-raising swing in Texas. That evening after a dinner at a private residence in Dallas, about 9:30 p.m., he rose to speak. The remarks went unnoticed by the media.

"But in some ways," the president said, "the biggest battles are yet to be fought, because sometimes when people enjoy a great deal of success, it makes them downright dumb. How many of us—haven't all of you been—had at least a moment of being downright dumb when you were really successful? Is there a person who is here who can say with a straight face you never had one moment of stupidity in the aftermath of some success you enjoy? Nobody can say that."

Around this time, staffers close to the Clintons, even the White House photographers, noticed that Hillary grew cold toward her husband. It was as if a wall had gone up. Suddenly, she would not touch him in public. She wasn't looking at him. They seemed estranged, as if the president had lost the support of his wife.

Lewinsky went to Cacheris's office the next day, June 3, for an eight-hour debriefing. Lewinsky provided what seemed almost frightening detail about her one-way oral sex relationship with the president. She had a near-photographic memory for objects, what people were wearing, colors, dialogue, placement of furniture in a room.

Preston Burton, Cacheris's 35-year-old partner, thought it was almost too much. His father, also a lawyer, had taught him to presume clients were lying. But a lot of the detail was so specific that it could be checked. What Lewinsky didn't say happened was almost as important as what she did. As she had written in her February 1 proffer, she maintained that neither the president nor Jordan had asked her to lie. She had not been threatened. Jordan's substantial efforts to get her a job, she said, were not connected to her decision to sign a false affidavit in the Jones case. They were not made for her silence. In short, evidence of serious felonies by the president, Jordan or others was missing.

On June 4, the Supreme Court rejected Starr's unusual request to bypass the normal appeals courts process and hear the White House privilege claims on an emergency basis. Starr invoked Nixon and Watergate. The high court said no, use the ordinary route. Starr worried the decision would add months to the delay.

Lewinsky's new lawyers debriefed her again that day and the next, June 5. Cacheris called in Sydney Hoffman, a younger female attorney he had worked with for a year. She was a petite, smart 46-year-old with two young children who worked out of an attic office in her Chevy Chase home.

Cacheris explained that there was an age and gender differential that he wanted to close with Lewinsky.

On Monday, June 8, Hoffman spent five hours listening to Lewinsky's story. The rush of detail seemed unreal. Hoffman thought that Lewinsky seemed delusional. Her story was a bizarre reconstruction, and it reflected a deep obsession on Lewinsky's part.

Afterwards, Hoffman consulted with some psychiatrists. Based on the description, she concluded it was highly possible that Lewinsky had a form of Clara Bow syndrome, named after the famous silent film actress who couldn't say no. Or perhaps Lewinsky had erotomania, an abnormally strong sexual desire. The relationship with Clinton made up a big piece of Lewinsky's emotional life. It was a relationship that Clinton dominated and in which Lewinsky had virtually no control. She had talked to so many friends about it because that was a way of regaining power. Under these circumstances it was going to be difficult to sort out fact from fancy. Yet Hoffman believed some part of the story was true. In some form, if only in a few sexual encounters, Lewinsky had the best known boyfriend in the world.

Cacheris and Stein both felt there was a core truth to Lewinsky's story. Through their extensive debriefing they thought they had already sorted out the truth and would quickly be able to make her a solid witness. They called Starr and made an appointment to see him at 2 p.m. on June 9. Starr, Bittman, Jackie Bennett and another prosecutor, Sol Wisenberg, greeted them.

We want to resolve this situation quickly, Cacheris said. That was their first goal. "Second, Monica Lewinsky is a truthful witness," he said. "Three, there are matters that are unpleasant subject matters for her involving intimate relations which we want handled sensitively." Fourth, knowing Starr's intense hostility toward Ginsburg, Cacheris promised he and Stein would deal honorably with Starr and his deputies.

Stein added, "We don't think that you'll need to polygraph Ms. Lewinsky. She's not the type of person who will respond well to a polygraph." He said as Lewinsky's lawyers they were willing to negotiate an immunity deal, but Lewinsky would not plead to any charge.

"We want you to think about a plea bargain," Bittman countered.

"I want you to know I have one good trial left in me," Stein said, challenging the prosecutors to indict Lewinsky.

Starr let the discussion flow by without reacting.

Bittman said they were interested in a number of physical items of evidence: a dress that reportedly might contain the president's semen;

personal diaries that Lewinsky might have kept; gifts the president gave to her; recordings of the president's voice from Lewinsky's answering machine.

Cacheris and Stein sat silently as Bittman rattled off his list.

Bittman said they had offered Ginsburg a plea bargain. Lewinsky would have to plead to a felony, but they would tell the sentencing judge that she was a cooperative witness so the tough sentencing guidelines would not have to be applied. They would also make a positive statement to the judge if she cooperated fully.

"We're definitely not interested in any kind of plea," Cacheris replied sharply. "That is off the table as far as we're concerned."

Starr and Bittman looked serious. The meeting was over. The new Lewinsky attorneys were playing hardball.

The next day, Bittman called Cacheris and Stein. He said Starr had requested that they bring Lewinsky in to make a formal proffer to detail her possible testimony.

No, Cacheris said, they had to have full immunity. "We want you to say that if you find her believable and credible, you will give her immunity." That agreement would have to be spelled out in any deal, he said.

After the phone call, Cacheris and Stein worried about what Starr might do next. They hoped to avoid a subpoena that would compel Lewinsky to testify with immunity.

Sydney Hoffman had a different view. If forced to testify as a hostile witness, Lewinsky could then limit what she said. She could have a kind of yes-and-no relationship with the grand jury and Starr. Given the nature of the relationship with the president, perhaps limited testimony was in Lewinsky's interest. Hoffman knew that prosecutors created a web and tried to draw cooperating witnesses into it. Starr was building one of the biggest webs ever assembled against a president, and he had to have Lewinsky in the middle of it. There was this big driverless truck, Hoffman believed, heading straight for Clinton. Starr needed Lewinsky to take the wheel. Protecting Lewinsky might entail keeping her out of that role. Stein agreed to a certain extent, but Cacheris thought it was in Lewinsky's best interest to do the negotiations quickly. An immunity deal would end it soonest.

On June 13, the first issue of *Brill's Content,* a new media magazine, was released. The magazine's editor, Steven Brill, wrote a long lead story called "Pressgate," alleging that Starr and his deputies regularly leaked grand jury information to the media. Brill quoted Starr saying, "I have talked with reporters on background on some occasions, but Jackie [Bennett] has been the primary person involved in that. He has spent much of his time talking to individual reporters." When the Lewinsky story broke in January, Jackie Bennett spent "much of the day briefing the press," Starr was quoted saying. Brill said the contacts between the independent counsel and the media violated Rule 6-E of the federal rules of criminal procedure, which prohibit prosecutors from disclosing grand jury material.

Kendall filed a motion on June 15 with the judge overseeing the grand jury investigation, saying they now had proof of official leaking.

About 5 p.m., Starr met in his conference room for the daily staff session with about 20 attorneys. Tension was high, with many of the prosecutors feeling that Starr had put Jackie Bennett in the crosshairs. The entire office seemed demoralized.

Starr was in serious distress.

"Steve Brill's been a friend of mine for 20 years," he began mournfully. "I advised him when he started his first magazine, *The American Lawyer.*" Brill had come to see him two months ago. "I thought he was coming to seek my advice on this endeavor, his new media magazine. He started firing 6-E questions at me. I feel terrible. I'm sorry." He had been used to launch Brill's new magazine, and he had given Kendall ammunition in their court fight about leaks. Starr said Brill had totally confused what he had said. He attempted to explain what he had meant, that he had been talking in general.

Charles Bakaly, who had attended most of the Starr-Brill interview, could see that Starr was contrite and embarrassed. During the interview, Starr had given one of his classic free-association lectures for 90 minutes on Rule 6-E.

By the end of the meeting Starr had dissipated his staff's anger by apologizing.

On June 25, almost two weeks later, the Supreme Court closed off the last possible avenue for Starr to get new information on the Vince Foster suicide. The Court ruled that James Hamilton, Foster's attorney, did not have to reveal notes or confidences he had shared with Foster nine days before his death. It was another setback for the independent counsel, who was having a difficult month.

Meanwhile work on Starr's draft referral to the House was proceeding. Starr had reviewed several hundred pages his staff had written on the evidence, which claimed that Clinton had lied and perhaps obstructed justice.

"This is good," Starr said. "This is strong."

Dash and Kavanaugh and some of the other experienced prosecutors tried to slow Starr down, since they did not have either Clinton or Lewinsky providing direct testimony.

"I've got a strong circumstantial case," Starr said. He reminded them of his reading of section 595(c) of the law, that he "shall" forward information if it "may" constitute impeachment grounds. "It would be improper to withhold it from Congress unless it was weightless."

Some of the attorneys argued against the significance of what they had at that point.

"I feel like I've been in 595(c) territory since the spring," Starr replied to their objections at one discussion, pounding the table for emphasis, "and I have a statutory obligation to get this to Congress." It was now summer. Starr said the White House strategy was to delay so any referral would not be ready until fall, to force him to put off sending the referral until after the November elections.

Starr recalled the controversy in 1992 when Iran-contra Independent Counsel Lawrence Walsh had released material adverse to President Bush—the famous "VP favored"—just five days before the election. "I don't want to do what Judge Walsh did," he said. "The electorate did not have time to absorb the significance of it." Starr, who at the time was solicitor general, felt Walsh's action had unfairly harmed President Bush's bid for a second term. He was deeply concerned that he would be accused of interfering with the 1998 congressional elections. Kavanaugh thought that Starr seemed panicked over the issue.

Suddenly speed was paramount. On July 2, Starr filed a secret request with the three-judge panel asking for approval to disclose grand jury material in a referral to Congress. Five days later, the court issued a sealed order "permitting disclosure of all grand jury material that the independent counsel deems necessary." It was a blank check.

Starr had set July 31 as the deadline to send the referral to the House.

On July 15, Kavanaugh sent Starr a long memo questioning the decision. Lewinsky was within their grasp. It would make little sense without her firsthand account. The draft of the referral alleged that Clinton had made a series of false statements in his Jones deposition on January 17 about his relationship with Lewinsky. Kavanaugh attempted to tear each one apart. None of the evidence came from either Lewinsky or Clinton. Suppose both of them eventually said the opposite in public or under oath?

Dash was outraged when he learned that Starr had made July 31 a final deadline for the referral. Other attorneys told him that Starr had actually preferred to send it up in June but had delayed it. They also told Dash that unnamed members of the Republican leadership had told Starr that if Congress didn't get the referral by July 31, action would have to wait until after the election. Dash wrote Starr a memo arguing that the important portion of 595(c) was not the "may," but the provision that said the independent counsel should send information if it was "substantial and credible." Circumstantial evidence by definition, Dash argued, was not "substantial and credible," not sufficient to trigger impeachment of the president.

Starr rebuffed Kavanaugh and Dash. "We're sending it up July 31," he said again. He cited senior members of his staff. "Tom Bienert says I have an overwhelming case. Ronald Mann says I have an overwhelming case. I have a duty."

Kavanaugh checked with Bienert and Mann. They said it was a strong circumstantial case, but only that.

Dash told Starr he would resign if they sent up a flimsy referral without solid evidence.

The arguments grew more heated. As Kavanaugh listened, he thought that Starr spoke as if he knew what had happened between Clinton and Lewinsky. He seemed to construe his burden under the law to show what he thought happened, not to prove it.

Michael Emmick, the expert on Lewinsky, also said it would be a mistake to send up a referral without Lewinsky's direct version.

If the referral was sent without Lewinsky's testimony, Kavanaugh asked Starr, what would happen?

The House could then have Lewinsky testify before the Judiciary Committee, Starr said.

Then, Kavanaugh said, why not just send up the evidence that had been gathered without an argument about the grounds for impeachment? In Watergate, Judge John Sirica had forwarded evidence from Special Prosecutor Leon Jaworski to the House Judiciary Committee. It contained a roadmap but no argument.

"I've got this statute," Starr said. He said his reading of 595(c), which didn't exist during Watergate, required him to relate the evidence to the possible grounds for impeachment. "I'm not just sending boxes." He pounded the table. "I have an obligation."

Starr found the evidence more conclusive than anyone else in the office. The sheer weight of the facts about the president's relationship with Lewinsky, Starr believed, was inconsistent with Clinton remaining president.

At almost every independent counsel staff meeting, they continued to discuss how and when to get the president's testimony. Many prosecutors continued to urge a subpoena, but Starr remained reluctant. From January to April they had issued six invitations. Kendall had rebuffed them.

Now the circumstances had changed. If they were going to send a referral to the House by July 31, they had to try to get the president on record some way, a number of Starr's deputies argued. They would look silly sending a referral to the House without having done everything in their power to obtain Clinton's testimony.

Starr was the last holdout on the subpoena. On Friday, July 17, he finally agreed. The subpoena was issued that day. It required Clinton to appear before the grand jury, third floor of the federal courthouse, at 9:15 a.m. the Tuesday after next, July 28.

Kendall received the subpoena about 5:45 p.m. What had provoked it? he wondered. Three months had passed since the last grand jury invitation. It was probably payback for the leak investigation that he had forced on Starr, Kendall thought. Since the summer, Judge Norma Johnson, chief judge of the U.S. District Court in Washington, D.C., had ruled in increasingly tough sealed orders that Kendall could cross-examine Starr and his deputies under oath about press leaks. Kendall was relishing the prospect, but the previous week a federal court of appeals had stayed the order temporarily. A panel of three appeals court judges highly favorable to Starr was going to make a final decision. Kendall believed that Starr now felt free to subpoena the president.

Kendall had examined the Supreme Court law. He too realized that the Nixon case and the Paula Jones ruling made a court battle to oppose a subpoena in a criminal case unwinnable.

34

DASH HAD LUNCH with one of Stein's law partners, who told him that Lewinsky's lawyers were amenable to an immunity deal.

On July 21, Starr called Stein and proposed

a meeting. They agreed to have coffee at 10 a.m. July 23 at Dash's Chevy Chase home.

Earlier that morning Cacheris played tennis at his home with his young partner Preston Burton. They called it the John Mitchell Memorial Tennis Court because Cacheris had paid for it with money from helping Bill Hundley represent Mitchell during Watergate. Afterwards, he drove over to pick up Stein and they went to Dash's home. Juice, bagels and coffee were set out in the family room as Dash and Starr greeted them.

Almost at once, Starr proposed a "Queen for a Day" agreement. His prosecutors would interview Lewinsky for a day with a promise that nothing she said could be used against her. The prosecutors would weigh the value and credibility of her possible testimony. "If that's successful," Starr added, "she would be out of harm's way."

Stein and Cacheris realized that Starr was virtually agreeing to their terms—if they believed her, they would give her immunity.

Cacheris said they also required immunity for Lewinsky's mother, who had been dragged before the grand jury and didn't want to testify against her daughter.

Starr indicated he was willing.

Okay, both Lewinsky attorneys said, when should the prosecutor get together with Lewinsky?

"Now," Starr said.

Lewinsky was in California visiting her father, Cacheris said. If they brought her back to Washington, the whole world would know.

"How about New York?" Starr proposed.

His mother-in-law had an apartment on East 56th Street in Manhattan they could use. He called it "Grandma's place."

"I want you to know she has a great distrust of your office," Cacheris said. They would have to have a signed proffer agreement spelling out the terms.

Starr agreed. He was in a hurry. He asked Dash to be there in New York.

Dash's wife, Sara, was ready to serve lunch, expecting a protracted negotiation, but they were done in an hour and everyone left.

Kendall told the president there were three options for dealing with Starr's subpoena. The president could accept the subpoena and try to cut a deal, limiting the time and insisting that his testimony be taken at the White House. He could fight the subpoena and file a lawsuit, but that would eventually be a loser. Or he could invoke the Fifth Amendment, permitting him not to testify on the grounds he might incriminate himself.

For Kendall, taking the Fifth was a real alternative. He could write a letter to Starr saying the lawyers insisted. According to the Justice Department guidelines, a subpoenaed witness who was going to take the Fifth would not be forced before the grand jury to go through the embarrassing formality of invoking the privilege.

Mickey Kantor disagreed strongly. Fighting a subpoena or taking the Fifth would look awful. The Democrats and the public would be outraged. The negatives could build with time. Losing in court would only be worse.

Chuck Ruff said the question was whether Clinton could testify and avoid being indicted by Starr after he left office in 2001. Contesting the subpoena in court or taking the Fifth would be a political disaster, he said.

The attorneys had the final debate Thursday night, July 23.

Clinton sided with Kantor. Fighting was not a real option if he would eventually lose, and a sitting president couldn't invoke the Fifth Amendment and survive.

The next day, July 24, Kendall sent a hand-delivered confidential letter to Bittman. "The president is willing to provide testimony for the grand jury," he wrote. The details would have to be worked out.

It was a big day for Starr. He and Lewinsky's attorneys also settled on a two-page agreement for her New York interview. Starr was in a generous mood. In final form, the agreement said Lewinsky "may decline to answer any questions posed to her" and "if the OIC [Office of Independent Counsel] is satisfied that the statements Ms. Lewinsky makes during the interview are truthful and sufficiently complete, the OIC will enter into an immunity agreement with Ms. Lewinsky." Starr, Stein and Cacheris signed it that day. Hoffman dropped her objections since it was potentially a total walk, full and complete legal protection from prosecution if Lewinsky told the truth. It would have been legal malpractice to turn it down, she felt. The New York meeting was set for Monday, July 27.

Hoffman had spent the weekend reviewing all the debriefing notes and documents. She tried to come up with what she called "Monica's Greatest Hits," the information she would be able to give the prosecutors.

On Sunday, Lewinsky, cloaked in a baseball cap and sunglasses, flew to New York. Stein, Cacheris and Hoffman sat down with her for a final discussion.

Hoffman told Lewinsky that she was magnetic in part because she was a pleaser. She should not provide long answers the next day with Starr's people. "Don't volunteer things," Hoffman said.

"I know," Lewinsky said.

"You've got to figure out who you care about, and who you love, and think about what you're going to say about those people," Hoffman said.

Lewinsky said she felt terrible about her family and friends who had been dragged into this spectacle.

It wasn't just the family and friends, Hoffman said. "If you want to hurt Clinton, go ahead. You can. But much will depend on how you say things."

Cacheris and Stein said there were 100 or more ways to answer a question truthfully. Every word uttered had a tone and secondary meaning that was often more important than the literal words. She needed to be vividly aware of what that spin was, and to control it.

"I know, I know," Lewinsky said.

"You have to think about what you want it all to look like at the end," Hoffman said.

Lewinsky was paying close attention.

"You have to think about how you are going

to structure your answers and what your contact and relationship is going to be with the Office of Independent Counsel." They were experienced prosecutors, and they wanted the story to come out a certain way. They might be subtle about it, or not subtle at all, but they would be directing and focusing her testimony.

They reminded her that she had to be truthful.

"How much damage do you want to do?" Hoffman asked. That was a question Lewinsky had to think about and answer.

Lewinsky indicated that she had.

The lawyers told her that her interpretation or impression of what other people were thinking, their state of mind, or their apparent reaction was not fact. Lewinsky did not have to testify to that, and she shouldn't. What you thought the president knew or what Vernon Jordan knew is not a fact. The facts were what people said and did.

"I know," Lewinsky said. "I know, I know."

The attorneys summarized. It was better to give a short answer than a long answer. Don't lose your temper and don't cry.

Starr went up to New York City and stayed the night at Grandma's place. He decided he wasn't going to be present for the "Queen for a Day" meeting with Lewinsky. She didn't like him personally, and he didn't want to aggravate the situation or upset her. He rose early, tidied up the apartment and left. He went to a midtown hotel to wait with three of his deputies. He hoped they would be able to cut a deal that day.

That morning, Monday, July 27, the attorneys picked up Lewinsky, drove over to the 56th Street apartment and went up to the 33rd floor. Bittman, Wisenberg, and Mary Anne Wirth, another of Starr's deputies, were there from Starr's office. Lewinsky, her three attorneys and Starr's prosecutors crowded around a dining-room table. There was art on the walls, and the room was small and confined. Sam Dash pulled up a chair at the edge of the room, where he could monitor what was being said. He had jokingly proposed to the members of Starr's team that since the meeting was being held at Grandma's place, they call it "Operation Red Riding Hood." No one saw the humor. Dash planned not to say anything unless the session got out of hand.

Lewinsky signed the two-page agreement promising to provide truthful information for a day in exchange for a pledge that none of her statements could be used against her. She said she understood she had to tell the truth.

"I want to catch the two o'clock shuttle," Cacheris joked.

Are you on any medication? Hoffman asked Lewinsky.

Lewinsky said she had used two prescription antidepressants, Effexor and Serzone.

Does it affect your memory?

Not in a significant way, Lewinsky replied, although at times it seemed to cause her not to remember certain words.

"Let's now turn to the events that are of interest to the people here at the table," Hoffman said. She noticed the suppressed laughs from several of the prosecutors.

Did there come a time when you became personally involved with President Clinton?

Yes.

Everyone started to take notes.

When was that? Hoffman asked.

November 15, 1995.

What happened?

We had a sexual encounter.

Did you perform oral sex on him?

Yes.

Was there kissing?

Yes.

Was there sexual touching?

Yes.

Was there sexual intercourse?

No.

How many total occasions did you see Mr. Clinton where there was some sexual component in your contacts?

Fourteen, Lewinsky replied. She defined sexual encounter to include one or more of the following: kissing, hugging, touching, oral sex on the president, but not intercourse.

Turning to the crucial month of December 1997 when Lewinsky was subpoenaed in the Jones case, Hoffman asked when and from whom Lewinsky first learned of it.

The president had telephoned her at home late on December 17.

Did you ever tell anyone about this relationship?

Yes. Lewinsky listed ten people, including Tripp.

Did you always give truthful answers to Tripp? Hoffman asked.

No, Lewinsky said, casting a blanket of doubt on information and tapes from the prosecutor's chief witness.

After about 30 minutes, the questioning was turned over to Mary Anne Wirth. One of her first questions was about the gifts Lewinsky had received from the president. Why had some been turned over and why did you keep others? Why did you, for example, keep the copy of Walt Whitman's *Leaves of Grass* from the president?

Lewinsky burst into tears.

Bittman interjected. "Sydney didn't make her cry," he said.

The book was one of the most treasured of the gifts. Lewinsky had crossed a line: she was ratting out the president, giving him up to the dreaded Starr team to save herself.

Hoffman asked for a break and took Lewinsky alone into another room. Can you continue?

Yes.

"You've done a perfect job," Hoffman said. "If you want to continue, you're going to have to pull yourself together."

Lewinsky said she was okay. They went back into the dining room.

Soon Bittman and Wisenberg took over the questioning. They bore in hard on possible physical evidence, especially the gifts. The tension between the two prosecutors was obvious as they regularly interrupted each other.

"What about the dress?" Bittman asked. Tripp had told them about a dress that might contain the president's semen stain.

"We're not talking about the dress now," Cacheris said, invoking the provision in their agreement that Lewinsky could decline to answer specific questions. Cacheris was making sure they did not give everything. Lewinsky had told her attorneys that the dress might contain the president's semen, but she also said the stains might be salad dressing or dip from a dinner she had attended wearing the same dress.

As the questioning proceeded, Lewinsky ceded control to the prosecutors. She volunteered information, showed her considerable memory for detail. When they asked about specific people in the White House, she revealed that she knew the schedules of key staffers—Clinton aide Nancy Hernreich's yoga night—their locations, normal movements, work hours, habits.

Hoffman was worried that it made Lewinsky look like a stalker. She made a "T" with her hands for time-out. They agreed to break for lunch. Sandwiches were served. Conversation turned to the backgrounds of the various lawyers on both sides, where they had grown up, what schools they had attended, what courses Dash was teaching at Georgetown.

One of the prosecutors phoned Starr. It's going well. They all believed her.

After lunch, Lewinsky warmed more to the process. The prosecutors hung on every word. In their questions, they were looking for evidence of active obstruction by the president. The closest Lewinsky came concerned the gifts. At her final meeting with Clinton on December 28, 1997, she had expressed concern about the gifts and had asked the president if she should give them to someone else. "I don't know," the president had replied. Then hours later Currie called Lewinsky and said, "You have some things to give me?" Currie came that afternoon and retrieved some of the gifts. The prosecutors knew that Currie had testified to the contrary, that Lewinsky had initiated their return.

Lewinsky provided a detailed list of 30 gifts she had given to the president and listed the 13 gifts she had received from him.

"Let's call a halt to this now," Cacheris finally said about 3:30 p.m. Lewinsky was visibly exhausted.

Bittman proposed that all the lawyers for both sides have a conference. Lewinsky went to the living room, and all the lawyers crowded into a bedroom.

Cacheris, Stein and Hoffman were optimistic. Obviously Lewinsky was an impressive witness.

"We'll get back to you," Bittman said. "We want to talk to her tomorrow."

"This is it!" Cacheris shouted, blowing up. "That's all you get! You've had more than ample time. It's clear she's a credible witness."

Dash nodded.

Bittman said they preferred to proceed carefully. He seemed hesitant.

Stein stepped forward. "It would be very good if we could walk out of here and announce that a deal has been struck," he said. "The press is going to learn of this. They find out about everything else, and it's only a matter of hours before this gets out."

Bittman said he was impressed with Lewinsky as a witness. He seemed to suggest that he didn't have the authority to make the deal. Starr would have to be briefed. He said Starr would call them the next day.

Lewinsky's attorneys escorted her out and took her back to an apartment where she was staying.

Stein said she had been stellar.

"You did terrific," Cacheris said. "Everything's going to be fine."

Hoffman thought that the Starr prosecutors were hound dogs with no noses, unable to distinguish a rabbit from a rock. Lewinsky was not able to give them hard evidence of obstruction. There had been no request that she lie. She had known what to say for herself. She had not been threatened, intimidated, offered money or a job for her silence—the components of heavy felonies. But she had given them chapter, verse, time, date and type on the sex. It was enough to nail Clinton, deliver a brutal political if not legal punch, if that was what they chose to do. Hoffman had no doubt they would. But was this evidence worthy of impeachment?

Bittman, Wisenberg and Wirth told Starr that they found Lewinsky credible.

"She's probably not giving us 100 percent," Wisenberg said, "but you never get 100 percent. The real test is she is telling us things that we did not know." Specifically, he cited the December 17 conversation with the president notifying Lewinsky of her subpoena in the Jones case, and the critical statement that Currie had phoned Lewinsky on December 28 about retrieving the gifts.

Starr called Stein that night and asked him

and Cacheris to come see him the next day, Tuesday, July 28, at 10 a.m.

That morning Starr had one of the easiest meetings with his staff. It took little time to draft an immunity agreement with Lewinsky. In Watergate and Iran-contra, the congressional investigating committees had granted more limited use immunity to witnesses such as John Dean, the Nixon counsel, and Oliver North, the Reagan National Security Council aide. It had meant their own testimony could not be used against them, but prosecutors could and did use other evidence gathered independently to bring charges. Since a federal court of appeals decision in Iran-contra had virtually eliminated any difference in the kinds of immunity, Starr agreed to provide full transactional immunity to Lewinsky in exchange for her cooperation. She could not be prosecuted as long as she told the truth. In addition, both her mother and father would be granted full immunity if they cooperated fully.

Starr, Lewinsky and the lawyers signed a formal three-page agreement.

Cacheris, Stein and Hoffman were delighted. Cacheris said they planned to have the briefest press conference announcing the agreement. Starr didn't object. After signing, his spirits improved. Finally they had a firsthand witness. Perhaps, he told several of his deputies, the president would come in and testify and say his testimony in the Jones case had not been complete. Clinton might now make an effort to rectify his obvious perjury.

• • •

Lewinsky, dressed in a powder-blue suit, her makeup and hair done perfectly, took a taxi over to her lawyers' offices. Escorted by her spokeswoman Judy Smith, Lewinsky emerged with a movie-star look of indifference. Her weight was down, and she had the pout for the part she was playing—America's woman-of-the-moment with the power of political life or death over the president of the United States. Just before 2 p.m., Cacheris and Stein appeared before the cameras, microphones and a mob of reporters. In one sentence, Cacheris announced the deal and declined to take additional questions.

Over at the White House, reporters asked McCurry about the president's reaction to the news.

"I think that he's pleased that things are working out for her," McCurry said.

The questioners expressed bafflement. Grim-faced, McCurry held the line as he was pounded with questions. ABC's Sam Donaldson put it the most directly. "But Mike, if they work out for her, it could sink him. He can't be pleased about that."

McCurry held his shaky ground. "Her lawyer indicated that she is going to testify truthfully and accurately. So why would that pose any problem to the president?"

The consensus in the press room was that the White House had lost touch with reality.

When McCurry had taken over as press secretary to Clinton in January 1995, Marlin Fitzwater, the Reagan and Bush press secretary, had warned him, "The most important thing you have to do is ensure the integrity of the information." Fitzwater had advised, "Not only the stuff you put out, but the stuff that goes to the president. Don't even for a minute think that everything the president knows or has been told is honest or straight or true, because it isn't." Fitzwater said it was important to have informants and spies all around the White House and government to cross-check.

McCurry didn't trust the information he was getting—from anyone, including the president. There wasn't enough information. No one, including the president, was trying to tell him the truth. The fragments always came framed, what was *not* the truth, what to deny. It was not a good place to be.

Kendall and Bittman opened negotiations on the president's grand jury testimony. In a July 27 letter, Kendall laid out his conditions: The subpoena would have to be withdrawn so the president could appear voluntarily; the testimony would have to be given in the White House with a time limit; because of an upcoming vacation, foreign trip and necessary preparation, the earliest the president could testify would be Sunday, September 13.

Starr felt that the delay was a maneuver to push his impeachment referral into the election cycle. With the Lewinsky immunity deal, he already could not make the July 31 deadline for the referral. He had set a new deadline for August 31.

Starr and Bittman came up with an initial position: They would accept voluntary, sworn testimony in the White House; the president would have to appear the first week of August for at least two days of testimony; they would be allowed to make a videotape of the testimony for any absent grand juror.

On July 28, Judge Johnson held a closed hearing on the subpoena issue. She said she was prepared to rule right then but would withhold her decision to encourage a compromise. Serious negotiations followed. Bittman said it was a deal-breaker if they could not have the testimony in mid-August. Kendall finally agreed when Bittman said testimony would be limited to four hours on a single day.

The next afternoon, July 29, Kendall appeared before the cameras outside the White House.

"In an effort to achieve a prompt resolution of this entire matter," he announced, "the president will voluntarily provide his testimony on August 17, 1998, to the Office of Independent Counsel, as he has on prior occasions."

Emmick called Cacheris and said he would be the prosecutor working with Lewinsky. He asked for any physical articles or evidence that she might have.

Lewinsky packed up the Gap dress and some other gifts she had retained from the president, put them in a sewing bag and brought them to Cacheris's office.

35

UNDER CAREFUL SECURITY, Starr sent Lewinsky's Gap dress to the FBI lab for tests. The dress was logged in as item Q3243. "Semen was identified on specimen Q3243," the results stated. Starr restricted knowledge of this finding to himself, Bittman and Wisenberg.

Bittman tried to reach Kendall twice on the morning of July 31 without success. That afternoon, he sent him a letter stating, "Investigative demands require that President Clinton provide this office as soon as possible with a blood sample to be taken under our supervision." Kendall wrote back that he had to be made aware of the test results so he could respond to false leaks if they occurred, as he expected. In a letter, still the same day, Bittman replied that the prosecutors had a "substantial" and "powerful" reason to request the blood sample. He did not promise that they would share the results with Kendall.

It could be a bluff, Kendall thought. Obviously, the prosecutors wanted blood to compare Clinton's DNA with the DNA that might be on the dress. The court decisions on requests for handwriting, hair or blood samples from prosecutors made it clear that there was no way to resist effectively. Fighting and losing in court, as they surely would, would make matters worse.

But the possibility that the dress contained

the president's semen was a terrifying proposition. It would provide everyone with what Kendall referred to as "an outside reality check." And it could give Starr another weapon.

On August 3, Kendall agreed that the president would provide a blood sample that evening. At 10:10 p.m., Clinton, Kendall, White House physician Dr. Connie Mariano, Bittman and an FBI agent met in the White House Map Room, where President Franklin Roosevelt monitored the course of World War II.

Kendall made a weak joke about having always wanted one of his clients to give blood. Clinton shot him a look that could freeze water.

The president rolled up his right sleeve and Dr. Mariano extracted approximately 4 milliliters of blood.

It was a painful invasion of Clinton's privacy. The president showed his unhappiness.

The tube was sealed with evidence tape. By 10:30 p.m., the FBI agent had delivered it to the FBI's DNA Analysis Unit I. A quick, comparatively unsophisticated test showed a match between the DNA from the dress semen and the president's DNA with a 1 in 43,000 chance of error. Later tests showed a match with what the FBI report called "a reasonable degree of scientific certainty," or a 1 in 7.87 trillion chance of error.

Starr, Bittman and Wisenberg knew the results. No one else was told, including Kendall. There was no leak.

Ordinary witnesses were not allowed to have counsel in the grand jury, but Kendall was going to have the unusual opportunity to attend. This arrangement was somewhat of a burden. As a lawyer and officer of the court, Kendall could not permit testimony that he knew to be false. His obligation was to his client and the truth. Because of the dress and the leaked news stories that Lewinsky would testify to a sexual relationship with the president, Kendall was going to have to find out what had happened between the two. The reality check would have to be total.

"We're going to have to prepare you like no witness has ever been prepared," Kendall told Clinton. Ruff did not have an ironclad lawyer-client privilege with the president, so he could not attend even the preparation sessions.

That first weekend after the agreement on testimony with Starr, Kendall and his partner, Nicole Seligman, commenced a series of sessions with Clinton at the White House residence. They worked with him in the president's study and the solarium, the summer room with large bay windows that sits perched on top of the White House.

One of the most powerful weapons that Starr possessed was the Lewinsky-Tripp audiotapes. Kendall did not know precisely what they contained, though there had been many leaks. He was convinced that Starr would play the actual tapes during the president's grand jury appearance, and he didn't want the president to be surprised. He gathered everything that had been printed or broadcast about the women's conversations. *Newsweek* had printed some verbatim excerpts. Kendall assigned two young women attorneys from his law firm, Williams

& Connolly, to play their roles, one Lewinsky, the other Tripp. They recorded portions of the conversations based on the best information they had. During the preparation sessions, Kendall played the recordings, some running several minutes or more, for the president.

On one, Tripp asks Lewinsky about Clinton. "Well, does he think you're going to tell the truth?"

"No," Lewinsky answers. "Oh, Jesus."

Playing Starr's interrogators, Kendall and Seligman assumed prosecutorial styles, ranging from seductive to combative, to break his defenses. It was brutal. In the president's mind he had not had sexual relations with Lewinsky as defined in the Jones case. Clinton gave ground slowly. There had been some intimate relationship, he admitted finally. The lawyers and the president began to work on how to square that admission with his public denials.

When he heard that Clinton had agreed to testify before Starr's grand jury, Bob Bennett could scarcely believe it. It was madness, he thought. Bennett felt cut off. Either he or one of the other lawyers in his firm participated in the daily White House conference call about the Lewinsky investigation. But discussion focused on what journalists seemed to be working on or were on the verge of reporting. Important matters, such as the July 17 subpoena to the president, were concealed, not addressed until they leaked.

Bennett called Mickey Kantor to express his

concern about the president going before the grand jury.

"He's got to go in," Kantor said. He said the politics and the polling supported it. He wouldn't be any more specific.

"Mickey," Bennett said, "what the fuck are you talking about?"

Kantor wouldn't say.

"I know I'm right on the law and the legal issues," Bennett said. A target should not testify. "But I think I'm also right on the politics."

Because there was an appeal pending in the Jones case, Bennett still had direct access to the president. He called and was given an appointment to see Clinton alone. Bennett didn't want his advice filtered through Kantor or anyone else, and he wished to confront the president directly.

On Wednesday, August 5, he sat across from Clinton.

Mr. President, Bennett said, you should not go to the grand jury, period. To do so would bring the entire Paula Jones case into the criminal realm. Enough of it was there already. He should not appear unless he could testify honestly that there was nothing to the relationship with Lewinsky. If he couldn't, better to take the Fifth Amendment and blame the decision on the lawyers' advice.

Bennett urged the president to write a 10- to 12-page letter stating, "I'm not above the law and I'm not beneath the law," and complain about the investigation of his personal life and the illegal leaks. Then the president should give a public statement blaming the lawyers, saying they had instructed him not to go before the grand jury. He felt strongly about this strategy, felt it in every bone of his body, Bennett said. Testifying would legitimize the grand jury's and Starr's entire Lewinsky investigation. By accepting this process, Clinton would jeopardize the effective efforts that Carville and others had made to undermine Starr.

Bennett felt it was like fly-fishing for trout with light tackle. The trout was a smart customer. He couldn't be horsed in, the line would break. The tension has to be maintained at a certain level at all times or the trout throws the lure. The president's grand jury testimony would remove the pressure, the tension on Starr.

As always, Clinton listened intently, nodding, drawing out the lawyer. It seemed to Bennett that he was inclined to agree, but Bennett knew that Clinton listening was not Clinton agreeing, although it might appear so to anyone who had no experience with him.

Bennett said the president would not be going before amateurs like Jim Fisher of the Jones legal team. Starr would have experienced prosecutors and interrogators in the grand jury to grill him. As Bennett argued, he grew hotter and hotter. By this point he was on fire. "You cannot go into the grand jury," he said loudly, "unless you can go in and answer truthfully and answer all the questions." The Starr team would get specific. What Fisher had not asked would be covered in great and humiliating detail. How would you answer these questions? Bennett asked.

Clinton didn't answer.

Bennett continued to push hard on his argument. It could be a disaster legally and politically with little or no offsetting benefits. Bennett felt he couldn't be more aggressive without becoming disrespectful. Starr had said he wanted to videotape Clinton's grand jury appearance. Bennett said he found the idea unsound. That video would surface somehow, some day. Starr would release it in his report to Congress. What did the president think his enemies would do with that? The testimony could become the president's legacy! The idea of videotape should be a deal-breaker all by itself.

Clinton seemed to respond to this argument a little more.

Even though the president had agreed to testify, he could argue convincingly that the situation had changed, Bennett said. Lewinsky had made the sweetest deal for herself, and her story had immediately leaked. That alone was grounds for canceling.

In the end, Clinton didn't agree or disagree.

Bennett left feeling that he may have scored some points. Maybe the president would find a way or reason to change his mind. He knew that Clinton and Hillary made all the decisions themselves. They were not legal practitioners, and they had little real-world legal experience. Good legal decisions started out by facing the facts, getting all the known facts laid out, and then, and only then, developing the strategy. But all the lawyers, including himself, were giving advice on legal strategy without having the facts. Bennett had a sinking feeling. He also had come to the conclusion that Clinton took his legal advice from the latest polls, and the polls said the president should testify.

Later, Kantor told Bennett on the phone

they were considering a strategy that would make a distinction between sexual intercourse and oral sex.

Bennett was disbelieving.

Kantor said they owed it all to Bennett's objection to the broader definition of sexual relations that the Jones attorneys had presented in Clinton's deposition. Bennett was a genius to have forced a narrower definition, Kantor said.

"I had no plan," Bennett said. "These distinctions are absurd. This crap won't fly with anyone." Bennett said he had been simply mucking up the record, a standard technique.

No, Kantor explained. Technically, the definition of sexual relations used by the Jones lawyers could be read to exclude oral sex. Under the portion of the definition allowed by the judge, Clinton would have had to have contact with Lewinsky's private parts to arouse or gratify her.

"It's fucking nuts," Bennett said. "It's awful, awful advice. I know this business. I'll defer to you on the politics, even though I believe it is crazy fucking politics, but on the legal issue this is just terrible. You can't do this. It's insanity."

Kantor didn't agree.

"How would you answer the question, 'Did she give you a blow job?' " Bennett asked.

Kantor didn't answer.

After the conversation was over, Bennett's wife tried to calm her husband down. "Stop," she said. "It's not your case. Let's go to the movies."

Jack Quinn called the president. He knew that Kendall and Bennett had recommended against the grand jury.

"Don't testify," Quinn also urged. "Don't do it. It will be a disservice to the presidency." The president had a strong separation of powers argument. "They can't constitutionally compel you."

"No one thinks I can get away with it politically," Clinton replied.

The summer became more stressful for the president. He had read some of the histories of the final year of both the Nixon presidency, mired in Watergate, and the Johnson presidency, caught in Vietnam. Clinton realized that Nixon and Johnson had not only lost their presidencies in disgrace, they had almost lost their sanity. He recalled his mother's reaction to Vince Foster's suicide: "Every man has his breaking point. We just don't know where it is." Nixon and Johnson had reached their breaking points, the point where the load on a man could just snap him in half. As Clinton saw it, Starr and his deputies were probing not just to break his presidency but to break him.

"Those fuckers, one of their goals," Clinton told one of his close White House aides, "is to get me to lose it, to blow, to lose my cool, to lose my mind." It was a victory, the president said, he was not going to let "those fuckers" ever have.

On August 6, Monica Lewinsky testified before the grand jury. She stuck to her story. Starr had ten attorneys go through her testimony and attempt to game out what the president might say in response.

Hickman Ewing, the deputy in Arkansas,

came to Washington and assumed the role of Clinton in a series of four-hour sessions. In one, he played Clinton in total denial, refusing to acknowledge anything. Ewing did a great job, but it was clear that total denial would not work. In another, he presented a Clinton refusing to answer anything, citing privacy and the dignity of his office. That didn't work well either. In a third, Ewing had Clinton acknowledging that he had received oral sex from Lewinsky but denying that constituted sexual relations as outlined in the Jones case. That still seemed a stretch.

Starr outlined the strategy he thought they should adopt. "Let's give him the information we have," Starr said. "Let's let him respond." The president surely would give some speeches, but it was going to be his version anyhow, his show. "I do not want to be disrespectful of the president," Starr said.

Clinton continued to prepare with Kendall and Seligman. He worked out a dozen major points or set pieces. After considerable debate, the lawyers agreed that Clinton would read a statement at the beginning. They spent time working out the proper euphemism for the relationship, finally deciding that he would call his conduct with Lewinsky "inappropriate intimate contact." He would acknowledge that it was "wrong" but refuse to answer detailed questions. He would deny that he committed perjury in the Jones civil deposition.

After some ten days of preparation, 40 or so hours, the reality check was nearly finished.

• • •

Late Thursday night, August 13, McCurry received a copy of the lead story in the early editions of the next day's *New York Times*. Headlined "Clinton Weighs Admitting He Had Sexual Contacts," the story said that according to a member of the president's "inner circle," Clinton was considering changing his story and testifying that he had some sort of sexual relationship with Lewinsky.

McCurry was baffled. He spoke with the lawyers—Kendall, Kantor and Ruff. They each denied they were behind the story. The *Times* article had four bylines. McCurry talked with some of the reporters.

"Look, Mike," one of the reporters told the press secretary, "you know we wouldn't have put a story out there unless we were absolutely, positively confident of its truth."

McCurry was going crazy. "Unless Clinton is picking up the phone and calling these guys himself," he told Joe Lockhart, his deputy, "these lawyers for some bizarre reason are just lying to us straight through their teeth."

At Friday's meeting with Ruff and his assistants, McCurry tried again. "Somebody, somewhere, has got a PR strategy here," he said, "and the rest of us would like to know what it is. You know, it's fine if you guys have got a strategy, just tell us what it is so we don't screw it up."

Ruff and the others said they had no idea.

Frustrated to the core, McCurry called Kendall.

"David," he pleaded, "99 percent of Washington believes that we're sending signals out about the president's forthcoming testimony. Can you help me out here?" Did he want the White House and the press secretary to be operating in total darkness?

There was a long pause.

"Mike," Kendall replied carefully, "you'll appreciate this. The last thing I, as his attorney, want is for Ken Starr to have a roadmap into the president's testimony, so I can't tell you where it's coming from, but it's surely not from anyone who is working off the same playbook that I am."

The *Times* story was carefully hedged. At that time, I spoke with someone who could definitively answer questions for the president and the legal team. Not only was the president considering the change of story, I was told, but he had decided to do it. "He has not prepared the family," the person said. "He has got a lot of work to do with the family." Mrs. Clinton "knows, but she doesn't know," the person said. I had to protect my source, but I wrote the story for the *Post*.

"President's Lawyers Brace for Change in Story," said the banner headline in Sunday's *Post*.

That day, Kendall told Ruff for the first time that, yes, the president was going to change his story.

Starr and his prosecutors read the news accounts with great interest. Starr had thought for some time that Clinton was going to have to admit to some sort of relationship, but he didn't know what to make of the news leaks.

• • •

On Monday morning, August 17, Clinton's advisers met to discuss whether the president should give a nationally televised speech after his testimony and what he should say if he did. Kantor and Kendall thought he should attack Starr.

"If you do that," McCurry said, "there's only going to be one thing that's heard about that speech and that's whatever he says about Starr. For what it's worth, my two cents is you're going to screw it up unless you're very factual and straightforward and just say, 'Here's what I said. Here's what I'm going to do.' "

That afternoon, Jackie Bennett, Bittman, Wisenberg and three others from Starr's staff went to the White House. Kendall, in what he called "a walk in the woods," took Starr aside.

"You're going to get what you need," Kendall said. The president was going to read a statement acknowledging "inappropriate intimate contact" with Lewinsky. He was not going to go into detail. "If you try to humiliate and embarrass him, I'll fight you to the knife."

The video hookup to the grand jury was tested. One grand juror was absent—it had been Starr's justification for making a videotape. The grand juror could view the tape later. Eight Starr deputies watched from the grand jury room.

In the Map Room, Clinton was sworn in. Bittman began.

"Mr. President, were you physically intimate with Monica Lewinsky?"

Clinton asked permission to read his statement, which said he had "inappropriate intimate contact" with her. "This is all I will say about the specifics of these particular matters."

The president was able early on to deliver one of his rehearsed set pieces—sexual relations only means intercourse. "I'll bet the grand jurors, if they were talking about two people they know, and said they have a sexual relationship, they meant they were sleeping together; they meant they were having intercourse."

As Bittman attempted to press him on his Jones deposition, in which he'd denied sexual relations, the president launched into a practiced speech about the Jones lawyers. "Their strategy, since they were being funded by my political opponents, was to have this dragnet of discovery.

"How could they know whether there had been any sexual harassment, unless they first knew whether there had been any sex? And so, with that broad mandate limited by time and employment in the federal or state government, they proceeded to cross the country and try to turn up whatever they could..."

"With all respect, Mister...," Bittman attempted to interrupt.

"Now let me finish," Clinton said. "I mean you brought this up." He went on for paragraphs. "I've been subject to quite a lot of illegal leaking, and they had a very determined deliberate strategy, because their real goal was to hurt me. When they knew they couldn't win the lawsuit, they thought, well, maybe we can pummel him." The Jones lawyers and their supporters had a political vendetta against him. "And so they just thought they would take a wrecking ball to me and see if they could do some damage." He returned to the theme repeatedly.

When Bittman turned to the gifts, the president began another speech. "I gave dozens of personal gifts to people last Christmas. I give gifts to people all the time. Friends of mine give me gifts all the time, give me ties, give me books, give me other things. So, it was just not a big deal."

After an hour, the president asked for a ten-minute break.

Wisenberg was up next. He brought up Bob Bennett's statement during the Jones deposition that Lewinsky's affidavit said in effect, "there is absolutely no sex of any kind in any manner, shape or form, with President Clinton." Wisenberg asked, "That statement is a completely false statement?"

Clinton paused briefly and smiled slightly. "It depends on what the meaning of the word 'is' is."

He and Lewinsky had discontinued their intimate relationship for nearly a year.

Round and round they went, debating tenses. Wisenberg asked about the December 19 meeting with Vernon Jordan.

"I do not remember exactly what the nature of the conversation was. I do remember that I told him that there was no sexual relationship between me and Monica Lewinsky, which was true."

Wisenberg reminded Clinton that his Jones

deposition had taken place three weeks after his meeting with Jordan, and yet the president had not remembered the details of that meeting in the deposition.

The Jones lawyers could have asked follow-up questions, Clinton said. It was not his job to do their work for them. "Now, they'd been up all night with Linda Tripp, who had betrayed her friend, Monica Lewinsky, stabbed her in the back and given them all this information....If they wanted to ask me follow-up questions they could. They didn't, I'm sorry. I did the best I could."

Wisenberg pressed again on the same question.

"I didn't have a perfect memory," Clinton said, "of all these events that have now, in the last seven months, since Ms. Lewinsky was kept for several hours by four or five of your lawyers and four or five FBI agents, as if she were a serious felon, these things have become the most important matters in the world. At the moment they were occurring many other things were going on."

If Jordan had testified that Clinton had an extraordinary memory, would Clinton dispute that? Wisenberg inquired.

He would not, Clinton said. "If I could say one thing about my memory," he said. It was time for another soliloquy. "Now, I have been shocked, and so have members of my family and friends of mine, at how many things that I have forgotten in the last six years. I think because of the pressure and the pace and the volume of events in the president's life, compounded by the pressure of your four-year inquiry, and all the other things that have happened, I'm amazed there are lots of times when I literally can't remember last week."

When Wisenberg pressed again, Clinton talked for paragraphs about the political nature of the Jones case—"thanks to Linda Tripp's work with you and with the Jones lawyers."

Wisenberg asked more questions about the Jones deposition.

"My goal in this deposition was to be truthful, but not particularly helpful," Clinton replied.

They called a break at 3:38 p.m. until just after 4 p.m., when Wisenberg said he was going to ask questions that came from the grand jurors. "You referred to what you did with Ms. Lewinsky as inappropriate contact; what do you mean by that?"

"I do not want to discuss something that is intensely painful to me," the president responded. "This has been tough enough already on me and on my family, although I take responsibility for it. I have no one to blame but myself."

"Is oral sex performed on you within that definition?"

"As I understood it, it was not, no."

"The grand jurors would like to know upon what basis, what legal basis you are declining to answer more specific questions?" he asked. Jurors were sending questions by phone during the breaks.

Clinton said the prosecutors would have to ask the questions, as they had with oral sex, and he would answer whether he believed they fell within the Jones definition.

Wisenberg felt he had no alternative, so he went along and asked: "If the person being deposed kissed the breast of another person, would that be in the definition of sexual relations as you understand it when you were under oath in the Jones case?"

"Yes," Clinton testified, "that would constitute contact."

"And you testified that you didn't have sexual relations with Monica Lewinsky in the Jones deposition, under that definition, correct?"

"That's correct, sir," the president replied.

The same with the genitalia? Wisenberg asked.

"Yes, sir."

"So you didn't do any of those things with Monica Lewinsky?"

"You are free to infer that my testimony is that I did not have sexual relations, as I understood this term to be defined," the president said.

"Including touching her breast, kissing her breast, or touching her genitalia?"

"That's correct."

He declined to go further. He looked pained as he answered these questions.

"I need to inform you that the grand jury will consider your not answering the questions more directly in the determination of whether or not they are going to issue another subpoena," Wisenberg said.

Kendall was not surprised. He expected another subpoena.

Questioned again on specifics of the relationship, the president referred to his statement. He said he had read news accounts of what was supposedly said on the Tripp-Lewinsky tapes and what Lewinsky had supposedly testified. "This reminds me, to some extent, of the hearings when Clarence Thomas and Anita Hill were both testifying under oath," Clinton said, beginning his version of Kendall's theory of good faith difference of recollections. "Now, in some rational way, they could not have both been telling the truth, since they had directly different accounts of a shared set of facts. Fortunately, or maybe you think unfortunately, there was no special prosecutor to try to go after one or the other of them, to take sides and try to prove one was a liar. And so Judge Thomas was able to go on and serve on the Supreme Court. What I learned from that, I can tell you that I was a citizen out there just listening. And when I heard both of them testify, what I believed after it was over, I believed that they both thought they were telling the truth.

"This is—you're dealing with, in some way, the most mysterious area of human life. I'm doing the best I can to give you honest recollections."

"Mr. President..." Wisenberg tried to get in a question.

Clinton went on and on and concluded, "So maybe Ms. Lewinsky believes she's telling the truth."

Wisenberg asked if Clinton saw a problem with having his powerful friend Vernon Jordan helping someone "who had some kind of sex with you" get a job and a lawyer at a time when the person had been subpoenaed in the Jones case?

"No," Clinton said. "Would you like to know why?"

Wisenberg said he would.

Clinton had another rehearsed speech ready. "I had already proved in two ways that I was not trying to influence her testimony. I didn't order her to be hired at the White House. I could have done so. I wouldn't do it." Second, he didn't see her as often as she wanted. "And thirdly," he said.

Wisenberg tried to interrupt.

"Let me finish the sentence," Clinton said. It was two long paragraphs. "I knew that the minute there was no longer any contact, she would talk about this. She would have to. She couldn't help it. It was, it was a part of her psyche. So, I had put myself at risk, sir."

"It's time for a break," Wisenberg said.

After a 15-minute break, Kendall announced that they had one hour and five minutes left of the four-hour session.

Jackie Bennett asked, "The grand jury would like to know, Mr. President, why it is that you think that oral sex performed on you does not fall within the definition of sexual relations as used in your deposition."

"If the deponent is the person who has oral sex performed on him, then the contact is with not anything on that list, but with the lips of another person. It seems to be self-evident." Clinton reminded everyone that he had read the definition carefully and had thought about it. "And I had to admit under this definition that I'd actually had sexual relations with Gennifer Flowers. Now, I would rather have taken a whipping than done that." He said the Jones lawyers were trying to make him bleed. "I'd give anything in the world not to be here talking about it. I'd be giving—I'd give anything in the world not to have to admit what I've had to admit today."

With 12 minutes left, Starr took over the questioning and asked three questions about executive privilege. "In none of those cases did I actually have any worry about what the people involved would say," Clinton said. Invoking executive or attorney-client privilege was a matter of principle. "I did not want to put the presidency at risk of being weakened as an institution, without having those matters litigated."

At the end, Clinton said, "Most of my time and energy in the last five and a half years have been devoted to my job. I have also had to contend with things no previous president has ever had to contend with." The Jones case had cost him a fortune and Starr's inquiry had gone on for a long time and also cost a great deal of money, he said. "And, during this whole time, I have tried as best I could to keep my mind on the job the American people gave me."

The prosecutors and the grand jury asked for more time. Kendall said no, and the session concluded at 6:25 p.m.

Clinton shook Starr's hand and put his other hand on Starr's shoulder.

Hillary had sent word to Carville that she needed him back at the White House. Carville returned from Brazil, where he was consulting in a campaign, and reached the White House about 5 p.m. He was one of the first to see Clinton emerge from the Map Room.

"I couldn't tell what the grand jurors' response

was," the president said. He had felt cut off. It was the only time he had performed for hours without being able to gauge the audience response.

Starr and his deputies met about 7 p.m. in the fourth-floor conference room. They were exhausted. Wisenberg and Emmick were down in the dumps. Perhaps Clinton had outfoxed them. He had constructed artful responses to acknowledge what he had to face and dodged the rest. "He did a superb job," Wisenberg said. Clinton hadn't provided the kind of testimony that contradicted the other witnesses—Currie or Jordan. The only dispute with Lewinsky concerned whether he had touched her in a sexual way.

Starr said he thought Clinton had been impressive. But the way Clinton parsed the definition of sexual relations was not going to work. "That's sophistry," he said.

There was some criticism that Bittman had not been aggressive enough in challenging the president.

The point of the grand jury appearance, Bittman said, was to let Clinton explain, lock down his position under oath. It was not to get in his face.

Starr agreed. He said they had done as well as possible with a sophisticated witness.

The president had the most difficulty answering the questions about whether he ever touched Lewinsky. They agreed it was absurd for Clinton to claim he had an exclusively one-way sexual relationship. But that way he was able to acknowledge an inappropriate relationship, explain the semen on the dress and say he had not perjured himself. He had denied the obvious touching and tried to ride it through. On one level it seemed trivial, but it was so revealing, so cynical and calculated.

Bakaly, who had watched from the grand jury room, wondered if Clinton were not the perfect liar. He wanted to lift the group up, so he said he thought it had gone well. "We really need to get the transcript and look at it," he said. There were some strong elements.

What next? What did they need to ask Lewinsky?

The details of the touching were already in the FBI reports of the extensive interviews with her, but Kavanaugh noted they had learned painfully in the Foster suicide investigation that the FBI 302s were often wrong and had gotten them in trouble. "You can't rely on the 302s as evidence," he said. "We've got to get her sworn testimony."

Starr and the others agreed. They decided to call Lewinsky back before the grand jury right away.

Without Starr, about ten of the attorneys went to dinner at Sam & Harry's Restaurant, where they had a private room. Bakaly told them that he had heard from a reporter that Clinton was going to give a speech to the nation and that he was going to be contrite.

Later, Carville saw Hillary in the solarium. She seemed torn up. "It's a very difficult time," she said to him. He was going to have to help her get through this mess. She looked straight at him. "I hope we can count on you to help *us*."

Clinton took a shower and went to caucus in the same solarium with his advisers on what kind of speech to give. He was tight, tired, and to some of them he seemed angry.

"These are sick folks," Clinton said, referring to his interrogators.

A speech to the nation was still in a tentative stage. Kantor was coordinating various approaches. Clinton was ready to attack Starr. Kendall and Kantor agreed. Others had drafts of a short mea culpa speech that expressed remorse and asked for forgiveness.

"Do you want to go ahead with this?" McCurry asked the president, adding that it had already been a long day.

"Yeah," Clinton said, "we should go ahead and do it."

"Say what you feel," Hillary told him, "what you want to say."

Clinton took the drafts and ideas and ordered a final blending. He went back to the Map Room. Begala arranged the clip-on microphone on Clinton's aqua-blue and silver tie. The president was nervous and kept asking if it was time to go live. Told it wasn't, he flipped his head back as if he were trying to shake off something. Just after 10 p.m. he began:

"Good evening. This afternoon in this room, from this chair, I testified before the Office of Independent Counsel and a grand jury. I answered their questions truthfully, including questions about my private life, questions no American citizen would ever want to answer."

In the January Jones case deposition, he said he had given "legally accurate" answers. But he did in fact have a relationship with Lewinsky that was "not appropriate" and was "wrong." He added, "I misled people, including even my wife. I deeply regret that." He was as unrelaxed as he had ever been on television as president. He was angry.

"This has gone on too long, cost too much, and hurt too many innocent people. Now this matter is between me, the two people I love most, my wife and our daughter, and our God....I intend to reclaim my family life for my family. It's nobody's business but ours. Even presidents have private lives. It is time to stop the pursuit of personal destruction and the prying into private lives and get on with our national life."

"Well, that wasn't very contrite!" shouted Jackie Bennett from Sam & Harry's private room, where the lawyers were watching. Several joked that their questions to the president had been too hard.

Carville appeared on *Larry King Live* that night as one of the lone voices defending Clinton unconditionally. "You judge somebody by the context of everything that they've done, and this man's had a hard day. I'm not going to jump on his back." Carville said Clinton's sex life should not be criminalized. "This is hardly the first powerful brilliant man that has made an error in judgment when it comes to a woman," Carville said. He said the president would spend some time in "the woodshed" on vacation with his family in Martha's Vineyard, Massachusetts, because of the affair. Hillary was upset. "To paraphrase Queen Victoria, I don't think she is amused," Carville said.

36

KENDALL REALIZED that he would never in his career have a witness as good, or clever, as Clinton. The president had turned it into a four-hour debate. The session was a laboratory test of Kendall's basic view of the case: the average person, the guy in the bowling alley, as he thought of it, already believed that there was sex but no obstruction of justice. It wasn't a lofty view, but that's where Kendall hoped public opinion remained.

Starr returned to work at 5:30 a.m. the next morning. He told his staff that the target date for the impeachment referral to Congress was still August 31. With Lewinsky and the president on the record before the grand jury, they could now use their firsthand testimony as grounds for impeachment. The information from the Tripp tapes and other documents could be moved mostly into the footnotes.

Hillary had her press secretary issue a public statement that the first lady was committed to her marriage and loved her husband. The statement also said, "She believes in the president and her love for him is compassionate and steadfast, and she's very uncomfortable with her personal life being made public." The media was playing the Hillary story second only to the details of the president's behavior and his acknowledgment about Lewinsky. Hillary was going down in the world record book for public marital humiliation.

From the White House, the president called key Democrats who were friends. The news was not good. The attack on Starr and the appeal for presidential privacy had not worked.

On an August 18 helicopter ride out to Andrews Air Force Base to catch a plane to Martha's Vineyard, the Clintons basically were not speaking to each other. McCurry and Doug Sosnik, the political aide, were traveling with them. Sosnik found it brutal, chilly, like sitting in the middle of an ice cube.

McCurry, whose job included studying the president's demeanor and moods, noticed that Clinton looked as if he didn't know what to expect from his own family. Hillary appeared drained. Chelsea looked so sad that McCurry thought he did not want to ever see a kid look like that again in his life.

"You guys need to help me out," McCurry said, trying to fill the void, comfortably going into his chatterbox mode, "I've never been to Martha's Vineyard before. What should I do?"

Chelsea told him her plans, as did Hillary. The president kind of entered the conversation, getting everyone through the helicopter ride.

On the plane, Clinton read a mystery novel, Hillary took a nap.

In the early evening, Clinton, Hillary and Chelsea stepped off Air Force One in the Vineyard. Vernon Jordan, wearing a golf hat, greeted the president at the bottom of the steps with a giant bear hug.

The next day was Clinton's 52nd birthday. It was one of his darkest and most lonely days. He went for a five-mile walk on the beach, accompanied only by his dog Buddy.

One of the few people the president spoke with regularly was Terrence "Terry" McAuliffe, the chief fund-raiser for the Democrats. McAuliffe, 41, a boyish, outgoing entrepreneur, was Clinton's primary money man. Even though Clinton had no political campaign in his future, fund-raising was more important than ever. McAuliffe, the biggest fund-raiser for the Democrats in the 1990s, was in charge of raising money for the Clintons' legal defense fund, which had recently collected a much needed $2.2 million. McAuliffe was also going to be responsible for raising $125 million for the Clinton presidential library—a key component to establishing Clinton's historical legacy.

McAuliffe, the first cheerleader, tried to keep Clinton in a fighting mood. "I'm with you," he said in a phone conversation. "People support you, love you, sir. We're going to get through this."

"I fucked it up," the president said. "I was mad. You won't believe the questions they asked me.... A fucking witch-hunt." Despondent, brooding, Clinton referred to reports that he was in a state of denial. "Goddamn it, I'm not in denial. I got my ass kicked. There's no denial here."

McAuliffe was planning to come to the Vineyard for three days. The president and McAuliffe had hoped to hit the links together. No, the president now said, there was going to be no golf on this vacation. Hillary wasn't objecting, but the political advisers were. They had agreed that the president had to be seen taking his medicine—the isolation of contrition or redemption or whatever it might be. Clinton indicated that his own political gut told him the same.

For McAuliffe, a vacation without golf was almost unthinkable. He decided to cancel his trip to the Vineyard. There was no real point. He realized that he was probably the last guy that the president wanted to know the true facts about Lewinsky. In some respects the serious fund-raising was in the future. Money and a dedicated fund-raiser were going to be as important as ever to Clinton. "I am his future," McAuliffe believed.

McCurry finally had some time alone with Hillary in Martha's Vineyard. She had been instrumental in his hiring. He had always tried to support her.

Showing emotion, the first lady said to McCurry that there was no way to understand what she was going through. As a woman, she said, as a spouse, and as a mother, it was complex. She offered a glimpse into her pain and asked five questions:

"Do I feel angry?"

"Do I feel betrayed?"

"Do I feel lonely?"

"Do I feel exasperated?"

"And humiliated?"

McCurry gasped, nearly whispered thank you. There it all was in those five questions. This great public drama was, to the first lady, something more real and personal—anger, betrayal, loneliness, exasperation and humiliation. McCurry's fondness and empathy for her ascended off the charts. The one-dimensional portraits of Hillary in the media—whatever version anyone might pick—were unfair, shallow, missed the layers. Here was this woman, almost frail and breakable, but still standing, mustering whatever dignity was left her. Any question of punishment, which McCurry felt the president richly deserved, seemed beside the point in the face of her endurance. Could there be nobility amid this squalor? She was there before him wrestling with the enormity—so much more complex than anyone had imagined.

In her heart, she said, she still believed in the work Bill was doing as president.

The question of forgiveness arose.

No, she said, she was not at the point emotionally where she *wanted* to forgive him.

Traditionally in his years as president, Clinton had celebrated his birthday with a giant bash, usually a fund-raiser or a large dinner. But that evening, Wednesday, August 19, his birthday, Clinton was only going to Vernon and Ann Jordan's place on the Vineyard.

"Is she coming?" one of Jordan's friends asked.

"Oh yeah, oh yeah," Jordan replied. It was going to be just the two couples. The good news was that Chelsea was joining them as a welcome fifth person. The bad news was that after the dinner of barbecued chicken and coconut cake, Chelsea left to see friends.

Back at their vacation residence, the president was on the phone until about 3 a.m. He was going to order the U.S. military to attack targets in Afghanistan and Sudan used by the Osama bin Ladin terrorist organization. The network was suspected of masterminding the bombings of two U.S. embassies in Africa earlier in the month.

Later in August, Clinton called Carville from the Vineyard.

"Good God," the president said. He was as down as Carville had ever heard him.

Carville tried to reassure him. They had to reinforce the political imperatives—maintain their standing in the polls, hold the Democrats. He praised Clinton's accomplishments, the support of world leaders.

Finally, the president admitted his chief concern.

"She is not going to forgive me," Clinton said.

Mark Penn, Clinton's pollster, told a dozen of Clinton's senior advisers that roughly 60 to 70 percent of the people blamed Starr for the prolonged investigation. About 60 to 70 percent thought the president's speech was sufficient and they did not want more from him on the topic. Although the polling ratings of Clinton's personal character were relatively low, that always had been the case.

Lanny Davis was one of the few Clinton supporters who had taken to the airwaves to defend him. On Friday, August 21, about 12:30 p.m., the president reached Davis at his office at George Washington University, where Davis was teaching a course titled "Scandal, Damage Control and American Politics."

Clinton thanked him and asked for a candid assessment.

Davis, who had made the rounds of nearly every television talk show, said it was ugly out there, as the president surely knew. The speech had not worked. "You were tired and you were in distress." The judgments the president made would not necessarily have been the same if he had had a good night's sleep.

Clinton did not agree. He had to use the speech to protest the unfairness, call Starr what he was. Even his own mention of Starr set Clinton off. He immediately let loose about the ignominies he was suffering. The FBI director's name came up. In a confidential memo to Attorney General Reno, Freeh had argued for the appointment of yet another independent counsel to investigate Clinton's 1996 campaign fund-raising. Freeh's memo had leaked. Charles LaBella, Reno's handpicked chief of the Justice Department's own campaign finance task force, had agreed with Freeh and also had argued for giving the inquiry to an independent counsel. Davis and Clinton agreed that the FBI director was so totally immune from any political control that he had become like the legendary baron, FBI Director J. Edgar Hoover.

"Louis Freeh is a goddamn, fucking asshole!" Clinton said.

Freeh's alienation with Clinton was so great that the FBI director refused to have a permanent White House access badge. When one had been sent to him, he sent it back with a note saying he would come as a visitor. He was the only major administration figure without a White House pass.

Clinton's distaste for Freeh and Starr was not the issue, Davis argued. "You're acting like a defendant and not like a president. You're listening to lawyers rather than to your political gut and to your political advisers. This must change."

Davis told Clinton to return to that basic strategy of telling the whole story, disclosing everything. Get credit and force everyone to embrace the presumption that the situation is not so bad, he said.

Give me an example, the president said.

Release all your grand jury testimony, even a full transcript of the entire four or five hours if you can.

"You really think I should?" Clinton asked.

"Here's the reason you shouldn't," Davis said. "There's probably really bad stuff in that grand jury testimony, and really embarrassing stuff, stuff that could really get you into trouble. No one is ever going to find out, of course. It would never leak. It won't be in the Starr report to Congress."

The president seemed to get the point but only promised to speak to Kendall about the issue.

On August 25, House Minority Leader Richard A. Gephardt, a Missouri Democrat, said Clinton's behavior was "reprehensible." He was out on a national campaign swing to help Democrats in important House races that would be decided in ten weeks. The top Democrat in the House spoke almost glowingly about the constitutional importance of impeachment as a test for the House. He did not rule it out.

Clinton was furious when he read the remarks. He made a late night call to McAuliffe. They agreed that Gephardt wanted to be president so badly that he would stab anyone and everyone in the back.

McAuliffe, who had been Gephardt's fund-raiser in 1988 when Gephardt had run unsuccessfully for president, called his old friend.

"Dick," McAuliffe said, "explain to me how this helps you win House seats?"

Hillary considered the vacation on the Vineyard the dark days. With some women friends she tried to sort it out. She insisted that she did not view Lewinsky as a real threat. It was only sex, not partnership. She had the partnership—the real friendship and love with him. Her friends thought that Hillary had used to be a wallflower. She had blossomed in the White House years. Several close friends believed that Hillary filled so many roles in her husband's life: the mother he didn't have any longer, the sister who had never existed, the chief adviser he didn't have any more and perhaps had never had. She was the smartest person in the room. Incongruously, her humiliation gave her status—in the relationship and in the world. Now she could do anything she wanted.

Hillary retreated to her religious and spiritual convictions. "I've got to take this," she told one friend. "I have to take this punishment. I don't know why God has chosen this for me. But

He has, and it will be revealed to me. God is doing this, and He knows the reason. There is some reason."

37

THE PROSECUTORS brought Lewinsky back on August 26. Cacheris took her over to Starr's office about noon. They met with Karin Immergut, an experienced prosecutor Starr had hired from Oregon.

"Why do you need this?" Cacheris asked. "We kind of agreed on only one day of grand jury appearance."

Immergut said they required a sworn statement or deposition in lieu of another grand jury appearance. They wanted details about the sexual relationship.

Why?

"She's told this story," Immergut said, "and we want it under oath."

Immergut, Mary Anne Wirth and Lewinsky went into the conference room. The only other person was a female court reporter. Cacheris waited outside and read magazines.

Immergut produced a chart of the dates when Lewinsky had sexual contact with the president. She said she wanted to get into some more detail about each incident. She asked Lewinsky what part of her body the president touched, what part of his body he used to touch her, when he touched her, what was unzipped and unbuttoned, and how many times she was touched, kissed or fondled.

"Oh God," Lewinsky said at one point. At another she said, "It's just hard thinking my dad might see this."

The narrative of the Clinton-Lewinsky relationship that a team in Starr's office had worked on for months had grown to more than 200 pages, with 1,000 footnotes.

Brett Kavanaugh now thought they had a case, given the testimony of Lewinsky and Clinton. He and William Kelley, a Notre Dame law professor and former law clerk to Starr, were spending day and night drafting specific grounds for possible impeachment. They had come up with 11—all tied to Clinton's lying in the Jones deposition, before the grand jury, and his alleged attempts to obstruct justice with Lewinsky, Vernon Jordan and Betty Currie.

When they saw the narrative that the team had produced, Kavanaugh and Kelley went to Starr to object. It had grown into an explicit account, sexual encounter by sexual encounter. They had moral, not legal objections. There was detail that was not needed. Kavanaugh pointed out that they should not be trapped by earlier drafts, when Clinton was still denying any relationship with Lewinsky. They didn't need to prove what Clinton no longer denied. The grounds section they were drafting was going to relate all the evidence to specific charges of perjury and obstruction. Each piece of evidence—admittedly some of it salacious—was going to be linked to a specific charge or ground for impeachment in their section, a more classic and traditional approach, much like an expanded indictment. The narrative was extraneous.

"No," Starr said, "we need to have an encyclopedia. It will show all the information. It will show how much work we did."

Kavanaugh was concerned that Starr thought it was the catalogue of Clinton's sexual behavior that provided a basis for recommending that Clinton should be bounced out of office, rather than the alleged crimes. The narrative was going to give ammunition to Starr's critics that he was a sex-crazed prosecutor.

All the attorneys continued to discuss the role of the independent counsel in an impeachment. Was it to remove Clinton from office, try to convict him as a regular prosecutor might? Or was it to provide information to the House? Jackie Bennett, Bittman and Wisenberg argued that there were crimes and that impeachment was the proper vehicle to try a president.

"The narrative shows how pathetic Clinton is," Kavanaugh argued, "that he needs therapy, not removal. It's a sad story. Our job is not to get Clinton out. It is just to give information."

Starr was becoming increasingly hard-line.

In late August, Kavanaugh and Kelley proposed to Starr that their grounds section be placed before the long narrative in the formal referral document. That would emphasize the grounds, not the lascivious narrative, which had expanded to novel length. The narrative was called "Nature of President Clinton's Relationship with Monica Lewinsky." But the sex was not the reason to recommend impeachment. The crimes were the basis—the lies, the perjury and the president's efforts to obstruct the Jones case and Starr's grand jury inquiry.

Starr rejected their suggestion. "I love the narrative!" Starr said.

Senator Joseph I. Lieberman, the Connecticut Democrat who was the informal rabbi to Clinton and the Senate, was troubled by Clinton's relationship with Lewinsky. As a Yale Law student, Clinton had worked on Lieberman's successful race for the Connecticut Senate in the early 1970s, and the two talked often. They were ideological allies from the centrist New Democrat wing of the party. They spoke frequently by phone at night. Clinton at times woke up Lieberman from a deep sleep. Lieberman joked that he felt like a fireman.

In the late summer, when Lieberman spoke with Clinton, he found the president in a dangerous self-denial. According to the president, the scandal was everyone else's fault—Starr's, the Republicans', the scandalmongering media's, Tripp's.

Lieberman tried to tell the president that he had missed an opportunity in his August 17 speech. He should have acknowledged his wrongdoing more fully, apologized, sought forgiveness.

Clinton disagreed.

Lieberman began drafting a long, highly critical speech. He could not allow the Democratic Party to cede the moral high ground to the Republicans. The White House got word and tried to persuade him to hold off. Lieberman said no.

On Thursday, September 3, just before the long Labor Day weekend, Lieberman went to the floor of the nearly empty Senate chamber and delivered a 24-minute speech admonishing Clinton for "disgraceful" and "immoral" behavior.

"It is wrong and unacceptable, and should be followed by some measure of public rebuke and accountability." Many had recommended that Congress formally censure the president for his behavior. But Lieberman said consideration of censure was premature. They should await Starr's report. He added, "Talk of impeachment and resignation at this time is unjust and unwise."

Two key Senate Democrats who had forced Clinton in 1994 to seek a Whitewater special counsel, Pat Moynihan of New York and Bob Kerrey of Nebraska, rose on the Senate floor to embrace Lieberman's speech and offer stinging words of their own.

During Watergate, a key turning point had been when senators in Nixon's own party had begun abandoning him. Clinton's advisers worried that Lieberman's remarks would start an avalanche of defections among Democrats.

The president was in Ireland. Asked by reporters what he thought of Lieberman's speech, an unusually subdued Clinton replied, "Basically I agree with what he said. I've already said that I made a bad mistake, it was indefensible, and I'm sorry about it....I'm very sorry about it."

The statement was Clinton's first public apology.

Clinton played golf with McAuliffe at the Army & Navy Club on Labor Day, September 7. Clinton hit exceptionally well, and McAuliffe was amazed the president could find the concentration. On the 18th hole, a short par 3, Clinton hit a six-iron within several feet of the pin and putted it in for a birdie. About 100 people watched from around the hole and cheered. Under Clinton's highly suspect and loose scoring, he shot an 80, one of his best scores ever.

Kendall was at work Labor Day drafting a lawsuit to stop Starr from sending a referral to Congress. He had researched the Independent Counsel Act, and it was clear to him that its purpose in a possible impeachment was to endorse what Judge Sirica had done in Watergate. In 1974, when Special Prosecutor Jaworski sent his information to the House, he had Judge Sirica review it to ensure that it "contained no recommendations, advice or judgment that would infringe on the prerogatives of the legislative branch," Kendall wrote. Unfortunately, the drafting of section 595(c) of the act was broad and fuzzy, Kendall thought, directing an independent counsel to forward "any" information that "may" constitute possible grounds for impeachment. It was enough for Starr to drive a truck through. Kendall didn't rate the chances of stopping or delaying the referral as high, but he finished the lawsuit and had the certificate of service on Starr ready to go.

Both Gephardt and Ruff argued that a lawsuit wouldn't work and would look as if the president were afraid. No one on the Clinton team, including Kendall, wanted to do anything that didn't have the political support of the Democrats. So the lawsuit was not filed. Instead, Kendall sent a letter to Starr requesting a week to review a draft referral.

Starr responded with a five-page letter the next day, September 8, stating that one apparent purpose of the law was to eliminate the issues "that complicated the delivery of Mr. Jaworski's report in the Watergate investigation." Citing the dictionary, Starr made it clear he read the statute broadly "to comfortably encompass some analysis of the underlying facts" and to "oblige the independent counsel to exercise judgment."

Kendall had no doubt Starr was going to send a referral. He was hearing through the legal grapevine that it would come in about a week. Anticipating the central allegations, Kendall and a team of lawyers from his law firm and the White House began drafting a written rebuttal.

Jack Quinn was keeping in close touch with Vice President Gore from his 12th-floor Washington office at the law firm of Arnold & Porter. Gore had expressed a welter of feelings about the scandal. On one hand it conceivably could elevate him to the presidency, on the other it could inflict a deep political wound on him as Clinton's number two. Gore said he felt his honor was at stake, and he had to remain loyal. Clinton had given him unprecedented authority as vice president and the two had become friends. He could not back away from the president or be seen as backing away, he said. He made it clear that he did not understand the sexual relationship with Lewinsky at all. He was baffled that Clinton would take the risk. His wife, Tipper, however, was unforgiving of Clinton, and Gore said he kept hearing about it at home. Overall, Gore seemed determined to remain stoic. "I'm powerless over this situation," he told Quinn, "and I can't try to deal with what I have no control over."

The president, meanwhile, had told his lawyers and political advisers that he knew he was going to have to make a greater acknowledgment of wrongdoing and apologize formally. The August 17 speech disaster and Lieberman's rebuke, he feared, could start a movement against him. He wanted to find a natural setting that was dramatic but not staged. One of his calls after Labor Day for advice was to Quinn.

Quinn encouraged him to apologize in biblical terms, to quote from scripture. The president, he noted, knew the language of the fundamentalist Christian community well, and he should use it. "Dig deep, speak contritely and publicly," Quinn recommended. "Lawyers don't give you what you need."

Conversation turned to a possible new chief of staff. Quinn said since the battle was moving to Congress, the president needed a former House member or senator as chief of staff, someone like Howard Baker, the former Republican majority leader, who had gone to help President Reagan in the middle of Iran-contra. Quinn suggested former Democratic Majority Leader George Mitchell or somebody like him as an ideal candidate for chief of staff or special counsel defending the president. Mitchell would be important in any role. "You need George Mitchell or his like to stand shoulder to shoulder with you," Quinn said. "You do not need to get him to take a job, you just want him visibly advising you and supporting you."

Clinton indicated he was going to talk with Mitchell.

Quinn asked how everything else was going.

"You know," the president said, "there are even rumors out there about a second intern."

Quinn was aware of the rumors.

"It's ridiculous," the president said, scoffing and deriding the possibility. He thanked Quinn and hung up.

Clinton's denial was unequivocal, but Quinn had heard that before. He could imagine Clinton quibbling along the lines, "Well, it depends on how you define intern."

The morning of September 9 was D-Day for Starr, the latest final deadline for completion of the referral. As far as Starr was concerned, this was the last opportunity to deliver their findings to Congress without seeming to interfere with the coming election.

Worried that Kendall would go to court to try to delay the referral and force the issue into the 1998 election cycle or beyond, Starr had one of his attorneys prepare and have ready a motion to file in court to oppose any steps that Kendall might take or motions he might file to interfere.

About 9 a.m., Lewinsky's lawyers paid a visit to Starr's office. They had forced a meeting after learning that Starr planned to send the Tripp tapes to Congress as part of his referral. Hoffman and Lewinsky had listened to the 14 hours of Tripp tapes over a three-day period. Lewinsky had made some outrageous statements that would be embarrassing for her.

Cacheris, Stein and Hoffman sat down with Starr, Bittman and Immergut.

There was derogatory information about the family, nicknames Monica used for family members, Cacheris and Stein said. There were rank sexual references in maybe a dozen places, all of which had nothing to do with Starr's investigation. None should go in the material Starr was sending to Congress, they argued.

"We don't want to leave stuff out because it will look like we are concealing or not giving them all of the facts," Starr said as he folded his hands and rubbed them together. All the truth and all the facts need to come out, Starr said. Details were part of the story.

Cacheris and Stein asked about a discussion Lewinsky and Tripp made on the tapes about a tomato and a penis. It was a joke the two women were making. It's not at all relevant. It doesn't connect to anything. These were among the obvious things that did not belong in any report to Congress.

"I believe we can remove the reference to genitalia and the to-MA-to," Starr said.

Starr said the other items would remain. He had to be thorough and comprehensive.

"I know we can't get all of the fucks out of this," Sydney Hoffman said, "but we at least ought to remove the personal items."

"I don't think we can remove all of the F-words," Starr answered prissily.

Cacheris and Stein laughed. Hoffman was more offended.

Starr said he would leave the detailed negotiating to Immergut.

Hoffman and Immergut eventually agreed to exclude some more of the information the Lewinsky lawyers found objectionable, including the nicknames that she used for family members. Immergut insisted on keeping in Monica's discussion of six boyfriends and her evaluations of them.

The goal had been to deliver the referral that morning, but these last-minute changes delayed the process. The prosecutor's lawyers were tired, operating on little sleep. Tensions were high. Starr had read through the entire referral a number of times, giving or withholding his approval for all the changes. The referral language was getting stronger. Sam Dash came in for the final review.

"The president repeatedly invoked the executive privilege to conceal evidence of his personal misconduct from the grand jury," Dash read of the 11th ground advocating Clinton's possible removal from office. It wasn't strong enough, he felt. He called over to Kavanaugh, who had written and edited the section. You've got to put in an "unlawfully," Dash said.

"Unlawful?" Kavanaugh asked. "There's no law being violated here. How can it be called unlawful?"

Dash insisted. He said Kavanaugh had to make two other changes. The report had to call the president's claims of executive privilege for five White House officials "patently groundless," and it had to say Clinton's assertion of privilege for his aide Nancy Hernreich was "frivolous."

Kavanaugh felt Dash was throwing his weight around unfairly. He appealed to Starr, who met with Dash in private. Dash threatened to quit if his suggestions were not followed.

"Make the changes," Starr told Kavanaugh. He couldn't afford to have his ethics adviser resigning on the most important day of his investigation.

Kavanaugh did as he was told.

Just after 3 p.m., the report was ready to go. Two copies of the final edited versions were run off on the office word processor: a 252-page narrative that included 1,123 footnotes and a 162-page section with 488 footnotes on the grounds for possible impeachment. A 16-page table of contents, chronology and table of names was included, as well as a 21-page introduction and the last page, which Starr signed. The total was 452 pages, three-hole-punched and put in a three-ring binder.

Two copies of the supplementary material, documents, FBI interviews, grand jury testimony and the Tripp-Lewinsky tapes were packed up and sealed in boxes to accompany the referral—18 boxes per set.

Starr wanted one copy of the referral and one set of the 18 boxes for the Republican majority and another for the Democratic minority. In a letter to Gingrich and Gephardt, Starr distinguished the 452-page referral from the supplementary material.

"The contents of the referral may not be

publicly disclosed unless and until authorized by the House of Representatives," he wrote, essentially inviting release of the document. "Many of the supporting materials contain information of a personal nature that I respectfully urge the House to treat as confidential."

At 3:45 p.m., Jackie Bennett called the House sergeant-at-arms and the House Judiciary Committee staffs. The report was on the way. Bennett said two vans, one blue and one white, would be at the front door of the House side of the Capitol in about 15 minutes. Television networks covered the arrival of the vans live at 4 p.m. The House sergeant-at-arms reloaded the boxes into Chevy Suburbans and sent the evidence to the Gerald R. Ford House Office Building.

Charles Bakaly and Bob Bittman walked to the steps of the Capitol.

"As required by the Ethics in Government Act and with the authorization of the court supervising independent counsels," Bakaly said, "the Office of Independent Counsel submitted a referral to the House of Representatives containing substantial and credible information that may constitute grounds for impeachment of the president of the United States." He said any further action was up to the Congress. "We have fulfilled our duty." It was the sound bite broadcast around the world.

Bakaly walked away from the cameras worried about his two children, ages eight and nine. He was supposed to pick them up at their school, but the delay had left him stranded.

Instead, he had sent a chauffeured sedan that Starr used to pick them up so he could make the announcement. He wondered what their reaction would be when a stranger showed up at school instead of him.

That evening, Bakaly took his children out to dinner at the Capital Grille four blocks from Starr's offices on Pennsylvania Avenue. A loud cheer arose from one section of the restaurant as he entered.

Terry McAuliffe was sitting in another section of the restaurant. He glanced up and instantly recognized they were cheering for Bakaly. He was with a group of Democratic fundraisers he was trying to keep happy in these trying times. He couldn't believe the celebration for Bakaly and the way the tables had been turned. It seemed like only yesterday that McAuliffe, who had been the chairman of Clinton's second inaugural, was riding down the middle of this same Pennsylvania Avenue. As chairman he had led the Inaugural Parade, seated in the first car with his family, proud and along with Clinton on top of the world. The cheering had been for them. No longer. Now with the scandal McAuliffe's wife Dorothy had half-humorously issued a personal definition of sexual relations: "Honey, kissing on the lips as far as I'm concerned is adultery. Just remember."

Over at his table, Bakaly was experiencing immense relief. He had felt under siege for so many months that he believed that the evidence would be safer with Congress. There, he hoped, the facts would be judged on their merits, rendering the White House–Kendall attacks less effective.

· · ·

Representative Henry Hyde, the Republican chairman of the House Judiciary Committee, sat in his congressional office nibbling on a doctor-forbidden chocolate chip cookie. Hyde, 74, weighed nearly 300 pounds. His doctor was trying to save Hyde's life by getting his weight down. All summer Hyde had expected that Starr would send a formal referral to the House with possible impeachment information. Hyde considered Kenneth Starr a serious person and a good lawyer who would not spend his time chasing shadows.

Hyde had said for months that he didn't want to preside over a partisan witch-hunt. Republicans had played key roles in Congress's impeachment investigation of Nixon. A serious impeachment investigation of Clinton would require similar support from some of the Democrats. But Hyde wasn't getting to first base with them. Hyde had a number of other serious problems. The Republican Party, especially in the House, was leaderless. Speaker Newt Gingrich, himself fined because of an ethics investigation, would never rehabilitate himself, Hyde believed. Never. Dick Armey, the acerbic Republican majority leader, was inadequate. The confrontational whip, Tom DeLay, was less than adequate. The bottom line was that there was little political muscle in the party, which gave Hyde unusual power.

Hyde had a reputation for fairness, but he was a Republican partisan. Using his big booming voice, giant physical presence and occasional eloquence, he promoted primarily the interests of his party. "Maybe we will cut Clinton down some," he said. He half-joked that his first witness could be Gennifer Flowers. He didn't want his committee to drive any impeachment. He would respond only and exclusively to Starr's report. Obviously the president was hiding a lot. The question would be simple if Starr had come up with hard evidence of crimes. It would rally and unite the Republicans.

Clinton asked for forgiveness and the support of his cabinet on Thursday, September 10. With tears in his eyes he said he would spend the rest of his life trying to redeem himself.

Secretary of Health and Human Services Donna Shalala said harshly that he had a responsibility to provide moral leadership.

Clinton defended himself.

After the long meeting, Clinton hugged Shalala.

"You're always on my ass," he said.

"Yes," she said, "and about the right things."

Hyde and John Conyers, the Michigan Democrat who headed the minority on Judiciary, had agreed to meet with Clinton's lawyers at 2 p.m. that afternoon. Kendall and Ruff arrived in Hyde's office. To the discomfort of the others, Hyde and Kendall both lit up cigars. Kendall was hoping to bond with the chairman. He had been up until 2 a.m. working on a rebuttal, and the smoke would at least keep him awake. They were having a peace conference before the war.

Ruff and Kendall argued that fundamental

fairness required that they get an advance look at the referral.

Hyde said no one, including himself, Conyers or their staffs, had read a word or looked at anything. It was still sealed, and the House would decide the next steps.

Clinton's lawyers pressed. Starr had sent the first impeachment referral under the Ethics in Government Act, and everyone should proceed carefully.

"You'll see it," Hyde promised. "We'll get it to you as soon as possible." He said he understood the history of impeachment. "If there is not a bipartisan majority, impeachment shouldn't go forward." If the House impeached, he said he understood the tremendous burden of a two-thirds majority in the Senate. "If there are not two-thirds in the Senate likely to vote for a conviction," Hyde said, "this won't go forward." He didn't want a "scorched earth" partisan war.

Kendall was satisfied that Hyde was at least making the right noises. He couldn't assess Hyde's sincerity. After decades in Washington and years representing Clinton, he found it difficult to take the measure of any politician's sincerity.

The House Rules Committee met that night to decide what to do with the 452-page referral. The Democrats tried unsuccessfully to give Clinton and his lawyers 48 hours to review the Starr Report but offered little opposition when the motion failed. By a unanimous voice vote, the Rules Committee recommended that the full House immediately release Starr's report without anyone reading it. The House prepared to debate the issue the next morning, Friday, September 11.

Clinton looked drawn as he stepped to the podium in the East Room for a breakfast with more than 100 religious leaders at 9:40 Friday morning. He had stayed up until 4 a.m. agonizing about what to say. He had no finished text.

"I have been on quite a journey these last few weeks to get to the end of this, to the rock bottom truth of where I am and where we all are," the president said. "I agree with those who have said that in my first statement after I testified I was not contrite enough. I don't think there is a fancy way to say that I have sinned." He bit his lip and tears came to his eyes.

"It is important to me that everybody who has been hurt know that the sorrow I feel is genuine: first and most important, my family, also my friends, my staff, my cabinet, Monica Lewinsky and her family, and the American people. I have asked all for their forgiveness.

"But I believe that to be forgiven, more than sorrow is required—at least two more things. First, genuine repentance—a determination to change and to repair breaches of my own making. I have repented. Second, what my Bible calls a 'broken spirit,' an understanding that I must have God's help to be the person that I want to be; a willingness to give the very forgiveness I seek; a renunciation of the pride and the anger which cloud judgment, lead people to excuse and compare and to blame and complain."

He was not bowing out. "I will instruct my lawyers to mount a vigorous defense, using all available appropriate arguments. But legal language must not obscure the fact that I have done wrong."

"If my repentance is genuine and sustained, and if I can maintain both a broken spirit and a strong heart, then good can come of this for our country as well as for me and my family. The children of this country can learn in a profound way that integrity is important and selfishness is wrong, but God can change us and make us strong at the broken places."

"This is really bad, and we're going to get blamed," Kavanaugh told Starr early Friday morning when he heard that the House was going to release the referral without reading it.

Starr agreed. Draft another letter warning Gingrich and Gephardt about the explicit material, Starr said.

"I caution against a blanket release of the referral without an initial review by some members of the Congress," Kavanaugh drafted for Starr. It was "almost certainly inappropriate for wide public dissemination." "We believe the nation and all parties involved would be best served by such a measured approach," the draft letter concluded.

Kavanaugh brought a computer disk containing the draft to Starr's secretary. The House was voting at this point on whether to release the referral.

Starr began editing. He added "highly" so that a sentence in the letter read, "Certain matters in the narrative and grounds sections are highly explicit."

They had a mini-conference to discuss whether to send the warning. Bittman and Jackie Bennett agreed with Kavanaugh. But the main author of the report, Stephen Bates, disagreed. Paul Rosenzweig, the prosecutor who had the first contact with the Jones legal team in January, was quite vocal. "Look, it's out of our hands," he said. "They know it's about sex. You've got to let them handle it."

"You're right," Starr said, changing his mind, "It's in their hands." He would not send the letter.

Bakaly knew Starr's position: Whatever the House did might be unfortunate, but it was necessary. People needed the facts.

Kavanaugh had an uneasy feeling that Starr was going to get blamed for the release of the most detailed, pornographic government report in history. The House was going to disseminate a report that not a single member had read.

Just after 12 p.m., the House voted 363–63 to release the report and it was posted on the Internet. Millions of Americans clicked on to read the explicit details.

Mike McCurry could not believe that Clinton had acted so recklessly. All along, McCurry expected the relationship had been dangerous or provocative. The leaks had been one thing, but the report documented oral sex in the hallway pantry off the Oval Office many times. It was beyond his imagination. McCurry knew the place well. He walked in to heat his coffee in the microwave three or four times a day, so he knew where to click the button and open the door. He didn't want an apology from the president because, like Hillary, he wasn't ready to accept one.

In conversations with others on the staff, McCurry found basically the same attitude. Among the senior political advisers there was a collective primal scream of rage. They told the lawyers to go do the Sunday television talk shows to defend the president. "We're not going out," McCurry announced.

Ruff too was astonished. It was about the worst behavior possible on the president's part. But Starr's referral was as bad. The notion that anyone would write an event-by-event narrative running hundreds of pages had never entered his mind. It never should have been put on paper, let alone released. He was appalled. As a matter of tactics, Ruff felt Starr had overreached.

David Kendall saw the referral as diabolical. Starr wanted to maximize the president's embarrassment, obviously believing that once it was all public, Clinton would be finished. The method was underhanded. Send it to the House and let them carry out the dirty work. An image of man at his most calculating and abhorrent formed in Kendall's mind. It was of Pontius Pilate washing his hands before the crucifixion.

But there was still the legal battle. Seeking to capitalize on a possible backlash, Kendall immediately released a 78-page rebuttal. "This private mistake does not amount to an impeachable offense," Kendall argued. He followed with another 42-page rebuttal, attacking the Starr Report as "pornographic" and a "hit-and-run smear campaign...that no prosecutor would present to any jury."

At a White House dinner that night, Clinton was given the Paul O'Dwyer Peace and Justice Award by a group of Irish Americans.

As Senator Ted Kennedy and others spoke about Clinton on the South Lawn, an audience of hundreds greeted the president with thunderous ovations, whooping and cheering. Side by side, the president and Hillary laughed, waved at people and had whispered interchanges.

"Hillary and I have been over there just lapping this up," Clinton said when he rose to speak about 7 p.m. "We don't want this to ever end." Laughter. "But I'm afraid you're going to get dizzy if you keep getting up and down." The audience laughed nine more times during his remarks.

Later that evening, the president was in despair. He had learned that Chelsea had read the Starr Report on the Internet.

38

SENATE JUDICIARY COMMITTEE Chairman Orrin G. Hatch pulled into the CBS parking lot early Sunday morning, September 13. He was scheduled to appear on the network's *Face the Nation* television talk show.

"The president's trying to reach you," said

Paul Smith, Hatch's press secretary. "He called the studio."

Hatch, a 64-year-old Utah Republican, called the White House switchboard from his cell phone. "Well, I finally did what you said I should do, what you asked me to do," Clinton said. His tone was amiable.

Since the summer, Hatch had called on Clinton to admit he had lied about Lewinsky, apologize to the nation for his affair and ask for forgiveness. Of the senior Republicans, he had been the most sympathetic. Hatch had been upset when Clinton attacked Starr on August 17 after his appearance before the grand jury, but he thought the president was sounding more contrite in his remarks lately, most recently at Friday's White House Prayer Breakfast.

"How did you think it was?" Clinton asked. "Did you accept my apology?"

"Well, of course I did," Hatch replied. "I thought it was a very good apology. But Mr. President, a repentance is more than just saying you're sorry."

Clinton hesitated.

Hatch, a Mormon Church bishop, offered a kind of religious sermon on repentance. "To really repent you've got to have four Rs," Hatch said. "One, you have to really recognize what you did is wrong. Number two, you should have remorse for it and feel sorry about what you did. Number three, you ought to refrain from ever doing it again, because that's what true repentance is. Number four, you ought to make a restitution."

Clinton listened quietly on the other end.

"You can't make a restitution to Monica Lewinsky," Hatch continued, "you can't restore what you took away from her, but you certainly can to the American people."

"I have tried to make amends," the president replied.

Two nights earlier, Hatch had voiced support on *Larry King Live* for Chelsea Clinton. "Well, if anybody mistreats her, they're going to hear from me," Hatch had said, "because I'll tell you, she's a very nice young woman."

"You know, Senator," Clinton told Hatch, "I heard what you said on the Larry King show about my daughter. I'll never forget that. I will always respect and appreciate you for that."

"Well, I meant it," Hatch replied. "I think you and your wife are good parents. I think you've done a good job with your daughter."

After 15 minutes, the call ended with friendly good-byes. Hatch found Clinton transparent. The president was trying to make a sale, and possibly feared that Hatch might call for the president's resignation or prosecution.

On the CBS show, Hatch said the president "ought to quit splitting legal hairs." He was critical of the president's claim that his answers in the Jones case were "legally correct."

"Nobody wants to hear that," Hatch said. "What they want to hear is the president who is truly contrite. I think he went a long way last Friday towards that."

The president's lawyers blanketed the same Sunday talk shows, attempting to stop a formal

House impeachment inquiry. Kendall took the hardest line. On ABC's *This Week,* he kept interrupting Sam Donaldson, the show's moderator. Five times he declared that the president did not commit perjury. Kendall's natural expression is a frown, and he didn't give an inch. His intellectual confidence radiated. He knew the facts. He knew the law. Technically, he was correct. It would be extremely difficult to prove perjury in a case that had been dismissed. But he lost on style points. He was the guy in the high school algebra class that everyone hated because he always had the answers.

At the end, Donaldson said with some scorn, "Mr. Kendall, many people believe you're very skillful and the president is lucky to have you. Because I take it your case is, the president of the United States may be a liar, but he is not a perjurer."

"The president of the United States has acknowledged wrongdoing and is trying to make up for it," Kendall said in response, perhaps sensing that his appearance had gone poorly. "He has committed no impeachable offenses, and none are in the report."

The next day, Senator Thomas A. Daschle, the Senate minority leader, and Gephardt in similar statements condemned the president's "hairsplitting" legal defense. *Washington Post* columnist David Broder scolded Kendall for "smugly and condescendingly twisting words," adding, "I can understand what drove Starr to dump every bit of trash he had collected onto the president's head."

It was the lowest, most miserable point for

Kendall. He was offending Democrats and the leading mainstream columnist. He had become the symbol of the Clinton administration's legal evasion, upstaging even the president.

Recognizing that Kendall had fallen short in the public relations battle, the White House immediately brought in Gregory Craig, a former law partner of Kendall's and the current director of the policy planning staff at the State Department, to be the new public face of the impeachment defense. Craig, who had attended law school with the Clintons, was a genial, more youthful, gray-haired version of the president himself.

Early in the week, James Carville had arranged confidentially for a focus group to discuss where Clinton stood. He was worried less about the mood in the White House—it fluctuated—than the strategy—there was none.

Do you share the president's moral values? the group was asked.

The president's support on that question was in the basement. But the group said basically they trusted the president to lead and be honest about the interests of the country. They saw him working to their overall benefit on the economy and foreign affairs. Carville was surprised that the overall rating didn't break against Clinton. He thought there was a point when moral values became more important than leadership. A *Washington Post* poll that week validated the focus group. The front-page headline made the critical point: "Poll Finds Approval of Job, Not of Person."

"A majority of Americans now believe President Clinton probably broke the law and should be censured but not forced from office for lying about his sexual relationship," the story said. Job approval was at 59 percent, according to the *Post* story, "and his ratings for honesty, integrity and personal morality fell to record lows."

Daschle, the leader of the 45 Democrats in the Senate, had a secret and a problem. The slight, 50-year-old South Dakotan was a good listener. Within the inner sanctum of the Senate club, the Democratic senators tended to confide in him. The conversations were sensitive and would be denied because they were tentative and exploratory. But Daschle counted as many as seven Democrats who were running around with speeches or statements in various stages of completion calling for Clinton to resign for the good of the party. One senator seemed to have a speech in his pocket and was itching to read it on the Senate floor. Others had just expressed a strong personal view. The list of possible defections included Senator Robert Byrd, the former Democratic leader and senior eminence from West Virginia, Bob Graham of Florida, Dianne Feinstein of California, Harry Reid of Nevada, Russell Feingold of Wisconsin, Fritz Hollings of South Carolina, and Joseph R. Biden of Delaware. Daschle urged them to be patient. But it was a volatile situation. One forceful public request for the president's voluntary resignation by a Democratic senator could start a panic.

Daschle invited Erskine Bowles and John Podesta to the Tuesday, September 15, Senate Democratic caucus lunch. He wanted them to hear the party distress for themselves. It would be a rude awakening to see firsthand the anger at the president from those in his own party.

Biden said their party would be better off in the coming elections if Clinton resigned. He was not necessarily advocating resignation, he said, but making clear it was his preference. Nonetheless, he said he was sure that Clinton never would quit anyway.

"He lied to me too," Bowles acknowledged, offering a meager defense. Many of the Democratic senators were furious that in private conversations Clinton was still lashing out at Starr. Few had heard any expression of genuine remorse from the president.

Another important factor for a number of the male Democratic senators was the reaction of their wives. Clinton's behavior was a nightmare for the wife of a politician, and the scorn, ridicule and dread some of the wives expressed to their husbands became a constant theme at home. The intensity and depth of negative feelings toward Clinton were so great that the senators would only repeat it to their closest friends or off the record. In all, it looked like maybe as many as half the Democratic senators privately wanted or would prefer that Clinton resign.

The center of power in a possible impeachment and trial was with the Senate Democrats— 34 of the 45 voting for acquittal would keep Clinton in office. But if a dozen or more favored resignation, the situation could reach critical mass—55 Republican senators plus 12 Democrats was enough to remove Clinton. Several senators could envision a replay of the end of the Nixon presidency. In August 1974, Republican senators, led by conservative Barry Goldwater, the party's presidential candidate in 1964, had gone to the White House to inform Nixon that he would lose an impeachment trial in the Senate because his own party had deserted him. A day after the Goldwater visit, Nixon had announced his resignation.

Senator Kent Conrad, the North Dakota Democrat, warned Greg Craig of the trouble, saying, "You're about three days away from having a senior delegation of Democratic senators going to the White House to ask for the president's resignation."

Back at the White House, Podesta reported, "There isn't much holding them together. There could be a stampede."

Bowles had reached the point of no return. "I just want you to know that I'm not going up and doing any more defense of the president on the Hill," he told Mike McCurry. Never again. "I can't do what I did this week. I also want you to leak it out somewhere that I'm going to be leaving when Congress leaves."

Daschle told several Senate Democrats that it might reach a point where it would be best for everyone if Clinton resigned. We're not there yet, he said, repeating his mantra, "Be patient, hold your fire."

Clinton gathered with his senior staff to prepare for a joint press conference he was to have the afternoon of Wednesday, September 16, with Czech President Vaclav Havel.

At the end of the session, McCurry, who was living with five rumors a day, said one question from reporters might be, "Are there other women out there, other women you've had an improper relationship with while you have been president?" He reminded Clinton that the president had assured the Senate Democratic leaders six days earlier that there wouldn't be any more surprises. Can the senators rely on that?

"Well," Clinton responded, "how would you answer that?" He often threw back the hard questions in a preparation session.

"It's a little unfair to ask us," McCurry replied lightly, looking around at the others.

Everyone laughed.

The president said he did not want to say something that would send every reporter off on a new chase, to issue a dare or an absolute declaration. On the other hand he wasn't going to say something that suggested there might be. He settled on something that went like, "I have addressed that to the satisfaction of the Senate, and I don't have anything else to say."

That might not satisfy the media, McCurry said. "You need to go work out with your lawyers what the answer to that question is," McCurry added, "just in case it comes."

"All right," the president said, "we will."

At the press conference, reporters beat up on Clinton about whether he had the moral authority to lead, but no one asked him about the possibility of another woman.

Clinton had understood the message from Carville's focus group.

"I have never stopped leading this country in foreign affairs in this entire year, and I never will." Later he said, "I'm determined to lead this country and to focus on the issues that are before us."

Salon, an online magazine, posted an article that day reporting that Henry Hyde had a five-year affair in the 1960s when he was married. "The statute of limitations has long since passed on my youthful indiscretions," Hyde, who was 41 years old when the affair began, said in a statement. Now a widower, he noted that his marriage had stayed intact. "The only purpose for this being dredged up now is an obvious attempt to intimidate me and it won't work. I intend to fulfill my constitutional duty and deal judiciously with the serious felony allegations presented to Congress in the Starr report."

Kendall realized immediately that Hyde's reference the previous week in their private meeting about "scorched earth" had undoubtedly been in anticipation of this story. Obviously, Hyde felt the White House or Clinton supporters were behind it. Kendall spent some time trying to reassure himself that no one associated with the president had anything to do with the story, but he feared the disclosure was going to help convert the House Judiciary chairman into an impeachment advocate.

Back in his office, Hyde was in near despair. He felt humiliated, degraded, sad for his children to know of his affair which was so dark and so wrong. He felt shame. Three decades ago, the woman's husband had confronted Hyde's wife. Hyde had accepted responsibility, broken off the relationship and begged his wife for forgiveness. After a difficult period, he and his wife had reconciled. Later she became seriously ill and he spent days at her bedside until she died in July 1992. He decided to grit his teeth and take it now. He had known something like this story would be dug up. He had seen James Carville on Sunday morning television enough to know the tactics were to destroy the opposition.

Still, it was a shock and surprise when it surfaced. He'd had only 30 minutes to respond to *Salon* with his statement. As he read it over, he realized his reference to "youthful indiscretions" looked cute and calculated. He wished he could take those words back. He had never lied about the affair or denied it. He had tried to make sure his remorse had tangibility to it. Now his image of rectitude was tainted, he realized. The story of the affair would be used against him the rest of his life. There would not be a major story or profile of him that did not contain it. What an awful price to pay. Maybe someone could learn from his sad experience.

Ever since Watergate, and several years later when in a congressional sex scandal Democratic Representative Wayne Hays of Ohio had his mistress on the payroll, everyone had been turning over rocks. On balance, Hyde concluded, this new era was not a good thing. He didn't like being judged by one event in his life, one mistake.

He didn't blame the White House, although he was sure they were taking pleasure in the disclosure. No, Hyde knew that his ex-mistress's husband had nurtured the grudge for decades and had released the story.

Hyde had never accused President Clinton of adultery, never accused him of marital infidelity. Never. The issues in the impeachment investigation were public acts in a lawsuit that were potential felonies. The subject of the cover-up was not relevant. Hyde wondered if the distinction would be lost.

He called Gingrich and said he didn't want to taint the Judiciary investigation. Would Gingrich accept his resignation?

"I wouldn't consider it," Gingrich said, dismissing the suggestion. "Absolutely not."

On September 20, *The New York Times* ran a long, front-page story portraying the Whitewater-Lewinsky investigation as a personal war between Clinton and Starr, fueled by deep animosity.

Later, in a discussion with some of his attorneys, Starr said the *Times* story was wrong. He was saddened by the perception that he had a vendetta against Clinton, he said. He was nonjudgmental about the president, he maintained, except for the lying and the obstruction of justice they had found in their investigation. He believed that the president had done wrong in the other parts of their investigation, and the only difference in the Lewinsky inquiry was that they had better proof. He turned to his upbringing in Texas. "My mother taught me never to hate anyone," Starr said. "You can hate what they do, but don't hate the person."

• • •

Hyde's committee voted 21 to 16 in party-line votes to release most of the Starr evidence and testimony publicly, including the video of Clinton's grand jury appearance. Kendall had tried but failed to stop release of the video, arguing that release was designed to embarrass the president. Advance news stories quoted sources saying the video showed Clinton at times in a rage and blind fury. The expectation was that the public was going to witness one of the president's famed purple fits.

Kendall was among the millions who sat glued to his television set the morning of Monday, September 21, when the tape was played on national television. He had attended the event, had taken detailed notes and had reviewed a transcript that had been released three days earlier. Still, as he watched, it was quite different. The tight camera focus on the president amplified his every gesture, facial expression and body language. The prosecutors were disembodied voices, as was Kendall's own voice the few times he interjected.

Clinton came across as beleaguered and alone, ashen and uncomfortable at first, but never erupting as the news previews had declared. In Kendall's view, Clinton also was heroic, acknowledging an inappropriate sexual relationship, bowing to the embarrassment and humiliation of that acknowledgment, but adamantly denying any perjury, witness tampering or obstruction of justice.

Kendall realized the public reaction would provide a laboratory test of the Clinton legal and political defense team's view that the average person, the guy in the bowling alley, already knew this story.

Ruff watched some of the video testimony on the television in his second-floor West Wing office as he did other work. He felt trepidation. But in the afternoon, press calls came in to the White House that seemed to reflect that Clinton had pulled it off. The president was not arrogant but besieged. Few could miss a sense that Clinton had experienced the worst hours of his life. By that evening, Ruff was thinking of the replay as a magic moment.

The next day's media coverage characterized the president's video testimony as surprisingly favorable to Clinton. *Washington Post* television critic Tom Shales, no Clinton fan, wrote, "Viewers who sat through it may well have emerged with a new or renewed feeling of sympathy for the president."

Carville was sure that the public wanted Clinton to be punished. Maybe time served before Starr's grand jury would be considered enough.

Later that day, Kendall and Ruff capitalized on Starr's failure to include some of Lewinsky's exculpatory statements in his formal referral. During her second grand jury appearance, a grand juror had asked Lewinsky if she had anything to add.

"I would just like to say that no one ever asked me to lie, and I was never promised a job for my silence," Lewinsky had testified. In the referral, Starr had paraphrased this statement, and Kendall charged publicly that Starr had deliberately concealed evidence beneficial to Clinton.

The president continued his fund-raising schedule. The evening of Wednesday, October 7, he attended a fund-raising dinner at the home of Ronald and Beth Dozoretz, top party fund-raisers and givers, at their home in Wesley Heights, a plush, wooded area of northwest Washington.

About 10:15 p.m., the president spoke to the Democratic group. Convinced that his survival hinged on continuing to function as president, he spoke about foreign affairs and his domestic program. His Republican opposition, he said, had a strategy designed to inflame. "You know what I think our strategy should be? The do-right rule, almost a nonpolitical strategy."

"If you look at every major conflict we face," he said, "it is essentially being driven by people who feel compelled to define themselves by what they are against, rather than by what they are for, and who seek conquest over reconciliation."

"But I'm telling you, based on my experience, the right thing to do is the right thing to do."

Hillary was still uncertain about her own course. A close friend told her about a high-profile, public couple. They had been married 40 years, the friend told Hillary. The man had lots of affairs and the woman finally caught him. "She was devastated," the friend said, "but she thought hard about it. They had a great friendship, and she decided he is worth fighting for, and it would be unwise to turn him out or to give him to someone else. Her decision was that it was better to fight for him and to fight for the relationship."

"Man," Hillary said, "that's exactly what I'm thinking now."

A therapist can stop the bleeding, Hillary's friend said. That was the key to making progress and saving the marriage.

Hillary said she and Bill knew that counseling was the right thing to do. Consciously or unconsciously, she echoed her husband's remarks, adding, "We are doing the right thing."

The next day, October 8, Carville was watching the television coverage of the House debate. The Republicans were proposing an open-ended impeachment inquiry. The Democrats wished to limit the scope and time frame of an investigation and determine before continuing if the facts in Starr's referral constituted grounds for impeachment. Carville called Rahm Emanuel, Clinton's senior policy adviser who had taken Stephanopoulos's place in the White House.

"You bastard," Carville screamed, "you stupid fools! The motherfuckers are going to come down and accept this." In the effort to be reasonable, the Democratic alternative had been crafted to be as attractive as possible. Since the Republicans had the controlling majority, they could simply take the limited inquiry, which was all they needed to get started, and expand the scope or the time as other matters arose. "Don't let them start a bipartisan investigation!"

"They are so driven," Emanuel replied, "they will not take anything any Democrat proposes. Shut up and don't worry."

Panicked, Carville continued to watch the debate on television. If the Republicans were smart enough to embrace the Democratic proposal, Carville thought they could undermine his core charge that it was a partisan witch-hunt. "How am I going to answer?" he thought to himself. He was scheduled to appear on television in full attack mode. He'd have to pretend he had the flu. But the Republicans didn't budge, and the House passed the open-ended inquiry 258 to 176. Although 31 Democrats defected and joined the Republicans, Carville felt his stomach ease. He could still claim partisanship. The Republicans seemed to be saying, "You don't understand how much we hate Bill Clinton." Carville's response was, "Here, tell me, right into this microphone." His plan was to keep it as political and partisan as possible. Relieved, he felt his own voice regain confidence.

He was still privately confident. "The core of the entire conspiracy lies in a few blow jobs," he said. "No phone was tapped, no one's office burglarized, no tax return audited. You can't elevate a blow job to anything more than a blow job."

In the cabinet room at 5 p.m. before a meeting with his economic advisers, Clinton told reporters, "It is not in my hands; it is in the hands of Congress, and the people of this country—ultimately, in the hands of God."

When pressed, the president added, "I have surrendered....What I can do is to do my job for the American people. I trust the American people."

The Republicans decided to spend an additional $10 million on an advertising blitz for the coming November 3 elections. The campaign attacked Clinton for lying. It was designed to boost the Republican gains in the House and Senate that every political analyst was forecasting.

Clinton privately expected that he and his party would do better. His job approval rating was still near 60 percent, Starr's was in the basement, and impeachment was the major issue on the table. It made no sense for the public, which basically supported him, to turn on him now.

About 9 p.m. on election day, Clinton showed up in the chief of staff's office, now occupied by John Podesta, who had replaced Bowles. White House political director Craig Smith showed the president how to use the computer and get CNN's online race-by-race update. The exit polling was more favorable than expected. Clinton began clicking around with about 20 people gathered nearby. Pizza was served.

D'Amato defeated! shouted Clinton. His old Whitewater nemesis from New York was booted from office.

A huge cheer went up.

Faircloth defeated! Clinton announced, referring to the conservative North Carolina Republican senator who had lunched with Judge Sentelle in the summer of 1994 right before Sentelle's panel replaced Robert Fiske with Starr.

Another cheer. The atmosphere was festive.

Clinton didn't leave until 2:30 a.m. It was a giant victory. The Senate would remain the same, 55 Republicans to 45 Democrats. In the House, Democrats gained an astonishing 5 seats, narrowing the Republican majority to 11 seats, 223 to 212. The president gave the few aides who were still standing a hug before going up to the residence.

It was almost an unprecedented triumph in an off-year election. Hyde met with Republicans and outlined a truncated investigation. Starr would be the only witness before his committee, and impeachment would be resolved by the end of the year.

"The American people sent us a message that would break the eardrums of anyone who was listening," the president said on November 5.

The next day, Speaker Newt Gingrich took responsibility for his party's losses. In a surprise announcement, he said he would not only step down as speaker but would resign from the House. There was general merriment in the Clinton camp. Many felt that the bad witch was dead. Kendall joked that a new book about Clinton by David Maraniss, author of the Clinton biography *First in His Class,* should be called *Still First in His Class.* Kendall was in buoyant spirits. The impeachment drive would conclude soon. "The troops will be home by Christmas," he said. The only problem was Starr, who he felt would cling to his investigation until the day Clinton left office. "I fully expect Starr to indict William Jefferson Clinton January 21, 2001," Kendall told his associates.

For Clinton, the Gingrich resignation was not good news. He was not happy. He didn't want a precedent of resignation set.

39

FOR A MONTH, Bob Bennett had been receiving feelers from lawyers for Paula Jones that she was interested in settling for $1 million. She was desperate for money. Bennett feared that the court of appeals might reinstate the case. He began negotiating. Clinton's insurance company agreed to pay $475,000. Jones reduced her demand to $850,000. The president finally said he would pay, and Hillary indicated that she no longer opposed a settlement. Bennett announced the terms on November 13. "The president has decided he is not prepared to spend one more hour on this matter," he said.

For Bennett, it was a bittersweet moment. The case had little or no legal merit, and it should have gone away or been settled years ago. He was caught between his defensive bluster, insisting that he had done everything possible, and the obvious conclusion that he had not done enough to protect his renowned client from his now infamous weakness. God, he had tried. For all his toughness, Bennett may not have been tough enough.

Starr saw with increasing clarity that he had no natural constituency. He had to build one.

The chance to testify before Hyde's Judiciary Committee provided one major opportunity to explain and defend his tactics and the referral. He prepared to tell the story his way.

For two weeks, Starr practiced—briefings, review of the records and sessions with his staff. He sat before a panel of his deputies, who played congressmen. It was their chance to take a free shot at the boss. The deputies gave three- or four-minute speeches and cut him off when he tried to answer. Starr's intention was to become acclimated to the frustrations of testifying in the most highly charged political atmosphere. The sessions were savage. He had to show he could sit there and take the best and cheapest attacks.

In particular, Starr practiced responding to Kendall, who was going to have at least 30 minutes to interrogate him.

His deputies convinced Starr that if he botched his appearance, he would taint their entire effort and damage the referral irreparably. The weight of the evidence could fall if he were not credible.

The deputies told him the Democrats would ask about Whitewater, the travel office and the FBI files investigations. Since they had gone nowhere, at least as applied to the president, he ought to exonerate Clinton, they argued. With immense reluctance, Starr agreed to clear the president in these cases in his opening statement. He insisted, however, that he state that the investigations continued actively with respect to other individuals.

Dash came in to urge Starr not to testify

before Hyde's committee as an advocate for impeachment. The Constitution gives the impeachment power solely to the House. Starr was in the executive branch. He had properly, in Dash's view, sent the referral and made his arguments to support his judgment that the information was "substantial and credible." He did not belong before the committee as an accuser. In Watergate, Special Prosecutor Jaworski had never appeared before the Judiciary Committee to testify or argue. That had been the role of the committee's chief counsel, John Doar.

Starr said he had to testify. To refuse would suggest that he could not defend his work.

Dash told Starr he was going to quit in protest, but that he would delay the announcement until after the testimony.

On Thursday, November 19, Starr met with Bakaly before going up to the House. Bakaly warned that the Democrats, or Kendall, would try to trick him into revealing something about secret grand jury testimony or sealed proceedings. "Be careful and watch your emotions," he advised. "Kendall is finally going to get his free shot at the piñata without a blindfold after four years of war."

Just before Starr's testimony, Kendall heard that Dash was resigning. He thought it could be great ammunition against Starr—the independent counsel's own ethics adviser thought Starr had gone too far. But he couldn't confirm it, so he decided not to use it. Nevertheless, Kendall was excited at the prospect of interrogating Starr. He had to calm his expectations. Starr would not break down or take it all back, Kendall knew. Cross-examination is the most dangerous but rewarding part of trial work. He would have to discredit a sophisticated witness who was there to destroy his client. He had assembled five volumes of documents. His game plan was to show the unfairness of Starr's investigation.

Starr began reading a 58-page opening statement that Thursday at 10 a.m. He highlighted the critical turning points in the Jones case, when the president had a chance to tell the truth but instead chose to conceal. He spent most of the day deflecting hostile questions from the Democrats and expanding on his themes during friendly questions from Republicans.

It was not until 8:40 p.m. that Kendall had his chance to question Starr. Hyde initially gave Kendall only 30 minutes. Kendall took out a press release that Starr had issued two weeks after the Lewinsky investigation became public. He had complained in the statement that they had not been able to talk to Lewinsky. Kendall read the release: "We cannot responsibly determine whether she is telling the truth without speaking directly to her. We have found that there is no substitute for looking a witness in the eye...."

Kendall asked if Starr had ever met, questioned or looked Lewinsky in the eye?

Starr conceded that he had not. He was not defensive, he did not argue. Kendall had wanted him to rise to the bait, but Starr did not.

Kendall questioned Starr's inconsistent press policies. In his opening statement, Starr had said,

"We go to court and not on the talk show circuit." Kendall read it and then pointed out that Bakaly, who was sitting behind Starr, had appeared on ten talk shows. Kendall hoped that it showed the hypocrisy. Again Starr did not argue.

Next, Kendall read Starr's first press release after the Lewinsky story had broken on January 21. "Because of confidentiality requirements we are unable to comment on any aspect of our work," it stated. Starr repudiated his own press release, citing "the duty of a prosecutor to provide appropriate and lawful public information."

Kendall raised the events of January 16, when Starr's prosecutors had approached Lewinsky at the Ritz-Carlton. He noted that Starr had denied that they had asked her to tape conversations or wear a body wire in discussions with the president, Jordan or Currie.

Starr repeated that denial.

Kendall cited the FBI report made by the agent at the Ritz-Carlton that night: "Cooperation, interview, telephone calls, body wires and testimony were mentioned." Kendall believed he had dropped an anvil on Starr's head.

But Starr's distance from the investigative details gave him an out. He accepted the inconsistency and again he didn't argue with Kendall.

Kendall wished he had done better. He lost a bit of his composure and raced rapidly through too many questions. Hyde was hovering, watching for the moment to gavel him off-stage. After little more than an hour, he did so.

"I would come back tomorrow," Kendall asked, too anxious.

"I don't think many of us want to come back tomorrow," Hyde answered.

Kendall put his glasses away, signaling his withdrawal.

Starr announced that it was almost his bedtime.

"We are at mine, I can assure you," Hyde said.

David Schippers, Hyde's chief counsel, had waited all day to question Starr. After Kendall finished, he threw softball after softball to the independent counsel. At the end, the Republican members and staffers gave Starr a standing ovation.

In a holding room, Starr hugged each of his staff members who had attended the hearing. He felt that he was on the road to recovering some of his reputation.

The next day, Dash officially resigned and released a letter accusing Starr of "unlawfully" intruding into impeachment and "abuse of your office."

Most of Starr's deputies were furious. Despite his delay, Dash seemed to be making an effort to undercut Starr at an important moment.

"Sam will be Sam," Starr said, reflecting on one of the legendary self-important egos of Washington. He called Dash to explain that he was not going to take their disagreement on the law personally. "I don't want this to interfere with our friendship. I realize you acted on principle."

Control of Clinton's defense had quietly shifted to Charles Ruff. There was no meeting and little discussion. As the White House counsel, he represented the institutional presidency. At 59, he was the senior member of the team. Confined to a wheelchair for the last 34 years because of a rare leg-crippling disease, Ruff had overcome his disability and had a remarkable public career. He had been the fourth and final Watergate special prosecutor from October 1975 to June 1977; had served as U.S. attorney for the District of Columbia, the chief federal prosecutor, from 1979 to 1982; and then practiced law for more than a dozen years as a partner at Covington & Burling.

Ruff had an unusual grasp of political advocacy and negotiation. He understood how to extricate well-known political figures from trouble and also how to put them in jail. A diffident and introspective man, Ruff preferred to work behind the scenes. He had learned not to take legal battles personally. He was trying not to allow his repugnance at Clinton's behavior to interfere with his efforts to defend the president, as many on the White House staff had. He also wasn't permitting himself to demonize Starr as Kendall had.

He was planning to give the president's closing defense before Hyde's committee on December 9. Hyde and the Republicans were not going to be stopped. It was 21 Republicans versus 16 Democrats, a sure loser. So the committee proceeding was going to be a sham. Since the committee Republicans were already lost, it was useless, Ruff thought, to address them. In his presentation, Ruff planned to address the two remaining and important audiences: the Democrats and the public. They needed a

747

defense, a rationale they could understand for why Clinton's behavior, however unseemly, was not enough for impeachment. He went to see the president.

Clinton seemed oddly detached.

Ruff outlined his plan and sought instructions and guidance.

The president indicated that he wanted Ruff to be contrite but not to roll over; to lower the temperature and, if possible, take the edge off the proceeding.

Ruff said he could not go in there and say the president had done nothing wrong when the president himself had said he had done wrong.

"You got to do what you got to do," Clinton said icily.

On Wednesday afternoon, December 9, Hyde swore in Ruff as a witness in the president's defense.

"Neither the president nor anyone speaking on his behalf will defend the morality of his personal conduct," Ruff said, reading from his statement, head slightly down, looking up only occasionally. "The president had a wrongful relationship with Monica Lewinsky. He violated his sacred obligations to his wife and daughter." He betrayed the trust placed in him by the American people, Ruff said, and his conduct was "morally reprehensible." But he should not be impeached.

"No one can claim to be free from doubt," he said. He attempted to strike a tone different from Kendall's but make essentially the same arguments. "I am worried that our sometimes irresistible urge to practice our profession will stand in the way of securing a just result." Ruff then went on to practice kinder, gentler "legalisms" to show that the president did not perjure himself because of "a truncated artificial definition of sexual relations" used in the Jones deposition.

During questioning, Ruff said "reasonable people" could conclude the president "crossed over the line" into perjury. "But in his mind—and that's the heart and soul of perjury—he thought and he believed that what he was doing was being evasive but truthful."

The news accounts and reviews described Ruff's presentation as somber, respectful, reserved, grave and serious.

Just as he was finishing, Hyde released the four proposed articles of impeachment, charging Clinton on two counts of perjury, obstruction of justice and abuse of power. For months, the committee Republicans and their staff had drafted a large number of proposed articles. The final number and precise wording totally swamped Ruff's defense in the news accounts.

On Friday, December 11, Hyde's committee debated all day before voting.

At the White House, Clinton examined the signals that Republicans seemed to be sending. If he publicly went a step further and acknowledged that he had not just misled but lied, he might be censured instead of impeached.

"I can't," the president told his aides, "I didn't lie."

At 4:10 p.m., Clinton went to the Rose Garden to make yet another contrite statement. "I am profoundly sorry for all I have done wrong in words and deeds," he said. "Quite simply, I gave in to my shame." He invited "rebuke and censure" by the Congress.

Within ten minutes the Judiciary Committee, on party lines, voted the first article of impeachment, 21 to 16, charging the president with perjury before the grand jury. A second article was approved by the committee alleging perjury in the Jones deposition with a lone Republican defecting. Lindsey Graham of South Carolina opposed it because the Jones case had been settled. A third article alleging obstruction of justice passed 21–16 also.

On Saturday, December 12, about 20 minutes before the vote on the fourth and final article of impeachment, Hyde waved over Democrat Howard Berman. Of all the Democrats on the committee, Hyde felt closest to Berman, 57, a soft-spoken colleague who had represented his Los Angeles district since 1983. Over the years, Hyde and Berman had formed an odd-couple relationship, the avuncular conservative Catholic from the Chicago suburbs and the amiable Jewish liberal from California. They had traveled abroad together on junkets, both enjoying and suffering through long transatlantic flights, endless dinners and inevitable sightseeing that can form friendships across the partisan divide. The House of Representatives is a club, and together they sponsored a popular antiterrorism bill and unpopular Russian aid legislation. As Judiciary chairman, Hyde gave unusual deference to some of Berman's ideas and bills, allowing them to pass through the committee to the floor. Hyde thought Berman was the most likely Democrat on the committee to vote for impeachment. During the summer, Hyde had told Berman, "Howard, if you're not voting for impeachment, it's not going to happen." Berman, however, had voted against impeachment across the board. In Berman's view, Starr had nailed Clinton's ass, but the charges didn't rise to the level of impeachment. Nonetheless, Berman shared Hyde's loathing for two aspects of the Clinton defense: one, the assertion that Clinton didn't lie, which Berman felt he obviously had; and two, the effort to paint Starr as evil and therefore excuse the president's conduct.

"Oh, you want me to speak five minutes more?" Berman joked as he approached the chairman. Committee members had been limited in their time to talk or question witnesses.

"No, I don't," Hyde replied. "I want you to come here."

Berman approached.

"Where are you going to be tonight?" Hyde inquired.

"I'm going to be out," Berman said.

"Well, can you call me?" the chairman asked deferentially. He wrote out his home phone number and handed it to Berman.

At 2:45 p.m., the committee passed the fourth article, alleging that Clinton had abused his power by making false statements to Congress. The vote was along party lines, 21 to 16, with Hyde voting yes and Berman voting no. Hyde then allowed three and a half hours of debate on the Democratic censure resolution, which declared that the president "dishon-ored" his office. The Democrats were pre-senting it as an alternative to impeachment. It failed to pass by a vote of 22 to 14.

About 9 p.m. Berman, who was at a party given by a television journalist, called Hyde's condo in Falls Church, Virginia, a Washington suburb.

The chairman answered. Berman wanted to have a serious conversation, but he thought he heard a click suggesting someone else might have picked up an extension at the party. Berman said he would call later in the evening when he was home.

After the party, Berman called Hyde again.

"Howard," Hyde said, sounding wiped out, "everyone thinks this is some DeLay thing or a Gingrich or Livingston thing." Livingston was speaker-elect of the House. It was not true that he was being pressured by the Republican leadership. "I'm stuck with every decision," he complained. He had to decide when, how, why and what to do in the hearings. The real source of the pressure to impeach Clinton was coming from his constituents in his conservative sub-urban Illinois district. "In my district they want this guy," Hyde said. "They want this guy's head."

Berman wasn't sure where the conversation was heading.

"What you've got to do is get to Bob Strauss," Hyde said, referring to the former Democratic National Committee chairman and eminence grise, "and get him to go visit Bob Dole and Bob Michel. Then they can go to Bob Livingston and say, 'We've got to have a censure option for the good of the party.' Then Livingston will visit me and I won't put up much of a fight."

Now let me get this straight, Berman asked. He should go to Strauss, who in turn would talk to former Republican Senate Majority Leader Dole, whom Clinton had defeated in 1996, and former Republican House Minority Leader Michel. Then Dole and Michel would make the for-the-good-of-the-party argument to Livingston, who would then get Hyde to go along with a censure?

Yes, Hyde said. He could in effect then say to Livingston: "Well, if this is what you really want to do. You're going to be the speaker. Okay. I'll go along with it." The heat would be off him. Hyde said he had to work through back channels because of the disappearance of the House Republican leadership. "My fingerprints can never be on this," he added. He still thought that Clinton was a bad man, and he still wanted to hold the president accountable. "I want to shame him," Hyde said.

Berman promised he would consider some way of making an approach to Strauss, perhaps indirectly. After Hyde hung up, Berman wasn't sure what to make of it. It was an offer of a straight deal, a way out of the mess. Everyone, including Hyde and Berman, was looking for an opportunity to be a hero and broker a compromise. Was this approach it? Despite his genuine friendship with Hyde, Berman knew that the chairman was well past his prime, not in good health and had a tendency to be lazy. This overture showed weakness, an unwillingness to stand up to his people whether back in Illinois or in Washington.

Berman thought a weak backbone would probably be the one thing that Hyde would not want to show, especially to a Democrat. He could not tell how deep Hyde's doubts were. Did Hyde think impeachment would be wrong? Did he think that a one-party impeachment would be bad for Republicans? For the country? Or, improbable as it was, was it Hyde's desire to show that he was a reasonable guy in private to one of his Democratic friends? Berman went to bed mystified. Was this proposal an opportunity or some kind of trap? Dole and Michel were suspect within the right wing of their party. Any effort on their part could backfire and harden the Republican conservatives.

Berman had to fly to Los Angeles early Sunday. On the plane he was surprised to read in the newspapers that Hyde had written a letter to Livingston opposing a censure resolution debate on the House floor. Berman read Hyde's letter: "It is my view that a resolution or amendment proposing censure of the president in lieu of impeachment violates the rules of the House, threatens the separation of powers and fails to meet constitutional muster."

Livingston in turn had written a letter declaring his opposition to censure or even a censure debate on the House floor. Upon arriving in Los Angeles, Berman called Hyde again at home and asked about the apparent contradiction. Had not Hyde's and Livingston's letters foreclosed the options? Had Hyde been serious the night before?

Hyde said he was. It was important that any effort to get the censure resolution to the floor not be traced to him. "I have to be against censure," he said, "or I'll get killed." He mentioned again the pressure from his district and referred to the conservative newsletter *Human Events.* "The *Human Events* crowd would kill me." Hyde reiterated that he wanted Berman to go to Strauss with the plan. If Livingston said he'd allow a censure resolution on the floor, Hyde said again he would acquiesce. Hyde mentioned other alternatives. "Maybe there is some parliamentary way to force a censure resolution on the floor." He suggested that Berman call an expert on House parliamentary rules.

Assured that Hyde meant it, Berman decided to get the White House involved. He began thinking of Hyde's suggestion as the "Plan of the Four Bobs," Bob Strauss to Bob Dole and Bob Michel—and then to Bob Livingston.

That night, Berman decided to work through the White House rather than to approach Strauss directly. The White House had the most at stake, and frankly the staff there seemed to like Clinton more than Berman did. Let them do the work, he figured. He reached chief of staff John Podesta.

"I can't tell you where this came from," Berman told Podesta, "but I'm told if you get Bob Strauss...." He then explained the "Plan of the Four Bobs." He added, "That will improve the chances of censure being available on the House floor. I have no idea whether it's true or not, but that's the message I got from a good source." He didn't want to make any promises, but he realized that the press references to his friendship with Hyde would make it obvious who that source was. To establish his bona fides, Berman added, "You guys can figure out whatever you want to assume from this, but I can't tell you where it came from."

"Well," Podesta said, "it's certainly worth trying. We might be able to get Michel, but I don't know about Dole."

On Monday morning, December 14, Gregory Craig, the special counsel to Clinton, called Berman. Craig had talked to Lloyd Cutler, who was also working hard to broker a censure compromise. Cutler had developed a close relationship with Hyde when he had represented the congressman in a federal court challenge to a state term limits law. "Lloyd Cutler says Henry Hyde was talking to him about a way out of this, and Hyde said something about he's talked to Howard Berman." Craig said he had been unable to find out the details. "Could you tell me what it was?"

"I've already talked to John about this," Berman replied, referring to his conversation with Podesta. He realized that Hyde had put his fingerprints on the "Plan of the Four Bobs." Berman outlined the plan to Craig.

Craig called Strauss. He said he was calling for himself and Podesta. Hyde has made an overture, Craig said, and he described it. Strauss would have to talk to Michel and to Dole, who was one of Strauss's best friends.

Strauss called Michel. Like Hyde, Michel was from Illinois, and the two had been close in the House. Strauss outlined the plan.

Michel couldn't quite believe that Hyde

would operate this way. He said he wanted to talk to Hyde directly. "If there is anything there, I'll call you," he told Strauss.

A week earlier, Cutler had visited Michel and pushed censure. Michel had told Cutler he was opposed and that if he were still in the House he probably would vote for impeachment. But obviously something was stirring, so Michel left several messages for Hyde to call him. He did not hear back.

Cutler also had met privately with Hyde on December 8 to push censure. Hyde had said he would not oppose it if Livingston wanted a censure motion on the floor.

Strauss passed the idea along to Dole. They talked nearly every day, another bipartisan friendship.

Dole, the 76-year-old GOP warhorse, was settled in a vast suite of offices at a law firm in downtown Washington. The Republican Party was in trouble on the impeachment issue, he realized. Only the true Clinton haters wanted it to go on and on. Bitterness and retribution were not the way to electoral success or happiness, he had concluded after his 1996 loss. The last thing people wanted was for the loser to go out and try to do in the winner. Dole decided to try to help Clinton. He was convinced that the route to censure was not through Livingston. Dole had talked with the speaker-designate a month before. Livingston didn't want anything to do with impeachment, and in effect had said, Get this dead cat out of here.

Dole had already test-marketed a censure option in a speech in Chicago to a group that was 90 percent Republican. The audience had seemed to agree. So he began writing it out as a formal proposal that might appear in an opinion piece in *The New York Times*—the current display window of choice for Republican elders.

Convinced that impeachment was too far down the road to stop completely, Dole proposed that a motion to censure come only after the full House voted on the articles of impeachment. Clinton then would have to sign the censure resolution, he suggested. He sent it to the *Times* late Monday, December 14, for publication the next day.

Neither Dole nor Michel contacted Livingston. The speaker-designate had his own problems. *Hustler* publisher Larry Flynt had threatened to publish allegations about Livingston's marital infidelities. In response, Livingston had publicly acknowledged that he had "on occasion strayed from my marriage."

Clinton read Dole's op-ed piece, headlined "A Tough but Responsible Solution." He phoned his former opponent to thank him.

"It might have some possibility," the president said, but he did not embrace the specifics.

"Just my thoughts," Dole said. "May not be worth anything."

The president then went on to give his legal argument as to why he had not committed perjury. He kept trying to explain perjury law.

Dole was not interested. "How can we get this over?" Dole asked. That was the point. That was in the interest of everyone. The president didn't have to make technical legal arguments to him.

Clinton returned to the perjury question and wouldn't let it go.

"You know," Dole said finally, "if I hear anything, I'll certainly be in touch."

Several moderate House Republicans called Dole, but his main inquiries came from Democrats wondering if censure were going to take hold. Podesta reached Dole to say he appreciated the effort and thought it was written in the spirit of trying to get the matter resolved.

Daschle called Dole to see if there were any serious nibbles. He gave Dole his home phone number.

Berman heard not one more word from Hyde and he didn't inquire. He assumed it had been a serious impulse on Hyde's part. Was it hypocrisy? Berman wondered if it was the lawyer in Hyde or the politician exploring all alternatives. Or maybe Hyde was just trying to survive. Berman was no big Clinton fan. He thought to himself and laughed, "What do I want to happen, by the way?"

The Republicans were able to take the high road. DeLay went on *Meet the Press,* Sunday, December 13, and wrapped himself in the Constitution and the rule of law. Tim Russert, the moderator, played a video clip of the president that morning responding to a question about censure. "Around three-quarters of the American people think that's the right thing to do," Clinton said.

Censure was not in the Constitution, DeLay said. Impeachment was. "This is a constitutional process. The president of the United States has been charged with breaking the law, and he has been charged with obstructing justice, and he has been charged with abuse of power. If we just forgave it and pushed it aside, we would be violating our oath of office.... This is too important to worry about politics and polls."

Democrats were forced into the position of acknowledging the bad conduct but insisting that it was not that bad. They had no clear principle to embrace.

On Tuesday, December 15, nine more moderate Republicans bailed out on Clinton and said they would vote for impeachment.

40

SECRETARY OF DEFENSE William S. Cohen rose early on Wednesday, December 16, as he did most mornings. He tried to wake up at 4:30 a.m. for a half hour of exercise to keep his 58-year-old body in shape. A serious man with an intellectual bent, he had written books of sentimental poetry and spy novels. In nearly two years, he had discovered the job of defense secretary required extraordinary discipline even for an already disciplined man. Time, words, thought, each had to be carefully measured.

It was a troubling, lonely time for Cohen, the only Republican in Clinton's cabinet. He had built his political reputation on Watergate. As a freshman congressman from Maine in 1974,

Cohen had been a leader among the Republicans on the House Judiciary Committee who had broken party ranks to vote to recommend Nixon's impeachment. Afterward, he had pushed for the Ethics in Government Act that included the special prosecutor provision. With his reputation for independence firmly established, he was elected in 1978 to the Senate. There he served on committees that focused on the CIA, the military and post-Watergate investigations.

Two scandals during his Senate years reshaped his thinking about the presidency. In 1987, one of his closest friends, Colorado Senator Gary Hart, was forced out of the Democratic presidential primary race when his extramarital relationship with a model, Donna Rice, was exposed. The same year, Cohen participated in the congressional investigation of Iran-contra and was horrified by the excesses of Reagan's men, especially Lieutenant Colonel Oliver North. The two events left a deep impression on Cohen, who came to realize how modern presidents are vulnerable both to their own temptations and to their staffs.

A meticulous, cautious man, Cohen grew disillusioned with the partisan politics and unrestrained campaign fund-raising of the 1990s. In 1996, he had chosen not to seek reelection to a fourth term. He was packing up his Senate office after the November elections when President Clinton called. The president said he hoped to bring some Republicans into his second administration. After several conversations as they got to know one another,

Cohen said he would join the administration if the president understood that he would quit if a matter of principle arose, or if he were undermined.

Clinton agreed.

Cohen recalled Nixon's and Reagan's missteps during Watergate and Iran-contra. The only way for Clinton to dispose of Whitewater and the coming campaign fund-raising investigations was to investigate himself and release all the findings publicly. "Nothing held back," he recommended to the president. Clinton would have to give a nationally televised address that might include a "mea culpa." But that should put an end to the investigations. There would be no further surprises. "It would be tragic for the country to go through four more years of investigations," he told the president. The main resemblance between Watergate and the present scandals seemed to be the "circle the wagons" mentality. It was time to uncircle them.

Clinton hadn't responded. But several days later, the president formally asked Cohen to become defense secretary and promised him total authority at the Pentagon.

"Look," Cohen said, "I've been independent. I never signed on to the Republican social agenda." He accepted and promised "absolute fidelity" to the president unless there was a matter of principle as they had previously discussed. "I don't intend to be a Lone Ranger."

A year later, when the Lewinsky scandal broke, Cohen was shocked that the independent counsel had strayed so far afield. Compared to Watergate, the Lewinsky matter, although troubling, seemed trivial. Lewinsky had worked as a secretary to Cohen's spokesman, Ken Bacon, in the Pentagon, and she had traveled with Cohen on some trips abroad. His impression was that the young woman was immature. But he didn't believe he should talk to Clinton about her.

On this December morning in 1998, Cohen was faced with a more serious matter. Iraqi President Saddam Hussein had repeatedly refused to allow United Nations inspections of facilities that were suspected of making weapons of mass destruction. It had been a frustrating cat-and-mouse game as the United States regularly threatened new bombing if Saddam did not comply with the agreement on inspections. In October, Iraq had shut down the UN inspections. The next month, in mid-November, Clinton had approved a substantial bombing raid in Iraq, but the operation did not go forward when Saddam blinked and promised to comply. Cohen and Secretary of State Madeleine Albright had advocated proceeding with the bombing anyway, but Clinton had aborted the raid at the last minute, conferring almost exclusively with national security adviser Sandy Berger. Although Cohen disagreed, he backed the president's decision. He had always felt there was a bit of the peacenik in Clinton.

After the November attack had been called off, Cohen sat down with his chairman of the Joint Chiefs of Staff, Army General H. Henry "Hugh" Shelton. They had to figure out how to array their forces so that attacks against Iraq could be launched with almost no advance notice. The UN inspectors were going to return to Iraq during the first two weeks of December. Cohen assumed that Saddam would comply just enough to make it appear that he was cooperating. But if Iraq did not, the United States had to be ready to act. As far as Cohen was concerned, they were facing a test of U.S. credibility. "The Last Chance Saloon," he called it.

On December 13, the day after the House Judiciary Committee voted its final impeachment article against Clinton, Cohen had received word that the UN inspectors were about to report that Saddam had not complied. Some inspections had been carried out, since the Iraqis were blocking only about half a dozen out of some 300 inspections. It did not represent an absolute shutdown of inspections as had occurred in October. With the president's permission, Cohen ordered the positioning of forces to attack on 24 hours' notice. That decision placed the likely air raids on the day the full House of Representatives was scheduled to open its impeachment debate.

General Shelton had reservations. The timing was too weird. At some point, the United States was going to lose planes and pilots. If there were prisoners of war, the media would become obsessed and it would probably leak that the military had reservations or had opposed the raids. When Cohen learned of General Shelton's concerns, he met privately with the chairman for 30 minutes. Shelton left the meeting a supporter of the plan to bomb. There were unusual circumstances that favored an immediate operation against Iraq. Routine exercises and normal duty tours of major forces would give them the right firepower in the region. The window of opportunity was now, before the Muslim holy month of Ramadan.

By 7 a.m. December 16, Cohen was seated in the White House Situation Room with the principals of the national security team. They reviewed the UN inspection report. It was strongly worded. Saddam was again not complying. President Clinton joined the group a little later.

All the advisers recommended that the president give final approval for the attack to begin about 5 p.m. that day, the eve of the impeachment debate.

"A failure to take action now will undercut our credibility," Secretary Cohen told President Clinton. "Our word is at stake. If we don't carry it out, we're going to be tested in the future." Weakness would be met by more of Saddam's defiance. "If you don't act here, the next argument will be that you're paralyzed," he said. Cohen didn't say who might make the argument, only that it would be made. Impeachment had been interjected—and not subtly—into the decision-making process. Cohen was pressuring the president on what he was convinced was a vital national interest.

"I can't consider anything else," Clinton said. "I have no choice."

He asked the members of the National Security Council if they would make the same recommendation if there were no impeachment pending.

All said they would.

The president seemed to take comfort in that. When he had made private phone calls seeking advice, one of the former presidents had told him, "Bill, either put up or shut up."

About 7:30 a.m., the president directed Cohen to sign the order so the first missiles and bombs would strike Iraq in a little more than eight hours. The Desert Fox operation would amount to 650 bomber or missile sorties against fewer than 100 targets during 70 hours. Thousands of Iraqis could be killed, as Saddam's elite Republican Guard units were specifically targeted. Overall the bombing would constitute between 1 and 2 percent of the air war in the 1991 Persian Gulf War.

A brief flap followed after the president announced the operation. Senate Majority Leader Trent Lott said, "Both the timing and the policy are open to question." Criticism was focused on the possibility that Clinton had ordered military action primarily to postpone or frustrate the impeachment proceedings. There were references to a popular movie, *Wag the Dog,* a comedy about a president and his advisers who manufacture a war to distract the nation from a sex scandal. In fact, the opposite had occurred. The Lewinsky scandal had sufficiently weakened Clinton so that the advocates for the strike had their way. Although the advocates might have prevailed no matter what, the president was not in a position to contest his advisers' recommendations.

A president faces a serious dilemma when presented with a recommendation that goes something along the lines of, "It is the unanimous recommendation of your advisers." In these situations, especially those involving military action, the president is supposed to have a real choice. The Constitution designates one person the commander in chief of the armed forces. There are no committees, no votes, no review. Weighing all arguments and factors, the commander in chief decides. By Clinton's own admission, however, he didn't decide. He ratified. Maybe it was just the language he used to embrace his advisers' unanimous recommendation. Maybe it was the right decision. It was certainly justified. But he had lost some of his power to say no, to overrule the experts and the committed cabinet members convinced they were correct. Clinton's strategy to hold on to office rested on his pledge to continue doing his job. Any suggestion that he could not would be potentially devastating. One fact is inescapable: Clinton ordered the biggest military action of his presidency up to that time when he could least afford to seem paralyzed.

The air strikes on Iraq caused the opening of the impeachment debate to be postponed by a single day.

"I wish to talk to you about the rule of law," Hyde said on Friday, December 18, opening 12 hours of initial debate. Representative Robert Menendez of New Jersey summarized the Democratic defense: "Monica Lewinsky is not Watergate." The words from both sides revealed how partisan positions had hardened.

House Republicans had been urged to review secret documents from the Starr inquiry that had not been made public. A woman subpoenaed in the Paula Jones case, Juanita Broaddrick, had denied under oath that Clinton had made unwanted sexual advances in 1978 when he was attorney general of Arkansas. She had changed her story in April 1998, telling FBI agents working for Starr that Clinton had raped her in a Little Rock hotel. Stories circulated that this allegation made a number of moderate Republicans more inclined to vote against Clinton, but of the 45 Republicans who saw the secret documents, only two were undecided. Although Democrats were outraged that secret evidence was being trotted out at the last minute, the Broaddrick allegations apparently had little impact.

That morning, Hillary Clinton broke weeks of public silence. She walked outside the White House to the South Portico to address reporters. She looked drawn and was unsmiling as she stood with her hands folded together.

"I think the vast majority of Americans share my approval and pride in the job that the president's been doing," she said tepidly. "We in our country ought to practice reconciliation, and we ought to bring our country together."

She mentioned Social Security, pensions, education and the environment—hers and the president's core issues. "So I hope that this holiday season is a very happy and blessed one for everyone."

"Goddamn, fuck it!" Clinton told one friend that night. He said no one could conceivably understand how he was suffering because no one had ever been subjected to such a public evisceration. "I'm dying a thousand cuts. It's like someone kicked me in the stomach. I've had a knot in my stomach for months!" He was in a rage. No person, no human being, no public figure, no politician, no president ever had such an investigation into his personal life, Clinton said. "No one has raw grand jury material put on the street for everyone to read, including his family." The Starr Report was an ugly counterpoint to whatever he did.

On Saturday, just after 10 a.m., dozens of staff and visitors crowded into the Oval Office to listen to the president's weekly radio address. He said the air strikes on Iraq were continuing and going well.

At the same time, the House opened its final debate before the vote, which would come later that afternoon. But there was a surprise when Speaker-elect Bob Livingston announced that he would resign from Congress. "I must set the example that I hope President Clinton will follow."

In the afternoon, formal voting began on the first article, which alleged that the president lied before Starr's grand jury. Hyde had not been able to get a good count in advance, and felt unsure of the outcome. He looked up at the vote board. It passed 228–206 on virtually a straight party-line vote, with five Democrats in favor and five Republicans against it. "There is a God in heaven," Hyde thought, "and justice is not illusory." He felt it was possible to win in the Senate if they could undo the White House spin and tell the story in full. But whatever happened, Clinton would always be an impeached president.

Clinton was in the Oval Office with the Reverend Tony Campolo, one of the ministers he had been consulting.

It took the House about 20 minutes to vote on the second article charging perjury in the Jones deposition—the allegation that Kendall and Ruff believed was Clinton's greatest vulnerability. The article was defeated 229 to 205, with a total of 28 Republicans voting against it.

Article Three, charging obstruction of justice, passed by a narrower, 221-to-212 margin. Then at 2:15, the fourth article, charging abuse of power stemming from written answers Clinton had given to the House Judiciary Committee, failed decisively, 285 to 148. Nearly a third of the House Republicans, 81, voted against it.

The passage of two articles meant that Clinton would stand trial in the Senate, the second presidential impeachment trial in U.S. history.

Gore was with Clinton during the last vote. "It's not fair, what they've done to you," Gore said.

Ruff watched the vote on television from his second-floor White House office. The defeat of the Jones deposition perjury article was a huge plus, he thought. He could see the outlines of a defense forming. He received word that his first grandchild had been born. He left the White House to visit his daughter and the new baby.

Before 4 p.m., television cameras caught Clinton leaving the Oval Office. He quickly wiped each eye. Then with Hillary on his arm and Gore attending, he walked onto the South Lawn to speak to the television cameras and Democratic House members who had taken two buses to a rally at the White House. His left eye was slightly closed. He looked gray and worn, but he pulled himself together to deliver a forceful speech.

"We still have to keep working to build that elusive 'one America' I have talked so much about.

"Just as America is coming together, it must look—from the country's point of view—like Washington is coming apart," the president said. "We must stop the politics of personal destruction. We must get rid of the poisonous venom of excessive partisanship, obsessive animosity, and uncontrolled anger." He called for "some sense of proportionality and balance," and pledged to serve "until the last hour of the last day of my term."

Despite his strong performance, friends and longtime aides could see that the president was shaken.

Two hours later, he announced the end of the air strikes. "I am confident we have achieved our mission," he said. "We have inflicted significant damage on Saddam's weapons of mass destruction programs."

At a black-tie White House party for 500 important campaign donors that night, the president tried to be upbeat. "We had a great day," he maintained at one point. "We did better than expected."

Clinton had to deal with two struggles—the turmoil within himself and the trial in the

Senate. The next day, Sunday, he expressed his regret to several allies that he had no true friends in the Congress. "For six years, I have not been out there with the Congress," he said; "maybe I should have."

Some 150 friends came to the White House for a Christmas party that night. Chelsea attended with her father. Hillary didn't appear. She was lying down flat because of back pain.

"It's probably stress," a friend said.

"No, it's physical," Hillary insisted.

"This is God's way of telling you to lie down," the friend said.

At the party, the president told a group of friends that he had learned from South African President Nelson Mandela to purge himself of hatred. Years earlier, Mandela had recounted to him how he had spent nearly three decades as a political prisoner hammering limestone. He had lost his youth, his marriage and his eyesight. All that was left were his mind and heart. When he left prison, he understood he would not be free if he let his anger accompany him. During the summer, Mandela's deputy had visited him, the president said, and had brought one question from Mandela, "Did you give your heart or mind to them?"

Clinton said he knew public approval depended on daily proof that he was doing his job. If he stopped to act as his own defense lawyer rather than function as president, his popularity would sink, he said.

Carville had gone public promising retribution at the polling places. "These people are going to pay for what they did," he said.

Clinton told Carville to back off. "Daschle wants everyone to go slow," he said. "Let's wait until it's over."

Gerald Ford had been traveling from California to Colorado when impeachment was voted but saw the gathering on the White House South Lawn on television. He was offended. It looked like a pep rally. It was another Clinton stunt. Ford liked Clinton personally but was wary of him. In the summer of 1993, Clinton and Ford had spent several days together in Colorado on vacation. They played golf one day with Jack Nicklaus. Clinton claimed he shot something like an 80.

Ford was shocked. Golf was a matter of honor, even for old duffers, and Clinton had repeatedly taken second shots called mulligans.

Nicklaus leaned over to Ford and whispered in disgust, "Eighty with fifty floating mulligans."

Both Ford and Jimmy Carter had agreed to speak jointly on impeachment because the issue had so many consequences for the presidency. Carter had faxed a draft statement. Ford and his staff had gone to work. After six drafts, the two ex-presidents sent a statement to the op-ed page of *The New York Times*.

Clinton read it on Monday, December 21.

"A Time to Heal Our Nation," by Gerald Ford and Jimmy Carter.

Citing the Nixon pardon and Carter's grant of amnesty for those who had avoided the Vietnam draft, they called for reconciliation— Senate censure without a trial. They proposed a bipartisan resolution that would require Clinton to acknowledge publicly that "he did not tell the truth under oath." They wanted an agreement that his acknowledgment could not "be used in any future criminal trial."

On Wednesday afternoon, December 30, Clinton called Ford.

Ford repeated his position. The Republicans were committed and would need a significant concession to keep the Senate trial from going forward. For censure to be feasible and practical at this point, Bill, you'll have to concede perjury.

I can't do that, Clinton said. He was firm. Those were hard, impossible terms. He made a presentation that mirrored his grand jury argument. He believed he had not lied. His lawyers supported him. He said he had told the painful truth to the grand jury—the only issue in the impeachment charge of perjury now.

If nothing else, Clinton was articulate and smooth. But Ford said he couldn't agree.

Their proposal provides for immunity from prosecution, Ford reminded Clinton. Bill, he said, Congress could provide for immunity.

"They can't do that," Clinton said. His lawyers had researched the matter. Prosecution of an individual was an executive branch function that the Congress could not determine or prohibit.

"Bill," Ford said, "the Congress has pretty broad jurisdiction, and I've seen them do things before where the experts said they couldn't. And I happen to believe very strongly that this is an area where the Congress could affirmatively act to give you immunity."

Clinton didn't want immunity.

So it looks like a Senate trial, Ford said. A long, drawn-out trial would be a disaster.

Jerry, Clinton said, why not call Trent Lott and remind him of the advantages of a short trial.

Ford promised that he would do just that.

He reached Lott and reported that Clinton was not going to concede perjury. "Therefore I'm stepping back from doing anything," Ford told him. But he advised Lott to keep the trial short. The party could not afford to be defined as the party of impeachment.

Lott was hoping to avoid a chaotic Senate trial. He had worked actively to encourage a bipartisan plan, developed by his close friend Slade Gorton, a Washington Republican, and Joe Lieberman, the Democrat from Connecticut. As it emerged, the essence of the Gorton-Lieberman plan called for about the shortest trial imaginable, less than the Senate might spend on a highway bill. There would be three days of arguments and questions, and then a preliminary test vote. If the measure failed to receive two-thirds, the Senate would terminate the trial and consider censure. Lott liked the idea and gave it all the offstage encouragement he could. Under Senate rules, the plan would have to be agreed to unanimously. When it surfaced in the media, however, Senate Republican conservatives gave it an emphatic no.

At 10 a.m. Thursday, January 7, 1999, Hyde and the dozen Republican House impeachment managers filed over to the Senate. Hyde lumbered in, tilted forward, his white hair flowing longish. On the Senate floor, he stepped slowly to the wooden lectern in the well. Head down, reading every word carefully, without any expression on his face, he formally charged Clinton with perjury and obstruction of justice.

The brief opening ceremony left senators with time on their hands. They milled around like students at school on the opening day, gravitating to their leaders, Lott and Daschle. The question of whether to call live witnesses had not been settled. Ten days of private and public haggling still left most Republicans in favor of live witnesses at the trial and most Democrats opposing them. Two Democrats, Joseph Biden of Delaware and John Kerry of Massachusetts, joined Republican Don Nickles of Oklahoma. Several dozen senators pressed forward. Soon 40 were gathered in a spontaneous meeting. Some arms flew high in the air as they argued.

"This is an issue that affects me," Senator Phil Gramm, the conservative Texas Republican, pleaded above the crowd. He was not a popular figure, bright but overbearing. His own presidential ambitions had gone up in flames in 1996. Although he had raised tons of money, he had ended up with little public support. "And it affects all 100 senators," he added. His head stuck forward like a turtle, and his voice was pitched with a hard-edged Southern accent. "It shouldn't be decided by the leadership."

Yeah, another senator said, tantalized by the hint of rebellion. They all had their chestnuts in the fire.

What about a meeting of all 100 senators, an informal gathering off the floor, perhaps in the Old Senate Chamber where the protocols and rules wouldn't drag them down? Nickles proposed. Where they could talk straight, make it Trent and Tom and Phil and Orrin and Ted, and not the gentleman from Mississippi or the distinguished gentleman from South Dakota?

Most seemed to agree, but it was hard to tell because the leadership had set all the rules so far.

"I think we're there," Nickles said of the proposed meeting, putting his hand on Daschle's shoulder. "We can do this."

"That might be a good idea," Daschle said tentatively as he left to meet with his fellow Democrats.

Lott told reporters, "It was one of the most bipartisan committee meetings I had ever seen, right in the well of the Senate." He said he favored a private discussion of the issue.

Then, at 1 p.m., the Senate reconvened for the formal opening of the trial. Chief Justice William Rehnquist appeared in his black robe, adorned with four nonregulation gold stripes on the sleeves. He took the oath himself and then administered it to 100 senators, who swore to do "impartial justice" as jurors.

Later, after some uncertainty, Lott convinced Daschle to agree to the joint meeting.

"It's done!" Lott announced at an early evening news conference with Daschle at his side.

After 6 p.m., the Senate majority leader went to meet with Hyde and the other House managers. For two hours, Hyde and his group argued that they had to have witnesses. Lott insisted that the House was going to have to let the Senate set the rules for the trial.

The next morning, Friday, January 8, at 9:30 a.m., all 100 senators gathered in the Old Senate Chamber. There weren't enough seats at the desks because the last time it had been used as the Senate Chamber—in 1859—there were far fewer members of the Senate.

Senator Robert Byrd, the 81-year-old West Virginia Democratic patriarch, rose first.

"The White House has sullied itself," he said unsteadily, his voice unsure but forging ahead as his hands shook. "The House has fallen into the black pit of partisan self-indulgence. The Senate is teetering on the brink of that same black pit."

Byrd said the Senate must stop "the anger that has overtaken this country and the chaos which threatens this city.

"At this moment, we look very bad," he said. "We appear to be dithering and posturing and slowly disintegrating into the political quicksand."

There was a road back to sanity. He reminded them of the Pardoner's Tale from Chaucer's *Canterbury Tales:* three men who find a pot of gold only to kill one another to get it all.

"We can start by disdaining any more of the salacious muck which has already soiled the gowns of too many."

Senator Christopher Dodd, the Connecticut Democrat, told a story which had unfolded in the room in which they were meeting. In 1856,

Senator Charles Sumner of Massachusetts denounced Southern leaders. Two days later, a congressman who was the nephew of one of those denounced entered the Senate Chamber and struck Sumner on the neck and shoulders with a heavy walking stick. Serious injury kept Sumner from the Senate for three and a half years. It was the end of civility and the effective beginning of the Civil War, Dodd asserted.

Then it was Gramm's turn. He quoted from Daniel Webster's famous speech, "The Constitution and the Union," about the necessity to rise above state and region to be American. The Senate was once again being tested.

"I am one who is not at all convinced that the House needs witnesses," he said. Witnesses could harm the case the House managers might make. It could turn out to be a mistake for them. But let me tell you why we will have witnesses.

"If the president or his lawyers came to us and said, 'The president wants witnesses,' not a senator here would deny him that right, not even his worst enemies.

"I would not deny him that right," Gramm continued. "I say, how can you treat the House differently and not permit them witnesses?"

Democrats like Byrd and Pat Moynihan of New York seemed to be listening with unusual attentiveness.

"There is no practical difference between the plan of the Democrats and the Republicans." Under the Democratic plan, witnesses can be called and under the Republican plan they can be called. We're going to have to vote on witnesses one way or the other, Gramm said, and besides, the Senate rules in an impeachment trial explicitly call for a vote on witnesses.

"I've read the two resolutions," Senator Ted Kennedy of Massachusetts said, taking the floor. "They are almost identical up to this point." He pointed out where the two draft resolutions were about the same. That would take them to first base and second base, he said. "We could see later on how we're going to get to third." Why not agree up to the point where they are identical? That way the trial, the presentation by both sides, could move forward, and the witness vote be taken afterwards. Kennedy saw not so much the logic as the votes behind what Gramm was saying. Better to embrace the Republican position and call it a bipartisan compromise than lose.

"So moved!" yelled one senator. Others called out "Deal!" in one form or another. Several pounded the old desks.

Seizing the momentum, Lott called out, "We have the Kennedy-Gramm solution!"

It was the most improbable pair. The two were ideological and personal foes.

There was enough consensus and no apparent objection.

"We have a deal!" Lott shouted.

Voices were raised.

"Let's not kill it by talking about it," Lott said as the senators were carried on the wave of a rare collective enthusiasm.

Some Republicans believed that Daschle had slipped off the White House leash for a dangerous instant.

The details were quickly worked out: 24

hours of Senate time for each side to present its case—the House, led by Hyde, for the prosecution, the White House for the defense. The senators would then have 16 hours to ask questions, which under the rules had to be asked through the chief justice. Then the Senate would take up the unresolved question of possible witnesses.

The vote was 100 to 0 in favor.

Bipartisanship and unanimity were Clinton's and Carville's nightmare. But Daschle convinced Clinton that the road to acquittal was not to further enflame the Republicans. He could hold the Democrats, but he would have to do it his way.

41

AS THE SENATE PROCEEDED with the impeachment trial, Ken Starr was not closing down. He planned to indict Julie Hiatt Steele, a woman whose testimony contradicted Kathleen Willey's allegation that the president groped her.

Brett Kavanaugh was appalled. Steele was so tangential—she had nothing to do with Clinton or Lewinsky. An indictment of Steele, Kavanaugh wrote in a memo to Starr, would win the "trifecta" for abuse of the independent counsel law. It would be too hard on a bit player, too late in the investigation, and not weighty enough, he argued.

On January 7, 1999, the same day that the Senate trial began, Starr indicted Steele, the only person formally charged in the sex scandal. He claimed he had a duty.

The independent counsel would not let go of the investigation into the documents in Vince Foster's office, now in its sixth year. His staff had delivered a 330-page memo to him showing there was no case.

Starr said he believed Henry O'Neill, the uniformed Secret Service officer who had testified that he had seen Maggie Williams with a box. "He is a sworn, trained law enforcement officer!" Starr said, pounding the desk.

His deputies reminded Starr that O'Neill's job was to escort the White House janitors removing the trash on the midnight shift.

Starr did not accept that. The investigation would remain open.

He said he had the same obligation with the travel office investigation. Yes, the president was cleared, but not Hillary Clinton, he said. He recited David Watkins's "cleansing" memo that claimed Mrs. Clinton was behind the firings. The inquiry would remain open.

He also would proceed with the FBI files probe. Again, Clinton was absolved. His staff had written a 400-page memo showing that they had no evidence tying Clinton to the files. Why continue?

"My order says I have to focus on Anthony Marceca and others!" Starr said in protest. That investigation would remain open, too. He had a duty.

The president spoke at a Democratic National Committee fund-raising dinner Friday night,

January 15, at the Corcoran Gallery of Art in Washington.

"Of course," he said, "I don't even know how to talk about what I believe Hillary has meant to the success of our endeavors. She's been on every continent. She's gone to places most people in her position don't go." He listed trips to Africa, Asia and Latin America. "And just a thousand other things. And she has done it under circumstances I think are probably more difficult than anyone who has ever done it before."

Hillary, sitting nearby, wiped her eyes.

"I love her for it, but our country should love her for it as well. It's been remarkable."

On Saturday, January 16, at 2:30 p.m., Henry Hyde stepped to the podium to sum up the arguments made by House managers advocating impeachment. He believed the managers presenting the case against Clinton had made strong arguments. The polls showed that a large majority of the public believed Clinton had lied and obstructed justice. Now all Hyde had to do was convince them and the senators that the president should be removed for these acts. He said the president had broken faith and trust by lying and obstructing justice.

"Some of us have been called 'Clinton haters,' " he said. "I must tell you, distinguished senators, that this impeachment trial is not for those of us from the House a question of hating anyone. This is not a question of who we hate. It's a question of what we love. And among the things we love are the rule of law."

Hyde invoked the Bible, the Magna Carta, the Declaration of Independence, the Revolutionary War, and D-Day. He said he had walked to the cemetery area at Normandy in 1994 on the 50th anniversary of the Allied landings. He had found a cross marking a grave with only the epitaph: "Here lies in honored glory a comrade in arms known but to God." Hyde looked directly at the senators. "How do we keep faith with that comrade in arms?"

Hyde said he had an answer. "We work to make this country the kind of America they were willing to die for. That's an America where the idea of sacred honor still has the power to stir men's souls."

Ruff had listened intently to Hyde and the Republican managers. He thought there were four core issues: Lewinsky's false affidavit; Jordan's extraordinary job assistance to Lewinsky; the return of the gifts to Currie; and Clinton's alleged coaching of Currie. The managers were making a kind of "Are you kidding me?" argument. Clinton was the guiding hand, they had argued, his actions carefully premeditated and clever.

Ruff had to put more distance between the president and what Lewinsky, Jordan and Currie had done and said. Two issues were most troubling. How did the box of gifts the president had given a former intern wind up under the bed of his personal secretary? How was that innocent? Second, why did the president call his secretary into the White House on a Sunday to refresh his recollection about what was surely memorable?

For two weeks, Ruff had worked on an opening argument. He planned to deliver part of it. The rest would be given by former Senate Majority Leader George Mitchell, the Maine Democrat who had recently brokered the Irish peace agreement. Mitchell, a former federal judge, could make the case to the most important audience—the 45 Senate Democrats. The Senate could convict only with Democratic support, since a two-thirds vote is required.

Mitchell backed out at the last minute. So Ruff had to prepare a two- to three-hour opening defense for the afternoon of Tuesday, January 19. Six hours later, the president would be giving his State of the Union Address to Congress and the nation. The counterpoint was crucial: the lawyer defending, the president governing.

Working alone, Ruff built his arguments from four months of total immersion in the facts and a year in the legal combat. He submitted his statement to no one for review or comment—not to the president, not to any White House political advisers, not to Kendall or the other lawyers on the team, not to his wife. He didn't like to be edited. There were no practice sessions. "If you give it twice, you lose the edge the second time," he said. It was a stunning delegation of authority by the president.

Ruff had never spoken uninterrupted for that length of time in court or elsewhere. But he had, he thought, some surprises. Surprise was critical to good advocacy, to destroy the appearance of reality that the other side had constructed.

Just after 1 p.m. on Tuesday, Ruff rolled his wheelchair slowly to the center of the well of the Senate and turned to face the 100 senators.

"William Jefferson Clinton is not guilty of the charges that have been preferred against him," he said, slightly hunched, reading but then looking up and adding in a strong voice, "He did not commit perjury; he did not obstruct justice; he must not be removed from office."

"There is no one who does not feel the weight of this moment," he said. His nervousness was visible, but his voice remained strong.

The House Republican managers are caught in a stark inconsistency, Ruff said. On one hand, they insist that witnesses be called to prove their case and resolve conflicts in the evidence. "Tell me, then, how is it that the managers can be so certain of the strength of their case? They didn't hear any of these witnesses.

"Yet they appeared before you to tell you that they are convinced of the president's guilt, and that they are prepared to demand his removal from office.

"What you have before you is the product of nothing more than a rush to judgment.

"Impeachment is not a remedy for private wrongs."

Ruff had discovered in the Nixon impeachment case a report made by ten Republicans from the House Judiciary Committee. The group included Trent Lott, who was then a congressman. Ruff read it aloud. Removal of a president was "only for serious misconduct, dangerous to the system of government."

Ruff explained that the charge of perjury did not specify the exact alleged false statements the president was supposed to have made. Any perjury indictment of any citizen would do so, he noted. The perjury charge was a "witch's brew," unfair. He quoted from the Supreme Court: " 'Equally honest witnesses may well have different recollections of the same event, and thus, a conviction for perjury ought not to rest entirely upon an oath against an oath.' "

"To conclude that the president lied to the grand jury about his relationship with Ms. Lewinsky, you must determine—forgive me—that he touched certain parts of her body, but for proof you have only her oath against his oath."

Senators who had served as prosecutors or criminal defense attorneys would know that no prosecutor would bring a perjury case on such weak evidence, he said.

Ruff had worked hard to find a Perry Mason moment or two.

"I want to talk first about what has become known as the concealment of gifts theory." He noted that the Judiciary Committee had discovered a cell phone record, unknown even to the independent counsel, showing that Betty Currie had called Lewinsky at 3:32 p.m. on the afternoon of December 28, 1997, when the gifts were handed over to Currie. He read the House Republican report: this phone record "proves conclusively" that the call began the chain of events that led to the return of the gifts.

"Does this timing fit with the rest of the testimony?" he asked. "Well, the answer is no, it doesn't, because on three separate occasions,

Ms. Lewinsky testified that Mrs. Currie came over to pick up the gifts at 2 o'clock in the afternoon."

A phone call that had occurred 1 hour and 32 minutes after the return of the gifts could not have caused their return, Ruff said. He knew it was a minor point, but he intended to attack the trustworthiness of the managers.

He said the Republican managers' case was "constructed out of sealing wax and string and spiders' webs."

Next, Ruff reminded everyone that on December 11 Judge Wright had ruled that the Jones lawyers were allowed to seek information about female government employees with whom the president had sexual relations. It was also the day that Vernon Jordan stepped up his efforts to get Lewinsky a job.

Ruff brought up the words of Representative Asa Hutchinson, the 48-year-old Republican from Arkansas. Hutchinson had made by far the best arguments of the House impeachment managers, Ruff felt. He was glad that 13 Republicans had argued and not just Hutchinson, a tall, sober Southerner.

Ruff quoted Hutchinson: "The judge's order came in, that triggered the president into action and the president triggered Vernon Jordan into action. That chain reaction here is what moved the job search along."

Ruff then went through a supposed interrogation that the managers might make of Jordan, all leading to what was in the record. The judge, it turned out, according to the court record, did not rule until 6:33 p.m. Washington time on December 11. Jordan had departed from Dulles Airport for Europe at 5:55 p.m., landing in Amsterdam the next morning. Ruff showed the record, which revealed that Jordan's efforts to get Lewinsky a job took place from 9:45 a.m. to 1:45 p.m.—hours before the judge ruled. The accelerated job search could not have been caused by what had not yet occurred. Since the Republican managers proposed to call Jordan as a witness before the Senate, a matter that was still unresolved, Ruff added, "Do any of you think that you need to look Mr. Jordan in the eye and hear his tone of voice to understand that the prosecutors have it wrong?"

"So much for obstruction by job search," he declared.

"We are not here to defend William Clinton, the man. He, like all of us, will find his judges elsewhere. We are here to defend William Clinton, the President of the United States."

For three days, Ruff had stewed privately about Hyde's invocation of what the soldiers on the beaches at Normandy would have thought of Clinton. He detested Hyde's flag-waving. Ruff's father had been at Omaha Beach during the June 6, 1944, landing. His father had recently died and he was on his son's mind. In the long drafting sessions, Ruff had written out some lines about this theme. They were risky. He had consulted no one, but as he neared the end he felt he might as well proceed.

"I am never certain how to respond when an advocate on the other side of a case calls up images of patriots over the centuries sacrificing themselves to preserve our democracy," he said. "I have no personal experience with war. I have only visited Normandy as a tourist." He choked up for an instant. "I do know this: My father was on the beach 55 years ago." Ruff's voice quavered. "If you want to know how he would feel if he were here today, he wouldn't fight—no one fought—for one side of this case or the other."

When the president speaks tonight, Ruff said, people would see the state of the Union. "It stands strong, vibrant and free." He repeated his assertion that Clinton was not guilty. "He must not be removed from office."

Fred Thompson, a Tennessee Republican, was among the 100 senators who would have to vote. Thompson, 56, the Republican counsel for the Senate Watergate Committee a quarter of a century earlier, believed that Ruff's presentation pointed to what the Republican managers *didn't* have. They had no tapes, no eyewitnesses, no confession, and no resignations. Watergate had raised the standard of proof on every scandal to a new height, an unattainable standard of the "smoking gun." That meant absolute proof, not beyond a reasonable doubt but beyond any doubt. Ruff was saying it didn't meet the necessary threshold.

Watergate had taught Thompson how difficult it is to remove a president. Four elements had to be present: low public opinion polls, a bad economy, a hostile media, and incontrovertible evidence, such as tapes with the president ordering illegal activity. All had been present for Nixon. In Thompson's view, none were here in the Clinton case. But ordinary citizens are convicted all the time, even in capital cases, on circumstantial evidence, Thompson, a former prosecutor, realized. Watergate was saving Clinton.

In his private room on the fifth floor of the Senate Dirksen Office Building, Thompson had consulted the law, history and evidence many times. He disliked the perjury article. It didn't specify the exact charge. The accused deserved to know the exact alleged offenses for the purposes of his defense. That was what the rule of law was about. What if it were a Republican president on trial?

Thompson realized that none of the Democrats were leaving the reservation. But some Republicans were leaving theirs, including himself on the perjury article.

That night, President Clinton delivered the State of the Union Address, an almost joyful summary of the nation's economic prosperity. He made dozens of proposals for new programs. He spoke for 77 minutes and was interrupted by applause 98 times, mostly by Democrats. At one point he mouthed "I love you" toward his wife in the gallery.

After the speech, the Clintons held a reception for about 100 friends on the main floor of the State Dining Room in the White House. Clinton worked the room and then, exhausted, he went upstairs to bed. Hillary stayed, outlasting him at a party for one of the few times in their lives together.

Clinton reached Ruff by telephone. The

president, who often spent hours replaying or plotting strategy in the smallest political fight, briefly thanked his counsel. "I'm getting good reports," he said. "People were impressed and happy." The conversation lasted about two minutes.

The president had retired from his own defense. Despite the public face of an engaged president, the president's advisers, including Carville, found Clinton withdrawn. The phone conversations were much shorter.

Three days later, on Friday, January 22, on the Senate floor Robert Byrd handed Hyde a copy of a press release. Hyde read that Byrd was offering a motion to dismiss the charges against Clinton. Hyde was thunderstruck. Words could not express his disappointment and rage. Byrd was the potential leader of an anti-Clinton faction. For weeks, Byrd had been making ominous comments. Even Clinton's advisers worried that he might favor conviction. Now Hyde feared that barring new evidence, it was over. The public wanted Clinton to remain in office, according to the latest polls. "Politicians live and die by the polls," Hyde said privately. "It's that simple."

Ruff and Kendall, too, realized that Byrd's dismissal motion could mean they had won. They passed around a "Don't gloat" message at their table on the Senate floor. Four days later, the motion failed, 56 to 44. A single Democrat, Russell Feingold of Wisconsin, joined the Republicans. The 44 votes—10 more than the 34 that would ensure Clinton stayed in office—provided a firewall that would prevent removal, if no one lost their equilibrium, Ruff felt.

The Republican House managers were still demanding that they depose witnesses. Lott would allow only closed-door depositions from three—Lewinsky, Jordan and White House aide Sidney Blumenthal.

Ruff and Kendall put up a somewhat deceptive protest. Witnesses were not needed, the record was clear enough, they would only prolong the trial and potentially could drag the Senate into the muck. Among themselves the lawyers privately called it a modified "briar patch strategy." They would protest, "Don't throw us in that briar patch, my God, we don't want witnesses!" But they well knew that the witnesses were not at all hostile. Loyalty and old ties bound Jordan and Blumenthal to Clinton. Her previous testimony constrained Lewinsky. If she changed her story, Starr could prosecute and send her to prison. The witnesses would not help the Republicans, and they didn't.

When Ruff clipped on the microphone on Monday, February 8, and rolled himself to the center of the Senate well for the closing argument, he could afford to toy with his opportunity.

"I thought about what I was going to say today, and how I could be of most help to you," he began. "I momentarily considered whether the answer to that question was simply to yield back my time, but I weighed that against the special pleasure of stretching out our last hours with you."

The senators laughed hard.

"Or as Ernie Banks would have said, 'It's such a nice day, let's play two.' "

More laughter.

The managers did not understand, he said. "I believe their vision could be too dark, a vision too little attuned to the needs of the people, too little sensitive to the needs of our democracy. I believe it to be a vision more focused on retribution, more designed to achieve partisan ends, more uncaring about the future we face together."

To the charge that Clinton could not represent the United States abroad, Ruff struck a distinctively political note. Ask those who live in places where the president has helped make peace, Ireland or the Middle East, whether the president should be removed. In a brazen reminder to the senators of public opinion, he added, "If you doubt whether he should, here at home, continue in office, ask the parent whose child walks safer streets or the men and women who go off to work in the morning to good jobs."

Hyde rose for his summation. He had suffered through "the media condemnations, the patronizing editorials, the hate mail, the insults hurled in public, the attempts at intimidation, the death threats." Cynicism had infected everyone. "That cynicism is an acid eating away at the vital organs of American public life." He suggested that he was a victim of it. "I wonder if after this culture war is over that we're engaged in, if an America will survive that's worth fighting to defend."

The Senate adjourned for three days of closed

deliberations and statements before a final vote that was expected on Friday.

The president's present for Terry McAuliffe, his chief fund-raiser, and his wife Dorothy was a night in the Lincoln Bedroom, Tuesday, February 9, McAuliffe's 42nd birthday. Overnights in the bedroom for $50,000 or $100,000 campaign donors had become one of the symbols of Clinton's 1996 campaign fundraising zeal. About 9 p.m., the president and Hillary arrived with a birthday cake and Dom Pérignon Champagne.

Clinton was upbeat. He hoped to get back to legislative business. The Republicans would need some legislation to dig themselves out of the impeachment hole. There was good interaction between the Clintons. The four partied for several hours into the night, almost like any two couples, relatively carefree. It looked like not only acquittal, the relieved president said, but no censure, no fine.

"I'll survive, but it will never be the same," the president said to a friend Thursday afternoon, February 11, the day before the expected vote. He meant his family, the presidency—his life. A price had been paid, he said. The loss is forever. Acquittal would be a hollow victory. He wondered if Starr would keep going. The damage is done, distrust is deep, betrayal is the order of the day, and there are bad feelings everywhere. He would go back and do the job. He would have another 700 days as president, but it would be tough. "If there is one victory," he added, "it will be a lot."

People magazine had published a cover story on Chelsea that the president and Hillary had tried to stop. Hillary had called Norman Pearlstine, the editor in chief of Time publications, in a futile effort to kill the story. The article had portrayed their mother-daughter relationship glowingly.

"We hate to have her so exposed," the president told his friend. "It was good for the two of them. It painted me out to be a bad father."

"I don't know where the hell you read that," the friend said. There was no hint or inference in the article. Insecurity and guilt seemed to color Clinton's remarks. Their discussion turned to whether the president should make a public statement after the vote. Most advisers and friends he had consulted had said no, he reported. Most of his public statements on the scandal since August 17 had not worked or had been disastrous.

"You owe the country a few words," his friend suggested.

"They'll kill me," Clinton said, meaning the critics, the press, the enemies.

"No," the friend said, "you'll be talking to your friends, not your enemies."

"I have to take the heat," Clinton replied. Nothing was resolved. His family situation was unsettled, his legal difficulties uncertain. He was a chastened man.

They discussed the need for him to relax, to play golf.

The president said he had lots of advice strongly suggesting he not play golf.

"Where are you getting your relief?" the

friend asked, recommending a golf outing. "Who can you spill your guts to? Who can you cry with?"

Clinton didn't answer.

At 12:09 p.m. the next day, the roll call began on Article One, charging perjury. All 45 Democrats and 10 Republicans, including Fred Thompson, voted not guilty, and 45 Republicans voted guilty. The 55-to-45 vote was 22 short of the necessary two-thirds.

All 45 Democrats and 5 Republicans voted not guilty on Article Two, and 50 Republicans voted guilty. The 50-to-50 vote was 17 short.

"Acquitted of the charges," Chief Justice Rehnquist declared at 12:39 p.m.

Two hours later, Clinton appeared in the Rose Garden before the cameras, alone. It was a windy, springlike day.

"I want to say again to the American people how profoundly sorry I am for what I said and did to trigger these events," he said solemnly. He thanked everyone for their support and prayers. "This can be and this must be a time of reconciliation and renewal for America." He turned and walked away.

"In your heart," Sam Donaldson shouted, "sir, can you forgive and forget?"

The president turned slowly around and stepped back to the podium. He paused. It was a dangerous moment. He had a lot of pent-up feelings and could say anything, take his shot.

"I believe any person who asks forgiveness has to be prepared to give it," the president said. He turned away again.

"Do you feel vindicated, sir?" another reporter shouted.

The president did not answer.

Ruff and the other lawyers went to see the president; Kendall was on a train to New York City. The president thanked them graciously. There were many smiles. Pictures were taken. There was no outpouring of emotion. It was a win but no victory.

Hillary went to Ruff's office on the second floor of the West Wing.

"Thank you," the first lady said. "I want to give you these as a token of my appreciation." She handed Ruff a pair of eagle cufflinks.

Ruff tried to make sense of it all. He had always thought that Nixon could have avoided resignation or being ousted. "If he could have brought himself to the point of public embarrassment involved in a straightforward explanation," Ruff had said, "even as late as 1974, if he had given a sort of mea culpa kind of speech, even then he could have saved himself." Clinton had come late in the game with his mea culpa, delivered in four or five public variations, and he had saved himself.

The presidency has so much weight, Ruff concluded, that any president, if his mind is made up and he is determined, can use it to achieve nearly anything.

Clinton drew his own conclusion. A president could do a lot, but to do big things even a president needed public support.

Lawyering, contrition, parsing the language,

political hardball, trying to change the subject wouldn't work by themselves.

To his closest advisers, Clinton said, "Thank God for public opinion."

EPILOGUE

AFTER WATERGATE, I never expected another impeachment investigation of a president in my lifetime, let alone an actual impeachment and a Senate trial. Nixon's successors, I thought, would recognize the price of scandal and learn the two fundamental lessons of Watergate. First, if there is questionable activity, release the facts, whatever they are, as early and completely as possible. Second, do not allow outside inquiries, whether conducted by prosecutors, congressmen or reporters, to harden into a permanent state of suspicion and warfare.

But the overwhelming evidence is that five presidents after Nixon didn't understand those lessons. It wasn't that they lacked the political skill. Four of these presidents had mastered American electoral politics to win political power, and Ford almost did. Of the five, Reagan managed his problems best, although belatedly, when, after three months of Iran-contra, he permitted a broad internal White House investigation of his own actions.

Why did they not see that they would be held fully accountable for their exercise of power?

Historians and psychiatrists will have their own answers to that question, but I have one preliminary conclusion. They have become victims of the myth of the big-time president. As successors to George Washington and Franklin Roosevelt, they expect to rule. But after

Vietnam and Watergate, the modern presidency has been limited and diminished. Its inner workings and the behavior of the presidents are fully exposed.

The men who followed Nixon are like addicts who have been denied their supply of drugs, in this case the alluring narcotic of presidential power. The myth of the big-time president persists, the longing for someone with heroic energy, someone who can take the air out of a room, who can define an era worth living in. That is not only what these presidents hope to see in themselves, it is what the public wants and what the press holds up as the standard against which they will be judged. But the post-Watergate conditions have made the emergence of such a leader increasingly unlikely, and the presidents, in frustration, have been in rebellion.

Clinton's rebellion was the greatest and the most self-defeating.

Faced with exposure of his relationship with a White House staffer half his age, Clinton panicked. He was embarrassed. If we are to believe him, he felt shame. He saw the possible jeopardy to his presidency.

Based on the available evidence, he confided in no one and conspired with no one. As many others, including Nixon, have said, the cover-up is worse than the crime. But in the Lewinsky affair, the cover-up was a one-man operation. There was no conspiracy. Clinton concealed and dodged shamelessly. He enlisted his personal secretary, Betty Currie, and best friend, Vernon Jordan, to help him. They certainly realized his desperation. But no one pulled the trigger: there were no orders, in clear or unambiguous language, to lie or obstruct justice. Or at least neither Jordan nor Currie provided any testimony suggesting Watergate-style crimes.

To convince the public or the Senate that a president should be removed from office, there would have to be testimony from close aides or friends that the president participated in or ordered illegal actions. Nixon's White House counsel, John Dean, was a potent witness in Watergate because he not only incriminated Nixon, he testified that he himself had a corrupt motive to obstruct the Watergate investigation. He blew himself up and took Nixon with him when the tapes corroborated his testimony.

In the Lewinsky investigation, it was the underlying activity, the sexual relationship, that was the problem. The cover-up was Clinton's lonely effort to save face and embarrassment. Whether instinctively or by design, Clinton did not enter into a conspiracy that might eventually produce witnesses who might testify against him.

During the pre-Lewinsky phase of the Whitewater investigations, from 1994 to early 1998, the Clintons and their attorney David Kendall reacted too many times as if the scandal were Watergate. They seemed to be hiding. Scrambling for cover, the Clintons and their lawyers played their parts too well. The forest is full of wolves, Kendall said. He believed that some of Starr's deputies were so hostile and aggressive that they had to be beaten into the ground. He had a strong case after 1996. But earlier, in 1994 and 1995, the president, Kendall and Starr should have worked out an arrangement to end the investigation at any reasonable cost. The prolonged investigation became an abuse in itself. Starr's decision to send a massive narrative of the Clinton-Lewinsky sexual relationship to Congress as part of his impeachment referral was pathetic and unwise. His determination to continue the marginal investigations and prosecutions after he had essentially completed his Clinton inquiries made no sense. Starr had lost his way.

For years, Clinton went into a full Watergate defense. He denied, stonewalled, parsed the language, belittled and attacked. In the course of defending himself, he lost control of his presidency.

That is the price he, and the American public, paid.

Clinton has great talent for the presidency—uncommon intellect, astonishing communication and political skills. Instead of harnessing himself to define the next stage of good—and progress—for a majority of people in the country and charting a way to get there, Clinton wound up living a self-inflicted melodrama he had not intended.

After his acquittal by the Senate, Clinton still had to manage his embarrassment and regret. He continued to acknowledge he had done wrong. "But I do not regard this impeachment vote as some great badge of shame," he said in a March 31, 1999, CBS Television interview with Dan Rather. The impeachment was not warranted, he said. It was political. By defending himself, he had defended the Constitution and the presidency. The larger wrong to the legal and constitutional system, he said, had been Starr's investigation.

Clinton also made it clear in the Rather interview that he had set out to drive his impeachment from the first paragraph of his obituary. Somehow he would remove the shadow. Nixon spent 20 years trying to rehabilitate himself. Clinton seemed determined to launch his comeback while still in office. In one sense, this is admirable, but it is also worrisome.

In pursuit of this goal, he has turned to foreign affairs, where a president has his greatest power and leverage. It would provide the possibility for a personal legacy of accomplishment. The first public hint of his plans came in October 1998, between the release of the Starr referral and the House impeachment vote. Clinton spent 85 hours over nine days fashioning a peace accord between the Israelis and the Palestinians. He stayed up until 2 a.m. or 3 a.m. with Israeli Prime Minister Benjamin Netanyahu and Yasser Arafat at the Wye River plantation on Maryland's Eastern Shore to work out an agreement. It was late night at the dorm, and Clinton had pulled an all-nighter the last day.

After the accord was signed on Friday afternoon, October 23, Clinton spoke that night to the Metropolitan African Methodist Episcopal Church's 160th anniversary celebration. He quoted scripture—"Let us not grow weary in doing good"—and explained his drive to negotiate the peace accord in a statement that seems to have gone largely unnoticed.

"I felt that it was a part of my job as president, my mission as a Christian, and my personal journey of atonement."

Peace is indeed part of his job as president, but there is something troubling about his willingness to link his peacemaking efforts to a "journey of atonement." Foreign policy should not be an instrument of a president's personal or historical redemption, whether he is making peace or waging war.

In March of 1999, when President Clinton led the NATO alliance to attack Yugoslavia to stop the ethnic cleansing in Kosovo, he voiced the right humanitarian motives. Yet there was a careless, ad hoc quality to the decision making. The clearest lesson of Vietnam and the Gulf War seemed to have been ignored. When going to war, state clear political objectives and ensure that enough military force is committed to guarantee success. Yet, because of his own words, lingering in the background were the unavoidable suggestions that Clinton's actions were influenced by his need for personal atonement and his political desire to do something big and bold so historians would concentrate less on his impeachment. Had the scandals and investigations so defined and crippled the president, ingrained a sense of desperate struggle and blind determination, that he had lost his way?

NOTES

Gerald Ford and Jimmy Carter were interviewed for this book; Ronald Reagan could not be because of his health; George Bush answered by letter; and Bill Clinton declined to be interviewed.

PART ONE. GERALD FORD: 1974–77

CHAPTER 1

August 1, 1974, was a hot: Haig-Nixon meeting quoted from author's interviews with Alexander Haig, November 6, 1997, and February 5, 1998; Alexander Haig, *Inner Circles* (1992), 478–479; Richard Nixon, *RN: The Memoirs of Richard Nixon* (1978), 1057. Nixon died in 1994.

"We've got to quietly bring": Kissinger quoted from Chuck Wardell contemporaneous diary entry, August 11, 1974, referring to an August 1, 1974, Kissinger to Haig conversation. Confirmed in author's interview with Wardell, March 19, 1998. Wardell was Haig's aide. This contemporaneous entry contradicts Haig's account of the meeting. Haig wrote in his memoir (p. 477), "Kissinger did not utter a single word in reply to what I had said to him. Certainly he did not advise me, as has been written, to nudge the president toward resignation."

Before he saw Ford: Buzhardt's meeting with Haig quoted from author's interviews with Haig, November 6, 1997, and February 5, 1998; Haig memoir, 481. See also James Cannon, *Time and Chance: Gerald Ford's Appointment with History* (1998 edn.), 291. Buzhardt died in 1978. For Buzhardt's interpretation of a president's power to pardon, see handwritten notes, folder 19, J. Fred Buzhardt Jr. Papers, Special Collections, Strom Thurmond Institute, Clemson University; "Memorandum on Presidential Power to Grant Reprieves and Pardons," "Correspondence and Memos," folder 6, J. Fred Buzhardt Jr. Papers.

Before 9 a.m., Haig went to Ford's office: First Haig-Ford meeting quoted from author's interview with Gerald Ford, September 22, 1997; author's interviews with Haig, November 6, 1997, and February 5, 1998; Haig memoir, 480–481; Robert Hartmann, *Palace Politics* (1979), 126–127; Gerald Ford, *A Time to Heal* (1980), 1–3.

"This left Jerry Ford": The top three candidates for vice president after Agnew's resignation were John Connally, Ronald Reagan and Nelson Rockefeller. Connally was Nixon's choice, but Nixon concluded Democrats would block his confirmation. Nixon decided that nominating the conservative Reagan or the moderate Rockefeller would split the Republican Party and weaken its chances in the 1976 presidential election. See Nixon memoir, 925–926.

Haig detested and distrusted Hartmann: Author's interview with Haig, November 6, 1997; author's interview with Wardell, March 19, 1998.

Later in the day Haig called: Second Haig-Ford meeting quoted from author's interview with Gerald Ford, September 22, 1997; author's interviews with Haig, November 6, 1997, and February 5, 1998; author's interview with Robert Hartmann, December 10, 1997; Gerald Ford's opening statement, "Pardon of Richard M. Nixon and Related Matters, Thursday, October 17, 1974, House of Representatives Subcommittee on Criminal Justice of the Committee on the Judiciary" report, 153–154; Ford memoir, 1–5; Haig memoir, 482–484. See also James Cannon, 292–294. For a transcript of the June 23, 1972, "smoking gun" conversation, see Stanley Kutler, *Abuse of Power: The New Nixon Tapes* (1997), 67–70.

Haig then reported to Nixon: Author's interview with Haig, November 6, 1997. Haig contradicts what he wrote in his memoirs: "As for Nixon, he never knew from anything I told him that the subject of presidential pardons had come up in my conversation with the vice president. The explanation for this is a simple one: It would have been a cruel insult even to mention such talk to Nixon in his agony, and I never for a moment considered doing so." Haig memoir, 486.

Ford summoned Hartmann: Ford-Hartmann meeting quoted from author's interviews with Hartmann, December 10, 1997, and January 7, 1998; author's interview with Ford, September 22, 1997; Hartmann memoir, 131; Ford memoir, 6. See also James Cannon, 295–296.

Ford didn't agree: Author's interview with Ford, September 22, 1997; author's interview with Hartmann, December 10, 1997; Ford memoir, 9–10.

About 1:30 a.m., a late hour: Author's interview with Haig, November 6, 1997; author's interview with Hartmann, December 10, 1997; Haig memoir, 485; Hartmann memoir, 135n. In his autobiography, *A Time to Heal* (pp. 9–10), Ford claims that Haig made the call. But in interviews and in their memoirs Haig and Hartmann—whom Ford told about the phone call the following morning—say Ford phoned Haig after talking to Betty. See also James Cannon, 299.

Haig concluded there was somebody: Author's interviews with Haig, November 6, 1997, and February 5, 1998.

The next morning, Friday, August 2: Author's interviews with Haig, November 6, 1997, and February 5, 1998.

Over in the vice president's suite: Marsh-Ford meeting quoted from author's and Jeff Glasser's interviews with Jack Marsh, October 23, 1997, and March 18, 1998; author's interview with Ford, September 22, 1997.

Marsh and Hartmann talked again: Hartmann-Marsh-Ford discussions quoted from author's and Glasser's interview with Marsh, October 23, 1997; author's interview with Hartmann, December 10, 1997; Hartmann memoir, 134–136.

At their request, Ford agreed: Harlow-Ford-Hartmann-Marsh meeting quoted from author's interview with Hartmann, December 10, 1997; author's interview with Ford, September 22, 1997; author's and Glasser's interview with Marsh, October 23, 1997; Ford memoir, 13; Hartmann memoir, 136–137. See also James Cannon, 306–308.

Ford called Haig: Ford-Haig conversation quoted from author's interview with Haig, November 6, 1997; author's interview with Ford, September 22,

1997; author's interview with Hartmann, December 10, 1997; author's and Glasser's interview with Marsh, October 23, 1997; Ford memoir, 13; Hartmann memoir, 137; Haig memoir, 485. See also James Cannon, 307.

Hartmann was convinced that Ford: Author's interview with Hartmann, December 10, 1997.

Ford still didn't want: Author's interview with Ford, September 22, 1997. Phil Buchen, Ford's former law partner and oldest friend, felt that Haig planted the seed in Ford's mind to grant Nixon a pardon. "Well, I think Ford wouldn't have gotten the idea if it hadn't been for those meetings with Haig," Buchen said. Author's interview with Buchen, April 8, 1998.

"Let them impeach me": Haig-Nixon exchange quoted from Haig memoir, 487; Nixon memoir, 1061.

The next day, August 3: Transcripts, Ford's August 3, 1974, press conferences in Hattiesburg, Mississippi, and New Orleans, Louisiana, found in folder "Nixon Pardon Hungate Subcommittee: Background Material (2)," Phil Buchen files, Box 33, Gerald R. Ford Presidential Library. Asked at the press conference for his opinion on a congressional censure of Nixon instead of impeachment, Ford answered, "If I had my druthers, I would rather have the House of Representatives vote as I think the facts justify, which is acquittal." He made this comment while knowing about the "smoking gun" tape.

CHAPTER 2

At 3 a.m. Wednesday: Author's interview with Hartmann, January 7, 1998; Hartmann memoir, 159–160. Ford omits this scene from his autobiography. "Our national nightmare" is one of two Ford phrases that appear in *Bartlett's Familiar Quotations*. "I am a Ford, not a Lincoln," made after Ford's nomination for the vice presidency, is the other.

"I feel it is my first duty": Ford's inauguration speech found in Public Papers of the Presidents, Gerald R. Ford, August 9, 1974, 1.

The muffins and the "Michigan Fight Song": Ford memoir, 126; Hartmann memoir, 181.

On August 27, Leonard Garment: Garment memo scene quoted from Bob Woodward & Carl Bernstein, "Ford Disputed on Events Preceding Nixon Pardon," *The Washington Post*, December 18, 1975, A1; author's interview with Buchen, April 8, 1998; author's interviews with Haig, November 6, 1997, and February 5, 1998. See also James Cannon, 370.

"In the last ten days or two weeks": Ford quoted from "The President's News Conference of August 28, 1974," Public Papers of the Presidents, Gerald R. Ford, 56–66.

Hartmann's stomach turned: Hartmann memoir, 252, 255.

After the press conference: Author's interview with Ford, September 22, 1997.

Later that night, Ford was up: Author's interview with close Ford adviser who witnessed the event firsthand.

Although nine of the 28 questions: Author's interview with Ford, September 22, 1997.

Two days after the press conference: Meeting quoted from author's interview with Ford, September 22, 1997; author's interview with Hartmann, December 10, 1997; author's and Glasser's interview with Marsh, October 23, 1997; author's interviews with Haig, November 6, 1997, and February 5, 1998; Hartmann memoir, 257–261; Haig memoir, 513; Ford memoir, 161–162. See also James Cannon, 375. Ford had a prior meeting with Haig, Hartmann, Buchen and Henry Kissinger on August 29, 1974, in which he said he was inclined to pardon Nixon. See Benton L. Becker, "Memorandum: History and Background of Nixon Pardon," September 9, 1974, Box 2, Benton L. Becker Papers, Gerald R. Ford Presidential Library, 6.

Marsh too was deeply worried: Marsh-Ford meeting quoted from author's and Glasser's interview with Marsh, October 23, 1997; author's interview with Ford, September 22, 1997. In addition to Marsh, Ford called in Hartmann, Kissinger and Buchen to discuss a pardon for Nixon. Ford said he is not certain if he raised the pardon with Nixon, but he believes he probably did. In his memoirs (p. 161), Ford writes, "Haig was for it too, although he never said as much. He laid out the pros and cons, then stepped back and said, 'It's your decision, sir.'" Haig writes in his memoir (p. 513), "Sometime during this period, Ford asked me . . . for an opinion on the pardon. I laid out the pros and cons as I saw them but declined to make a recommendation."

Ford called in Benton Becker: Ford-Becker meeting quoted from author's interview with Benton Becker, April 22, 1998.

Nixon wanted them shipped: Nixon's old staff felt Nixon should have his papers like any other president. The attorney general also had issued an opinion to Ford saying a failure to send the papers to Nixon "would be to reverse what has apparently been the almost unvaried understanding of all three branches of the government since the beginning of the Republic." Attorney General William Saxbe had informally notified Ford through his advisers earlier in the month that it was his opinion that Nixon owned his papers and tapes. In addition, before the opinion was issued, Haig had told the Watergate special prosecutor, Leon Jaworski, that Saxbe's opinion would be that Nixon owned his papers. Antonin Scalia, later a Supreme Court justice, drafted Saxbe's opinion. President Ford requested the opinion on August 22, 1974. See William Saxbe, "Text of a Legal Opinion by the Attorney General," September 6, 1974; Becker memorandum; draft of Saxbe opinion, Antonin Scalia to Deputy Attorney General, found in folder "Nixon Papers: Saxbe Opinion Re: Ownership," Phil Buchen files, Box 32, Gerald R. Ford Presidential Library; August 22, 1974, letter Gerald R. Ford to Mr. Attorney General, folder "Nixon Papers: Saxbe Opinion Re: Ownership," Phil Buchen files, Box 32, Gerald R. Ford Presidential Library.

In his research on presidential: Becker research quoted from author's interview with Becker, April 22, 1998; Becker memorandum; Supreme Court decision in *George Burdick* v. *United States,* January 15, 1915, October 1914 Term *Supreme Court Reporter,* 267–271. Burdick was a newspaper editor at the *New York Tribune* who had run a series of articles detailing customs frauds by U.S. Treasury Department employees. A federal grand jury investigation began, and Burdick was called before the grand jury. He refused to answer questions about the sources of his newspaper's information, invoking his constitutional right against self-incrimination. One month later, Burdick was subpoenaed again. He again refused to answer. The U.S. attorney pulled out a piece of paper signed by Woodrow Wilson granting "a full and unconditional pardon for offenses against the United States which he, the said George Burdick, has committed or may have committed or taken part in." The result was that Burdick could no longer claim Fifth Amendment rights. He would have to respond to the questions. Burdick, however, objected and he tried to decline the pardon. When he continued to refuse to cooperate, he was sent to jail in contempt of court. The Supreme Court reversed that conviction and set Burdick free on the grounds that a pardon can be rejected. The case set a number of precedents, including "A pardon is a deed, to the validity of which delivery is essential, and delivery is not complete without acceptance"; "The President has power to pardon for a crime of which the individual has not been convicted and which he does not admit"; and, a pardon "carries an imputation of guilt: confession an acceptance of it."

Herbert J. Miller: Scenes quoted from author's interview with Herbert J. Miller, May 19, 1998.

A few days later: Becker-Miller-Ziegler scenes in San Clemente quoted from author's interview with Becker, April 22, 1998; Becker memorandum, 9–10, 14–16; author's interview with Miller, May 19, 1998; drafts of Nixon acceptance statement, Box 2, Benton L. Becker Papers, Gerald R. Ford Library.

Becker thought Haig had tipped off Ziegler to Ford's instructions. Becker wrote in the contemporaneous memorandum, "I learned later, what I had suspected at the time, that Ziegler had had telephone contact with General Haig regarding GRF's [Ford's] position on pardon, GRF's reliance on me and my report to him upon my return to D.C. which could 'tip' the decision either way and GRF's position of not imposing a statement of contrition upon President Nixon before granting, if to be granted at all, the pardon. Armed with what he apparently considered to be 'inside' information, Ziegler immediately attempted to seize the initiative and 'upperhand' in the negotiations." Haig denied that he ever talked to Ziegler or Diane Sawyer, then a Nixon aide, during the period between Nixon's resignation and the pardon. He said he did talk to President Nixon once or twice during that time, and Nixon complained bitterly that Ford had put a lock on his records. Author's interview with Haig, February 5, 1998.

Becker walked alone: Nixon-Becker meetings quoted from author's interview with Becker, April 22, 1998; author's interview with Miller, May 19, 1998; Becker memorandum, 16–18. See also James Cannon, 381; Ford memoir, 170–171.

After returning to Washington: Becker-Ford meeting quoted from author's interview with Becker, April 22, 1998; Ford memoir, 171–172; draft statement, Box 2, Benton L. Becker Papers, Gerald R. Ford Library.

"Did you put a gun to his head": Haig quoted from author's interview with Becker, April 22, 1998.

Hartmann persisted: Hartmann-Ford discussion quoted from author's interview with Hartmann, December 10, 1997; Hartmann memoir, 264.

Taking a felt-tip pen: Reading copy of Ford's statement with Ford's insertion, folder "Sept. 8, 1974 Presidential Pardon Message," Office of the Editorial Staff, Reading Copies of Presidential Speeches and Statements, 1974–1977, Box 1, Gerald R. Ford Library, 7; author's interview with Hartmann, December 10, 1997.

An hour before Ford was to go: TerHorst letter quoted from Ford memoir, 175–176; Jerald F. terHorst, *Gerald Ford and the Future of the Presidency* (1974), 236–237.

"Theirs is an American tragedy": Gerald R. Ford, "Remarks on Signing a Proclamation Granting Pardon to Richard Nixon," September 8, 1974, Public Papers of the President, 101–103.

One day not long after: Kennerly-Ford discussions quoted from author's interview with David Kennerly, May 14, 1998.

On September 16, eight days: Gerald R. Ford, "The President's News Conference of September 16, 1974," Public Papers of the President, 146–156.

"Did you ever discuss the pardon": Questions quoted from privileged resolution, U.S. House of Representatives, September 12, 1974, Bella Abzug.

Jack Marsh saw the draft answers: Ford-Marsh exchange quoted from author's and Glasser's interviews with Marsh, October 23, 1997, and March 18, 1998; author's interview with Ford, September 22, 1997; Ford memoir, 196–197. See also James Cannon, 388.

Marsh felt that Albert's recommendation: Author's and Glasser's interview with Marsh, October 23, 1997. Nixon in his memoirs (p. 925) writes, "Among the 400 top party leaders from all sections of the country and from Congress, the Cabinet, and the White House staff whose recommendations I had solicited, Rockefeller and Reagan were in a virtual tie for first choice; Connally was third; Ford was fourth. Ford, however, was first choice among members of Congress, and they were the ones who would have to approve the man I nominated."

Marsh prepared a one-page summary: Marsh-Albert meeting quoted from author's and Glasser's interview with Marsh, October 23, 1997; Ford memoir, 197. See also James Cannon, 389–390.

Marsh next went to see Hungate: Author's and Glasser's interview with Marsh, October 23, 1997. See also James Cannon, 388.

Marsh had significant missionary work: Marsh-Buchen-Ford exchanges quoted from author's and Glasser's interview with Marsh, October 23, 1997; author's interview with Buchen, April 8, 1998. See also James Cannon, 388.

Fred Buzhardt . . . read the prepared testimony: Buzhardt-Haig phone call quoted from author's interview with Haig, November 6, 1997.

"Whoever wrote this testimony": Haig quoted from author's interviews with Haig, November 6, 1997, and February 8, 1998.

Marsh said there was no reason: Author's interview with Haig, November 6, 1997; author's and Glasser's interview with Marsh, October 23, 1997.

Within minutes Haig was in: Haig-Ford discussion quoted from author's interview with Haig, November 6, 1997. Ford omits this scene from his memoirs.

Ford and Marsh worked almost: Author's and Glasser's interview with Marsh, October 23, 1997; Ford memoir, 197.

"I was determined not to make": Ford testimony quoted from "Pardon of Richard M. Nixon, and Related Matters," Hearings before the Subcommittee on Criminal Justice of the Committee on the Judiciary, House of Representatives, October 17, 1974, 95.

The stakes couldn't be higher: Author's and Glasser's interview with Marsh, October 23, 1997.

It was the first documented appearance: Jeff Glasser's October 19, 1998, interview with Stephen Lynch; Bernard J. Firestone and Alexej Ugrinsky, *Gerald R. Ford and the Politics of Post-Watergate America* (1993), 67. Lynch did the research for the subcommittee on presidential appearances before Congress. He could not find any record at the Library of Congress or the National Archives of the two alleged prior appearances of presidents at congressional hearings. The two were George Washington appearing at an appropriations hearing, and Abraham Lincoln demanding to speak at hearings defending his wife from charges that she was a conspirator with the South. Lynch concluded that they were undocumented legends.

The Firestone and Ugrinsky book is a final report from a Hofstra University conference on President Ford. Hungate was one of the participants, and a transcript of what he said at the conference appears in the book.

"President Denies Any Deal": Richard L. Lyons, "President Denies Any Deal on Pardon," *The Washington Post*, October 18, 1974, A1.

But on November 22, the Republicans: *New York Times*, November 23, 1974, A14.

CHAPTER 3

He was used to a congressional: Ford's drinking scenes quoted from author's interview with Wardell, March 19, 1998; Jeff Glasser's interview with Don Penny, June 2, 1998. Lukash died in February 1998. In a March 31, 1999, interview, Ford said he didn't recall Lukash's specific warning. "I will admit it was good advice if it took place," he said. "The truth is I haven't had a drink for 20 years. Betty stopped 21 years ago this week or next week, and I drank by myself for a year and then I said, 'Hell, why am I doing this?' I'm living better and feeling better."

"Why'd you pardon Nixon?": Penny-Ford exchange on the pardon quoted from Glasser's interview with Penny, June 2, 1998.

Congress had passed bills: In the midst of Watergate in November 1973, Congress passed the War Powers Act, which required the president to consult Congress before introducing U.S. forces into hostilities. Military action had to be terminated within 60 days unless Congress approved. Nixon vetoed the bill, but the Democratic Congress overrode the veto. Ford chafed under the restrictions, finding them impractical. See Ford memoir, 249–252, 280–281.

Congress further constrained executive authority with the 1974 Budget and Impoundment Act, ending the president's ability to refuse to spend funds—called impounding—that Congress had allocated. The act set up a Congressional Budget Office, two budget committees on the Hill, and strict deadlines. See John Robert Greene, *The Presidency of Gerald R. Ford* (1995 edn.), 54.

One of the most shocking: Ford-Schlesinger section quoted from author's interviews with Ford, September 22, 1997, and May 20, 1998; author's interview with James Schlesinger, July 31, 1989; author's interview with Haig, November 6, 1997. In his memoirs, Ford wrote extensively of his distaste for Schlesinger. But the closest he came to actually stating that Schlesinger disobeyed his orders was when he wrote, "I could never be sure he was leveling with me." See Ford memoir, 320–324. The press later dubbed the weekend firings of Schlesinger and CIA Director William Colby the "Sunday Morning Massacre." See John Robert Greene, 161–162.

In the case of Vietnam, Ford wrote that in the first week of April Schlesinger had ordered the flight of empty or near-empty planes in and out of Saigon to establish that it would not be his fault if the United States failed to remove its people. Ford had refused to evacuate at that point (Ford memoir, p. 253).

In the case of the *Mayaguez*, Ford wrote coyly (p. 282), "The first strike never took place, although we were told it had been 'completed.' . . . What is harder for me to understand is why the fourth air strike—and I specifically ordered four—was never carried out. I hadn't told anyone to cancel that attack. Apparently, someone had, and I was anxious to find out who had contravened my authority. The explanations I had received from the Pentagon were not satisfactory at all, and direct answers kept eluding me. Perhaps I should have pursued my inquiry, but since we had achieved our objective, I let the matter drop." There was no mention of Schlesinger in this passage.

For his part, Schlesinger was concerned about the military risk of a U.S. operation into Cambodia. As was borne out, more military personnel died in the assault than were retrieved from the ship. Schlesinger also was against punitive strikes in the absence of hard information that the Cambodian leadership in Phnom Penh was responsible. See John Robert Greene, 143–155.

"Well, it's my judgment": Ford quoted from "The President's News Conference of April 29, 1976," Public Papers of the President, April 29, 1976, 1298.

"The director of the FBI": Carter quoted from Jules Witcover, *Marathon 1972–1976: The Pursuit of the Presidency* (1977), 547–548.

The Watergate shadow got worse: 1976 Ford probe quoted from author's interview with Ford, May 20, 1998; author's interview with James Cannon, October 14, 1997; author's interview with Jack Marsh, March 18, 1998; Ford memoir, 418; John Robert Greene, 182–186.

Ford wrote of the union investigation, "I failed to see how the story would build and inject the foul aroma of Watergate into the closing weeks of the campaign."

At the debate, Carter answered Ford's claim that Eastern Europe was free by saying, "I'd like to see Mr. Ford convince Polish-Americans and Hungarian-Americans in this country that those countries don't live under the domination of the Soviet Union." There were, of course, Soviet troops all over Eastern Europe, including Poland.

After the election, Ford had: Ford-Haig meeting after the election quoted from author's interview with Haig, November 6, 1997.

He thought that all anyone: Hartmann quoted from author's interviews with Hartmann, December 10, 1997, and January 7, 1998.

In the years afterwards: Nixon quoted from David Frost, *"I Gave Them a Sword": Behind the Scenes of the Nixon Interviews* (1978), 268, 272; author's interview with Miller, May 19, 1998. Nixon claimed in the Frost interview, "I want to say right here and now, I said things that were not true. Most of them were fundamentally true on the big issues, but without going as far as I should have gone and saying, perhaps, that I had considered other things but not done them."

In the end, Ford wasn't sure: Author's interviews with Ford, September 22, 1997, and May 20, 1998.

I arranged to go see Ford: Author's interview with Ford, September 22, 1997.

Ten months later: Author's interview with Ford, May 20, 1998.

In our second interview: Author's interview with Ford, May 20, 1998.

PART TWO. JIMMY CARTER: 1977–81
CHAPTER 4

He set up in a hotel room: Carter-Powell campaign scenes quoted from author's interview with Jimmy Carter, September 18, 1997; author's interviews with Jody Powell, October 14, 1997, and April 14, 1998.

No one came: Author's interview with Jimmy Carter, September 18, 1997; author' sinterviews with Powell, October 14, 1997, and April 14, 1998. Although Carter and Powell said no one showed up, Kandy Stroud in her book on the 1976 campaign writes that four people attended a Carter breakfast in Des Moines in March 1975. "We were very apologetic," Elaine Baxter, who organized the event, told Stroud. "But he said not to worry, that he'd come back again and he would win. He knew next time there would be more people. Well, everything he said came true. The next time four hundred people showed up to see him." Kandy Stroud, *How Jimmy Won: The Victory Campaign from Plains to the White House* (1977), 238.

"I'll never lie to you": Author's interview with Carter, September 18, 1997.

"I'll never mislead you": Stroud, 136. In *Dasher*, Jim Wooten's book on the roots and rising of Jimmy Carter, Carter is quoted as saying, "If I ever lie to you, if I ever mislead you, if I ever avoid a controversial issue, then don't vote for me, because I won't be worthy of your vote if I'm not worthy of my trust." James Wooten, *Dasher: The Roots and the Rising of Jimmy Carter* (1978), 244.

Carter's mother: Author's interview with Carter, September 18, 1997.

Charles Kirbo . . . also told him: Author's interview with Carter, September 18, 1997.

Powell thought the plain statement: Author's interview with Powell, October 14, 1997.

But Carter saw the no-lie: Author's interview with Carter, September 18, 1997. The promise to tell the truth became the centerpiece of Carter's campaign. In 1975, Carter released an autobiography called *Why Not the Best?* Carter argued that the shocks and embarrassments of Vietnam and Watergate could be overcome if the government was as honest and as good as the American people. "I respectfully dedicate this book to the American people who have been hurt, embarrassed and disappointed, but retain a basic faith in the ideals of decency, equality and freedom. Americans are a good, honest, hardworking and unselfish people with a vast reservoir of compassion and concern for those less fortunate. Almost without exception, the mistakes and failings of our government have resulted from indifference to these fundamental characteristics of our citizens. I make this dedication in the firm belief that a renewed commitment to excellence by all of us to what is good and decent and honorable can result in a government as good and fine as our people." See Jimmy Carter, *Why Not the Best? Why One Man Is Optimistic About America's Third Century*(1975), 1.

When Senator Vance Hartke: Author's interview with James Wooten, December 28, 1998. In 1976, Hartke led all other candidates with $245,000 in interest group donations. Hartke was also criticized for spending more than $14,000 in government money to travel abroad, ostensibly to study veterans' problems. Senate aides twice voted him "the senator with the least integrity." See David Alpern, "Questions of Ethics," *Newsweek*, June 14, 1976, 21; L. L. L. Golden, "A Dangerous Rush to Political Action," *BusinessWeek*, September 25, 1978, 14; Susan Fraker and Henry W. Hubbard, "The Choice Races; Eagle Scout," *Newsweek*, November 1, 1976, 36. "Eagle Scout" referred to Hartke's opponent, Richard Lugar, who defeated him that year.

Patrick Caddell: Caddell's analysis quoted from author's interviews with Patrick Caddell, November 28, 1997, and December 3, 1997.

On December 22, 1974: Seymour Hersh, "Huge CIA Operation Reported in U.S. Against Antiwar Forces, Other Dissidents in Nixon Years," *New York Times*, December 22, 1974, A1, A16.

"If the CIA ever": Jimmy Carter, February 11, 1976, campaign stop in Manchester, N.H., quoted from Richard E. Meyer, Associated Press, February 23, 1977.

Carter gained national attention: In Iowa, Carter won 27.6 percent of the vote. Indiana Senator Birch Bayh came in second with 13.1 percent. In New Hampshire, Carter prevailed with just under 30 percent of the vote, and Arizona Representative Morris Udall finished second, with 24 percent. Carter locked up the nomination on Super Tuesday, June 8, 1976, winning 218 out of 540 delegates and scoring a crucial victory in Ohio. See Witcover, 214, 237, 350.

"We have just lived": Mondale speech quoted from "Text of Sen. Walter Mondale's Acceptance Speech," *Facts on File World News Digest*, July 17, 1976, B1; Witcover, 368.

"It is time": Carter speech quoted from Witcover, 369.

In Carter's view, the good guys: Author's interview with Carter, September 18, 1997.

Caddell was certain: Caddell's analysis and meeting with Carter quoted from author's interviews with Caddell, November 28, 1997, and December 3, 1997.

"We're going to govern": Carter quoted from author's interviews with Caddell, November 28, 1997, and December 3, 1997. Carter was fond of using variations on the expression, Do the best that you can. His son had once asked,

"And what if that doesn't work?" "Well Jack," Carter had replied, "that probably means you haven't done your best." See Wooten, 29.

In February 1977: The King Hussein story quoted from author's contemporaneous notes; author's interview with Carter, September 18, 1997; author's interviews with Powell, October 14, 1997, and April 14, 1998. See also Bob Woodward, "CIA Paid Millions to King Hussein," *The Washington Post*, February 18, 1977, A1; Bob Woodward, "White House Reviewing Intelligence Operations," *The Washington Post*, February 19, 1977, A1; George Lardner, "CIA Is Tightlipped and Congress Is Reluctant to Pry," *The Washington Post*, February 19, 1977, A8. The Carter memorandum to Congress is quoted from Peggy Simpson, Associated Press, February 25, 1977.

I decided to turn: See Bob Woodward and Scott Armstrong, *The Brethren* (1979).

CHAPTER 5

In the spring of 1977: Author's interview with Wooten, December 28, 1998; James Wooten, "Carter's Style Making Aides Apprehensive, Ways Discourage Dissent, Isolate Office, Some Say," *New York Times*, April 25, 1977, A1. Wooten said he was disclosing his initial source for the first time.

While in the Navy: Carter, *Why Not the Best?*, 57. "Admiral Rickover had a profound effect on my life—perhaps more than anyone except my own parents," Carter wrote in the book.

"The absence of a comment": Quoted from Carter, *Why Not the Best?*, 57.

Gerald Rafshoon: Author's interviews with three former Carter aides.

Katharine Graham: Scene quoted from author's and Jeff Glasser's interviews with two participants.

After several of these dinners: Author's interview with former Carter aide.

Rafshoon saw that Carter: Author's interview with former Carter aide. See also Carter, *Why Not the Best?*, 139. Carter admitted in his campaign book, "A fault: I don't know how to compromise on any principle I believe is right." One of Carter's friends, Georgia Secretary of State Ben Fortson, called Carter "as stubborn as a South Georgia turtle."

Representative Jim Wright: Wright, then the House majority leader, and the Democratic Congress had passed a $10.1 billion public works bill that included five major water projects in Texas. Carter, calling the bill wasteful and inflationary, vetoed it. Democratic House Speaker Tip O'Neill said Carter was acting like an "ostrich" in ignoring America's water needs. O'Neill and Wright tried to round up enough votes to override the veto, but on October 4, 1978, the House sustained it, 223 to 190. After the vote, Wright said, "Carter made Lyndon Johnson look like a Sunday school teacher." See Mary Russell, "House Sustains Carter's Veto," *The Washington Post*, October 6, 1978, A1; Mary Russell, "Hill Leaders Hit Promised Veto of Water Projects," *The Washington Post*, October 5, 1978.

"Every time I see Carter": Wright quoted from author's interview with former Carter aide.

"You are running the risk": Quoted from Memo "Image," Gerald Rafshoon to Jimmy Carter, June 14, 1977, in "Chief of Staff: Jordan" collection, Box 34, Jimmy Carter Presidential Library. Carter wrote in his own pen on the memo, "CC: Jody & Ham Good Advice J." (Jody and Ham refer to press secretary Powell and Jordan, his top White House aide.) "Truthfully," Rafshoon wrote frankly to Carter, "you are being overexposed in an area that is very dangerous. An occasional fireside chat is O.K.; bi-weekly press conferences necessary; a town meeting, perhaps. But it is not necessary to have a T.V. event every few weeks just to show that you are close to the American people. And this is happening."

At one critical juncture: The following Carter scenes quoted from author's interviews with former Carter aide.

In June 1977, Bert Lance: Lance-Carter meeting quoted from author's interview with Bert Lance, February 3, 1999; Bert Lance, *The Truth of the Matter* (1991), 133–135. "I remember that like it was yesterday," Lance said in an interview. Carter said he didn't recall such an early warning. The description of Lance and Carter and their relationship is quoted from author's interview with Carter, September 18, 1997; author's interview with Lance, February 3, 1999; Jimmy Carter, *Keeping Faith: Memoirs of a President* (1995 edn.), 133–134; Lance memoir, 133–135.

William Safire: Section quoted from author's interview with William Safire, February 16, 1998; William Safire, "Carter's Broken Lance," *New York Times*, July 21, 1977, A23; William Safire, "Lancegate," *New York Times*, August 11, 1977, A17; Michael Schudson, *Watergate in American Memory* (1992), 78.

Hamilton Jordan: Author's interview with Hamilton Jordan, August 21, 1997; memo, Hamilton Jordan to President Carter Re: Bert Lance Situation, folder "Lance, Bert 1977," "Chief of Staff: Jordan" collection, Box 35, Jimmy Carter Presidential Library, 1–7.

Carter was worried: Author's interview with Carter, September 18, 1997.

He realized that the Watergate: Author's interview with Carter, September 18, 1998; Carter, *Keeping Faith*, 132.

"My faith in the character": Carter quoted from Edward Walsh, "Investigation Clears Lance of Wrongdoing; President Dramatically Endorses OMB Director," *The Washington Post*, August 19, 1977, A1.

Reporters soon discovered: John F. Berry and Jack Egan, "Comptroller Outlines Some Questionable Practices," *The Washington Post*, August 19, 1977, A1; Michael Ruby, "What the Report Says," *Newsweek*, August 29, 1977, 18; Haynes Johnson and George Lardner Jr., "Carter and Lance: The Political Price of Friendship," *The Washington Post*, September 25, 1977, C1; William Safire, "Lancegate: Why Carter Stuck It Out," *New York Times Magazine*, October 16, 1977, 111. Lance also had made interest-free deposits at banks where he held personal loans. "This recurring pattern of shifting bank relationships and personal borrowing raises unresolved questions as to what constitutes acceptable banking practices," the comptroller, John Heimann, wrote.

On September 1, Carter picked up: Carter diary entry quoted from Carter, *Keeping Faith*, 136.

Carter had overcounted: A search of a computer database found five *Washington Post* stories mentioning Lance on September 1, 1977.

Carter realized it was seriously: Author's interview with Carter, September 18, 1997; Carter, *Keeping Faith*, 138.

Early the morning of his testimony: Lance-Carter meeting quoted from Bert Lance memoir, 138.

"Is it part of our American": Lance testimony quoted from Bert Lance memoir, 139.

Carter summoned Lance: Carter-Lance meeting quoted from author's interview with Carter, September 18, 1997; author's interview with Lance, September 18, 1999; Carter, *Keeping Faith*, 139–140.

On September 21, he brought: Lance–LaBelle Lance–Carter meeting in study quoted from author's interview with Lance, February 3, 1999; Bert Lance memoir, 148; LaBelle Lance, *This Too Shall Pass* (1978), 11–13.

"You have stabbed": LaBelle Lance quoted from author's interview with Carter, September 18, 1997.

She refused to help: Bert Lance memoir, 149; LaBelle Lance memoir, 13.

"I want to tell you": LaBelle Lance quoted from author's interview with Lance, February 3, 1999; Bert Lance memoir, 130.

They then watched: Author's interview with Lance, February 3, 1999; Bert Lance memoir, 150; LaBelle Lance memoir, 15.

"I accept Bert's resignation": "Excerpts from Text of President Carter's Press Conference," *The Washington Post*, September 22, 1977, A16.

"Your phone call": Lance quoted from Bert Lance memoir, 150.

Lance went back: Author's interview with Lance, February 3, 1999.

Carter realized he had: Author's interview with Carter, September 18, 1997; Carter, *Keeping Faith*, 131.

Carter felt it was impossible: Author's interview with Carter, September 18, 1997; Carter, *Keeping Faith*, 132.

But to Carter it didn't: Carter, *Keeping Faith*, 142.

CHAPTER 6

Four months into his presidency: Carter quoted from "Ethics Message Text," *Congressional Quarterly*, May 7, 1977, 865, 866. Carter explained why he supported special prosecutor reform in his 1975 autobiography: "Following recent presidential elections, our U.S. attorney general has replaced the postmaster general as the chief political appointee; and we have recently witnessed the prostitution of this most important law enforcement office. Special prosecutors had to be appointed simply to insure enforcement of the law! The attorney general should be removed from politics." Carter, *Why Not the Best?*, 151.

Over at the Georgetown: Author's interview with Samuel Dash, October 27, 1998.

As Dash saw it: Author's interview with Dash, October 27, 1998; Samuel Dash, "Independent Counsel: No More, No Less a Federal Prosecutor," *Georgetown Law Journal* (July 1998), 2077–2098. For an overview of the Saturday Night Massacre, see Ken Gormley, *Conscience of a Nation: Archibald Cox* (1997), 338–359; Bob Woodward and Carl Bernstein, *The Final Days* (1976), 50–76; Haig, *Inner Circles*, 382–409.

Ervin and Dash felt: Author's interview with Dash, October 27, 1998; Samuel Dash, *Chief Counsel: Inside the Ervin Committee—The Untold Story of Watergate* (1976), 212; Dash, "Independent Counsel," 2077–2098.

"If the many allegations made": Ervin quoted from Dash memoir, 127–128.

Ervin realized that his Watergate: Ervin-Dash meeting about ending the hearings quoted from author's interview with Dash, October 27, 1998.

Dash wanted Ervin's weight: Author's interview with Dash, October 27, 1998; Dash memoir, 249.

The centerpiece was a proposal: "Watergate Reform Act," *Congressional Quarterly*, August 2, 1975, 1688; Dash memoir, 252.

The first bills introduced: Congressman John C. Culver, an Iowa Democrat, introduced a plan on October 23, 1973, for a judicially appointed prosecutor, based on recommendations by a Democratic study group. The bill had 105 sponsors. At least eight bills were introduced in the fall of 1973. Quoted from Jeff Glasser's interview with Stephen Lynch, October 19, 1998; Katy Harriger, *Independent Justice: The Federal Special Prosecutor in American Politics* (1992), 43; Terry Eastland, *Ethics, Politics, and the Independent Counsel* (1989), 35. Lynch worked on the staff of the committee which handled the different bills that were proposed in the wake of the Saturday Night Massacre.

The federal courts in the past: Author's interview with Dash, October 27, 1998; Jeff Glasser's interview with David Schaefer, October 27, 1998. Schaefer worked on the Watergate reform legislation as a Senate aide and ally of Senator Abraham Ribicoff, the Connecticut Democrat who chaired the Government Operations Committee.

The Ervin-Dash proposal: Dash, "Independent Counsel," 2078n.

Dash felt their proposal: Dash "Independent Counsel," 2094.

Ervin and Dash released: Dash memoir, 251. Nixon's press secretary had declared that the report would be "full of baloney," so a Watergate Committee staffer, Scott Armstrong, bought a giant, 20–pound kosher baloney, and Ervin held it high over his head.

Dash appeared in favor: Dash memoir, 252. Dash was responding to Senator Howard Baker, the Tennessee Republican and Senate Watergate Committee vice chairman, who said at the hearings, "I think sometimes that the country is tired of being outraged and indignant."

"As special prosecutor now": Ruth quoted from "Witnesses Disagree on Watergate Reform Bill," *Congressional Quarterly*, August 9, 1975, 1786.

Eventually, President Ford: "Senate Passes Watergate Reform Measure with Administration Changes," *Congressional Quarterly*, July 24, 1976, 1953. Ford overruled his own Justice Department, which had opposed the special prosecutor reform provisions. Under Ford's plan, the president would appoint the prosecutor for a three-year term and the prosecutor would be subject to Senate confirmation, rather than court review.

Dash felt that reform: Author's interview with Dash, October 27, 1998; Dash memoir, 253.

In 1976, the Senate voted out: "Senate Passes Watergate Reform," 1953; Harriger, 57–58.

Finally, after almost five years: Jeff Glasser's interview with Schaefer, October 27, 1998.

In 1978, as the November election: Author's interview with Dash, October 27, 1998.

"I will be very candid": Hyde quoted from *Congressional Record*—House, October 12, 1978, 36463.

"I believe that this act": Carter quoted from Associated Press, October 26, 1978; Fred Barbash, "President Signs for U.S. Workers Disclosure Bill," *The Washington Post*, October 27, 1978, A1.Dash later spoke by phone: Dash-Ervin conversation quoted from author's interview with Dash, October 27, 1998.

CHAPTER 7

"We need a special prosecutor": Lumbard-Christy phone call and meeting with judges quoted from author's interview with Arthur Christy, March 9, 1998; Arthur H. Christy, "Trials and Tribulations of the First Special Prosecutor Under the Ethics in Government Act of 1978," *Georgetown Law Journal*, July 1998, 2287–2288; George Lardner Jr. and Howard Kurtz, "Lawmakers Warn Meese Not to Limit Counsel's Role," *The Washington Post*, December 4, 1986, A56. The ABC *20/20* program aired on October 4, 1979.

Christy was reluctant: Author's interview with Christy, March 9, 1998.

Attorney General Benjamin Civiletti: Civiletti-Carter meeting quoted from author's interview with Benjamin Civiletti, September 28, 1998.

Christy consulted his partners: Author's interview with Christy, March 9, 1998; Christy, "Trials and Tribulations," 2288.

That afternoon Christy: Order quoted from Arthur Christy, Report of Special Prosecutor on Alleged Possession of Cocaine by Hamilton Jordan in Violation of 21 U.S.C. 844(a), 2.

At a press conference: Tom Morganthau, "Ham Jordan's Prosecutor," *Newsweek*, December 10, 1979, 55; George Lardner Jr., "Prosecutor Appointed in Jordan Case," *The Washington Post*, November 30, 1979, A1.

He vividly recalled: FBI interview quoted from FBI 302 interview transcript, Hamilton Jordan, August 24, 1979, Records Relating to the Hamilton Jordan Investigation, Records of the Independent Counsels, National Archives II, RB 449, Box 2.

In the summer of 1979: Christy report, 3–11. The problems for Rubell and Schrager began when an employee they fired, Donald Moon, went to federal prosecutors and said they were running a large tax-skimming operation. Then Rubell bragged in the November 7, 1978, edition of *New York* magazine, "Profits are astronomical. Only the Mafia does better." A little more than a month later, on December 12, 1978, the Feds raided Studio 54. In the walls, behind the pipes and up in the roof they found nearly $1 million in cash stashed in Hefty garbage bags. Another $100,000 was discovered in the trunk of Schrager's car. Rubell and Schrager had filed a Studio 54 tax return for 1977 listing net taxable income of $47,000. They had paid just $8,000 altogether in taxes. At the end of June 1979, Rubell and Schrager were charged with skimming $2.5 million net income. The two began plea-bargaining, which led to the

820

August 1979 Jordan accusations. Of the tax evasion operation, the assistant U.S. attorney handling the case, Peter Sudler, later said he believed they had shielded $5 million. "Normally, if people skim from a cash business, they'll skim 10 percent, or 15 percent, or 25 percent at the most. These guys skimmed $5 million in one year. Probably 80 percent of their gross. It was ridiculous, what they did." See Anthony Haden-Guest, *The Last Party: Studio 54, Disco, and the Culture of the Night* (1997), 76–78, 111, 130–131, 144–145.

"We have damaging information": Rogovin quoted from Jody Powell, *The Other Side of the Story* (1984), 152. Rogovin claimed he had brokered a similar deal for a client in the intelligence community in the spring of 1979. Rogovin told Steven Brill, "Well, it turned out he had information about some serious wrongdoing—breaches of security—in the intelligence community. The kind of thing that the government wouldn't want to prosecute but would want to take care of very quietly. We offered the information to the government, and in return . . . they very quietly decided not to indict.

"Here," Rogovin continued, referring to the Studio 54 case, "we had information that wasn't necessarily prosecutable—that the chief of staff to the president was using cocaine in public. But I can tell you from my CIA background that it's the kind of thing the government would want to know, because the Russians might try to blackmail Jordan if they knew." See Steven Brill, "How a Legal Ploy Backfired," *The Washington Post*, November 4, 1979, C1. The article was reprinted from *The American Lawyer*, which at the time Brill edited.

Attorney General Civiletti declined: Civiletti quoted from author's interview with Civiletti, September 28, 1998; Powell memoir, 152.

The investigation leaked: Christy report, 10; Powell memoir, 144–150. Roy Cohn leaked it to the *Times* as part of a dispute he was having with Rogovin. See Brill article.

"No, that would be an admission": Jordan-Carter exchange quoted from author's interview with Hamilton Jordan, August 21, 1997.

Publicly Carter expressed: Tom Morganthau, "Ham Jordan's Prosecutor," *Newsweek*, December 10, 1979, 55; "Accusers Lied About Jordan, President Says," *The Washington Post*, September 2, 1979, A1. "I think they just dreamed up the story and now they're getting caught telling all kinds of lies," Carter said of the Studio 54 owners. Rubell later said, "When Jimmy Carter called me a liar I was insulted." See Haden-Guest, 145.

After some soul-searching: Author's interview with Jordan, August 21, 1997.

During late 1977: Sally Quinn, "Where Did All the Good Times Go? Where Have All the Good Times Gone? The Carter Crowd and the Washingtonians; The Trials and Separations of the Carter Crowd and the Washingtonians," *The Washington Post*, December 18, 1977, G1.

The second exhibit: Rudy Maxa, front-page People column, *The Washington Post Magazine*, February 19, 1978; Dan Morgan, "The Jordan Encounter: White House Paper Contradicts Report on Jordan Bar Incident; White House Issues 33-Page Rebuttal," *The Washington Post*, February 21, 1978, A1. The alleged Amaretto and cream incident took place one month after Jordan announced he had separated from his wife, Nancy, who also worked for the

Carter administration, after eight years of marriage. The pyramids incident took place one month prior to that announcement. See Garrett Epps, "The Myth of Hamilton Jordan," *The Washington Post Magazine*, December 17, 1978, 10.

Jordan himself realized: Author's interview with Jordan, August 21, 1997.

Christy tried to figure out: Christy, "Trials and Tribulations," 2289.

He requested a meeting: Christy-Civiletti discussion quoted from author's interview with Christy, March 9, 1998; author's interview with Civiletti, September 28, 1998; Christy, "Trials and Tribulations," 2289.

Within a week, Christy was: Author's interview with Christy; Christy, "Trials and Tribulations," 2289.

Would you like me to give: Christy-Robb meeting quoted from author's interview with Christy, March 9, 1998.

Christy began assembling: Section quoted from author's interview with Christy, March 9, 1998; Jeff Glasser's interview with Terri Duggan, September 23, 1998; Christy, "Trials and Tribulations," 2290–2292; Christy report, 50; letter, Arthur Christy to Violet Collins, Administrative Office of the U.S. Courts, January 28, 1980, folder "H.J. Investigation—Staff (2)," Records Relating to the Hamilton Jordan Investigation, Records of the Independent Counsels, National Archives II, RB 449, Box 10b.

One of the first was: Christy's questioning of Landau quoted from author's interview with Christy, March 9, 1998; transcripts of independent counsel's interviews of Landau for January 29, 1980, February 1, 1980, February 6, 1980, February 13, 1980, and March 28, 1980, folder "Witness Interviews," Records Related to the Hamilton Jordan Investigation, Records of the Independent Counsels, National Archives II, RB 449, Box 3. For more on Roy Cohn allegations, see Maxine Cheshire, "Barry Landau and the $12,000 Jewelry Deal," *The Washington Post*, April 22, 1980, B1. See also Christy report, 26–33.

Christy went to work: Christy-Rubell scenes quoted from author's interview with Christy, March 9, 1998; FBI 302 interview and polygraph examination of Steve Rubell, February 26, 1980, folder "Addendum to Report of Special Prosecutor 5/28/80," Records Relating to the Hamilton Jordan Investigation, Records of the Independent Counsels, National Archives II, RB 449, Box 6; letter, Arthur Christy to Robert Kasanof, April 7, 1980, folder "Correspondence, March to April 1980," Records Relating to the Hamilton Jordan Investigation, Records of the Independent Counsels, National Archives II, RB 449, Box 4; witness interview of Dr. Herbert Speigel for March 11, 1980, Records Relating to the Hamilton Jordan Investigation, Records of the Independent Counsels, National Archives II, RB 449, Box 3. See also Christy report, 14–20.

Speigel, an expert in hypnosis from Columbia University, told Christy and his prosecutors that hypnosis could elicit suppressed details from a witness who had honestly forgotten them. If a witness was determined to lie, however, hypnosis would not necessarily expose the lie and might even enable the patient to lie better by embellishing his story with additional false details. Speigel said about 30 percent of the population cannot be hypnotized at all. After an examination, he claimed that Christy and one of the assistants could be hypnotized, but another assistant could not.

Rubell and Schrager were sentenced January 18, 1980. Even the prosecutor, Peter Sudler, thought it was a stiff sentence. The judge criticized Rubell and Schrager for "tremendous arrogance." See Haden-Guest, 145.

At 3:45 p.m. on January 18, 1980: Christy–Johnny C scenes quoted from author's interview with Christy, March 9, 1998; transcripts of independent counsel's interviews with John "Johnny C" Conaghan for January 18, 1980, January 25, 1980, February 6, 1980, and May 20, 1980, Records Relating to the Hamilton Jordan Investigation, Records of the Independent Counsels, National Archives II, RB 449, Box 3. See also Christy report, 21–25.

Maxine Cheshire: Memorandum "Conversation with Maxine Cheshire," March 13, 1980, folder "Witness Interviews ABC," Records Relating to the Hamilton Jordan Investigation, Records of the Independent Counsels, RB 449, Box 3. See also Christy June 22, 1981, letter to Sen. William S. Cohen, folder "Administrative Records of the Division for the Purpose of Appointing Special Prosecutors, 1979–1982 (1)," Records Relating to Hamilton Jordan Investigation, Records of the Independent Counsels, National Archives II, RB 449, Box 1. "A member of the press kept calling me, telling me that there was at least one person on the West Coast who could tell me about Mr. Jordan using cocaine," Christy wrote in the 1981 letter. "When I did locate the person who was supposed to be able to support the allegations, it turned out that the member of the press had been badly misinformed, and there was no substance to the allegations."

Within two weeks, he had learned: Christy-prosecutors-Alksne scenes quoted from memo "Interview of Cynthia Alksne on 3/27/80," folder "Witness Interviews ABC," Records Relating to the Hamilton Jordan Investigation, Records of the Independent Counsels, National Archives II, RB 449, Box 3.

In the interest of a complete: Rawls-Christy section quoted from Christy report, 45–46. Christy later learned that Rawls had been upset at one of the members of Carter's administration who had attended the party because she thought he had stolen her coat. See transcript of Jordan interview, March 27, 1980, "Witness Interviews," Records Relating to the Hamilton Jordan Investigation, Records of the Independent Counsels, National Archives II, RB 449, Box 3.

As Christy dug into: For a description of the events of June 27–28, see Christy report, 11–13.

Christy soon established: Author's interview with Christy, March 9, 1998.

Christy thought the Studio 54: Author's interview with Christy, March 9, 1998.

McCleary and his lawyer: Christy-prosecutors-McCleary scenes quoted from author's interview with Joel McCleary, April 19, 1999. Also see transcripts of independent counsel's interviews with McCleary for January 28, 1980, February 1, 1980, and May 20, 1980, folder "Witness Interviews," Records Relating to the Hamilton Jordan Investigation, Records of the Independent Counsels, National Archives II, RB 449, Box 3.

Christy also learned: Kraft-Christy scenes quoted from author's interview with Christy, March 9, 1998; Christy report, 37; Christy June 22, 1981 letter to Sen. Wiliam S. Cohen and "Petition of the Attorney General" for special prosecutor in Kraft allegations, folder "Administrative Records of the Division for the Purpose of Appointing Special Prosecutors, 1979–1982 (1)," Records Relating to Hamilton Jordan Investigation, Records of the Independent Counsels, National Archives II, RB 449, Box 1; transcripts of independent counsel interview with Evan Dobelle, January 31, 1980, and with Timothy Kraft on the same date, folder "Witness Interviews," Records Relating to the Hamilton Jordan Investigation, Records of the Independent Counsels, National Archives II, RB 449, Box 3; transcript of phone interview with Kraft's lawyer, February 28, 1980, folder "Witness Interviews," Records Relating to the Hamilton Jordan Investigation, Records of the Independent Counsels, National Archives II, RB 449, Box 3.

Christy called Henry Ruth: Author's interview with Christy, March 9, 1998.

Jordan was wary: Hamilton Jordan, *Crisis: The True Story of an Unforgettable Year in the White House* (1983 edn.), 223.

On Thursday, March 27: Christy-Jordan meeting quoted from author's interview with Christy, March 9, 1998; transcript of Jordan interview, March 27, 1980, "Witness Interviews," Records Relating to the Hamilton Jordan Investigation, Records of the Independent Counsels, National Archives II, RB 449, Box 3. See also Christy report, 42.

Judge Lumbard called Christy: Author's interview with Christy, March 9, 1998. Judge Lumbard, who is now 97 years old, had no independent recollection of the call. "I would not disagree with it," Lumbard said, if that was Christy's recollection. Jeff Glasser's interview with J. Edward Lumbard, September 24, 1998.

On May 21, 1980: Christy grand jury instructions quoted from author's interview with Christy, March 9, 1998; Christy report, 3, 52.

He instructed his deputies: Jeff Glasser's interview with Duggan, September 23, 1998.

"Where's all the dirt?": Kempton quoted from Glasser's interview with Duggan, September 23, 1998.

President Carter attended: "Ham Jordan Gets His Vindication," *Newsweek*, June 9, 1980, 43; Jordan memoir, 251.

"All you've got": Jordan quoted from "Ham Jordan Gets No Case Verdict," *U.S. News & World Report*, June 9, 1980, 11.

Jordan damn sure didn't: Author's interview with Jordan, August 21, 1997.

All the stories: For example, the *Post* wrote an editorial asserting, "The charge that Mr. Jordan snorted cocaine in a New York disco in 1978 looked weak from the moment it was first made." *Newsweek* wrote, "The charges seemed flimsy to begin with." See "The End of the Jordan Affair," editorial, *The Washington Post*, May 30, 1980, A12; "Ham Jordan Gets His Vindication," *Newsweek*, June 9, 1980, 43.

The taxpayers paid: Christy letter to Judge Roger Robb, May 27, 1982, folder "Administration Records for the Division for the Purpose of Appointing Special Prosecutors, 1979–1982 (1)," Records Relating to the Hamilton Jordan Investigation, Records of the Independent Counsels, National Archives II, RB 449, Box 1; Henry Ruth and Stephen Pollak (Jordan's attorneys), July 21, 1980, letter to Hamilton Jordan re: attorneys fees, folder "Original Records Relating to Jordan's Application for Reimbursement of Attorney's Fees (4)," Records Relating to the Hamilton Jordan Investigation, Records of the Independent Counsels, National Archives II, RB 449, Box 1.

He spent the next half dozen: In 1983, Congress changed the law so that targets who were not indicted—like Jordan—could recover their attorneys' fees. The amendment was not retroactive, however. In December 1985, the House passed a bill 347–40 that would have allowed Jordan to be reimbursed for his legal bills. Jordan asked his friends in Congress to hold off, however, when he entered the 1986 U.S. Senate race in Georgia. After Jordan lost the Democratic primary, Senator Sam Nunn revived the measure and it passed both the Senate and the House. But the bill died in the final hours of the 1986 congressional session when Representative James Sensenbrenner, a Wisconsin Republican, put a hold on it. See "House OKs Paying Hamilton Jordan's Cocaine Probe Costs," United Press International, December 17, 1985; Phil Gailey, "Talking Politics; No Reimbursement," *New York Times*, October 21, 1986, B8.

As part of the 1983 reforms, Congress tightened the statute so that only felonies—not misdemeanors like those alleged in the Jordan case—would be prosecuted. The new law also changed the name of the position from special prosecutor to independent counsel, an effort to destigmatize the office and its Watergate origins.

Years later, I went to see: Author's interview with Jordan, August 21, 1997.

President Carter later concluded: Author's interview with Carter, September 18, 1997.

CHAPTER 8

The 1970s energy crisis: In an April 18, 1977, address to the nation, Carter called his energy conservation efforts "the moral equivalent of war," a phrase coined by William James and suggested by his mentor, Admiral Rickover. See Carter, *Keeping Faith*, 96–129.

The treaty giving the Panama: Carter called the battle to persuade Congress to ratify the treaties "one of the most onerous political ordeals of my life." "It's hard to concentrate on anything except Panama," Carter wrote in his diary on March 13, 1978. The treaty was finally signed into law on September 27, 1979, returning control to Panama on December 31, 1999. See Carter, *Keeping Faith*, 156–189.

On November 4, 1979: Hostage crisis scenes quoted from Carter, *Keeping Faith*, 5–16.

On the Fourth of July: "After Rosalynn and I read it over, I told her I couldn't deliver it, that I had already made four speeches to the nation on energy and that they had increasingly been ignored. . . . I had to do something to get the attention of the news media and the public," Carter wrote in his diary on July 4, 1979. Carter, *Keeping Faith*, 120–121.

Finally, Carter came down: He told the nation, "We were sure that ours was a nation of the ballot, not the bullet, until the murders of John F. Kennedy, Robert Kennedy, and Martin Luther King Jr. We were taught that our armies were always invincible and our causes always just, only to suffer the agony of Vietnam. We respected the presidency as a place of honor until the shock of Watergate. We remember the phrase 'sound as a dollar' was an expression of absolute dependability, until ten years of inflation began to shrink our dollar and our savings. We believed that our nation's resources were limitless until 1973, when we had to face a growing dependence on foreign oil. These wounds are very deep. They have never been healed." "Text of President Carter's Address to the Nation," *The Washington Post*, July 16, 1979, A14; Haynes Johnson, *In the Absence of Power* (1980), 311–313.

The summary action created: Carter acknowledged in his memoir, "I handled the Cabinet changes very poorly." See Carter, *Keeping Faith*, 127.

Carter summoned his health: Carter-Califano scenes quoted from author's contemporaneous discussions with Califano; Joseph A. Califano Jr., *Governing America: An Insider's Report from the White House and the Cabinet* (1981), 427–448.

PART THREE. RONALD REAGAN: 1981–89
CHAPTER 9

On April 22, 1986, Theodore B. Olson: In a case that Olson had argued, the Supreme Court ruled 8 to 0 that Aetna Life Insurance would not have to pay $3.5 million in punitive damages because the Alabama judge who cast the deciding vote and wrote the opinion had a personal stake in the outcome. See "Court Upsets Alabama Award As Tainted By Judge," *New York Times*, April 23, 1986, A11.

MacKinnon had sworn: Office of Legal Counsel was the elite, 20-lawyer legal braintrust and legal conscience for the attorney general and administration, outlining positions on the most critical issues involving presidential power and constitutional law.

"You know": MacKinnon-Olson phone call quoted from author's interview with Ted Olson, October 29, 1998.

Olson, who had returned: Olson left the Justice Department in the fall of 1984 for a job at the law firm Gibson, Dunn & Crutcher. He took over as head of the firm's Washington office.

A House committee had alleged: In December 1985, the House Judiciary Committee released a 1,200-page report contending that Olson and other top Justice and White House officials may have lied to Congress about the decision to withhold the EPA documents from two House subcommittees. Attorney General Meese, however, recommended to the three-judge panel that only the allegations against Olson should be investigated by an independent counsel. See Philip Shenon, "Independent Counsel Is Named in Inquiry Over E.P.A. Documents," *New York Times*, April 25, 1986, A13.

It was a political wrangle: The Reagan Environmental Protection Agency hadn't yet referred a single case against polluters to the Justice Department under the Superfund law. Environmental activists were accusing agency leaders of dragging their feet on prosecuting hazardous waste dumpers. See Alison

Frankel, "Ted Olson's Five Years in Purgatory," *The American Lawyer* (December 1988), 68.

The judge's wife: MacKinnon-Olson meeting at MacKinnon home quoted from author's interview with Olson, October 29, 1998. MacKinnon was an old Washington hand. Having been elected to Congress for one term in 1946, he had worked with Nixon on the Alger Hiss case. In 1969, Nixon had appointed him to the appeals court. MacKinnon died May 1, 1995.

Olson had once done a chart: Author's interview with Olson, October 29, 1998. The four independent counsels up to that point were Arthur Christy with the Hamilton Jordan case, Gerald Gallinghouse looking at whether Carter aide Tim Kraft used cocaine, Leon Silverman probing Reagan Secretary of Labor Raymond Donovan's alleged organized crime ties, and Jake Stein investigating Reagan adviser Ed Meese for possible conflicts of interest.

All of the investigations: Although Donovan's original special prosecutor case ended within six months, he was under investigation by the Justice Department, the FBI and local authorities for a much longer period of time, and he was later tried in New York State Court. After the more than six-year ordeal ended in his acquittal in a Bronx courtroom, Donovan asked, "Which office do I go to, to get my reputation back?"

Two days later the three-judge: McKay was a trial lawyer who had worked as an assistant U.S. attorney in the 1940s and was a partner with the law firm of Covington & Burling. See Howard Kurtz, "Independent Counsel Is Named in EPA Documents Case," *The Washington Post*, April 25, 1986, A1; Philip Shenon, "Independent Counsel Is Named in Inquiry Over E.P.A. Documents," *New York Times*, April 25, 1986, A13.

Five weeks later: Mary Thornton, "Independent Counsel Quits to Avoid Conflict; Deputy Will Pursue Case of Withheld EPA Documents," *The Washington Post*, May 30, 1986, A17.

The three-judge panel assigned: Morrison was the former chief litigation counsel at the Securities and Exchange Commission.

He had made comments: Author's interview with Olson, October 29, 1998.

While at the Justice Department: Author's interview with Olson, October 29, 1998.

Olson, Attorney General William: The Senate considered the Justice Department's objections during April 1982 hearings, but it unanimously passed an amended version of the law, and the House soon followed with a 347–37 vote in favor of reenactment. Faced with likely veto-proof majorities, Reagan signed the bill renewing the act on January 3, 1983. Five years later, in the midst of Iran-contra, the House voted by 322–90 and the Senate by 85–7 to renew the law for another five years. On December 15, 1987, again facing veto-proof majorities, Reagan signed the act into law. He said he had "very strong doubts about its constitutionality." But, he said, he signed the bill "in order to ensure that public confidence in government not be eroded while the courts are in the process" of ruling on the constitutional issue. See William French Smith, *Law and Justice in the Reagan Administration: Memoirs of an Attorney General* (1991), 175–190; George Lardner Jr., "Administration, Senators Air Ethics Law

Changes," *The Washington Post*, April 29, 1982, A5; "Reagan Signs Extension of Ethics Law," United Press International; January 3, 1983; Tom Seppy, "Senate Joins House in Passing Independent Counsel Renewal," Associated Press, November 4, 1987; George Lardner Jr., "Renewal of Special-Counsel Law Advances," *The Washington Post*, November 21, 1987, A4; "Independent Prosecutor Law Renewed," *Facts on File World News Digest*, December 25, 1987.

But on January 22, 1988: Ruth Marcus, "Court Strikes Down Counsel Law," *The Washington Post*, January 23, 1988, A1.

Olson was elated: Author's interview with Olson, October 29, 1998.

As he read Rehnquist's: "Most importantly," Rehnquist's opinion stated, "the attorney general retains the power to remove the counsel for 'good cause.' ... No independent counsel may be appointed without specific request by the attorney general." The attorney general's determination that "no reasonable ground to believe that further investigation is warranted" is absolute and "unreviewable." The independent counsel jurisdiction stems from the attorney general's application to the three-judge panel, and the independent counsel was forced to abide by Justice Department policy. Quoted from the Supreme Court decision *Morrison* v. *Olson*, 487 U.S. 654 (1988).

"Power": Scalia's dissent quoted from *Morrison* v. *Olson*, 487 U.S. 654 (1988).

Fearing that Independent Counsel Morrison: Author's interview with Olson, October 29, 1998.

Two months later, Morrison announced: Bill McAllister and Ruth Marcus, "Olson's Indictment Won't Be Sought; Counsel Ends 29-Month Probe of Ex-Assistant Attorney General," *The Washington Post*, August 27, 1988, A1; Philip Shenon, "Special Prosecutor Drops E.P.A. Case Without Indictment," *New York Times*, August 27, 1988, A1.

Six months after that, her 225-page: Morrison accepted Olson's claim that he had forgotten about one memo when he testified. "As unappealing as this explanation may appear," the Morrison report said, "we have been unable to develop evidence to support a contrary conclusion." Ruth Marcus, "Ex-Official's Testimony Not 'Designed to Conceal'; Decision Against Prosecuting Olson Explained," *The Washington Post*, March 21, 1989, A4; Dale Russakoff, "Theodore Olson Is Free At Last," *The Washington Post*, March 23, 1989, A25; Alison Frankel, "Ted Olson's Five Years in Purgatory," *The American Lawyer* (December 1988), 68.

The investigation infected: Author's interview with Olson, October 29, 1998.

CHAPTER 10

"We have not dealt directly": Reagan's meeting with key advisers quoted from author's interview with George Shultz, November 3, 1997; handwritten notes of Don Regan, Alton Keel and Caspar Weinberger, folder "11/10/86 White House Meeting," John Q. Barrett general investigative files, Office of Independent Counsel Lawrence Walsh, National Archives II, Box 55; Charles Hill (Shultz's executive assistant) handwritten notes of November 10, 1986, meeting, Ronald Reagan 1992 exhibit binder (folder 1), Christina Spaulding attorney files, Office of Independent Counsel Lawrence Walsh, National Archives II, Box 2; Report of the Congressional Committees Investigating the Iran Contra Affair, November 1987, 295; George Shultz, *Turmoil and Triumph* (1993), 810, 812–813, 814; Jane Mayer and Doyle McManus, *Landslide: The Unmaking of the President 1984–1988* (1988), 298.

"I can't help but feel": The Israelis had quietly sold U.S. arms to Iran since Iraq had invaded Iran in September 1980, even though Iran held 52 Americans hostage at that time. The Israelis considered Iraq, which had sent troops marching toward Israel in 1948 and 1967, more of a menace than Iran. The Iran-Iraq War, it was thought, enhanced Israel's security. Since the two countries were fighting one another, they wouldn't attack Israel.

Later that afternoon: Poindexter quoted from Hill November 10, 1986, handwritten notes; Shultz memoir, 815; Report of the Congressional Committees Investigating the Iran-Contra Affair, 295.

He sent the text to Shultz's plane: Report of the Congressional Committees Investigating the Iran-Contra Affair, 295.

"That's a lie": Shultz quoted from Hill handwritten notes; Shultz memoir, 815.

By cable, Shultz told Poindexter: Hill handwritten notes; Shultz memoir, 815.

Hill . . . believed in Ralph Waldo Emerson's: Jeff Glasser's interview with Charles Hill, May 8, 1998.

"They are distorting": Hill's handwritten notes give a somewhat different account than found in Shultz's memoir on 815–816. Specifically, in the book Shultz omitted the statement, "They will ruin a beautiful president, let alone policy. So I have to call it to account and say I can't be part of it." In the book, Shultz wrote, "They are distorting the record, and there's no end to it. They are lying to me and others in the cabinet right now."

In Shultz's view, Casey and Poindexter: Author's interview with Shultz, November 3, 1997.

Just three months earlier: Hill handwritten notes; Shultz memoir, 816.

"This has earmarks of Nixon": Shultz quoted from Hill handwritten notes.

"It would put me in the position": Nixon quoted from J. Anthony Lukas, *Nightmare: The Underside of the Nixon Years* (1976), 25.

"This is an example": Shultz quoted from Hill notes.

"It's not even a hard": Shultz quoted from Hill notes.

"Let me talk to you": Bush quoted from November 10, 1986, diary entry. "Was Vice President Bush in the Loop? You Make the Call," *The Washington Post*, January 31, 1993, C6.

The night before: Bush November 9, 1986, diary entry; Shultz memoir, 808.

"He feels he's been cut out": Bush November 10, 1986, diary entry.

"Good things, such as the release": Bush November 10, 1986, diary entry.

"a Watergate syndrome": Bush November 10, 1986, diary entry.

"George does not want this": Bush November 10, 1986, diary entry.

Shultz felt he had been rough: Author's November 3, 1997, interview with Shultz.

"I don't believe we can stonewall": Regan quoted from Don Regan, *For the Record: From Wall Street to Washington* (1988), 26; author's interview with Don Regan, April 9, 1999. "They may not have liked me," Regan said. "But no one has ever disputed the facts in the book." He also said he had "buried the hatchet" with Nancy Reagan in 1996. "Time heals all wounds," he said.

"He's not going to talk": Don Regan/Nancy Reagan phone call quoted from Regan memoir, 28.

Green ink was used: Regan memoir, 3–4, 359; Nancy Reagan, *My Turn: The Memoirs of Nancy Reagan* (1989), 44, 46, 49. Nancy Reagan had turned to Quigley, who was from San Francisco, after the March 30, 1981, assassination attempt on her husband. The president should have stayed home because the astrology charts showed it was a dangerous day for him, Quigley told the first lady. Nancy was impressed and enlisted Quigley to phone in regular charts. She found Quigley's astrology predictions a way of coping with fear about another possible assassination attempt on her husband. It was a superstitious precaution, a way to hedge their bets. Quigley sent monthly bills to the White House with Nancy's personal five-digit code on the envelope to ensure it was sorted out from the general White House mail and delivered to the first lady. Aware of the potential risk if the relationship was disclosed publicly, Nancy, forever the natural intelligence agent, used another friend as a cutout to make the payments to Quigley. Nancy then reimbursed her friend.

In meticulous handwriting: Author's interviews with Bill Lytton, February 20, 1998, and April 23, 1998. Lytton, a lawyer, later became a special counsel to the president for Iran-contra.

"This whole irresponsible": Reagan diary entry quoted from Ronald Reagan, *An American Life: The Autobiography* (1990), 528.

"The appearance of things": Buchanan quoted from Mayer & McManus, 300.

"I agree, and have so advocated": Regan quoted from Regan memoir, 29–30.

"I remember Watergate": Bush quoted from Bush diary entry referring to November 13, 1986.

"I KNOW YOU HAVE BEEN": Speech draft, Ronald Reagan to Pat Buchanan via David L. Chew, folder " 'Address to the Nation on Iran, Nov. 13, 1986' (NSC/Buchanan) (Research Staff) [3 of 4]," White House Office of Speechwriting, Box OA12890, Ronald Reagan Presidential Library.

"WE DID NOT": Reagan November 13, 1986, speech draft. Reagan also added language contending that the weapons that had been sold to Iran could not have had "ANY" impact on the seven-year war between Iran and Iraq. Following that reference he inserted the sentence, "NOR COULD THEY IN ANY WAY AFFECT THE MILITARY BALANCE BETWEEN THE 2 COUNTRIES."

In an accompanying note: Note, Ronald Reagan to David L. Chew, folder " 'Address to the Nation on Iran, Nov. 13, 1986' (NSC/Buchanan) (Research Staff) [3 of 4]," White House Office of Speechwriting, Box OA12890, Ronald Reagan Presidential Library.

At 8:01 p.m. that night: Past accounts have tended to blame Oliver North for the inaccuracies in Reagan's speech. North supplied a false chronology that excluded many details and distorted others. For example, North told Buchanan that the "modest delivery" of "defensive weapons and spare parts" to Iran could fit "on a single cargo plane." The statement was foolish. The "modest delivery" actually consisted of 2,004 TOW antitank missiles and Hawk antiaircraft missiles. A C-4 cargo plane could not hold that amount of arms. But as Reagan's handwritten insertions show, the president was not a passive player.

The lead quote: David Hoffman, "Reagan Denies 'Ransom' Was Paid for Hostages," *The Washington Post*, November 14, 1986, A1.

A *Los Angeles Times* poll: Regan memoir, 32.

Don Regan noticed: Regan memoir, 32.

Shultz went to see Reagan: Shultz-Reagan meeting quoted from author's November 3, 1997, interview with Shultz; Shultz memoir, 820.

The next day, Saturday: Report of the Congressional Committees Investigating the Iran-Contra Affair, 296.

On Sunday, November 16: Shultz quoted from transcript, *Face the Nation*, CBS, November 16, 1986; Shultz memoir, 821–824.

Shultz now fully expected: Author's November 3, 1997, interview with Shultz.

"The president has no desire": Statement quoted from Shultz memoir, 823; Larry Speakes, *Speaking Out: Inside the Reagan White House* (1988), 292.

For the moment, Shultz felt: Author's November 3, 1997, interview with Shultz.

Nancy Reagan cleared the date: Regan memoir, 35.

That morning, Bush went: Bush November 20, 1986, diary entry.

Shultz put his argument: Reagan-Shultz meeting quoted from author's November 3, 1997, interview with Shultz; Charles Hill November 19, 1986, handwritten notes, Ronald Reagan 1992 exhibit binder (folder 2), Christina Spaulding attorney files, Office of Independent Counsel Lawrence Walsh, National Archives, Box 2; Shultz memoir, 827–828; Report of the Congressional Committees Investigating the Iran-Contra Affair, 298.

"It's not so": Hill handwritten notes. In Shultz's book, (p. 828), he put these remarks a little differently. "Even if the Iranians agreed to cease targeting Americans in return for arms—which, in reality, they have not—that's a terrible deal to make!"

Shultz said he remembered: Hill handwritten notes. The national security adviser at that time, Robert C. "Bud" McFarlane, had called Shultz on November 19, 1985, in Geneva, Switzerland, where Shultz was attending the summit meeting with the Soviets. According to Shultz, McFarlane said, "The Israelis would send a plane with 100 Hawk anti-aircraft missiles to Portugal, where they would transfer them to another aircraft. If the hostages were released, the airplane would fly to Iran. If not, it would fly to Israel. Israel would buy replacements for the Hawks from the U.S., and they would be paid by Iran." See Shultz memoir, 797–798.

The president disclosed none: "Transcript of President Reagan's Press Conference," *The Washington Post*, November 20, 1986, A20.

Shultz watched from his: Reagan-Shultz exchange quoted from author's November 3, 1997, interview with Shultz; Charles Hill November 20, 1986, handwritten notes; Shultz memoir, 830–831. Shultz met with Hill at 7:30 a.m.

on November 20, 1986, for a debriefing on the prior night's phone conversation with Reagan after the president's press conference.

"Congress is going to tear": Shultz-Regan meeting quoted from Shultz memoir, 831.

Regan left the meeting for lunch: Bush November 20, 1986, diary entry.

Shaken, the president: Bush November 20, 1986, diary entry.

At his State Department office: Shultz memoir, 831. Michael Armacost, a senior State Department officer, was the staff member who noticed that the contractor, Southern Air Transport, was the same for the Iran and contra initiatives.

He directed Hill to dig out: Jeff Glasser's May 8, 1998, interview with Hill.

At 5:15 p.m. that evening: Shultz-Reagan meeting quoted from Hill November 20, 1986, handwritten notes; author's November 3, 1997, interview with Shultz; Shultz memoir, 832–833.

He told Reagan he was concerned: Meese-Reagan meeting quoted from Reagan memoir, 529; Edwin Meese III, *With Reagan: The Inside Story* (1992), 297.

"A shipment like that": Peter Wallison diary entry for November 21, 1986, in Ronald Reagan 1992 exhibit binder (folder 2), Christina Spaulding attorney files, Records of Independent Counsel Lawrence Walsh, National Archives, Box 2.

Just after 8 a.m. Saturday: Meese-Shultz meeting quoted from Charles Hill November 22, 1986, handwritten notes; Shultz memoir, 835; Meese memoir, 298.

Meese went to lunch: Meese-Reynolds meeting quoted from Meese memoir, 242–244, 298; Mayer & McManus, 334.

CIA Director Casey later sat down: Casey letter quoted from Shultz memoir, 837.

Reagan received the letter: Reagan's burning of the letter quoted from Bill Lytton 1987 handwritten notes and author's interviews with Lytton, February 20, 1998, and April 23, 1998.

On Monday at 2 p.m.: This meeting quoted from handwritten notes of Don Regan, Alton Keel, Caspar Weinberger, and Charles Hill, folder "11/24/86 NSPG Meeting," John Q. Barrett general investigative files, Records of Independent Counsel Lawrence Walsh, National Archives II, Box 55; Shultz memoir, 838.

At 4:30 p.m., Meese told Reagan: Reagan-Meese meeting about diversion quoted from Reagan memoir, 530; Meese memoir, 300. See also Mayer & McManus, 342–343.

"After the meeting": Reagan journal quoted from Reagan memoir, 530.

CHAPTER 11

Don Regan felt that the press: Regan memoir, 43.

His suspicions confirmed: Author's November 3, 1997, interview with Shultz; Shultz memoir, 841.

Reagan responded that he would now: Reagan quoted from Shultz memoir, 841.

Shultz noticed that the president: Shultz memoir, 841, 850.

Casey's men had even used: The ambassador in Lebanon, John Kelly, had had numerous contacts with the National Security Council staff regarding arms for hostages without informing Shultz. Shultz memoir, 845.

"We must have a clear chain": Shultz memoir, 851. Shultz wanted to fire Kelly, the ambassador in Lebanon, but Reagan and Shultz later settled on admonishing him officially. Shultz memoir, 851, 853–854.

Reagan reacted as if someone: Shultz memoir, 851.

"I'm glad to be in the position": Shultz memoir, 851.

"Mr. President, you must be decisive!": Shultz memoir, 852.

"Bill Casey is bad news": Shultz memoir, 853.

They released a statement: The statement perplexed Regan, who realized Casey was unlikely to recover. Regan memoir, 65.

Nancy Reagan had distrusted: Nancy Reagan memoir, 322–324.

The first lady called Don Regan: Regan memoir, 66.

What had the chief of staff: Regan-Nancy Reagan exchange quoted from Regan memoir, 66–67; Nancy Reagan memoir, 323.

With Casey out of action: Shultz memoir, 857; author's interview with Regan, April 9, 1999.

They concluded after looking at the record: Author's November 3, 1997, interview with Shultz; Shultz memoir, 845; author's interview with Regan, April 9, 1999.

Don Regan told the president: Meeting about Jack Miller quoted from Regan memoir, 63–64.

Reagan and Nancy attended: The Reagans-Shultz New Year's Eve meetings quoted from author's November 3, 1997, interview with Shultz; Shultz memoir, 863.

When the president returned: Regan memoir, 68.

"No press conference": Regan memoir, 68.

The astrologer's charts: Regan memoir, 70, 367. Nancy Reagan in her memoir(p. 319) gave a different reason for preventing Reagan from holding a press conference. She wrote that Reagan didn't want to be put in the position of responding to information that may well be contradicted in the future, as had happened at his November 13 press conference.

"What are we going to do": Regan memoir, 69.

"Ronnie could just send him": Regan memoir, 69.

"I wish that you were as": Nancy Reagan memoir, 323; Regan memoir, 72.

She proposed Edward Bennett Williams: Regan memoir, 75. Their first candidate for director of central intelligence, former Tennessee Senator Howard Baker, the former Republican majority leader, declined the job.

"What we're going to have to do": Regan memoir, 77.

"What's the news on Casey?": Regan memoir, 79.

"It looks like we're shielding": Don Regan/Nancy Reagan exchange quoted from Regan memoir, 90, 91.

That same evening: McFarlane-Nixon meeting quoted from Robert C. McFarlane, *Special Trust* (1994), 341–342.

Michael Deaver: Deaver-Reagan meetings quoted from author's July 17, 1997, interview with Michael Deaver. Deaver knew that Reagan didn't respond well to scandals. Back in 1973 when Reagan was governor of California, Deaver was at a luncheon around the large cabinet table waiting for Reagan to arrive. The big news was that Vice President Agnew had resigned in a plea-bargain deal. Agnew had accepted illegal bribes years before as governor of Maryland.

"Gosh," Reagan said. Agnew and his wife had left Washington and come to California. "They've just arrived at Palm Springs, and they have no help. I feel so sorry for them."

"If it had been a Democrat you wouldn't feel sorry for him," Deaver said. "I mean he sold his office. Pat Brown you used to harangue against because he sold savings and loan charters."

Reagan had a set of keys in his hand and he threw them across the table, hitting Deaver squarely in the chest. The governor then blew up about the way Agnew had been hounded from office.

At 10:10 a.m. on February 23: Reagan-Regan meeting quoted from Regan memoir, 96–98.

CHAPTER 12

"He must bear primary": Report of the President's Special Review Board, February 26, 1987, pp. IV–11. The paragraph on Regan said, "More than any other chief of staff in recent memory, [Regan] asserted personal control over the White House staff and sought to extend this control to the national security advisor. He was personally active in national security affairs and attended almost all of the relevant meetings regarding the Iran initiative. He, as much as anyone, should have insisted that an orderly process be observed. In addition, he especially should have ensured that plans were made for handling public disclosure of the initiative. He must bear primary responsibility for the chaos that descended upon the White House when such disclosure did occur." In Regan's defense, the board found no evidence to suggest that he was aware of the diversion. For his reaction, see Regan memoir, 364.

Bush summoned Regan: Bush-Regan meeting quoted from Regan memoir, 368–371.

Baker was smart, personable: Ronald Reagan memoir, 540.

Late Thursday afternoon: Regan–Joy Baker phone call quoted from author's interviews with Howard Baker, November 24, 1997, and December 9, 1997.

Reagan thought Baker accepted: Reagan memoir, 538–539.

Baker believed he had only agreed: Author's interviews with Baker, November 24, 1997, and December 9, 1997.

He had been bitten: Author's interviews with Baker, November 24, 1997, and December 9, 1997.

Baker felt he was ready: Author's interviews with Baker, November 24, 1997, and December 9, 1997.

In early 1973 after he had: Baker-Nixon meeting quoted from author's interviews with Baker, November 24, 1997, and December 9, 1997.

Years later Baker read a transcript: Author's interviews with Baker, November 24, 1997, and December 9, 1997. The transcript is printed in Kutler, *Abuse of Power*, 212–213.

He was shocked to see: Author's interviews with Baker, November 24, 1997, and December 9, 1997; Kutler, 631. Nixon called Baker a "simpering asshole" during a July 12, 1973, meeting with Alexander Haig, Nixon's chief of staff. Baker had asked John Dean on June 25, 1973, during the televised Watergate hearings the famous question: "What did the president know and when did he know it?"

"Baker will not be in this office": Nixon quoted from Kutler, 631.

"Never be in the White House": Nixon quoted from conversation with Bill Timmons, his head of congressional relations. See Kutler, 633.

"I don't want anybody": Nixon quoted from Kutler, 634.

"Howard Baker, Rose": Nixon quoted from Kutler, 634.

It was almost the kind of knowledge: Author's interviews with Baker, November 24, 1997, and December 9, 1997.

The next month, Baker came home: Burglary of Baker's house quoted from author's interviews with Baker, November 24, 1997, and December 9, 1997.

After the break-in: Baker's story about the FBI file quoted from author's interviews with Baker, November 24, 1997, and December 9, 1997.

Baker worried that he actually: Author's interviews with Baker, November 24, 1997, and December 9, 1997.

The next morning Baker went straight: Baker-Reagan meeting at residence quoted from author's interviews with Baker, November 24, 1997, and December 9, 1997.

News that Reagan had selected: CNN broadcast a report, and the staff told Regan that it was accurate. "There's been a deliberate leak, and it's been done to humiliate me," Regan said upon learning that he was ousted. See Regan memoir, 372–373.

It was the bitterest event: Regan memoir, 375–377.

"The president has asked me": Baker-Culvahouse phone call quoted from author's interview with A. B. Culvahouse, December 30, 1997; author's interviews with Baker, November 24, 1997, and December 9, 1997.

On Sunday, March 1: The meeting at Baker's house quoted from author's interviews with Baker, November 24, 1997, and December 9, 1997; author's interview with Culvahouse, December 30, 1997; author's interview with James Cannon, October 14, 1997. See also Mayer & McManus, vii–xi.

Even Cannon agreed: Author's interview with Cannon, October 14, 1997; Mayer & McManus, xi.

Baker introduced Reagan: Baker-Reagan-Culvahouse meeting quoted from author's interviews with Baker, November 24, 1997, and December 9, 1997; author's interview with Culvahouse, December 30, 1997.

"A few months ago I told": Reagan quoted from "The President's Speech," editorial, *The Washington Post*, March 5, 1987. Nancy Reagan had given Parvin the idea for the speech. In a phone conversation before the Tower Report, the first lady told Parvin that the president had not intended to trade arms for hostages, "but in the execution this is what happened." Parvin then wrote the speech incorporating Nancy's idea. See Lou Cannon, *President Reagan: The Role of a Lifetime* (1991), 735–738.

Culvahouse saw they were fighting: Author's interview with Culvahouse, December 30, 1997.

Marlin Fitzwater: Section quoted from author's interviews with Marlin Fitzwater, December 8, 1997, and January 13, 1998; author's interview with Culvahouse, December 30, 1998.

CHAPTER 13

Walsh respected what Reagan: Walsh quoted from author's interview with Lawrence Walsh, February 18, 1998.

At the White House: Culvahouse-Lytton phone call quoted from author's interview with Culvahouse, December 30, 1997; author's interviews with Bill Lytton, February 20, 1998, and April 23, 1998.

Lytton arrived at the White House: Baker-Culvahouse-Lytton meeting quoted from author's interviews with Baker, November 24, 1997, and December 9, 1997; author's interview with Culvahouse, December 30, 1997; and author's interviews with Lytton, February 20, 1998, and April 23, 1998.

Culvahouse and Lytton tried: Author's interview with Culvahouse, December 30, 1997; author's interviews with Lytton, February 20, 1998, and April 23, 1998.

Finding personnel: Author's interview with Culvahouse, December 30, 1997. The intelligence agencies were deeply concerned that North and Poindexter, who had access to the most sensitive communications and other intelligence-gathering operations, would reveal top-secret national security information as part of their defense or out of angst. Culvahouse was able to play on this anxiety to obtain personnel and lawyers, especially from the National Security Agency, which runs the communications interception and cryptographic code-breaking programs.

Someone mentioned that the National: Author's interviews with Lytton, February 20, 1998, and April 23, 1998.

Lytton discovered: Author's interviews with Lytton, February 20, 1998, and April 23, 1998.

By March 25, Lytton had completed: Memo, "Proposed Organization of Iran-Contra Legal Task Force," William B. Lytton to Arthur B. Culvahouse, March 25, 1987.

"The president has said": Lytton quoted from Lytton's contemporaneous notes and chronology and author's interviews with Lytton, February 20, 1998, and April 23, 1998.

"If we find a document": Lytton quoted from Lytton's contemporaneous notes and chronology and author's interviews with Lytton, February 20, 1998, and April 23, 1998.

Baker came over: Baker's remarks quoted from Lytton's contemporaneous notes and chronology and author's interviews with Lytton, February 20, 1998, and April 23, 1998; author's interviews with Baker, November 24, 1997, and December 9, 1997.

On April 6, Culvahouse and: Culvahouse-Lytton-Walsh meeting quoted from Lytton's contemporaneous notes and chronology and author's interviews with Lytton, February 20, 1998, and April 23, 1998; author's interview with Walsh, February 18, 1998.

On April 13, when Culvahouse: Culvahouse-Reagan meeting and reading of the diaries quoted from author's interview with Culvahouse, December 30, 1997; Lytton's contemporaneous notes and chronology and author's interviews with Lytton, February 20, 1998, and April 23, 1998.

On April 30, six days: Baker-Culvahouse-Lytton-Reagan meeting quoted from author's interviews with Baker, November 24, 1997, and December 9, 1997; author's interview with Culvahouse, December 30, 1997; Lytton's contemporaneous notes and chronology and author's interviews with Lytton, February 20, 1998, and April 23, 1998.

The next day, William J. Casey: In January 1987, I interviewed Casey in his hospital room. I asked him if he knew all along about the diversion of funds, and he nodded his head yes. Why? I asked. "I believed," he said. See Bob Woodward, *Veil: The Secret Wars of the CIA* (1987), 507.

Reagan was to hold: Events at meeting quoted from author's interviews with Baker, November 24, 1997, and December 9, 1997; author's interview with Culvahouse, December 30, 1997; Lytton's contemporaneous notes and chronology and author's interviews with Lytton, February 20, 1998, and April 23, 1998.

"take care that the laws": Laurence H. Tribe, "Reagan Ignites a Constitutional Crisis," opinion piece, *New York Times*, May 20, 1987, A31. Tribe wrote that the restrictions on using government funds for the contras applied to the president, who could not resort to private fund-raising. Reagan had personally persuaded Saudi Arabia's King Fahd to double the Saudis' clandestine aid to the contras to $2 million a month after Congress cut off U.S. funding.

Three days later, May 29: Quoted from author's interviews with Baker, November 24, 1997, and December 9, 1997; author's interview with Culvahouse, December 30, 1997; Lytton's contemporaneous notes and chronology and author's interviews with Lytton, February 20, 1998, and April 23, 1998; Report of the Congressional Committees Investigating the Iran-Contra Affair, 197–199; "Text of North's April 1986 Memo on Iran Negotiations," *The Washington Post*, March 1, 1987, A22; Report of the Tower Board.

They asked about a May 16, 1986, meeting: Alan Fiers, the CIA Central America task force chief, later disclosed to investigators that Reagan had startled them at the meeting by asking, "Can't Ollie find funds until we get the hundred million dollars?" This meeting came as Congress was cutting off the funding for the contras. Author's and Jeff Glasser's interview with John Q. Barrett, June 18, 1998; Walsh memoir, 286. Barrett was a prosecutor on Walsh's team.

On June 10, Culvahouse and Lytton: Lytton's contemporaneous notes and chronology and author's interviews with Lytton, February 20, 1998, and April 23, 1998.

Eight days later, the attorneys: Quoted from Lytton's contemporaneous notes and chronology and author's interviews with Lytton, February 20, 1998, and April 23, 1998; author's interview with Culvahouse, December 30, 1997. In the meeting, the lawyers also said the records showed that Reagan had met alone briefly with Poindexter six or possibly seven times. Reagan said he didn't recall any specific one-on-one meetings with Poindexter ever. Usually the chief of staff or Poindexter's deputy or often Vice President Bush were present. "It's possible he might have come in, dropped off a memo," Reagan said.

On June 23, Baker: Meeting quoted from Lytton's contemporaneous notes and chronology and author's interviews with Lytton, February 20, 1998, and April 23, 1998; author's interview with Culvahouse, December 30, 1997. See also minutes "National Security Planning Group Meeting June 25, 1984," folder "Files of the Office of the Vice President Bush, George (3)," John Q. Barrett attorney files, Records of Independent Counsel Lawrence Walsh, National Archives II, Box 2; Walsh memoir, 194.

Reagan allegedly made the comment that until funding was restored, Bud McFarlane, the NSC adviser, was "to hold them body and soul together," Mc-Farlane later testified. See Haynes Johnson, "A Somber Recounting of a Secret Policy and Its 'Fatal Risks,' " *The Washington Post*, May 12, 1987, A14; "The Iran-Contra Hearings: Excerpts: 'Hold Body and Soul Together,' " testimony of Robert C. "Bud" McFarlane, *Los Angeles Times*, May 12, 1987, 15; Walsh memoir, 119.

The next morning, June 24: Meeting quoted from Lytton's contemporaneous notes and chronology and author's interviews with Lytton, February 20, 1998, and April 23, 1998; author's interview with Culvahouse, December 30, 1997.

In the 11 days between: According to the final report of the congressional committees, the only change was the insertion of the words "third parties" in the list of entities to be assisted by the CIA. See Report of the Congressional Committees Investigating the Iran-Contra Affair, 208–211.

The three came back at 10 a.m.: Meeting quoted from Lytton's contemporaneous notes and chronology and author's interviews with Lytton, February 20, 1998, and April 23, 1998; author's interview with Culvahouse, December 30, 1997; author's interviews with Baker, November 24, 1997, and December 9, 1997. See also Woodward, *Veil: The Secret Wars of the CIA*, for an account of Casey's involvement in Iran-contra, which contradicts Reagan's statement that "Casey had very little involvement in it."

On June 30 at 11 a.m.: Meeting quoted from Lytton's contemporaneous notes and chronology and author's interviews with Lytton, February 20, 1998, and April 23, 1998; author's interview with Culvahouse, December 30, 1997; author's interviews with Baker, November 24, 1997, and December 9, 1997; David Halevy and Neil C. Livingstone, "The Ollie We Knew," *Washingtonian* magazine (July 1987), 77–79, 140–158. See also Charles R. Babcock and Joe Pichirallo, "North Hoped to Sway '96 Election Hill Told; Hill Panel Votes to Compel North to Give Testimony," *The Washington Post*, June 5, 1987, A1; Dan Morgan and Walter Pincus, "North, Panels Agree on Terms for Public, Private Testimony," *The Washington Post*, June 25, 1987, A1.

On July 2, just after 10 a.m.: Meeting quoted from Lytton's contemporaneous notes and chronology and author's interviews with Lytton, February 20, 1998, and April 23, 1998; author's interview with Culvahouse, December 30, 1997; author's interviews with Baker, November 24, 1997, and December 9, 1997. For more information on the 1985 finding, see Report of the Congressional Committees Investigating the Iran-Contra Affair, 186, 196–197.

Five days later, Oliver North: North congressional appearance quoted from Oliver North, *Under Fire: An American Story* (1991), 12; Oliver North, *Taking the Stand: The Testimony of Lieutenant Colonel Oliver L. North* (1987), 13; author's interviews with knowledgeable source close to North. North later wrote, "The administration chose to focus almost exclusively on the 'diversion,' and there was certainly a lot to be gained by presenting it that way. This particular detail was so dramatic, so sexy, that it might actually—well, divert public attention from other, even more important aspects of the story, such as what else the president and his top advisers had known about and approved. And if it could be insinuated that this supposedly terrible deed was the exclusive responsibility of one mid-level staff assistant at the National Security Council (and perhaps his immediate superior, the national security adviser), and that this staffer had acted on his own (however unlikely that might be) and that, now that you mention it, his activities might even be criminal—if the public and the press focused on that, then maybe you didn't have another Watergate on your hands after all. Especially if you insisted that the president knew nothing about it." See North, *Under Fire*, 6–7.

"We're glad to be able to bring": Meeting quoted from Lytton's contemporaneous notes and chronology and author's interviews with Lytton, February 20, 1998, and April 23, 1998; author's interview with Culvahouse, December 30, 1997; author's interviews with Baker, November 24, 1997, and December 9, 1997.

On July 10, they came back: Meeting quoted from Lytton's contemporaneous notes and chronology and author's interviews with Lytton, February 20, 1998, and April 23, 1998; author's interview with Culvahouse, December 30, 1997; author's interviews with Baker, November 24, 1997, and December 9, 1997. See also "The Iran-Contra Hearings: Excerpts: 'Hold Body and Soul Together,'" testimony of Robert C. "Bud" McFarlane, *Los Angeles Times*, May 12, 1987, 15; Walsh memoir, 119. Also see "Text of North's April 1986 Memo on Iran Negotiations," *The Washington Post*, March 1, 1987, A22.

Baker had arranged: Meeting quoted from Lytton's contemporaneous notes and chronology and author's interviews with Lytton, February 20, 1998, and April 23, 1998; author's interview with Culvahouse, December 30, 1997; author's interviews with Baker, November 24, 1997, and December 9, 1997. See also folder "White House Residence Visitor Logs," John Q. Barrett general investigative files, Records of Independent Counsel Lawrence Walsh, Records of the Independent Counsels, National Archives II, Box 39.

The morning of July 15: Meeting quoted from Lytton's contemporaneous notes and chronology and author's interviews with Lytton, February 20, 1998, and April 23, 1998; author's interview with Culvahouse, December 30, 1997; author's interviews with Baker, November 24, 1997, and December 9, 1997.

What do you have with a lawyer: Meeting quoted from Lytton's contemporaneous notes and chronology and author's interviews with Lytton, February 20, 1998, and April 23, 1998; author's interview with Culvahouse, December 30, 1997; author's interviews with Baker, November 24, 1997, and December 9, 1997. See also Report of the Congressional Committees Investigating the Iran-Contra Affair, 197–199; David Hoffman, "Reagan's 'Worst' Speech; How Talk on Arms Deal Went Wrong," *The Washington Post*, July 20, 1987, A1. Hoffman wrote, "The basic premise of the talk—that the Iran effort was essentially a diplomatic enterprise aimed at establishing a relationship with moderate groups in that country and not an arms-for-hostages swap—was undermined this week by the revelation that Reagan had signed a presidential 'finding' on Dec. 5, 1985, explicitly authorizing a trade of arms for hostages. . . . Reagan now asserts that he forgot about the original finding, but does not dispute signing it."

That evening Baker, Culvahouse: Lytton's contemporaneous notes and chronology and author's interviews with Lytton, February 20, 1998, and April 23, 1998.

CHAPTER 14

"I developed a very clear": Shultz quoted from Shultz memoir, 914.

Shultz recounted that: Shultz's comments about Bryce Harlow quoted from Shultz memoir, 917. Harlow had been the key person to convince Vice President Gerald Ford that Haig was offering him a deal on the pardon back in August 1974.

There was an explanation: Author's interview with Shultz, November 3, 1997.

Lawrence Walsh, television clicker: Quoted from author's interview with Walsh, February 18, 1998; Walsh memoir, 143–144; "Transcript of President Reagan's Address to the Nation," *The Washington Post*, August 13, 1987, A18.

Richard Nixon, in the 13th year: Nixon letter to Reagan in Ronald Reagan Presidential Library, file 533859, SP 1169. On the letter is the notation, "No reply—phoned."

Poindexter and North were tried: In May 1989, North was convicted of obstructing Congress, illegally aiding and abetting the destruction of government documents and taking an illegal gratuity from one of his confederates. In April 1990, Poindexter was convicted of lying to Congress, destroying official documents and obstructing congressional inquiries into the Iran-contra affair. The U.S. Court of Appeals for the District of Columbia set aside both Poindexter's and North's convictions in separate rulings because the witnesses against them may have been "tainted" by immunized testimony to Congress.

He felt bad: Author's interview with Walsh, February 18, 1998.

John Barrett, a young prosecutor: Author's and Jeff Glasser's interview with Barrett, June 18, 1998.

According to Shultz, Weinberger: Walsh memoir, 336.

Walsh tried to subpoena: Walsh memoir, 338.

Weinberger repeated his earlier: Walsh memoir, 339. Weinberger claimed he largely discontinued the practice of taking notes after the first year because he did not have time to consolidate notes at meetings.

Walsh sent a young associate: Walsh memoir, 340. When the associate, Greg Mark, asked to look through other parts of Weinberger's papers, the librarian told him he could see only those items that specified Iran or a Central American country in the register. Weinberger's longtime secretary, Kay Leisz, stood sentry over Mark, preventing him from going to the unclassified section.

840

Finally, in November 1991: Walsh memoir, 340. Tom Baker found a different librarian, who was less overbearing.

In all there were 7,000 pages: Walsh memoir, 342.

"Very smart": Author's interview with Walsh, February 18, 1998.

"I argued strongly": Weinberger's notes for December 7, 1985, quoted from Ronald Reagan 1992 exhibit binder (folder 1), Christina Spaulding attorney files, Office of Independent Counsel Lawrence Walsh, National Archives II, Box 2.

Robert Bennett, Weinberger's lawyer: Quoted from Walsh memoir, 398, 401.

Walsh was amused and astounded: Walsh memoir, 398. Walsh wrote, "Even though we might actually forget brushing our teeth, we would hardly deny ever having brushed them."

"Of course, you know this means": Bennett quoted from Walsh memoir, 410.

More than five and a half years: Author's interview with Walsh, February 18, 1998; author's and Jeff Glasser's interview with Barrett, June 18, 1998.

The Weinberger indictment was designed: Walsh memoir, 408–410; author's interview with Walsh, February 18, 1998. Walsh felt betrayed by Weinberger. "I was his advocate within our group, defending him. The last thing I want to do is take on a guy who's got the Medal of Freedom and all the other things that the fellow has earned. But it becomes so clear that he's a liar that you have to," Walsh said.

In the summer of 1992: Walsh-Olson meeting quoted from author's and Jeff Glasser's interview with Barrett, June 18, 1998; author's interview with Ted Olson, October 29, 1998. Walsh also was interested in obtaining information from Nancy Reagan for the Weinberger trial, notwithstanding the spousal privilege that normally would shield her. "The spousal privilege does not serve as a bar to an OIC interview of Mrs. Reagan," a member of Walsh's staff argued in a memo. They apparently did not pursue it. See memo, "Spousal Privilege—Nancy Reagan," Jeffrey Harleston to Judge Walsh, Craig Gillen, folder "General Investigative, Reagan 7/24/92 Interview," John Q. Barrett attorney files, Records of Independent Counsel Lawrence Walsh, National Archives II, Box 39.

Walsh would not back down: Walsh memoir, 420.

Walsh alternately felt a drive: Author's interview with Walsh, February 18, 1998.

Barrett was assigned the task: Author's and Glasser's interview with Barrett, June 18, 1998. Barrett, seeing the value of a verbatim, real-time account that Hill had provided, started filling his notebooks for June and July 1992 with dozens of conversations with Olson.

As a preliminary step: Barrett's vetting of the diary quoted from author's and Glasser's interview with John Barrett, June 18, 1998.

Walsh and Barrett continued to insist: The exchanges between Olson and Walsh-Barrett quoted from author's and Glasser's interview with Barrett, June 18, 1998; author's interview with Olson, October 29, 1998.

Olson felt like he was handling: Author's interview with Olson, October 29, 1998.

The agreement was signed July 21: It stated, "You have said that he is not a 'target' of your investigation, as that term is defined in the U.S. attorneys' manual, and that he is not a putative defendant. You have also stated that it is highly unlikely that you will seek further interviews or testimony from President Reagan and that your request to interview President Reagan should not be perceived as a hostile act." See July 21 letter of agreement and drafts, folder "General Investigative, Reagan 7/24/92 Interview," John Q. Barrett attorney files, Records of Independent Counsel Lawrence Walsh, National Archives II, Box 39.

At a 3 p.m. meeting with the lawyers: Author's interview with Olson, October 29, 1998; author's and Glasser's interview with Barrett, June 18, 1998.

In an accompanying note: Note, Olson to Barrett, folder "General Investigative, Reagan 7/24/92 Interview," John Q. Barrett attorney files, Records of Independent Counsel Lawrence Walsh, National Archives II, Box 39.

Two days later, Walsh: Scene quoted from transcript, folder "Reagan Deposition 7/4/92," Christina Spaulding attorney files, Records of Independent Counsel Lawrence Walsh, National Archives II, Box 5; author's and Glasser's interview with Barrett, June 18, 1998; author's interview with Olson, October 29, 1998; author's interview with Walsh, February 18, 1998. See also Walsh memoir for a partial account of the meeting, 420–421.

Barrett prepared a rough: Outline, "A" list and Barrett notes, folder "General Investigative, Reagan 7/24/92 Interview," John Q. Barrett Attorney Files, Records of Independent Counsel Lawrence Walsh, National Archives II, Box 39.

What are we going to do: Quoted from author's and Glasser's interview with Barrett, June 18, 1998.

For Walsh, the Reagan interview: Walsh memoir, 421; author's interview with Walsh, February 18, 1998.

Two days later, on July 26: Walter Pincus, "Walsh May Seek Indictment of Reagan in Iran-Contra; Meese, Shultz, Regan Also Seen Targeted," *The Washington Post*, July 26, 1992, A1.

Mrs. Reagan was hysterical: Author's and Glasser's interview with Barrett, June 18, 1998; author's interview with Olson, October 29, 1998; Walsh memoir, 421–422.

"It's not true": Author's interview with Olson, October 29, 1998; Walsh memoir, 421–422.

A few days after the article: Author's and Glasser's interview with Barrett, June 18, 1998. See also Walter Pincus, "Iran-Contra Probe Focuses on Meese; Reagan and Regan Are Not Under Investigation, Lawyer Says," *The Washington Post*, August 6, 1992, A1.

On August 17, more than three: Speech quoted from transcript, "Reagan: 'What We Should Change Is a Democratic Congress,' " *The Washington Post*, August 18, 1992, A19.

Olson almost wept: Author's interview with Olson, October 29, 1998.

"Gippericious": Tom Shales, "Reagan, Back in from the Sunset," *The Washington Post*, August 18, 1992, D1.

Were we had?: Barrett-Spaulding-Walsh meeting quoted from author's and Glasser's interview with Barrett, June 18, 1998.

"My fellow Americans": "Text of Letter from Former President Reagan to the American People," Associated Press, November 5, 1994. Reagan also wrote, "In closing, let me thank you, the American people, for giving me the great honor of allowing me to serve as your president. When the Lord calls me home, whenever that may be, I will leave with the greatest love for this country of ours and eternal optimism for its future."

On February 18, 1998, I went to see: Quoted from author's interview with Walsh, February 18, 1998.

PART FOUR. GEORGE BUSH: 1989–93
CHAPTER 15

"The news is *not* encouraging": Bush quoted from memo, "George Bush to Alexander M. Haig Jr.," July 10, 1974, Alexander M. Haig Jr. files, Richard Nixon collection, National Archives II.

One Friday night near the end: Haig-Bush exchange quoted from author's interviews with Haig, November 6, 1997, and February 5, 1998.

Haig thought Bush was weak: In 1988, Haig ran against Bush for president. At a primary debate, Haig quipped, "I never heard a wimp out of you" about an arms control treaty with the Soviet Union in 1982 when Haig was secretary of state. See David S. Broder and David Hoffman, "Bush Deflects Attacks During GOP Debate; Vice President Alone Defends INF Pact," *The Washington Post*, October 29, 1987, A1.

"He broke out into assholes": Bush's reactions in August 1974 quoted from author's interviews with two sources who were present when Burch made the remark. See Woodward and Bernstein, *The Final Days*, 369.

Bush was often tagged: When Bush announced his candidacy for the presidency in 1988, *Newsweek* ran a cover story with the headline "Fighting the 'Wimp' Label." Furious, Bush's son, George W. Bush, called *Newsweek*'s Washington bureau and threatened that Bush would freeze out the magazine for the rest of the campaign. See Margaret Garrard Warner, "Bush Battles the 'Wimp Factor,'" *Newsweek*, October 19, 1987, 28; Maralee Schwartz, "Bush Jr. vs. Newsweek," *The Washington Post*, October 16, 1987, A11.

George Will wrote, "The unpleasant sound Bush is emitting as he traipses from one conservative gathering to another is a thin, tinny 'arf'—the sound of a lapdog." See George F. Will, "George Bush: The Sound of a Lapdog," *The Washington Post*, January 30, 1986, A25.

Publicly, he backed Reagan: Bush told David Broder in August 1987, "If I'd have sat there and heard George Shultz and Cap express it strongly, maybe I would have had a stronger view," referring to Secretary of State Shultz's and Secretary of Defense Caspar Weinberger's opposition. "But when you don't know something it's hard to react. . . . We were not in the loop." See David S. Broder, "Bush Asserts Vindication in Iran Affair; Says Key Facts Were Denied Him," *The Washington Post*, August 6, 1987, A1.

On Friday, February 6, 1987, Bush: Bush's planting of the Iran arms deals story quoted from author's interview with knowledgeable source; Bob Wood-

843

ward and David Hoffman, "Bush Told U.S. Arms Deals Were with Iran Radicals," *The Washington Post*, February 8, 1987, A1.

The records showed that: Author's interview with Walsh, February 18, 1998.

In interviews outside the grand jury: Author's and Glasser's interview with Barrett, June 18, 1998.

"How would you like it": The "seven minutes" Bush referred to was by most accounts six, and it happened when Rather exited the set while in Miami, not New York. But few focused on these details, and the attack helped Bush beat the wimp factor. See Tom Shales, "Rather, Bush and the Nine-Minute War; On CBS, a Fiery Lesson in News Through Confrontation," *The Washington Post*, January 26, 1988, E1.

One of his first decisions: Bush-Tower section quoted from author's interviews with knowledgeable source; John Tower, *Consequences* (1991), 336–337. Bush's diary entries are quoted from Herbert S. Parmet, *George Bush: The Life of a Lone Star Yankee* (1998), 371–375. I wrote five stories in this period about Tower's background and his FBI file. The most controversial of these was an account from a retired Air Force sergeant, Bob Jackson, who said he observed Tower fondle two women on separate occasions, and that Tower appeared to be drunk both times. The next day, Tower and other senators disputed the sergeant's claims. The Senate released a letter saying Jackson had been treated for psychological problems before he retired. Since the allegations were not corroborated, I wish in hindsight that I had not published that particular story.

Bush asked Marlin Fitzwater: Bush-Fitzwater section quoted from author's interviews with Fitzwater, December 8, 1997, and January 13, 1998.

Bush's third son, Neil: Neil Bush section quoted from author's interview with Fitzwater, December 8, 1997; author's interview with knowledgeable source; Barbara Bush, *A Memoir* (1994 paperback edn.), 59, 344–346.

Who is your candidate?: Souter section quoted from author's interviews with knowledgeable source; Margaret Carlson, "An 18th Century Man," *Time*, August 6, 1990; Roxanne Roberts, "The Bachelors; They Say Power Corrupts. In Washington It Also Seduces," *The Washington Post*, October 3, 1990, C1. For a partial account, see Warren Rudman, *Combat: Twelve Years in the Senate* (1996), 152–194.

The next summer, 1991: Thomas confirmation section quoted from author's interviews with knowledgeable source; Christopher Connell, "Bush Denounces Thomas Hearings," Associated Press, October 13, 1991.

In August 1990: Bush-Scowcroft-Powell-Baker scene quoted from author's interviews with knowledgeable source.

Fitzwater realized the box: Fitzwater-Bush exchange quoted from author's interviews with Fitzwater, December 8, 1997, and January 13, 1998.

Bush had written his five children: Letter quoted from George Bush and Brent Scowcroft, *A World Transformed* (1998), 434–435.

Again the issue of half measures: Meeting quoted from author's interview with knowledgeable source.

"It hasn't been a clean": Bush diary entry quoted from Bush and Scowcroft memoir, 486–487.

Bush didn't want the turmoil: For a book I was writing on the Gulf War and the Pentagon, I had requested an interview with the president. Bush declined through Fitzwater, who told me in a February 19, 1991, letter that Bush had "a general policy of declining book interviews because of their commercial value."

"This is not something I want": Bush quoted from author's interviews with Fitzwater, December 8, 1997, and January 13, 1998.

In their book: In a portion of the book written only by Scowcroft, the former Bush national security adviser gave a partial explanation of their dilemma. He wrote, "There was absolutely no doubt that Jim Baker was a brilliant negotiator. But I also had no doubt that he would do everything possible to attain our demands by persuasion rather than force. The unhappy reality of the situation, from my perspective, was that an Iraqi withdrawal would leave us in a most difficult position. Saddam could pull his forces back just north of the border and leave them there, poised for attack. U.S. forces, on the other hand, could not long remain in place. The force exceeded our capability to rotate it and, in any event, it would not be tolerable for the Saudis to have such a large foreign force indefinitely on their territory." Bush and Scowcroft memoir, 437–438.

the "sniping, carping, bitching": Bush diary entries quoted from Parmet biography, 488.

CHAPTER 16

In April 1991, Patty Presock: The questions about Bush's health quoted from author's interviews with Fitzwater, December 8, 1997, and January 13, 1998; Parmet biography, 490.

"This office has been in business": Stein's meeting with Walsh prosecutors quoted from memo, John Q. Barrett to Judge Walsh et al., December 13, 1990, folder "Files of the Office of the Vice President Bush, George (1)," John Q. Barrett attorney files, Records of Independent Counsel Lawrence Walsh, National Archives II, Box 1.

By April 1991, Boyden Gray: Bush-Gray-Lytton meetings quoted from Lytton's contemporaneous notes and chronology and author's interviews with Lytton, February 20, 1998, and April 23, 1998; author's interviews with knowledgeable source.

In the middle of the summer of 1991: Meeting quoted from author's interview with knowledgeable source and source's contemporaneous handwritten notes.

Since the spring: Sununu section quoted from author's interviews with Fitzwater, December 8, 1997, and January 13, 1998. Sununu claimed it was essential to use military planes even on private trips because he needed secure communications in an emergency or he might have to come back to the White House on short notice. See also Marlin Fitzwater, *Call the Briefing: Reagan and Bush, Sam and Helen: A Decade with Presidents and the Press* (1995), 176–178, 179, 187, 189.

After finally declaring: New Hampshire primary scene quoted from author's interview with knowledgeable source. Also see Jack W. Germond and Jules Witcover, *Mad as Hell: Revolt at the Ballot Box* (1992), 149–152.

In the summer of 1992, the U.S. Navy: Tailhook section quoted from author's interview with knowledgeable source; author's interview with Fitzwater, January 13, 1998; transcript, *ABC World News Tonight with Peter Jennings*, June 24, 1992.

On July 24, Bush snapped: Members of POW-MIA families had shouted down a Bush speech when the president yelled, "Would you please shut up and sit down?" See Ann Devroy, "Bush Cites His Patriotism, War Record in Response to MIA Families' Heckling," *The Washington Post*, July 25, 1992, A1.

Later that day, campaigning: Concerns about Bush's health quoted from author's interviews with Fitzwater, December 8, 1997, and January 13, 1998.

On September 24, two months: Transcript of independent counsel interview of Patty Presock, January 26, 1993, Records of Independent Counsel Lawrence Walsh, National Archives II.

Bush disagreed and called Gray: Quoted from author's interview with knowledgeable source.

Nine days later, on Sunday: See press release "Who Tampered with Bill Clinton's Passport File?", *Newsweek*, October 4, 1992.

Bush dictated in his diary: Bush diary entries quoted from file "Baker 9/10/93, 12/9/93," Records of Independent Counsel Joseph diGenova, National Archives II, Box 190.

Afterwards, Jim Baker: Bush-Baker-Bond exchanges quoted from author's interviews with knowledgeable source. See also Germond & Witcover campaign book, 495–496.

Iran-contra would not go away: Debate about Weinberger reindictment quoted from author's interview with Walsh, February 18, 1998; author's and Glasser's interview with Barrett, June 18, 1998; author's interview with Stephen Ellis, November 2, 1998; Glasser's interview with Ken Parsigian, January 25, 1999; Glasser's interview with James Brosnahan, April 21, 1999.

The polling showed: Political controversy over reindictment quoted from author's interview with Walsh, February 18, 1998; author's interviews with two participants; transcript, *Larry King Live*, CNN, October 30, 1992; Robert Pear, " '86 Weinberger Notes Contradict Bush Account on Iran Arms Deal," *New York Times*, October 31, 1992, 1; Walter Pincus and George Lardner Jr., "Bush Stance, Iran-Contra Note at Odds; Weinberger Memo Says President 'Favored' Arms-Hostage Plan," *The Washington Post*, October 31, 1992, A1; Germond and Witcover campaign book, 495, 498, 501–502.

"You don't live or die": Bush quoted from transcript, *Newsmaker Sunday*, CNN, November 1, 1992.

He was cranky: Author's interviews with knowledgeable source.

On Monday, November 2: Nixon quoted from Parmet biography, 506.

"Let's finish this job": Bush quoted from Ann Devroy and Mary Jordan, "White House 'Family' Embraces Bush," *The Washington Post*, November 5, 1992, A1.

With an index finger motion: Meeting quoted from author's interviews with knowledgeable source.

"I'm not going to mind": Baker quoted from author's interview with knowledgeable source.

Walsh voted against Bush: Author's interview with Walsh, February 18, 1998.

"Walsh had that phony": Bush quoted from author's interview with Fitzwater, December 8, 1997.

After the election: Passportgate section quoted from FBI 302 interview with President Bush, November 8, 1993, Records of Independent Counsel Joseph diGenova, National Archives II, Box 190; diary entries, folder "Baker 9/10/93, 12/9/93," Records of Independent Counsel Joseph diGenova, National Archives II, Box 190; Walter Pincus, "White House Tied to Passport Search," *The Washington Post*, November 16, 1992, A1. See also Barbara Bush memoir, 530.

In December, Gray realized: Lytton's contemporaneous notes and chronology and author's interviews with Lytton, February 20, 1998, and April 23, 1998; author's and Glasser's interview with Barrett, June 18, 1998; author's interview with Walsh, February 18, 1998.

CHAPTER 17

"This is a load of bullshit!": Author's interviews with knowledgeable source. Barr had refused to seek independent counsels in two cases, the so-called Iraqgate and Inslaw scandals, and instead had appointed special counsels answerable to him and the Justice Department. Neither investigation led to criminal charges.

"Jim Baker is still all": Bush quoted from his Passportgate diary entries for December 9, 1992, Records of Independent Counsel Joseph diGenova, National Archives II, Box 190.

The next day, December 10: Author's interviews with knowledgeable source. See also Joseph E. diGenova, Final Report of the Independent Counsel in Re: Janet G. Mullins, November 30, 1995, Vol. I, 6.

Three days later, Joseph E. diGenova: Meeting with the judges quoted from author's interview with Joseph diGenova, January 27, 1998.

"Jim Baker has lost all interest": Bush quoted from December 15, 1992, Passportgate diary entry in diGenova's files.

"Baker is a nervous wreck": Bush quoted from December 17, 1992, Passportgate diary entry in diGenova's files.

Bush met with Gray: Author's interview with knowledgeable source.

"It's ruining Jim Baker's life": Bush quoted from December 18, 1992, Passportgate diary entry in diGenova's files.

Bush arranged to have a meeting: Bush-Gray-Barr meeting quoted from author's interviews with knowledgeable sources.

Bush read Mary McGrory's: Mary McGrory, "Missing and Presumed Injured," *The Washington Post*, December 22, 1992, A2; Bush quoted from December 22, 1992, Passportgate diary entry in diGenova's files.

Walsh was determined to proceed: Author's interview with Walsh, February 18, 1998; Walsh memoir, 485; Walter Pincus, " 'Mock Trial' of Weinberger Is Staged by Independent Counsel's Prosecutors," *The Washington Post*, December 15, 1992, A5. After the *Post* reported on the mock trials, Senate Minority Leader Bob Dole, the Republican from Kansas, called for Walsh's resignation. "Their 'mock trial' is a mockery of the taxpayer and is the latest arrogance from Lawrence Walsh's outrageous . . . political persecution of Republicans," Dole said.

Many Republicans were now publicly: Dole and Vice President Dan Quayle came out in favor of a pardon for Weinberger right after the election. See Ann Devroy and Walter Pincus, "Bush Urged to Grant Pardons; Aides Advise Action on Iran-Contra Cases, Including Weinberger's," *The Washington Post*, November 7, 1992, A1; "Dole Urges Inquiry About Prosecutor," Associated Press, November 8, 1992; David Johnston, "Pardon Is Sought for Weinberger," *New York Times*, November 8, 1992, 31.

"What can I do?": Bennett quoted from author's interviews with knowledgeable sources.

"The pardon of Weinberger": Bush quoted from December 22, 1992, Passportgate diary entry in diGenova's files.

"Okay, Marlin": Bush-Fitzwater meeting quoted from author's interviews with Fitzwater, December 8, 1997, and January 13, 1998.

Gray was strongly in favor: Author's interviews with knowledgeable source.

"I am pardoning him": Bush's statements on the pardons quoted from "Text of President Bush's Statement on the Pardon of Weinberger and Others," Associated Press, December 25, 1992.

At midafternoon, Gray called: Gray-Parsigian exchange quoted from Glasser's interview with Parsigian, January 25, 1999.

Half-laughing, Gray said: Author's interview with Walsh, February 18, 1998; Walsh memoir, 492.

Walsh thought it was just: Author's interview with Walsh, February 18, 1998; Walsh memoir, 500–503.

Bush found no joy: Bush quoted from December 29, 1992, Passportgate diary entry in diGenova's files.

On January 15, 1993: King & Spaulding, Report to President Bush, January 15, 1993. Bush's lawyers also attached to the report a 45-page extract from Bush's diary entries related to Iran-contra for the period November 4, 1986–January 2, 1987.

The real problem was: Author's interview with Walsh, February 18, 1998.

Walsh called a meeting: Glasser's interview with Parsigian, January 15, 1999; memo, "Possible use of grand jury in Bush investigation," Ken Parsigian to Judge Walsh, April 2, 1993, folder "Lawrence Walsh—Miscellaneous George Bush," Records of Independent Counsel Walsh, National Archives II, Box 5. Walsh wrote on the memo in his own handwriting about his deputy Gillen, "Craig's position was based on the assumption Bush would deny (falsely) any recollection." Walsh also wrote, "Again because Bush will not be forthcoming."

Walsh in his memoir (p. 515) wrote a partial account of this meeting: "My immediate instinct was to use the grand jury and subpoena Bush; he was no longer in a position to set the terms for his deposition. In this I was alone. The staff unanimously opposed the use of the grand jury, arguing that to do so would exaggerate public expectations and would appear retaliatory. Underlying this position was the legal question of whether there was a sufficient likelihood of indictable criminal conduct to supply an appropriate basis for a grand jury proceeding."

The same day, two of his other: Memo, "Factual Findings of the Bush Investigation," Jeffrey Harleston, Sam Wilkins III to Judge Walsh, Craig Gillen, Jim Weighart, Mary Belcher, April 2, 1993, folder "Files of the Office of the Vice President Bush—1993 Investigative Work Product," John Q. Barrett files, Records of Independent Counsel Lawrence Walsh, National Archives II, Box 2.

Despite this conclusion, Walsh: Author's interview with Walsh, February 18, 1998; Walsh memoir, 515.

"I think President Bush": Walsh quoted from George Lardner Jr. and Walter Pincus, "Iran-Contra Report Castigates Reagan," *The Washington Post*, January 19, 1994, A1.

Passportgate still lingered: Bush-diGenova section quoted from author's interview with diGenova, January 27, 1998; Bush Passportgate diary entries; FBI 302 record of Bush interview, October 28, 1993. On the Perot FBI sting, also see Germond & Witcover campaign book, 489–490. DiGenova had already discovered that Perot secretly taped conversations with Scowcroft and Eagleburger. Perot's lawyer turned the tapes over to diGenova. DiGenova went over them with Scowcroft and Eagleburger, and they were appalled.

It took three years: Joseph E. diGenova, Final Report of the Independent Counsel in Re: Janet G. Mullins, November 30, 1995.

But diGenova realized that given: Author's interview with diGenova, January 27, 1998.

In early 1998, I talked with: Letter, George Bush to Bob Woodward, January 27, 1998.

Bush had declined numerous requests: Bush declined to be interviewed for the second Watergate book that Carl Bernstein and I wrote and published in 1976, *The Final Days*; for an October 1988 *Washington Post* series of articles on Bush's life; for my 1991 book, *The Commanders*, on the military and the Gulf War; for an early 1992 *Washington Post* series on Vice President Dan Quayle, which I wrote with David Broder; and for an October 1992 preelection *Washington Post* series on Bush's economic policy making.

PART FIVE. BILL CLINTON: 1993–

CHAPTER 18

Bernie Nussbaum: Nussbaum-Hillary-Clinton scenes quoted from author's interviews with knowledgeable source. See also James Stewart, *Blood Sport: The President and His Adversaries* (1996), 237–242.

Watergate was ingrained: During the fall of 1973 and the spring of 1974, Clinton was teaching law at the University of Arkansas, Fayetteville. He often would turn the discussion in class to whether the people involved in Watergate were agents of the president. In the summer of 1974, Clinton was running for Congress from Arkansas's third district, which included Fayetteville. He used Richard Nixon as a campaign issue. "I think it's plain that the president should resign and spare the country the agony of this impeachment and removal proceeding," Clinton told the *Arkansas Gazette* in 1974. "I think the country could be spared a lot of agony and the government could worry about inflation and a lot of other problems if he'd go on and resign." See Deb Riechmann, "First Lady Helped Craft Impeachment Procedures Being Weighed Today," Associated Press, October 1, 1998; David Maraniss, *First in His Class: A Biography of Bill Clinton* (1995), 291–292, 297–306, 313–315.

"We killed": Quoted from author's interviews with Barr, January 19 and 26, 1999; Panel, "The Independent Counsel Process: Is It Broken and How Should It Be Fixed?" *Washington and Lee Law Review* (Fall 1997), 1534.

"We have got a problem": Meeting on Baird quoted from author's interviews with participants.

During the next months: Guinier section quoted from author's interviews with participants. Lani Guinier, *Lift Every Voice: Turning a Civil Rights Setback into a New Vision of Social Justice* (1998), 114–131; Al Kamen, "Nussbaum Sized Up for the Blindfold," *The Washington Post*, June 7, 1993, A17.

That spring seven members: Five of the seven employees were later reinstated and placed in other jobs. Billy Dale's case went to trial, and he was acquitted. Quoted from author's interviews with knowledgeable source; Ann Devroy and Michael Isikoff, "Clinton Staff Went Past Reno to FBI," *The Washington Post*, May 25, 1993, A1; Thomas L. Friedman, "White House Asked Aid of F.B.I. in Dismissals," *New York Times*, May 25, 1993, A18; Paul Richter and Ronald J. Ostrow, "Travel Flap Stirs In-House Probe; 5 to Regain Pay," *Los Angeles Times*, May 26, 1993, A1; Ann Devroy, "Clinton Friends Cited in Travel Staff Purge; Report Says First Lady Monitored Actions," *The Washington Post*, July 3, 1993, A1. See also Stewart book, 258–278.

On July 20, Foster was found: Reaction to Foster suicide quoted from author's interviews with participants. See also Jeff Gerth, "Clintons Joined S&L Venture in an Ozark Real Estate Venture," *New York Times*, March 8, 1992, A1.

By the fall of 1993: Susan Schmidt, "U.S. Is Asked to Probe Failed Arkansas S&L; RTC Questions Thrift's Mid-80s Check Flow," *The Washington Post*, October 31, 1993, A1.

With a possible criminal investigation: Kendall section quoted from author's interviews with knowledgeable source; David Von Drehle, *Among the Lowest of the Dead: The Culture of Death Row* (1995), 6–9, 15–20, 44–51, 61–62, 68–78.

The story alleged: Jerry Seper, "Clinton Papers Lifted After Aide's Suicide," *The Washington Times*, December 20, 1993, A1.

Certain key Republicans began: On January 2, 1994, Senate Minority Leader Bob Dole and House Minority Leader Newt Gingrich called for an outside counsel to review Whitewater. On January 9, Senator Daniel Patrick Moynihan, the Democrat from New York, announced that he favored a special counsel. See Helen Dewar, "Independent Counsel Urged in Arkansas Probe; GOP Leaders' Call Rebuffed by White House Aide George Stephanopoulos as

Politically Inspired," *The Washington Post*, January 3, 1994, A5; Gwen Ifill, "Moynihan Urges Prosecutor to Study Clinton Land Deal," *New York Times*, January 10, 1994, A8.

"Here is an institution": Nussbaum quoted from author's interviews with knowledgeable source.

"Those guys are fucking": Ickes quoted from author's interview with knowledgeable source.

"We need a plan": Hillary quoted from author's interview with knowledgeable source.

The article was titled: David Brock, "His Cheatin' Heart: Living with the Clintons," *American Spectator* (January 1994), 18–30.

Hillary vetoed: Author's interviews with participants.

Stephanopoulos was convinced: Author's interview with knowledgeable source.

The evening of January 5: Earlier that day, I went to the White House for a background interview with President Clinton for the book I was writing on the making of economic policy—*The Agenda*, published in 1994. The interview gave Clinton a chance to respond to what others had said. He added little of substance. At the end of the hour, he voiced concern about the scenes in the book in which he had lost his temper. "I'm afraid you're going to make me look like a madman," he said. Like others, I was struck by Clinton's ability to leave the impression he was agreeing with me without really saying so. His talent for maintaining eye contact was breathtaking. During the interview I thought I was getting significant new information critical to my reporting. I thought his answers better and more useful than they were in fact when I later read the transcript and listened to the tape.

Within hours: Quoted from "Senator Bob Dole, Senate Minority Leader, Discusses the Clinton Investigation," *CBS This Morning*, January 6, 1994; Bob Woodward, *The Choice* (1996), 16.

Calls for an independent: Michael Isikoff and Ann Devroy, "9 Democrats Join Call for Prosecutor; Clinton Aides Reconsider Whitewater Stance," *The Washington Post*, January 12, 1994, A1.

The next day, Clinton was: Meeting of the Whitewater Response Team quoted from author's interviews with three participants. See also Stewart book, 373–376.

The next morning, Hillary walked: Author's interview with knowledgeable source.

Nussbaum drafted: Text of letter from Bernard W. Nussbaum to Madam Attorney General, Associated Press, January 13, 1994.

CHAPTER 19

At the Justice Department: Reno-Fiske section quoted from author's interviews with participants; transcript "Fiske Expects to Question Both Clintons Under Oath," CNN, January 20, 1994; Michael Isikoff, "Whitewater Special Counsel Promises 'Thorough' Probe," *The Washington Post*, January 21, 1994, A1.

David Hale: Hale-Fiske attorneys section quoted from author's interviews with knowledgeable source.

The *American Spectator* editors: Quoted from author's interview with Terry Eastland, October 27, 1998. Referring to the inclusion of "Paula" in the story, Eastland said, "It escaped the editors' radar."

In February, *The New York Times:* Neil A. Lewis, "Litigator on a Tightrope," *New York Times*, February 5, 1994, A9. Hazard is now a professor at the University of Pennsylvania School of Law. In 1994, he taught at Yale.

By early March 1994, news stories: Ann Devroy and Susan Schmidt, "Treasury Officials Told White House Status of S&L Probe," *The Washington Post*, March 3, 1994, A1.

Nussbaum insisted: Author's interviews with knowledgeable source.

"I think it would be better": Clinton quoted from Ann Devroy and Ruth Marcus, "Clinton Faults Contacts with Officials on Probe; White House Counsel Considers Resigning," *The Washington Post*, March 4, 1994, A1.

Nussbaum talked with Hillary: Author's interviews with knowledgeable source.

One of the first indications: Nussbaum-Klein-Gore scene quoted from author's interviews with knowledgeable sources.

Nussbaum knew his head: Nussbaum-Clinton discussion quoted from author's interviews with knowledgeable source. For a partial account of this meeting, see Stewart book, 412–414.

Kendall called Clinton: Author's interview with knowledgeable source.

Several hours later McLarty told: Author's interview with knowledgeable source.

The next day, Nussbaum wrote: Author's interview with knowledgeable source. Later, when Nussbaum testified publicly before a congressional committee about the Foster suicide and other Whitewater matters, both Clintons made separate calls to him.

"You were great," Hillary said. "You were terrific, you did a fantastic job."

In his call, the president only coldly dissected the Republicans. "They've got nothing," Clinton said. "There's nothing there."

CHAPTER 20

One call Cutler received: Cutler-Jordan call and discussion quoted from author's interviews with knowledgeable source.

At 8 p.m. Sunday: Cutler-Clinton meeting quoted from author's interviews with knowledgeable source. Cutler's wife, Polly Kraft, a well-regarded still life painter, had been married to the political columnist Joseph Kraft until his death in 1986.

At 4:15 Tuesday afternoon: Cutler-Clinton press conference quoted from "Remarks Announcing the Appointment of Lloyd Cutler as Special Counsel to the President and an Exchange with Reporters," Public Papers of the Presidents, March 8, 1994; author's interview with knowledgeable source; Paul Richter, "Ex Carter Aide Named White House Counsel," *Los Angeles Times*, March 9, 1994, A1.

Cutler felt the guts: Author's interviews with two knowledgeable sources.

Cutler met with Fiske: Author's interviews with two knowledgeable sources.

David Kendall argued: Author's interviews with knowledgeable source.

Cutler reviewed the material: Author's interviews with two knowledgeable sources.

Hillary Clinton: Author's interviews with two knowledgeable sources; Dean Baquet, Jeff Gerth and Stephen Labaton, "Top Arkansas Lawyer Helped Hillary Clinton Turn Big Profit," *New York Times*, March 18, 1999, A1.

An argument: Author's interviews with two knowledgeable sources.

Clinton sided with Cutler: Author's interviews with two knowledgeable sources.

Cutler wanted to go: Author's interviews with knowledgeable source.

On Thursday, April 21: Ronald Brownstein, "The Times Poll; Enthusiasm for Clinton's Health Reform Is Waning," *Los Angeles Times*, April 21, 1994, A1. In the poll, 32 percent said the Whitewater controversy had diminished their assessment of Hillary.

She would answer any: Hillary Pink Press Conference quoted from transcript "Hillary Clinton Press Conference on Whitewater," ABC News, April 22, 1994. The reaction to the press conference among the public and most of the White House press corps was positive, although a handful of reporters who covered the details were not satisfied. Tom Shales, *Washington Post* television critic, wrote, "Hillary Rodham Clinton came through like a champ yesterday. . . . She was masterful at not seeming in the least irked. . . . There was also a self-effacing candor to her performance. . . . Not once did she seem to be at a loss or in need of assistance. . . . She seems much smarter than the man she married. . . . Sometimes this woman is so unflappable, it's a little scary." See Tom Shales, "The First Lady, On the Spot—And Hitting It," *The Washington Post*, April 23, 1994, G1; Susan Schmidt and Charles R. Babcock, "First Lady's Explanations Yield Little Information," *The Washington Post*, April 23, 1994, A11; Gwen Ifill, "Hillary Clinton Takes Questions on Whitewater," *New York Times*, April 23, 1994, 1.

Nixon died that evening: "Text of President Clinton's Statement on Nixon's Death," Associated Press, April 23, 1994.

In private to his staff: Clinton-Stephanopoulos exchanges quoted from author's interview with knowledgeable source. See also George Stephanopoulos, *All Too Human: A Political Education* (1999), 264-265.

David Kendall wanted to handle: Author's interviews with two knowledgeable sources.

He told the president: Cutler-Clinton meeting quoted from author's interviews with knowledgeable source.

Cutler invited Bennett: Cutler-Bennett lunch quoted from author's interviews with knowledgeable source. Deputy Chief of Staff Harold Ickes also strongly recommended Bennett to Clinton. Bennett had represented Ickes in Whitewater and in a New York investigation of alleged organized crime union ties to his law firm. No charges were brought.

"I want you": Clinton-Bennett meeting quoted from author's interviews with knowledgeable source.

On April 30, he spent: Author's interviews with knowledgeable source.

Bennett called one: Bennett-Davis negotiations section quoted from author's interviews with knowledgeable source. Davis confirmed the substance of the conversations in a March 1, 1999, interview with Jeff Glasser. See also Michael Isikoff, "Clinton's Accuser 'Smelled Money' in Charges; Woman Was Not Sexually Harassed in Hotel Room in 1991, Her Sister Asserts," *The Washington Post*, May 6, 1994, A8.

"The president adamantly denies": Bennett quoted from transcript "News Conference by Robert Bennett, Attorney for President Bill Clinton Regarding Sexual Harassment Lawsuit Filed Against President Clinton," Federal News Service, May 6, 1994.

Bennett met with Clinton: Bennett-Clinton-Cutler meeting quoted from author's interviews with two knowledgeable sources.

On June 27, Bennett filed: Joel Williams, "Clinton Seeking Harassment Suit Delay Till He Leaves Office," Associated Press, June 27, 1994.

Bennett began meeting frequently: Meetings quoted from author's interviews with knowledgeable source.

CHAPTER 21

One component of Fiske's: Author's interviews with knowledgeable source.

In May, Fiske met with: Meeting with the pathologists quoted from author's interviews with knowledgeable source. Hirsch confirmed the substance of his remarks in a March 2, 1999, interview with Jeff Glasser.

Fiske spoke with David: Conversation quoted from author's interviews with two knowledgeable sources.

On Sunday, June 12: Fiske interview of Clintons quoted from author's interviews with three knowledgeable sources.

On Thursday, June 30: Robert B. Fiske Jr., Report of the Independent Counsel In Re Vincent W. Foster Jr., June 30, 1994; Robert B. Fiske Jr., "Statement on Washington, D.C. Investigations," June 30, 1994.

Cutler was pleased: Author's interviews with knowledgeable source.

"This should put to rest": Cutler quoted from transcript "Special White House Briefing," Federal News Service, June 30, 1994.

"Do I have to?": Clinton-Panetta meeting about Independent Counsel Act quoted from author's interview with Leon Panetta, March 16, 1998. Clinton had supported the law in the 1992 campaign, and he agreed that it had been an effective political weapon Democrats had used against Republicans, most notably in the seven-year Iran-contra investigation.

The previous year, Senate Majority Leader George Mitchell had privately told Clinton, "This can be put on the back burner." Some Republicans and moderate Democrats were also apparently looking for the slightest indirect signal from the White House that Clinton didn't support the new law. But the administration publicly supported reenactment of the law, with Attorney General Reno publicly speaking out in favor of it for the administration.

On June 21, the House passed the independent counsel reauthorization legislation, 317–105; the Senate had passed the bill 76–21 on November 18, 1993.

On May 25, 1994, the Senate agreed to adopt the conference report by a voice vote. See "Independent Counsel Law Renewed," *CQ Almanac* (1994), 295–298; Larry Margasak, "Independent Counsel Law Headed to Clinton," Associated Press, June 21, 1994.

A statement was handed out: Clinton also said, "Regrettably this statute was permitted to lapse when its reauthorization became mired in a partisan dispute in the Congress. In fact, the independent counsel statute has been in the past and is today a force for government integrity and public confidence." See Tom Raum, "Clinton Signs Bill Reauthorizing Special Counsel Act," Associated Press, June 30, 1994. The *Post* ran a short, six-paragraph story on the development: "Independent Counsel Law Reauthorized," *The Washington Post*, July 1, 1994, A16.

Afterwards, Clinton asked: Author's interview with Panetta, July 16, 1998.

The next day, Attorney General Reno: The new law contained a special waiver to allow Fiske to stay on if the three-judge panel agreed. See Carolyn Skorneck, "Reno Asks Appeals Court to Make Fiske More Independent," Associated Press, July 1, 1994; "Justice Department Releases Application to Court for Independent Counsel in Matter of Madison Guaranty Savings & Loan," U.S. Newswire, July 5, 1994.

Senator Lauch Faircloth: Howard Schneider, "Judge Met Senator Faircloth Before Fiske Was Ousted; Sentelle Says Special Counsel Wasn't Discussed," *The Washington Post*, August 12, 1994, A1.

Indiana Representative Dan Burton: Howard Schneider, "Judge Met Senator Faircloth Before Fiske Was Ousted; Sentelle Says Special Counsel Wasn't Discussed," *The Washington Post*, August 12, 1994, A1.

Despite the partisan objection: Author's interviews with knowledgeable source.

On August 5, Fiske arrived: Author's interviews with knowledgeable source.

The three-judge panel: Susan Schmidt, "Judges Replace Fiske as Whitewater Counsel; Ex-Solicitor General Starr to Take Over Probe," *The Washington Post*, August 6, 1994, A1.

He not only thought: Starr's view of the act quoted from author's interviews with two knowledgeable sources.

Kendall read the order: Author's interviews with knowledgeable source.

Kendall had represented: "The record abounds with uncontradicted evidence of nepotism," Starr wrote in the Mobil case decision. The *Post* published "the article in good faith." Starr went further and endorsed aggressive investigative reporting. The adversarial statements made by one of the *Post* reporters, he ruled, are similar to ones a lawyer might make. "As in other professions, an adversarial stance is fully consistent with professional, investigative reporting." The author was also a defendant in the suit because he had been an editor on the Mobil story. He too was impressed with the Starr decision. United States Court of Appeals for the District of Columbia, No. 83-1605, decided March 13, 1987.

"Who is Ken Starr?": Ickes quoted from author's interviews with knowledgeable source.

Panetta convened a meeting: Author's interviews with knowledgeable source; author's interview with Panetta, July 16, 1998.

"Wait a minute!": Author's interviews with knowledgeable source.

Sentelle's patron had been: In addition to Helms, Faircloth, a fierce critic of Fiske, lunched with Judge Sentelle on July 14, less than a month before the three-judge panel appointed Starr in Fiske's place. See Howard Schneider, "Judge Met Senator Faircloth Before Fiske Was Ousted; Sentelle Says Special Counsel Wasn't Discussed," *The Washington Post*, August 12, 1994, A1. Sentelle later testified on April 14, 1999, that there may have been "one sentence" of discussion with the senators.

Clinton called Bob Bennett: Author's interviews with knowledgeable source.

Kendall soon called Bennett: Author's interview with two knowledgeable sources.

"I think Starr should": Bennett quoted from Ruth Marcus and Rebecca Fowler, "Starr Urged to Decline Counsel Post; Clinton's Lawyer Criticizes Appointee's Stance on Jones Suit," *The Washington Post*, August 8, 1994, A1.

Attending the American Bar Association's: Starr quoted from Ruth Marcus and Rebecca Fowler, "Starr Urged to Decline Counsel Post; Clinton's Lawyer Criticizes Appointee's Stance on Jones Suit," *The Washington Post*, August 8, 1994, A1.

Cutler, upset, argued: Author's interviews with knowledgeable source.

"We have no reason": Cutler quoted from Howard Schneider and Ruth Marcus, "White House Supports Staff; Despite Misgivings, Aides Express Acceptance," *The Washington Post*, August 9, 1994, A1. "Those are his comments," Cutler said about Bennett's weekend remarks calling on Starr to decline the appointment.

He had a letter hand-delivered: Copy of August 9, 1994, letter from James Carville to Leon Panetta obtained by the author.

Panetta showed the letter: Author's interview with Panetta, July 16, 1998; author's interviews with two knowledgeable sources.

Panetta and Stephanopoulos concluded: Author's interview with Panetta, July 16, 1998; author's interviews with knowledgeable source.

Panetta talked to Clinton: Author's interview with Panetta, July 16, 1998.

Carville had drafted: Author's interviews with knowledgeable source.

"Please, God": Stephanopoulos quoted from author's interviews with two knowledgeable sources.

He attacked Starr publicly: The Texas Republican, Tex Lezar, was running "Whitewater Update" ads in support of his Texas lieutenant governor campaign. In one ad, Lezar said that Deputy Treasury Secretary Roger C. Altman "is caught in the middle of an apparent cover-up by the Clinton administration." See Ruth Marcus, "Starr, Fiske Meet as Democrats Continue to Protest Appointment," *The Washington Post*, August 10, 1994.

On Sunday, August 7: Author's interviews with knowledgeable source.

"My people are going": Fiske-Starr meeting quoted from author's interviews with knowledgeable source.

"Everybody else has talked": Clinton quoted from "Remarks on Health

Care Legislation and an Exchange with Reporters," *Public Papers of the President*, August 10, 1994.

He increased the number of lawyers: Starr quoted from knowledgeable lawyer who worked in Starr's office.

As Cutler's six-month tenure: Author's interviews with knowledgeable source.

Cutler began to search: Author's interviews with two knowledgeable sources.

During a transition: Author's interviews with two knowledgeable sources. Because the White House counsel was on the public payroll, he effectively had no confidential attorney-client relationship with the president. If the independent counsel or Congress came seeking documents or testimony, he probably would have to comply.

The president told Mikva: Author's interviews with knowledgeable source.

CHAPTER 22

It was a devastating defeat: The Republicans gained a 53-to-47 majority in the Senate and a 230-to-204 majority, with one independent, in the House. It gave Republicans control of the House for the first time in 40 years, and a majority in the Senate for the first time in eight years.

Harold Ickes was deeply worried: Author's interviews with knowledgeable source.

"Washington just can't imagine": Gingrich quoted from Ann Devroy and Charles R. Babcock, "Gingrich Foresees Corruption Probe by a GOP House; Party Could Wield Subpoenas Against 'Enemy Administration,' " *The Washington Post*, October 14, 1994, A1.

On the day after the Republican victory, Gingrich said that contrary to his prior remarks, he would not terrorize the Democratic administration with "witch hunts." He promised, instead, "legitimate" investigations.

"I want you to come back": Ickes-Sherburne conversation quoted from author's interviews with knowledgeable source.

Kendall liked the idea: Author's interview with knowledgeable source.

"Nothing to hide": Sherburne's notes, House Government Reform and Oversight Committee.

Sherburne went to see Ickes: Meeting quoted from author's interviews with knowledgeable source.

Sherburne conceived of: Author's interviews with knowledgeable source.

Ickes arranged for: Author's interviews with two knowledgeable sources.

Early in 1995, Sherburne went to see: Meeting quoted from author's interviews with knowledgeable source.

Ickes asked Fabiani to: Meeting quoted from author's interviews with Mark Fabiani, July 7, 1998, and July 9, 1998.

Mikva asked what she was doing: Author's interviews with knowledgeable source.

Ickes arrived in Mikva's office: Meeting quoted from author's interviews with two knowledgeable sources.

Ickes later told Sherburne: Author's interviews with knowledgeable source.

"Why doesn't Jane get": Hillary quoted from author's interviews with knowledgeable source.

"You can't do that!": Meeting quoted from author's interview with knowledgeable source.

"The sad truth": Douglas Jehl, "Clinton and G.O.P. Spar Over Nominee," *New York Times*, March 12, 1995, A28.

"Oh my God": Clinton quoted from author's interview with Panetta, July 16, 1998. Cisneros was caught up in a tawdry scandal that vaguely echoed Clinton's problems with the Gennifer Flowers allegations. The previous summer Cisneros's former mistress, Linda Medlar, had sold her story and four years of secretly recorded phone conversations to a television tabloid program. In the phone conversations, Cisneros and she discussed monthly $4,000 payments that Cisneros was making to her.

Justice had launched an investigation because in Cisneros's background interview with the FBI, he had said that he never paid her more than $10,000 a year. An agonizing debate raged in the Justice Department about what to do after the investigators determined that Cisneros had paid between $42,000 and $60,000 a year—way more than he had acknowledged.

On March 13, 1995, Reno formally applied for the appointment of an independent counsel to investigate Cisneros, concluding that "Cisneros made false statements to the FBI." See Pierre Thomas and Guy Gugliotta, "Special Counsel Sought to Investigate Cisneros," *The Washington Post*, March 15, 1995, A1; David Johnston, "Concluding That Cisneros Lied, Reno Urges a Special Prosecutor," *New York Times*, March 15, 1995, A1.

Mikva said his hands: Author's interviews with knowledgeable source.

They should stick together: Clinton quoted from David Johnston, "Concluding That Cisneros Lied, Reno Urges a Special Prosecutor," *New York Times*, March 15, 1995, A1.

Mikva began privately calling: Author's interviews with knowledgeable source.

"Your friend Ken": Hillary quoted from author's interviews with knowledgeable source.

He called Mark Tuohey: Conversation quoted from author's interviews with two knowledgeable sources.

We would like to examine: Phone call and Clinton testimony quoted from author's interviews with two knowledgeable sources.

The president was disbelieving: Author's interviews with knowledgeable source. The allegations focused on $500,000 that Brown had made by selling his share of a business in which he had not invested any money. Clinton issued a strong statement of support, declaring, "I am confident at the conclusion of the process, the independent counsel will find no wrongdoing by Secretary Brown." See John F. Harris, "Special Counsel to Probe Brown; Clinton Stands by Commerce Chief," *The Washington Post*, May 18, 1995, A1.

Sherburne heard: Author's interviews with knowledgeable source.

Mark Fabiani had spent: Author's interviews with Fabiani, July 7, 1998, and July 9, 1998. Fabiani had determined that the true origin of the Whitewater scandal could be traced back to December 1993. On December 20, 1993, *The Washington Times*, the conservative newspaper owned by the Reverend Moon, ran a banner headline story, "CLINTON PAPERS LIFTED AFTER AIDE'S SUICIDE." It was the first article substantively linking Foster and Whitewater. Three days later, the Clintons turned Foster's Whitewater documents over to the Justice Department, which had begun an inquiry. David Kendall had arranged to get a subpoena for the documents so the papers wouldn't have to be made public. The White House announcement, however, stressed that the documents had been given voluntarily, giving the appearance that the Clintons were fully cooperating with the investigation. The *Washington Times* story and the surrender of the documents were the gasoline and the match that ignited the Whitewater story. Without them, Fabiani concluded, there would have been no Whitewater Special Counsel Fiske or the follow-on investigation of Independent Counsel Starr.

"Let's get this stuff": Fabiani-Kendall-Hillary scenes quoted from author's interviews with Fabiani, July 7, 1998, and July 9, 1998; author's interviews with knowledgeable legal source.

Why would you want: Mikva quoted from author's interviews with knowledgeable source.

Kendall finally agreed: Author's interviews with two knowledgeable sources; author's interviews with Fabiani, July 7, 1998, and July 9, 1998.

Fabiani decided that one: Author's interviews with Fabiani, July 7, 1998, and July 9, 1998.

Stephanopoulos called Fabiani: Author's interviews with Fabiani, July 7, 1998, and July 9, 1998; author's interview with knowledgeable source.

They wrote a script: Author's interviews with Fabiani, July 7, 1998, and July 9, 1998; author's interviews with knowledgeable source.

On Sunday, July 9: Michael Isikoff, "The Night Foster Died," *Newsweek*, July 17, 1995, 20; author's interviews with Fabiani, July 7, 1998, and July 9, 1998; author's interviews with knowledgeable source.

Still, in the White House on Monday: Author's interviews with Fabiani, July 7, 1998, and July 9, 1998; author's interviews with knowledgeable source.

"Of course," Hillary said: Sherburne-Hillary conversation and meeting quoted from author's interviews with knowledgeable source.

D'Amato was livid: author's interview with knowledgeable source.

He went back to Kendall: Author's interviews with Fabiani, July 7, 1998, and July 9, 1998.

Foster's notes showed: Copy of Foster's handwritten notes.

"Poor Michael Isikoff": Editorial "Nothing but the Truth," *Washington Times*, July 17, 1995, A20.

Time **magazine's story:** James Carney, "Whitewater Tricks; New Hearings Prompt the Clintons to Make New Revelations—Only to Be Caught Short Again," *Time*, July 24, 1995, 32.

The New York Post **headline:** Thomas Galvin, "TARGET HILLARY: New Charges Put the First Lady at the Center of W'water Probe," *New York Post*, July 17, 1998, 4–5.

"Well," Ickes told Fabiani: Fabiani-Ickes exchange quoted from author's interviews with Fabiani, July 7, 1998, and July 9, 1998.

After the short-lived success: Fabiani-Kendall discussion quoted from author's interviews with Fabiani, July 7, 1998, and July 9, 1998.

Starr requested a second session: Meeting and Mikva-Starr exchange quoted from author's interviews with knowledgeable source.

Hillary picked up: Author's interviews with knowledgeable source; Joe Klein, "The Body Count, The Real Whitewater Scandal May Be How the Clintons Treat Their Friends," *Newsweek*, August 7, 1995, 34. Klein is the author of the popular novel *Primary Colors*, a thinly disguised *roman à clef* about a Southern governor who becomes president after overcoming a sex scandal.

Hillary was sobbing: Author's interviews with knowledgeable source.

Kendall was against it: Author's interviews with two knowledgeable sources.

Mikva's relationship with Sherburne: Author's interviews with knowledgeable source.

On Wednesday, September 20: Ann Devroy, "Mikva Will Step Down as White House Counsel," *The Washington Post*, September 21, 1995, A29.

Starr's conflicts of interest: Fabiani-Sherburne discussions quoted from author's interviews with Fabiani, July 7, 1998, and July 9, 1998; author's interviews with knowledgeable source; Sam Skolnik, "Kenneth Starr's Conservative Conflict?" *Legal Times*, October 23, 1995, 1.

In the fall, Fabiani called in: Author's interview with knowledgeable source; author's interviews with Fabiani, July 7, 1998, and July 9, 1998.

CHAPTER 23

In mid-November 1995: The six-day shutdown ended on November 20, 1995.

They began flirting: Independent Counsel, Referral to the United States House of Representatives pursuant to Title 28, United States Code, 595(C), September 9, 1998, 37–52.

Jane Sherburne was enjoying: Williams-Sherburne scenes quoted from author's and Jeff Glasser's interviews with two knowledgeable sources.

"This is a soul cleansing": Memo draft, David Watkins, "Response to Internal White House Travel Office Management Review," House Government Reform and Oversight Committee.

"Make a copy of it": Author's and Glasser's interviews with two knowledgeable sources.

She went home and called: Author's interviews with knowledgeable source.

Sherburne called Maggie Williams: Author's interviews with knowledgeable source; Hillary Rodham Clinton, *It Takes a Village and Other Lessons Children Teach Us* (1996).

"Man, how are we going to": Author's interviews with knowledgeable source.

"You just better get back": Author's interviews with Fabiani, July 7, 1998, and July 9, 1998; author's interviews with knowledgeable source.

Hillary dismissed the memo: Author's interviews with knowledgeable source.

It was her practice not to produce: Author's interviews with knowledgeable source.

Fabiani bet that the memo: Author's interviews with Fabiani, July 7, 1998, and July 9, 1998.

Fabiani called the Associated Press: Pete Yost, Associated Press, January 3, 1996.

Oh, no! she realized: Sherburne quoted from author's interviews with knowledgeable source.

"There was a cover-up here": David Johnston, "Memo Places Hillary Clinton at Core of Travel Office Case," *New York Times*, January 5, 1996, A1.

D'Amato cited a "troubling": Susan Schmidt and Toni Locy, "Travel Office Memo Draws Probers' Ire; Ex-Aide Contradicts Hillary Clinton on Firings," *The Washington Post*, January 5, 1996, A1.

Starr and John Bates: Author's interviews with knowledgeable source.

"The White House had an obligation": Susan Schmidt and Toni Locy, "Travel Office Memo Draws Probers' Ire; Ex-Aide Contradicts Hillary Clinton on Firings," *The Washington Post*, January 5, 1996, A1.

Bates didn't think: Author's interview with knowledgeable source.

"Goddamn you": Sherburne-Bates conversation quoted from author's interviews with two knowledgeable sources.

Fabiani was unsure about how: Author's interviews with Fabiani, July 7, 1998, and July 9, 1998.

Before noon on January 4: Discovery of billing records scenes quoted from author's interviews with three knowledgeable sources; author's interviews with Fabiani, July 7, 1998, and July 9, 1998; Deposition of David E. Kendall, Senate Special Committee to Investigate Whitewater and Other Matters, February 7, 1996, Vol. XV, 2441–2490; Deposition of Jane Sherburne, Senate Special Committee to Investigate Whitewater and Other Matters, February 6, 1996, Vol. XV, 2357–2436; Deposition of Carolyn Huber, Senate Special Committee to Investigate Whitewater and Other Matters, January 17, 1996, Vol. XIV, 1113–1190; "Who Is Hillary Clinton?" *Wall Street Journal*, January 5, 1996, A8.

CHAPTER 24

Mike McCurry wanted Kendall: Author's interviews with two knowledgeable sources.

Finally Kendall appeared: Susan Schmidt, "White House Locates 'Missing' Law Firm Records; Billing Documents Under Subpoena, Detail Hillary Clinton's Work for S&L Involved in Whitewater," *The Washington Post*, January 6, 1996, A1.

Starr and Bates met with: Meeting quoted from author's interviews with knowledgeable source.

"If you do this": Kendall quoted from author's interviews with knowledgeable source.

He told his deputies that Mrs. Clinton: Author's interviews with knowledgeable source.

Around this time Hillary: Meeting quoted from author's interviews with knowledgeable source; transcript, *This Week With David Brinkley*, ABC News, January 7, 1996.

"Where did these come from?": Discussion about whether to have a self-investigation quoted from author's interview with Panetta, July 16, 1998; author's interviews with Fabiani, July 7, 1998, and July 9, 1998; author's interviews with two knowledgeable sources.

Carolyn Huber testified: Deposition of Carolyn Huber, Senate Special Committee to Investigate Whitewater and Other Matters, January 17, 1996, Vol. XIV, 1113–1190.

Mrs. Clinton, Sherburne and Fabiani concluded: Author's interviews with Fabiani, July 7, 1998, and July 9, 1998; author's interviews with knowledgeable source.

Fabiani felt that the search: Author's interviews with Fabiani, July 7, 1998, and July 9, 1998; author's interviews with two knowledgeable sources.

On January 8, a *Newsweek*: Martha Brant and Evan Thomas, "Saint or Sinner?" *Newsweek*, January 15, 1996, 20–33; William Safire, "Blizzard of Lies," *New York Times*, January 8, 1996, A27; Neil Lewis, "White House Says President Would Like to Punch Safire," *New York Times*, January 10, 1996, A11.

"in good faith": Hillary quoted from transcript "Interview with Hillary Rodham Clinton," The Diane Rehm Show, Federal News Service, January 15, 1996.

The *New York Times* Washington bureau: Author's interviews with two knowledgeable sources; author's interviews with Fabiani, July 7, 1998, and July 9, 1998.

Sherburne called Susan Thomases: Author's interviews with knowledgeable source.

Sherburne and Fabiani reviewed: Author's interviews with Fabiani, July 7, 1998, and July 9, 1998; author's interviews with knowledgeable source.

Sherburne had to phone Hillary: Author's interviews with knowledgeable source; Stephen Labaton, "Aides Say Mrs. Clinton Erred in Claiming Press Got All Files," *New York Times*, January 20, 1996, A10.

For the election year: Author's interviews with knowledgeable source; Hearing transcript, Senate Special Committee to Investigate Whitewater and Other Matters, August 7, 1995, Vol. II, 1031–1035.

"There is nothing there": Mikva quoted from author's interviews with two knowledgeable sources.

Kendall wanted a meeting: Section quoted from author's interviews with five knowledgeable sources.

They felt a leak: Author's interviews with Fabiani, July 7, 1998, and July 9, 1998;author's interviews with knowledgeable source.

Bob Bennett learned about: Author's interviews with knowledgeable source.

He was continuing to urge: Author's interviews with two knowledgeable sources.

Kendall was opposed: Author's interviews with knowledgeable source.

Maggie Williams, however, forced: Meeting quoted from author's interviews with three knowledgeable sources; author's interviews with Fabiani, July 7, 1998, and July 9, 1998.

"Then I'll get ready": Hillary quoted from author's interviews with knowledgeable source.

she chose a fashionable: "It wasn't a dragon," Robin Givhan began her Style column in *The Washington Post*. "It is an abstract design that resembles an art deco rendering of seashells. That flourish, however, turned into a Washington political Rorschach test. People saw what they wanted to see. There probably are some folks who would swear they saw flames shooting out of the imaginary dragon's mouth." Robin D. Givhan, "Her True Colors," *The Washington Post*, February 4, 1996, F3.

She and Sherburne were lingering: Author's interviews with knowledgeable source.

Inside the grand jury room: Author's interviews with knowledgeable source.

"Well, you are all still here": David Maraniss, "A Solitary Figure Enters New Territory," *The Washington Post*, January 27, 1996, A1.

"Why is Starr getting": Author's interviews with knowledgeable source.

Fabiani did not believe they: Author's interviews with Fabiani, July 7, 1998, and July 9, 1998.

Sherburne decided not to tell: Author's interviews with knowledgeable source.

On March 15, Starr got word: Author's interviews with knowledgeable source; author's interview with Henry Woods, April 2, 1998; author's interviews with judicial source; *United States of America, Appellant, v. Jim Guy Tucker et al.*, No. 95-3268, Decided March 15, 1996.

"I admire Mrs. Clinton very much—a fine lawyer and a brilliant woman," Judge Woods said in an interview. In 1994, on the day of the midterm election, he planned to have a cup of coffee with Mrs. Clinton at the White House when he was in Washington attending a conference on law and religion. "Why don't you spend the night?" Hillary asked. Woods accepted, and he and his wife stayed in the Lincoln Bedroom. They joined key Democrats for a buffet dinner that night. The next morning they talked with the president. The Democrats had lost both the Senate and House. "I saw him the next morning," Woods said. "Clinton is good at masking his feelings. I admire the way he took it." Woods didn't have the Tucker case at that point. He categorically said he never discussed the case with either of the Clintons.

On September 5, 1995, Woods held a hearing on the motion by Tucker and the others to dismiss one of the indictments against him. Starr argued that the case was properly within his jurisdiction and outlined the careful steps he had taken. He had the best authority on his side, the Supreme Court case (*Morrison* v. *Olson*) upholding the independent counsel law on precisely this and other issues. Woods didn't ask a single question of Starr. Two hours after the argument, Woods issued a 21-page opinion.

Woods later in an interview outlined his reasoning for dismissing the indictment. Tucker was charged with fraudulently obtaining government-backed loans, using the money to buy a Florida cable company, then selling it and conspiring to evade taxes on as much as $4 million by conducting a "sham bankruptcy." Woods thought it was a weak case because Tucker paid back the loans—with interest—within a year. More important, Woods acknowledged that he engaged in judicial nullification. He thought the tax issue was not related at all to Whitewater. Even though the independent counsel was authorized to investigate and prosecute wrongdoing he found in the course of his investigation, Woods didn't like the sweeping jurisdiction. "I didn't think that ought to be the law," he said. His ruling cited no constitutional or other legal reason. He simply substituted his judgment for that of the Congress. It was one of the more breathless declarations of a judge legislating.

Starr appealed, and Judge Pasco M. Bowman II and two other judges on the 8th Circuit Court of Appeals heard oral argument, December 12, 1995. They later met in closed conference to consider what to do about Starr's appeal. All three found Woods's opinion in total contradiction of the Supreme Court ruling that had upheld the constitutionality of the independent counsel law. They quickly decided to reverse Woods.

On the more complicated question of ordering Woods off the case, they felt that Woods should have automatically recused himself, as had a number of federal judges from Arkansas in Clinton-related cases, because of his friendship with Hillary. But they didn't want to embarrass Woods. "It is the appearance of bias or partiality that matters here, not actual bias," Bowman wrote in his opinion for himself and the other two judges. "The OIC's request for reassignment is granted, not because we believe Judge Woods would not handle the case in a fair and impartial manner (we have every confidence that he would), but only because we believe that this step is necessary in order to preserve the appearance as well as the reality of impartial justice."

Starr asked for the first lady's: Author's interviews with two knowledgeable sources; author's interviews with Fabiani, July 7, 1998, and July 9, 1998.

In May, John Bates called: Search of White House residence scenes quoted from author's interview with Gary Walters, April 27, 1999; author's interviews with two knowledgeable sources. For a partial account, see Jeffrey Toobin, "Starr Can't Help It," *The New Yorker*, May 18, 1998, 35.

CHAPTER 25

In early May 1996: Dispute between Quinn and Sherburne and response to congressional travel office investigation quoted from author's interview with Panetta, July 16, 1998; author's interviews with three knowledgeable sources; letters, Jack Quinn to William F. Clinger, May 2, 1996, and May 9, 1996, provided by House Committee on Government Reform and Oversight; Susan Schmidt, "House Prober Presses Demand for Travel Office Documents; Contempt Citation Against White House Is Threatened," *The Washington Post*, May 3, 1996, A2; R. H. Melton, "House Panel Votes for Contempt Citation; Action Against White House Counsel Stems from Travel Office Probe," *The Washington Post*, May 10,1996, A4.

On Tuesday, June 4, Sherburne: Susan Schmidt, "FBI Analysis Sheds Little Light on Rose File Mystery; Fingerprints of Hillary Clinton, Foster, and 2

864

Paralegals Found on Long-Missing Records," *The Washington Post*, June 5, 1996, A8.

"Yet another Whitewater allegation": Neil A. Lewis, "Hillary Clinton's Fingerprints Among Those Found on Papers," *New York Times*, June 5, 1996, A18.

At 8 p.m., Sherburne was reading: Author's interview with knowledgeable source.

Just that day they had turned: Ann Devroy and John E. Yang, "White House Gives Congress 1,000 Pages of Travel Office Papers," *The Washington Post*, May 31, 1996.

She threw it in the pile: Author's interviews with knowledgeable source.

It listed 21 categories: Subpoena provided by House Committee on Government Reform and Oversight.

The next morning, June 5: Author's interviews with knowledgeable source.

Sherburne went upstairs: Author's interviews with knowledgeable source.

Bernie Nussbaum's name appeared: Request provided by House Committee on Government Reform and Oversight.

"You mean that requests": Quinn quoted from author's interviews with knowledgeable source.

Sherburne reached Shapiro: Author's interviews with knowledgeable source.

Next, Sherburne called Paxton: Author's interviews with knowledgeable source.

"What!" Clinton said: Meeting with Clinton quoted from author's interviews with two knowledgeable sources; author's interview with Panetta, July 16, 1998.

Mark Fabiani was worried: Author's interviews with Fabiani, July 7, 1998, and July 9, 1998.

"We believe Mr. Dale's records": Sherburne statement quoted from Bryan Sierra, "Background Information on Dale Scrutinized," United Press International, June 5, 1996.

Sherburne informed Hillary: Author's interviews with knowledgeable source.

"Why aren't we investigating": Author's interviews with knowledgeable source.

Gorelick had been a white-collar: Author's interview with knowledgeable source.

"Unfortunately, the FBI and I": Freeh quoted from George Lardner and John Harris, "FBI Chief Says Request for Files Was Unjustified; Freeh Tightens Disclosure Policy for White House," *The Washington Post*, June 15, 1996, A1.

The Republicans were already having: On June 8, Republican presidential candidate Bob Dole called the file-gathering a "Clinton enemies list" at a campaign stop in Marietta, Georgia. The next day, Clinton conceded that Panetta was correct in saying an apology was owed to the Republicans, but he called the episode a "completely honest bureaucratic snafu." See Kevin Merida, "Dole Compares White House's File Gathering to Watergate," *The Washington Post*, June 9, 1996, A12; George Lardner Jr. and John F. Harris, "Panetta Offers

Apology Over Files 'Mistake'; Reports on GOP Ex-Aides Were Not Misused, Says White House Chief of Staff," *The Washington Post*, June 10, 1996, A1.

The White House was stunned: George Lardner Jr. and John F. Harris, "FBI Chief Says Request for Files Was Unjustified; Freeh Tightens Disclosure Policy for White House," *The Washington Post*, June 15, 1996, A1.

"This is not right!": Gorelick-Freeh exchange quoted from author's interview with knowledgeable source.

"The FBI and I fell victim": George Lardner Jr. and John F. Harris, "FBI Chief Says Request for Files Was Unjustified; Freeh Tightens Disclosure Policy for White House," *The Washington Post*, June 15, 1996, A1.

Starr decided he didn't want: Author's interviews with two knowledgeable sources.

Reno and Gorelick concluded that: Author's interviews with knowledgeable source.

At 7 a.m., Gorelick called: Author's interviews with two knowledgeable sources.

On June 20, Reno made application: John F. Harris and George Lardner Jr., "Reno Seeks Starr Probe of FBI Files," *The Washington Post*, June 21, 1996, A1; George Lardner Jr., "Starr Gets Authority for FBI Files Probe; Court Gives Independent Counsel Broad Mandate," *The Washington Post*, June 22, 1996, A9.

On July 15, the FBI passed on: Section quoted from author's interviews with knowledgeable source. See also George Lardner Jr., "Clinger, White House Battle Over File Allegations; FBI Agent's Account of Ex-Security Chief's Ties to First Lady Draws Administration Denials," *The Washington Post*, July 26, 1996, A19.

Over in the scandal management: Author's interview with knowledgeable source.

"the ultimate master of the Western World": George Stephanopoulos, *All Too Human*, 385.

A total of 52 percent: Dick Morris, *Behind the Oval Office: Getting Re-elected Against All Odds* (1999 edn.), 570.

Morris had used the Republican: Morris section quoted from author's interviews with knowledgeable source. See also Morris memoir (1997 edn.), 64–66, 324, 330, 333; Maraniss biography, 455.

CHAPTER 26

Six weeks before the election: "Interview with President Clinton," *The NewsHour With Jim Lehrer*, PBS, September 23, 1996.

When Starr saw Clinton's words: Starr's reaction quoted from author's interviews with three knowledgeable sources.

"Upon careful reflection, we are concerned that President Clinton, by his public statements, has reinforced Ms. McDougal's unlawful intransigence. I am writing to ask that the president remove this serious obstacle to our inquiry," Starr wrote in a February 14, 1997, letter to Clinton's counsel, Charles Ruff. ". . . We request that the president publicly urge Ms. McDougal to testify truthfully before the federal grand jury in Little Rock."

In reply, Ruff wrote on April 4, 1997, "The president has neither said nor done, wittingly or unwittingly, anything in the slightest degree improper, and I reject the suggestion that he has somehow encouraged Ms. McDougal to violate the law." The back-and-forth continued through the spring of 1998.

A number of the contributions were: Scenes about the Riadys and Sherburne's departure quoted from author's interviews with four knowledgeable sources; author's interviews with Fabiani, July 7, 1998, and July 9, 1998; copies of November 26, 1996, letter from Sherburne to Leon Panetta provided by House Committee on Government Reform and Oversight; Jeff Gerth and Stephen Labaton, "Wealthy Indonesian Has Strong Ties to Clinton," *New York Times*, October 11, 1996, A1; Jim Mann and Glenn F. Bunting, "Clinton Aided Indonesia Regime; Large Donations Raise Questions of Connection Between Money, Policies. Kantor Denies Any Link," *Los Angeles Times*, October 16, 1996, A1; David E. Sanger, "President Admits He and Indonesian Had Policy Talks," *New York Times*, November 16, 1996, A1; Jeff Gerth and Stephen Labaton, "Close Aide to Clinton Urged Less Candor Over Indonesian," *New York Times*, November 19, 1996, A1; "Text of President Clinton's News Conference," *The Washington Post*, January 29, 1997, A12; William Safire, "Hush Money?" *New York Times*, January 30, 1998, A21; Stephen Labaton and Jeff Gerth, "Asian Paid $100,000 to Hubbell Days After Visits to White House," *New York Times*, March 20, 1997, A1.

Bowles, a tall, calm: Author's interview with knowledgeable source.

CHAPTER 27

"Good luck": Clinton's comments to Rehnquist and discussion with Quinn quoted from author's interviews with knowledgeable source.

Quinn preferred to settle: Author's interviews with knowledgeable source.

For months Clinton and Bennett: Author's interviews with knowledgeable source.

"We'll hear argument now": Oral arguments in front of the Supreme Court quoted from *Clinton* v. *Jones* No. 95–1853, January 13, 1997.

Later in January 1997: Author's interviews with knowledgeable source.

In February, Starr met: Debate about Pepperdine scenes quoted from author's interviews with two knowledgeable sources; Susan Schmidt, "Some Starr Allies Say Departure Means No Clinton Charges," *The Washington Post*, February 19, 1997, A7; "Just a Minute, Mr. Starr," *New York Times*, February 19, 1997, A20; Susan Schmidt, "Starr Appears to Waver on Timing of Departure; August Date Is Counsel's 'Current Understanding,' " *The Washington Post*, February 20, 1997, A4; "Excerpts from News Conference: 'It Was a Mistake,' " *New York Times*, February 22, 1997, A9. "There's joy in Mudville" was the lead quote from a White House official in *The Washington Post* the day Starr announced his intention to resign. See Susan Schmidt, "Starr Will Leave Whitewater Post; Prosecutor Becomes Law School Dean in August," February 18, 1997, A1.

Despite the skepticism: Author's interviews with knowledgeable source; Supreme Court decision in *Clinton* v. *Jones* No. 95–1853, decided May 13, 1997.

For three years, Starr: Scenes about Starr quoted from author's interviews with three knowledgeable sources. Also see Susan Schmidt, "White House Notes Are Given to Starr," *The Washington Post*, June 24, 1997, A1.

In June 1997, I received: Section about the troopers quoted from author's interview with Ronald B. Anderson, June 19, 1997; author's interviews with Roger Perry, June 20, 1997; author's interview with John Bates, June 24, 1997; author's interviews with four knowledgeable sources. See Bob Woodward and Susan Schmidt, "Starr Probes Clinton Personal Life," *The Washington Post*, June 25, 1997, A1; copy of Starr June 25, 1997, press release.

That same month, Anthony Lewis, the *New York Times* columnist, criticized our story in a column, claiming it was exaggerated. "It distorted and vastly over-played what was actually involved."

In October 1998, I received a letter from Lewis. "I have just had occasion to reread that column, and I did so with chagrin," he wrote. "I wrote it at a time when I still had some faith in Starr, and I believed people who explained his actions on his behalf. I see now, all too well, that your story was an important clue to what had happened to the Starr I knew: the judge who decided *Tavoulareas* and other cases with sound judgment. So: my belated apologies. You were right. Best wishes—Tony."

In July, Starr announced: Kenneth Starr, Summary Report on Vincent W. Foster Jr., released October 10, 1997; Susan Schmidt, "Starr Probe Reaffirms Foster Killed Himself; Forensic Details Counter Conspiracy Theories," *The Washington Post*, October 11, 1997, A4.

CHAPTER 28

In late September 1997: Section quoted from author's interviews with legal source.

"I'll kill her": Bennett quoted from author's interviews with knowledgeable source.

On October 1, the new: Interrogatories quoted from court records in Jones Civil Action, No. LR-C-94-290 (E.D. Ark.).

"It's a sham": transcript "Robert Bennett, Attorney, Discusses the Investigation into Campaign Fund-Raising Activities and the Paula Jones Case," *Face the Nation*, CBS, October 12, 1997.

But it was not: Court records in Jones case.

They came up with a broad list: Author's interviews with legal source. For example, they listed witness number 101 as Jane Doe 101 and described her only as the young woman lawyer mentioned on page 238 of Roger Morris's book, *Partners in Power*.

One possible witness: Author's interviews with legal source. The Jones attorneys filed a notice of Tripp's deposition on November 25, 1997, to be taken on December 18. The date was later changed to January 23, 1998.

In the fall, Clinton: Independent Counsel, Referral to the United States House of Representatives Pursuant to Title 28, United States Code, 595(c), September 9, 1998, 138–139, 141–142 (based on Lewinsky-Tripp phone conversation recorded by Tripp).

At 5:40 p.m.: Author's interviews with knowledgeable source; Jones court records.

Bennett immediately sent a copy: Author's interviews with knowledgeable source. Also see Starr Referral, 173.

Betty Currie called Vernon: Author's interviews with knowledgeable source; Starr Referral, 174–177.

Later that day, December 11: Jones court records.

Jim Fisher and his partners: Author's interviews with knowledgeable source.

About 2 a.m. on December 17: Starr Referral, 177–179 (based on Lewinsky and Clinton grand jury testimony).

After 3 p.m. on Friday: Starr Referral, 181–187 (based on Lewinsky, Jordan and Clinton grand jury testimony).

In one way or another: Jordan had been called twice to testify before the grand jury investigating former Agriculture Secretary Mike Espy, another friend under investigation. He had to provide records to the independent counsel investigating former Housing Secretary Henry Cisneros. The FBI had interviewed Jordan about the investigation of former Commerce Secretary Ron Brown, another friend. Jordan had arranged for Webster Hubbell to be hired under a $100,000-a-year contract with Revlon, and the FBI had questioned him about that. The various congressional committees also demanded his testimony.

"You aren't boffing": Jordan quoted from author's interviews with knowledgeable source.

On Monday, December 22: Starr Referral, 188–190; author's interviews with knowledgeable source.

The next day, December 23: Author's interviews with knowledgeable source.

That day Clinton reviewed: Starr Referral, 191; Jones court records.

On Sunday, December 28: Starr Referral, 191–194.

CHAPTER 29

On January 7, 1998: Starr Referral, 209–215 (based on grand jury testimony of Lewinsky, Jordan and Clinton).

On Saturday, January 10: Jones court documents.

The Jones lawyers were elated: Author's interviews with knowledgeable source.

On Monday, January 12—five days: Author's interviews with two knowledgeable sources and notes of a participant; Jones court documents.

He went back to Washington: Author's interviews with knowledgeable source.

Paul Rosenzweig: Michael Isikoff, "The Right Wing Web," *Newsweek*, February 22, 1999, 32–34.

On Monday, January 12, Tripp called: Tripp January 12, 1998, FBI 302 interview report, Starr Referral Supplemental Materials, Part 3, released September 28, 1998, 3753.

Back at Starr's office: Author's interviews with two knowledgeable sources.

The next day, January 13: Body wire transcript, Starr Referral Supplemental Materials, Part 2, released September 28, 1998, 2762.

The next night, Wednesday: Author's interviews with knowledgeable source. Also see Michael Isikoff, *Uncovering Clinton: A Reporter's Story* (1999), 277, 293, 312–313.

On Friday, January 16: Author's interviews with knowledgeable source.

No, Bennett believed: Jenkins's attorneys made an extraordinary effort to keep her out of the Jones case. Referred to in court filings as Jane Doe #1, Jenkins refused to answer questions about sexual relations with Clinton or whether she had ridden in limos or cars with state troopers, claiming a constitutional privilege of privacy, at a deposition on November 18, 1997. In response, the Jones legal team adjourned the deposition and had a conference call with Judge Wright. Later, Jenkins's attorney advised that his client was too ill to return for the deposition.

Two days later, Jenkins's attorney filed a motion to terminate or limit her examination based on the privacy claim. The "disclosure of Jane Doe's identification and the information sought from her could very well devastate her life as she knows it," her attorney argued.

The next day, the Jones legal team filed a motion in opposition saying they had a right to take the testimony because "the conduct being discovered was not marital but adulterous." The Jones lawyers claimed that Jenkins's counsel was making up a privilege in a desperate attempt not to answer their questions. "Because it was adulterous, the activity we seek to discover is proscribed, not protected, by state law. It is therefore ineligible for constitutional protection."

The Jenkins lawyers later that day filed another motion and supporting brief claiming that "Jane Doe has never at any time had sexual relations with President Clinton," and asserting that she "has never been offered a state job or other benefits in exchange for having sexual relations with President Clinton." She "has no information regarding any *nonconsensual* touching or sexual advances made by Clinton against herself or any other woman."

The sparring continued, and on December 3, the Jones lawyers were allowed to continue taking Jenkins's deposition, although Wright would rule later on whether disputed questions were admissible.

On December 12, Clinton's attorneys filed a motion in support of three Jane Does, including Jenkins, who were seeking to stop the Jones lawyers from asking whether they had sexual relations with Clinton. "This case is not about whether President Clinton had female friends, or whether he had a consensual relationship with any woman other than his wife," Clinton's attorneys argued. "Any such relationship would in no way be germane to the allegations advanced in this case."

Six days later, on December 18, Judge Wright ordered one of the three Jane Does to answer the questions about sexual relations, but she did not compel the other two Jane Does.

This legal battle is quoted from Jones legal case documents.

Danny Ferguson, the Arkansas trooper: Transcript of Ferguson deposition in the Jones case.

Bennett had learned: Author's interviews with two knowledgeable sources.

The judges later in the day: Starr Referral Supplemental Materials, Part 1, released September 18, 1998, 6–7.

That morning Tripp, once again wired: Starr Referral Supplemental Materials, Part 1, released September 18, 1998, 1375–1380.

Ginsburg: Author's interview with William Ginsburg, January 28, 1998.

That night Tripp had met: Peter Baker, "Linda Tripp Briefed Jones Team on Tapes," *The Washington Post*, February 14, 1998, A1.

CHAPTER 30

Bennett had decided: Author's interviews with three knowledgeable sources.

Bennett arrived early: Author's interview with knowledgeable source.

About 10:25 a.m.: Transcript of Videotaped Oral Deposition of William Jefferson Clinton, January 17, 1998, District Court of the United States for the Eastern District of Arkansas, Western Division, Civil Action, No. LR-C-94–290 (E.D. Ark.), 1–218.

Gathering in Bennett's 11th-floor conference room for the closed, sealed proceeding were 19 people: Clinton, Bennett and three associates, Ruff, Jones herself (now age 31), six of her attorneys, the attorney for Arkansas state trooper Danny Ferguson, Judge Wright, two video-camera operators, a court reporter and the head of the president's Secret Service detail, Larry L. Cockell.

"How do you think it went?": Author's interviews with two knowledgeable sources.

After the deposition, Paula: Author's interviews with knowledgeable source.

David Kendall was in New York: Author's interviews with knowledgeable source.

Just after midnight: Matt Drudge, "BLOCKBUSTER REPORT: 23-YEAR-OLD, FORMER WHITE HOUSE INTERN, SEX RELATIONSHIP WITH PRESIDENT," the Drudge Report, January 18, 1998.

At 5 p.m. Sunday: Starr Referral, 224–235 (based on Currie and Clinton grand jury testimony).

CHAPTER 31

Kendall had been out: Author's interviews with knowledgeable source.

"Jesus! Jesus! Jesus!": Author's interviews with knowledgeable source.

The *Post* story: Susan Schmidt, Peter Baker and Toni Locy, "Clinton Accused of Urging Aide to Lie," *The Washington Post*, January 21, 1998, A1.

Since the White House lawyers: Author's interviews with two knowledgeable sources.

Ruff drafted a statement: Author's interviews with knowledgeable source.

His press briefing was disastrous: Michael McCurry, "The White House Regular Briefing," Federal News Service, January 21, 1998.

Clinton told Bowles: Starr Referral, 241, 242–243.

Dick Morris had left a message: Starr Referral, 247–248.

That afternoon, the president: Clinton interview transcript, *The NewsHour with Jim Lehrer*, PBS, January 21, 1998.

Listening, McCurry was confused: Author's interviews with knowledgeable source.

An hour later: Ed Henry and Morton Kondracke, "Clinton: Relationship Was Not 'Sexual,' Intern Allegations Won't Lead to Impeachment, President Tells *Roll Call*," *Roll Call*, January 22, 1998, 1.

In Los Angeles, James Carville: Author's interviews with knowledgeable source.

"I think in the end": Carville quoted from transcript, *Larry King Live*, January 21, 1998.

Carville talked to all: Author's interviews with knowledgeable source.

At 11:30 p.m. that night: Starr Referral Supplemental Materials, Part 2, released September 28, 1998, 2929.

The next morning, January 22: Meeting quoted from author's interviews with two knowledgeable sources.

Just after 10 a.m.: "Remarks Prior to Discussions with Chairman Yasser Arafat of the Palestinian Authority and an Exchange with Reporters," Public Papers of the Presidents, January 22, 1998, 124.

McCurry, Begala and Emanuel: Author's interviews with two knowledgeable sources.

McCurry didn't like it: Author's interviews with knowledgeable source.

Sam Dash read: Author's interviews with two knowledgeable sources.

Harry Thomason: Starr Referral Supplemental Materials, Part 3, released September 28, 1998, 3727–3750.

On Monday morning, January 26: "Remarks on the After-School Child Care Initiative," Public Papers of the Presidents, January 26, 1998, 129.

At 5 a.m., Tuesday: David Maraniss, "First Lady Launches Counter-attack; Prosecutor Called 'Politically Motivated' Ally of 'Right Wing Conspiracy,' " *The Washington Post*, January 28, 1998, A1.

"We appreciate you honoring": Transcript, "Hillary Rodham Clinton Discusses Allegations Against Her Husband, Child Care, State of the Union Address," *Today Show*, NBC, January 27, 1998.

"Just remember, you've got": Thomason quoted from Jeffrey Toobin, "Circling the Wagons," *The New Yorker*, July 6, 1998, 28–33.

The next day, Starr: Author's interviews with knowledgeable source.

"The first lady today": Text of Starr statement, January 27, 1998.

Two of Starr's deputies: Author's interviews with two knowledgeable sources.

Clinton grew more emphatic: Author's interview with knowledgeable source.

CHAPTER 32

William Ginsburg submitted: Starr Referral Supplemental Materials, Part 1, released September 18, 1998, 709–718.

On February 5, Starr: Letter provided by knowledgeable legal source.

Kendall courted Ginsburg: Author's interview with knowledgeable source.

Starr heard about: Author's interviews with knowledgeable source.

At a White House dinner: Author's interviews with knowledgeable source; Jeff Gerth, Stephen Labaton and Don Van Natta Jr., "Aide's Statements Are Said to Differ from President's," *New York Times*, February 6, 1998, A1.

Kendall was sure: Author's interviews with knowledgeable source; copy of February 6, 1998, statement by Kendall.

Carville was dancing: Author's interviews with knowledgeable source.

In the White House: Author's interviews with knowledgeable source; Richard Morin and Claudia Deane, "President's Popularity Hits New Highs," *The Washington Post*, February 1, 1999, A1; "Leaks Involving White House Sex Scandal Create Controversy," *NBC Nightly News*, February 8, 1998. The 79 percent approval rating for Clinton came from an NBC News/*Wall Street Journal* poll.

Starr issued: Starr Referral Supplemental Materials, Part 2, released September 18, 1998, 2295–2296.

The letter was greeted: Author's interviews with two knowledgeable sources.

A fifth invitation was sent: Starr Referral Supplemental Materials, Part 2, released September 18, 1998, 2298–2299.

Bill Hundley spent days: Author's interviews with knowledgeable source.

About 9:50 a.m., Jordan: Starr Referral Supplemental Materials, Part 2, released September 28, 1998, 1700–1732.

"To those of you": Jordan quoted from Peter Baker and Toni Locy, "Jordan Reaffirms Clinton Friendship," *The Washington Post*, March 4, 1998, A1.

Kendall continued with his strategy: Author's interviews with knowledgeable source. The letter is quoted from Starr Referral Supplemental Materials, Part 2, released September 18, 1998, 2300–2326.

On Wednesday, April 1: Author's interviews with knowledgeable source.

He was photographed chewing: Peter Baker, "Judge Dismisses *Jones* v. *Clinton* Lawsuit," *The Washington Post*, April 2, 1998, A1.

Ginsburg was still spending: Author's interview with Carol Joynt, January 23, 1999.

Starr realized: Bakaly-Starr section quoted from author's interviews with knowledgeable source.

Starr reacted emotionally: Author's interviews with two knowledgeable sources.

Moving on the live witnesses: Steve Barnes, "McDougal Trial Sees Mrs. Clinton's Videotape," *New York Times*, March 17, 1999, A18.

On May 25, Memorial Day: Author's interviews with knowledgeable source.

"I'm having the time": Clinton quoted from Joseph White, "Clinton Takes In Memorial Day Hockey Game," Associated Press, May 25, 1998.

CHAPTER 33

Starr had carefully studied: Author's interviews with two knowledgeable sources.

Kavanaugh had sometimes wondered: Author's interview with knowledgeable source.

"At what point": Transcript, "Remarks by Whitewater Independent Counsel Kenneth Starr at Mecklenburg Bar Foundation, Charlotte, North Carolina," Federal News Service, June 1, 1998.

My God, Kendall thought: Author's interviews with knowledgeable source; David Kendall, "To Distort a Mockingbird," *New York Times*, June 3, 1998, A25.

Over in Starr's office: Author's interviews with two knowledgeable sources.

Plato Cacheris: Author's interviews with knowledgeable source and lawyer's chronology.

"Thank God": Author's interviews with knowledgeable source; Peter Baker, "Ginsburg Replaced as Lewinsky Counsel," *The Washington Post*, June 3, 1998, A1.

Lewinsky came up: Author's interviews with two knowledgeable legal sources; William Ginsburg, "An Open Letter to Kenneth Starr," *California Lawyer*, June 1998, 23.

Clinton was on a: Bill Clinton, "Remarks at a Democratic National Committee Dinner in Dallas, Texas," Public Papers of the Presidents, June 2, 1998, 1024.

Around this time, staffers: Author's interviews with two knowledgeable sources.

Lewinsky went to Cacheris's office: Author's interviews with two knowledgeable sources.

On June 4: Susan Schmidt and Joan Biskupic, "High Court Rejects Starr Plea for Ruling; Appeals Panel to Consider Privilege Issues," *The Washington Post*, June 5, 1998, A1.

Lewinsky's new lawyers: Author's interviews with three knowledgeable sources.

Afterwards, Hoffman consulted: Author's interviews with knowledgeable source.

Cacheris and Stein both felt: Author's interviews with knowledgeable source.

The next day, Bittman: Author's interviews with two knowledgeable sources.

"I have talked": Starr quoted from Steven Brill, "PRESSGATE," *Brill's Content*, August 1998, 122–151.

Kendall filed a motion: Ruth Marcus, "Starr Defends Discussions with Reporters," *The Washington Post*, June 16, 1998, A8.

About 5 p.m., Starr: Author's interviews with two knowledgeable sources.

On June 25: Ruth Marcus and Susan Schmidt, "Attorney-Client Privilege After Death Is Upheld," *The Washington Post*, June 26, 1998, A1.

Meanwhile work on Starr's: Author's interviews with two knowledgeable sources.

On July 2: Starr Referral Supplemental Materials, Part 1, released September 18, 1998, 10.

Starr had set July 31: Author's interviews with two knowledgeable sources.

From January to April: Starr Referral Supplemental Materials, Part 2, released September 18, 1998, 2316, 2329.

Starr was the last holdout: Author's interviews with two knowledgeable sources.

The subpoena was issued: Starr Referral Supplemental Materials, Part 2, September 18, 1998, 2330.

Kendall received the subpoena: Author's interviews with knowledgeable source.

CHAPTER 34

Dash had lunch: Author's interviews with two knowledgeable sources.

Kendall told the president: Author's interviews with three knowledgeable sources.

"The president is willing": Starr Referral Supplemental Materials, Part 2, released September 18, 1998, 2339.

In final form, the agreement: Copy provided by knowledgeable source.

Hoffman dropped her objections: Author's interviews with knowledgeable source.

Hoffman had spent the weekend: Author's interviews with two knowledgeable sources.

She didn't like him: Author's interviews with knowledgeable source.

That morning, Monday, July 27: Author's interviews with three knowledgeable sources and notes of participants.

"She's probably not giving": Author's interviews with two knowledgeable sources.

That morning Starr had: Author's interviews with knowledgeable source.

Over at the White House: Transcript, Michael McCurry, "The White House, Washington, D.C., Regular Briefing," Federal News Service, June 28, 1998.

"The most important thing": Author's interviews with Fitzwater, December 8, 1997, and January 13, 1998.

McCurry didn't trust the information: Author's interviews with knowledgeable source.

Kendall and Bittman opened: Starr Referral Supplemental Materials, Part 2, released September 18, 1998, 2347–2351, 2355.

Starr felt that the delay: Author's interviews with knowledgeable source.

On July 28, Judge Johnson: Starr Referral Supplemental Materials, Part 2, released September 18, 1998, 2369–2404.

Serious negotiations followed: Author's interviews with knowledgeable source.

"In an effort": Transcript of Kendall press conference, July 29, 1998.

Emmick called Cacheris: Author's interviews with knowledgeable source.

CHAPTER 35

The dress was logged in: Starr Referral Supplemental Materials, Part 2, released September 18, 1998, 2433.

Bittman tried to reach: Starr Referral Supplemental Materials, Part 2, released September 18, 1998, 2411, 2415–2416, 2419–2420.

It could be a bluff: Author's interviews with knowledgeable source.

On August 3, Kendall agreed: Author's interviews with two knowledgeable sources; Starr Referral Supplemental Materials, Part 2, released September 18, 1998, 2423–2424, 2427.

Ordinary witnesses were not: Author's interviews with knowledgeable source; Lewinsky-Tripp transcript, " 'This Is Sick, This Is Sick,' " *Newsweek*, February 2, 1998, 35.

When he heard: Author's interviews with knowledgeable source.

Jack Quinn called: Author's interviews with knowledgeable source.

Clinton realized that Nixon: Author's interview with knowledgeable source.

"Every man has his": Virginia Kelley, *Leading with My Heart* (1994), 278.

"Those fuckers": Author's interviews with knowledgeable source.

On August 6, Monica: Starr Referral Supplemental Materials, Part 1, released September 18, 1998, 721–961.

Hickman Ewing: Author's interviews with knowledgeable source.

Clinton continued to prepare: Author's interviews with knowledgeable source.

Late Thursday night: Author's interviews with knowledgeable source; Richard L. Berke, Neil A. Lewis, James Bennet and David E. Sanger, "Clinton Weighs Admitting He Had Sexual Contacts," *New York Times*, August 14, 1998, A1; Bob Woodward, "President's Lawyers Brace for Change in Story," *The Washington Post*, August 16, 1998, A1.

On Monday morning: Author's interviews with two knowledgeable sources.

The video hookup: Starr Referral Supplemental Materials, Part 1, released September 18, 1998, 453–628; author's interviews with knowledgeable source.

Hillary had sent word: Author's interviews with knowledgeable source.

Starr and his deputies: Author's interviews with two knowledgeable sources.

Later, Carville saw Hillary: Author's interviews with two knowledgeable sources.

"Good evening": Bill Clinton, "Address to the Nation on Testimony Before the Independent Counsel's Grand Jury," Public Papers of the Presidents, August 17, 1998, 1638–1639.

"Well, that wasn't very contrite!": Author's interviews with two knowledgeable sources.

Carville appeared: Transcript, *Larry King Live*, CNN, August 17, 1998.

CHAPTER 36

Kendall realized: Author's interviews with knowledgeable source.

Starr returned to work: Author's interviews with knowledgeable source.

Hillary had her press secretary: Statement quoted from Sandra Sobieraj,

"Clintons Head for Island Vacation, Escaping Washington's Tensions," Associated Press, August 18, 1998.

From the White House: Author's interviews with knowledgeable source.

One of the few people: Author's interviews with knowledgeable source.

McCurry finally had some: Author's interviews with knowledgeable source.

Traditionally, in his years: Author's interviews with knowledgeable source; Annie Groer and Ann Gerhart, "The Reliable Source," *The Washington Post*, August 21, 1998, B3. Clinton received a lone gift at the birthday party: "A beautiful wool sweater made from wool taken from the sheep that live right there on the Allen farm," where the Jordans were staying, McCurry told the White House press corps.

The network was suspected: The terrorists attacked U.S. embassies in Nairobi, Kenya, and Dar es Salaam, Kenya, killing 263 and wounding more than 5,500.

Later in August, Clinton: Author's interviews with knowledgeable source.

Mark Penn, Clinton's pollster: Author's interviews with knowledgeable source.

Lanny Davis was one: Author's interviews with knowledgeable source.

Freeh's alienation with Clinton: Author's interview with knowledgeable source.

"You're acting like a defendant": Author's interview with knowledgeable source.

On August 25: Ceci Connolly, "Gephardt Says Clinton Could Be Impeached; House Leader Won't Rule Out Process," *The Washington Post*, August 26, 1998, A1. Gephardt said impeaching the president was a serious matter. "That doesn't mean it can't be done or shouldn't be done; you just better be sure you do it the right way." If Clinton were to leave office, "We'll get through this," Gephardt said.

Clinton was furious: Author's interviews with knowledgeable source.

Hillary considered the vacation: Author's interviews with knowledgeable source.

CHAPTER 37

The prosecutors brought Lewinsky back: Author's interviews with two knowledgeable sources.

Immergut produced a chart: Starr Referral Supplemental Materials, Part 1, released September 18, 1998, 1281–1350.

The narrative: Author's interviews with two knowledgeable sources.

Senator Joseph I. Lieberman: Author's interview with knowledgeable source; transcript, "Lieberman's Remarks," Federal News Service, September 3, 1998.

The president was in Ireland: Bill Clinton, "Exchange with Reporters Prior to Discussions with Prime Minister Bertie Ahern of Ireland in Dublin," Public Papers of the Presidents, September 3, 1998, 1720.

Clinton hit exceptionally well: Author's interviews with knowledgeable source.

Kendall was at work: Author's interviews with knowledgeable source.

Instead, Kendall sent a letter: Copy of Kendall letter, September 7, 1998. Kendall asked for the one-week delay so there would be "due consideration for fundamental fairness. This concern for fairness was shared by then-Chief Judge Sirica 24 years ago, when he was presented with a report of the Watergate grand jury. . . . Chief Judge Sirica's desire to ensure that the Watergate report was fair, and, in particular, that it contained no recommendations, advice or judgments that would infringe on the prerogatives of the legislative branch parallels our concern. . . ."

Starr responded: Copy of Starr letter, September 8, 1998.

Kendall had no doubt: Author's interviews with knowledgeable source.

Jack Quinn was keeping: Author's interviews with knowledgeable source.

The morning of September 9: Author's interviews with knowledgeable source.

About 9 a.m.: Author's interviews with two knowledgeable sources.

The goal had been: Author's interviews with two knowledgeable sources; Starr Referral.

At 3:45 p.m.: Guy Gugliotta and Juliet Eilperin, "Delivery Catches the Hill by Surprise," *The Washington Post*, September 10, 1998, A12.

"As required": Transcript, "Stakeout with Starr Spokesperson Charles Bakaly and Deputy Independent Counsel Robert Bittman," Federal News Service, September 9, 1998.

Bakaly walked away: Author's interviews with two knowledgeable sources.

Terry McAuliffe was sitting: Author's interviews with knowledgeable source.

Representative Henry Hyde: Author's interviews with knowledgeable source.

Clinton asked for forgiveness: Author's interview with knowledgeable source.

Hyde and John Conyers: Author's interviews with four knowledgeable sources.

The House Rules Committee: Edward Walsh and Juliet Eilperin, "Vote Sets Capitol Process in Motion," *The Washington Post*, September 11, 1998, A1.

Clinton looked drawn: Bill Clinton, "Remarks at a Breakfast with Religious Leaders," Public Papers of the Presidents, September 11, 1998, 1762–1763.

"This is really bad": Author's interviews with two knowledgeable sources.

Mike McCurry could not: Author's interviews with knowledgeable source.

Ruff too was astonished: Author's interview with knowledgeable source.

David Kendall saw the referral: Author's interviews with knowledgeable source.

"This private mistake": David E. Kendall et al., "Preliminary Memorandum Concerning Referral of Office of Independent Counsel," September 12, 1998, 1–78; David Kendall, Second Memorandum, September 12, 1998, 1–42.

At a White House dinner: Bill Clinton, "Remarks on Receiving the Paul O'Dwyer Peace and Justice Award," Public Papers of the Presidents, September 11, 1998, 1769–1772.

Later that evening, the president: Author's interviews with two knowledgeable sources.

CHAPTER 38

Senate Judiciary Committee Chairman: Author's interviews with knowledgeable source.

Of the senior Republicans: In August, Hatch had said, "I don't know anybody at the top of the system—like, take Chairman Hyde, take myself as chairman of the respective Judiciary Committees—who really wants to see the president hurt in this matter." See transcript, "Senator Orrin Hatch Discusses Ken Starr's Investigation of President Clinton," *Meet the Press*, NBC, August 2, 1998.

"How did you think": Author's interviews with knowledgeable source.

Two nights earlier, Hatch: Transcript, *Larry King Live*, CNN, September 11, 1998. Hatch also said, "When you look at what a fine young woman, you have to say, 'Hey, there's something right about that couple.' I mean, they're doing some things right."

"You know, Senator": Author's interviews with knowledgeable source.

On the CBS show: Transcript, *Face the Nation*, CBS, September 13, 1998. The moderator, Bob Schieffer, asked Hatch on the air about his conversation with Clinton. The Utah senator confirmed that he had talked with the president but would not elaborate. "Well, I'd rather keep that conversation just between the two of us," Hatch told Schieffer.

Kendall took the hardest line: Transcript, *This Week*, ABC, September 13, 1998.

The next day: Thomas Daschle, "Statement on the Starr Report," September 14, 1998; Richard Gephardt, "Statement on Report of the Independent Counsel," September 14, 1998; David S. Broder, "With 28 Months to Go," *The Washington Post*, September 15, 1998, A21.

Recognizing that Kendall had fallen: Author's interviews with knowledgeable source.

Early in the week: Author's interviews with knowledgeable source.

A *Washington Post* poll: Richard Morin and Claudia Deane, "Poll Finds Approval of Job, Not of Person," *The Washington Post*, September 14, 1998, A1.

Daschle, the leader: Section quoted from author's interviews with two senators; author's interviews with three knowledgeable sources.

Clinton gathered: Author's interviews with knowledgeable source; Robert Burns, "President Apologizes to Senate Democrats, Assures Them 'No Surprises,' " Associated Press, September 10, 1998.

At the press conference: Bill Clinton, "The President's News Conference with President Havel," Public Papers of the Presidents, September 16, 1998, 1803–1808.

***Salon*, an online magazine:** Section quoted from author's interview with two knowledgeable sources; David Talbot, " 'This Hypocrite Broke Up My Family,' " *Salon*, September 16, 1998; David Talbot, "Hyde Lied, Says Former Lover," *Salon*, September 18, 1998.

Kendall realized immediately: Author's interviews with knowledgeable source.

On September 20: John M. Broder and Don Van Natta Jr., "Clinton and Starr, a Mutual Admonition Society," *New York Times*, September 20, 1998, A1.

Later, in a discussion: Author's interviews with two knowledgeable sources.

Hyde's committee voted: Juliet Eilperin and Dan Morgan, "Clinton Videotape Set for Release," *The Washington Post*, September 19, 1998, A1.

Kendall had tried: Author's interviews with knowledgeable source.

Advance news stories quoted sources: "Today, millions of people will see Clinton's anger," John Harris wrote in the *Post*, "though these glimpses will only hint at the eruptions to which he is sometimes prone." The *New York Times* wrote that Clinton would deliver "a diatribe," criticizing prosecutors for the way in which they confronted Lewinsky. See John Harris, "View of a President Prone to Pique," *The Washington Post*, September 21, 1998, A1; James Bennet and Jill Abramson, "Lawyers Say Tape of Clinton Shows Regret and Anger," *New York Times*, September 20, 1998, A1.

Kendall was among: Author's interviews with knowledgeable source.

Ruff watched: Author's interviews with knowledgeable source.

"Viewers who sat through": Tom Shales, "Clinton and the Kenneth Inquisition," *The Washington Post*, September 22, 1998, E1.

Carville was sure: Author's interviews with knowledgeable source.

Later that day: Author's interviews with two knowledgeable sources; Starr Referral Supplemental Material, Part 1, released September 18, 1998, 1161.

The president continued: Bill Clinton, "Remarks at a Democratic National Committee Dinner," Public Papers of the Presidents, October 7, 1998, 2002–2006.

Hillary was still uncertain: Author's interviews with knowledgeable source.

The next day, October 8: Author's interviews with knowledgeable source.

In the cabinet room: Bill Clinton, "Remarks Prior to a Meeting with the Economic Team and an Exchange with Reporters," Public Papers of the Presidents, October 8, 1998, 2010–2011.

The Republicans decided to spend: Ceci Connolly, "GOP Spends Millions on TV Ads Attacking President's Conduct," *The Washington Post*, October 28, 1998, A5.

Clinton privately expected: Author's interviews with two knowledgeable sources.

"The American people sent": Bill Clinton, "Remarks Following a Meeting with Congressional Leaders and an Exchange with Reporters," Public Papers of the Presidents, November 5, 1998, 2252.

The next day, Speaker Newt: "Today, I have reached a difficult decision," Gingrich said in the statement. "The Republican Conference needs to be unified, and it is time for me to move forward where I believe I still have a significant role to play for our country and our party." Copy of Gingrich statement, November 6, 1998.

Kendall joked: Author's interviews with knowledgeable source.

CHAPTER 39

For a month, Bob Bennett: Author's interviews with knowledgeable source; Peter Baker, "Clinton, Jones Reach Settlement," *The Washington Post*, November 14, 1998, A1.

Starr saw with increasing clarity: Author's interviews with two knowledgeable sources.

Just before Starr's testimony: Author's interviews with knowledgeable source; House Judiciary Committee hearing, "Appearance of Independent Counsel, Impeachment Inquiry, William Jefferson Clinton, President of the United States," November 19, 1998, 170–189.

In a holding room: Author's interviews with knowledgeable source.

The next day, Dash: "Text of Dash Resignation Letter," Associated Press, November 20, 1998. "You have no right or authority under the law, as independent counsel, to advocate for a particular position on the evidence before the Judiciary Committee or to argue that the evidence in your referral is strong enough to justify the decision by the committee to recommend impeachment," Dash wrote. He called Starr's appearance before Congress "an abuse of your office." He also wrote, "Indeed, the committee does not have a right to impose upon you as independent counsel to be its prosecuting counsel for impeachment."

Most of Starr's deputies: Author's interviews with two knowledgeable sources.

Control of Clinton's defense: Author's interviews with knowledgeable source.

On Wednesday afternoon: Transcript, "December 9 Statement by White House Counsel Charles F. C. Ruff," Federal News Service, December 9, 1998. For news media reviews of Ruff's performance, see Melinda Henneberger, "Dripping with Charm, Clinton's 'Clean-Up Hitter' Seems to Soothe Ardent Critics," *New York Times*, December 10, 1998, A25; Ruth Marcus, "A Conciliatory, Constitutional Appeal by Ruff," *The Washington Post*, December 10, 1998, A33; "The Effectiveness of Charles Ruff," "Investigating the President," CNN, December 9, 1998.

At the White House, Clinton: Author's interviews with knowledgeable source.

At 4:10 p.m., Clinton: Bill Clinton, "Remarks Prior to the House Judiciary Committee Vote on the First Article of Impeachment," Public Papers of the Presidents, December 11, 1998, 2465–2466.

On Saturday, December 12: Section quoted from author's interviews with four knowledgeable sources; author's interviews with Bob Michel, January 8, 1999; Eric Schmitt, "Speaker-Elect Says Censure Is Not an Option for House," *New York Times*, December 13, 1998, A1; Robert Dole, "A Tough but Responsible Solution," *New York Times*, December 15, 1998, A27.

In the wake of Iran-contra, Hyde and Berman sponsored legislation in 1988 that tightened laws banning the sale of weapons to countries that sponsor terrorism. "I was surprised that officials would come up here and deliberately lie to Congress in the wake of Watergate," Hyde said at the end of the Iran-contra hearings. "I thought that was [as unfashionable as] wearing a hoop skirt." See Karen Tumulty and Sara Fritz, "President, Panel Agree on Covert Action Rules; Foreign Policy to Feel Effect on Iran Scandal," *The Washington Post*, August 8, 1987, 1; Jim Drinkard, "House Passes Bill to Tighten Laws on Arms Sales to Terrorists," Associated Press, April 19, 1988.

In 1993, Hyde said of the proposed assistance to Russia, "Foreign aid is about as unpopular a program as there is. But I think there will be some aid. We have to convince the American people. I think most members of Congress understand the stakes—that if Russia reverts, it would be very dangerous for the whole world." See Melissa Healy and Edwin Chen, "Lawmakers See Need to Sell Public on Aid Plan," *Los Angeles Times*, April 4, 1993, A18.

Cutler represented Hyde in a 1994 term limits case in Washington State in opposition to an amendment that could have barred then House Speaker Tom Foley, the Washington Democrat, from office. Cutler won the case when a federal judge in Washington State declared the law unconstitutional. Rory Marshall, "Federal Judge Declares Washington State Term Limits Unconstitutional," Associated Press, February 10, 1994.

"Around three-quarters": DeLay quoted from transcript, *Meet the Press*, NBC, December 13, 1998.

On Tuesday, December 15: The nine were Nancy Johnson (Connecticut), Anne Northup (Kentucky), Michael P. Forbes (New York), John McHugh (New York), Sue W. Kelly (New York), Tom Campbell (California), E. Clay Shaw Jr. (Florida), Gerald Weller (Illinois), and Fred Upton (Michigan). See Peter Baker and Juliet Eilperin, "Clinton's Chances Dimming in House," *The Washington Post*, December 16, 1998, A1.

CHAPTER 40

Secretary of Defense: Section quoted from author's interviews with two knowledgeable sources. In the early 1980s, Cohen had chaired the committee that recommended changing the name of the office from special prosecutor to independent counsel in the effort to reduce the Watergate stigma.

"I wish to talk": Text of Hyde statement, Federal Document Clearing House, December 18, 1998.

"Monica Lewinsky is not Watergate": Menendez quoted from Peter Baker and Juliet Eilperin, "Partisan Bitterness Infuses Historic Debate," *The Washington Post*, December 19, 1998, A1.

Stories circulated that: Author's interviews with two knowledgeable sources and contemporaneous records.

That morning, Hillary Clinton: Text of Hillary Rodham Clinton remarks, Associated Press, December 18, 1998.

"Goddamn, fuck it": Clinton quoted from author's interviews with knowledgeable source.

On Saturday, just after: Bill Clinton, "The President's Radio Address," Public Papers of the Presidents, December 19, 1998, 2514–2515. "As we enter the season of peace, we remain ever hopeful that one day all nations and all communities will actually live in peace, with tolerance, respect and civility," Clinton said.

"I must set the example": Text of Livingston statement, Associated Press, December 19, 1998. The prior night, Livingston had issued the following statement on his affair: "When I did an early interview with the media after announcing my candidacy for speaker, I told a reporter that I was running for speaker, *not* sainthood. There was a reason for those words." He also stated, "This chapter was a small but painful part of the past in an otherwise wonderful marriage." "Text of Livingston Statement," *washingtonpost.com*, December 17, 1998.

Hyde had not been: Author's interviews with two knowledgeable sources.

Clinton was in the: John F. Harris, "Clinton Vows to Finish Term," *The Washington Post*, December 20, 1998, A1.

Gore was with Clinton: John F. Harris, "Clinton Vows to Finish Term," *The Washington Post*, December 20, 1998, A1.

Ruff watched the vote: Author's interviews with knowledgeable source.

"We still have to": Bill Clinton, "Remarks Following the House of Representatives Vote on Impeachment," Public Papers of the Presidents, December 19, 1998, 2515–2516.

Despite his strong performance: Author's interviews with two knowledgeable sources.

Two hours later, he announced: Bill Clinton, "Address to the Nation on Completion of Military Strikes in Iraq," Public Papers of the Presidents, December 19, 1998, 2516–2518.

At a black-tie White House party: Author's interviews with knowledgeable source.

"For six years": Clinton quoted from author's interviews with knowledgeable source.

Hillary didn't appear: Author's interviews with knowledgeable source.

At the party, the president: Elizabeth Shogren, "Clinton Puts His Faith in History," *Los Angeles Times*, December 22, 1998, A1. Clinton also told Shogren that it felt "not bad" to have been impeached. He claimed that within 10 or 20 years he would be on the right side of history, that historians would not give undue weight to impeachment when they analyzed his presidency.

Carville had gone public: He also said, "This was a cowardly, dastardly thing that they did, and there's going to be retribution, and the retribution is going to be at the polling place." Transcript, *Meet the Press*, NBC, December 20, 1998.

Clinton told Carville: Author's interviews with knowledgeable source.

Gerald Ford had been: Author's interview with Gerald Ford, March 31, 1999; author's interview with knowledgeable source; Gerald Ford and Jimmy Carter, "A Time to Heal Our Nation," *New York Times*, December 21, 1998, A29. *A Time to Heal* is the name of Ford's memoir.

Lott was hoping: John F. Harris and Juliet Eilperin, "Lott Searching for Consensus," *The Washington Post*, January 1, 1999; Guy Gugliotta, "Two Senators Drew Up Plan for Trial Hoping to Rise Above Partisan Rancor," *The Washington Post*, December 5, 1999, A5; Eric Pianin, "Prospects Dim for Avoiding Long Clinton Trial," *The Washington Post*, January 6, 1999, A1.

"This is an issue": Spontaneous meeting quoted from author's interviews with two knowledgeable sources.

Later, after some uncertainty: "News Conference with Senate Majority Leader Trent Lott and Senate Minority Leader Tom Daschle," Federal News Service, January 7, 1999; "Stakeout Remarks by Senate Majority Leader Trent

Lott Following Opening Session of U.S. Senate Impeachment Proceedings Against President Clinton," January 7, 1999.

The next morning: Author's interviews with two senators; Robert C. Byrd, "Conference in the Old Senate Chamber," Congressional Press Releases, January 8, 1999.

Bipartisanship and unanimity: Author's interviews with knowledgeable source.

CHAPTER 41

As the Senate proceeded: Author's interviews with knowledgeable source.

The president spoke: Bill Clinton, "Remarks at a Democratic National Committee Dinner," Public Papers of the Presidents, January 15, 1999, 70–73.

He believed the managers: Author's interviews with two knowledgeable sources.

"Some of us": Henry Hyde, Summation, Federal Document Clearing House Political Transcripts, January 16, 1999.

Ruff had listened intently: Author's interviews with knowledgeable source.

"William Jefferson Clinton is not guilty": Charles F. C. Ruff, Opening Statement, *Congressional Record*, January 19, 1999; author's interviews with knowledgeable source.

Fred Thompson: Author's interviews with knowledgeable source.

That night, President Clinton: Bill Clinton, "Address Before a Joint Session of the Congress on the State of the Union," Public Papers of the Presidents, January 19, 1999, 78–88.

Clinton worked the room: Author's interviews with knowledgeable source.

Clinton reached Ruff: Author's interviews with knowledgeable source.

The president had retired: Author's interviews with two knowledgeable sources.

Three days later: Author's interviews with two knowledgeable sources; copy of Byrd January 22, 1999, press release announcing his intention to offer a motion to dismiss the charges.

Ruff and Kendall, too: Author's interviews with two knowledgeable sources.

Ruff and Kendall put up: Author's interviews with two knowledgeable sources.

When Ruff clipped on: Charles F. C. Ruff, Closing Statement, *Congressional Record*, February 8, 1999.

Hyde rose: Henry Hyde, Closing Statement, *Congressional Record*, February 8, 1999.

The president's present for Terry: Author's interviews with two knowledgeable sources.

"I'll survive": Author's interviews with knowledgeable source; Susan Schindehette, "Hillary & Chelsea, Grace Under Fire: An Intimate Look at the Deep Bond of Love That Sustains the Clinton Women Through Their Painful Family Ordeal," *People*, February 15, 1999, 78–88.

Two hours later, Clinton appeared: Bill Clinton, "Remarks on the

884

Conclusion of the Senate Impeachment Trial and an Exchange with Reporters," Public Papers of the Presidents, February 12, 1999, 225.

Ruff and the other lawyers: Author's interviews with two knowledgeable sources.

Hillary went to Ruff's: Author's interview with knowledgeable source.

He had always thought: Ruff quoted from Bob Woodward, "The Last Prosecutor; Special Watergate Force Is Going Out of Business," *The Washington Post*, June 19, 1977, A1.

Clinton drew his own: Author's interviews with three knowledgeable sources.

ACKNOWLEDGMENTS

Simon & Schuster and *The Washington Post* again backed this project—my ninth book in 25 years done under their gracious auspices.

Alice Mayhew, vice president and editorial director at Simon & Schuster, threw herself and her considerable energies into the work. She rekindled my interest in presidents I had written about from 1974 to the present. We agreed it would be possible to interrogate the historical record, return to the major players and then try to sort out what had happened and find some of its meaning. A force of nature in book publishing, Alice lives two lives, at least. In her day job, she acquires, manages and coordinates her books. At night and on the weekends, she edits. She has my gratitude and greatest respect.

Carolyn K. Reidy, president and publisher at Simon & Schuster, performed another publishing miracle to get the book out in nearly record time.

Leonard Downie Jr., *The Washington Post*'s executive editor, and Steve Coll, its new managing editor, gave me the freedom to make this independent inquiry. Many thanks also to Steve Luxenberg, now the Outlook editor of the *Post*, and to the *Post*'s owners, Katharine Graham and Don Graham.

There are dozens of people at the *Post* who assisted me. Jennifer Belton, director of news research, oversees the best library and photo library in the business. I owe a special thanks to Melody Blake, Alice Crites, Richard Drezen, Madonna Lebling, Ruth Leonard, Bob Lyford, Roland Matifas, Heming Nelson, Bobbye Pratt, Nancy Shiner, Rob Thomason, Mary Lou White and others on the news research staff who answered our research requests.

Olwen Price transcribed many interviews, from former presidents to obscure aides. Joe Elbert and his photo staff at the Post provided most of the pictures in this book.

At Simon & Schuster, I thank Jonathan Newcomb, the chairman; Jack Romanos, the president and chief operating officer; David Rosenthal, the publisher; Elisa Rivlin, the general counsel; director of publicity Victoria Meyer; associate director of publicity Aileen Boyle; art director and jacket designer Jackie Seow; copyediting director Marcia Peterson; production manager John Wahler; designer Edith Fowler and Alice Mayhew's skillful and always cheerful editorial assistant, Layla Hearth. All our gratitude to copy supervisor Stephen Messina for his extraordinary professional care under deadline pressure.

Ann Adelman traveled to Washington to copyedit the manuscript. I thank her for her keen eye, thoughtfulness and friendship.

During and after important events, Jeff Glasser and I relied on *The Washington Post*, *The New York Times*, the *Los Angeles Times*, *The Wall Street Journal*, *Time*, *Newsweek*, *U.S. News & World Report*, *National Journal*, *The New Yorker* and the *Associated Press*.

We used many presidential memoirs and

biographies, but the work of James Cannon and Robert Hartmann on Ford, Haynes Johnson and Jules Witcover on Carter, Lou Cannon and Jane Mayer & Doyle McManus on Reagan, Herbert S. Parmet on Bush, and James B. Stewart on the Clintons was particularly noteworthy.

William F. Powers Jr., media columnist for the *National Journal* and a longtime friend, read and offered valuable advice on the early chapters.

David Maraniss, my colleague at the *Post*, provided special encouragement and assistance. His book on President Clinton *First in His Class* still stands as the definitive biography. The work of the following editors, columnists and reporters at the *Post* helped immeasurably: Nathan Abse, Rick Atkinson, Peter Baker, David Broder, Richard Cohen, Helen Dewar, Karen DeYoung, Juliet Eilperin, Susan Glasser, Guy Gugliotta, Bill Hamilton, John Harris, Al Kamen, George Lardner, Ruth Marcus, John Mintz, Dan Morgan, Eric Pianin, Walter Pincus, Susan Schmidt, Roberto Suro, David von Drehle and dozens of others.

Carl Bernstein, my friend and former colleague, provided advice and guidance as always.

Larry King at CNN and his staff of talented producers offered many assists and insights, particularly during 1998, the year of Monica. Jim Wooten of ABC gave important information and conclusions. My regards to the remarkable news team at NBC, especially Andy Lack, Tom Brokaw, Tim Russert, Lisa Myers, and Pete Williams.

Elizabeth Lockwood provided invaluable assistance at the National Archives II in College Park, Maryland, working tirelessly to process our FOIA requests on the independent counsels. Richard Norton Smith and David Horrocks at the Ford Museum and Library; Donald Schewe, Robert Bohanon and James Yancey at the Carter Library; Diane Barrie, Larry Bumgardner and Sherrie Fletcher at the Reagan Library and their staffs guided us expertly through the extensive presidential paper trail.

Robert B. Barnett was again my agent and counselor in the Edward Bennett Williams tradition. Because of his professional association with President and Mrs. Clinton, he did not read the book until it was finished and printed.

Special thanks to Rosa Criollo, Norma Gianelloni, and Jackie Crowe.

Elsa Walsh, my wife and best friend, once again provided the comfort, sober advice, good sense and love to guide me and our household through this latest book.

PHOTO CREDITS